ALBERT E. HARTUNG

GENERAL EDITOR

A Manual of the Writings in Middle English

1050-1500

ALBERT E. HARTUNG
GENERAL EDITOR

A Manual of the Writings in Middle English

1050-1500

*By members of the Middle English Group of the
Modern Language Association
of America*

Based upon
A Manual of the Writings in Middle English 1050–1400
by John Edwin Wells, New Haven, 1916
and Supplements 1–9, 1919–1951

THE CONNECTICUT ACADEMY OF ARTS AND SCIENCES, NEW HAVEN, CONNECTICUT
MDCCCCLXXIII

Library of Congress Cataloging in Publication Data
Main entry under title:

A Manual of the writings in Middle English, 1050–1500.

"Based upon A manual of the writings in Middle
English 1050–1400, by John Edwin Wells, New Haven,
1916, and supplements 1–9, 1919–1951."
  Includes bibliographies.
  CONTENTS: v. 1 Romances, by M. J. Donovan,
and others.—v. 2 The Pearl poet, by M. P. Hamilton.
Wyclyf and his followers, by E. W. Talbert and S. H.
Thomson. Translations and paraphrases of the Bible, and
commentaries, by L. Muir. Saints' legends by C. D'Evelyn
and F. A. Foster. Instruction for religious, by C. D'Evelyn.
v. 3. Dialogues, Debates, and Catechisms, by F. L. Utley,
Thomas Hoccleve, by W. Matthews, Malory and Caxton,
by R. H. Wilson, [etc.]
  1. English literature—Middle English (1100–1500)—
History and criticism. 2. English literature—Middle English
(1100–1500)—Bibliography. I. Severs, Jonathan Burke, ed.
II. Wells, John Edwin, 1875–1943. A manual of the writings
in Middle English, 1050–1400. III. Hartung, Albert E.,
1923–   ed. IV. Modern Language Association of
America. Middle English Group.
PR255.M3   016.82′09′001   67–7687
ISBN 0–208–01342–3 (v. 4)

© 1973 by The Connecticut Academy of Arts and Sciences
Published for The Connecticut Academy of Arts and
Sciences by Archon Books / The Shoe String Press, Inc.
Hamden, Connecticut 06514

Printed in the United States of America

Volume 4

X. MIDDLE SCOTS WRITERS

by

Florence H. Ridley

XI. THE CHAUCERIAN APOCRYPHA

by

Rossell Hope Robbins

PREFACE

This manual of Middle English literature is a collaborative project of the Middle English Group of the Modern Language Association of America. Printed in parts as the various chapters of the work are completed, the *Manual* already comprises three volumes: Volume 1 on the Romances; Volume 2 on the *Pearl* Poet, Wyclyf and His Followers, Translations and Paraphrases of the Bible, Saints' Legends, and Instructions for Religious; Volume 3 on Dialogues, Debates, and Catechisms, Thomas Hoccleve, and Malory and Caxton. The present Volume 4 deals with Middle Scots Writers and The Chaucerian Apocrypha. Originally intended to be complete to 1955 with selected important studies after that date up to the time of going to press for each volume, the Bibliography has been modified in the direction of a more recent cut-off date. The two chapters in the present volume are intended to be complete for all serious studies to 1971 with selected important studies to the time of going to press (October 20, 1972, for Volume 4). A full account of the principles followed by the editors of the work will be found in the Preface to Volume 1.

For help in the editorial work on this fourth volume, the General Editor wishes to express appreciation to his able secretaries, Mrs. Elizabeth J. Salay and Mrs. Beatrice Buck, who assisted in the preparation of copy for the printer. In addition, he particularly should like to thank his editorial assistant, Mrs. Marilyn C. Dunlap, whose capable aid was made possible by financial support from the American Council of Learned Societies and from Lehigh University. Her work was indispensable in the completion of the present volume. And for unfailing help with copy, proof, and index in meeting deadlines he must mention his wife, Ruth.

Finally, on behalf of the Middle English Group and on his own behalf, the General Editor is deeply grateful to the Connecticut Academy of Arts and Sciences for undertaking the publication of this revised *Manual*, as it had undertaken publication of the original.

Albert E. Hartung
General Editor

CONTENTS

X. MIDDLE SCOTS WRITERS

by

Florence H. Ridley

1. JAMES I

The term "Scottish Chaucerians" has in the past been applied to four major poets of the late medieval period who are related by nationality, language, and to a varying degree by the influence of Chaucer upon their work. However, it is now generally though not universally recognized as applicable to only one of them, the author of *The Kingis Quair*, who may or may not have been James I of Scotland. Details of this king's life are contained in public records of Scotland and England and in accounts by his contemporaries, Walter Bower and Æneas Sylvius; they are clearly presented in E. W. M. Balfour-Melville's comprehensive biography, *James I King of Scots*. Born the son of Queen Annabella and Robert III at Dunfermline Abbey in July 1394, James was sent out of the country in March 1406 for safekeeping, but en route to France was captured by pirates and delivered into the hands of Henry IV of England. Bower reports that from the time Robert received news of his son's capture he refused all food until he died on April fourth, leaving James I king of Scotland.

Evidence indicates that during his imprisonment the English treated James well and trained him thoroughly in both arms and books. He was, of course, a valuable political pawn, and at the time of his release in 1423 his English captors insisted that he marry some highborn English lady as one means of strengthening the union between their country and Scotland. The story of James' wooing of such a lady, be it fact or fiction, is told in *The Kingis Quair*. He had been imprisoned for a time at Windsor, and it is not impossible that one May morning he looked from a tower window there to see and fall in love with his future queen, Joan

Beaufort, walking in the garden below. However, that he wrote a poem describing the event is highly problematical. Neither James' poetic canon nor even the fact of his ever having been a poet has yet been established. Walter Bower and Æneas Sylvius, both of whom describe the king from personal observation, do not speak of him as a poet. John Major, writing in the century following the king's death, says that James, "In vernacula lingua artificiosissimus compositor: cuius codices plurimi & cantilenae . . . ." Among them, "Artificiosum libellum de Regina dum captivus erat composuit, antequam eam in coniugem duceret; & aliam artificiosam cantilenam eiusdem. *Yas sen* & c. & iucundum artificiosumque illum cantum: *at beltayn* & etc. quem alii de Dalketh & Gargeil, mutare studuerunt . . ." *Yas sen* and *At Beltayn* have been tentatively identified as poems in MS Pepys 2553, respectively the anonymous *Sang on Absence,* which contains "Yas" in its first line, and *Peblis to the Play,* which begins "At Beltane quhen ilk bodie bownis." Although such resemblance in wording would seem too meager to be accepted as evidence in identifying the poems cited by Major, and the meter and style of *Peblis* are obviously later than the period of James I, a number of literary historians have attributed not only *Peblis* and *Sang on Absence* to James I, but *Christis Kirk* as well on the basis of its similarity in style, tone, meter, language, and content to *Peblis* and of its being signed "Quod James I" in MS National Library Scotland 1.1.6. But MS Pepys 2553, which dates from the same period as MS National Library Scotland 1.1.6 and also contains *Christis Kirk,* does not assign it to the king; nor does the poem fit the description of any of those which Major specifically assigned him. Skeat dated *Christis Kirk* no earlier than the end of the fifteenth or beginning of the sixteenth century, probably some time during the reign of James V to whom the poem's first three editors attributed it. Thus even if we accept the relatively late testimony of John Major that James I wrote poetry, we cannot say conclusively that any of what might be considered the king's minor works, the "aliam artificiosam cantilenam eiusdem . . . & iucundum artificiosumque," have survived. There is little question, however, that the "artificiosum libellum de Regina dum captivus erat composuit," also listed by Major, is *The Kingis Quair,* whether or not written by James.

THE KINGIS QUAIR [1]. 197 rime royal stanzas in the Northern dialect with an admixture of Midland and Southern forms.

One midnight the poet, unable to sleep, reads the *Consolation of Philosophy*, muses upon his own past fortune, then roused by the matin bell, which seems to say "tell on what befell you," begins to write. In March when he was about ten, on the advice of those who had care of him, the poet passed out of his country by sea, was captured and imprisoned in enemy country for eighteen years. Continually he lamented, questioning his evil fortune, until one morning he heard nightingales singing hymns of praise to love, wondered about its nature, and prayed to be taken into love's service. At that moment he saw beneath his prison tower a beautiful, richly-clad lady with whom he promptly fell in love. He chided the silent nightingale, bidding it sing for his lady, wondering how and whether to attract her attention; and when the lady sang, directed a prayer for mercy to her, commanding his heart to follow. But then the lady departed, leaving the poet to bewail his helpless pain alone. Since she had gone, all good for him was changed to evil.

Throughout the day he lamented, then at night in a vision was taken on an aerial journey to the courts of Venus and Minerva, who instructed him further in the nature of true love. Both deities touched upon the question of Fortune's rule, Venus pointing out that though she had power over love, eternal ordinance bound her influence to that of other planets; thus while she could foresee events, she could not direct them alone. By other's influence the poet had been imprisoned, and although she would in time be benevolent to him, she could not until a certain period had passed and he had won his lady's grace by true service. Since he needed the help of other goddesses, Venus sent him to Minerva with Good Hope as guide, instructing the lover to chide men for their neglect of her when he returned to earth. Minerva cautioned that she would aid the poet only if his love proved worthy, he followed good rather than evil love, and grounded his heart firmly in God's law. When the dreamer declared the honorableness and enduring fidelity of his love, Minerva took compassion upon him, promised to pray Fortune to favor him, then explained something of the workings of Fortune, predestination, and necessity, warning that whereas he who knew what was to come was less subject to Fortune's rule, the dreamer, being weak in wit and learning, was more tied to her and should pray to her for aid.

Passing then down a light beam he crossed a flowering plain filled with animals, and came at last to the court of Fortune, at her feet the wheel upon which folk swarmed to climb, rise, and fall; beneath, a deep pit from which none ever returned. To his plea for aid in love, Fortune replied that he was too feeble from imprisonment, sadness, and oppressed youth to mount her wheel alone, and bidding him learn to climb and from the fate of others see that the nature of the wheel was to bring one from high to low, took him by the ear so earnestly that he woke.

The poet muses over man's spirit, restless until it return whence it came, troubled by the flesh sleeping or waking, as was his own spirit which had been vexed in the dream but was twenty times more troubled on waking, with only dreams to gladden him. If his had been a vision of the future sent by the gods for comfort, he humbly asked for more tokens; and suddenly a turtle dove came bearing a message written in gold that he was to rejoice, for in heaven his cure had been decreed. From that time the pain passed away, and the poet came to bliss with his lady.

Should any wonder, "Why write all this upon so small a subject," he answers "Who, having passed from hell to heaven, would say just one thanks?" What greater pleasure is there than to pass to largess from pain through love? He prays Venus to help lovers of diverse kind, God to bless each being and thing that aided his love, his poor, bare treatise to seek readers' patience with and remedying of its faults and acceptance because of their good will. Thus ends the influence exerted from heaven where the power of government is committed by God, Who many a year ago has written our life. The poet recommends his book to the hymns of his masters, Gower and Chaucer, and their souls to heaven.

This dream vision embodies most of the genre's conventions, showing markedly the influence of Chaucer on meter, wording, situation, and of Boethius on action and thought. The central section in particular seems to draw upon Lydgate's *Temple of Glass*. The poem's tone is more that of a sermon than of an allegory of love; it contains no characterization to speak of and the story line is slight, being designed principally to serve the ends of moral allegory. The greatest difficulties in interpretation have arisen from an apparent inconsistency between the Boethian musings on the nature of Fortune and God's governance, and the personal love story. However, recent critics have to some extent resolved this inconsistency by interpreting the poem as an allegory of the acceptance of and reconciliation to divine order through the power of love, rather than as an autobiographical account of courtship and marriage. The work's poetic high points, notably descriptions of garden and flowering plain, of singing birds, lovely lady, and the restless state of man's spirit, "ay flikering to and fro," have been widely praised. But on the whole, had *The Kingis Quair* never been associated with James I, it would doubtless have fared better than many other anonymous poems, *The Quair of Jelousy* or *The Court of Love,* for instance, to which it is akin, but scarcely better or worse than the dream visions of Lydgate.

There is serious question as to James' authorship, the most telling evidence against it being the failure of people whom one might expect to acknowledge the king's poetic ability and to praise him for this poem to do so. Neither Walter Bower nor Æneas Sylvius mentions *The Kingis Quair*. William Dunbar, although dependent upon the patronage of one of James' descendants, does not include the king in his roll call of dead "makars" in *Lament for the Makaris,* [29] below. David Lindsay names eight Scots poets in *The Testament of the Papyngo,* but not James I. James VI discusses Scottish poems at length in his *Reulis and Cautelis,* but none by his own forebear.

The evidence for James I's authorship consists of the poem's auto-biographical content, its title and colophon in the unique manuscript, Bodleian 3354, and John Major's attribution to the king of a poem about his queen. However, an autobiographical pose may be assumed by any poet for the creation of any story. The evidence of MS Bodleian 3354 cannot be accepted as conclusive for it was compiled about 1490, thus not by anyone who could have vouched personally for James' authorship; and of the twelve poems which it contains one has an illegible signature, five are correctly, five incorrectly attributed to Chaucer, and *The Kingis Quair* to James. If half of the manuscript's attributions which can be verified are wrong, those which cannot be verified are, of course, open to question. Finally, it is impossible to evaluate Major's testimony accurately since its source is unknown. He may well have been simply drawing upon the Bodleian 3354. Thus although from the time of Major's history in the early sixteenth century until the last decade most commentators have attributed *The Kingis Quair* to James I, there was never much reason to do so, and few critics now accept the poem as James' personal account of his wooing of Joan.

GOOD COUNSEL [2]. Two rime royal stanzas with refrain in one version, three stanzas in other versions.

A moral exhortation, modeled on Chaucer's *Truth*, advising the reader to follow virtue and truth; avoid pride remembering that life is short; restrain both tongue and lust; love God putting trust and faith in Him; and be repaid multifold.

The authorship of the poem is unknown. It has been attributed to James I only on the grounds that its style is assertedly similar to that of *The Kingis Quair* and its dialect is Northern.

2. HENRYSON

The only facts definitely known about Robert Henryson are that he was a poet who lived in Dunfermline and died before the end of 1508. In *Lament for the Makaris*, [29] below, printed in 1508, Dunbar says that death, "In Dunfermlyne . . . hes done roune / With Maister Robert

Henrisoun." Douglas, commenting upon the term "Muse" in *Eneados,*
[19] below, speaks of "Mastir Robert Hendirson," who has something of
the nine Muses in "New Orpheus." Lindsay in *The Testament of the
Papyngo* groups Henryson with other poets who, "Thocht thay be deed,
thar libells bene levand, / Quhilk to reheirs makeith redaris to rejoise."
In the 1570, 1571, and 1621 editions of *The Fables,* [3] below, and in the
1593 and 1663 editions of *The Testament of Cresseid,* [4] below, Henryson is called a schoolmaster of Dunfermline; and from his *Abbay Walk,*
[11] below, it has been surmised that he taught in the Grammar and Song
School of the Benedictine Abbey at Dunfermline. It has also been suggested that he spent his life in the general area of Dunfermline because
of the reference to "fra lawdian to lundin" in *Sum Practysis of Medecyne,*
[15] below, and to "master Robert hendersonnis Dreme On fut by forth,"
a poem listed in the Asloan MS table of contents but now lost. Since,
however, the first reference may have been simply a conventional phrase
indicating comprehensiveness, like Chaucer's "Hulle to Cartage" or
"Dover unto Ware," and the second could have been to a person other
than the poet, neither tells us anything definite about his movements. Sir
Francis Kynaston relates a highly entertaining story about the manner of
his dying; but as Kynaston was writing at least 130 years after Henryson's
death and the source of the story is unknown, it cannot be accepted as
authoritative. David Laing believed the poet to have been the "vir
Magister Robertus Henrisone in Artibus Licentiatus et in Decretis Bach-
alarius" admitted as a member of the University of Glasgow in September 1462; George Chalmers, that he was the "Magister Robertus Henrison
notarius publicus" named in the Chartulary of Dunfermline in 1477–78
as a witness. He could have been either or both; but many "Henrysons,"
even many "Robert Henrysons," appear in the public records of fifteenth-
century Scotland, and there seems no way of knowing which if any of
them is the poet. When we look at the poems themselves, their author
emerges as a good pastor, moral, of a markedly didactic turn, with an
abundant store of common sense, humor, wit, and folk wisdom; a university man, trained in rhetoric, logic, music, astrology, etc., well read in
Aristotle, Boethius, the church fathers, the Vulgate and its commentaries.
On the basis of evidence in his poetry it has been suggested that Henry-

son studied either medicine or law—possibly at Bologna—or both; but the evidence cited is by no means conclusive.

The titles and order of the poems adopted here are those of the PSTS edition.

THE FABLES [3]. A prologue and thirteen tales each with a moralitas, in rime royal except for the moralitas to *The Uponlandis Mous and the Burges Mous* which is in eight-line stanzas, ababbcbc, and three similar stanzas in the moralitas to *The Paddock and the Mous*.

(a) *Prolog* (in MS National Library Scotland 1.1.6 placed between *The Parliament of fourfuttit Beistis* and *The Cok and the Iasp*): nine stanzas.

> Though old fables are not all grounded upon truth, they are pleasant to hear and teach a moral lesson effectively by embodying it in a poetic fiction. Just so the shell holds fruit, and the mind benefits from a mixture of earnestness and merriment. The poet translates from Aesop at the request of an anonymous lord, and apologizing for his homely language and rude terms prays the audience to amend his work's deficiencies. Aesop tells how beasts spoke, understood, disputed, proposed syllogisms, drew conclusions. No marvel it is if a man who loves carnality so much that shame cannot restrain him is like a beast. By habit, lust and appetite become so rooted in men's minds that they are transformed into beasts. Aesop wrote in gay meter and figurative language to avoid the disdain of high and low, and began with the tale of a cock and a stone.

Despite Henryson's reference to translating, his work is by no means a direct translation of any of his various sources. The prologue and seven of the fables are based upon the *Romulus* of Gualterus Anglicus from whom Henryson quotes a line and borrows the images—flower and fruit, the nut's hard shell and sweet kernel—representative of moral poetry. His apology for unpolished language and reference to Aesop as poet laureate have been cited as evidence of Lydgate's influence. But such apologies were commonplace; and the poet laureate reference may not, in fact, be Henryson's since it does not appear in the best text of *The Fables*, MS National Library Scotland 1.1.6. The lord who requested the poem has never been identified, and it has been suggested that Henryson conjured up a hypothetical patron hoping thus either to procure a real one or to lend his work an air of greater objectivity.

(b) *The Cok and the Iasp*: fourteen stanzas.

A cock, merry, confident, but poor, seeking his dinner finds a jewel on a dungheap, swept out perhaps by some careless maid. He muses on the fact that he should find this precious stone, fit for a king, but useless to him who loves food far better; and bidding it seek a more suitable setting, leaves the jewel upon the ground. It has color like fire and sky, power to make a man strong, victorious, safe, likely to succeed, and unafraid of fire or water. Moralitas: The jewel betokens virtuous prudence and cunning, which make men rule honorably, happy, and strong to conquer all vice. The cock is like a fool who scorns knowledge, precious beyond price, as a sow does jewels. The man who spends his life seeking knowledge needs nothing more; but now the jewel is lost; we value only riches. To speak of this matter is vain. Let who will seek the jewel.

The interpretation actually begins at line 120 with description of the jasp's properties; and there in MS National Library Scotland 1.1.6, although not in other early texts, the "Taill" proper ends and the Moralitas begins. Various critics have attempted to reconcile the cock's seemingly sympathetic portrayal with the poet's derogatory interpretation of him. The most plausible suggestion to date is that he is the figurative embodiment of sensuous man who, having permitted himself to descend to the level of beasts, is incapable of pursuing and utilizing true wisdom rather than succumbing to appetite. The bird in the "Taill" acting naturally on his sub-human level is not culpable; while the same figure in the Moralitas as a representative of bestial man is.

   (c) *The Uponlandis Mous and the Burges Mous*: twenty-eight stanzas in Charteris *The Morall Fabillis*, twenty-nine in other texts.

Once a town mouse who lives the life of a guild brother, a burgess, free of toll, going where she will among the cheese and meal, visits her sister, a country mouse who lives the solitary, hard life of an outlaw. The town mouse scorns the plain fare and lodging most generously offered, and invites the country mouse to town. There they find rich food enough, without grace wash and go to dinner. But the country mouse, frightened into a faint by the steward, then tormented by the cat, at last defies all such feasts and returns to her simple, but warm, well-stocked, quiet home. She visits her sister no more. Moralitas: Joy is ever mingled with adversity and none are free of trouble, especially those who climb highest and are not content with little. Blessed be the simple, fearless life, the sober quiet feast. Let wanton, gluttonous man beware, for the cat may come, and feast and royalty with dread avail nothing. The best life is that of security, honesty, and blitheness with small possession.

One of the fables most frequently praised for the richness of its information about life in Henryson's day. One stanza and the burden of the Moralitas suggest Lydgate's influence; while Henryson's poem in turn seems to have influenced *The Mean and Sure Estate* of Thomas Wyatt.

(d) *Schir Chantecleir and the Foxe*: thirty stanzas in Harley 3865, thirty-one in other texts.

Though beasts are irrational each has its characteristics—the bear strength, the lion wildness, etc.—unknown to man, so infinite, so diverse that the poet cannot write of them. A widow who lives by spinning and her flock of chickens once suffered from a poultry-stealing fox. One dawn this hungry Lawrence greets the cock of the flock; tells in highly ambiguous terms of his devotion to Chantecleir's father, which should lead the son to trust him; and praises Chantecleir's appearance, although suggesting that he scarcely equals his father, who had excelled in crowing as he winked and turned about. Filled with vainglory, Chantecleir crows, winks, and the fox snatches him away, leaving the hens to hold a disputation. Pertok first laments their loss as a widow should, then agrees with Sprutok that Chantecleir was a most unsatisfactory husband; Toppok intones that his fate is heavenly vengeance for sin. Here the widow sets dogs after Lawrence, whom Chantecleir advises to tell the dogs that they two are friends. At the fox's first cry the cock breaks loose and spurning all further overtures from his enemy, flies away to the widow's barn. Moralitas: This cock represents foolish men, proud of their kin; the fox, dangerous, wicked flatterers who delight in lying. Vainglory and flattery are venomous; let good folk flee them.

The fable's ultimate source appears to be the *Roman de Renart,* while certain details, such as names of the fox, hens, dogs, derive from popular tradition. Its immediate source is *"The Nun's Priest's Tale,"* which it resembles in action, mock heroic treatment, and the objects of its satire: pride and flattery. There is also a noticeable resemblance between Sprutok and the Wife of Bath. "Reylock" (robbery), which occurs in line 90 of the National Library Scotland 1.1.6 text, has been identified as a legal term and taken as evidence of Henryson's legal training. For more extensive evidence, cf. *The Scheip and the Doig, Of the Foxe that begylit the Uolf in the Schadow of the Mone,* and *Of the Uolf and the Lamb.*

(e) *How this foirsaid Tod maid his Confessioun to Freir Wolf Waitskaith*: twenty-six stanzas.

At night the fox reads in the stars his future, one mingled with mischief unless he amend, determines to seek a confessor and be shriven. Seeing Friar Wolf Waitskaith, he flatters the worthy doctor of divinity for his holiness until, pleased by such a proper attitude, the wolf agrees to hear Lawrence's confession. But the would-be penitent is not contrite: hens and lambs being so honey-sweet he repents only that he has slain so few; ashamed to beg, unable to work, yet pretending to gentle estate, how can he live save by theft? Lacking then, says the Wolf, two points of perfect confession, will he accept the third (Satisfactio)? For the sake of his soul the fox will forgo flesh till Easter, if he may eat puddings, blood, head, feet, or paunches twice a week. But then, prevented from fishing by wild water and lack of equipment, he drowns a kid, rechristening it "Sir Salmon" eats his fill of new-made fish, and basks his belly in the sun. As he muses that an arrow therein would be most fitting, Lawrence is pinned to the ground by an arrow from the kid's owner, and dying sadly reflects that no one may speak a word in play nowadays but it is taken in earnest. His skin is taken by the goatherd in recompense for the kid. Moralitas: The fate of the tod should exhort folk to amend, repent sincerely, resist sensuality, and since all must die, beware the sudden shot, examine their conscience, obey God, and so pass to endless bliss.

A satire on the laxness of the contemporary clergy. Henryson's sources have been identified as *De Lupo et Mutone* in the *Romulus* of Gualterus, and Caxton's *History of Reynard the Fox* from which apparently came the name and ecclesiastical role of Wolf Waitskaith. There has been some discussion as to which two points of confession the fox lacks, most critics agreeing that they are *contritio* and *confessio* of the Catholic sacrament of penance.

(f) *Of the Sone and Air of the foirsaid Foxe, callit Father-wer: alswa the Parliament of fourfuttit Beistis haldin be the Lyoun*: forty-eight stanzas in National Library Scotland 1.1.6, fifty in other versions.

Lawrence had a bastard son called "Father War" (worse) appropriately, since from evil comes worse, from worse worst of all. Naturally false as were his forebears, this fox thanked God for the death of his father, whose territory he can now hunt, throws the corpse into a peat-hole, then sees a unicorn pursuivant bound up to summon all beasts to a parliament. Next morning at King Lion's command, the animals, minotaur, werewolf, lynx, tiger, etc., gather; the king declares that he will defend and be merciful to those who submit, will rend those who do not; and the court is called into session. Fearful that this parliament is designed to ruin misdoers like himself, the fox tries to hide, but is dispatched with the wolf to summon an absent mare. She is in contempt of law, the fox tells her, and must come to the king. But the mare refusing, cites an exemption written on the bottom of her hoof, and kicks off the crown of the wolf's head when he attempts to read it. On their homeward journey the fox fetching water to wash the wolf's bloody head kills a lamb. All the parliament laugh at the wolf—his red cap proves that "the greatest clerks are not the wisest men." But their merriment is interrupted by the sorrowful ewe, come to ask justice for her slain lamb; and the fox, tried and convicted of murder, is shriven by Doctor Wolf, then hanged by Executioner Ape. Moralitas: The lion is the world to whom all bow, thinking to prosper; the mare, good men withdrawn from the world, seeking only to please God; the wolf, the sensuality of worshipping worldly vanity; the hoof, remembrance of death by which we break sensuality's head and flee lust; the fox, temptation, ever ready to trap us but failing if we see sensuality nearly slain and death at hand. God defend us from pain and peril and help us all to heaven.

The fable considered most indebted to Caxton's *Reynard*. However, the lion's pronouncement, "The greatest clerks are not the wisest men," cited as evidence of this indebtedness, is a proverb which appears not only in Caxton and Henryson but almost verbatim in Chaucer's *Reeve's Tale*; the animals' description is clearly influenced both by terms of heraldry and by the bestiaries; and their cataloguing was a medieval common-place (cf. *The Kingis Quair*, [1] above, *The Palice of Honour*, [20] below, and Chaucer's *Parliament of Fowls*). The meaning of certain terms in that catalogue, "sparth," "bowranban," etc., has been debated at length but as yet inconclusively. The parliament of animals has been taken to represent one of James III's, on the somewhat tenuous grounds of the precision with which it is assembled.

(g) *The Scheip and the Doig*: twenty-five stanzas.

A poor dog, to get bread, calls a sheep before a consistory court corrupt in every way: judge a fradulent wolf; sumnor, Corbie ravin, who picks out sheep's eyes; clerk of the court, the fox; dog's advocates, the kite and vulture who are agreed on procuring a sentence, however false, against the sheep. But though the sheep objects to the judge, the time—sundown in vacation, and the remote place where the court is held as being suspect and unlawful, after pouring over legal volumes, the arbiters, bear and badger, say he must stand trial. Despite his denial of wrongfully withholding bread from the dog the sheep is convicted against good faith, law, and conscience, forced to sell his wool to recompense the dog, and returns naked to the field. Moralitas: This sheep represents the oppressed commons; the wolf, a sheriff who buys a forfeit from the king, then indicts poor innocent men who are slain unless they settle with the judge; the raven, a coroner who gets bribes by false indictments. Hearing the sheep ask in the midst of winter why God does not see his undeserved misery, the poet compares his state to man's. Covetousness has ruined loyalty and law; few or none execute justice and thus the poor man is overthrown—if the judge knows the truth, for might he lets right fail. Does God not see the world overturned, the poor stripped, the lord unblamed? Simony is unpunished; the successful usurer happy; generosity slain; pity gone. Why does God suffer it? For our sins He sends hunger, war, pestilence. Oppressed on earth we can only pray for rest in heaven.

One of Henryson's most direct attacks on contemporary corruption, this fable satirizes the miscarriage of justice in both ecclesiastical and civil courts and has been cited as evidence of the poet's possible training in law (cf. also *Of the Foxe that begylit the Uolf in the Schadow of the Mone* and *Of the Uolf and the Lamb*). The outspoken remonstrance against divinely countenanced but unjust human suffering reflects sentiments implicit in both *The Testament of Cresseid* [4] and *Orpheus and Eurydice* [5] (cf. also *Ane Prayer for the Pest* [17]).

(h) *The Lyoun and the Mous*: forty-three stanzas.

In June the poet dreams that Aesop, who says he is a native of Rome and studied law there, at his request tells this moral fable. Once a flock of mice danced to and fro over a sleeping lion until he woke, seized the head mouse, and demanded if the caitiff wretch did not know that he ruled all beasts? Yes, she knew; but she had mistaken the king who lay so low; and she pleaded, consider her poverty, his magnificence. Mere negligence should be forgiven, and the mice would not have danced upon the lion had they not thought him dead. And if he had been dead, rejoined the lion, they should have respected his image; the mouse shall hang. But begging for the mercy without which justice is mere cruelty, the mouse pointed out that the conquest of a thousand mice would bring little worship to a lion, that the meat of a mouse would be a tainted meal for him, and that perchance she might help the king—little men have rescued lords. Persuaded, the lion released her. Later the lion, trapped in a net by hunters, was rescued by the mouse who with her fellows cut the ropes that bound him. Because he had shown pity, the lion was again safe and free. Moralitas: As Aesop explains, the lion is the ruler who should be wakeful but sleeps in lust; the forest, the prosperous world, sure to fade; mice, the wanton, unwise commons who, seeing their ruler fail to do justice, do not know, have awe of, or fear to rebel against him. From this fable lords may learn to be merciful, for a little man often repays harshness or grace. Fortune may destroy a lustful lord and blind unjust men till they fail to provide against peril. The hunters sought redress; for injured men remember, as king and lord will understand. Aesop beseeches all men to pray that treason be exiled, justice reign, and lords keep faith with their king, then vanishes; and the poet turns homeward.

Despite its conventional dream framework this fable has particularly appealing and realistic characterization. Efforts have been made to link the characters with historical figures, the lion being identified variously as Robert III, James I, or James III, the hunters as nobles who once imprisoned James III. The vagueness of Henryson's references, perhaps deliberately assumed for his own protection, would seem to render any attempt at such definite identification futile; although the last stanza, with its plea regarding conditions in "this country," seems clearly enough to refer to the poet's own day.

(i) *The Preiching of the Swallow*: forty-seven stanzas.

The poet praises God's omnipotent wisdom, pointing out that man, oppressed by sensuality and fantasy, has limited understanding and should not seek the secrets of the Trinity, but rely upon the goodness, beauty, wisdom, and benignity of God as evidenced in His creations. In spring the poet sees men ditching, plowing, sowing seed, and hears a swallow advise a flock of birds to eat the seed before it can grow into flax for nets—prudence makes a man consider the end and thus better avoid peril. But all the birds scorn the swallow. In June she urges them to pull up the growing flax while it is yet small, warning that its owner, a fowler, has slain many of their kin. But the birds protest that the flax will give them food and refuse to think of any possible peril. So the flax ripens; the fowler harvests and prepares it; his wife spins it into thread and he makes his nets. With winter he sets them out; and the birds thinking the chaff with which they are concealed is corn, and despite the swallow's loud warnings, busily scrape in the chaff, are caught and brutally slaughtered. The swallow muses: thus it often happens to those who will not be counseled. Thrice the birds were warned; now they are dead. And off she flies to be seen no more. Moralitas: The flax sower is the fiend, ever sowing wicked thoughts in man's soul. When the soul consents to delectation, thought sprouts in sin and ripens, reason is blinded, lust grows, the fiend weaves his nets and hides them under the chaff of lust and vain prosperity. The birds are wretches scraping in vain pleasure, greedy to gather goods worthless as chaff; the swallow, a preacher exhorting folk to beware of the fiend. To perceive his nets and chaff, beware in greatest prosperity, for nothing in this world lasts and no man knows after death whither he goes. While alive let us pray that we leave sin, have peace, charity, love, and reach the bliss of heaven.

The most explicitly homiletic of the fables. The description of the seasons is reminiscent of those in *Sir Gawain and the Green Knight* and Douglas' Prolougs 7 and 12, *Eneados*, [19] below. The detailed description of the processing of flax has been taken as evidence of Henryson's firsthand acquaintance with the industry. Late fifteenth-century records indicate that during the poet's lifetime there were weavers in Dunfermline, and their raw material may indeed have been grown and processed in the vicinity.

(j) *Of the Uolf that gat the Nekhering throw the Wrinkis of the Foxe that begylit the Cadgear*: forty stanzas.

A wolf forces an unwilling fox, Lawrence, to become his steward. Seeing a cadger approach with a creel full of herring, the fox circles ahead of the man; then stretched out in the road plays dead and the delighted cadger, thinking to make mittens from his skin, swings him up on the creel. After Lawrence lets the fish fall out to be gathered up by the wolf, the cadger, discovering his loss, shouts to the escaping fox that he shall have a nekherring (blow on the neck) and cuts a stout stick. This "nek-herring," Lawrence explains to the admiring, greedy wolf, is a fish so huge he had been unable to heave it out of the creel, but the wolf could get it in the same way as he himself had gotten all the others. So the wolf stretches himself in the road and the cadger, not to be fooled twice, beats him blind while the laughing fox takes all the fish. He has betrayed both his master and the man; one runs with blood, the other has lost his herring. Moralitas: The fox is the world; the wolf, man; the cadger, death. The world makes man forget death. Gold, the herring, causes him to put his head in peril and blinds avaricious men, making them forget that the cadger strikes, whatever their state. Let mighty men remember the nekherring.

Of Henryson's fables this is perhaps second only to *The Uponlandis Mous and the Burges Mous* in popularity, in large part because of its vivid, sensuous description and the humor which derives from sensitive perception of human nature and its depiction in animal form. There has been some discussion of Henryson's source, which is now generally accepted as having been the *Roman de Renart*, perhaps with influence from Caxton's *Reynard* and European oral tradition.

(k) *Of the Foxe that begylit the Uolf in the Schadow of the Mone*: thirty-two stanzas.

A plowman's furrow is so ruined by his skittish team of oxen that he angrily vows to give them to the wolf, who together with a fox overhears the vow. That evening the wolf demands the oxen; but the plowman protests that he had spoken in anger and not being a king may gainsay his words; and the disputants agree to let the fox decide between them. First the fox goes to the farmer, who promises him a bribe of fat hens; then to the wolf, who reluctantly agrees to relinquish his claim in exchange for a big, beautiful, summer cheese. After showing the wolf the moon's reflection, which he claims is the cheese, in a well, the fox rides down in one of two buckets ostensibly to bring up this magnificent prize. But then he calls that its weight is so great he needs help in raising the cheese, worthy of a king. Worthy, then, says the wolf, for me; and into the other bucket he leaps. As his weight carries the wolf down, the fox up, the fox explains that it is ever thus with Fortune: one comes up, the other goes down; and he leaves the wolf in the well. Moralitas: The wolf is like a wicked oppressor picking every possible quarrel with the poor; the fox, the fiend urging men into evil; the plowman, a godly man whom the fiend tempts; the hens, good works proceeding from faith which thwart the fiend; the woods haunted by the wolf, riches sought by all men, the devil's net; the cheese, covetousness which draws men down to hell. Christ keep all men from that wicked well.

While the plowman's thoughtless consigning of his team to the wolf and its consequences are somewhat similar to actions in Chaucer's *Friar's Tale*, the main sources of this fable appear to be the *Roman de Renart*, Caxton's *Aesop*, and his *Reynard*.

(l) *Of the Uolf and the Uedder*: twenty-three stanzas.

A faithful dog who diligently guarded his master's sheep dies, and the shepherd, despairing, thinks to give up his unprotected flock until a wether suggests that he be sewn into the dog's skin and replace him. The shepherd agrees and for a time the ruse succeeds, the disguised wether chasing away all would-be predators. At last, however, a desperately hungry wolf runs off with a lamb and is so fiercely pursued by the wether that he befouls the ground from fear. But when his disguise is torn away by briars, the wether is recognized by the wolf, who, outraged, breaks his neck. Moralitas: Rich array causes poor men to be presumptuous, to counterfeit lords and fail in deference to their betters. Some have such good fortune that they disparage lords and forget their own lineage, though none knows how long that fortune may last. Let all men know themselves and to whom they should defer, neither oppose their superior nor climb so high they fall.

The principal source here has been identified as Caxton's *Aesop* on the grounds that, among the earlier versions of the story, Caxton's alone contains certain details which are also found in Henryson's fable.

(m) *Of the Uolf and the Lamb*: twenty-three stanzas.

A wolf drinking upstream from a lamb accuses him of defiling the water. But the lamb points out that a stream cannot run backward; nor have his lips ever touched a thing contagious. Well then, says the wolf, he must pay for the misdeeds of his father, who had tried to poison the wolf. Though the lamb cites scripture—each man should pay for his own deeds, and pleads for due process of law, the wolf will take vengeance on the child for the father's offense. Rejecting reason and mercy, asserting the rule of wrong, he kills and eats the lamb. Moralitas: The lamb signifies poor people, their life half purgatory, trying to win an honest living; the wolf, false extortioners such as corrupt lawyers and powerful landowners who oppress the poor in various ways. These wicked men should fear God's righteous wrath, remembering that for their oppression they shall suffer. God keep the innocent lamb from the wolf, let wrongful men be punished, save the king, and give him heart and hand to banish all such wolves.

This fable has been cited as evidence of Henryson's familiarity with contemporary legal practises (cf. *The Scheip and the Doig*, which contains a similar protest against oppression of the poor). It has been suggested that the concluding prayer is for Scotland's relief from the troubles which beset her during the reign of James III. But the prayer is conventional and does not contain sufficient enough or precise enough detail to place it in any given period.

(n) *Of the Paddok and the Mous:* twenty-six stanzas plus one line in Charteris, *The Morall Fabillis*; twenty-eight stanzas in other versions.

A mouse coming to a river cries for help to reach a field of grain on the other side, and a paddock offers to bring her across. Although the mouse distrusts the paddock's ugliness—clerks say a crooked will goes with a crooked physiognomy, the paddock points out that fair things are often false; one should not judge a man by his face; God, not she, caused her beauty; and she swears to ferry the mouse over safely. With their legs bound together, the two leap in; but half way across, the paddock tries to drown the mouse. They struggle, plunging up and down, until a kite carries them ashore, devours both, and flies away. Moralitas: A wicked mind and fair, sly words surpass pestilence. Do not trust fair speakers too quickly, or join with a crooked, feigned companion, or bind yourself in such a way that you can protect neither life nor liberty. The paddock is man's body; the mouse his soul; the two bound together till death breaks the thread of life. The water is the world wherein the soul, pressing up and striving to reach the shore of heaven beyond, struggles with the body, pressing down because of lust. The kite is death. Since you know not when he comes, be ready and trust in Christ. If any ask for more of this fable, let the friars make an exemplum.

Here Henryson has greatly expanded the material of his source, apparently Gualterus rather than Caxton, to make the "Taill" accord particularly well with its Moralitas.

In similar fashion throughout *The Fables* Henryson expands by adding irony, literary commonplaces, and much detail from contemporary life. Each tale is an exemplum whose lesson may be driven home in a variety of ways: by an introductory didactic statement, interspersed stanzas of moralizing, or proverbs, as well as by the concluding moralitas. The moralitas does not in every case seem applicable to the tale it accompanies, a fact which has occasioned numerous attempts to interpret the more seemingly inconsistent pairs in such a way as to bring them into accord (cf. especially criticism of *The Cok and the Iasp*). *The Fables* as a whole make an effective attack on abuses both timeless and contemporary with Henryson. Their reflection of life in fifteenth-century Scotland has been commented upon at length, while rather surprisingly their intrinsic literary merit has not. They often achieve realism as a result of the poet's intimate knowledge of and ability to delineate accurately the haunts and actions of animals, and to create well-rounded characters and vivid pictures. They have, moreover, pervasive humor which derives not only from the assigning of human attributes to beasts, but from the presentation of characters whose lofty sentiments contrast startlingly with their true natures, whose self delusion brings disaster, or who make candid, rueful self appraisals. They have a wide variety of tone—pathos, brutality, cynicism, grim absurdity, and irony created by interjections of the narrator, by misapplied honorifics and proverbs, extravagant misinterpretations, inappropriate reactions (cf. the song of Pertok, "Was never widow so gay," with which she greets the news of her husband's impending death), and by the drama of fate all too clearly foreseen by the reader but hidden from the animal actor.

THE TESTAMENT OF CRESSEID [4]. Seventy-nine rime royal stanzas and a complaint of seven nine-line stanzas, aabaabbab.

A sorrowful season should match a sorrowful tale, and on a bitter cold night in Lent the poet began to write this tragedy. He had thought to ask Venus to make his faded heart green again, but cold drove him back to the fire where to shorten the night he read Chaucer's account of Cresseid's forsaking Troilus. Who knows if all that Chaucer wrote was true? He himself does not know if the tale he read in another book of Cresseid's wretched end be true. This second book tells how Diomede satiated with Cresseid turns her out—some men say she became a prostitute; but her father, Calchas, keeper of the temple of Venus and Cupid, welcomes her. One feast day while others sacrifice to the gods, Cresseid blames them for the loss of her lovers, and falling into a swoon sees the planets who guide all created things appear before Cupid. He explains that Cresseid has shamefully blasphemed against her own gods, blaming Venus and himself for the sad results of her own lechery, and must be punished. Saturn and Cynthia, highest and lowest of the planets, mete out the punishment: Cresseid shall henceforth suffer pain and incurable sickness, be abominable to lovers, lose all beauty, mirth, moisture, heat, and riches, be afflicted with leprosy and the life and death of a beggar. Waking from the vision Cresseid sees her face in a glass and weeps. In her can be seen what it means to anger the gods. With her father she mourns, then secretly enters a leper house and there laments her loss of pleasure, renown, and beauty, cautioning other ladies to learn from her to be prepared for similar loss. A leper admonishes Cresseid to follow the law of the lepers, and she goes forth with them as a beggar. Returning victorious from battle, Troilus rides by. He does not recognize Cresseid; yet the sight of her brings his lost love to mind for an image may be so deeply imprinted in the imagination as to make a different outward image seem similar to that already in the mind. Swept by a sudden fever of love, Troilus throws down rich alms for pity and remembrance. A leper identifies her benefactor, and Cresseid swoons, then lamenting her falsity and lechery, Troilus' truth, honor, and chasteness, admonishes lovers to beware whom they love, for few love truly in return. Let every man who finds a faithful lady praise her. Cresseid accuses only herself, then makes her testament, leaving body, cup, clapper, gold, etc. to their appropriate recipients. She dies; and a leper takes the ruby ring, once given her as a love token by Troilus, to him and tells of her death. The prince swoons, then says, "I can do no more; she was untrue, and for that woe is me"; and some say he built a tomb for her with an epitaph in gold telling of her end. Women, for whose instruction this ballad was made, be true, remembering Cresseid.

It is principally upon the basis of this poem that the term "Scots Chaucerian" has often been applied to Henryson. *The Testament of Cresseid* was attributed to Chaucer by early bibliographers largely as a result of its having been first printed at the end of *Troilus and Criseyde* and introduced as if it were a sixth book of that work. As a continuation of Chaucer's narrative, Henryson's does gain irony and poignance from contrast with the earlier poem and repetition of certain of its details. The Scots poet also draws here, though less extensively, upon other works of Chaucer—*The Legend of Good Women, Anelida and Arcite, The Canterbury Tales*, and, for his astrological depictions of the planet gods, *The Knight's Tale*, although he seems indebted as well to similar depictions in *The Assembly of the Gods* and Boccaccio's *De Genealogia Deorum*. The other book wherein Henryson purports to have found the story of

Cresseid's prostitution has been tentatively identified as the now lost source of the same story in *The Spektakle of Lufe*," a work translated, its author says, from Latin into the vulgar tongue in 1492. However it has been pointed out, first, that if there were once a Latin version of the story translated in 1492 its author could have borrowed information from *The Testament of Cresseid* rather than vice versa since the date of Henryson's poem is unknown; and second, that both the author of *The Spektakle of Lufe* and Henryson may have been citing a nonexistent source to give their fictions the weight of authority. At any rate, no such Latin account of Cresseid's tragic end has ever been found.

The description of her physical affliction may have been taken from life, for the details Henryson cites accord exactly with a type of leprosy prevalent in fifteenth-century Scotland, and apparently there was a lepers' house in Dunfermline. A few critics have, however, identified the disease as syphilis, which would be a more dramatically appropriate punishment for Cresseid's sins against love. As a whole, *The Testament of Cresseid* is almost a pastiche of literary conventions: the introductory seasonal description, offense against Venus and Cupid, vision and trial of the offender, complaint on the *ubi sunt* theme, testament, etc. The poem has been variously interpreted as a study of sin, punishment, and regeneration transcending courtly love; a study of blasphemy against courtly love; an exercise in irony, Cresseid being punished merely for errors of judgment in choosing sexual partners; as a questioning of theological order in which Henryson attacks divine justice untempered by mercy; as a medieval tragedy illustrating the turn of Fortune's wheel which brings the heroine from high to low; and more recently as an allegory depicting the interplay of appetite, moral virtue, and intellect.

ORPHEUS AND EURYDICE [5]. Fifty-two rime royal stanzas and five ten-line stanzas, aabaabbcbc, plus 218 lines of heroic couplets in MS National Library Scotland 1.1.6, 163 such lines in MS National Library Scotland 19.1.16.

To magnify the nobility and magnificence of a prince, extol his ancestors. It is unnatural for a nobleman not to follow the nobility of his progenitor. Thus Greek lords sought to follow their fathers, increasing the worship of their lineage, and sober

old men instructed the young to make them virtuous, each youth assuming the quality
of his forebears. One such lord, not surprisingly replete with excellences in view of
his ancestry, was Orpheus, grandson of Jupiter and Memoria, son of Phoebus and
Calliope, and nephew of the other eight muses. When Orpheus grew to be a fair,
famous man, Eurydice, queen of Thrace, married him, and their love increased daily.
But one May morning Aristaeus, a rough herdsman, tried to ravish Eurydice and in
fleeing she was stung by a serpent, then called away to Hades by Proserpina. Learning
of this and half mad with grief, Orpheus made a Complaint, attempting in vain to
gladden himself with music, taking leave of all delights and royal trappings, and
asking Phoebus for light, Jupiter for strength to find his lady. He sought her in the
heavens among the planets, then returned to earth, on the way learning the music
of the spheres. At last Orpheus came to the gate of hell, by means of his music slipped
past Cerberus, crossed the bridge of the Furies, and ended the torment of Ixion,
Tantalus, and Tytius. At the end of a dark street in hell's house he saw many a once
rich and powerful person suffering for his sins—Alexander, Antiochus, pope, cardinal,
etc. Then lower down in the company of Pluto and Proserpina, Orpheus recognized
his pale, deathlike Eurydice and played his harp until the gods of hell, weeping,
granted what he asked. With his wife he might pass out of hell, but must not once
look back. So Orpheus and Eurydice passed almost to the outward gate when, blinded
by great affection, he glanced back; and Pluto carried Eurydice away to hell again
leaving Orpheus to cry out against the hard law of love. Wherever love goes, perforce
the eye must turn. For a look he had lost his lady; and home he went, a woeful
widower. Moralitas: Phoebus, wisdom, and Calliope, eloquence, beget Orpheus, understanding or the intellectual part of the soul separate from sensuality. Eurydice, affection, flees Aristaeus, virtue; but then the serpent's sting, sin, poisons the soul and thus
affection dies, borne down to worldly lust, and wisdom vainly seeks her in heaven, the
contemplative life. Reason plays his harp, eloquence, subduing in turn Cerberus, sin
and foul delight; the furies, wicked thought, ill word, crooked deed; and the respective
causes of the suffering of Ixion, fleshly appetites, Tantalus, greed and covetousness,
and Tytius, pursuit of wrongful knowledge. Wisdom with his music turns us from
the false to the true. The street of hell is the blinding with ignorance of the spirit
which, tied to vain pleasance and temporality, stumbles after affection, going down
into despair through long indulgence in sin until reason calls a halt to desire and
appetite. When desire makes peace with reason and detesting sin seeks to rise to con-
templation, Orpheus has won Eurydice. But if a man look back, reason consents to
and finds delectation in lust, affection sinking backward to lust is slain, Eurydice is
lost and Orpheus, reason, becomes a widower.

Orpheus and Eurydice has some detail suggestive of the story as told
by Ovid and Virgil, particularly in its descriptions of the suffering of the
damned and the second loss of Eurydice; but it lacks the essential point
of the classical myth, the agony and irony of a man's daring hell for his
beloved, only to lose her again through ineluctable human weakness.
Certain of the poem's details are also drawn from medieval romance
versions; but again the effect is quite different, as for example from that
of *Sir Orfeo* (see I [86] in the first volume of this series). Henryson's poem
is in the tradition of Boethius' *Consolatione* and Nicholas Trivet's com-

mentary thereon, being a moral allegory which comprises a slender exemplum with minimum characterization and action, and a moralitas which constitutes one-third of the whole. The moralitas occasionally clashes with the narrative, most noticeably in depicting a would-be rapist as Virtue. Henryson's much-discussed interpretation of Aristaeus was not, however, original with him, but as has been pointed out dated from some 250 years earlier. Although the wording, particularly of the moralitas, is sometimes confusing, the lesson of the poem is clear enough and seems to encompass not only the allegory explicated in the moralitas, but in the narrative proper the same kind of veiled questioning of divine providence implicit in *The Testament of Cresseid* and *The Scheip and the Doig*. The poem's lyric passages have been highly praised, especially the Complaint of Orpheus, which is often excerpted and printed alone.

ROBENE AND MAKYNE [6]. Sixteen stanzas of alternate tetrameter and trimeter lines, abababab.

As Robene was keeping his sheep, Makyne begged for his love, explaining its law to him. He protested ignorance of the emotion, marveled at her unhappiness, rejoiced in the fair weather, refused to offend his sheep or risk their going astray by dallying with the maiden, and bidding her cheer up and love where she would, left her alone to weep. Then Robene began to feel something of Makyne's malady and returning pressed his love upon her. But "The man that will nocht quhen he may / sall haif nocht quhen he wald." Mending rapidly, laughing and singing, Makyne left Robene alone to mourn with his sheep among the hoary woods.

Robene and Makyne is generally akin to the French pastourelle, has something of the structure of a debate or disputation, and the narrative technique, simple rime, pronounced rhythm, and alliterative formulas of a ballad. Its sources have been discussed at some length, but none has yet been found for the poem as a whole. Its basic situation is the same as that of a thirteenth-century poem attributed to Baudes de la Kakerie, although the telling use of the sheep to emphasize Robene's boorishness and the age of the woods to emphasize the timelessness of his lesson seems to have been original with Henryson. The concluding proverb which by its very form, one natural for dispensing folk wisdom, also emphasizes the lesson's timelessness, has been current since the tenth century and reappears as late as the end of the nineteenth.

THE BLUDY SERK [7]. Fifteen stanzas of alternate tetrameter and trimeter lines, abababab.

A giant once imprisoned a king's daughter in a dark dungeon. A prince rescued her, in the process being so sorely wounded that, giving the lady his bloody shirt and asking her to look upon it and remember him when wooers came, he died. The princess did as the knight had asked, prayed for him and loved his memory so well that she never took a man. Thus should we love and pray to God day and night. Moralitas: The king is the Trinity; the lady, man's soul, daughter and handiwork of God; the giant, Lucifer, who betrayed that soul; the knight, Christ, Who ransomed it with His death; the dungeon, hell; the wooers, sin. As the lady refused those wooers, so should we drive all sin away. Christ Who bled for us help us at Doomsday. Good men, for His love think on the bloody shirt.

There is some question as to whether this version of *The Tale of Emperor Frederick's Daughter* had a Latin or English source. Either is possible, for the Latin *Gesta Romanorum* in which the story originally appears had circulated in England and had been translated into English at least three times before the end of the fifteenth century. It has been suggested that Henryson was familiar with the version of the tale in MS Harley 7333 both because that is the only English version to use the words "blody serke" and because the manuscript contains other material with which the poet was undoubtedly familiar, such as *The Canterbury Tales*. Whatever his immediate source, Henryson would seem to have romanticized and vivified it, for example making his villain not the faceless earl of the Harleian story, but a foul giant with fingernails like crooks of hell, five quarters long.

THE GARMONT OF GUD LADEIS [8]. Ten stanzas of alternate tetrameter and trimeter lines, abab (cf. [7]).

In return for his lady's love and obedience the poet would make her the best of garments whose details he lists in a catalogue of virtues: hood of honor garnished with good government, shirt of chastity mingled with modesty and fear of dishonor, kirtle of constancy laced with lawful life through eyelets of permanence, etc. If she would don this garment, he dares swear she wore never green nor gray that became her half so well.

In their moral theme, allegorical method, and ballad-like stanza, this poem and *The Bludy Serk* [7] are companion pieces. The allegory here could have been suggested by either 1 Timothy 2:9–11 and Ephesians 6:13–17, or the *Triumphe des Dames* of Olivier de la Marche, who seems to have been the first to deal in such a way with woman's attire. However, the allegorical concept of dress, or more often armor, was widespread, and Henryson need not have drawn upon any one source. If he did actually use de La Marche's work, he altered it considerably, condensing a tedious mixture of verse and prose in which each garment is described, made a virtue, and exemplified by a story, to ten succinct stanzas which have the concreteness, color, and pace of a ballad.

THE PRAIS OF AIGE [9]. Four pentameter-line stanzas with refrain, ababbcbc.

Within a garden under a rose tree the poet heard an old man sing that he would not be young for all the world, for the older a man, the nearer he is to heaven. Cupidity, he said, has made the world false, changeable, a prey to sin, sorrow, and guile, without freedom or wealth, and has banished lords. Youth he does not esteem, for in youth without grace none can withstand the raging blood until he is old; then what he enjoyed most shall vanish, being only vanity. None should trust the world, whose joy ends in sorrow. God grant us grace, which alone can defend us, that we may amend and reach heaven.

For similar meditations cf. Dunbar, *Of Manis Mortalitie*, [95] below, *Of the Warldis Vanitie* [96], and *Doun by ane Rever as I red* [109]; the latter particularly seems to reflect the situation of Henryson's poem. The musing upon Fortune's fickleness and the vanity of earthly joy and the reconciliation resulting from Boethian and Christian ethics are to some slight degree reminiscent of *Troilus and Criseyde*. Although the thought is relatively commonplace, it is given an effective statement by means of the poem's pervasive sense of serene joy at the approach of death, and its contrast between a setting appropriate to love, rebirth, and youth, and a speaker who is old.

THE RESSONING BETUIX AIGE AND YOWTH [10]. Five pentameter-line stanzas in MS Laing 149, nine in other texts, ababbcbc, with alternating refrains (cf. [9]).

A descriptive introduction, alternate speeches by Youth and Age, and a concluding comment by the narrator. One morning the poet meets a merry man who sings, "O youth, rejoice in your green flowers"; boasts of his strength and unfading comeliness; thinks to tarry awhile with love, swaggering at court; and feeling sound in body, wits, and spirits, rejects the admonitions of an old man who bears a document warning that youth's flowers fade desperately soon. This old man sings that he too had once been strong, noble, gay, and young; but as his appearance shows, all is past. He refutes the youth who for his swaggering shall cower, renounce lust, and cease to succeed in love. However bold, he shall obey this warning and himself grow old. So Youth and Age depart, one grieving and angry, the other somber; and the poet sees the truth of both their views.

The Ressoning Betuix Aige and Yowth, The Ressoning Betwixt Deth and Man [12], and The Thre Deid Pollis [16] are all meditations on mortality of the kind given widespread representation in various medieval art forms. This particular allegorical debate is a modified expression of the motif of the three living and the three dead, current as early as the thirteenth century, in which corpses warn men, "As we are now, so shall you be." The memento mori is reminiscent of that conveyed in The Prais of Aige, [9] above, here made particularly effective by Henryson's use of alliteration, refrains, and nature imagery to emphasize the contrast between youth and age.

THE ABBAY WALK [11]. Seven tetrameter-line stanzas with refrain, ababbcbc (cf. [9] and [10]).

Walking alone in an abbey, thinking what consolation was best in adversity, the poet saw written on a wall a series of admonitions to obey and thank God for all. Power and wealth pass when fortune pleases; Job and Tobit patiently bore adversity. Physical defects which come not through one's own fault should not be reproved; nor should God be blamed for adversity, Who by justice must correct, by mercy, have pity. He punishes and saves lord and begger, varying earthly estates by His providence. In wealth be meek, in poverty, glad, for power and riches are vanity. Remember Christ, Who suffered for you, Who elevates low hearts and humbles proud.

Although certain of its imagery and attitudes suggest Chaucer's influence, The Abbay Walk seems to have been based upon an anonymous poem found in several early manuscripts (Brown-Robbins, no. 562). Henryson's poem, in turn, served as a model for the seventeenth-century Obey and Thank Thy God of All, which is similar to but not a modernization of it as has been thought. Since only the National Library Scotland 1.1.6 proper, not the draft section of that manuscript, attributes the poem to Henryson, his authorship has been questioned. However, the attribution

is supported by both style and cast of thought. Here as in the poet's unquestioned work alliteration, assonance, and refrain serve not merely for
poetic effect, but to emphasize a moral lesson. Moreover, the contrast
between God's justice and His mercy suggests *Ane Prayer for the Pest*
[17]; the theme of *sic transit gloria mundi* suggests *The Prais of Aige*
[9]; and the theme of the necessity of accepting God's providence without
question, *The Testament of Cresseid* [4].

THE RESSONING BETWIXT DETH AND MAN [12]. Six pentam-
eter-line stanzas, ababbcbc (cf. [9], [10], and [11]).

Alternating speeches by Death and Man. Death warns man that all who live must
die, tells of his irresistible power to call all people to their biers, and advises Man to
repent, examine his conscience, and prepare to die. Man boasts that none dare menace
or fight him or can withstand his might; but then recognizing Death's omnipotence,
repents of the misguided youth he had thought would last forever, defies the wretched
world and, offering himself to Death, beseeches God to save his soul, Jesus to have
mercy upon him on judgment day.

A debate which, in its process of question and answer, allegorical figures,
and concluding renunciation of the world, has a certain affinity with
Everyman. Although here the warning characteristic of the three living
and the three dead is joined to a rudimentary dance of death, the allegory
is even barer than in *The Ressoning Betuix Aige and Yowth* [10]. As in
the case of *The Abbay Walk* [11], though only National Library Scotland
1.1.6 proper, not the draft section of the manuscript, attributes *The Ressoning Betwixt Deth and Man* to Henryson, in view of the poem's style
and intellectual content there seems little reason to question his authorship.

AGANIS HAISTY CREDENCE OF TITLARIS [13]. Seven pentam-
eter-line stanzas, ababbcbc, each ending in the same word or words (cf.
[10], [11], and [12]).

Many false, uncharitable tattlers now hope to curry favor by lies. A lord should
consider if a tale be true, who tells it and why, about whom, and if the teller will
abide by it, then listen to both parties, not giving hasty credence at first. It is no
honor for a lord because of the tattlers' false tale to slight a true, innocent man without hearing his defense. Tattlers cause strife, make lords angry with, perhaps even

banish, their innocent servants. Flatterers and liars are more dangerous than the plague. Before judging a flatterer's tale against the innocent, the wise lord should hear both sides and soberly consider; else he may repent. Tattlers and those who listen to them shall go to hell. Backbiters, who slay themselves, the hearer, and the innocent with a word, are excommunicated everywhere. God grant lords grace not to give tales hasty credence.

In subject and vehemence this poem anticipates certain of Dunbar's satires (cf. particularly *None May Assure in this Warld*, [43] below, and *Complaint to the King* [41]). It contains echoes of Lydgate's *The Churl and the Bird*; but its main source appears to be the same poet's *Danger of Hasty Credance* from *The Fall of Princes*.

THE ANNUNCIATION [14]. Six stanzas of tetrameter lines.

Strong as death is pleasing love which makes the bitter sweet and all things easy. Love relieved us from trouble when Gabriel brought the annunciation to Mary and returned to heaven, leaving her happy, honored to be both maiden and mother of God's son. The miracles of love are great: its flame burns unburnt; Aaron's dry rod buds; the flesh within is moist while without it is dry. Just so was the virgin made a mother, God preserving her maidenhead and keeping her divinity undoubted. Fearless of death, He bought us with His blood, His charity manifest abroad when He rose. The poet prays the Virgin to free him from sin and bring him to heaven.

This poem is anticipatory of some of Dunbar's work not only in subject, but in its lyricism and measured grace which result from alliteration, restricted rime, and the varied rhythm of its short lines. The power of the climax seems, in fact, due more to sound and movement than to the rising tension which accompanies the progression of thought from annunciation to resurrection to salvation. It has been suggested that *The Annunciation* is a recast of an older poem, but none of the many lyrics to Mary which are similar to Henryson's poem has yet been identified as its specific source. Much of the subject matter was, of course, commonplace: the apostrophe to love and its power—a reflection of 1 Corinthians 13:4–7, Aaron's rod as a symbol of Mary; the prayer for her aid, here rather like the prayer and absolution of Matins, etc. Possibly Henryson was influenced by the prologues to Chaucer's *Prioress's* and *Second Nun's Tales*; but the ideas found there occur in many hymns, and his wording in this instance is not strikingly similar to that of Chaucer.

SUM PRACTYSIS OF MEDECYNE [15]. Seven stanzas of nine irregular tetrameter and pentameter lines with a four trimeter and dimeter line tail, ababababcdddc.

To demonstrate his skill to a critic, an apothecary sets forth four mock prescriptions —for colic, insomnia, hasty flight, and coughing—compounded of exotic, often scatological ingredients, such as seven sobs of a seal and a double handful of cuckoo fart. He then bids his listener good-night, assuring him that this medicine will make patients bless or curse the doctor since it will cause them to fly out of the world (an ambiguity perhaps for being either transported with joy or poisoned by the apothecary's concoctions).

This exercise in grotesquerie and abuse is of the same type as Dunbar's *Flyting*, [28] below, and *The Manere of Crying of Ane Play* [117], like them achieving its effect of burlesque extravagance from pell-mell rhythm, continuous alliteration, and the heaping up of gross, fantastic detail. It has been suggested that the poem is nonsense verse, or, more plausibly, a parody of a physician comparable to Chaucer's parody of a knight in *Sir Thopas*.

THE THRE DEID POLLIS [16]. Eight pentameter-line stanzas, ababbcbc (cf. [9], [10], [11], [12], and [13]).

Three skulls, whose example should cause all men to flee vice, admonish sinful man, youth, gallants, lovely ladies, to behold them who once were as the living, and remember that all must come to the same end, though the hour and place of death be uncertain. Who now can tell which of the skulls was once fairest, gentlest of kin, most learned? Let Pride meditate upon them, Age behold the skulls and pray for mercy, man ask mercy for his sin and pray for the salvation of all.

A meditation on mortality whose lesson is given considerable dramatic force by its sharp visual contrast between the hollow, peeled skulls, and the lavish color and richness of youth. In MS National Library Scotland 1.1.6 the poem is ascribed to "patrik Iohinstoun" (possibly the dead poet named by Dunbar in *Lament for the Makaris* [29] and to Henryson in MS Pepys 2553. However, it is generally accepted as Henryson's because of its similarity in tone, theme, and metrical structure to some of his unquestioned work. Like *The Ressoning Betuix Aige and Yowth* [10] and *The Ressoning Betwixt Deth and Man* [12], *The Thre Deid Pollis* suggests a dance of death and develops, though more fully, the theme of the three living and the three dead.

ANE PRAYER FOR THE PEST [17]. Eleven pentameter-line stanzas, ababbcbc (cf. [10], [11], [12], [13], and [16]). The first five stanzas have one refrain, the last three another; the first nine stanzas end with the same word, the last three have two to three words of internal rime per line.

The poet prays all-powerful God mercifully to preserve himself and others from the pestilence which is justly visited upon them for their sins. God is their only help; they would gladly accept any other punishment. Though their sin is vexatious, their death will not make recompense for it. As He bought them so dearly He should redeem them and punish with pity not violence, though they be undeserving. God grant them grace to amend and evade this cruel death, caused by their sin. Legally God's justice must punish. The lack of justice brings His wrath; but if the leaders would enforce earthly justice, He would have no cause for wrath. Now the leaders are so oppressive that God justly punishes all for disobedience. Were they contrite their suffering would cease, for God never casts away those who beseech Him. May He have pity, not let sloth destroy them. Unless He have pity and forgive their sin, they die. Justice must correct their vice; but may God pacify His wrath and though their sin be huge, help them. They repent. Glory to God; may He not let what He so dearly bought be lost.

The phraseology of this poem is unusually difficult, the literal meaning of certain lines being still open to question; but the essential meaning and development of the line of reasoning are clear enough. Although *Ane Prayer for the Pest* is attributed to Henryson only in National Library Scotland 1.1.6 proper, not in the draft section of the manuscript, there seems little reason to question his authorship in view of the poem's theme and form. Throughout a sharp contrast is drawn between God's strength and man's weakness, between justice and mercy—man's only defense and the poet's best argument for relief. For a similarly legalistic argument and another remonstrance against divine passivity in the face of human suffering, cf. Henryson's *The Scheip and the Doig*, [3] above, item (g). For a display of metrical gymnastics comparable to the complex stanzas which here provide a climax of pleading and praise, cf. Dunbar's *Ane Ballat of Our Lady* [103] and the concluding stanzas of Douglas's *Palice of Honour* [20].

THE WANT OF WYSE MEN [18]. Nine pentameter-line stanzas, ababbcbc, with refrain (cf. [9], [10], [11], [12], and [13]).

The poet marvels at the confused, upside-down state of the world which has resulted since lack of wise men put fools in power, then describes this state in detail, citing the virtues—constancy, trust, wealth, wit, happiness, peace, etc.—now lost, and the vices—sorrow, falseness, ignorance, terror, avarice, etc.—which rule. May God have compassion and reform these things!

The poem is ascribed to Henryson in neither of its early texts. However, in MS National Library Scotland 19.1.16 it is printed without a separate heading in a tract with *Orpheus and Eurydice* [15] which is ascribed to Henryson, and thus would seem to have been considered to be his by early compilers. Moreover, its attack upon contemporary abuses and plea to God for remedy are similar to those in *The Scheip and the Doig*, [3] above, item (g), and *Ane Prayer for the Pest* [17]. It has been suggested that *The Want of Wyse Men* belongs to the reign of James III since it deals with the kind of unsettled conditions then prevalent. But the evidence contained within the poem is not specific enough to identify the precise period of its composition. The objects of its attack are, in fact, quite similar to those in the satires of Dunbar, particularly *None May Assure in this Warld*, [43] below, and *A General Satyre* [98], which were written during the reign of James IV.

3. DOUGLAS

Details of the life of Gawin Douglas are contained in the public records of England and Scotland, in his correspondence and that of his contemporaries, and in early accounts such as Myln's *Lives of the Bishops of Dunkeld* and the histories of Major, Leslie, Drummond of Hawthornden, and Hume of Godscroft. His life falls roughly into three periods: that of childhood, education, and poetic creativity, ending with the battle of Flodden in 1513; of struggle for political and ecclesiastical power initiated by the alliance between the Douglases and Queen Margaret, culminating in his ordination as Bishop of Dunkeld; and of his decline in power due largely to the disaffection of the Queen, ending with his exile and death in England in 1522.

The poet was the third son of Elizabeth Boyd and Archibald, the great Earl of Angus, called "Bell-the-Cat" from his role in an attack upon favorites of James III. Although nothing definite is known about the date and place of Gawin Douglas's birth, it is thought to have occurred in the mid 1470's at one of the family residences in Lanarkshire, East Lothian, Angus, or Strathearn. Little is known of his early education except that it was of a nature to prepare him for the university course then required for ecclesiastical advancement. Records show that in 1492 Douglas became a Bachelor, in 1494 a Master of Arts at the University of St. Andrews; but he subsequently disappears from the public records for three years during which time he is conjectured to have studied in Paris. John Major says he did so, giving an account of a disputation held there in which Douglas took part; and the close ties between France and Scotland, the fifteenth-century Scotsman's custom of financing his education abroad, and the evidence of pervasive French influence in *The Palice of Honour* tend to support Major's testimony.

Douglas's ecclesiastical career had begun by 1497 when he held the living of Monymusk in Aberdeenshire and the deanship of Dunkeld. By 1498 he had been presented the parsonage of Glenquhom, by 1503 the provostship of St. Giles in Edinburgh. Save for the Chapel Royal at Stirling, St. Giles was Scotland's most extensive collegiate church; and it is possible that *The Palice of Honour*, completed in 1501 with its effusive dedication to "The Rich Nobill and Illuster Prince Iames the Feird, King of Scottis," helped obtain for the poet his appointment there. In 1513 he completed the *Eneados* and in September of that year, perhaps in part because of his growing literary eminence, was created a burgess of Edinburgh. But just at this point, when he seemed destined for a distinguished, peaceful career as a man of religion, letters and minor activity in public affairs, Douglas became involved in the violent struggle for political and ecclesiastical power which was to last the rest of his life.

At the battle of Flodden the poet's two older brothers died, and shortly afterward his father, leaving the title to a grandson. Before a year had elapsed this newly designated young Earl of Angus had married the dowager Queen Margaret, and in his rise to power carried his uncle, Gawin Douglas, with him. In August 1514, the very month of her marriage, Margaret wrote Pope Leo X urging him to give her new uncle-in-law the Abbey of Arbroath; and in November further recommended Douglas for the Archbishopric of St. Andrews. But the influence of neither the Queen nor her brother, Henry VIII, who at her instigation also wrote the Pope in Douglas's behalf, was sufficient to overcome his formidable rivals, Andrew Forman, Bishop of Moray, and John Hepburn, Prior of St. Andrews. Forman was given the post at Arbroath; while Hepburn, who had been elected to the Archbishopric of St. Andrews by his canons, seized and held the castle there. Lacking money and men to combat such formidable opponents, Douglas was forced to withdraw from the competition. Although the poem is undated, it may well be that at this time he composed *Conscience*, his biting little satire on ecclesiastical preferment.

By September 18, 1514, however, he had become the Queen's representative before the Scottish Lords of Council, and shortly thereafter seems to have assumed the role of Chancellor, for by the twenty-first of September the Great Seal of Scotland was in his possession and in November 1514 the title of Chancellor was being applied to him. In January 1515, Margaret nominated Douglas to the Bishopric of Dunkeld, and this time was successful in procuring from the Pope a bull in his favor. But once again his advancement was checked. First, Andrew Stewart compelled the canons of Dunkeld to elect him their bishop and drew to himself all those nobles hostile to Margaret or to the Douglases. Then in an apparent attempt to prevent the family from increasing its power further, the Regent, Albany, caused Douglas's correspondence to be watched and certain letters damaging to him were intercepted. On charges of seeking aid from a foreign king and papal bulls in his own favor, Douglas was arraigned before the Lords of Council in July 1515, convicted and imprisoned.

There has been some debate as to the justice of his conviction and the reprehensibleness of his political negotiations both at this time and later. His own correspondence, that of his agents Adam Williamson and Alexander Turnbull, of the Queen and of Lord Thomas Dacre, Warden of the Marches, show clearly enough that Douglas both petitioned Henry VIII to exert influence upon the Pope in his own behalf and sought to purchase preferment at Rome. Although there were laws in Scotland prohibiting such actions, they had not been strictly enforced before; and without doubt they were upon this occasion only at the instigation of Douglas's enemies. In 1515 and 1522 he did seek Henry VIII's intervention in Scotland; but there is no evidence that he did not believe such action was for the best interest of the Scottish people who "ar sa oppressyt," he wrote, "for lak of justyce by thevys, rubry and other extortiones that thai wald be glayd to leyf ondyr the gret Turk to haf justyce." Very likely Douglas saw the welfare of his country, his clan, and himself as interdependent; and from that point of view, at least, his negotiations with England and Rome were well justified.

By the end of July 1516, after more than a year's imprisonment Douglas was freed, and with the aid of Albany who wishing to placate Margaret now befriended him, was ordained Bishop of Dunkeld. The ensuing four years were, on the whole, peaceful ones for the poet-bishop. He supervised repairs of the cathedral of Dunkeld and its buildings, attended to his clerical duties, participated in meetings of the Lords of Council and in negotiations with France which led to the Treaty of Rouen in 1517. As early as 1519, however, Douglas seems to have lost the favor of Queen Margaret, by that time disenchanted with her husband, Angus, the poet's nephew, and anxious for divorce. In order to control "Anguish," as she called him, Margaret instigated the return of Albany from France where he had been since 1517, and when the Regent reached Scotland in November 1521, the Earl of Angus was forced to take refuge in a church on the Border and send his uncle to seek the aid of Henry VIII. But despite submitting a lengthy memorial of charges against Albany and several petitions to Henry's minister, Wolsey, Douglas was unable to obtain the assistance of the English, was declared a traitor and deprived of his bishopric by the Scots, and Angus was exiled to France.

Still Gawin Douglas retained a certain influence. Polydore Vergil wrote of him as "virque summa nobilitate & virtute." Lord Dacre, in March 1522, urged Wolsey to support his nomination by the Pope to the Archbishopric of St. Andrews; and James Beaton, a candidate for the same post, considered Douglas a formidable enough rival to seek the aid of Christian II of Denmark in attempting to turn the Pope against him.

Beaton's measure proved unnecessary. In September 1522, at the house of Lord Dacre in London Douglas died, of the plague according to Polydore Vergil, and was buried in the Hospital Church of the Savoy with the epitaph, "cui laevus conditur Gavanus Dowglas natione Scotus Dunkeldensis praesul, patria Sua exul."

The canon of Douglas's writings has not been finally established. In the epilogue to *Eneados*, book 12, he says that he translated "Of Lundeys Lufe the Remeid," then wrote "off hie Honour the Palyce." It has been suggested that the first is a misreading for Ovid's "Of Love the Remedy"; but no translation of the *Remedia amores* by the Scots poet has yet been discovered. David Lindsay, in *The Testament of the Papyngo*, says that Douglas's "works are more than five"; and Thomas Tanner names six, *Palatium honoris, Aureas narrationes, Comoedias aliquot, De rebus Scoticis*, and translations of *Aeneidas Virgilii Maronis* and *Ovidium de remedio amoris*. *De rebus Scoticis* was probably the brief commentary on Scottish history which Polydore Vergil says Douglas wrote for his use, but what the *Aureas narrationes* and the *Comoedias aliquot* may have been is still unknown.

ENEADOS [19]. A translation in heroic couplets of the twelve books of Virgil's *Aeneid* and the 13th book by Polydore Vergil, with an original prologue for each and miscellaneous passages of identification, direction, etc. following books 12 and 13.

Proloug 1: 511 lines of heroic couplets.

The poet praises Virgil, whose *Aeneid* he, though most unworthy, shall write in his own idiom, dedicating the work to Lord Henry Sinclair at whose request it is written. He explains his choice of language and method of translation, attacks Caxton's *Eneydos* for errors and omissions, even remonstrates with Chaucer the master poet for saying he could follow Virgil word for word and that Aeneas was forsworn. He does not shrink from informed criticism although rejecting crude interference, acknowledges his inferiority to Virgil, asks forgiveness of his mistakes, and bids his readers to reprove his work if he has failed, but not before studying it thoroughly.

First of the three prologues (1, 5, 9) concerned with literary criticism and theory. The modesty topos, the praise of Virgil and Chaucer and the aureate language in which it is couched were common conventions. Douglas's discussion of translating and his attack upon Caxton's *Eneydos* are among those aspects of his prologues which have received the most attention from commentators.

Proloug 2: three rime royal stanzas.

The poet invokes God for grace to follow Virgil worthily, Saturn for guidance of his woeful pen, bids ladies, knights, and wise men to attend, deceivers to read of their own art. Here the proverb is proven, "All earthly gladness finishes with woe."

Proloug 3: five stanzas of iambic pentameter lines, aabaabbab.

The poet prays for cunning to write the strange courses of the moon (a possible reference to the journeys of Aeneas). Dull of wit, he must describe strange, unknown dangers called fables by ignoramuses, and dismissing petty, ineffectual faultfinders he asks for the attention of readers of good will. As this text has strange things enough to make the eye whirl, none ought blame his small mistakes. May the Virgin save him from Harpies, Cyclopes, and the Scylla and Charybdis of hell.

The modesty topos, similar to that of Proloug 1, and the use of mythological figures as symbols for Christian concepts were literary conventions.

Proloug 4: thirty-two rime royal stanzas, and six stanzas of iambic pentameter lines, one abaabcc, one aaaaabb, four ababbcbc.

A sermon against unrestrained carnal love whose vicious aspects the poet lists in detail. He attacks drunkenness and lust; explains the nature of false love and true, whose purpose is the begetting of children, and the necessity of directing love toward God; rebukes old lechers, bawds, those who boast of Venus's works and provoke others to sin; bids unwed maidens remain chaste, gallants restrain their lust; and leaves to Gower's confession the condemning of deceit. He then turns to the tragic story of Dido which illustrates the evils of false love and should lead ladies to beware of lascivious strangers.

Possible sources for many of the topics touched upon in this prologue have been pointed out, but most of them—the contradictory effects of love, list of sufferers from love, the begetting of children as the only proper end of sexual love, the relation between lust and drink, etc.—were commonplaces or literary conventions.

Proloug 5: six stanzas of iambic pentameter lines, aabaabbcc, two of rime royal.

Different things please different people—books the clerk, his lady the lover, game and play young folk—and pleasure is beneficial. Virgil skillfully adapts his style to each subject and to each man's taste, writing now [in book five] of sports and mirth never known to Caxton who errs, whose writing is feeble and maimed while that of Douglas is fresh, original. Rejecting Bacchus and Proserpina, the poet calls on God for help to resist temporal joy and thus gain eternal joy undiminished.

Second of the prologues (cf. 1 and 9) to be concerned with literary criticism and theory.

Proloug 6: twenty-one stanzas of iambic pentameter lines, ababbcbc.

The poet invokes Pluto for aid in writing this book, which fools think full of lies and idolatries. Virgil has great meaning everywhere as Servius, Augustine, Ascensius attest. Having described man's life and death in the first five books, he writes of the afterlife in the sixth and includes many things, which Douglas lists, in keeping with our faith, thus strengthening it with precious speeches, as in the bucolics when he prophesies Christ. There are many passages in Virgil which seem Christian, although being a pagan at times he departs from our faith. Since to write all of his thoughts would be impossible, suffice it to say Virgil suggests that One Mover, One Beginner, sustains all things and exists continually. Not everything he writes is perfect; thus Douglas rejects transmigration and multiple gods, interprets the Cumean Sibyl as Mary, Pluto as Satan, and defying Satan, calls on Mary for aid in assaying gloomy Dis, or its likeness, in this misty poetry.

Here Douglas carries much further the interpreting of mythology in Christian terms begun in Proloug 3. The interpretation of Virgil as a prophet of Christ's coming and the golden age thereby initiated, particularly in the Messianic Eclogue, IV, was widespread in the Middle Ages.

Proloug 7: 168 lines of heroic couplets.

The poet describes a December day, its storms, floods, faded fields, etc., which lead to thoughts of age and death. In bed at night he hears the clacking of geese, then near dawn wakes to the cry of other birds. He blesses himself, dresses, looks out at the wintery day, then hastily retreating to the fire sees his Virgil and, annoyed that so great a part of the work remains undone, at once begins to write the next book, telling of Aeneas's warfare, to which he has appropriately annexed this dreary prologue.

First of the nature prologues (cf. 12 and 13). The mirroring of man's emotions in the seasons was, of course, a commonplace. In detail and situation this prologue is highly reminiscent of the opening scene of *The Testament of Cresseid* [4]; but Douglas's recounting of winter's sights, sounds, and sensations is much more comprehensive than that of Henryson and constitutes some of the most graphic, original nature description to be found in medieval British literature.

Proloug 8: fourteen bob-and-wheel stanzas of long, usually eleven or

twelve syllable, alliterative lines, abababab, followed by a wheel of
shorter lines, dddc.

   The poet dreams that he sees a man attacking the state of the land by cataloguing
its ills: its abuse of reason and faith, its dishonesty, lust, strife, etc. He enumerates
many people all of whom desire something, many of whom seek it shamefully. Vice
and dishonesty prevail. Priests are wicked. No one is content. The complainer asks
the poet why he lies there idly and what it is everyone wants. Different people,
different things, replies the poet; he wants to finish his book. But he is told his book
is wretchedness; for aid he is given a roll inscribed with doggerel dealing with all the
tricks of the world, the movement of the heavenly bodies, why the corn has chaff,
etc.; and when he protests that these are riddles, is shown a hoard of pennies which
vanishes as he wakes. Angry for having attended to such meaningless, shameful fantasies
as dreams and for listening like a sluggard to ignorance, he leaps up and begins the
eighth book.

Neither the prologue's subject matter nor its alliterative stanza were
unusual in the period, although this appears to represent the sole occur-
rence of either in Douglas's poetry. Chaucer's discussion of the nature
of dreams in *The House of Fame* perhaps influenced the Scots poet here,
particularly in his last stanza; but the social criticism presented in a
catalogue of tumbling detail is like that of Henryson's *The Want of
Wyse Men* [18], Dunbar's *Remonstrance to the King* [39] and *Complaint
to the King* [41].

   Prologue 9: three stanzas of iambic pentameter lines, ababba, with
internal interlocking rime, eighty lines of heroic couplets.

   Worthy clerks write of nobility, wisdom, utility, not villainy. The poet exhorts men
to virtuous action, then discusses the suiting of style to subject and the nature of the
heroic style. An author should consider his subject and to whom the work is dedicated.
Virgil's noble book, for its qualities called the imperial work, was composed for the
emperor Octavian, and this translation is dedicated to a knight; thus Douglas will the
more gladly employ the heroic style. Though his own terms be not always polished,
he will keep Virgil's sense as best he can, letting the Roman poet be thanked for
what is good, himself blamed for what is bad. Hoping to follow Virgil as closely as
his own rough idiom permits, he begins.

The third discussion of literary style, second of the translator's technique
(cf. Prologues 1 and 5). The Polonius-like moralizing of stanzas 1–16 is
reminiscent of Henryson's *The Abbay Walk* [11], and more particularly
of Dunbar's *Gude Counsale* [89]; but metrical display such as that
achieved by the interlocking rimes of these stanzas was by no means

uncommon (cf. Dunbar's *Of the Ladyis Solistaris at Court* [69]). It has been suggested that in advocating the suiting of style to subject Douglas was influenced by either the *Ars poetica* of Horace or Virgil's second *Georgic*. The poet's acceptance of blame for his mistakes and of correction represents another instance of the modesty topos frequently found in Chaucer.

Proloug 10: thirty-five stanzas of iambic pentameter lines, aabba.

A hymn in praise of God Whose works are incomprehensible, Who assigns to every-thing its proper office and creates all things only so that they might share His goodness, His Godhead being neither richer nor poorer for it. The supreme indivisible, eternal, unvarying substance, one nature in three persons, Father, Son, and Holy Ghost. Gen-erated of none, He engenders His only Son of His substance, without diminution or change; and from both proceeds the Holy Ghost, each of one substance, equal though separate, like the soul of man with its understanding, reason, memory, and like fire with its flame, light, heat. Man with his feeble reason cannot comprehend the measure-less, omnipresent, all-encompassing God Who for man underwent incarnation and crucifixion, harrowed hell, gave His flesh and blood in pledge for glory and in memory of His passion and death. For such bounty how may the sinful poet give thanks? Let Virgil keep his pagan gods for there is but one God, to Whom are united all who keep His mandate, and Whom the poet prays to bring us all to heaven.

A homily, with its conventional theology in the tradition of numberless religious lyrics, as is Proloug 11.

Proloug 11: twenty-five stanzas of iambic pentameter lines, ababbccb.

An exaltation of prowess, for which, moved by the example of our elders, we should strive. Virtuous prowess is lawful, just, a sovereign virtue between foolhardiness and cowardice. To be Christ's faithful knights we must be bold and stand firm. Such men alone, Paul says, win the crown of bliss. Their armor is spiritual; their force directed against demons; their foes, flesh and the world. Master the flesh, resist the fiend and the world. Arm yourself in faith, hope, charity, prayer; stand firm in the field of grace thinking of martyrs, hell's pain, eternal glory, Christ's sacrifice, the ruin inevitable without Him, the puniness of our pain compared to His, and of Mary; none can then overcome you. Never consent, and you will never be lost. A faithful servant who at last commits treason must crave mercy and be pardoned by his prince or die; so may we be forgiven. Since a virtuous man who falls will burn, and though by grace and free will may recover merit but never his former degree of grace, do not fall and ruin your labor, but learn from Aeneas, who endured much for a temporal kingdom. Surely these virtuous pagans who suffered for short renown should shame us. May we strive to possess, and God grant us, the realm promised Abraham and his seed.

A homily (cf. Prolougs 6 and 10) developing the not uncommon concept of the church militant. For similar religious-military terminology cf. *The*

Book of the Ordre of Chyualry, The Kingly Wooer, and Henryson's
Bludy Serk [7].
  Proloug 12: 310 lines of heroic couplets.

  An elaborate, aureate description of spring. The poet tells, in terms of classical
gods and goddesses, of the coming of dawn on a calm, bright May morning, of the
rising mists, glittering waters, silver fish, gleaming banks, blossoming earth, etc., of
the birds building their nests, rejoicing in their mates, of the spider, deer, new lambs
and calves. Nymphs wander through the groves singing of love, and he speaks of
lovers, their pain, fluctuation, and the shameful play of some, inappropriate to wholesome May when new courage rouses all gentle hearts and causes each thing to be
renewed. To cure lovers of their nightly sorrow a host of birds sing until the rivers,
woods, and vales resound. They praise Nature and Venus, welcome the sun whose
gladdening beams chide sluggards. On this ninth of May the poet leaps up determined
to complete his long work, blesses himself, dresses, and begins the twelfth book with
its Proloug entitled "Pearl of May," whose capital letters in sign of royal state must
be illuminated.

Despite the poet's closing admonition, the prologue's capitals are not
illuminated in any of the surviving manuscripts, though its style is
certainly gilded enough throughout. Descriptions of May and sluggard
poets, catalogues of plants, birds, and spices, apostrophes to Phoebus and
other rhetorical devices such as the *repetitio* found here were conventional, and Douglas's conclusion seems clearly to have been influenced
by *The Parliament of Fowls*. Yet like Proloug 7, this prologue contains
some of the best nature description in early British poetry, its freshness
and unusual sensuous appeal resulting from detail such as the varying
play of light and shadow, the suggested color and fragrance of warm,
dewy earth and flowers. The Middle English poem, *Pearl* (see II [2]),
contains description somewhat similar and may have suggested Proloug
12's title.

  "Heir the translatour of this buk makis mensioun of thre of hys pryn-
cipall warkis": in four of the manuscripts eight lines of heroic couplets
immediately following book 12.

  The poet has now translated the *Aeneid,* as in his undisciplined youth he had
translated "Of Lundeys Lufe the Remeid," and then written *The Palice of Honour.*

That Douglas's earlier translation was, as has been suggested, "Of Ovideis
Lufe the Remeid" with a faultily transcribed title seems doubtful in view

of his subsequent challenge in "Heir the translatar direkkis hys buk" (see below), "Let others attempt to translate Ovid as I have Virgil."

"To knaw that naym of the translatour": a 5 line acrostic, aabab, identifying "Gawwyne Dowglass."

Proloug 13: 198 lines of heroic couplets.

On a June evening the poet walks about the fields rich with grain, fruit, cattle, etc., sees the sun set, the evening star and mists rise, the dew fall, and the world become shrouded in night. All creatures prepare for rest except the nightingale; so sitting under a laurel to hear her, he watches the stars then falls asleep. Aged Mapheus Vegius appears crowned with laurel, chides Douglas for being under his tree and for translating the *Aeneid* without taking notice of the thirteenth book added by Mapheus, then despite the poet's protests, beats him until crying for mercy he swears to translate the thirteenth book. Mollified, Mapheus departs; and waking for fear the poet sees the dawn, heralded by a lark and the cries of steward, herdsman, peasant's wife, etc. He will keep his promise, end this work, then think only on grave matters. His tongue and pen being no worse than before, many will like his text, although Mapheus's style is not Virgil's. Let clerks know that the poets are different; unlearned men heed the translator's work.

The dream vision wherein some figure admonishes a poet is conventional —cf. especially Henryson's *Lyoun and the Mous*, [3] above, item (h), which seems directly to have influenced this interview with Mapheus, Chaucer's *The Legend of Good Women*, and Lydgate's *Fall of Princes*— as is the description of evening and morning. However, as in Prolougs 7 and 12, here Douglas's nature description is highly original, containing detail striking in its vividness and precision—a bat with her peeled leathern flight, midges and restless flies, the valley swimming in sops of mist, and the simultaneous fading down of the evening light and springing up of dawn, whose effect is enhanced by the poet's reaction, "plesans, and half wondir."

"Conclusio": twenty-four lines of heroic couplets. A passage on the immortality of poetry, translated from Ovid's *Metamorphoses* and applied to Douglas's own work, and a farewell to secular writing and the observances of youth. The reference herein to "my days neir passyt the half dait" has been taken as an indication that the poet was about thirty-five when he completed the *Eneados*.

"Heir the translatar direkkis hys buk": 148 lines of heroic couplets.

The poet asks his kinsman who commissioned this work and to whom it is dedicated for protection against those who cannot amend it, but criticize it. Having been mocked for creating only fables, lies, and sins, he cries *mea culpa* where time was wasted—though his critics exaggerate. His work has notable doctrines; it will aid folk to eschew idleness, teachers to explain Virgil, whose meaning Douglas's verses contain almost word for word, and, being a translation of the best poet, should not be considered unprofitable. After looking over the book, let Sinclair judge if it offends Virgil, as the critics say. For his sake the poet has exposed himself to such pursuers. But he is careless of the opinion of fools, having made his book only for Sinclair, with whom he would share all he has, so that Virgil may be read correctly in their vulgar tongue. To this end he has used only plain, familiar terms, writing not as he should but as he can, for the matter is so profound and strange. Let he who thinks the poet speaks in vain now translate Ovid, as Douglas has Virgil. May Sinclair receive this work, promised Venus twelve years before in *The Palice of Honour*; Aeneas, whose renown will be spread abroad, be glad. The poet bids Venus adieu, mentions a commentary he has compiled on strange histories and terms, and promises that if anything is lacking it shall be soon written at his patron's desire.

The commentary referred to here has never been identified, but may be the marginal notes found in the Gale 0.3.12 manuscript of the *Eneydos* and believed to be in Douglas's hand.

"Ane exclamation aganyst detractouris and oncurtass redaris": five stanzas of pentameter lines, aabaabcc. The long work is ended and may be read in the poet's vulgar tongue as Virgil is sung in Latin. Malicious detractors seek faults; but let his work, which lacks none of Virgil's meaning, be compared to the original, and let who can do better. Some pick out another's faults, then write perfectly; others are so accustomed to faultfinding that they must ruin someone or burst. Let this vernacular Virgil, accurately translated, seek correction from nobles and be unashamed. Now can the work, comprehended before only by clerks, be known to every gentle Scot and read aloud to the unlearned.

"Heir followys the tyme, space and dait of the translatioun"; twenty-six lines of heroic couplets. The work was completed on the feast of Mary Magdalene, 1513, in eighteen months during which the poet often neglected it for more serious matters, thus leaving it more obscure and less pleasant than it ought to be. May his readers pardon him, take good notice, and neither mismeter his rime nor alter his words.

"Mantua me genuit": an epitaph of three heroic couplets translated from Suetonius, giving Virgil's place of birth, death, and burial, and listing his three notable works, of pastorage, husbandry, and chivalrous chieftains.

There has been much discussion as to whether Douglas's translation is medieval or renaissance in nature. The poet's purpose and period seem to have made the work, which can most accurately be described as transitional, something of both. First, his hero is cast in the mold of the renaissance prince, a benevolent despot, dedicated to the service of the state. Second, since Douglas's reiterated purpose was to enable his countrymen to understand Virgil's poem, he augments the original in such a way as to make it more readily comprehensible to them, explaining unfamiliar concepts, giving Scottish spellings of classical names, replacing classical figures or objects with more familiar ones: a ship becomes a ballingaire, a bacchante, Bacchus nun. Changes such as these give the translation a medieval flavor. At times, apparently in an effort to make the meaning completely clear, Douglas becomes more explicit than Virgil and loses something of the original's rich connotations. He expands when the limitations of Scots force him to do so, or in order to give a scene greater reality. Thus though on the whole Douglas translated accurately, it was not word for word; and he does commit errors, a number of which seem to result from his use of an imperfect Latin text, or of commentaries such as those of Servius and Badius Ascensius.

Attempts have been made to gauge the relative nearness of Douglas's effect and that of others, particularly Surrey, to Virgil's. However, this is difficult for the modern critic since the effect of poetry has to be judged in relation to the reaction of the audience and there is today no comprehensive, precise information as to the reaction of the audience of either Virgil or Douglas. Nevertheless it is possible to see that the effect of Douglas's diction and meter is somewhat at variance with that of Virgil's. The Scots poet says he sacrificed "eloquence" for "sentence," choosing plain terms in place of "facund rethoryk castis fair." His diction gives an impression of freshness, naturalness, and of belonging generally not to the high style but to the low; and low style is, of course, in no way characteristic of Virgil. Nor was Douglas's meter particularly well suited for translating the Latin epic. The conciseness of Latin is difficult enough to maintain in Middle Scots, and the couplet form too often requires, or at least encourages, padding; its rhythm and tendency to express thought in two-line units too easily becomes monotonous. Douglas did attempt to offset monotony by varying line length, omitting a syllable or using an extra one, employing frequent enjambment and an occasional alexandrine; but on the whole his Scots heroic couplets were not capable of reproducing the effect of Virgil's unrimed Latin hexameters.

The *Eneados* has been praised particularly for the zest and immediacy of its descriptions of action and of the sea. Historically it is important as the first translation of the *Aeneid* to be made in English, as a departure from the practice of building a romance upon the epic as Caxton and others had done, and for its influence upon Surrey, whose translation of books two and four draws throughout upon that of Douglas.

THE PALICE OF HONOUR [20]. 240 stanzas of iambic pentameter lines, riming aabaabbab, aabaabbaba, or aabaabbcbc.

Proloug: On a May morning the poet hears a voice praising the season. Frightened he calls on Nature and May for comfort so that he may sing their praise, then struck by a sudden gleam of light, swoons.

Part I: After invoking wit for aid the poet recounts his vision. In a fearful desert place, he cries out on fickle Fortune, hears a great noise, hides in a tree, and sees three courts pass. The first is that of Minerva, with figures from classical and biblical tradition, some vicious, some virtuous, all wise, on their way to the Palace of Honour; the second, a small company, is that of Diana; the third, heralded by angelic music, is that of Venus. The poet describes the transmission of sound, then the goddess of love and her varied company with their music, and is moved to sing a ballad of inconstant love. At that, Venus's followers angrily bind and lead him to their goddess's throne where the clerk Varius accuses him of blasphemy against love. Though he pleads for mercy and objects to the secular court and feminine judge on the grounds that he is a spiritual man, he is tried by Venus who attacks all clerks as enemies of love and commands Varius to write the poet's sentence. Filled with terror of being transformed into a beast, for the gods have wrought other such transformations, he remains hopeless, friendless, without wit, and wretched.

Part II: God now sends hope in the form of a court of the Muses, its members drawn from the classical and modern worlds, singing ancient histories and myths. When Calliope points out how degrading it would be to slay a man for so small a crime or to bandy words with a frightened wretch, Venus pardons the poet on condition that he write her praises and obey her next reasonable command. With thanks he writes a ballad bidding his rescued wit rejoice, serve love, and praise Venus always; and the mollified goddess departs. Calliope delivers the poet to a nymph who is to show more wonders, and with the Muses's company he flies on horseback above the world, finally alighting by the Hippocrene fountain whose water the crowd prevents him from even tasting. There ladies play, sing, dance, then in a pavilion hold a feast where they pose problems, asking who have been best in their day, who the truest lovers. At Calliope's command, Ovid tells his tales; Virgil, Terence, Juvenal, and other Latin writers speak; and the company remounts to ride again, coming at last to a rock in a pleasant plain. Now the poet because of backbiters fears to write, for the joy he saw was unimaginable, untellable, and he knows not whether his vision was of the soul or body. Yet trusting in God, he hopes to describe at least part of the heavenly pleasure, and bids his dull pen be diligent.

Part III: Having invoked the Muses, the poet continues his story. Fearfully he climbs the one high, straight path up Honour's rock, led by his nymph and carried by her across the burning abyss of care. Below he sees the world engulfed in a stormy sea with the Ship of Grace wrecked in sin, the survivors brought to land by faith, Christ, and good works. In a verdant plain his nymph directs the poet to the palace of Honour, a worthy crowd before it, within its outer walls deeds of arms being done for ladies. Bidding him attend and afterwards write what he sees, she then leads him to the garden of Venus where hangs a mirror reflecting the deeds and fates, which he recites at some length, of every man. Venus gives him a book to put into rime and with his nymph he passes to the palace which many strive in vain to enter. Its keeper is Loyalty, its porter Patience, its prince Honour, etc.; and on its golden gate are engraved all natural things. Annoyed by his doting over these wonders, the nymph bids him be brave and shoves the poet into the rich interior whose walls shine so brightly he cannot see how they are wrought. Then through a hole in a closed door he sees princes in jeweled armor and a god whose brightness smites them down. The nymph restores him to consciousness, chides him until he becomes angry, which rather pleases her, and laughing promises to show him no more fearful pleasure. Leading him toward the Muses's garden, she explains that those bejeweled men were the most valiant and virtuous in their lives. Earthly glory passes while virtuous honour endures and is, thus, the only sure way to lasting honour. She lists some of the folk from biblical, classical, and Scottish history who may be found in the land of honour. Were it not for the poet's fear and dullness, he should have seen how the heavenly conversed and the vicious were punished; but he shall see it all after a visit to the Muses's garden. In attempting to cross the tree bridge to this garden he falls, and what with fright and birds' song, wakes, finding the real arbor where he lies a hell compared to that of his vision. Always he thinks of the pleasant island where he would have liked to dwell, perhaps there to find something of rhetoric, grieved most that he woke before seeing enough to be able to describe the torment of wretches who mangle honour. Since all that visionary happiness has vanished, with a lavish praise of honour he concludes.

"The Author directis his Buik": two stanzas of dedication and encomium to James IV, one in which the poet disowns this book, bare of eloquence, rustic in dress, imperfect in sentence, and admonishes it to ask each man for correction.

An allegory of the various paths to honour, *The Palice of Honour* might serve as a text for the study of literary influences current in Douglas's day. The poem is a dream vision in the tradition of the *Roman de la rose*, exhibiting virtually every feature of the genre. Some critics have suggested that it was directly modelled on *Le séjour d'honneur* of Octavien de St. Gelais; and obviously it does draw upon the school of French poets influenced by the Rhétoriqueurs to which St. Gelais belonged. The numberless allusions are taken from popular biblical and classical tradition, from the folklore, history, or pseudo-science of Douglas's own day; a few details of setting or action perhaps from Ovid and Dante; the discussion of the transcience of earthly glory and the permanence of moral virtue from Boethius. However, the most significant source for *The Palice of Honour* seems to have been *The House of Fame*, from which not only certain details could have come, such as the desert from which the dreamer departs, the helpful guide, the difficult ascent of a slippery rock to a supernatural palace, the throng of suppliants at its gate, the rich interior of the palace and high enthroned deity, but also suggestions for the humorous characterization of narrator and guide, which is somewhat unusual for a dream vision. Despite its rambling, digressive pace and endless catalogues, the poem has energy, wit, and a certain philosophic wisdom. Its diction provides an excellent example of the aureate style popular in the sixteenth century, and its verse at times displays the skillful gymnastics in rime advocated by the Rhétoriqueurs and practised by British as well as French poets (cf. especially *Anelida and Arcite,* and Dunbar's *Ane Ballat of Our Lady* [103]). *The Palice of Honour* as a whole is, in fact, a tribute to Douglas's ability as a metricist; its basic pattern of a nine-line stanza built on two rimes is one exceedingly difficult to maintain in the relatively limited "Scottis."

KING HART [21]. 121 stanzas of alliterative pentameter lines, ababbcbc.

An allegory of human life in which the heart represents man. Young King Hart in his strong castle, surrounded by servants—the attributes of youth—and watchmen—the five senses—thinks he will always live in joy and revelry. Honour, refused admittance by the King's company, enters by a trick, bringing fresh delight; and those within make such melody they do not hear the sinister black water rising without. Dame Plesance, who dwells nearby in a well-fortified castle with a court of fitting attributes, goes hunting one day; and her company, seen by watchers on the King's wall, promptly capture Youth and Delight, who come out to reconnoiter. Receiving no message from his warriors, the King first sends others who are also captured despite the warning of Dread of Disdain, then himself boldly attacks with all his host only to be overthrown, wounded by Plesance, and delivered to Beauty for nursing, which only increases his pain. The King yields to Plesance. His men are captured or slain; his castle left desolate, with Heaviness, Fear, Langour and Ire in possession. Jealousy as a spy follows King Hart to Plesance's prison, and there finds many a creature: some, like Green Love, fettered; others, like Youth, free; Discretion blinded by Lust. In the courtyard the Queen with her officers, attributes suited to youth and/or pleasure, and her singing ladies, commands the prisoners to do homage while King Hart listens, painfully wounded. Danger has made him a pavilion of sorrow; Youth, a coat of green and a visor of red and white. The King cries for aid to Pity who is held by Danger until, drugged by Fair Calling, Danger sleeps and Pity slipping out is seized by Business. Plesance becomes a prisoner of Lust and other forces of King Hart, who now puts on his amorous cloak; and as the company feasts, Plesance drinks of Venus's tun and Chastity departs. For seven years Hart lives with Liking and Love, until Age comes, followed by Conscience, Reason, and Wit, who help the King atone for his misdeeds. One by one the attributes of youth and pleasure depart, Delight, Strength, finally Queen Plesance herself, leaving the King asleep to be joined forthwith by Disease and Jealousy. Reason, Wisdom, and Sadness advise the King to leave Love and return to his own castle. Heaviness welcomes him, wondering at his changed face; and at last the King is left with only the likes of Desire, Jealousy, Ire, Wretchedness, and Ease as his best-loved companion. Worship of War would serve him, but now that Strength has gone cannot stay. Decrepitude captures the castle, and as the ailments of old age rush in, sorely wounds the King, whose last servants now become ineffectual. Sending for Death, King Hart makes his testament. To his evil companions he bequeaths appropriate characteristics: to Plesance, faithlessness; to Beauty, appetite; to Gluttony, a rotten liver, etc. To Chastity he leaves his conscience for scouring, to Generosity a threadbare cloak, to Business a stool to rest upon, and to Danger, a spear, once stiff and stout, but now broken and headless.

This moral allegory is suggestive of a variety of genres: morality play, sermon, debate, etc. It is said to have been influenced by St. Gelais's *Le séjour d'honneur*, or Rene of Anjou's *Le livre de cuer d'amour esprins*. Queen Plesance, with her court of attributes suitable to courtly love, clearly owes something to the *Roman de la rose*. However, unlike *The Palice of Honour, King Hart* exhibits no pervasive French influence and lacks the aureate diction, rhetorical devices, ornamental description, and metrical gymnastics advocated by the Rhétoriqueurs. Its allegorical and rhetorical devices—the struggle between personifications of virtue and vice for a man's soul, the body presented in terms of a building and physical attributes in terms of clothing, the *ubi sunt* lamentation, listing of contraries, and testament—are conventional ones, widely used in the medieval period. Yet the poem displays considerable originality in their use, despite its allegorical structure, achieving real dramatic suspense, pathos, and realism, as for example in the petulancy of Queen Plesance or the brutal onslaught of Decrepitude. In addition it has a terse, swift pace whose movement is facilitated by prosody simpler than that of *The Palice of Honour*, the stanza being built on three rimes instead of two with little if any internal rime and alliteration used structurally rather than for ornamentation. Although its story is perhaps more interesting, *King Hart* is more difficult for the modern reader than *The Palice of Honour* because of its relatively obscure diction, anacolutha, and frequent metrically or grammatically incomplete lines. Because of the radical difference in style between *King Hart* and Douglas's unquestioned work, the lack of any contemporary ascription of it to him, and his failure to list it among his other works at the end of the *Eneados*, the poem is generally no longer attributed to him.

CONSCIENCE [22]. Four stanzas of pentameter lines, ababbab.

    When the church was young, prelates were perfect, being chosen by Conscience; and though Conscience then was clipped to Science, still the church was well served by men of wit and learning. But now Science has been reduced to Ens (riches and possessions) which drives out grace, corrupts Science and Conscience, makes every clerk false, and poisons Justice. Let Ens depart, God send us Defense with Conscience.

Although this punning satire is not included in Douglas's list of works at the end of the *Eneados* [19] there seems little reason to question its authorship. It is ascribed to him by the same sixteenth-century hand which copied the poem into its unique manuscript, and it could very plausibly have been written after completion of the *Eneados* in 1513 for its subject and tone seem to reflect the kind of disillusionment with ecclesiastical preferment which Douglas may well have felt after, though scarcely before, his unsuccessful attempt to procure the Archbishopric of St. Andrews in 1514.

4. Dunbar

Accounts of the life of William Dunbar are at best conjectural, being based principally upon evidence in his poems, with some assistance from the public records of Scotland for the years 1500–1513. It has been assumed from Kennedy's reference in *The Flyting of Dunbar and Kennedie* [28], "Thou was consavit in the grete eclips," that the poet was born shortly after July 18, 1460, when such an eclipse did occur. If, however, he were the William Dunbar named in the roll of licentiates at St. Andrews in 1479, he would seem to have been born at an earlier date, possibly 1455–57. Judging from a reference in *To the King—Schir yit remembir* [42] the poet was intended for an ecclesiastical career from an early age; and Kennedy suggests something of such a career in *The Flyting*, telling how Dunbar travelled as a pardoner from Ettrick Forest in the north to Dumfrieshire in the south, then abroad through France as far south as the foot of the Alps, north through Paris, and up into Denmark. *How Dumbar wes Desyrd to be Ane Freir* [26] seems to confirm this testimony as to his ecclesiastical travels, but says it was as a friar he preached, in pulpits in England and once at Canterbury, then crossed the channel on a ferry from Dover to Picardy. He also says, in *The Flyting*, that he travelled by sea past Holland, Zeeland, Jutland, and the Norway coast. *Dunbar at Oxinfurde* [74] suggests that he studied, or simply resided for a time, at Oxford; and a William Dunbar, who may have been the poet, was awarded the Bachelor of Arts Degree at St. Andrews in 1477, the Masters two years later. Since an entry in the Register of the Privy Seal indicates that James IV granted Dunbar a pension in August 1500, he must have joined the King's retinue at some time prior to that date. And judging from subsequent references to payments made him by the King and the number of his poems which deal with court life, he remained at court at least until 1513, possibly in a capacity approximating that of poet laureate. Dunbar may have been the Protonotary of Scotland who accompanied a mission to London to arrange the marriage of Margaret Tudor and James IV, delivered *To the City of London* [123] at a reception for that mission, and as Rhymer of Scotland was rewarded by Henry VII on December 31, 1501, and January 7, 1502. On March 14, 1503, James IV made an offering at the poet's first Mass, so it would seem he had by that time been ordained. He last appears in the public records as recipient of a pension paid on May 14, 1513; but there is some question as to the precise date on which he died. Certain commentators believe that Dunbar fought with the King at Flodden and fell beside him. However, nowhere does the poet give any indication of being militarily inclined; and attitudes implicit in *The Flyting* [28], *That the King War Johne Thomsounis Man* [40], *Of a*

Dance in the Quenis Chalmer [53], *Of James Dog* [54], *Gladethe Thoue Queyne of Scottis Regioun* [114], and *To the Princess Margaret* [125] suggest that his sympathies might have lain as much with the English countrymen of the Queen as with the Scottish followers of the King. *Quhen the Governour Past in France* [86] and *To the Queen Dowager* [126] are sometimes cited as evidence of his having been alive after the battle of Flodden, although the authorship of both poems is open to doubt. If Dunbar did live on after Flodden, it is not known how or where. He was, at all events, dead by 1530 when David Lindsay speaks of his poetic career as past.

Most editors group the Dunbar poems by subject, attempting to arrange them chronologically as well, on the assumption that chronology is to some extent suggested by subject. The following classifications and titles are those used in the most recent edition, Mackenzie's. Poems which Mackenzie omits are listed below among Attributions and designated by their first line.

I. Personal

The richest source of information about Dunbar, his lineage, stature, and career both as an ecclesiastic and poet. The accuracy of the information is as yet undetermined.

TO THE KING [23]. Seven stanzas with refrain, of tetrameter lines, aabab, in which the poet laments the painful state of his purse, which deprives him of charity, the ability to write, of pleasure, drink, and food, and hints that the King might remedy matters. Possibly influenced by *The Complaint of Chaucer to His Purse* and Lydgate's *Letter to Gloucester*, both pleas for funds. This humorous rueful acknowledgement of financial straits is similar in subject and tone to *Welcome to the Lord Treasurer* [45] and *To the Lordis of the Kingis Chalker* [46], and might well be listed with them among the Petitions below.

ANE HIS AWIN ENNEMY [24]. Five stanzas with refrain (cf. *To the King* [23]).

The man who is rich and expels gladness, who is single and marries, who is healthy and contracts venereal disease, or who serves an ungrateful master works sorrow to himself. The devil take a man who worries dry bread when there is good wine to sell.

A light, alliterative drinking song, reminiscent of goliardic verse.

ON HIS HEID-AKE [25]. Three stanzas of tetrameter lines, aabba. A severe headache prevents the poet from writing, dulls all his thought, and makes his spirit sleep. Description of a mental state similar to Dunbar's has been pointed out in Chaucer's *Knight's Tale*.

HOW DUMBAR WES DESYRD TO BE ANE FREIR [26]. Nine stanzas in Pepys 2553, ten in National Library Scotland 1.1.6, of pentameter lines, aabba. A dream vision in which St. Francis appears to the poet, demanding that he don the habit of a friar and preach. But though he had done so long ago, he now refuses, and the saint, a fiend in disguise, vanishes in smoke. One of the poems thought to shed light on Dunbar's early life and his attitude toward friars.

COMPLAINT TO THE KING AGANIS MURE [27]. Four stanzas of tetrameter lines, aabbcbc, each stanza ending with the same word. The poet demands that the King punish Mure for mangling his work by adding lying, slanderous, treasonable verses to it. The poem suggests something of Dunbar's position at court: evidently his poetry was popular enough to be plagiarized, and he himself in sufficient favor to expect protection for it from the King.

THE FLYTING OF DUNBAR AND KENNEDIE [28]. Sixty-nine stanzas of irregular pentameter lines, ababbccb or -cbc, with internal rime and heavy alliteration.

A compendium of abuse which achieves something of the effect of a formal ceremony because of its structure. In three stanzas Dunbar threatens Kennedy and Quentin, who have boasted of their work and whose backbiting could make him attack them, and in three Kennedy accepts the challenge, bidding Dunbar leave his riming and make amends to Quentin. Each poet then has a long speech attacking, in language obscene and scurrilous in the extreme, the other's ancestry, intelligence, moral character, appearance, poverty, unsavory activities past and present, and demanding that his opponent acknowledge defeat.

The richest source of personal detail about Dunbar, none of which, unfortunately, can be accepted as reliable since in this conventional literary performance fact cannot be disentangled from fiction. It has been suggested that the poem shows the influence of the *jeu-parti* of Northern France, the *tenso* and *sirvente* of Provence, more specifically of the letters of Poggio against Philelfo and Lorenzo Valla, and of a Latin Carolingian poem, *Ecloga Theoduli*. Quite possibly there was no one main source. The practice of verbal combat was a very old, widespread one going back to Ovid and found among the French, Italian, Anglo-Saxon, and Celtic writers; moreover the opposition between the two poets of racial, political, and religious attitudes could have made it natural for them to engage in a flyting.

LAMENT FOR THE MAKARIS [29]. Twenty-five stanzas of two tetrameter couplets each, the old French Kyrielle form, with a Latin refrain. A development of the dance of death comparable to Henryson's *The Ressoning Betwixt Deth and Man* [12] and *The Thre Deid Pollis* [16], employing as refrain a line from the Response to the seventh lesson in the Office of the Dead.

In his sickness the poet laments the transience of earthly life. All ranks, all professions, his brother poets, whom he names one by one, are subject to death, for which we should prepare in order to gain eternal life. Fear of death confounds him.

The poem's somberness has led to the assumption that it was written in Dunbar's old age; but such a tone could, of course, have been occasioned as readily by illness as by age. In any case it could not have been written before 1490 when the Treasurer's Accounts last refer to "Patrik Johnson," a player at court during the 1480's, but in Dunbar's poem found among the dead.

OF DEMING [30]. Ten stanzas, each ending with the same word, in National Library Scotland 1.1.6, eleven in Pepys 2553 (cf. *To the King* [23]).

No one remains unjudged: king, lord, lady, courtier, knight, little man, big man, ornate speaker. But if the judges knew how their words were judged, some would cease;

and if they did not, save that it would worsen matters, the poet would do vengeance upon them. In youth the King advised, "Ignore judging, for no man shall be unjudged." With God's grace the poet will keep his command [whether a reference to the King's or to God's is not clear], praying to have a place in heaven where no man will be judged.

The poem is attributed to Dunbar in MS National Library Scotland 1.1.6 but to Stewart in Pepys 2553. However, it closely resembles *How Sall I Governe Me?* [31] in thought and method; its meter, rime, cataloguing technique, condemnation of a universal human weakness, reference to small stature and to ornate speech—both of which might be the speaker's own—are in keeping with Dunbar's acknowledged work, and the poem is commonly accepted as his.

HOW SALL I GOVERNE ME? [31]. Ten stanzas with slightly varying refrain (cf. *To the King* [23]). A companion piece to [30].

However the poet governs himself, be he merry or sad, well or poorly dressed, etc., he cannot escape censure. Since all actions, good or ill, are judged, he determines to do the best and leave his governing to God.

Possibly influenced by Lydgate's *A Wicked Tunge Wille Sey Amys.*

MEDITATION IN WYNTIR [32]. Ten stanzas (cf. *On His Heid-ake* [25]).

In the dark, wet days and long nights of winter the poet, unable to write, despondent and sleepless, is counselled by Despair to provide a livelihood, by Patience not to fear, by Prudence not to desire what must pass, by Age to remember he must make an accounting, by Death, that he must die, which thought no pleasure can blot from memory. Yet as the night grows shorter his spirit is somewhat comforted, and he bids summer come with its flowers to cheer him.

The tone of this beautiful meditation, whose somberness is skillfully evoked by the description of winter, then lightened by the anticipation of summer, has been interpreted as an indication of the poet's old age, as in the case of *Lament for the Makaris* [29]; but here the indication is strengthened by references to the necessity of providing something to live on in time and to Age's taking his hand.

II. Petitions

A good source of information about the practice of patronage at the court of James IV, Dunbar's attitudes toward the King and Queen, toward his own deserts and those of others, rank and privilege, the oppression of the poor, and toward greed and corruption among the clergy. The nature of these poems and their number, second only to those on Court Life, have led to Dunbar's being charged with sycophancy; but in view of their frequent bluntness the charge seems unjustified. With the exception of *That the King War Johne Thomsounis Man* [40], *Welcome to the Lord Treasurer* [45], and *To the Lordis of the Kingis Chalker* [46], which combine whimsey with urgency, the Petitions suggest indignation and disillusionment rather than servile begging, and the majority are harsh, outspoken attacks upon contemporary abuses.

QUHONE MONY BENEFICES VAKIT [33]. Three stanzas (cf. *On His Heid-ake* [25]).

A plea for equal distribution of benefices, which will content the reasonable man, be an act of merit—not filling the full man to bursting but giving the thirsty drink—forestall the sadness unequal distribution brings, and win the company's blessing. (Cf. [34].)

TO THE KING—OFF BENEFICE SCHIR [34]. Six stanzas with a half-line refrain (cf. *To the King* [23]).

At every feast of benefice they who have the most request the most and feel wronged if they do not get everything to divide among them. While they swell, the poet fasts, singing "Charitas pro Dei amore"; but in this world, who has nothing gets nothing. Those who rule the church think not of its welfare or that of the poor, but only whether they have the pelf to divide. This world's profits are cursed: none bring content; after death, who have the most shall repent the most, for they shall have the largest account to divide among themselves.

A companion piece to [33]; in view of their identical subjects the two poems seem to have been composed during the same period.

OF THE WARLDIS INSTABILITIE [35]. Twenty-five stanzas with slightly varying refrain (cf. *Lament for the Makaris* [29]).

To consider the world's wretchedness, its ingratitude, transitory joy, feigned love, hypocrisy—not only here but in other countries as well, the loss of honorable custom, of belief, good rule, and manners, the fruitless earth and infected air, unfilial sons and conscienceless clergy, the unjust distribution of benefices, causes the poet pain. Painful to him as well is his own long wait for a little church, which is to come from King or Queen, but has been delayed so long it might by this time have come from the ends of the earth; he fears it has turned back again. Experience having wearied him of this false, changeable world, his chief hope now lies in the King, which is some lessening of his pain.

The description of his long wait and weariness suggests that this poem was a product of Dunbar's old age, as perhaps was *Meditatioun in Wyntir* [32]; but all that is definitely known regarding its date is that it must have been composed after 1492 because of its reference to "the new fund Yle," America.

OF DISCRETIOUN IN ASKING [36]. Eight stanzas with refrain in Pepys 2553, nine in National Library Scotland 1.1.6 (cf. *To the King* [23]). First of three poems, [36], [37], [38], similar in title and form but quite different in purpose.

The poet gives advice as to effective asking, since reward does not follow every request: have a cause, do not bore the listener by repetition, ask neither for too little nor too much, be not ashamed as is the poet to ask, for to serve yet live in beggary shames both man and master. Do not boast, use few but sufficient words, choose a convenient place and time then ask without haste or crowd in neither an abashed nor reckless manner. A lord will sometime reward long service; if he does not, what remedy? It is witless to fight with fortune.

OF DISCRETIOUN IN GEVING [37]. Eleven stanzas with refrain in Pepys 2553, twelve in National Library Scotland 1.1.6 (cf. *To the King* [23]).

In large part an attack on indiscreet giving. People give for reasons good and bad; some wait so long the asker grows tired and ungrateful; some give too little, some too much. Some, neglecting the poor or old servants, give to those who do not need or deserve it: rich men, strangers who flew from Flanders (possibly a reference to Damian, Abbot of Tungland, cf. *The Fenyeit Freir of Tungland* [59] and *The Birth of Antichrist* [60]), crafty complainers, flatterers, knaves. Some give to honest, good men; and to ecclesiastics lacking wit even to guide themselves, some give wide parishes to govern.

OF DISCRETIOUN IN TAKING [38]. Eight stanzas with refrain in National Library Scotland 1.1.6, ten in Pepys 2553 (cf. *To the King* [23]).

An attack on evil taking: of too little authority or too much; of benefices by clerics who care only for rents; by landlords who beggar their tenants, or dishonest merchants who do not enrich their posterity; by robbers on sea and land who forget death until they swing from gallows or tree. Some man would take his neighbor's all, if he feared man as little as he does God. Were the poet in awe of neither, he would take everything—but that is justice not worth a clod. Some would take the world's bread and be unsatisfied; others take little and cannot advance. Great men for their taking are famous, seated at the Session; poor men for theirs are hanged, they and their descendants shamed forever.

REMONSTRANCE TO THE KING [39]. Eighty-eight lines of tetrameter couplets.

The King has servants who are cunning, industrious members of various professions and crafts, well deserving of thanks, reward, and cherishing; and the poet's work shall last as long as any of theirs, though his reward be small. But the King has another sort of follower: parasites, fools, evil speakers and doers who have no cunning and know no craft; and while it is reasonable that the first sort be rewarded, when the latter are and the poet is not, either his heart must break or he must avenge himself with his pen—which he shall do unless reward come quickly.

This poem and *Complaint to the King* [41], two of the most impassioned and direct of Dunbar's protests against his treatment by the King, achieve their effect of vehemence largely by means of alliterative catalogues and the swift movement of the short lines with their occasional enjambment. Together they present a striking picture of the court of James IV, subsequent to 1507 if the poet's reference to "Pryntouris" meant operators of a printing press, for it was in that year that the printers, Andrew Myllar and Walter Chepman, were granted a patent by James IV.

THAT THE KING WAR JOHNE THOMSOUNIS MAN [40]. Eight stanzas with slightly varying refrain (cf. *Lament for the Makaris* [29]).

The poet prays that the King become Joan Thomson's man, i.e., be subservient to his wife, for if he were, Dunbar would not lack a benefice. It would do no harm for the fairest and best in Britain to achieve such worship; the King would be merciful, the rose would soften the thistle and speed in the poet's behalf. Whenever he finds the King harsh he prays to God and St. Ann that James become Joan Thomson's man.

The poem has something of the rueful whimsey of *The Petition of the Gray Horse Auld Dunbar* [44], *Welcome to the Lord Treasurer* [45], and *To the Lordis of the Kingis Chalker* [46]; the gentleness and grace of *The Thrissil and the Rois* [76], *Gladethe Thoue Queyne of Scottis Regioun*

[114], and *To the Princess Margaret* [125], wherein the poet also speaks of Margaret. It is one of those poems which suggest that from the time of her arrival in Scotland, Dunbar was more the Queen's man than the King's (cf. *Of a Dance in the Quenis Chalmer* [53], *Of James Dog* [54], *Of the Said James* [55], *The Thrissil and the Rois* [76], and *To the Princess Margaret* [125]).

COMPLAINT TO THE KING [41]. Seventy-six lines (cf. *Remonstrance to the King* [39]).

The poet would complain, if he knew to whom, of injuries endured by nobles of virtue and wisdom who win nothing in the court for their loyalty, love, or service, while lackies and rascals, dullards and thieves rise to the rule of convent or bishopric, or, spurning a parsonage, do not rest content until they become a lord. How content is the learned son of a noble who serves an ignorant, undeserving, misshapened, greedy peasant, one promoted above him, who despises and helps keep down nobles of blood? Let the prince be merciful and remember old servants who have long trusted him. Whether or not the poet has been such a servant has been told through all regions; his writing bears witness to it. The poem, after rising to an outcry of bitter remonstrance, closes on a muted, somewhat hopeful note: though the prince's "danger" ever injures the poet, after "danger" comes grace, as has been heard in many a place.

From its reference to old servants, among whom is Dunbar, who have long trusted the King, this poem is usually thought to have been written in his old age (cf. *Meditatioun in Wyntir* [32] and *Of the Warldis Instabilitie* [35]). It has been suggested that the poem's piling up of abusive epithets, many of them obscure, represents an exercise in fifteenth-century nonsense such as a medieval Lewis Carroll might have composed. Not impossibly, a number of these terms, and of those in *The Flyting of Dunbar and Kennedie* [28], were actually neologisms, coined for the sake of verbal attack and highly suited for it because of the harsh, contemptuous effect they create even when their literal meaning is unknown— if it ever existed. However, it is difficult to see how this vehement excoriation could ever have been judged to be primarily nonsense verse. Cf. *Remonstrance to the King* [39].

TO THE KING—SCHIR YIT REMEMBIR [42]. Seventeen stanzas with refrain (cf. *To the King* [23]).

A stern remonstrance to the King, each accusation being followed by the cry, "Excess of thought does me mischief." The King should remember the poet's youth spent in his service; it deserves reward. But noble birds are now forgotten; neglected; ignoble ones cosseted. How can this gentle eagle not cherish his lieges properly? While all men are served, the poet, who would fain live too, gets nothing. If it were not an offense to God, he would be one of the pickthanks; they lack no pleasure. When others flatter and feign, he, simple as a child, can only write ballads. Since his service is light, he asks only, for the sake of mercy, a benefice. But he who in youth was called "bishop," now cannot be even a vicar. One cattle boy, with a trick worth all the poet's ballads, gets churches; another, curacies; Dunbar, nothing. How can he live without land or benefice? Not speaking to reprove the King, the poet comes close to it, like a soul in purgatory living in hope of heaven.

The poem is interesting for what it suggests about Dunbar's early and lasting ecclesiastical ambitions, his attitude toward the advancement of low-born men, and his relations with James IV, which were either so intimate or so misguided that he felt he could reprove the King in most outspoken terms. *To the King—Schir yit remembir* alone should be sufficient to offset the charge that Dunbar was a whining beggar at court (cf. also [39] and [41]).

NONE MAY ASSURE IN THIS WARLD [43]. Seventeen stanzas with slightly varying refrain (cf. *To the King* [23]).

The poet knows not to whom to complain nor how to employ his days, for none may trust this world with its hypocrisy, ingratitude, falseness, abuse of truth, injustice, contempt for virtue, unfitting promotion, loss of nobility and of pity in princes, etc. Yet since all must die and make an accounting before God, who should trust this transitory world or by means of oppression seek its wrongful wealth, which if unrestored represents sin that no confession helps, cannot save one from hell, and shall be swept away? Since he must die so soon, the poet prays for no earthly curacy, but to be received into the kingdom of God—for in this world none may assure.

One of the most effective of Dunbar's poems, with its apt, evocative imagery; passion intensified by alliteration; and climax made particularly dramatic by the use of phrases from the Vulgate and a refrain whose reiteration of the vanity of all earthly concerns controls both the rush of the verse and the poet's agonized protest. To see the poet's increase in skill and power, compare this piece to *How Sall I Governe Me?* [31]. It would seem to be the last, or one of the last, of Dunbar's petitions, not only because here he has achieved complete mastery of his art, but also because he no longer requests any earthly office and no longer addresses the King, but God.

THE PETITION OF THE GRAY HORSE AULD DUNBAR [44]. Two lines and five stanzas with double refrain, of tetrameter lines riming aaabbb in Pepys 2553; in Cambridge University Library Ll.5.10, ten similar stanzas in three fragments, the last two being in reversed order and followed by the "Respontio Regis," eight lines of tetrameter couplets. Although the majority of editors have assigned this stanza to James IV, it may have been written by Dunbar himself in a final attempt to sway the King by depicting him engaged in an action which would be to the poet's mind highly desirable. In Pepys 2553 the poem begins with what seems obviously meant to be, and usually is printed as, the double refrain for each stanza, though its second line is not actually repeated as a refrain in either manuscript.

Why should not palfreys be proud when mares, ridden by high and low, are shorn and adorned? Let the King not permit the poet to be called a Youllis yald [one who lacks new clothes at Christmas]. In youth he could have been bought in neighboring realms; now he is driven away from gentle horses to join coal nags; and lacking the stall and silk of a courser, would be happy with a new horse blanket. He would be housed, though he is just an old horse as the King knows; but he is put from the stall by great court horses. Now for age he might be taken in from the bare pastures where he has long run. His mane is white (thanks to the King), he is fed only grass, never petted; his life so miserable all he can offer to get straw is his skin, he yet prays the King not to let cobblers gnaw that skin after his death. Made a worn-out mule by the court, still if he could wear trappings at Christmas, he would be spurred in every limb.

Despite the whimsey of its consistently maintained metaphor, the meagerness of the poet's request (no longer for a benefice but only Christmas trappings), the evidences of old age, and the glaring discrepancy between the poet's service and its reward give the poem a certain bitter pathos.

WELCOME TO THE LORD TREASURER [45]. Eight stanzas with refrain (cf. *Lament for the Makaris* [29]).

Having thought it long till some lord returned from whom he could claim comfort, the poet now welcomes the Lord Treasurer, most powerful and renowned, who had promised to return to Edinburgh speedily and has kept the promise, proving true as steel. The poet had feared lest the Treasurer pass from Stirling to the courts of justice; his writing would have been sad had he lacked his wage till Yule. But now he sings happily and heartily, "Welcome" to benefice, rent, livelihood, pension; "Welcome" from personal servant to dear master.

Similar to *To the King* [23] and *To the Lordis of the Kingis Chalker* [46] in subject and rueful effect, the poem has an air of formality enhanced by its ceremonious refrain covering, but just barely, a most urgent need of money. The result seems anticipatory of Gilbert and Sullivan.

TO THE LORDIS OF THE KINGIS CHALKER [46]. Four stanzas (cf. *On His Heid-ake* [25]).

The poet shall plainly state his account to the Lords of Exchequer: he has no money. They need not tire themselves reckoning up his rents, rooms, or sums. Though he took money from my Lord Treasurer trusting to enjoy it long, he cannot tell how but it has been spent, as his light purse proves.

In its combination of slight pomposity, down-to-earth urgency, and humor at the poet's own expense, here enhanced by occasional feminine rimes, the poem is similar to *To the King* [23] and to [45], above.

III. Court Life

A group interesting primarily for the light it sheds on the nature and moral tone of amusements popular at James' court. Adultery, lust, sycophancy, grossness, drunkenness, obscenity, mockery of aliens, of deformity, and of religion, would seem to have been the order of the day. The bulk of these poems, together with *Dance of the Sevin Deidly Synnis* [78] below, and *The Sowtar and Tailyouris War* [79], has caused considerable debate over Dunbar's possible immorality and obvious delight in obscenity.

A NEW YEAR'S GIFT TO THE KING [47]. Five stanzas with refrain (cf. *Lament for the Makaris* [29]).

As a gift for the New Year may God grant the King grace, joy, comfort, mirth, virtue, prosperity, fortune, as long as he lives; help him rule and defend the realm in peace and justice; grant him bliss, wealth, and liberality.

A graceful, light occasional piece reflecting a custom that went back to the days of the Roman Empire. Dunbar's prayer that the King be granted liberality might justify including this poem among the Petitions.

THE WOWING OF THE KING QUHEN HE WAS IN DUNFERM-LINE [48]. Ten stanzas with slightly varying refrain (cf. *Complaint to the King Aganis Mure* [27]).

Last night the poet was told a wonderful thing: how a fox played with and would have ravished a lamb, embracing her, then asking grace while she cried to Mary for help. The lusty red fox was too big for the white tender lamb, yet she did not flee but let him kiss her. He spoke fair, though falsely, swore he would not threaten her virginity, and the silly thing trusted him. The poet will not lie as janglers do, but will tell how these two were confounded. He knows not, when the lights were out and the doors barred, whether the fox granted the lamb grace; but when joy is most, woe comes—the wolf beset the house. The lamb cheeped like a mouse; the ewes were silent; and deep in the lamb's skin, the fox hid until the wolf thought all asleep and departed protesting. That is what happened at Dunfermline.

Although the precise occasion of this poem is not known, it is definitely thought to have been one of James IV's amorous escapades, and the poet's frankness in dealing with it suggests a familiar relationship between himself and the King. The poem's obscenity, like that of *In Secreit Place* [49], *To the Quene* [52], *Of a Dance in the Quenis Chalmer* [53], and *Of Ane Blak-Moir* [58], has been found reprehensible and especially surprising for one seeking ecclesiastical preferment, by critics who find such an element a means of marring rather than invigorating the verse.

IN SECREIT PLACE [49]. Nine stanzas with alternating refrains (cf. *Complaint to the King Aganis Mure* [27]). Often called *Ane Brash of Wooing*.

Last night the poet overheard an exchange between a town lout and a wench, the man pleading that he has long been a faithful lover without any comfort, and asking how long his bonny one will resist him, for she breaks his heart. He embraces, kisses, and would lie with her, he has never loved another, his stomach so full of love he trembles; let her not be hostile, aroused as he is to erection by her white throat, mouth, and pudendum. Laughing she bids her lover be quiet, assures him she has loved no other all week; his graceless face is dear to her, his musing would pierce a heart of stone, and she welcomes him, being of the same mind as he. He gives her an apple, and they begin the sexual dance; she protests mildly but now loves that graceless face.

Possibly another instance of the use of nonsense terms, since a number of the epithets are obscure, and seem here used for their effect of foolish endearment, or baby talk, rather than of savage abuse (cf. *The Flyting of Dunbar and Kennedie* [28] and *Complaint to the King* [41]). The poem has been both attacked for its indecency and defended as either a telling satire upon sexual corruption or an expression of Dunbar's delight in and sympathy with the uninhibited animality of the lower classes as opposed to the courtly code of the nobility. In MS National Library Scotland 1.1.6 it is ascribed to "Clerk" (cf. *Fane wald I luve but quhair abowt?* [111]), but in a later hand; and in the light of the ascriptions to Dunbar in MSS Pepys 2553 and Cambridge University L1.5.10 no editor has seriously questioned his authorship.

AGANIS THE SOLISTARIS IN COURT [50]. Twenty-six lines (cf. *Remonstrance to the King* [39].

The poet lists the ways men solicit at court: some by service, some by entertainment; some whisper, some for covetousness nearly swoon, others look as if they would go mad; some lose all devotion laboring for promotion, while others use advocates. His own simpleness knows of no way save humility to commend himself to the grace of the King, whose countenance is, for him, sufficient riches.

An indirect request which, despite its title, might be included among the Petitions. That it is an accurate reflection of at least one aspect of court life is borne out by the Treasurer's Accounts which list payment to just such entertainers as those whose activities Dunbar catalogues.

THE DREGY OF DUNBAR [51]. Eighty-four lines (cf. *Remonstrance to the King* [39]). Three four-line Responses, and two concluding Latin prayers, one of nine lines, the other of six. There has been some discussion as to the form of the Responses, the second having been identified as a type of tail-rime. However, though they are usually printed in three groups of four double lines with two rimes each, when printed in groups of eight single lines the Responses constitute perfect French triolets, with the rime scheme abaaabab. The poem is a parody of the Office of the Dead, "Dirge" being the first word of the antiphon at Matins in that Office.

The poet gives the reason for his dirge: we, in the paradise of Edinburgh, commend ourselves to you pleasureless hermits and anchorites in Sterling where you have neither restorative meat, comforting wine, nor good company, and shall beseech the Lord to deliver you from purgatory to the bliss of Edinburgh. He then prays for this deliverance in three lessons, each followed by a Response, the first two also by a Benediction, and concludes with prayers adapted from the Latin service: lead us not into the temptation of Sterling, but deliver us from its evil; give them the rest of Edinburgh and let its light shine upon them, etc.

Dunbar has been severely criticized for this profane employment of a form dedicated to sacred usage—the coupling of Latin phrases, ceremonious order and cadence, with secular content is admittedly humorous—and the sincerity of his religious commitment questioned. But it has been pointed out that similar violations of religious observances, as for example in the celebrations under the Lords of Misrule, were readily countenanced in his day; and it would seem that the number and power of his serious religious poems should allay any doubt as to his true devoutness.

TO THE QUENE [52]. Seven stanzas each ending with the same word (cf. *To the King* [23]).

On Fastern's Eve the Queen's men said they would ride, but their wives bade them stay at home and cure themselves of the pox [Dunbar's phrase, "lib tham of the pockis" is taken as a reference to a method of treating venereal disease by lancing the chancres]. Now since the Queen remains, they propose to take their fill of wenching, but prove inadequate; better had they gone than infect their wives. Some were so lusty they broke doors and locks to get a wench; some, before as riotous as rams or thinking themselves strong as a giant, are now tame as lambs, sit down like old ewes, and have forsaken all such games, or are skinny from too much of them. The poet saw harlots lure young men better off in the stocks, for some got the Spanish pox. He prays all of them to avoid harlots, or they shall repent, and beware that perilous game called curing the pox.

That Dunbar could address a poem upon such a subject to the Queen, or describe so gross an entertainment as that of *Of a Dance in the Quenis Chalmer* [53] taking place in her presence, has been interpreted as evidence of the moral deficiency of the age, of Margaret, or of the poet, in his case resulting in failure to achieve church preferment, or as evidence of the poet's intimacy with one of the rulers or of his tactlessness. *The Wowing of the King quhen he was in Dunfermline* [48] has given rise to similar interpretations.

OF A DANCE IN THE QUENIS CHALMER [53]. Seven stanzas with refrain (cf. *Complaint to the King Aganis Mure* [27]).

> The poet describes various dancers: Sir John Sinclair, newly come from France, whose feet could not agree; Master Robert Shaw, who looked as if he could teach them all, but staggered like a hobbled cart horse; Master Almaser, who befouled himself until John But, the fool, cried out upon him; Dunbar the maker dancing the "dirrye dantoun" and hopping like a wanton colt—for love of Musgrave, men say— till he lost his slipper; Musgrave herself, who might have taught them—for her sake the poet wished to be the greatest lord in France; sour Dame Dounteboir, at whom none could help but laugh, dancing so busily a blast of wind escaped her; and the Queen's Dog (cf. *Of James Dog* [54] and *Of the Said James* [55]), who went like a mastiff and stunk like a tyke. A merrier dance might no man see.

Cf. [52]. On the basis of this poem some commentators have concluded that Dunbar was in love with Mistress Musgrave and she, then, was the subject of *To a Ladye* [70] and *Quhone he List to Feyne* [71].

OF JAMES DOG KEPAR OF THE QUENIS WARDROP [54]. Six stanzas with refrain (cf. *Lament for the Makaris* [29]).

> An attack on the wardrober, a dangerous dog, as dour to give a doublet as if it were a long frock. When the poet shows him the Queen's seal or writing, or speaks in a friendly fashion to him, he barks as if worrying a hog or chasing cattle and grimaces as if to bite, and Dunbar wishes he had a heavy clog to wear. He is a mighty mastiff to keep a wardrobe, too big to be a lap dog; the Queen should get a smaller one, for his steps shake the chamber.

For another reference to Dog, see [53]; a servant first of the King, then of the Queen, he is mentioned in the Treasurer's Accounts, 1488–1527. It has been suggested that this poem and *Of the Said James* [55] attest to the favor in which Dunbar stood with Margaret: apparently she not only made him gifts of clothing, but let him criticize her servants and sometimes acted upon his suggestions as to how they should treat him.

OF THE SAID JAMES QUHEN HE HAD PLESETT HIM [55]. Six stanzas with refrain (cf. *Lament for the Makaris* [29]). A companion piece to [54].

> The poet now urges his princess to treat well her wardrober, no dog but a lamb, whose faithful brother and greatest friend the poet is. Only for her amusement did he in a ballad jest about this man, the best possible director of the wardrobe. May the wife who would break his shins be drowned; the one who would cuckold him be beaten. So well he has obeyed the poet in everything, may he never be sad.

OF SIR THOMAS NORNY [56]. Nine tail-rime stanzas of tetrameter and trimeter b lines riming aabccb.

> A satiric encomium of a knight, wise, strong, chivalric, born of a giant and a fairy queen, chaser of thieves, highland ghosts, and twenty score of the Clan Chattan—though no man knows of it. He won the prize at feasts and upland bridals, best dancer, undefeated wrestler—he knows if this is a lie—who outstripped legendary heroes and always won at joust or tournament. Quentin was an idler to call him a full jordan, fouler than a fool, a lecherous bellowing bull. He would make Norny Currey's servant; but Norny never fouled a saddle while Currey fouled two. Therefore at Easter and Yule, the poet rightly cries him lord of every fool here; for of a renowned knight he lacks nothing but bells.

The poem is reminiscent both in form and content of Chaucer's burlesque of the romance hero, *Sir Thopas*. Some of the personages here mentioned have not been identified, but most seem to be figures from ballad or romance. The Treasurer's Accounts, 1504–12, cite Thomas Norny (or Norne[e]) a number of times among the king's attendants; and although it has been suggested that he was not a jester, since he lacked bells, and was perhaps simply some braggart Dunbar chose to pillory, he is spoken of specifically in one entry as "Thomas Norny, fule, . . . at his passage to Sanct James, iiij French crounis."

EPITAPHE FOR DONALD OWRE [57]. Eight tail-rime stanzas, each consisting of a tetrameter line couplet and a dimeter line wheel, riming aabbba. An attack on Donald of the Isles, whose adherents launched an unsuccessful revolt against James IV, and who was in prison by 1507, about which time it is conjectured the poem was written.

A traitor is most vicious, though pardoned, never free of shame and suspicion, odious, unnatural as a fiend in monk's garb. He beguiles himself, as now is proven in the Isles. That traitor, Donald Owre, falser than four others, yet glowers on gallows trees [the meaning of this reference has not as yet been made clear; as Owre did not die until long after the assumed date of the poem it could scarcely be "his corpse now hangs glowering"]. Falseness has no defense, for God will show the right with sore vengeance. Every thief and traitor is like the dissimulating fox. After respite, he works for spite by nature. If the fox be captured and forgiven a thousand times, when he is free, none may hold him from hens. A murderer murders until he is slain; a fox runs while he has a foot.

The poem proved prophetic, for some forty years later Donald led another revolt of the Isles.

OF ANE BLAK-MOIR [58]. Five stanzas with refrain (cf. *To the King* [23]).

Long has the poet written of white ladies, now he would describe a black one— my lady with the great lips. She has a mouth like an ape, gaping like a toad; a short cat nose; a shine like soap, or when she is richly clad, a bright tar barrel. At her birth the sun suffered eclipse, the night championed her. Who for her proves mightiest in the field shall kiss, embrace her, and control her love henceforth; and who loses, shall kiss her hips and never claim other comfort.

The possible subject and occasion of this poem have been discussed at some length. Perhaps Dunbar is here celebrating the tournament of "the black knight and the black lady" held in 1508, described at length in Pitscottie's *Chronicles* and the Treasurer's Accounts. The poem itself has been interpreted both as a broad but goodnatured caricature and as a display of unusual cruelty and inhumanity. On the whole it would seem that the poet was merely reflecting the normal attitudes of a court which would expend considerable money and effort to hold an entertainment such as the above-mentioned tournament.

THE FENYEIT FREIR OF TUNGLAND [59]. Seven tail-rime stanzas, the first and last consisting of twenty-four tetrameter and trimeter b lines, riming aaabcccbdddb, etc., the others of sixteen lines similar in length and rime. First of two burlesque dream visions (cf. *The Birth of Antichrist* [60]) attacking John Damian, a "French leich" or "medicinar" referred to a number of times in the Treasurer's Accounts, 1501–13, and possibly in *Of Discretioun in Geving* [37].

     The poet dreamt of a son of Satan, a Turk long an outlaw in Lombardy, who slew a religious man to escape baptism and, being literate, assumed his victim's habit. Discovered, he fled to France and though he had little medical learning, pretended to be a doctor, slaying so many that he had to flee to Scotland, where again he committed much murder with his medicine, crude instruments, powerful laxatives and purges. This ingenious pagan generated of giants, this new-made canon, neglected his duties for alchemy; but failing to make the quintessence put on a robe of feathers and flew off for Turkey. The birds first wondered what he was, then attacked him violently until, crying out on Fortune, he defecated for fear and slipping out of his feathers fell into the mud where he lay while the shrieking birds searched for him. Their hideous noise waked the poet who now wherever he goes curses the whole company.

Dunbar has been criticized for mocking the failure of this early attempt at flight rather than praising its ingenuity and daring.

THE BIRTH OF ANTICHRIST [60]. Ten stanzas (cf. *How Dumbar wes Desyrd to be Ane Freir* [26]).

     Oppressed, the poet goes to bed and having complained of contrary Fortune, dreamt that she advised him not to strive against her, that his trouble would be nearly over at a time—and he should never have a benefice until such time—when an abbot clothed in eagle feathers should fly among the cranes and as a gryphon meet a she-dragon in the air and there beget the Antichrist. Simon Magus, Mahoun, Merlin, and Jonet with her witches would then meet the Antichrist and preach his empire, and the world's end would be near. Fortune then vanished. Thus sleeping or waking the poet's desire was frustrated; and he hid his foolish dream until he heard that an abbot would fly in the sky, his feather robe perfectly made. Then he was comforted, for he had known he would never prosper until there were two moons in the sky, or an abbot flew above the moon.

Cf. [59]. Since the poem is an indirect plea for a benefice, it might be classified as a Petition, a later one judging both from the reference to Damian's exploit, which Leslie dates 1508, and the resignation with which the poet places his advancement among the impossibilities.

THE TESTAMENT OF MR ANDRO KENNEDY [61]. Fourteen stanzas, one of twelve, the others of eight tetrameter lines riming abababab (stanzas 1, 9, 10, 11), ababcdcd (stanzas 2, 4–8, 13), ababacac (stanza 3), ababbcbc (stanza 12), ababacacacac (stanza 14).

Kennedy, begotten by an incubus or a friar, not knowing where or how he was born but only that he is a devil incarnate, makes his testament. He leaves his soul to his lord's wine cellar, there to drink with Cuthbert till doomsday; his body to Ayre to lie in a midden heap receiving drink and malt refuse in his face each day; his varying heart to James; his best possession to the head of the family—though he knows not who that may be; his lying remedies to William Gray, Master of St. Anthony's and a liar; his false winnings to the false brothers who say they sing for men's souls; to Jok Fool, the rich swindler, his folly; to John Clark who killed him, God's curse and his own; all the rest of his goods to his lord to dispose of, with the guardianship of the boys. He would have his burial be in the new style, attended by his gang with two rustics to bear a barrel, with drinking such as he himself is accustomed to, singing and weeping, mixing drink with tears. He will have no priests sing or ring bells, but a dance by a bagpipe, an ale garland in place of banners, four flagons in place of the cross; then to escape the fiends, let "De terra plasmasti me" be heartily sung.

Not all of the recipients of these bequests have as yet been identified. The Pepys 2553 and Cambridge University L1.5.10 manuscripts give "Walter" instead of "Andro," apparently confusing the Kennedy of *The Flyting* [28] with that of [61]. Dunbar's attitude toward his victims seems the same in both poems, but the emphasis upon drunkenness and the reference to a practice of medicine which are found only in [61] suggest that they were different men. It has been suggested that the "Andro" named in National Library Scotland 19.1.16 and National Library Scotland 1.1.6 as the maker of the testament was some drunken court physician, now forgotten.

REWL OF ANIS SELF [62]. Six stanzas with refrain, of pentameter lines riming ababbcbc.

Polonius-like advice on dwelling at court: envy none; look, listen, but speak little; never lie; do not try to rule those who will not be ruled; beware in whom you confide, for appearances are deceiving and friend may turn to foe. Choose honorable companions, avoid evil ones; be patient even without a lordship, content with enough, for if you are not desire will drive you until death. Flee those of ill fame, flatterers, shrews, for you are known by your company; flee dangerous, envious gossip and arguments with willful men. Be not a whisperer, a scorner or a counselor or corrector of proud men, for that brings peril without profit. Since many things vary, attend to business and stand by God; be not spiteful to the poor nor do wrong to any man. He rules well that can guide himself so well.

The poem suggests the influence of Chaucer's *Truth* and the concluding stanzas of *Troilus and Criseyde*. Cf. *Best to be Blyth* [90], *Of Content* [91], *No Tressour Availis without Glaidnes* [94].

IV. Town Life

In large part attacks on contemporary abuses, interesting particularly for the light they shed on practices among the various crafts and professions of Dunbar's day.

THE DEVILLIS INQUEST [63]. Thirteen stanzas with refrain (cf. *To the King* [23]), in Pepys 2553, five of which are not in National Library Scotland 1.1.6; seventeen stanzas in National Library Scotland 1.1.6, nine of which are not in Pepys 2553. The text being obviously corrupt, different editors print the poem in the light of their own conjecture as to its original form.

> The poet dreamt that he saw the devil pass through the market, saying in turn to priest, courtier, goldsmith, commoner, merchant, tailor, brewer, etc., each person of all the crafts who blasphemed or perjured himself, "Renounce your God and come to me." And he thought the black devils, soliciting as thick as bees, ever tempted folk slyly, whispering to Robene and Dick, "Renounce your God and come to me."

TYDINGIS FRA THE SESSIOUN [64]. Eight stanzas with slightly varying refrain (cf. *Complaint to the King Aganis Mure* [27]).

> A highlander asks his neighbor for tidings, and the other tells, under seal of confession, what he has heard at the Session in Edinburgh: tidings of mistrust, successful transgression against innocence, hypocrisy, fawning, mortgaging, bribery, partiality, feigning. Litigants act in various ways, cases are variously decided; some make merry, some are robbed and dine on credit. Some forsake God; some cut throats, pick purses, or go to the gallows; some bless, some curse the court. Religious men come to woo, see fair faces, beget more friars, and are unmindful of their profession. The younger learn from the elder, subduing their hot flesh only with panting, so humble in intercession that all merciful women grant their errand. Such tidings he heard at the Session.

Since the date of the poem is unknown, there has been some question as to whether the poet is speaking of the Court of Session which was abolished in 1503–04, or of the Court of Daily Council which took its place and was also called "the Session."

TO THE MERCHANTIS OF EDINBURGH [65]. Eleven stanzas each consisting of tetrameter lines riming aaab, and a kind of bob-and-wheel consisting of a dimeter line and two tetrameter lines riming bab, lines five and seven serving as a double refrain throughout the poem.

An attack upon the merchants of Edinburgh in the form of a list of abuses which destroy the town's profit and fame, and a repeated question: are they not ashamed to have their name so dishonored? The streets are impassable because of stinking fish and people brawling; the stinking school [the meaning is debated; the "school" is now unknown and it has been suggested that "style" or "styll" was meant] darkens the parish church; outside stairs darken the houses, as in no other country. Junk is vended at High Cross and Trone [weighing machine]; minstrels sing only vulgar songs, while more clever men are slighted. The streets are defiled by craftsmen, merchants crammed into the Stinking Style, honest folk molested by beggars, the poor neglected. Merchants increase in profit, lessen in godly works; streets are full of the crooked, blind, and lame. The region's great assemblages for the Court and Session are here; if they pass to another town, the merchants of Edinburgh and their name will decay. Thus the merchants should mend all faults, entertain strangers and lieges, not overcharge or be proclaimed for extortion, keep order, supply the poor, and get a better name. Individual profit blinds them so that common profit fails. The poet prays God to find a remedy, to shame them, so reason may bind them and they have a good name.

The poem has been interpreted as an attack by Dunbar upon capitalism in general, but from the specific detail, it would seem to be directed rather at contemporary local ills, physical and moral.

V. Of Women

The attitude reflected by this group has been variously interpreted, recently as one of frustration resulting from the celibacy enforced by the poet-priest's calling. The bulk of the poems suggests that Dunbar was something of a misogynist, a suggestion substantiated by *Ballate against evil Women* [107], which may be his. However, it should be noted that *The Tua Mariit Wemen and the Wedo* [68] has been interpreted at least once as an exaltation of an ancient female cult.

IN PRAIS OF WEMEN [66]. Thirty-five lines in heroic couplets.

As far as the poet is concerned no earthly thing is better than women; men should worship and honor them above all. Who disparages them dishonors his source and therefore himself. Women are women and so will end and die. They suffer in our conception and birth, nourish and comfort us; no man may be half so dear. Who says one thing against them fouls his own nest, should be exiled from good company, and, lacking intelligence, received by no wise man. Since Christ had no man as father, and a woman bore Him, women should have worship, honor, service, love above all things.

It has been suggested that this poem, in the light of its poor quality, was not written by Dunbar. However, since it is ascribed to him in both the National Library Scotland 1.1.6 and Pepys 2553 manuscripts and possibly expresses not sincere praise but a heavy-handed irony in keeping with his characteristic attitude toward women, there is no real reason to question his authorship.

THE TWA CUMMERIS [67]. Six stanzas with refrain (cf. *To the King* [23]). The text has not been finally established, there being three versions which differ particularly in the refrain, and the refrain not being completely consistent with its context in any of them.

The poet's essential meaning would seem to be: early on Ash Wednesday as two gossips sat at wine, one, great and fat, feigning to be feeble, complained that the long Lent made her lean. The other said, you inherit that leanness from your mother, who disdained all wine save malmsey. Be glad; refrain from fasting; let your husband suffer; and Lent shall not make you lean. The first said, this counsel is good; everything I do is to plague him, for he is not worth a bean in bed; drink to me that Lent shall not make us lean. So thirsty they were, they drank two quarts hoping to mend and that Lent should not make them lean.

THE TRETIS OF THE TUA MARIIT WEMEN AND THE WEDO [68]. 530 unrimed alliterative lines, the only example among Dunbar's works of the use of alliteration as the governing metrical device.

Near midnight in midsummer the hidden poet overhears three beautiful, richly dressed ladies. To the widow's question, is marriage a blessed bond, one of the wives answers that it is bare of bliss, baleful, and causes great deceit. If she could, like the birds she would choose a new mate each year, go about to fairs, plays, preachings, pilgrimages, seeing new faces and showing herself off; and when she had chosen and then exhausted a lusty fellow in a month, she would look for another. Now she has an impotent, lustful, badtempered, jealous old carl, repulsive to her in every way, whom she makes pay handsomely for his abortive attempts at love-making. God save her sisters from such a husband. All laugh, pass the cup, and the second lady reveals that her husband was impotent from long lechery when he married her. Though he swaggers and seems lusty for love, he is a failure at it. An old man is no worse at Venus' work than he could be expected to be, but her husband had seemed a jewel and turned out to be a jet. If she could she would change for a fresh fellow she liked. She curses the kin who made the match; feigns tenderness for her husband, but wishes him bound to a tender maiden whom his love-making certainly could not hurt. The others laugh, praise her, drink, and talk more briskly. The widow prays that her preaching may make the others meeker to men. She has always been a deceitful shrew under seeming innocence and saintliness, and from her they can learn to be the same. She has had two husbands who loved her while she despised them, the first a loathsome old man whom she cuckolded and fooled until he gave her son, begotten after her husband was impotent, his chief mansion. The second was a merchant, unequal to her in rank or fairness, of which she constantly reminded him, letting him embrace her, as she told him often, only for pity and mercy—a great virtue in a woman, generated only in a gentle heart. The more he loved, the less did she, subjecting and humiliating him completely until he gave her all his wealth and managed it for her. Then she despised him, dressed her children like nobility, made fools of his first wife's fry, banished his brothers and friends. Now he is dead and she is merry, though playing the widow—weeping, sighing, saintly—as if finished with men, while at church she inspects them to find the likeliest lover. Women by their appearance deceive men, grieve for no evil deed if it be kept secret, and have ways to trick jealous husbands. Foolish damsels let the country know of their secret love; but the widow has a discreet servant to solace her and still is considered a holy wife, one who is piteous to the poor in public and goes on pilgrimages for company and not for pardon. Her best pleasure is to have all her lovers pay her various attentions at once while she, in various ways, comforts them all, so warmhearted that no fellow lusts for her unsatisfied, so merciful toward all men that her soul shall be safe at judgment. She admonishes the wives to learn her lessons. They laugh, praise her, say they will follow her teaching; and then these royal roses drink, gossip, pass the night with dances until dawn, then go home, leaving the poet to record their pastime and pose a question: which of the three would you choose for a wife?

The poem would seem to be in the anti-feminist tradition, and was obviously influenced by the characterizations of La Vielle in *Roman de la rose* and the Wife of Bath. It is usually accepted as a formal debate on love, beginning with one ironic *demaunde d'amor*, concluding with another and burlesquing the virtues and practices of courtly love. But A. D. Hope has offered the novel suggestion that the three ladies represent the survival of a woman's cult extending back to classical times. The poem embodies diction and devices of the alliterative revival whose traditional subject matter is of a serious, courtly nature. Its highly effective contrast between the aureate style, the beauty of surroundings and speakers, and the grossness of their sentiments has been discussed at length.

OF THE LADYIS SOLISTARIS AT COURT [69]. Usually printed as six eight-line stanzas of alternating tetrameter (with internal rime) and trimeter lines riming ababcdcd, but sometimes described as tail-rime stanzas of twelve dimeter and trimeter b lines riming aabaabccdccd.

Fair ladies accomplish more in three days at court than their good men in ten, so well they know when to make their complaint. With little annoyance quietly at evening, doing nothing amiss—if they kiss and confer who cares—they conclude a matter. They know well how to solicit, true as steel, nothing missed when they come home. Their lords are beholden to such ladies, and if they have a suit at court should send them as representatives gaily dressed. They can defend a matter; and if they spend it is unknown; their goods are not less. In a quiet place in less than two hours they can purchase grace, making the settlement expeditiously and fully, paying soberly, losing little, and getting their evidence wholly endorsed. Such wise ladies are to be prized, who can so devise without anyone's harming them or their honesty.

Whether the ladies are "soliciting" in a court of justice or that of the king is not clear; possibly both. It has been claimed that Dunbar does not pun, but this graceful minuet seems to be built upon just such a device. The tripping meter serves to intensify the irony, for it results in a rather dainty movement, one appropriate to woman's refinement but here used to describe her prostitution.

TO A LADYE [70]. Three stanzas (cf. *The Testament of Cresseid* [4]). Aureate praise largely in terms of garden imagery of a lady who lacks no virtue save mercy.

In her garden the poet saw fresh, lusty flowers and wholesome herbs, but no rue (possibly a pun; cf. [69]). He fears that March has slain that gentle, comforting herb, and so would plant it again.

It has been conjectured that Mrs. Musgrave (cf. *Of a Dance in the Quenis Chalmer* [53]) is the subject of this delicate piece, reminiscent of Chaucer's *Complaint unto Pity*.

QUHONE HE LIST TO FEYNE [71]. Seven rime royal stanzas.

A plea in ludicrously exaggerated terms that the lady who is slaying the poet by her cruelty have mercy. He has never deserved to be murdered; she should leave cruelty and save her man. His spirit, faint, frightened, kneels beseeching grace. His pain is intolerable—why does she slay him? Death, which no medicine save mercy may assuage, rages in his breast. How can any gentle heart look upon his hideous hue, woe, tears? Where is the humbleness of this white dove, the pity of this gentle turtle, the ruth, treasure of womanhood, and pity found in every gentle heart? When his tongue shall fail, then his mind shall cry for mercy until nature denies him sight, his eyes close for pain, death breaks his heart—or until his mind may think and tongue may stir. Then farewell, heart's lady dear!

A parody of courtly love, comparable in its irony to *The Tretis of the Tua Mariit Wemen and the Wedo* [68]. The last stanza has been interpreted as merely a continuation in the same vein as the rest, which necessitates reading "quhill" as "while." But the word more often means "until," which accords better with "syne" in the last line. Moreover, the poem seems influenced by Chaucer's *Mericles Beaute*; and there is little reason to think that Dunbar is not here doing what Chaucer had done, employing an adroit turn in the last stanza to make glaringly clear the unreality of the poem's exaggeration.

INCONSTANCY OF LUVE [72]. Four tail-rime stanzas of tetrameter and dimeter b lines riming aaabaaab, the same two rimes being carried throughout.

Love has a sweet deceiving countenance in which none may trust. It begins with inconstancy, ends with variance, never lasts, has no discretion or consideration and thus only brief pleasure. The poet gives it up. To love intemperately is ignorance; to be faithful as foolish as bid a dead man dance.

A polished little piece, whose quick, graceful rhythm with its turns is well adapted to the subject of fickleness.

OF LUVE ERDLY AND DIVINE [73]. Fifteen stanzas with double refrain (cf. *Petition of the Gray Horse Auld Dunbar* [44]). Development of a theme common in medieval and renaissance poetry: a farewell to physical, and praise of spiritual love.

As Venus' brand cools, the poet begins to understand what folly is in feigned love. Until that dies true love never burns boldly and no man desires to write of its pleasures, the two kinds of love being so contrary. The man is well off who turns to true love. For every joy the poet has experienced in earthly love he has found fifteen troubles. Before, he had doubt, displeasure, danger, disease, jealousy, shame, concealment; now he has hope, reward, ease, comfort, desire to share his love with all, pride in it, and indifference to his former lady's beauty. He has a fairer, perfect love, who entertains no danger, grants mercy, fully rewards and returns love, who is good, sweet, rich, merciful, most fit for man, most true—Christ, Who died for love of us and should be loved in return. To consider this in youth one must have grace, for then the deceptive world's bliss guides men. Now age comes where youth was before, and true love rises from the heart.

VI. Allegories and Addresses

A group lacking the customary logic and unity of Mackenzie's classifications. There is no plausible reason for combining allegories with
addresses, or for listing *The Sowtar and Tailyouris War* [79], *Amends to
the Telyouris and Sowtaris* [80]—or for that matter *Elegy on the death of
Lord Bernard Stewart* [83]—with either.

DUNBAR AT OXINFURDE [74]. Three stanzas with slightly varying
refrain (cf. *Rewl of Anis Self* [62]).

All learning is lost if not used as it should be or if the scholar does not lead a good
life. Vain prosperity is a perilous life. Therefore, learned clerks, be mirrors for us
in your governance, shining lamps, or your learning is in vain. If your words be contrary to your deeds, your own cunning will accuse you. Vain prosperity is a perilous
sickness.

In view of its content and the form of the first two stanzas, the poem
could as readily be classified among Moralizings. It has been said to
indicate that Dunbar studied or preached at Oxford, but no other
evidence of his presence there is known, and it may simply be an expression of his attitude toward scholars in general.

BEWTY AND THE PRESONEIR [75]. Fourteen stanzas, each ending
with the same word, of tetrameter lines riming ababbaba (stanza 1) and
ababbcbc.

The lover desires to remain a prisoner to the fairest and best. Captured by Sweet
Manner and Beauty, he had been led to the castle of penance where Strangeness was
porter, thrown into a dungeon, fettered and watched by the lady's servants. Advised
and helped by Good Hope, Humility, and Fair Service, he sent a letter to the lady
asking for pity; then his helpers besieged the castle, overcoming its defenders, drowning
Good Fame, and ransoming the prisoner. He was denounced by jealous folk and Envy
when Slander ranged the countryside after Lust's victory; but King Matrimony chased
Slander to the west coast and endorsed a bond between the new couple. By then the
heir of Good Fame had come to the court where Matrimony rules; he inherited his
mother's estate and remains still with Beauty and the prisoner.

An allegory of courtly love in the tradition of the *Roman de la rose* and
King Hart [21], unexceptional save for the innovation of Matrimony's

putting all to rights. It has been suggested that this is "Lady, help your prisoner," one of the songs mentioned in *The Complaynt of Scotlande*, and/or that it is a delineation of a pageant performed at court. Its authorship is to a degree questionable since the only complete version, that in National Library Scotland 1.1.6, is anonymous. However, it is usually printed as Dunbar's work because the first two stanzas, which are given in Cambridge University L1.5.10, are there ascribed to him; and the poem, evidently an early work, is in keeping in content and style with other of his allegories (cf. *The Thrissil and the Rois* [76] and *The Goldyn Targe* [77]).

THE THRISSIL AND THE ROIS [76]. Twenty-seven stanzas (cf. *Quhone he List to Feyne* [71]).

In spring Aurora greets the poet, May commands him to write something in her honor, and though he protests that the season is unfavorable bids him rise and describe the pleasant rose as he had promised. He follows May to a flowering garden, the sun comforts all the world, birds welcome day, Nature commands gods to keep the elements peaceful, then bids every beast, bird, and flower to do homage to her and sends messengers to summon them. She crowns the lion, standing on a field of gold encircled with lilies, king of beasts, and admonishes him to be just and merciful, protect the weak, and administer the law equitably. She then crowns the eagle king of birds, admonishing him as she had done the lion; and the thistle, king of flowers, bidding him to defend the rest, to be discreet, and to let no vile nettle be fellow to the lily, or any churlish weed compare herself to it, and to value no other flower as he does the peerless red and white rose. Nature praises the rose, which is above the lily in lineage, rising without stain from royal stock, and crowns her with polished jewels. Flowers hail the rose, their queen, and birds sing praise and welcome to this royal blossom, their princess, until with the noise the poet awakes to find the court gone. Up he gets, half frightened and writes of lusty May on the ninth morning.

An aureate celebration of the union of James IV and Margaret Tudor in 1503, employing heraldic imagery and suggesting the influence of Chaucer's *The Parliament of Fowls* and perhaps the *Parliament of four-futtit Beistis haldin be the Lyoun* in *The Fables*, [3] above, item (f). For allegories in a similar vein see the preceding and following items. That the poet should admonish James, who was given to amorous adventuring, to be faithful to his young Queen has been seen as an indication of Dunbar's closeness to the King and of his early sympathy with the Queen (cf. also *That the King War Johne Thomsounis Man* [40], *The Wowing of the King quhen he was in Dunfermline* [48], and *Of a Dance in the Quenis Chalmer* [53]).

THE GOLDYN TARGE [77]. Thirty-one stanzas of iambic pentameter lines riming aabaabbab, the stanza pattern of Chaucer's *Compleynt of Anelida.*

At dawn in a luminous rose garden beside a river the poet falls asleep to the singing of birds, and dreams he sees a white sail approach, a ship land, and a hundred lovely ladies disembark. He would describe the glittering fields, but even masters of rhetoric could not. He sees Nature, Venus, and a band of goddesses enter the park, birds and flowers salute and thank them and sing love ballads to Venus; then he sees the court of Cupid and a number of gods playing and singing as the ladies dance. But suddenly he is spied by Venus, who bids her archers arrest him. Reason with a golden shield defends the poet against Venus' band—Beauty, Tender Youth, etc.—until Presence blinds him with a powder; then like a drunken man Reason goes astray and is banished. The poet, wounded near to death, yields to Beauty, who seems lovelier now that Reason has lost his clear eyes; and a hell appears to be a paradise, mercy to be where there is none. Dissimulance misleads the poet, Fair Calling smiles, Cherishing feeds, and New Acquaintance embraces him for a while, then takes her leave, and Danger approaching at last delivers him to Heavyness. Eolus blows such a blast the leaves shake, and the company sailing away fires guns until the rocks resound and the frightened poet wakes from his dream, back in the beautiful world of May. He closes with an apostrophe to Chaucer, Gower, and Lydgate, and a directive to his little Quair, commanding it to be obedient, humble, simple. Having no rose of rhetoric but only a rude garment, well should it fear the light.

An allegory of courtly love, like the preceding two items, in the tradition of the *Roman de la rose*, Chaucer's *The Legend of Good Women,* and *King Hart* [21]. It has been suggested, however, that Dunbar is here actually attacking the tradition and bidding farewell to love and to romantic poetry. The poem is one of the best examples of the aureate style, and despite its artificiality of diction and action contains description which has been justifiably praised for its striking vividness. Some of the descriptive phrasing suggests the influence of Chaucer and Douglas, especially that of *The Knight's Tale, The Squire's Tale, The Parliament of Fowls, The Palice of Honour* [20], and Book 4 of *Eneados* [19]; some of the action, the influence of *King Hart* [21], the assembly of the gods in *The Testament of Cresseid* [4], and possibly the conclusion of *The Kingis Quair* [1].

THE DANCE OF THE SEVIN DEIDLY SYNNIS [78]. Eight tail-rime stanzas of tetrameter and trimeter b lines riming aabccbddbeeb, and two (possibly interpolations) which are similar in line length and rime but consist of only six lines each.

On the night of February 15th the poet in a vision saw Mahound order a dance for Fastern's Eve [preceding Lent]. The Seven Deadly Sins began, each described with its human followers: Pride, whose company skips through fire, all the fiends laughing when the priests come; Ire, with boasters and bullies dressed for war; Envy, trembling with secret hatred, followed by dissemblers of which, alas, royal courts are never free; Covetousness, whose wretches spit molten gold, of which fiends keep them full, upon each other; Sloth, drawing along idle gluttons and slatterns lashed by Belial; Lechery, led by Idleness, with a company of stinking corpses leading each other by the penis; Gluttony, whose drunkards crying for drink the fiends supply with hot lead. No minstrels played, for none were there, save one who by murder had won his heritage. Then Mahound cried for a highland pageant; MacFadden shouted the coronach, and a great crowd of Highlanders gathered, chattering and bawling until the Devil, deafened, smothered them with smoke in the deepest pit of hell.

The theme of the Seven Deadly Sins was common in various medieval art forms, but Dunbar makes novel use of it here by presenting the Sins in a dance in hell and turning it to an attack upon his enemies, the Highlanders. The allegory, which contrasts sharply with the courtly personifications in the preceding three items ([75], [76], [77]), anticipates the work of Spenser. Fastern's Eve fell upon February 16th in 1496, 1507, and 1518, and the poem has been tentatively assigned to one of the first two years.

THE SOWTAR AND TAILYOURIS WAR [79]. Nine tail-rime stanzas (cf. [78] of which [79] is a continuation, following that poem without a break in National Library Scotland 1.1.6 and beginning with its first and last stanzas in Pepys 2553).

Next a tournament was held before Mahound between a tailor and a cobbler. The tailor, with his company of knaves and banner of stolen rags, was knighted by Mahound. He promised to beat the cobbler, but the lists frightened him so that he was struck dumb and farted like thunder. The cobbler, with his lousy rascals, banner of tanned hide, oil oozing out between his armor plates, looked at the tailor and could neither sit upright nor digest his dinner. When the Devil made him a knight, for sorrow he spit and spewed leather blacking about the Devil's neck, thus repaying him in knightly fashion. The frightened jousters received their spears and ran together;

the tailor was unseated, leaving his saddle befouled and breaking his harness with such a rattle that the cobbler's frightened horse ran off to the Devil, who, turning his buttocks, befouled the cobbler completely. Swooning, the new-made knights forswore all arms; and the Devil put them in a dungeon, deprived them of knighthood, and made them rascals forever, which they much preferred. The poet thought the befouling of the cobbler so good a jest he laughed till he woke, and no man could stop his writing of this joust. Believe it if you please.

A burlesque similar to *Of Sir Thomas Norny* [56], possibly influenced by *The Taill of Rauf Coilyear* (see I [59]). Dunbar's principal object of attack here has been said to be the world of chivalry, soon to be routed by the lower classes. But the satire seems to be directed as much at the traditionally unreliable craftsmen as at knights.

AMENDS TO THE TELYOURIS AND SOWTARIS [80]. Ten stanzas with refrain (cf. *Lament for the Makaris* [29]).

Between twelve and eleven o'clock the poet dreamt that an angel blessed tailors and cobblers, who shall be next to God in heaven since they amend what He mismakes. They mend the faults of the ill-made, hiding knobbed toes and chilblains with shoes, making the worst-made man seemly with clothes. They can refashion God's misfashioned man three times better, covering even a broken back, and may claim great kindness of God for helping His people from deformity and lameness, showing such miracles on earth that in heaven they will be saints—though knaves here.

An ironic, but good-natured, sequel to [79] (cf. *Of James Dog* [54] and *Of the Said James* [55]), whose occasion is suggested by its colophon in Pepys 2553, "Quod Dumbar quhone he drank to ye Dekynnis [heads of the trade guilds] ffor amendis to ye bodeis of yair craftis."

THE DREAM [81]. Twenty-three stanzas (cf. *How Dumbar wes Desyrd to be Ane Freir* [26]).

Last night the poet thought that into his chamber, newly painted with noble stories, there entered a company, singing and dancing, whose merriment could not cheer him because of Distress, Heaviness, and Langour. Nobleness, Comfort, Pleasance, Perceiving, Discretion try to cheer him, Discretion saying that for him to recover Nobleness must appear with her in court where the poet has long served in vain. Consideration agrees and will help maintain the dance; but Blind Affection claims that he governs the court. Reason says, no longer; now he distributes everything, and it is time this man, who has long served the king without feigning or flattery, only humbly complaining in ballads, had something. Discretion agrees with Reason, valuable companion for lords at the Session. But Inopportunity insists he must be served—

a busy asker succeeds sooner than two busy servants; to ask is only to lose a word; to lose long service is no joke. Sir John Kirkpakar says he has seven churches and shall have eleven before the ballad maker has one; Sir Better-the-Church, that his servants wait on churchmen's deeds, and he expects tidings from them quickly; Reason, that the balance is uneven when one has seven churches, while seven as worthy have none; Temperance, that if a man take more than one curacy, he upsets proper balance. Patience advises the poet to be cheerful, depending upon the prince who even for a bishopric's rent would not leave him unrewarded half a year. Rushing to the door, the company fires a gun, and with the crack he wakes.

In its allegory, which has neither the courtliness of *Bewty and the Presoneir* [75], *The Thrissil and the Rois* [76], or *The Goldyn Targe* [77], nor the grotesquerie of *The Dance of the Sevin Deidly Synnis* [78], and in its moral tone, the poem somewhat resembles *Piers Plowman*. In purpose it belongs among the Petitions, its attack upon the greed of the clergy and some of its wording suggesting that it was written in the same period as a number of them (cf. *Quhone Mony Benefices Vakit* [33], *To the King—Off Benefice Schir* [34], *Of the Warldis Instabilitie* [35], *Of Discretioun in Asking* [36], particularly *Complaint to the King* [41] and *To the King—Schir yit remembir* [42]).

THE BALLADE OF LORD BERNARD STEWART [82]. Twelve stanzas with refrain (cf. *Rewl of Anis Self* [62]). An elaborate encomium on the occasion, which is identified in the poem's heading in National Library Scotland 19.1.16, of Aubigny's arrival in Scotland, May 9, 1508.

To the lord renowned, royal, reverent, peerless in lineage, military prowess, and wisdom, shield of Scotland in every realm, unfailing helper of the nation and Scotsmen, leader whom the faithful would die defending, welcome with glory, honour, praise, and reverence. He whose fame covers the earth, who is a replica of the great warriors, should be accorded the greatest honors. At his nativity Mars, Saturn, Venus, Mercury, and Fortuna Major exerted their influence. Only to avoid prolixity does the poet at present not tell of the fields Aubigny has won; later he shall; and he concludes by listing knightly qualities betokened by the letters of "Bernadvs" [Aubigny's name], which should be written in gold.

ELEGY ON THE DEATH OF LORD BERNARD STEWART [83]. Four stanzas with partial refrain (cf. *Rewl of Anis Self* [62]). Sequel to [82], Aubigny having died before June 8, 1508, a month after his arrival in Scotland, the occasion for that poem.

Illustrious King Louis of France well may lament the death of noble Bernard Stewart, warrior most mighty, wise, and worthy to guide the French. Every noble knight should complain of the death of this doughty warrior, dreaded to the Turkish sea, whose force magnified the fame of France. None shall equal him. Why did this peerless, famous knight die? Let all who loved him, especially the Scots whom most he did trust, pray for his soul.

THE MERLE AND THE NYCHTINGAILL [84]. Fifteen stanzas in National Library Scotland 1.1.6, thirteen in Pepys 2553, with alternating refrains (cf. *Rewl of Anis Self* [62]).

In May at dawn the poet heard a merle beside a river sing that a joyful life is in love's service, bid lovers awake, and argue that it is the nature of young folk to love; that God made ladies beautiful and gave them inclination to love, and would have put nothing in vain in any creature; that love, depending as it does upon charity, must be a virtue, contrary to envy; that God bade men to love their neighbors, of whom ladies are the sweetest; and that love is ever the cause of honour, bravery, largess, etc., changing vice to virtue. The nightingale on the river's other side sang that all love is lost but upon God alone, and argued that the love of God, Who made man in His image, died to save man, and is most true, should be most dear; that God gave beauty and goodness to ladies not so that they, but He, should have thanks; that a man may take such delight in his lady as to forget God, Who gave her virtue, and be blinded to perfect love; that vain love leads to loss of wit, worship, goods, and strength. The merle then confessed his error, and both birds singing the nightingale's song flew away. Now it comforts the poet, when he finds no love, to think how they sang, all love is lost but upon God alone.

A debate in the tradition of *The Owl and the Nightingale* (see VII [45]), which suggests the influence of Lydgate's *The Chorle and the Bird*. The poem is attributed to Dunbar in both its manuscripts, though in theme, method, and tone it seems more characteristic of Henryson than on Dunbar (cf. particularly *The Ressoning Betuix Aige and Yowth*, [10] above).

TO ABERDEIN [85]. Nine stanzas with refrain (cf. *Rewl of Anis Self* [62]). A conventional encomium of the city and description of its welcome to the Queen.

In Aberdeen Margaret was met by richly arrayed burgesses, four to bear a canopy above her, and a procession which depicted biblical scenes, the Bruce, the Stewarts, and twenty-four maidens marvelously clad, playing, singing, saluting the Queen. The streets, filled with people, were hung with tapestry; pageants were played; lieges bowed; barons and ladies conveyed the Queen; and the commons shouted welcome.

Wine flowed abundantly at the cross, and the town presented her a large, costly cup filled with gold. This potent princess, pleasant and famous, so long as she rules should be thankful to Aberdeen, which spared neither goods nor persons to honor, receive, and please her.

It is usually assumed that Dunbar was present at the Queen's reception, plans for which are recorded in the Council Register of Aberdeen, May 4, 1511; but there is no evidence of his presence other than the specificity and vividness of the description he gives in this poem.

QUHEN THE GOUVERNOUR PAST IN FRANCE [86]. Five stanzas with refrain (cf. *Rewl of Anis Self* [62]). Sometimes called *Ane Orisoun*.

May God, Who for our salvation made justice, mercy, and pity agree, sent Gabriel to Mary and Christ to become man, grant us—lacking in wit and prudence, beastly, ignorant, sinful, etc.—pity and protection, prudence, grace, mercy; may He succor the poor divided realm, sending grace to guide it, withhold His hand that has striken so sorely, and restore the people from care to comfort; for without His help, the kingdom is lost.

The authorship of this poem is questionable principally because of its date, no earlier than 1517, in which year the Duke of Albany as Governor first left Scotland, four years after both the last reference to Dunbar in the public records and the Battle of Flodden where a number of commentators believe the poet died. Then too, although its stanzaic pattern and use of a refrain are characteristic of Dunbar's work, its inversions, awkwardness, and roughness contrast sharply with his usual direct expression and smoothness, as do the abstract diction, lack of imagery, and deadly serious tone in treating a subject which lends itself to satire. Possibly it should be listed among the Attributions, despite the ascription to him in Pepys 2553. If it was written by Dunbar, it demonstrates a noticeable decline in his poetic ability.

VII. Moralizings

A heterogeneous group, though less so than Allegories and Addresses, which includes Boethian musings on the instability and falseness of

earthly pleasure, social protest like that of the Petitions, and moral exhortation like that of the Religious poems.

OF THE CHANGES OF LIFE [87]. Four stanzas (cf. *On His Heid-ake*
[25]).

> The truest thing the poet finds to say about the world is, it is deceitful; for yesterday
> was fair and flowers bloomed, while today stings like an adder, flowers are slain, and
> birds that sang before are now dreary and cold. Next to summer is winter, to comfort
> cares, to midnight morning, to joy sorrow; so the world has always been.

A delicate lyric with appealing imagery which seems somewhat indebted
to *The Pricke of Conscience.*

OF COVETYCE [88]. Eleven stanzas with refrain (cf. *Lament for the
Makaris* [29]).

> A catalogue of abuse caused by cupidity: virtues in court considered vice; welfare,
> wealth, and merriment become wretchedness; play discounted; honest sport changed
> to gambling; honorable households destroyed; lords counseled by rascals; pleasure and
> plenty in towns decayed; farmers with no beast but cats and mice; yeomen's garments
> but rags; lords dressed in silk while their tenants live on roots; the peaceful, charitable
> man held a fool; the exploiter of farmers and the poor, active and wise. Let man
> please his Maker, be merry, not value this world, but work for paradise where no
> covetousness reigns.

Cf. *Of the Warldis Instabilitie* [35], *Of Discretioun in Taking* [38], *None
May Assure in this Warld* [43], *To the Merchantis of Edinburgh* [65],
and *A General Satyre* [98]. The poem has been interpreted as an attack
upon capitalism; but its title and range would suggest that Dunbar's
subject was avarice in general rather than an economic system.

GUDE COUNSALE [89]. Three stanzas with refrain (cf. *Rewl of Anis
Self* [62]).

> Advice for a lover who should be well advised in his conduct, for if he is not it will
> be told. He should beware of misjudgment, be no wretch or niggard, but loath to do
> amiss; no liar, chatterer, wrangler, or thrall to vice; be master of his will, not talk
> too much or be dismayed by a wicked tongue, or be too proud. Let him be wise so
> that others may learn from him, but never a slanderer or friar-like preacher of his
> love. Let him ever be secret, true, increasing of his name.

This sententious piece, as it has been considered, is wholly in keeping with the tradition of courtly love (cf. *To a Ladye* [70], *Bewty and the Presoneir* [75], and *Gif ye wald lufe and luvit be* [113], which it resembles not only in sentiment but in its refrain).

BEST TO BE BLYTH [90]. Eight stanzas with refrain in National Library Scotland 1.1.6, seven in Pepys 2553 (cf. *To the King* [23]).

When the poet muses on the world's instability he always concludes it is best to be blithe. None should grieve over change, but keep in mind the transitoriness of earthly honour; his fall shall then be less painful. Who wrestles with the world and is doleful lives wretchedly. Of worldly goods the only fruit is merriness; without that, all is poverty. Why mourn to lose tinsel—compared to everlasting life, this life here is but the twinkling of an eye. Had the poet for the world's unkindness been sad, he had been long dead. Whatever the changes, never be sorry, but ever ready to pass out of this fraudulent fairyland.

Like *Rewl of Anis Self* [62], *Of Content* [91], and *No Tressour Availis without Glaidnes* [94], directly in the Boethian tradition and suggestive of the influence of Chaucer's *Truth*, possibly too of the conclusion of *Troilus and Criseyde*. The poem has been said to state Dunbar's maxim of life; but in view of the prevailing tone of his Personal poems this seems unlikely.

OF CONTENT [91]. Seven stanzas with refrain (cf. *To the King* [23]).

He has enough who is content: a contented man is never poor; a discontented man never rich. Thank God, therefore, for what is sent you and be happy with it. Defy the false world; who most serves it repents most, and its surplus is sour. If you have might, be gentle and generous; if you are poor, willingly consent and riches shall return. Let us who have small lordship not be languorous; if we do not climb we shall not fall. The most covetous is poorest and least successful, for nothing is his whom nothing contents.

Cf. *Rewl of Anis Self* [62], *Best to Be Blythe* [90], and *No Tressour Availis without Glaidnes* [94]. At least three of these poems, [90], [91], and [94], would seem to reflect Dunbar's reaction to the failure of his Petitions.

ALL ERDLY JOY RETURNIS IN PANE [92]. Ten stanzas with refrain in National Library Scotland 1.1.6, nine in Pepys 2553 (cf. *Lament for the Makaris* [29]).

At the first dawn of Lent a bird sang that all earthly joy returns in pain. Man should remember he is and must return to dust; age follows youth, death follows life; wealth, glory, rich array are but a snare; May is followed by January, drought by rain, joy by annoyance; health turns to sickness, mirth to heaviness, town to desert, etc. Since all earthly joy passes and is vain, work for that which is everlasting.

A *memento mori* in the same homiletic tradition as Henryson's *The Ressoning Betwixt Deth and Man* [12] and *The Thre Deid Pollis* [16], and Dunbar's *Of Manis Mortalitie* [95], *Of the Warldis Vanitie* [96], and *Of Lyfe* [97]. As miniature sermons the Dunbar poems might well be classified as Religious instead of Moralizings.

ADVICE TO SPEND ANIS AWIN GUDE [93]. Ten stanzas with refrain (cf. *Lament for the Makaris* [29]).

Since life is uncertain and death is sure, let man spend his goods himself while he has time, not leaving them to cause another to harm someone, or perhaps to permit heirs to squander merrily what he has gathered with pain and thrift. Only what you spend is yours, not your heirs'.

The poem's last two somewhat ambiguous stanzas have been variously interpreted. They seem to mean either that one should not give his heirs everything before his death, depending in King Lear fashion upon their generosity; or that one should not expect his heirs after he is dead to manage the inheritance as he would wish. The text has not been finally established, Pepys 2553 reversing these two stanzas as well as the second and third, and having a slightly different refrain. The Pepys 2553 version also lacks an ascription, and both for this reason and because of the poem's awkwardness and asserted incongruity in theme with Dunbar's usual utterance, there has been some question as to its authorship. However, it is ascribed to the poet in MS National Library Scotland 1.1.6 and its subject and somewhat cynical tone seem in no way incongruous with most of the Petitions, for example *Of Discretioun in Geving* [37], *Of Discretioun in Taking* [38], *Remonstrance to the King* [39], *That the King War Johne Thomsounis Man* [40], or *To the King—Schir yit remembir* [42], though certainly they are with the rest of the Moralizings. The theme, though with a different emphasis, one essentially moral, is akin to that of *Doun by ane Rever as I red* [109]—since death is sure to come, do for yourself (i.e., prepare for your soul's welfare) while you are here.

NO TRESSOUR AVAILIS WITHOUT GLAIDNES [94]. Five stanzas with refrain (cf. *Rewl of Anis Self* [62]). In National Library Scotland 1.1.6 called *Hermes the Philosopher*.

Let man be merry, remembering the transitoriness of the world; be humble to God, kind to his friend, glad to lend and borrow with neighbors, blithe whatever befalls; for without gladness no treasure profits. Be happy with what God sends; goods without welfare are nothing; only what one spends is his own, and he can enjoy but a remnant. Avoid dolour, which shortens life; follow pity, flee trouble, mingle with famous folk, be charitable, humble—for worldly honour is brief, and patient. With sorrow and care wretches all their lives gather goods of which they have only the keeping, others the spending; learn and spend merrily. Though you had all the wealth that any man ever had, no more would belong to you than meat, drink, clothes, and a sight of the rest; yet you must account to God for all. Be just, joyous, injure none, and truth shall make you strong.

In details of wording and thought this is a companion piece to [93], but one which, like *Rewl of Anis Self* [62], *Best to be Blyth* [90], and *Of Content* [91], develops the Boethian theme suggested by its title: happiness depends upon man's mind. The poem not only reflects the influence, but like *Rewl of Anis Self* achieves something of the effect of Chaucer's *Truth*.

OF MANIS MORTALITIE [95]. Six stanzas with Latin refrain (cf. *Bewty and the Presoneir* [75]). A *memento mori* whose exhortation and refrain are taken from the service for Ash Wednesday, probably, as has been pointed out, that of the Sarum use: *Memento, homo, quia cinis es et in cinerem reverteris.*

Let man not strive to dwell here long, for like heroes of the past he too must go. Though now he is most glad, fairest, pleasantest, yet within a year he may be a loathsome corpse. Life is ever in doubt; beauty and youth shall fade; inescapable death shall swallow him and though he possess all the world he shall take with him only good deeds. Let him, therefore, speed and confess humbly with sober tears; and may his Ransomer keep his soul alive when he returns to dust.

Cf. *All Erdly Joy Returnis in Pane* [92]. Although the *ubi sunt* passage dealing with dead heroes, the contrast between present beauty and its ultimate decay, and the final efficacy of good deeds alone were commonplaces, this emerges as one of Dunbar's more effective poems, as in the case of *None May Assure in this Warld* [43], largely because of its striking imagery.

OF THE WARLDIS VANITIE [96]. Three stanzas with refrain (cf. *Rewl of Anis Self* [62]). Like [95], an exhortation for man to prepare for death.

This world which has beguiled many an estate will pass, so let man trust his friend and not his foe, prepare in time for the journey, and provide his place. While there is daylight, speed home; night comes soon, and if death overtake him in trespass then he may well lament. This false world is ever changing, day, night, ebb, flood, etc. All is vanity.

Cf. *All Erdly Joy Returnis in Pane* [92]. Despite a certain similarity in the last stanza to *Of the Changes of Life* [87] and the influence of Chaucer, the poem has been justifiably criticized for its dull conventionality.

OF LYFE [97]. One stanza (cf. *Aganis the Solistaris in Court* [50]).

Life is but a way to death, with a set time to be passed, where none remain; a chance to win paradise or hell; a short torment or joy, for lasting gladness or sorrow.

The poem is attributed to Dunbar in only one of the two manuscripts; but as its concision, force, and polish are typical of the poet at his best (cf. for example *Meditatioun in Wyntir* [32] or *In Prais of Wemen* [66]) and the thought is quite in keeping with a number of his moral poems (cf. for example *All Erdly Joy Returnis in Pane* [92], *Of Manis Mortalitie* [95], and [96]), it seems reasonable to consider it his work.

A GENERAL SATYRE [98]. Sixteen stanzas with refrain, of pentameter lines riming aabab, frequent internal rime and rime between half lines. When the poem is arranged in stanzas of these half lines and the refrain, it follows the pattern ababbcbbc.

The poet dreams how the realm, for many years controlled by numberless nobles, has now great hunger, cowardice, and trouble, and he makes a repetitious catalogue of its corruptions: pride, negligence, lust, improper attire among the clergy; waste, spite, disease, stupidity of lords unfit to correct the sorrows of the commons, treason, lying, neglect of the common cause, disrespect for law, legal trickery, theft, collusion, empty threats of correction, quilted coats for some but rags for beggars, boasting, brawling, oppression of the poor by retailers, justices, landlords; so many new-made judges and lords, concern for rank not the common weal, gambling, begging, forsworn merchants, too much tennis, evil gossip, gluttons, dressed up sluts and stupid—such abuse and such a company of Satan within this land was never heard or seen.

There has been much discussion of the poem's authorship. It is attributed to Sir James Inglis in MS Pepys 2553 and its meter, internal rime, wording, and sentiments have been found uncharacteristic of Dunbar's work. However, it is attributed to him in MS National Library Scotland 1.1.6; the end rime pattern is one he most frequently employs (cf. *To the King* [23], *Ane His Awin Ennemy* [24], *Of Deming* [30], etc.); elsewhere he uses internal rime throughout (cf. *Ane Ballat of Our Lady* [103] and particularly *Of the Ladyis Solistaris at Court* [69], where the half lines have a regular rime scheme comparable to that in [98]). The catalogue method and the wording are reminiscent of the more vehement Petitions (cf. *Remonstrance to the King* [39] and *Complaint to the King* [41]); at least one expression is also found in *To the King—Off Benefice Schir* [34]; and the attack upon neglectful, sensual priests and new-made lords is one Dunbar quite often makes. Thus the grounds for rejecting it from his canon would appear to be inadequate. In light of its reference to recently created lords and to the King and Queen, the poem is dated between 1504 (when the Lords of Daily Council were established) and 1513 (when James IV died), or after 1532 (when the College of Justice or Court of Session was instituted), depending largely upon the commentator's opinion of its authorship.

VIII. Religious

ANE ORISOUN [99]. One stanza of pentameter lines riming ababbbbb. A Donne-like prayer comparable in conciseness and force to *Of Lyfe* [97].

If through sensuality the poet has often sinned, spirituality wakens and reason bids him rise. His corrupt conscience pleads for grace, time to amend, substance with honour, that he harm none, but have friends, prosperity, peace here, then heaven's bliss.

Cf. *Ballate against evil Women* [107], to which this is sometimes considered an epilogue, apparently as a concluding prayer for protection against sin such as is depicted in that poem, which immediately precedes [99] in the manuscripts. However, since the sin which the poet attacks in [107] is the sensuality of women, the two poems actually have little logical connection.

OF THE NATIVITIE OF CHRIST [100]. Seven stanzas with Latin refrain (cf. *Bewty and the Presoneir* [75]).

Let the heavens distill its showers, for Christ is born; let all orders and bodies of heaven and all elements love Him; sinners rejoice, do penance, and thank their Maker, Who only for His mercy has come to buy their souls and loose them from the fiend; let clergy bow to Him, incense His altar, read and sing, honouring Him; let fowls sing and rejoice, flowers spring up, the empyrean sing, fish and fowl rejoice and make melody. Let all things cry Glory in the highest, for to us a Child is born.

A conventional Nativity lyric whose refrain and other Latin phrases are taken from the services for Advent through Christmas Eve and Christmas Day. Cf. *Jerusalem reioss for joy* [116], *Now glaidith euery liffis creature* [118], and *The sterne is rissin of our Redemptioun* [121].

OF THE PASSIOUN OF CHRIST [101]. Eighteen stanzas in Pepys 2553, eleven with one refrain, three with another; sixteen stanzas in Arundel 285; eleven in Asloan (cf. *Bewty and the Presoneir* [75]).

In the oratory of a friary the poet knelt, and thinking on the passion said a pater noster, saluted Mary, then dreamt he saw in all their painful detail the torture and crucifixion of Christ, endured for the love of mankind. Through the allegorical action of Compassion, Contrition, Ruth, etc., he was prepared for the resurrection. Then the earth trembled for terror of Christ's death, waking the poet who wrote without delay this account of what befell him on Good Friday.

A change in the refrain underscores a turn in the poem's thought. Both the detailed account of the passion, with its brooding upon pain, and the allegory of repentance were conventional subjects of medieval verse (cf. *Piers Plowman*, B text, passus xviii).

ON THE RESURRECTION OF CHRIST [102]. Five stanzas with Latin refrain of irregular tetrameter or pentameter lines (cf. *Rewl of Anis Self* [62] and *Bewty and the Presoneir* [75]).

A cry of exultation reiterating Satan's defeat and Christ's victory, summed up in the refrain, *Surrexit Dominus de sepulchro*. The battle is done, the gates of hell broken, the triumphant cross raised, the souls ransomed, Lucifer—dragon, serpent, tiger— defeated by the Lord. Christ, Who for us suffered Himself to be sacrificed like a lamb, now rises like a lion, stretches like a giant. Dawn has come; our faith refound. Mercy sounds from heaven; Christians are delivered, Jews confounded. The prison is broken, the jailers banished, peace confirmed, the prisoners redeemed, and the foe despoiled of his treasure.

Perhaps the most powerful, certainly one of the most popular of Dunbar's poems, with both the force of the Anglo-Saxon alliterative line and the control of the French stanza form. Like *Of the Nativitie of Christ* [100] it embodies a Latin refrain taken from the Church, here matins for Easter Sunday; its animal imagery reflects the influence of the bestiaries. For a much inferior treatment of the same subject, see *Surrexit Dominus de sepulchro* [122].

ANE BALLAT OF OUR LADY [103]. Seven stanzas each consisting of alternating tetrameter and trimeter lines riming abababab, a Latin refrain, and a wheel riming bab, with internal rime in the a, alliteration in most of the b lines.

A lavish Ave Maria: star to shine eternally in God's sight, lamp discerned by glory and grace, everlasting queen; dwelling of Christ Who saved us, mother and maid matchless, etc. May she cherish, guide, and intercede for us; and until he is old the poet will praise her.

The poem is largely a repetitious heaping up of praise of Mary as pleader, mediatrix, salvatrix. Although in the tradition of the Latin hymns to the Virgin, in its aureate diction and internal rime it is reminiscent of the concluding stanzas of Henryson, *Ane Prayer for the Pest* [17] and Douglas, *The Palice of Honour* [20]. Its aureation, alliteration, and intricate rime make it one of the most artfully contrived of Scottish poems; and its sound, like a pealing of bells, has been justly praised.

THE TABILL OF CONFESSION [104]. Twenty-one stanzas with refrain (cf. *Rewl of Anis Self* [62]). Lines have been crossed out in both manuscripts, as a result, it is conjectured, of Reformation influences.

> The poet confesses to Jesus all the sins he has committed, enumerating them in detail by kinds: the wrong spending of his five wits, the seven deadly sins, abuse of the seven deeds of corporal mercy, neglect of the seven deeds of spiritual mercy and the sacraments, offense against the ten commandments and the articles of faith, failure to arm himself with the four cardinal virtues, breaking of the seven commands of the church, sins against the Holy Spirit, failure to thank his Creator and Saviour, viciousness, swearing, lying, blasphemy, words which are foolish, vile, or vain, praise of himself and condemnation of his neighbors, pride, folly, disobedience, disdain, robbery, oppression, prodigality without pity for the poor, deceit for his own gain, flattery and false solicitation for false judgments, cursed company. For his crimes by deed, counsel, or consent, the poet asks mercy, weeps like the Magdalen for his sins, and prays that Christ will forgive them as He did hers. Finally, so that he may remember Christ, the poet pleads to share the passion and feel its pain fully. For sins confessed and forgotten, he cries to God for mercy and leisure to repent.

The poem would seem to be both a confessional guide by a priest for his flock and a confession of personal sin. Although it has been considered merely a dull form of general confession according to the Catholic rite, it is a vehement, comprehensive summary of medieval Christian beliefs, which would seem to bear eloquent testimony to the sincerity of Dunbar's priestly dedication.

THE MANER OF PASSING TO CONFESSION [105]. Ten stanzas (cf. *Aganis the Solistaris in Court* [50]).

> In Lent every man should do penance, as did our example, Jesus. Let him shrive himself and confess, showing every sin, for one forgotten or concealed gets no remission. A wise, discreet confessor, when all is confessed, can discharge every doubt and have power over all sins. So let a man search his mind as to how the sins occurred, have them all in mind, not come to confession hastily, but with humility and contrition, and reveal his sins as only he may do. Infrequent or postponed confession is dangerous, for man forgets many a thing if he wait a year; and it is small merit to leave sin when one grows old and can commit none.

A sermon, suggesting the possible influence of Chaucer's *The Parson's*

Tale, on the same subject as *Elegy on the death of Lord Bernard Stewart* [83]. The tone and content—wise, fatherly, rather than impassioned, advice—seem more characteristic of Henryson than of Dunbar; however, the poem is ascribed to the latter poet in its only source and the ascription has never been questioned.

IX. Attributions

These poems differ widely in quality. Some of them seem clearly to be Dunbar's although their authorship has been questioned (cf. items [117], [119], [123], [125]). Others seem clearly not to be his because of their radical departure in style or subject matter from his usual practice, but are occasionally attributed to him (cf. items [106], [112], [115]), as are others which, though having no substantial claim to his authorship, are somewhat similar in form, method, theme, and/or wording to his unquestioned work or which first appear in company with that work (cf. items [107–111], [113], [114], [116], [118], [120–122], [124], [126]).

THE BALLAD OF KYND KYTTOK [106]. Three stanzas of long, usually twelve syllable, alliterative lines riming abababab, followed by a trimeter c and tetrameter line bob-and-wheel riming cdddc.

The poet's gay, simple, pretty grandmother, Kynd Kittok, on her way to heaven met a newt with whom she rode on a snail, coming at night to an alehouse. Having died of thirst she did not eat, but drank beyond measure, slept till noon, and then while God laughed His heart sore, stole past St. Peter into heaven, there to be our Lady's hen wife for seven years and fight with St. Peter. One day, since the ale of heaven was sour, Kittok went out to get a fresh drink; but when she returned at the bell's sound, St. Peter hit her with a club, and back she ran to the alehouse, there to pour pitchers, brew, and bake. The poet prays his friends, if they be dry, to drink with his grandmother once for his sake.

The poem is attributed to Dunbar in neither of its text sources, but is often included in his canon because it first appears with poems which are ascribed to him, and because both its content and novel use of a typical romance stanza are said to be characteristic of him. However, in none of his unquestioned poems does Dunbar display a comparable gentle good humor or narrative gift. With the possible exception of that in *The*

Wowing of the King quhen he was in Dunfermline [48], what meager plots there are among the Allegories and Court Life poems seem to exist for the sake of criticism or abuse or elaborate personification rather than for the interest of story or rounded characterization. And while the use of this type of stanza for comedy might suggest *Of Sir Thomas Norny* [56], where Dunbar apparently followed Chaucer's *Sir Thopas* in burlesquing tail-rime, the particular pattern of [106] is found nowhere among his unquestioned work. Especially in view of its good-natured tolerance and rapport with humble folk, the poem is really more characteristic of Henryson than of Dunbar.

BALLATE AGAINST EVIL WOMEN [107]. Six stanzas (cf. *Quhone he List to Feyne* [71]).

The beastly lusts of women that fear no shame and value neither God's nor man's blame have troubled them so that they trust only their god, Cupid. Just as the bitch in heat chooses not the greyhound but the foulest tyke, and the mare not the courser but a crooked, old horse, so women bestow their virginity on the unworthiest—even the pleasantest lady will suddenly take a crippled or deformed creature. Since it is their fate, who should blame them for serving their lust? Clerks have taught what injuries women do with colored eloquence. Had one the virtues of Solomon, Aristotle, Samson, and Hector, women's trickery should render them unavailing. Dissembling, false, known for deceit, teaching inconstancy, envy, and spite, women banish peace forever, which should make men leave subtle whores.

This has been interpreted as an attack only against that group of reprehensible women who should be censured by both sexes. However, viewed in its entirety the poem appears to be a misogynist diatribe against all womankind. It is attributed to Dunbar because *Ane Orisoun* [99], which immediately follows it in the manuscripts, is subscribed "Quod Dunbar," and is sometimes printed as an epilogue to the *Ballate*. However, *Ane Orisoun* is concerned with what would seem to be a quite different subject, the sensuality of the poet and not the sins of women, and employs a different stanzaic pattern. The *Ballate* proper concludes with "Explicit," and the majority of editors consider it anonymous.

CRISTES PASSIOUN [108]. Four stanzas, the last incomplete, of irregular tetrameter or pentameter lines riming ababbcc, ababbcbc, abaababc, abaababcd.

An address from the cross: to redeem man Christ undergoes the agonies of the crucifixion, which He enumerates, bidding man look on His wounds and think on His passion.

The poem is a rough, incomplete version of Lydgate's *Cristes Passioun*. It has been attributed to Dunbar on the following grounds: *Of the Passioun of Christ* [101], which seems unquestionably to be Dunbar's, has as refrain a line which is almost identical with one in Lydgate's poem, indicating that Dunbar was familiar enough with that English poem to have composed its Scottish version; and [108] resembles [101] sufficiently in subject, detail, and wording to suggest that the two poems had a common author.

DOUN BY ANE REVER AS I RED [109]. Ten stanzas with refrain (cf. *Bewty and the Presoneir* [75]).

A *memento mori* in which a bird counsels the poet: repent, confess, for the coming of death is sure, though its time is not; he can lengthen his life no more than could Solomon; he has seen many lords who feared neither heaven nor hell, they were so strong, no doubt. With the souls of such he and the bird will not meddle. If he be a merchant, let him spend part of his goods, being honest always; after his death his wife will have another mate. If he have a benefice, let him never hoard the church's goods, but give to the poor. A proud, wanton priest left money which strangers took, praying for him only ill; wise men said he did nothing wise. This priest, so rich in worldly trash, mended his friends no whit till he died. Since in no way may any man lengthen his life, and when he is buried others will take his goods, let the poet say a bird taught him: do for yourself while you are here.

Cf. *Advice to Spend anis Awin Gude* [93] and *Of Manis Mortalitie* [95] to which this poem has some general similarity in thought. On the whole, however, in tone, purpose, and method, it is less characteristic of Dunbar than of Henryson (cf. *The Prais of Aige* [9], *The Ressoning Betuix Aige and Yowth* [10], *The Abbay Walk* [11], *The Ressoning Betwixt Deth and Man* [12], and *The Thre Deid Pollis* [16]), though it has the consistency, polish, and power of neither poet's usual work.

FAINE WALD I WITH ALL DILIGENCE [110]. Seven stanzas with refrain (cf. *To the King* [23]).

The poet would make a song pleasant to all, but he knows not what to write. If he thought for seven years to write one thing, some men would despise it. If he speak in general, some take it specially; if of liberality, noble birth, nobility, they say he flatters, so few have those qualities; if of wretchedness, they say he backbites, so many wretched there are. If he writes not according to all men's mind—though some of them are evil—they find his poetry is worthless; none can write after the will of all.

This poem in method, form, and theme is of the same kind as *Of Deming* [30] and *How Sall I Governe Me?* [31], which state respectively that whatever a person is someone will judge him, and whatever he does someone will condemn him.

FANE WALD I LUVE BUT QUHAIR ABOWT [111]. Seven stanzas with half refrain (cf. *To the King* [23]).

The poet would love but tarries in doubt: he knows not where to love, so many love there is no place for him; so many write love ballads, he finds only mad conceits left to say; though some think their ladies peerless, some suffer painfully; some love long and fail, cannot find both love and friendship, cannot escape from love, or are blinded by it. Though young love is strong and difficult to assuage, its end is misery; a misgoverned youth brings a ghastly old age unless one leave love alone. He who would fix his affections perfectly will find a permanent love, God; treat himself well; be content; and let other lovers be.

In MS National Library Scotland 1.1.6 this poem follows *In Secreit Place* [49] and both are ascribed to "clerk"—possibly the "Johne Clerk" mentioned in *Lament for the Makaris* [29]—which suggests common authorship. However, there are two other early ascriptions of *In Secreit Place*, both to Dunbar, and none of *Fane Wald I luve*; and since its meter, though used by Dunbar a number of times, was not unusual, and its theme, though akin to that of *Inconstancy of Luve* [72] and *The Merle and the Nychtingaill* [84], was a medieval commonplace, there is little reason to conclude that he actually wrote it.

THE FREIRIS OF BERWICK [112]. 567 lines of heroic couplet in MS National Library Scotland 1.1.6 which appears to contain the better text, 564 lines in MS Pepys 2553.

Berwick, fairest and pleasantest of towns, had such strong fortifications that if those within should choose, none without might win it. Therein dwelt the four orders of friars. Once in May two Jacobins, Allan, old and sick, and Robert, young and strong, returning from a visit to their up-country brethren stopped outside the walls to rest at the hostel of Simon Lawlor. The hostler was away, but his fair wife, giving them bread, cheese, and drink, listened to their stories until the friars heard the abbey bell ring and knew the town gates were locked for the night. Then reluctantly, at Allan's plea, she made beds for them in the loft at the hall's end, and left them there—though Friar Robert promised to walk that night and perhaps see some sport. This good wife was happy to have them shut up for she was expecting her lover, John, rich abbot of the Gray Friars, who could issue from town undetected through a secret gate. She put fat capons and rabbits on the fire, left her maid to cook them, then decked herself gaily, covered the table with fine linen, and waited for her abbot, who soon arrived bringing a gallon of Gascon wine, new-slain partridges, and white bread. Through a hole in the wall Robert watched the lovers sporting together, the abbot revelling in the wife's endearments, until just as supper was ready they heard her husband at the gate. Since there was no way for John to escape, the good wife hid him in a meal trough, bade her maid remove all evidence of their feast, cast off her finery, and went to bed, leaving her husband to knock and at last call her by name, "Alison." At first she refused to recognize him or to admit anyone while her Simon was away; then she let him in, but offered only the plainest food for his supper, which she refused to share, saying it was fitter for them to be in bed. Thinking Simon's plight a shame, Robert coughed to make his and Allan's presence known; and despite Alison's protests, they were invited down to join her husband. Since Simon wished for good meat and drink, Robert promised to bring the best in the land; then pretended to conjure, bowing low to the locker where the lovers' feast was hidden and sorely frightening Alison. Having finished his spell Robert ordered her to bring forth the food and she did, pretending great amazement. Simon was truly amazed and thought Robert a man of great science who could do such things by his subtility and knowledge in philosophy. The men drank and sang, but the wife had little pleasure, despairing lest Robert betray her. As the wine passed around, the men grew merrier, and Robert explained to Simon that he had a secret servant whom he agreed to summon—in disguise since, he said, the servant's natural appearance was so ugly it might drive Simon mad. Since it would be a disgrace to the Jacobins for such a fellow to appear in their habit, as the hostler requested, he should come in the habit of a Gray Friar; and Robert bade Simon be brave, hide by the door, and when told, to strike with his staff. Then Robert conjured "Hurlybas" to rise silently from the trough in his gray habit with hands in sleeves, cowl over face, and to depart speedily, coming here no more save at Robert's bidding. Up rose Abbot John and went soberly toward the door. Robert told Simon to strike and the good man did, so fiercely that he fell breaking his head, while the abbot tumbled over the stair into the mire below, then ran and climbed over the wall, happy to escape. Bleeding, Simon was revived, bidden by Robert to be merry and, having struck the Gray Friar over the stair into the mire, to get to bed and let the graceless ghost go. The poet closes with an invocation to Christ.

Berwick having passed into English hands in 1482, the poem must have been written before 1539, by which time all the English monasteries had been disestablished. Although it has been included in every edition of Dunbar's work, it affords no evidence of his authorship. The use of a fabliau, and the lack of obscenity which might be expected of the genre;

the sympathetic, even admiring, presentation of two friars; the gusto with which food is described, are all completely uncharacteristic of Dunbar's acknowledged poems. Moreover, the heroic couplet occurs only once among those poems, in *In Prais of Wemen* [66] where it is used for a short expression of opinion rather than for a lengthy narrative. Dunbar, in fact, seems to have had little narrative gift. Only this poem, *The Wowing of the King quhen he was in Dunfermline* [48], which is relatively short, and *The Ballad of Kynd Kyttok* [106], which he probably did not write, could be said to tell a dramatic story whose action is of major importance, with a climax and denouement, and with clearly delineated, believable characters. Apparently Pinkerton, who first assigned the poem to Dunbar, did so only in the absence of any other likely candidate.

GIF YE WALD LUFE AND LUVIT BE [113]. Six stanzas with refrain (cf. *Lament for the Makaris* [29]).

If you would love and be loved, be ever secret, true, and patient. If one is not patient, he shall have displeasure; if not secret, he shall lack good fellowship and credence; if untrue, he shall lack fame. Lacking any of the three, he may never be a glad lover. Do not reveal the things you have by nature, for you would regret it.

In theme and certain wording, most noticeably in its refrain, similar to *Gude Counsale* [89].

GLADETHE THOUE QUEYNE OF SCOTTIS REGIOUN [114]. Five stanzas with refrain (cf. *Rewl of Anis Self* [62]).

An encomium, largely in terms of flowers and jewels, praising Queen Margaret's youth, beauty, lineage, sweetness, nobility, and womanliness; bidding her be glad; and praying that a plant may spring from her succession, his spirit inspired with all grace.

A repetitious, conventional performance, obviously written at some time between *The Thrissil and the Rois* [76] and *To the Princess Margaret* [125] on the one hand, and *To the Queen Dowager* [126] on the other, all three of which it resembles to some degree in subject, wording, and style, especially aureation and imagery.

IN ALL OURE GARDYN GROWIS THARE NA FLOURIS [115].

Two stanzas and three lines (cf. *Rewl of Anis Self* [62]).

Our garden is bare; Danger is gardener; Good Breeding out of service. The poet dare not say what he means, his heart is so sore; nor shall he take revenge save upon himself. Of her who was the goodliest, he can praise only her earthly beauty; and no earthly thing may last. Since in this world there is no security, he takes leave of all unsteadfastness.

The poem has been attributed to Dunbar apparently because it first appears in MS National Library Scotland 19.1.16 with his acknowledged work and touches upon a theme, *sic transit gloria mundi,* which he sometimes treats (cf. items [92], [93], [95–97]). But the major, though implicit, theme of the sadness of love's betrayal, the extended opening conceit, the lingering rhythm facilitated by an occasional extra light syllable, and even the form of its infinitive and past participle are completely uncharacteristic of Dunbar.

JERUSALEM REIOSS FOR JOY [116].

JERUSALEM REIOSS FOR JOY [116]. Eight stanzas with Latin refrain (cf. *Of James Dog* [54]). An exhortation in the manner and measure of *The Nativitie of Christ* [100], though lacking that poem's smoothness and power.

Jerusalem rejoice, for Jesus as King is born with angels' song, to illuminate the city and make it free. Angels' light illumines it; three richly garbed kings shout to the city, "Shine!" The tyrant, Herod, is exiled; the rightful King has risen. When men name Him, heaven, earth, and hell make obeisance. All the elements heralded His coming, as did the cross and stones. The long-dead knew Him Who rose upright; the crooked and blind declared His might That healed them; Nature, wondering at the virgin birth, and hell, when its gates were broken, knew Him. *Illuminare Jerusalem!*

This is the first of three unexceptional celebrations of the Nativity (cf. *Now glaidith euery liffis creature* [118] and *The sterne is rissin of our Redemptioun* [121]) which have been included in editions of Dunbar because they are written in the same measure as certain poems which are unquestionably his.

THE MANERE OF CRYING OF ANE PLAY [117].

THE MANERE OF CRYING OF ANE PLAY [117]. Eleven stanzas (cf. *The Fenyeit Freir of Tungland* [59]).

A cry, or announcement of a May play for the summer festival. The speaker comes on with a roar; identifies himself variously as a sultan, giant, Blind Harry, and/or the spirit of Guy; prays God to preserve the audience; and traces his lineage, which is of the race of giants beginning with Hercules. He describes the marvelous feats of his great-grandfather and grandfather; in more detail describes those of his grandmother —whose belch made the heavens roar, who urinated Craigforth, etc.—and those of his father. Generated a thousand years ago, he has been a bold warrior so long that now he is wasted for age and is small, as they may see. Having been long banished he, Wealth, has come with the wind to show them comfort, slay dearth, and dwell forever within the sound of St. Gelis' bell. Warfare makes him shun the lands of the Shah and Sultan, France, Denmark, Sweden, Norway, and the Netherlands; for its language he shuns Ireland, and so has come to peerless, merriest Edinburgh. Since Wealth has come, let the merchants in green with bow and arrow follow Robin Hood. He and his comrades, Welfare, Wantonness, and Play, shall remain and banish care and dearth. Since as they see he is a giant, where shall for him be gotten a suitable wife? Let Lothian and Fife be searched. He bids farewell, but not for long, prays Christ to preserve, God to bless them; and asks for a drink from the man who best knows he loves it.

Though in neither manuscript is the poem complete or ascribed (it has been attributed to David Lindsay), it is usually accepted as Dunbar's because of its similarity in form, content, and style to some of his un-questioned works (cf. *Of Sir Thomas Norny* [56], *The Fenyeit Freir of Tungland* [59], and *Inconstancy of Luve* [72]). The revelling in scatology is, of course, a Dunbar characteristic. In MS National Library Scotland 1.1.6 the poem is entitled "Ane litill interlud of the droichis part of the play," which has been interpreted as a reference to the stature of the poet, who it is surmised might have been Dunbar himself, particularly in view of the references to his dwarfish stature in *The Flyting of Dunbar and Kennedie* [28]. But the surmise both as to the poet's delivering the piece in person and to his small size have been attacked. The identity of personages in the poem has occasioned some comment: Blind Harry, for example, has been variously identified as author of *The Wallace,* re-cipient of gifts from the king recorded in the Treasurer's Accounts, and a character from folklore.

NOW GLAIDITH EUERY LIFFIS CREATURE [118]. Five stanzas with refrain (cf. *Rewl of Anis Self* [62]).

Every creature is glad, for the King of heaven, to ransom us from death, be the world's light, and banish grief, is born. He has come from His Father's throne with inestimable light and angels' sweet song. Whoever heard so happy a tale as how the

Garden of grace and glory, the Maker of all things, has for love and mercy and to defeat our foe taken on humanity and come as a babe. Sovereign of cherubims, Encompassor of all, without beginning or end, with Whom is all good and all men. He has come to wash away our sin. So sing, cast away care, cupidity, woe; be merry and virtuous, banish vice, despise fortune. Right now reigns and we welcome the Prince of paradise.

Cf. *Jerusalem reioss for joy* [116] and *The sterne is rissin of our Redemptioun* [121].

OF FOLKIS EVILL TO PLEIS [119]. Seven stanzas with partial refrain (cf. *Lament for the Makaris* [29]).

Four manner of folk are hard to please: the rich man and the powerful lord, both of whom would have more from others; the husband of a perfect lady, who would have another; and the man who drinks to satiety, yet is unsatisfied. No man has so great abundance but he would have more. Yet whoever has wealth, it is not the poet. At this Christmas he will ask no largess of Sir Gold, who goes from him to others.

Ascribed to Dunbar in MS Cambridge University L1.5.10, but not in MS National Library Scotland 1.1.6, which gives a defective version. Although the poem is not even printed as an Attribution in the Scottish Text Society edition, it seems unquestionably Dunbar's since the complete version is ascribed to him, its subject matter and attitude are both characteristic of his work, and there is a similar reference in *The Petition of the Gray Horse Auld Dunbar* [44] to largess at Christmas.

ROS MARY ANE BALLAT OF OUR LADY [120]. Six stanzas with refrain (cf. *Rewl of Anis Self* [62]).

A somewhat repetitious Ave Maria in which the poet praises Mary as flower, gem, source of refuge and mercy, empress of heaven and hell, star-blinding Phoebus, etc., and prays that she will intercede with her Son so that in heaven we may sing with Gabriel, *Benedicta tu in mulieribus, O mater Jhesu.*

In none of the manuscripts is this poem ascribed to Dunbar, and while its subject, imagery, diction, alliteration, Latin phrases, and meter are in keeping with his practice, it is noticeably inferior to *Ane Ballat of Our Lady* [103], the one of Dunbar's poems it most resembles. There seems, then, little reason to assign to him the poem proper, and none to assign him the four similar stanzas, with anglicized spelling and grammatical forms, which are added in a later manuscript.

THE STERNE IS RISSIN OF OUR REDEMPTION [121]. Five stanzas with refrain (cf. *Rewl of Anis Self* [62]).

Since our Redeemer has come let all earthly rulers abase themselves before this King of lasting life, of joy, and of every region, this Christian Conqueror, high Maker, etc., and to Him cry *Ave Redemptor Jesu*. We cannot abide in this dark valley, for the Star of glory is risen to guide us to the high, supernal, eternal regions where are no harmful skies. We follow with the three kings the brightest, supreme Star, Dispeller of darkness, beseeching Him to receive us with angels' sound into heaven.

Cf. *Jerusalem reioss for joy* [116] and *Now glaidith euery liffis creature* [118].

SURREXIT DOMINUS DE SEPULCHRO [122]. Five stanzas with Latin refrain (cf. *Rewl of Anis Self* [62]).

A rejoicing over the Resurrection, which first restates briefly Mark's and Matthew's account of the visit of the Marys to Christ's sepulchre. We honor the mighty Champion Who won victory over hell and brought souls to everlasting joy; may we, who lacked other aid, please this Lord, our shield, Whom the darkness of Phoebus revealed as God's Son, Who died triumphing, rose, and won the field. *Surrexit sicut dixit, allelulia!*

Possibly an imitation, adopting its first line, meter, theme, and occasionally wording from *On the Resurrection of Christ* [102], which comes just before it in MS National Library Scotland 1.1.6. However, despite the fact that [102] is ascribed to Dunbar and that [122] resembles it, there is little reason for considering the latter to be Dunbar's. It is not ascribed in the manuscript, and in power and general poetic competence is in no way comparable to the former.

TO THE CITY OF LONDON [123]. Seven stanzas with refrain (cf. *Rewl of Anis Self* [62]).

A lavish catalogue encomium of London, sovereign of cities, praising its fairness, renown, riches, pleasure, river, bridge, inhabitants, tower. May its walls be strong, its people wise, churches blithe, bells well-sounding, merchants rich, wives fair and loving, virgins beautiful. The prudent mayor, unrivalled by any lord of Paris, Venice, or Florence, is pattern and guide, worthy master of mayors. London, you are the flower of all cities.

Dunbar has been identified as author of this poem, on the basis of references in one of the manuscripts to the occasion of the poem and in English records to payments by Henry VII to the Rhymer of Scotland; on the basis of the evident relationship between James IV and the poet, which would have made natural Dunbar's presence on the embassy to London to arrange James' marriage and his role as poet-spokesman for the group; and on the basis of the resemblance between it and *To Aberdein* [85] in subject, form, tone, style, and a number of words and phrases. However, it is not ascribed; and an entry in the Scottish Treasurer's Accounts indicates, though not conclusively, that the poet was in Scotland during Christmas week, 1501. If he were, indeed, in Scotland, he could not have made this poem, as the manuscript asserts its author did, at the same time in London. Thus the question of authorship remains unsettled.

TO THE GOUVERNOUR IN FRANCE [124]. Five stanzas with refrain (cf. *Rewl of Anis Self* [62]).

A remonstrance to the marvelous chieftain who has left perplexed the lords who chose him, and does not intend to see the land or people, correct its faults or vice. Now lacking justice the land is ruined. Each man works to destroy the other, pleasing their old enemy and causing dissension, which is sad for their lord and guide to hear. He has abused his wit by absenting himself for gain, refusing to return, and causing theft, slaughter, and war. He should return in time to win the friendship of loyal lieges who pay dearly for his absence. Cupidity reigns among the clergy, who will debate over vacant benefices and oppose his bidding in his absence. Let him fulfill his bond soon. Great war and trouble have come about since his departure; more trouble approaches. Despairing of his return because of his tardiness, without government, depending ever on his state and grace, overcome with fear, they bid him speed.

The poem resembles *Quhen the Governour Past in France* [86] in subject and form, and like it was written after Albany's first departure from Scotland in 1517, the reference here to "Yeiris and dayis mo than two or thre" indicating 1519 as the earliest possible date. Its power, smoothness, irony, and satirical vehemence are in keeping with Dunbar's usual practice. Yet it is by no means certain that he wrote this poem, since several of its words are not found among his unquestioned work, and the references to "We Lordis" and "our auld innamy" (if this does, indeed, designate England) are totally uncharacteristic of him.

TO THE PRINCESS MARGARET [125]. Four stanzas with refrain (cf. *Lament for the Makaris* [29]). A lyrical encomium of Margaret, praising her beauty, fame, and lineage, and welcoming her as Queen of Scotland. This seems the most likely of the anonymous poems to have been written by Dunbar. It is the kind of composition which could have been expected from a poet living at the court of James IV, is on the same subject and obviously dates from the same period as *The Thrissil and the Rois* [76]. The aureate diction, ornamental alliteration, and metrical facility of this extremely musical piece—which may have been intended to be sung since one part of a setting for its words is given in the manu-script—are all characteristic of his poetry; and the pro-English sentiment and flattery of a princess who might, and did, become his patron are in keeping with attitudes expressed in his poetry.

TO THE QUEEN DOWAGER [126]. Five stanzas with refrain (cf. *Rewl of Anis Self* [62]). A lavish encomium of a lady, bidding her remove languor and live in joyfulness.

> Let this morning star, life and guide of love, whose brightness is our only comfort, banish all grief. Since she is pleasant, young, fair, virtuous, noble, wise, etc., why should she be sad? The poet, her faithful servant, commends himself to her, for whose comfort and joy he shall make songs; and he bids this blossom, whose lord death has devoured, not to fade her fair face with weeping, but to cast out care and sighing, having pity on her servant.

Somewhat similar to *Gladethe Thoue Queyne of Scottis Regioun* [114] in subject, form, imagery, and method of listing terms of praise, but less effective, lacking smoothness and consistent development of imagery and having an awkward abstraction for refrain. In the manuscript this poem has no title and has been attributed to Dunbar only on the insubstantial grounds of its reference to the death of the lady's husband, assumed to have been James IV.

XI. THE CHAUCERIAN APOCRYPHA

by

Rossell Hope Robbins

Some one hundred miscellaneous poems have been either ascribed to Chaucer in fifteenth- and sixteenth-century manuscripts, or printed with or as Chaucer's in the black-letter editions of the sixteenth century, or linked to Chaucer by later scholars in the eighteenth and nineteenth centuries. By 1900, stricter literary and linguistic rules had classified this material into three groups: an accepted Chaucer canon of minor poems, works by other known authors (such as Lydgate), and a small collection of formal poems (generally anonymous) on courtly love. Discussed in other chapters are Chaucer and the identified authors: the big three—Gower, Lydgate, and Hoccleve; the minor English Chaucerians—Burgh, Usk, Ashby, Bradshaw, Ripley and Norton, Walton, the translator of Palladius, and Bokenham; and the Scottish Chaucerians—James I, Robert Henryson, Gavin Douglas, and William Dunbar. The third group, the Chaucerian apocrypha, is the subject of this present chapter.

The following poems have all at one time or another been ascribed to Chaucer:

(1) Poems now accepted as by Chaucer: *Against Women Unconstant (Newfangelnesse); Compleint d'amours; A Balade of Compleynt; A Compleint to His Lady (Balade of Pity); Merciles Beaute; Chaucer's Proverbs; To Rosemounde; Womanly Noblesse; Romaunt of the Rose.* (On the other hand, the following seven poems have occasionally appeared as Chaucerian apocrypha: *Book of the Duchess; Complaint to His Purse; Fortune; Lak of Stedfastnesse; Envoy to Bukton; Envoy to Scogan;* and *Truth.*)

(2) Spurious Canterbury Tales: *Tale of Beryn* (Brown-Robbins, no.

3926); *Tale of Gamelyn* (Brown-Robbins, no. 1913; see I [9]); *Plowman's Tale* (Brown-Robbins, no. 3448).

(3) Poems by Lydgate: *Balade in Commendation of Our Lady* (Brown-Robbins, no. 99); *Wicked Tongue* (Brown-Robbins, no. 653); *Doubleness* (Brown-Robbins, no. 3656); *Instructions to the Estates* (Brown-Robbins, no. 920); *Four Things Making a Man a Fool* (Brown-Robbins, no. 3521 with 3523, 4230); *Sober Conversation* (Brown-Robbins, no. 1294); *Balade de bon conseil* (Brown-Robbins, no. 1419); *Flower of Courtesy* (Brown-Robbins, no. 1487); *Assembly of Gods* (Brown-Robbins, no. 4005); *Siege of Thebes* (Brown-Robbins, no. 3928); *Chastity* (an extract from *The Fall of Princes*; Brown-Robbins, no. 1592).

(4) Poems by Hoccleve: *Letter of Cupid* (VIII [1]); *Mother of God* (VIII [27]); *Balade au tres honourable compaignie du Garter* (VIII [23]).

(5) Poem by Gower: *In Praise of Peace* (Brown-Robbins, no. 2587).

(6) Poem by Henryson: *Testament of Cresseid* (X [4]).

(7) Prose by Usk: *Testament of Love*, perhaps the most firmly linked to Chaucer of any of these apocryphal pieces.

(8) Other poems of the Chaucerian apocrypha: *Rotheley's Praise of the House of Vere* (Brown-Robbins, no. 1087); *Jack Upland* (III [95]); *Lamentation of Mary Magdalen* (Brown-Robbins, no. 2759); *Ashby's Prisoner's Reflections* (Brown-Robbins, no. 437); *Speak No Evil* (Brown-Robbins, no. 1619 with 1618); *Beware of Deceitful Women* (Brown-Robbins, no. 1944); *Leaulte vault richesse* (Brown-Robbins, no. 3660); *Moral Proverbs of Christine* (Robbins-Cutler, no. 3372.1); *Advice Resented* (Brown-Robbins, no. 2594); *Cuckoo and the Nightingale* (VII [47]); *Letter to His Heart's Sovereign* (Brown-Robbins, no. 1238).

1. Evolution of the Chaucerian Apocrypha

I. The Influence of John Shirley

Among the first to link spurious secular poems with the prestige name of Chaucer was John Shirley (1366–1456), gradually emerging as an important manuscript distributor and littérateur in fifteenth-century London. For many of Chaucer's minor poems, Shirley is the sole authority; for Lydgate, too, as Hammond remarked, "Shirley did yeoman service," compounding confusion, however, by naming Lydgate as warranty for anonymous religious or moral pieces. Shirley's own verses are, at least in intention, Chaucerian imitations: "In Englische was neuer noon him lyke." For two of the volumes in what amounted to a circulating library, Shirley wrote rimed lists of contents. For two others, he appended a little book-plate (perhaps by Lydgate).

SHIRLEY'S METRICAL INDEX, I [1], 104 lines in doggerel couplets, of "no literary merit" (Hammond), is essentially a publisher's advertisement for a Shirley compilation of pieces by Chaucer, Lydgate, and others. It notes the variety of the contents and the difficulty of assembling them, and requests the borrower to return the manuscript to the lender (i.e., Shirley). Brown-Robbins, no. 1426.

SHIRLEY'S METRICAL INDEX, II [2], also 104 lines in doggerel couplets, copied by Stow in 1558 (in MS British Museum Additional 29729) from pages now lost from a Shirley manuscript, Trinity Cambridge 600. Like [1] above, a metrical calendar or list of contents for a codex, praising especially Lydgate's "sugared mouth," and concluding with a request that the borrower send it back to Shirley, who will be glad to be of service again in this capacity. Brown-Robbins, no. 2598.

SHIRLEY'S BOOK MOTTO [3], possibly by Lydgate (named in the rubric), in two of Shirley's own manuscripts (mid fifteenth-century), one rime royal stanza, requests readers who have enjoyed the stories to restore the collection again to John Shirley. Brown-Robbins, no. 4260.

CHAUCER'S CHRONICLE or THE NINE WORSHIPFULLEST LADIES [4] (Brown-Robbins, no. 1016), ascribed to Shirley, in MS Ashmole 59 (about 1450) headed "The Cronycle made by Chaucier," devotes nine eight-line stanzas (in couplets)—"wholly worthless" (Skeat)—to nine heroines constant in love, all celebrated in Chaucer's *Legend of Good Women*: Cleopatra, Ariadne, Dido, Lucretia, Phyllis, Thisbe, Hypsipyle,

Hypermnestra, with Alceste (in mistake for Alcyone) who replaces Philomela. The verses are purely descriptive and could serve as texts for tapestries, windows, or for mummings; since they appear in a manuscript written by John Shirley, Skeat and Gaertner assumed his authorship. A later synopsis of nine other feminine worthies (not derived from Chaucer) is the *Nine Ladies Worthy*, [28] below (Brown-Robbins, no. 2767).

Others works by Shirley, all in MS British Museum Additional 5467, include *The Lamentable Cronycle of the Dethe and False Murdere of James Stewarde, Late Kynge of Scotys; The Boke Cleped Les bones meures*, a translation of Jean Legrand, made about 1440; *Secrete of Secretes*; and *The Governance of Kynges and Prynces*, also from the French.

Among Shirley's friends were gentlemen authors. Toward the middle of the fifteenth century, one such, Richard Sellyng, requested Shirley's criticism of some of his verses:

SELLYNG'S EVIDENCE TO BEWARE [5], in a unique manuscript written by Shirley himself, 23 rime royal stanzas with concluding six couplets: In his old age, the poet reviews his past life and warns young men of the nearness of death. Although aureate and mannered, the poem introduces simple metaphors from farming and trading, and goes beyond the merely historic interest of its conclusion, wherein Sellyng asks Shirley "to amende where it is amisse." Brown-Robbins, no. 4074.

Squire Halsham's Balade (Brown-Robbins, no. 3504 with 3437), included by Shirley in three manuscripts, and also found elsewhere following *Chaucer's Proverbs* (Brown-Robbins, no. 3914), may be by another poetry-writing member of Shirley's circle; Bühler, however, rejects South's identification of "Johannes Halsham, armiger" (died 1415). *Impingham's Proverbs* (Brown-Robbins, no. 2290), containing lines from Chaucer, in a Shirley-influenced manuscript, Harley 7333, may have been compiled by another customer acquaintance, or, as Manly and Rickert suggest, by Benedict Burgh when Prebend of Impingham. Other writers whose names have become attached to miscellaneous moral verses include John Lucas (Brown-Robbins, nos. 2585, 3143), R. Stokys (Brown-Robbins, no. 3083)

—a man of this name served with Chaucer on an inquest in 1387—and Hichecocke (Brown-Robbins, no. 1261).

SCOGAN'S MORAL BALADE [6] (Brown-Robbins, no. 2264), 21 eight-line stanzas, ababbcbc, addressed to the four sons of Henry IV (Henry, Prince of Wales; Thomas, the future Duke of Clarence; John, the future Duke of Bedford; and Humfrey, the future Duke of Gloucester) by their tutor, Henry Scogan (1361–1407), misnamed by Caxton, John Scogan. The verses were to be read aloud at a public banquet of the Merchants Guild at the house of Lewis John, probably in 1406–07 (Skeat's conjecture), when the princes would have ranged in age from sixteen to nineteen.

Scogan, his health failing, wishes to impart some moral lessons: in their youth, the princes should plant the roots of virtue which flower in old age. Clerks have written that faith is dead without works, estate without intelligence, and that lordship without virtue perishes. True nobility comes not from lineage but from honest life. Take heed of the examples of Tullius Hostilius, Julius Caesar, Nero, Balthasar, and Antiochus. As their tutor, Scogan hopes the princes choose rightly, that God may confirm them "in vertuous noblesse."

Lines from works of "my mayster Chaucer"—*Wife of Bath's Tale, Boethius,* and the *Monk's Tale*—are freely quoted, as well as Chaucer's *Gentilesse* (Brown-Robbins, no. 3348), complete, between lines 105 and 125. The poem falls into the traditions of instructions to the estates and advice to young people.

PRISONER'S COMPLAINT AGAINST FORTUNE [7], 21 rime royal stanzas, is reminiscent of Chaucer's *Fortune* as well as Usk's *Testament of Love.* Preserved only in three Shirley manuscripts; in Harley 2251 and British Museum Additional 34260, it is contiguous to Chaucer's *Purse.* Hammond, following Speght (1598), suggests Usk as the author of this poem, which would make it written before 1388 (the date of his execution). Seaton, followed by Jacob, suggests Sir Richard Roos as author, and the occasion the imprisonment of Eleanor Cobham in 1441; Seaton erroneously links the verses in Paston Letter No. 870 (Robbins-Cutler, no. 2267.5) with the same event. The poet upbraids Fortune and the three Fates because he is a prisoner, contrasting former prosperity with present woe, and concluding with a prayer to Christ and the Virgin. Brown-Robbins, no. 860.

For similar complaints see Earl Rivers' *Virelai on Fickle Fortune* [22] below, George Ashby's *Prisoner's Reflections* (Brown-Robbins, no. 437), and "Ar ne kuthe ich sorghe non nu ich mot manen min mon" (Brown-Robbins, no. 322).

In addition to Anthony Woodville, Earl Rivers, the Chaucerian tradition was continued among the nobility who wrote poetry by Richard Beauchamp, Earl of Warwick (see [20] below), and William de la Pole, Duke of Suffolk, who married the poet's granddaughter Alice.

II. Other Manuscripts Containing Chaucerian Apocrypha

Several other late fifteenth-century manuscripts, like the Shirley manuscripts made to sell to the general public rather than designed for one particular nobleman or merchant, also disguised minor productions with the magic name of Chaucer. So MS Trinity Cambridge 599 assigned *The Craft of Lovers* ([43] below) to Chaucer, and called Chaucer's a composite poem on hypocritical women ([32] below), although its borrowed stanza came from Lydgate's *Pain and Sorrow of Evil Marriage* (Brown-Robbins, no. 919). *Virtuous Maidens but Wicked Wives* (Brown-Robbins, no. 679) and *The Complaint Against Hope* (Brown-Robbins, no. 370) are two others attributed in these manuscripts to Chaucer. Such manuscripts became the quarry for the publishers of the black-letter editions of Chaucer and for the nineteenth- and twentieth-century editors. Named as Chaucer's in these manuscripts were several of Lydgate's and Hoccleve's poems, and, of those pieces discussed in this chapter, items [10], [11], [12], [18], [21], [30], [33], [42], [43], and [49].

The professed design of the English Chaucerians to follow their exemplar is illustrated in a typical eulogy:

PRAISE AND COMMENDATION OF CHAUCER [8], one rime royal stanza, probably 1475–1500, appearing in two manuscripts at the end of the *Parlement of Foules,* praises Master Geoffrey Chaucer, now in his grave, as the first to distill and rain down the gold dewdrops of speech and eloquence into the English tongue. Skeat considered it "a poor imitation of the style of Lydgate." Brown-Robbins, no. 2128.

Other eulogies of Chaucer are found here in items [6], [24], [44], [53], and [55]. The three major English Chaucerians often paid homage to Chaucer. Gower in his *Confessio Amantis* (III. 2941–57) called him "the first fyndere of oure faire langage" and stressed his renown as the poet of courtly love; Lydgate in the *Fall of Princes* (Prologue, 274–357), the *Life of Our Lady*, and frequently elsewhere; and Hoccleve in his *De Regimine Principum* (I. 694–97) called him "master dere and fadre reuerent . . . floure of eloquence." James I praised him "as superlative as poetis laureate." Caxton in three rime royal stanzas in his *Book of Curtesye* (ca. 1477–78) referred to the "fader and founder of eternate eloquence," and Hawes in his *Pastime of Pleasure* ([54] below) listed his works. Dunbar's *Golden Targe* added Lydgate and Gower to its praise of Chaucer. The adulation culminated in Spenser's "well of English undefiled."

Although it does not mention Chaucer by name, *Partonope of Blois* (see Romances, I [99], for Lillian Hornstein's commentary and bibliography) is steeped in the writings of Chaucer, with very numerous parallels especially to Chaucer's love poetry. A retelling of the Legend of Ugolino (Robbins-Cutler, no. 28.8) in Chaucer's *Monk's Tale* draws heavily on the original.

Another poet generally associated with the Chaucerian apocrypha, Benedict Burgh (ca. 1413–83), praised Lydgate. Burgh's major works are treated elsewhere: his supposed completion of Lydgate's translation of the *Secrets of the Philosophers* (Brown-Robbins, no. 935), the *Distichs of Cato* (Brown-Robbins, nos. 854, 3955), and the *Christmas Game* (Brown-Robbins, no. 2749); his alliterative lines, *Aristotle's ABC* (Brown-Robbins, no. 4155), are now ascribed to Benedict of Norwich. See above for Burgh's suggested authorship of *Impingham's Proverbs*.

BURGH'S PRAISE OF LYDGATE [9], eight rime royal stanzas, although described by Hammond as "the least didactic and most living of [Burgh's] productions," is in fact tedious and unpoetic. The encomium was written on a December 11, "with frosty fingers." Förster postulates a year between 1433 and 1440, while Burgh was (supposedly) vicar of Maldon in Essex, a few miles from Hatfield Broadoak, where Lydgate was prior (1423–34). Brown-Robbins, no. 2284.

> Burgh pleads he is no author and has never sipped the great classics, twelve of which he gives as supposedly known to Lydgate—actually Lydgate quoted directly only Ovid. The list is, however, interesting for a mid fifteenth-century appraisal of the classics: Virgil, Homer, Boethius, Ovid, Terence, Porcius Latro, Lucan, Martianus Capella, Horace, Statius, Juvenal, and Boccaccio. Lydgate's words live; he is the Gold Bible (stanza 4), to see which is Burgh's heaven. Long life and the laurel of victory to Lydgate.

Praises of Lydgate, who was a more immediate influence on the English Chaucerians than Chaucer himself, also come in Hawes (items [53–55] below), and Nevill (item [56]). For a love song in reproof of Lydgate, perhaps by the Duke of Suffolk, see Brown-Robbins, no. 2178.

III. Black Letter Editions of Chaucer with Chaucerian Apocrypha

Some of the Chaucerian manuscripts, especially those owned by Shirley, later passed into the possession of John Stow, the celebrated but impoverished London antiquarian, who himself compiled manuscript collections of poetry, and published the famous editions of Chaucer and Chaucerian apocrypha.

The first printed book to add major apocrypha was Richard Pynson's *The Boke of Fame* (1526), which included *La belle dame* sans mercy [46] below, the *Letter of Dido to Aeneas* [52], Lydgate's advice on sober conversation (Brown-Robbins, no. 1294), and the *Lamentation of Mary Magdalene* (Brown-Robbins, no. 2759).

In 1532, Thynne appended to his Chaucer some twenty-three apocryphal items, nineteen appearing for the first time. (In the black-letter editions, there is occasionally some disparity in the item count, for several poems may be reckoned as one, e.g., *Chaucer's Prophecy* followed by two independent quatrains.) From Pynson, Thynne reprinted *La belle dame sans mercy* and *Lamentation of Mary Magdalene*; from de Worde,

Lydgate's *Black Knight* (Brown-Robbins, no. 1507) and *Instructions to the Estates* (Brown-Robbins, no. 920).

At this point, the confusion inherent in the Chaucerian apocrypha mounts, for of Thynne's twenty-three Chaucerian apocrypha only part of one belongs to Chaucer (*Romaunt of the Rose*), while one each is by Henryson (X [4]), Gower (Brown-Robbins, no. 2587), and Usk, two by Hoccleve (VIII [1], [23]), and some five by Lydgate (Brown-Robbins, nos. 99, 653, 920, 1487, 1507), leaving eleven spurious pieces, ten in the present chapter (items [6], [10–11], [15–17], [33–34], [46], [48]) and the *Cuckoo and the Nightingale* (see Dialogues, Debates, and Catechisms, VII [47], for Francis L. Utley's commentary and bibliography). In a later edition of 1542, Thynne added the *Plowman's Tale* (Brown-Robbins, no. 3448). By this date, the Chaucerian apocrypha amounted altogether to twenty-eight pieces.

Inasmuch as they do not closely relate to other Chaucerian apocrypha, the five items (three from Caxton) Thynne printed at the end of his table of contents are noted here:

EIGHT GOODLY QUESTIONS AND THEIR ANSWERS [10], nine rime royal stanzas, an expansion of the first seven lines of a Latin poem by Ausonius, *Eorundem septem sapientium sententiae*, forming proverbial maxims on the abuses of the age. The Latin reads:

Quaenam summa boni? Mens quae sibi conscia recti.
Pernicies homini quae maxima? Solus homo alter.
Quis dives? Qui nil cupiat. Quis pauper? Avarus.
Quae dos matronae pulcherrima? Vita pudica.
Quae casta est? De qua mentiri fama veretur.
Quod prudentis opus? Cum possit, nolle nocere.
Quid stulti proprium? Non posse, et velle nocere.

There is no clue to the authorship of this inconsequential item, although the Bannatyne manuscript adds "Finis quod Chawseir," and Skeat thought the style resembled Lydgate's. Brown-Robbins, no. 3183.

CHAUCER'S PROPHECY [11], attributed also to "Merlin" (as in Shakespeare's *King Lear* III. ii. 95), a very common tag of three couplets:

When these evil things come to pass, then the land of Albion shall be in great confusion. In addition to the printings by Caxton in *Queen Anelida* (1477) and in all the black-letter Chaucers, the little piece is found in seventeen manuscripts. Brown-Robbins, no. 3943. It is followed immediately by two quatrains:

Speak No Evil, two couplets beginning "It falleth for a gentleman," a brief exhortation to speak the best of a man in his absence and the truth in his presence. Brown-Robbins, no. 1619.

On Good Words, two couplets immediately following the preceding, as if a second stanza ("It cometh by kynde"). These two tags are not recorded in any manuscripts, but were first printed by Caxton in 1477 following [11].

Hoccleve's *Balade au tres honourable compaignie du Garter* is the fifth of the Thynne additions. See Hoccleve, VIII [23], for William Matthews' commentary and bibliography.

John Stow, ca. 1525–1605, in 1561 reprinted Thynne's addenda among the genuine poems of Chaucer, with two or three new items of Lydgate (Brown-Robbins, nos. 3521 and 3523, 1419), and the aforementioned [8]. Following the reprinted material, came a section entitled: "Certaine workes of Geffray Chaucer which hath not bene tofore printed," many from Stow's own manuscripts or those he had acquired from Shirley. Apart from Chaucer's own *Proverbs, Against Women Unconstant,* and *Pity,* Lydgate's *Doubleness* and the *Siege of Thebes* (Brown-Robbins, nos. 3656, 3928), previously printed separately by de Worde, and two short extracts from the *Fall of Princes* (Brown-Robbins, nos. 1592, 2661), the remaining eleven items are generally typical of the late fifteenth-century courtly love poetry, such as *The Craft of Lovers* [43], *Praise of Margaret the Daisy* [19], *Ten Commandments of Love* [40], and the *Court of Love* [37]; shorter items suitable for a mumming or pageant [28], [29]; short love lyrics [21], [23], a warning against deceitful women (Brown-Robbins, no. 1944), and two scurrilous poems [30], [31]. On this edition, Hammond commented: "It foisted upon Chaucer many poems which are obviously not his, and which it has cost a long struggle to remove from the Chaucer canon." By 1561, the Chaucerian apocrypha, with the items from Caxton [6], [11], now counted over fifty.

Late sixteenth- and seventeenth-century editions added a few more poems. Thomas Speght in 1598, as well as reprinting Thynne's prefatory poems and Stow's complete roster, included four courtly poems typical of the Chaucerian apocrypha: the *Prisoner's Complaint Against Fortune* [7] above, the famous *Flower and the Leaf* [50], and the *Isle of Ladies* [51] with its independent envoy [14]. In 1602, Speght added *Jack Upland* (see Wyclif and His Followers, III [95], for Ernest W. Talbert's commentary and bibliography).

IV. Later Editions of Chaucer with Chaucerian Apocrypha

Such was the core of the Chaucerian apocrypha, some 17,000 lines of verse, which, including Urry's addition of two pseudo-*Canterbury Tales* (*Beryn* and *Gamelyn*), remained standard, in spite of Tyrwhitt's revision in 1775, until as late as the 1810 edition of Chaucer by Alexander Chalmers. Among the "Genuine Poetical Works of Chaucer," Chalmers included such non-Chaucerian poems as *Mother of Nurture* [16] below, *Praise of Women* [33], *Court of Love* [37], *The Flower and the Leaf* [50], *The Cuckoo and the Nightingale* (see VII [47] in the third volume of this series), and *Instructions to the Estates* (Brown-Robbins, no. 920). Yet such a piece as Chaucer's *Purse* was printed among the "Poems imputed to Chaucer, or by Other Authors."

A few other eighteenth-century antiquaries in addition to Urry, printed short pieces they found in various manuscripts, e.g., Percy in his *Reliques* (1767)—Chaucer's *Merciles Beaute* and Pinkerton in his *Ancient Scotish Poems* (1786)—*Leaulte vault richesse* (Brown-Robbins, no. 3660). Nineteenth-century editors such as Skeat, who with Ellis, Furnivall, and Halliwell, examined the Shirley, Stow, and other repositories, together contributed further items to the apocrypha, e.g., [26], [27], [35], [36], [38], [39], [41], below. One of these additions is hardly typical:

WALTON'S PROSPERITY [12], a single eight-line stanza (lines 83–90) from Walton's Prologue to his translation (1410) of Boethius' *De consolatione philosophiae* (Brown-Robbins, no. 1597), appearing separately, on the evils of prosperity, especially money and women. In MS Selden B.24, the stanza is subscribed "Quod Chaucere," and in MS

Harley 2251 it appears as the last stanza of Lydgate's *Wicked Tongue* (Brown-Robbins, no. 653). Liddell in 1895 was the first to point out its true author. Brown-Robbins, no. 2820.

The later editors, however, rejected some of the early accretions, and Chalmers' edition of 1810 is the only one generally available for the Chaucerian apocrypha. Unfortunately, many of the famous nineteenth-century editions of Chaucer (with apocrypha) are now found only in major libraries. Editions after 1810 generally show a decrease in the spurious poems, and the classic edition of Skeat's *Chaucerian and Other Pieces* (1897) added to the *Oxford Chaucer* only 29 items. In her famous *Manual* (1908), Hammond entered 69 items from all previous sources as "Verse and Prose Printed with the Works of Chaucer." To these should be added those poems linked with the group after 1908, and other related items, bringing the total to about one hundred. In the forty years from 1930 to 1970, little research (save a few dissertations, an edition of two typical poems, and a few short articles) has been initiated on the Chaucerian apocrypha, and (Pearsall excepted) critical opinion still rests on Skeat, Hammond, and Berdan.

2. APOCRYPHAL LOVE LYRICS

What are essentially and typically the Chaucerian apocrypha comprise a relatively small group of fifteenth-century poems in the medieval tradition of courtly love, at this time a literary convention. This was the aspect of Chaucer that intrigued the later poets and justified their designation as Chaucerians. Especially influential were Chaucer's *Romaunt of the Rose, The Book of the Duchess, The Parliament of Foules,* the Prologue to *The Legend of Good Women,* and such minor poems as *The Hous of Fame, Against Women Unconstant, Compleint d'amours, Anelida and Arcite, Compleynt of Mars, Compleynt of Venus, A Compleint to His Lady, Compleynt unto Pite, Merciles Beaute, To Rosemounde,* and *Womanly Noblesse.* But this emphasis on Chaucer as the poet of love and love allegories did not distinguish his unique contributions to literature from the similar love allegories of Lydgate (especially his *Temple of Glass*) or Gower (*Confessio Amantis*). Consequently all three poets were regarded as a group, and any poem in this vein might be assigned to any one of them.

The parallelisms in the apocryphal love lyrics and the longer love visions or *dits amoreux* sparked the only extended study of this corpus by Ethel Seaton. Unfortunately, her penchant to unearth anagrams in every poem led her to see Sir Richard Roos, possibly the translator of *La belle dame sans mercy* [46] below, as the only begetter of "a corpus as large as that of Chaucer" of fifteenth-century court verse. The rejection of this view has regrettably downgraded Seaton's meticulous scholarship on fifteenth-century manuscripts, polite society in the later Middle Ages, English and French sources and analogues, and an apperceptive appreciation of the poems themselves. Any student who ignores her study does so to his own loss.

From this tradition of courtly love poetry, two literary forms evolved in the fifteenth century: the longer narrative poems or "love aunters" describing an erotic adventure with a full complement of literary conventions, leading into Spenser; and the shorter mannered love lyrics, deriving from Chaucer's own complaints or the lyrics intercalated into such works as *Troilus and Criseyde* (e.g., lines 1317–1421, 1590–1631), leading into Wyatt and Surrey.

The shorter love lyrics treated here are separated from the main corpus to be presented in the chapter on Lyrics only because of their continued association with the genuine works of Chaucer, or because of their affinity with Chaucerian styles and themes.

The mistress is fair but obdurate, and the poet languishes for her love. The diction is mannered and clichéd, the form rime royal or eight-line stanza. Variation depends on tricks of style—the employment of the less common French forms, balade or virelai, the introduction of macaronic lines, or the use of an acrostic. Later, some authors mock the conventions, using shorter lines or tail-rime stanzas, professing disinterest in their mistresses' moods, and even mocking or abusing their beauty.

These courtly love lyrics of the Chaucerian apocrypha are, in fact, little different from many other fifteenth-century formal poems, especially the lyrics of Charles d'Orleans, the lyrics in three major collections of secular poetry (MSS Rawlinson C.813, Bodleian Latin misc c.66, and Cambridge

University Ff.1.6), and poems in such manuscripts as Tanner 346 or Trinity Cambridge 599 (like Brown-Robbins, nos. 402, 1238). Moreover, these same manuscripts contain parallels to the longer love visions, such as Brown-Robbins, nos. 2496, 572, and poems by Charles d'Orleans (Brown-Robbins, nos. 4024, 3972, 2309). To complete the picture of fifteenth-century courtly love poetry, therefore, it is essential that the appropriate sections of the chapter on Lyrics be consulted. The availability of the Chaucerian apocryphal lyrics in printed books until the end of the nineteenth century was valuable, however, because critics could form from them accurate views of the nature of medieval court-coterie poetry. These views were not greatly changed by the much later publication of the hitherto unpublished fifteenth-century love lyrics.

THE LOVER'S MASS [13], entitled by its first editor *The Venus Mass*, is a cycle of seven short love lyrics (145 lines in all) and one prose piece, imitating the main sections of the Mass (as far as the Epistle, where the series ends), which supply the headings. Changes in tone are suggested by variations in the metrical forms. There are allusions to *The Legend of Good Women* and (possibly) to *Confessio Amantis*. The skill and good taste in handling the parody have brought high praise from most critics: Chambers called them "unusually good lyrics," and Hammond wrote that "Chaucer need not have been ashamed to sign [them]." Simmons and Neilson accepted Lydgate as the author; Hammond and Bennett rejected him. Brown-Robbins, no. 4186.

Introibo (seven tetrameter couplets): I will go to worship at the altar of the God of Love.
Confiteor (thirteen tetrameter couplets): I repent that in my youth I was slow in Love's service; but now I shall emulate the examples of Love's servants (cf. *Troilus and Criseyde*, II, 523–39).
Misereatur (eight tetrameter couplets): Love will forgive me the time I idly wasted in sleep and sloth.
Officium (a roundel in seventeen lines): Honor to Cupid: may he assist my suit.
Kyrie, Christe, Kyrie (a balade, three eight-line stanzas, aabaabab, in pentameters with double internal rimes changing with each line, and with stanza linking): 1. Lady, have pity on me; 2. I am desolate; 3. But I will serve her anyway (cf. Chaucer's *Anelida*, lines 272–78, 332–41; and triple internal rime in Brown-Robbins, no. 267).
Gloria (eight tetrameter quatrains with dimeter bob): My pains will give way to joys.
Oryson (one eight-line stanza, ababbcbc): Cupid, pity thy servants.
Epistle (about 500 words in prose): To all true lovers who shun deceit: The progress

of love is like a difficult pilgrimage, but it can be endured by remembering Love's heroes and heroines, Cupid's martyrs. Lovers, pray for my success with my lady. (The pilgrim simile is founded on Laurent's French prose version of Boccaccio's *De casibus*, Book III, rather than on Lydgate's *Fall of Princes*.)

Although there are comparable French and Latin parodies of the Mass (e.g., *Missa potatorum*), there are no similar works in Middle English. As yet, no source has been identified, though Hammond believes in Spanish origin.

For a parody of the burial services (incorporating key words into the text), see the satire on the death of the Duke of Suffolk in Works Dealing with Contemporary Conditions (Brown-Robbins, no. 1555), and for erotic parodies of church services see here [37] and [39], and Dunbar's *Dregy* (X [51] above). For a prose parody, see *The Gospelles of Dystaues* in Works Dealing with Contemporary Conditions.

BALADE TO HIS MISTRESS, FAIREST OF FAIR [14], a conventional formal love lyric of the early fifteenth century, follows without break *The Isle of Ladies*, [51] below. It has two distinct parts. The first ("Fayrest of fayer and goodleste on lyve") has been considered an envoy to the longer poem; it is a rime royal stanza (lacking the second line), a *salut d'amour* to his mistress on her power to heal or slay him. The second ("Go forth mine own true heart innocent") is a balade, three stanzas rime royal with refrain ("The bliss that thou desirest oft") enumerating the duties of the courtly lover. A later hand has added a doggerel couplet, possibly referring back to verse 25 ("Fayninge in love is breadinge of a fall"): "Ye that this balade read shall / I pray you keepe you from the fall." Skeat thought the balade "almost certainly by Lydgate." Brown-Robbins, no. 923.

BALADE AND ENVOY TO ALISON [15], in two manuscripts, mid fifteenth-century, printed in editions of Chaucer from 1532 to 1878 as an Envoy to *The Cuckoo and the Nightingale* (see VII [47]). In MS Fairfax it follows without break Chaucer's *The Book of the Duchess*. The author commends his book to Alison, whose name appears in an acrostic in a six-line envoy ("Aurore of gladness and day of lustinesse") following the balade, three rime royal stanzas ("O leud book with thy foule rudenesse"), all four stanzas using the same three rimes. Brown-Robbins, no. 2479.

A balade (three rime royal stanzas using the same three rimes) on fickleness, *Against Women Unconstant or Newfangelnesse*, is now accepted as Chaucer's.

A GOODLY BALADE TO HIS LADY MARGARET or MOTHER OF NURTURE [16], attributed to Chaucer by Thynne ("A Goodlie Balade of Chaucer") and Bale ("Carmen Chaucer"), and continued in the Chaucerian apocrypha through the nineteenth century (although Skeat called it "manifestly Lydgate's"). Originally a triple balade (the sixth stanza has been lost): three balades each of three rime royal stanzas with the same rimes and refrain, and concluding eight-line envoy, similar to Chaucer's *Fortune* or *Compleynt of Venus*. The unusual combination of initial letters beginning each stanza in the third balade, J, C, Q, with M, M, M, and D, D, D of the first and second, suggested to Skeat an anagram of Margaret, Dame Jacques—"daisy," the nickname of Margaret, appears throughout. The piece itself, couched in epistle form ("litel lettre") is a dull and worthless praise of his mistress, with the poet swearing his loyalty; the language and style are painfully inverted and tortuous. Brown-Robbins, no. 2223.

TO MY SOVEREIGN LADY [17], is a conventional and complimentary poem to a lady of high renown, whom the poet has chosen to be his Valentine. He cannot find words to express his devotion, but nevertheless ekes out sixteen rime royal stanzas with encomiums of his mistress, asseverations of his loyalty, and complaints of her disdain—some twelve lines are in French. The third stanza incorporates "Your eyen two wol slee me sodainly" from Chaucer's *Merciles Beaute*. Skeat hazarded "a pure guess" that the poem was written by Lydgate for Henry V to send to Queen Catherine when she was at Dover in February 1421. His evidence depends on taking conventional literary expressions as personal allusions, and it must remain merely an attractive speculation. Seaton suggests the marriage of Queen Margaret's sister, Yolande d'Anjou, to Ferry of Lorraine in 1445. In the black-letter editions of Chaucer, this piece is run without a break into the Lydgatian *Commendation of Our Lady* (Brown-Robbins, no. 99). To Rosemary Woolf, the poet's mistress is the Virgin Mary (cf. vv. 85–91), and the poem "a very supple and delicate handling of secular conventions for religious purposes."

EPISTLE TO HIS MISTRESS, SIGNED CHAUCER [18], ten rime royal stanzas (Brown-Robbins, no. 1838), one of the items in MS Trinity Cambridge 599 which Stow omitted from his 1561 Chaucer, is included here because of its manuscript heading ("Chaucer"), and its resemblance in tone and scope to Chaucer's *Compleint d'amours*. It is a competent minor poem, typical of the courtly poetry at the end of the fifteenth century, with classical and Biblical allusions, protestations of literary incompetence, and the formal diction of the psychology of love. Yet into this routine has crept a touch of humor and a homely proverb. Four of its stanzas (3, 4, 5, and 10), all quite aureated, are taken from *The Craft of Lovers* (see [43] below, stanzas 3, 7, 11, 15), but divorced from their context they lose their original satire against the courtly tradition. The use of metaphors essentially religious has sometimes caused doubt about the secular character of the poem (cf. [17] above), but it appears as one of a chain of similar aureate love lyrics, preceded by Brown-Robbins, nos. 1238, 267, 1562, and followed by nos. 2510, 3197.

PRAISE OF MARGARET THE DAISY [19], ("In the season of Feverere") in MS Trinity Cambridge 599, was first printed by Stow, and considered as Chaucer's until rejected by Tyrwhitt (1775). Its seven rime royal stanzas preserve the conventions of courtly love in an agreeable poem, somewhat clichéd and stylized (with a brief "O" anaphora), judged by Skeat "very poor." Brown-Robbins, no. 1562.

After an oblique gambit telling how the bad weather of February had given way to showery April, the herald of May, when all lovers should worship their ladies, the poet launches into the praise of la belle Margaret, referred to by the punning pet-name of daisy. His love pangs are mitigated by her proximity, and his woe becomes a pleasant pain. He will protect her good name, as should all who have joy of their mistresses.

WARWICK'S VIRELAI [20], "I can not half the woo compleyne,"

known only in the Shirley manuscript, British Museum Additional 16165, first printed in 1907, is a type of virelai in three groups each of five mono-riming short-lined quatrains (group 3 substitutes a couplet for its final line). The subject matter is a routine protestation of courtly love to his second wife, Isabella, Lady Despenser (whom he married in 1422), by Richard Beauchamp, Earl (1401–39) of Warwick. Brown-Robbins, no. 1288. Beauchamp was a patron of Lydgate, who wrote Brown-Robbins, no. 3808, at his order, and, according to Shirley, nos. 3440 and 447.

VIRELAI [21], in MS Trinity Cambridge 599 used by Stow, headed "Chaucer." Brown-Robbins, no. 267. A late fifteenth-century love poem, dialect East Anglian, unconventional only in its form, a virelai in five eight-line tail-rime stanzas, aaabaaab, with the b rime of one stanza interlocking to become the a rime of the following; the short four-syllabled lines became very popular at the end of the fifteenth century. The poet, desolate and of unfortunate fate, hates his desperate life and wishes for death. Virelais of any type are rare in Middle English; besides this poem, and items [20] and [22], there are only four by Hoccleve (VIII [15], [29], [32]), and the Envoy to De Regimine Principum (VIII [2]). In Chaucer's Anelida and Arcite lines 256–71 and 317–32 resemble a virelai, and the same pattern (aaab aaab bbba bbba) occurs in [24] below, lines 108–23, and in [25], lines 64–79, 160–75.

EARL RIVERS' VIRELAI ON FICKLE FORTUNE [22]. According to the historian John Rous, Earl Rivers, on the eve of his execution at Pontefract in 1483, composed a virelai to Fortune on his sorry plight. Like [21], it consists of five eight-line tail-rime stanzas with interlocking tail-rime. Robbins-Cutler, no. 3193.5.

The Complaint against Hope, mid fifteenth-century, a lover's confession, is described in Dialogues, Debates, and Catechisms, VII [50]. In all three manuscripts, this poem is followed by the Chaucerian Complaynt d'amours, similar in tone. See also Chaucer's A Balade of Complaint and A Complaint to His Lady.

O MERCIFUL AND O MERCIABLE [23] is a composite love poem,

first printed by Stow from MS Trinity Cambridge 599, thirteen rime royal stanzas, including stanzas 1–4 from the pseudo-Lydgatian *Court of Sapience* (Brown-Robbins, no. 168) and stanza 10 (omitted by Stow) from stanza 19 of the pseudo-Chaucerian *Craft of Lovers*, [43] below.

> The first four stanzas were originally religious (Peace's appeal to God), but are twisted to a secular use: God has the property of mercy, the poet is repentant, God should help him. A witty paradox is discussed: if there is no sin or trespass, then there is no need for mercy. Beginning at stanza 5, the poet turns to secular love. To his knowledge, he has not offended his lady. She should, nevertheless, show him mercy (though he has *not* sinned, offended, her). The concluding three-stanza Envoy, a "Go little bill" formula, continues to beg for mercy, and petitions God to show mercy (grace) to his mistress.

The poem is less disjointed than its hotch-potch composition would suggest. Brown-Robbins, no. 2510.

THE LOVER'S COMPLAINT AGAINST FORTUNE AND HIS LADY [24], late fifteenth-century, in a prologue of nine rime royal stanzas and twelve nine-line stanzas, aabaabbab (save the octosyllabic sixteen-line stanza 15), consists of a conventional complaint ("Quho may compleyne my langoure and distresse") of the lover against his mistress and Fortune (Prologue), followed by a love epistle appealing to various gods and heroes of antiquity (Oedipus, Adonis, Troilus, Jove, etc.) for help. "My hevyness is nothing less than hell." His pains are so great he will die. The Prologue includes a eulogy of Chaucer, "quhilk was of poetis the honour and the glore." Brown-Robbins, no. 564.

See Brown-Robbins, Robbins-Cutler, no. 572, in the chapter on Lyrics for sixteen quatrains by Humfrey Newton (1466–1536), which tell of the disillusioned lover whose disinterest provokes Venus to make him fall in love again; he immediately changes heart, pleads with his new mistress, and wins her favors. For a similar lyric by Charles d'Orleans see Brown-Robbins, no. 460.

THE LAY OF SORROW [25], 185 lines in nineteen stanzas, basically the decasyllabic aabaabbab of Dunbar's *Golden Targe* (X [77]), but in stanzas 8 and 18 a sixteen-line stanza with interlocking tail-rimes (cf.

[24] above), is a conventional complaint of the late fifteenth century (about 1500). The speaker is a woman, but there is no need to postulate a woman as author (cf. [49] and [50] below); the poem concludes with a dedication to the poet's patron, a princess. Brown-Robbins, no. 482.

The speaker laments her lover's desertion; her Christmas is turned into Lent, the ruby has dropped out of her wedding ring. He has broken faith with her; she can only die. She berates the man, branching into a tirade against men in general.

In the manuscript the poem is followed immediately by [24], possibly by the same author. The manuscript also contains *The Kingis Quair* [X [1]) and *The Quare of Jelusy* (Brown-Robbins, no. 325).

COMPLAINT TO MY MORTAL FOE [26], four eight-line stanzas, ababbcbc, appealing to St. Valentine, Cupid, and Venus to move his lady to show mercy and pity, headed in the unique manuscript (about 1450), "Balade." Skeat, who first printed the poem, was certain it was Chaucer's, but Kittredge thought this "more than doubtful." All later editors have omitted it from the canon, and Wells in the original *Manual* listed it as "Doubtful." The following poem in the manuscript, item [27] below, is also sometimes attributed to Chaucer. Brown-Robbins, no. 231.

COMPLAINT TO MY LODESTAR [27], seven rime royal stanzas, a formal love lyric, using fashionable clichés and paradoxes, affirming the poet's loyalty to his mistress and praying for her pity. Brown-Robbins, no. 2626. The lines are smooth, but, apart from a few verbal echoes from *Troilus and Criseyde* and *Anelida and Arcite,* there is little distinctively Chaucerian, and Skeat alone upholds this attribution. In the manuscript, it is followed without break by a dissimilar poem (Brown-Robbins, no. 551).

THE NINE LADIES WORTHY [28] is among the more worthless of the Chaucerian apocrypha preserved in MS Trinity Cambridge 599-Stow group (and consequently without authority for a date preceding 1500). Brown-Robbins, no. 2767. Its nine rime royal stanzas, in aureate and stilted diction, describe the Nine Feminine Worthies, "les neufs preuses," celebrated with their masculine counterparts by Eustache Deschamps (Balade 93): Sinope, Hippolyta, Deifyle, Teuca (French, Tantha), Penthesilea, Tomyris, Lampeto (French, Marsopye), Semiramis, and Melanippe. The combination of the brutal and the courteous aspects of each heroine is seldom synthesized, and the stanzas border on parody. The title recalls Chaucer's *Legend of Good Women*—also nine, if Alceste of the Prologue be omitted—itself headed in MS Bodley 638 "Nine Good Women." The composition was probably intended for a pageant or mumming (similar to that of the *Seven Philosophers* [Brown-Robbins, no. 3807] in this same Trinity MS, or *Dame Sapience and the Seven Arts* in Fabyan's Chronicle, or the *Nine Worthies* [Brown-Robbins, no. 3666] in MS Tanner 407), or perhaps, as Utley suggests, for a tapestry (like Lydgate's *Bycorne and Chichevache* [Brown-Robbins, no. 2541], also in this manuscript). This poem should not be confused with *Chaucer's Chronicle* [4].

For a translation of Boccaccio's *De Mulieribus Claris*, see Brown-Robbins, no. 2642. A late sixteenth-century list of Cupid's martyrs, George Turberville's *The Heroycall Epistles*, a translation of Ovid's *Heroides*, includes eight women not mentioned elsewhere.

THE JUDGMENT OF PARIS [29], also in MS Trinity Cambridge 599, first printed by Stow in 1561 and last by Chalmers in 1810, consists of four rime royal stanzas, probably designed for a pageant. "A very poor performance" (Skeat). Brown-Robbins, no. 3197.

Minerva (Pallas) tells Paris to take the apple and give it to the fairest of the three goddesses; Juno promises fame in battle, Venus in love, and Minerva herself fame in governing.

A longer poem, an extended complaint in letter form, stressing the qualities of Venus, occurs in Bodleian 12653 (Robbins-Cutler, no. 3917.8). For a fragment of five quatrains wherein Palamon, Ersyte, and Emlyn speak in the first person (not influenced by the *Knight's Tale*), see VII [59].

In addition to these shorter lyrics, a small contrasting group of little poems oppose or parody the ideals of courtly love, somewhat unexpected in Chaucerian-inspired formal poetry. Here the woman is no longer the traditional paragon of virtue and beauty, and the typical virtues are topsy-turvied. Lydgate himself is assigned at least one such production: if not the satirical *Hood of Green* (Brown-Robbins, no. 2237), and the parallel *To Say You Are Not Fair* (Robbins-Cutler, no. 3765.5), both attributed to Lydgate, *Doubleness* (Brown-Robbins, no. 3656) is surely his. Hoccleve followed the new vogue with a roundel, *Praise of His Lady*, VIII [18]. Included in this chapter are the comic ([30]) and the savage ([31]), both in MS Trinity Cambridge 599 and in Stow's 1561 edition of Chaucer; [35] and [36] in the Shirley manuscript, British Museum Additional 16165, with double entendre on the physical aspects of love.

THE DESCRIBING OF A FAIR LADY [30], headed "by Chaucer" in a later hand in MS Trinity Cambridge 599, and entitled by Stow a "Balade Pleasant," mocks the courtly panegyric listing the traditional charms, giving instead a catalogue of undesirable traits. His lady is of small stature, has little fingers, a skin as smooth as an ox's. A comic allusion to the marriage of Joan of Navarre to Henry IV in 1403 makes the lady's age (if the poem were written at the close of the fifteenth century, say, in 1488) one hundred, yet she has the intelligence of a silly child. The presence of these seven rime royal stanzas in the Leyden MS shows that at least one of the Chaucerian apocrypha in the sixteenth-century Trinity and Stow group is authentically medieval (and see below, *Beware of Deceitful Women*, dealt with under [31]). Brown-Robbins, no. 1300.

O MOSSIE QUINCE [31], a companion to [30], is a similar burlesque of the courtly love poems praising a beautiful and admired mistress. In the Trinity MS, Lydgate's *Four Things Making Man a Fool* (Brown-Robbins, no. 4230) is incorporated as the second stanza. Brown-Robbins, no. 2524. This little squib (two rime royal stanzas and concluding eight-line stanza) is a savage and heartless invective; it mocks the lady as a quince and a rotten apple; she has a swarthy complexion and a dried-out skin; she is fat-buttocked like a badger and is the foulest in the nation. In this catalogue there is nothing of the good-natured teasing that mellows similar flytings like Brown-Robbins, nos. 3832 and 2437 (see *Two Satirical Verse Epistles* in VII [60]).

Beware of Deceitful Women (Brown-Robbins, no. 1944) is classed with Proverbs, Precepts, and Monitory Pieces; although restrained, its scorn is no less bitter than that of the two foregoing poems. A text in the recently discovered Rome MS emphasizes its composition in the second half of the fifteenth century.

BALADE AGAINST HYPOCRITICAL WOMEN [32] takes stanza 16 of the Lydgatian *Pain and Sorrow of Evil Marriage* (Brown-Robbins, no. 919) for its opening, and in stanza 2 uses the "blind eats many a fly" refrain of the Chaucerian apocryphon, *Beware of Deceitful Women* (see above), four stanzas rime royal in all. Brown-Robbins, no. 2661. For a longer satire on women's inconstancy and desire for the mastery, see *Piers of Fulham* (Brown-Robbins, no. 71).

A PRAISE OF WOMEN [33], first attributed to Chaucer by Thynne (1532), followed by Stow and others; also in the sixteenth-century Bannatyne MS, rubricated "finis quod Chauseir." Now rejected from the Chaucer canon—Skeat (opposed by MacCracken) thought it probably Lydgate's. Brown-Robbins, no. 228.

The 25 rime royal stanzas, in an envelope pattern, give two traditional reasons for praising women: they bore and reared us, and our salvation came through a woman. Furthermore, women's follies are committed only at men's instigation: this major argument produces several lively vignettes (stanzas 6–10, 18–19) of the deceitful male pursuing the routine of courtly love—sighing, feigning illness, and like Troilus swearing fidelity. Yet all these manifestations are false, made solely to deceive the trusting female, the paragon of all virtues (stanzas 20–22). Stanza 25 returns to the main theme that men should cease slandering women and pray the Virgin to bring them to heaven where all good women will be found.

The effect of the poem is thus an indirect attack on the code of courtly love, and also, by its seeming straight-faced encomiums of women, an oblique attack on the parallel medieval convention of the all-virtuous woman. The doublets of stanza 4 (courteous and meek, glad and merry), the warning in stanza 13 not to blame all women for the errors of a few, the comment in stanza 15 that women never seek a lover (as men do), the sly observation in stanza 22 that women are right sorry when a man is sick, come too pat for the tongue of the poet not to be in cheek. A destroying refrain or burden would topple the whole structure.

Six short items in this same Bannatyne MS are rubricated "quod Chauseir," as well as Hoccleve's *Letter of Cupid* (see VIII [1]). There are two poems abusing women (Brown-Robbins, nos. 679, 2580), one praising women ([33] just dealt with), an extract abusing women from Lydgate's *Complaint of the Black Knight* (Robbins-Cutler, no. 3911.5), and two extracts from *The Remedy of Love* ([34] below): an excerpt, "Fle the mys-woman" (stanzas 1–9, 18), and "Gif all the erth war perchmene scribable" (stanza 15), another attack on women. Robbins-Cutler, nos. 3648.8 and 1409.3. For an acephalous poem praising women see Robbins-Cutler, no. 552.8.

THE REMEDY OF LOVE [34] entered the Chaucerian apocrypha by way of Thynne (1532), but since there is no manuscript the poem may not be medieval. Brown-Robbins, no. 3084. The piece is obviously not Chaucerian, although Utley notes three possible Chaucer allusions. Skeat considered it "poor and uninteresting."

The Remedy of Love is the garrulous versification of a cynical morality: it condemns alike promiscuity, courtly love, and married love, and it recommends a man treat a woman with canny unconcern combined with sneaking supervision—in this it certainly fulfills its title: a remedy against [passionate] love.

The Prologue (19 stanzas rime royal) is especially rambling and dull, passing from an implied epistle form in stanza 1 to a dialogue between the writer and his sovereign lord, Youth. The poet will advise on the dangerous emotional problems besetting young men from the malady of love—older people's problems are merely physical (stanzas 1–7). Youth answers that the advice of old people is prejudiced, and that their immoral actions belie their advice (stanzas 8–13). In five succeeding stanzas (14–18) the protagonists parry, and the writer invokes the Furies and jealous Juno to inspire him.

The 63 rime royal stanzas of the poem proper consist of "a warning to take heed of the deceitful company of women," such as the prostitute whose allure is wormwood (stanza 3), or the attractive pick-up (stanza 4). This sober counsel is illustrated by a traditional story of a woman who had three lovers. One day they all came to see her at the same time. She gave them dinner and flirted with each one. "Which of these three stood now in grace?" The poet, who unexpectedly turns out to be one of the three, has the answer: No one. So loathsome is the subject that he will dismiss the

Muses (stanza 11) and invoke the Furies (stanza 12) to inspire him to an appropriate memorial to women's falsehood. If all the earth were parchment he could not tell women's deceit (stanza 16). Steer clear of women: if you walk on hot coals, you get burned. Solomon (Proverbs 7:6–27) gave an apt example (stanzas 23–35): a lascivious wife, in the absence of her husband, seduced a young man and started him on the "ways of hell leading to death." The poet discusses this anecdote at length (stanzas 36–48), although his moral lacks conviction as much as his etymology of "cuckold"— a *c*old *o*ld *k*nave and a *c*alot [woman]*o*f *l*ewd *d*emeanor (stanzas 43–44). Yet the husband's jealousy provoked the infidelity. If a man is jealous, let him try to find a wife he can trust; even for jealous men, marriage is better than fornication (stanza 53). The best thing a man can do is to love his wife or mistress without emotional involvement, and keep her so busy she has no time for other love affairs. At this point, the poem breaks off, apparently unfinished (the piece is so formless even its conclusion is dubious).

A similar but shorter satire, seven eight-line stanzas, exists in the Bannatyne MS (ca. 1568), Alexander Scott's *The Slicht Remeid of Luve*, influenced by Ovid's *Remedia amoris*. Another warning against any amorous indulgence save that limited and regulated by marriage is the subject of a late fifteenth-century prose piece (ca. 1492) in the Asloan MS, *The Spektacle of Luf*, by "M. G. Myll." An English piece with the same title was written about 1520 and printed by de Worde (after 1529). For a warning against courtly love, where a lady keeps a page for fleshly love and disparages her blood, see Audelay's *Of the Decadence of Marriage* (Brown-Robbins, no. 1630).

BALADE BY CHAUCER [35], so headed in a Shirley manuscript, and entitled by Brusendorff (who accepted it as Chaucer's) "Balade of a Reeve," from the refrain. Any work of love, says the poet in three rime royal stanzas, is better than laboring like a reeve, and he will try his luck at it, even if he get caught like a hooked fish. The language is smooth, but the contents undistinguished. Brown-Robbins, no. 1635.

THE PLOWMAN'S SONG [36], in the Shirley manuscript, British Museum Additional 16165, two rime royal stanzas (space left in manuscript for a third stanza), full of indecent double entendre (*pace* Hammond), comparing a plowman making his furrow to a lover wooing his lady. Brown-Robbins, no. 2611.

Two mocking epistles by two lovers are discussed elsewhere (see VII [60]): the second notes that Chaucer's English was not on the mind of his derisive mistress. Related poems to be discussed in the chapter on Lyrics include Brown-Robbins, nos. 1280, 1957, 3180, 3879, 4090, and Robbins-Cutler, no. 1356.8, a brief parody of a courtly complaint.

3. COURTLY LOVE AUNTERS

The longer formal poems (often love visions) narrating courtly love adventures present enough points of resemblance to form a homogeneous literary group of about two dozen items. These are the poems which constitute the core of the Chaucerian apocrypha, and to which this term might best be restricted. For the French *dits amoreux*, there is unfortunately no comparable English designation.

Their poetic machinery (wrote Neilson) includes the following features: a spring setting in a meadow; the poet's dream or vision; a magnificent court of Cupid or Venus, organized on a feudal system; buildings often with walls of glass and gates of gold, and decorated with pictures of famous lovers; personified abstractions serving as courtiers; throngs of fair ladies; statutes or commandments of love; a guide or adviser to the poet on his journeyings; introduction of birds, often as attendant on the God of Love; the transfer of religious motifs to secular love (including parodies of religious services); a temple of Venus where prayers are said; the presentation of "bills" or complaints; swooning lovers and unusually stony-hearted mistresses (whose beauties are catalogued); and parliaments of love. The form is almost uniformly the rime royal stanza, with only an occasional piece in couplets or the eight-line Monk's Tale stanza, ababbcbc.

In addition to Chaucer's *Romaunt of the Rose* and his other poems mentioned previously, the paramount models of the Chaucerian apocrypha were Gower's *Confessio Amantis* (Brown-Robbins, no. 2662) and Lydgate's *Temple of Glass* (Brown-Robbins, no. 851). Other works by Lydgate influential in establishing the tradition were his *Flower of Courtesy*, *Complaint of the Black Knight*, and *The Assembly of Gods* (Brown-Robbins, nos. 1487, 1507, 4005)—all, incidentally, included as Chaucerian apocrypha in the black-letter editions.

Some are attractive poems, not unworthy of a Chaucer; their interest lies, however, as much in their acceptance of the courtly code as in their awareness that the code was bogus. It is easy to overlook the scepticism in some of these poems and see in the others only a parroting of discarded traditions and futile imitations. Yet the ironic or self-deprecating asides show that their authors as well as their audiences were questioning the standards of courtly love. These poems are therefore more subtle and satisfying than the outright lampoons against women discussed at the end of the previous section. Such an approach started, of course, with Chaucer himself in *Merciles Beaute*, but by the fifteenth century one poet could exempt a lover from performing his duty to his mistress twenty-one times a night! To enjoy only the graceful descriptions in these Chaucerian apocrypha and to ignore their amused worldliness is to lose the essence of the lively and pulsating fifteenth century, where new ways of thinking were ruffling the feudal image in even minor literary by-waters.

THE COURT OF LOVE [37], 1442 lines in 206 rime royal stanzas, although considered post 1500 (e.g., by Skeat, Neilson, Berdan, and Pearsall), is retained here because of its continuing association in the Chaucerian apocrypha from Stow (first in 1561) to Skeat (1897). Brown-Robbins, no. 4205. It is perhaps the most typical poem of the apocrypha. Stow took it from MS Trinity Cambridge 599, but the text is imperfect and weakened by scribal blunders (e.g., possible omissions after line 1316; Neilson suggested transfer of lines 1093–1176 to follow line 266). Linguistic forms are often incorrect conscious archaisms (in a pseudo-Midland dialect—Skeat and Lounsbury). The literary devices are based on medieval patterns: allegorical personifications, canons of love, complaints, parodies of religious services, etc. In addition to imitating Lydgate (especially his *Temple of Glass*, some lines being identical), the unknown poet (called by Skeat "one of the heralds of the Elizabethan poetry") was also influenced by *The Kingis Quair* (X [1]), rather than vice versa (as J. T. T. Brown held), by many works of Chaucer (*Anelida and Arcite, Complaint of Pity, Knight's Tale, Legend of Good Women, Troilus and Criseyde*), by Ovid and Maximian, and by Hoccleve's *Letter of Cupid* (VIII [1]), and by *The Cuckoo and the Nightingale* (VII [47]). In form, it resembles the Prologue to *The Court of Venus* [42].

Much controversy has attended the authorship: it was attributed to

Chaucer by Tyrwhitt and Godwin, then rejected by all later scholars, including Bradshaw, Ten Brink, Skeat, Furnivall, and Lounsbury. Brandl, refuted by Kittredge, suggested Scogan; Lange suggested Lydgate as author.

While the overall attitude is serious, there are several side comments so humorous as to become mocking and derisive of the courtly love traditions, e.g., in the Twenty Statutes: Women cannot be untrue (lines 406–20); believe whatever women say (lines 427–34); also, elsewhere, the dismissal of chastity (line 685), the leering implication of fat lips (lines 795–98), and especially Statute 16 and the author's broad comments thereon (lines 453–55 and 1013).

Many critics have praised the poem; although Skeat thought it "pleasing, but much over-rated," Berdan believed the poem was an imitation of older models, which, however, were "out of touch with the ideas of the new age," Bennett called it "a good example of the debilitating effect of a tradition that has lost its vigor," and Lewis wrote it "towers above most Drab Age verse by its sheer accomplishment."

The Court of Love falls into four main sections:

Prologue (lines 1–42). Wishing to please his lady, the poet invokes the Muses for help to write a love poem.

Allegory (lines 43–301, 505–1351). When eighteen, the poet was commanded by Mercury to appear at the Court of Love. Finally, he reaches a magnificent castle and sees King Admetus and Queen Alceste, vice-regents for Venus, attended by Danger and Disdain and surrounded by courtiers. Philobone, a gentlewoman of the court, reveals the king's displeasure with the poet who, although eighteen, had never served Love. Having visited the Temple of Venus, with its windows depicting celebrated lovers (e.g., Dido and Aeneas, Anelida and Arcite), the poet has audience with the king who, however, merely admonishes him to observe the Twenty Statutes of Love (modelled on Lydgate's *Temple of Glass*). Warned not to pry into the corresponding commandments for women (compare [40]), the poet visits the Temple of Venus again, where thousands of fellow neophytes are petitioning or praising the goddess. He asks for help, visits the shrine of Pity, and is directed to Rosiall, most beautiful of virgins, a prize for Jove himself. After penning her a "bill" of seven stanzas (lines 841–99: "O ye fresh, of beauty the root"), the poet reveals he is Philogenet, a clerk of Cambridge. Rosiall advises patience, but when Philogenet falls into a swoon revives him with promises and blushingly permits a relaxation of the sixteenth of the Statutes. The allegory starts again (line 1023) with Rosiall instructing Philobene to take Philogenet on a second tour of the Court of Love, where he meets personifications of facets of love (e.g., Shamefastness, Avaunter, Envy, Privy Thought), and monks and nuns (cf. Robbins-Cutler, no. 316.3), the poor and maimed, all bewailing their lack of opportunity to enjoy the solace of love. Rosiall finally lets the poet dwell with her until May, when the King of Love will hold a festival.

The Twenty Statutes of Love (lines 302–504), inserted in the allegory, are in part derived from Lydgate's *Temple of Glass*: (1) Be true and faithful to principles of [courtly] love, (2) secret, (3) constant, (4) praising love, (5) suffering love's torments and (6) wandering alone in despair. (7) Be obedient and (8) petition for love, (9) without offense and (10) never demanding. (11) Be discreet and (12) suffer love's wounds. (13) Send presents. (14) Dream about your love and think no evil; (15) uphold her reputation. (16) Please your mistress twenty-one times a night! (17) Continue talking about love even when doing is impossible. (18) Be clean and neat. (19) Fast for love, and (20) in her absence mourn for your mistress.

Bird Matins and Lauds (lines 1352–1442). On May Day all the birds sing a service in praise of love, a parody on matins and lauds (one section to each bird): nightingale, eagle, falcon, popinjay, goldfinch, wren, robin, turtle-dove, throstle-cock, peacock, linnet, owl, lark, kite and cuckoo and magpie, too. These lines are perhaps influenced by the thirteenth-century *Messe des oisiaus* of Jean de Condé. The poem ends here.

The Kingis Quair, by James I of Scotland, in the mainstream of the English Chaucerians, is discussed in X [1].

BIRDS' PRAISE OF LOVE [38], "a rather pretty poem" (Skeat), fifteen stanzas, ababbccb, tetrameters, the final line in each stanza in French and cleverly blended into the English, imitates Chaucer's *Parlement of Foules*. In May time, in a green arbor, the poet listens to the songs of Cupid's bird, the nightingale. Other birds, the robin, wren, pheasant, lark, titmouse, starling and throstle-cock all praise love, except the cuckoo and "the frosty feldefare." The poem is even-flowing and light-hearted, one of the more attractive of the Chaucerian apocrypha. Brown-Robbins, no. 1506.

BIRDS' DEVOTIONS [39], ten rime royal stanzas, sometimes taken as Lydgate's, is a religious poem in a secular setting. Brown-Robbins, no. 357.

The poet wanders in the sunshine and hears birds singing typical office hymns of the Christian season. The popinjay sings *A solis ortus cardine* (Christmas), the pelican the *Vexilla regis prodeunt* (Passiontide), the nightingale *Consurgat Christus altissime* (Eastertide), the dove *Veni creator spiritus* (Whitsuntide). All join in with *O lux beata Trinitas*.

The early sixteenth-century *Parlament of Byrdes*, modelled perhaps on Aesop's *Parliament of Beasts*, is a political moralizing allegory, unrelated to the Chaucerian tradition. The mid sixteenth-century macaronic

Armonye of Byrdes (ca. 1550) recalls Chaucer's *Parlement of Foules*, the anonymous *Parlament of Byrdes*, and *The Court of Love* [37]; it ascribes to the various birds pericopes in praise of Christ and the Trinity, all in a love-vision setting.

THE TEN COMMANDMENTS OF LOVE [40], fourteen rime royal stanzas, in two late manuscripts, Trinity Cambridge 599 and Fairfax 16 (added in seventeenth-century hand), first printed by Stow in 1561, and reprinted until 1810. Probably no earlier than 1500; certainly (as the hand shows) later than Skeat's 1450. Brown-Robbins, no. 590.

After two introductory stanzas, the poet instructs ladies to observe the Ten Commandments of [courtly] love. It thus relates to the Statutes for Women in [37], which the poet there is forbidden to read.
Exhibit (1) good faith, (2) intention to please, (3) discretion in assignation, (4) patience, (5) secretiveness, (6) prudence in good judgment, (7) constancy, (8) pity, (9) moderation in talking, and (10) mercy.
The piece concludes with a two-stanza Envoy: Accept, lady, this "balade" even though the devoted writer is devoid of literary skill.

In spite of its appeal to *The Romaunt of the Rose*, it is not dependent on it and can be linked only in a very general way to the commandments.

THE PARLIAMENT OF LOVE [41] is a late fifteenth-century courtly poem of 40 couplets (with four rime royal stanzas inserted) in praise of his mistress, using the device of a love adventure to give variety to an essentially stereotyped formula. Brown-Robbins, no. 2383.

At the opening of Love's Parliament, men and women (including merchants' wives) sing a ballad (one stanza rime royal) instead of Mass. The poet notices one lady who stands out above the rest; she is the typical paragon of courtly love. The poet withdraws to compose a little song in her honor (three rime royal stanzas).

The lines, even though routine, are pleasant and even. Neilson commented that it "is only one more proof of the familiarity of the Court of Love tradition in the 15th century."

THE COURT OF VENUS [42], a sixteenth-century production, survives in three different printed fragments, about 1535–64, comprising a prologue of fifteen rime royal stanzas (the complaint of the disconsolate lover to "Genius," who promises to intercede for him with Venus) and a sequence of short courtly poems in miscellaneous forms (at least five and possibly eight by Sir Thomas Wyatt). It was ascribed to Chaucer in John Bale's catalogue of British writers in 1548, but later (1557) Bale gave it to Robert Shyngleton. Not in Brown-Robbins, Robbins-Cutler.

John Rolland's *Court of Venus* (1575) is a late Scottish poem in the tradition of *The Court of Love* [37], *The Flower and the Leaf* [50], and Chaucer's *Parlement of Foules. The Cuckoo and the Nightingale*, "one of the most delightful pseudo-Chaucerian pieces" (Brusendorff), is described in VII [47]. For *The Eye and the Heart* in MS Longleat 258, another debate with the full Court of Love apparatus, see VII [28]. This is a translation of *Le débat du cueur et de l'oeil*, found *inter alia* in Royal 19.A-iii, ff 29ᵃ–41ᵇ, a manuscript which also contains the French original of *La belle dame sans mercy* [46].

THE CRAFT OF LOVERS [43] is an attractive English Chaucerian poem, if not for its execution (Skeat: "too bad even for Lydgate"), then for its realistic criticism of the dead artificialities of courtly love and obscure poetic diction. Its satire and irony link it with the tiny group of parodies on courtly love such as Hoccleve's *Praise of His Lady* (VIII [18]), Lydgate's *Doublenesse* (Brown-Robbins, no. 3656), the pseudo-Lydgate *Description of His Lady* (Brown-Robbins, no. 2237), Chaucer's own *To Rosemounde*, and items [30], [31], [35], and [36] above. The significance of this poem and of the whole group has been ably interpreted by Moore. Brown-Robbins, no. 3761.

Stanzas 1 and 2 introduce the topic: the significance of the code or craft of courtly love, believed a remedy for disease both of body and heart. The subject is then debated by a man and a woman (defined in MS British Museum Additional as Cupido and Diana), the man in the odd stanzas employing a rhetorical colored style, answered and ridiculed in the even stanzas by the woman in a direct style. Stanzas 3–6 show the woman hitting the obscurity of the man's pretensions and forcing him (stanza 7) to admit that his oblique approach masks his desire "to break the virginity of virgins" and have carnal copulation. Unexpectedly, the woman welcomes this frank statement, which, unlike the courtly circumlocutions, could convert (she thinks) every woman's heart (stanza 18). After demanding assurance of discretion, she accepts him as her lover. The final stanza (23) reports that the poet overheard this dialogue in 1459 (changed by Stow to 1348 in an effort to justify his ascription to Chaucer), and begs Venus' protection for all true lovers.

MS Trinity Cambridge 599 adds "Chaucer" in a sixteenth-century hand alongside the text, and MSS Harley and Additional add a three-stanza Envoy, *"Verba auctoris."* Four stanzas have been incorporated in [18], and one stanza in [23].

HOW A LOVER PRAISETH HIS LADY [44], 467 lines in pentameter couplets, first half fifteenth century, spends lines 1–246 in a seeming prologue to a love adventure—the spring setting, the garden, and extended lists of trees, herbs, and birds. The remainder of the poem, however, is simply an extremely detailed list of the beauties of his 21-inch waist mistress, summarizing the conventional attributes of woman in three white, three red, three long, three round, and three little. The poem is thus rooted in the courtly tradition and even digresses (lines 214–22) to pay tribute to "mayster Chauser sours and fundement / In englysshe tunge swetely to endyte." Yet it departs somewhat from conventional formulas and reveals the personality of a real writer by the continuous stress on the medical aspects of the garden, where herbs outrank flowers, by its insertion of an inverse Evils of the Age (lines 156–71, e.g., "there was without envy, religion"), and by its lively if clumsy observations from real life, which displace the poetic vocabularly (e.g., "Whos lyppys with chyld ben by maydenhede / Swol and engreyned wyth rosys rede" or "The [finger] nailys rede not peynted as in Spayne"). There are numerous miswritings and some obscurities. Brown-Robbins, no. 4043.

SUPPLICACIO AMANTIS [45], a lover's complaint, 628 lines in couplets, follows Lydgate's *Temple of Glass* in two manuscripts, but, says Schick, "not a shadow of doubt can remain that the Compleynt has [anything] whatever to do with *The Temple of Glass*". Although lengthy and introduced by the love-vision conventions, the poem is essentially an unhappy lover's description of his mistress, and as such it ranks among the better of the Chaucerian apocrypha. Brown-Robbins, no. 147.

The poem, according to Schick, "was written by a lover to express his feelings, when he took leave of his mistress Margaret (the day's eye), on the last day of March. In her presence, he cannot speak; she will not help him, or bid him do aught for her, tho' she sees his sorrow and love for her. On this March 31, the Sun rejoices because he'll spend the night with Diana; but the poet has left his love. He reproaches March for its changes, and describes the charms of his Mistress. He appeals to Fortune to let his Margaret, the day's eye, whose beauty he praises, give him her grace and love in April, for he is hers till death; she is his joy, his heart's rest, but alas also the cause of his woe. For her, he is in a fever, first hot, then cold; he ever burns like the lamp of Albiston in Venus' shrine. Never had he felt such pain till this last of March, when he parted from his love. So he writes her this Ditty to tell her his woe. He prays her to look at his little book; to tear it, if she will, with her soft hands: but rather look on it with her goodly face, and take heed of him, who is hers for ever."

LA BELLE DAME SANS MERCY [46] is one of the major poems in the Chaucerian apocrypha; it occurs in seven manuscripts, was printed as early as 1526 by Pynson and continued in the black-letter editions of Thynne, Stow, and Speght. The piece, by Sir Richard Ros of Leicestershire, is a translation of Alain Chartier's poem (written about 1424), according to one manuscript only, Harley 372, about the middle of the fifteenth century. The translator (whoever he was) added a brief introduction and conclusion, each of four stanzas rime royal; the body of the translation (100 stanzas), which is close to the French, uses the original eight-line stanza, ababbcbc, but with pentameter lines instead of tetrameters. Brown-Robbins, no. 1086.

The poet remembers he had promised to translate Chartier's poem; still half asleep he comes to a green valley full of flowers to begin his task (lines 1–28). The French poet (Chartier), sore languishing, mourns the death of his mistress. If he had to compose a love poem, he could only weep, for his inspiration is buried with his lady and he cares for nothing (lines 29–76). Riding along in this state, Chartier stumbles on a garden party, where two friends insist he stay, and the guests try to divert him. At the banquet, Chartier observes a gentleman so enamored of a beautiful young lady that he could not speak or take his eyes off her. After the dancing, the pair draw apart to an arbor, where Chartier inadvertently overhears their conversation (lines 77–196). Finally, the anguished lover overcomes his bashfulness and tells the lady of his pains of love and desire to serve as her man (lines 197–244).

From here on, the poem becomes a debate in alternating stanzas between La Dame and L'Amant on the reality and functions of courtly love. The lover puts forward all the old rules and conventions to show that the lady should accept him as her lover. With matter-of-fact commonsense, she brushes these aside: she is free to choose any one as her lover, she is quite indifferent to his misery, she did not ask him to love her, and she wishes to be left alone (lines 245–796). The disconsolate lover, having produced argument on argument without result, departs in a trance and dies soon afterward (lines 796–812). L'Envoy advises women not to be cruel like this Belle Dame sans mercy (lines 812–28). The conclusion (lines 829–56) is a conventional plea for a favorable reception for his translation, with a pious hope that men fare better than Chartier's protagonist.

While the poem is perhaps needlessly prolix, the lines are generally smooth, the dialogue well-handled, the descriptions pleasing, and the structure stanzaic (not lineal). Lewis thought it "an essentially second-rate theme redeemed by sheer good writing." In 1424, Chartier's original poem was protested "on the grounds he was reviling womankind" (Utley), but the English translation a few decades later seems closer to the viewpoint of [43], where the woman is to be praised for exposing the fatuity of *amor cortois*. The almost pathological grovelling of the lover was taken at its face value by some, however, and used to point a moral; Pynson, for example, added an envoy warning against loving to excess (cf [34]) and advised keeping carnal love confined to the marriage bed; and Bale (1557) called the poem *"Super impia domina."*

O BEWTIE PERELES [47] is an alternate envoy found on a separate sheet added to a manuscript of the French *La belle dame sans merci*, two stanzas rime royal requesting his lady to read the poet's work. Brown-Robbins, no. 2386.

FOR HE IS TRUE [48], one eight-line stanza exhorting to faithfulness in love, follows the preceding dedication [47]. These two lyrics may possibly be conceived as forming one poem. Brown-Robbins, no. 823.

For a translation of a balade perhaps by Chartier see Brown-Robbins, Robbins-Cutler, no. 3540. For the *Dialogue Between an Unhappy Lover and the Advocate of Venus* see Brown-Robbins, Robbins-Cutler, no. 2594. For the *Dialogue Between the Clerk and the Nightingale* see VII [48]. For the *Dialogue Between Palamon and Ersyte* see VII [59].

THE ASSEMBLY OF LADIES [49], 108 rime royal stanzas, late fifteenth-century, linked by Skeat without specific grounds to [50], loses the charm of the latter poem by rambling and prosy allegory, only coming alive where the poet occasionally draws on his own detailed knowledge of the life and manners of the court. Even with the allegory, it lacks the implicit morality of [50], and remains essentially a museum piece. Brewer notes stylistic parallels in *Generydes*. In MS Trinity Cambridge 599, a seventeenth-century hand has marked it "By Chaucer." Brown-Robbins, no. 1528.

The poet, speaking as a woman, tells a knight of her dream: with four of her friends she is summoned to the Castle of Pleasant Regard to present "bills" of their unhappiness in love before Lady Loyalty. They meet Countenance the porter, Perseverance the usher, Remembrance the chamberlain, Largess the steward, and other officers of the court—Diligence, Discretion, Acquaintance, Belchere, Advisedness, and Attemperance. Lady Loyalty examines the petitions and promises relief at the forthcoming "court of parliament." The poem ends in envelope fashion, with the lady and knight giving a title to this incident, *L'assemble de dames*.

THE FLOWER AND THE LEAF [50], late fifteenth century, survives only in Speght's printing of 1598, but with *La belle dame sans mercy* [46] ranks among the best and most familiar of the Chaucerian apocrypha. Brown-Robbins, no. 4026. It was modernized by Dryden, Keats praised its "honied lines—what mighty power has this gentle story," and Hazlitt quoted nine stanzas to illustrate Chaucer's power of describing nature scenery. Its 85 rime royal stanzas form a pleasing didactic allegory. Led by Diana, the white-clad followers of the Leaf—the chaste and steadfast lovers, symbolizing devotion and restraint, the serious and useful side of life—are contrasted with the green-clad adherents of the Flower, under Flora, representing frivolity and leisure, pleasure and indulgence, who cannot face the storms of life. To some extent, the poem invites comparison with the purely political *Winner and Waster* (Brown-Robbins, no. 3137; see Works Dealing with Contemporary Conditions), but the instruction is gracefully hidden under the jewelled allegory. The poem was ascribed to Chaucer on account of a passage in the Prologue (lines 184–89) to *The Legend of Good Women*, and so accepted by Sandras, Hall, Saintsbury, and Marsh. Gower, however, has similar lines in his *Confessio Amantis* (III.357–58). Godwin was the first to suggest a woman as author (the nouns and pronouns are feminine), but this view was largely propagated by Skeat, who furthermore believed *The Assembly of Ladies* [49] by the same writer. Seaton proposed Sir Richard Roos as author for this and many other poems of the Chaucerian apocrypha. Brewer, the latest editor of the present item and of [49] above, learnedly but sympathetically rejects Chaucer, Lydgate, Roos, or a woman, as author.

After a clear imitation of the spring opening of Chaucer's *Prologue*, the poet tells how, unable to sleep, "she" went to an arbor to hear the singing of a nightingale and a goldfinch (the equivalent of the cuckoo in *The Cuckoo and the Nightingale*), the bird of the Flower (stanzas 1–18). Here she views many lovely ladies coming from a grove to dance in a meadow, followed by their knights (the Knights of the Round Table, the Twelve Peers of Charlemagne, the Knights of the Garter, and the Nine Worthies), who stage a tournament in honor of the Leaf (stanzas 19–46). The descriptions of nature are leisurely and detailed, stressing color, light and shade; those of the costumes are similarly rich and delicious, so that the narrative progresses very slowly. Then another company of ladies with attendant lords, all in contrasting green, dance and kneel in honor of the Flower (the daisy or marguerite). Soon exhausted by the heat and drenched by sudden hail and rain (stanzas 47–54), this group is succored by those of the Leaf, who have been sheltered by a huge laurel tree. Finally, both groups depart, singing pleasantly together (stanzas 55–64). The explanation of the symbolism (as noted above) is given the poet by a tarrying lady. However, those of the Flower are censured only indirectly, and the new morality of the fifteenth century makes a compromise between the opposing views (stanzas 65–85). [Lewis sees in this a fusion of courtly and homiletic allegory.]

There is no direct source, but the poem is influenced by French and English poems on the cult of the daisy, e.g., *The Cuckoo and the Nightingale* (VII [47]), and [16] and [19] in the present chapter; the orders of the Flower and Leaf (in Chaucer, Deschamps, and Charles d'Orleans); and the friendly rivalry of two contrasting positions. The immediate models are Chaucer's Prologue to *The Legend of Good Women,* Lydgate's *Reson and Sensuality,* and Deschamps' cult poems.

The courtly games of Flower and Leaf in [50] permit mention of other games described in court-coterie verse: *Chance of the Dice, Ragman's Roll,* and *Le roi qui ne ment* (Brown-Robbins, nos. 803, 2251; Robbins-Cutler, no. 586.5).

THE ISLE OF LADIES [51], a long poem of 2206 short lines in couplets, within a framework of courtly love weaves elements of supernatural romance (magic apples, magic ships, and magic birdseed), under the influence of Marie de France's *Lai d'Eliduc* and perhaps *Lanval.* It was ascribed to Chaucer in the Longleat MS, falsely entitled *Chaucer's Dream* by Speght in 1598 (thereby confusing it with Chaucer's *Book of the Duchess,* which duplicated this title), but rejected from the Chaucer canon by most critics of the nineteenth-century (Hertzberg, Ellis, Ten Brink, and McClumpha). Brown-Robbins, no. 3947.

On a May night, thinking of his lady, the poet has a dream vision of an island with walls of glass and gates of gold, peopled by beautiful ladies having perpetual youth. Men are forbidden the island. As the poet cannot account for his presence, he becomes the ladies' prisoner. The queen, who has been away, returns to the island with a strange knight and the poet's lady, and explains how the knight tried to seize her while she was gathering the apples of eternal youth on a perilous rock. In a long speech, the knight complains of the merciless queen and swoons for love, but she revives him and then bids him leave the island. The God of Love approaches, with 10,000 ships surrounded by singing birds, to aid his stricken knight. Reproaching the queen for her long neglect of love's laws, he pierces her heart with his arrow; then he prophesies the knight's recovery and recommends the poet as his own true servant. The next day, after the queen's capitulation, the God of Love holds a council, in which everyone is reconciled, and the knight and poet promised success with their mistresses. The poet's lady sets sail, and the poet, rushing into the water, is rescued from drowning only by a magic apple given him by his now contrite lady. The poet and his lady-love reach her homeland. At this point, the poet awakens, his room full of smoke.

The poet falls asleep again, and returns in his dream to the isle, where he finds the queen and the knight about to be wed. The knight departs in a magic boat ("It needeth neither mast ne rother") to gather a retinue of 60,000 attendants sufficiently impressive for a noble ceremony, promising to return within ten days. However, it is not until fifteen days later that the whole company arrive on the one magic ship. On arrival, they are met by the news that the queen is dead, shamed by the knight's breaking his promise. Whereupon the knight kills himself. The bodies of the two lovers are put in a rich tomb, with prayers to the Holy Trinity. A blue and green bird sings over the corpses, but in trying to fly away beats its wings on the stained-glass windows of the church and falls down dead. Other birds bring seeds which restore its life. An abbess takes some of these bird seeds and similarly resuscitates the queen and the knight. The wedding is sumptuous, lasting three months. The poet and his lady are also married in a fitting ceremony, when the sound of the music wakens the poet once again, and "my dream seemed that was not." The poet vows his loyalty in real life to his mistress. Following immediately is an envoy and balade [14] not properly part of the poem.

Speght interpreted the allegory as a "covert report of the marriage of John of Gaunt, the King's son, with Blanche, the daughter of Henry, Duke of Lancaster." Hertzberg saw the alliance of John of Gaunt with Catherine Swynford; Brandl and Sherzer, the marriage of Henry V with Catherine of France. Skeat thought the poem written after 1450, Seaton between 1435 and 1438.

LETTER OF DIDO TO AENEAS [52], published only once in 1526 by Pynson, 242 lines in pentameter couplets, framed by a Translator's Prologue of nine rime royal stanzas and a Translator's Envoy of two stanzas. The verses in spirit are modern and show sympathetic understanding of a woman's problems. Robbins-Cutler, no. 811.5.

The Prologue ("Folks discomforted bere heuy countenance") advises against dissembling one's feelings; himself joyless, the poet will relate Dido's desertion by faithless

Aeneas (to pen whose name makes the hand quake with fury). Only Celeno, "full of enuyous yre," can inspire him, who, although he was never in France, will translate from the French Dido's letter to Aeneas. The letter itself ("Right as þe swan when her dethe is nye") describes Dido's feelings when she learns Aeneas is leaving her. Where will he find a fairer land or more devoted wife? How could sweet Venus bear such an unkind son? Don't go now, Aeneas, wait for calmer seas—waves swallow up faithless men. I love your life more than I want your death: tarry. You were a paragon in everything save pity. I will kill myself when you leave me.

The Envoy warns "good ladyes which be of tender age / Beware of love." Even when they promise marriage, men cannot be trusted. Avoid the heat of passion (cf. [34]). If a woman must take a lover, make sure he is steadfast and true!

A later lamentation of Dido, signed Thomas Pridioxe, appears with John Redford's *The Play of Wyt and Science* in MS British Museum Additional 15233 ("Behowlde of pensyfnes the pycture here in place").

Stephen Hawes (ca. 1474–1530) is in the tradition of the Chaucerian apocrypha although his work falls just outside the fifteenth century. He regarded himself as the disciple of Chaucer, Gower, and Lydgate, and frequently memorializes them in his writings. "More than any other writer of his time, [Hawes] represents the most characteristic features of the rapidly disappearing Middle Ages" (Mead). Hawes was born in Suffolk, and attended the University of Oxford. During the first decade of the sixteenth century, he lived in London as a courtier, and then retired to spend the last years of his life in Suffolk. While at Oxford, Hawes was exposed to Italian humanism, and after 1497 to the interest in reformed religion. Both these influences predominated in the Tudor court which Hawes frequented. The early *Example of Virtue*, written before his London life, is traditional and conservative; *The Pastime of Pleasure*, written a few years later, shows the impact of the New Learning; and *The Conversion of Swearers*, the influence of humanists turned reformers, in its insistence upon the importance of Christ as an example and upon a personal relationship of love between Christ and man.

THE EXAMPLE OF VIRTUE [53], published about 1503–04, in 300 stanzas rime royal, is in some ways a preliminary sketch for *The Pastime of Pleasure*. Robbins-Cutler, no. 3954.8.

In a spring dream, the poet meets Discretion and goes to a castle, where he finds the Nine Worthies and Lady Fortune. Nearby, Dame Hardiness tells of her achievements. Discretion thinks the poet should be married, and he must therefore win Dame Cleanness in a distant castle. To do so he must first kill a three-headed dragon. Finally, he meets and weds his lady, and at the age of sixty he and his wife die. The poem concludes with a prayer for King Henry VII, and a final tribute to Gower, Chaucer, and Lydgate.

THE PASTIME OF PLEASURE [54], published in 1509, in 5,816 lines in couplets and rime royal stanzas, is a moralizing allegory in which the perfect lover struggles to win the perfect lady. The poem, whose love-vision narrative collapses under the didacticism of the allegory, is influenced by de Guileville's *Pélérinage de l'âme humaine* (probably known to Hawes in Lydgate's translation), Lydgate's *Court of Sapience*, Chaucer's *Romaunt of the Rose*, and the *Margarita philosophica*. Thus the poem merely makes use of the machinery of love-vision poetry to enforce a didactic moral. Ferguson sees the poem as an allegorical romance disguising the education of a knight. Brown-Robbins, no. 4004.

The Prologue consists of a dedication to King Henry VII and an appeal to "my mayster Lydgate." The poet, named Graund Amour, on a spring morning walks in a meadow and follows the path of Active Life. Falling asleep, he is visited by Lady Fame and encouraged to woo La Belle Pucelle, symbolic of "the true aim of life, only attainable through many labors" (Morley). En route, Fame directs him to the Tower of Doctrine, leaving him two greyhounds, Governance and Grace. At the Tower, he is admitted by Porteress Countenance and asks aid of Dame Doctrine, who sends him to her seven daughters, Lady Grammar, Lady Logic, and Lady Rhetoric (who describes the five divisions of rhetoric, noting that Gower, Chaucer, and Lydgate are illustrious models). Next he visits the four other daughters representing the Quadrivium: Lady Arithmetic, Lady Music, Lady Geometry, and Lady Astronomy. Lady Music introduces the poet to La Belle Pucelle. As he dances with her, his passion increases, but fearing that she will read his thoughts, he sorrowfully departs to a temple. Here, a new acquaintance, Counsel, gives him hope. He returns to the Tower of Music, and having been admitted by the Porteress Courtesy, Graund Amour pleads his suit to La Belle Pucelle. She agrees to show him mercy, but first he has to follow her to the far north. For the perils of the trip, he learns knighthood at the Tower of Chivalry. He receives further help from Mars (who disputes with Fortune about their respective jurisdiction in battles) and is knighted by King Melezyus. Starting on his trip, he is joined for a short while by a grotesque dwarf, Godfrey Gobelyve, who is soon chased away by Lady Correction (this comic relief in couplets), and Graund Amour receives pledges of aid from Venus, who dispatches Cupid to tell La Belle Pucelle the excellent qualities of her suitor. Graund Amour kills the giant with the three heads (Falsehood, Imagination, Perjury) and is succored by three ladies (Verity, Good Operation, Fidelity) in their castle. Perseverance encourages him with news of Pucelle's devotion, in spite of the attacks by Disdain and Strangeness. Having visited the castle of Lady Comfort, Graund Amour overcomes the giant with seven allegorical heads and is greeted by seven more ladies. Then he conquers a monster with the aid of a magic ointment, and sees La Belle Pucelle in a high tower. Lex Ecclesiae unites the pair in marriage.

After many years happiness, Age comes to fetch Graund Amour, and he is buried by Mercy and Charity, and Remembrance (Fame) places a long epitaph on his grave. Time and Eternity pronounce the final exhortation.

THE COMFORT OF LOVERS [55], published in 1512, is a debate in 126 rime royal stanzas between Amour and Pucelle, similar to the themes of [53] and [54]. Hawes ends his allegory with the customary eulogy of Gower, Chaucer, and (especially) Lydgate. Robbins-Cutler, no. 3357.5.

Meditating in a meadow, the poet dreams of a palace garden. He tells an older lady that long ago he secretly loved a beautiful mistress, but somehow misfortune fell on him and he turned his thoughts to God. The lady shows him a tower with three magic crystals: in the first, he sees his past; in the second, his enemies' plots; and in the third, the dove of the Holy Ghost, with its emblems, the sword of prudence and the shield of perception. A bright star suggests the poet will finally gain his lady-love, who is shortly thereafter presented to him by Dame Diligence. Then Pucelle refers the case to Venus and Fortune. Hawes gives no key to this allegory.

THE CASTELL OF PLEASURE [56], by William Nevill, printed about 1517, in 971 lines, including six introductory twelve-line stanzas, ababbcbccdcd, of dialogue between Copland and the author, and another six similar concluding stanzas with envoy, Copland's Envoy, a Ballade Royale, and a stanza to the author, with the main body of the poem in eight-line stanzas, ababbcbc. Three rime royal stanzas are included at lines 802–22. The allegory belongs in the secular love tradition of the *Romaunt of the Rose* and *The Temple of Glass* rather than to the moralizing tradition of Barclay's *Castell of Labour* or Hawes' *Pastime of Pleasure*. In it are combined many literary motifs: dream setting, allegorical personifications, gorgeous palaces and meadows, debates, and illustrations from antiquity, with all the conventions of courtly love. Brown-Robbins, no. 3811.

Reading Ovid's story of Phoebus and Daphne, the poet (named Desire) dozes and finds himself locked in the library overnight. Obsessed by "many fantasyes," including his longing to serve the Lady Beauty, he is led by Morpheus on a perilous pilgrimage toward his goal. Desire, prompted by Morpheus, crosses the mountain of Courage, fords the dangerous river which drowns inconstant lovers, and sees Beauty's castle. Avoiding the pathway of worldly wealth and success, he is welcomed into the castle by Comfort. While viewing a lovely green court, Desire is turned over to Kindness, the sister of Comfort. The dreamer's next visit is to the lovely covert of Fantasy, who reassures him with the story of Hippomenes and Atlanta. Lady Eloquence next helps to "advance" Desire's cause with Lady Beauty. Fantasy pleads with Beauty and overcomes the opposition of Disdain. In a debate, Pity, assisted by Credence, also vanquishes Disdain. Beauty then promises not to forsake Desire, who in turn pledges fidelity. The poet awakens from his dream, lamenting the loss of his vision, and advises diligence and courage in love.

Bibliography

TABLE OF ABBREVIATIONS

For abbreviations and shortened forms not appearing in this table consult the list of background books at the beginning of the appropriate chapter of the Bibliography.

AAGRP	Ausgaben und Abhandlungen aus dem Gebiete der romanischen Philologie
AC	Archaeologica Cantiana
Acad	Academy
AEB	Kölbing E, Altenglische Bibliothek, Heilbronn 1883–
AELeg 1875	Horstmann C, Altenglische Legenden, Paderborn 1875
AELeg 1878	Horstmann C, Sammlung altenglischer Legenden, Heilbronn 1878
AELeg 1881	Horstmann C, Altenglische Lekenden (Neue Fogle), Heilbronn 1881
AESpr	Mätzner E, Altenglische Sprachproben, Berlin 1867–
AF	Anglistische Forschungen
AfDA	Anzeiger für deutsches Alterthum
AHR	American Historical Review
AJ	Ampleforth Journal
AJA	American Journal of Archaeology
AJP	American Journal of Philology
ALb	Allgemeines Literaturblatt
ALg	Archivum linguisticum
Allen WAR	Allen H E, Writings Ascribed to Richard Rolle

	Hermit of Hampole and Materials for His Biography, MLA Monograph Series 3, N Y 1927
Angl	Anglia, Zeitschrift für englische Philologie
AnglA	Anglia Anzeiger
AnglB	Beiblatt zur Anglia
AN&Q	American Notes and Queries
Antiq	Antiquity
APS	Acta philologica scandinavica
AQ	American Quarterly
AR	Antioch Review
Arch	Archiv für das Studium der neueren Sprachen und Literaturen
Archaeol	Archaeologia
Ashton	Ashton J, Romances of Chivalry, London 1890
ASp	American Speech
ASR	American Scandinavian Review
ASt	Aberystwyth Studies
Athen	Athenaeum
BA	Books Abroad
BARB	Bulletin de l'Académie royale de Belgique
Baugh LHE	Baugh A C, The Middle English Period, in A Literary History of England, N Y 1948; 2nd edn 1967
BB	Bulletin of Bibliography
BBA	Bonner Beiträge zur Anglistik
BBCS	Bulletin of the Board of Celtic Studies (Univ of Wales)
BBGRP	Berliner Beiträge zur germanischen und romanischen Philologie
BBSIA	Bulletin bibliographique de la Société internationale arthurienne
Bennett OHEL	Bennett H S, Chaucer and the Fifteenth Century, Oxford 1947
Best BIP	Best R I, Bibliography of Irish Philology, 2 vols, Dublin 1913

BGDSL	Beiträge zur Geschichte der deutschen Sprache und Literatur
BHR	Bibliothèque d'humanisme et renaissance
BIHR	Bulletin of the Institute of Historical Research
Billings	Billings A H, A Guide to the Middle English Metrical Romances, N Y 1901
Blackf	Blackfriars
Bloomfield SDS	Bloomfield M W, The Seven Deadly Sins, Michigan State College of Agriculture and Applied Science Studies in Language and Literature, 1952
BNYPL	Bulletin of the New York Public Library
Böddeker AED	Böddeker K, Altenglische Dichtungen des MS Harl 2253, Berlin 1878
Bossuat MBLF	Bossuat R, Manuel bibliographique de la littérature française du moyen âge, Paris 1951; supplément Paris 1955; deuxième supplément Paris 1961 [the item numbers run consecutively through the supplement]
BPLQ	Boston Public Library Quarterly
BQR	Bodleian Quarterly Record (sometimes Review)
Brandl	Brandl A, Mittelenglische Literatur, in Paul's Grundriss der germanische Philologie, 1st edn, Strassburg 1893, 2^1.609 ff, Index 2^2.345
Brown ELxiiiC	Brown C F, English Lyrics of the 13th Century, Oxford 1932
Brown Reg	Brown C, A Register of Middle English Religious and Didactic Verse, parts 1 and 2, Oxford (for the Bibliographical Society) 1916, 1920
Brown RLxivC	Brown C F, Religious Lyrics of the 14th Century, Oxford 1924
Brown RLxvC	Brown C F, Religious Lyrics of the 15th Century, Oxford 1939
Brown-Robbins	Brown C and R H Robbins, The Index of Middle English Verse, N Y 1943; see also Robbins-Cutler
Bryan-Dempster	Bryan W F and G Dempster, Sources and Ana-

	logues of Chaucer's Canterbury Tales, Chicago 1941
BrynMawrMon	Bryn Mawr College Monographs, Bryn Mawr 1905–
BSEP	Bonner Studien zur englischen Philologie
BUSE	Boston University Studies in English
CASP	Cambridge Antiquarian Society Publication
CBEL	Bateson F W, Cambridge Bibliography of English Literature, 5 vols, London and N Y 1941, 1957
CE	College English
CFMA	Les classiques français du moyen âge; collection de textes française et provençaux antérieurs a 1500, Paris 1910–
Chambers	Chambers E K, The Mediaeval Stage, 2 vols, Oxford 1903
Chambers OHEL	Chambers E K, English Literature at the Close of the Middle Ages, Oxford 1945
CHEL	Ward A W and A R Waller, The Cambridge History of English Literature, vols 1 and 2, Cambridge 1907, 1908
CHR	Catholic Historical Review
ChS	Publications of the Chaucer Society, London 1869–1924
Ch&Sidg	Chambers E K and F Sidgwick, Early English Lyrics, London 1907; numerous reprints
CJ	Classic Journal
CL	Comparative Literature
CMLR	Canadian Modern Language Review
Comper Spir Songs	Comper F M M, Spiritual Songs from English Manuscripts of Fourteenth to Sixteenth Centuries, London and N Y 1936
Conviv	Convivium
Courthope	Courthope W J, History of English Poetry, vol 1, London 1895
CP	Classical Philology
Craig HEL	Craig H, G K Anderson, L I Bredvold, J W Beach, History of English Literature, N Y 1950

Cross Mot Ind	Cross T P, Motif Index of Early Irish Literature Bloomington Ind 1951
Crotch PEWC	Crotch W J B, The Prologues and Epilogues of William Caxton, EETS 176, London 1928·
CUS	Columbia University Studies in English and in Comparative Literature, N Y 1899–
DA	Dissertation Abstracts
DANHSJ	Derbyshire Archaeological and Natural History Society Journal
de Julleville Hist	de Julleville L Petit, Histoire de la langue et de la littérature française, vols 1 and 2, Paris 1896–99
de Ricci Census	de Ricci S and W J Wilson, Census of Medieval and Renaissance Manuscripts in the United States of America and Canada, vols 1–3, N Y 1935, 1937, 1940
Dickins and Wilson	Dickins B and R M Wilson, Early Middle English Texts, Cambridge 1950
DLz	Deutsche Literaturzeitung
DNB	Stephen L and S Lee, Dictionary of National Biography, N Y and London 1885–1900, and supplements
DomS	Dominican Studies: An Annual Review, Blackfriars Publications, London
DUJ	Durham University Journal
EA	Études anglaises
EBEP	Erlanger Beiträge zur englischen Philologie
EC	Essays in Criticism
EETS	Publications of the Early English Text Society (Original Series), 1864–
EETSES	Publication of the Early English Text Society (Extra Series), 1867–
EG	Études germaniques
EGS	English and Germanic Studies
EHR	English Historical Review
EIE, EIA	English Institute Essays (Annual), N Y 1939–

EJ	English Journal
ELH	Journal of English Literary History
Ellis EEP	Ellis G, Specimens of Early English Poetry, 3 vols, London 1811
Ellis Spec	Ellis G, Specimens of Early English Metrical Romances, 3 vols, London 1805; rvsd Halliwell, 1 vol, Bohn edn 1848 (latter edn referred to, unless otherwise indicated)
Enc Brit	Encyclopaedia Britannica, 11th edn
Engl	English: The Magazine of the English Association
E&S	Essays and Studies by Members of the English Association, Oxford 1910–
E&S Brown	Essays and Studies in Honor of Carleton Brown, N Y 1940
Esdaile ETPR	Esdaile A, A List of English Tales and Prose Romances Printed before 1740, London 1912
EStn	Englische Studien
ESts	English Studies
ETB	Hoops J, Englische Textbibliothek, 21 vols, Heidelberg 1898–1935?
Expl	Explicator
Farrar-Evans	Farrar C P and A P Evans, Bibliography of English Translations from Medieval Sources, N Y 1946
FFC	Foklore Fellows Communications
FFK	Forschungen und Fortschritte: Korrespondenzblatt der deutschen Wissenschaft und Technik
Flügel NL	Flügel E, Neuenglisches Lesebuch, Halle 1895
FQ	French Quarterly
FR	French Review
FS	French Studies
Furnivall EEP	Furnivall F J, Early English Poems and Lives of Saints, Berlin 1862 (Transactions of Philological Society of London 1858)
Gautier Bibl	Gautier L, Bibliographie des chansons de geste, Paris 1897

Gayley	Gayley C M, Plays of Our Forefathers, N Y 1907
GdW	Gesamtkatalog der Wiegendrucke, Leipzig 1925–
Germ	Germania
Gerould S Leg	Gerould G H, Saints' Legends, Boston 1916
GGA	Göttingische gelehrte Anzeiger
GJ	Gutenberg Jahrbuch
GQ	German Quarterly
GR	Germanic Review
Greene E E Carols	Greene R L, The Early English Carols, Oxford 1935
GRM	Germanisch-Romanische Monatsschrift
Gröber	Gröber G, Grundriss der romanischen Philologie, Strassburg 1888–1902, new issue 1897–1906, 2nd edn 1904– (vol 2¹ 1902 referred to, unless otherwise indicated)
Gröber-Hofer	Hofer S, Geschichte der mittelfranzösischen Literatur, 2 vols, 2nd edn, Berlin and Leipzig 1933–37
Hall Selections	Hall J, Selections from Early Middle English 1130–1250, 2 parts, Oxford 1920
Hammond	Hammond E P, Chaucer: A Bibliographical Manual, N Y 1908
Hartshorne AMT	Hartshorne C H, Ancient Metrical Tales, London 1829
Hazlitt Rem	Hazlitt W C, Remains of the Early Popular Poetry of England, 4 vols, London 1864–66
Herbert	Herbert J A, Catalogue of Romances in the Department of MSS of the British Museum, London 1910 (vol 3 of Ward's Catalogue)
Hermes	Hermes
Hibbard Med Rom	Hibbard L, Medieval Romance in England, N Y 1924
HINL	History of Ideas News Letter
Hisp	Hispania
HispR	Hispanic Review
HJ	Hibbert Journal

HLB	Harvard Library Bulletin
HLF	Histoire littéraire de la France, Paris 1733–; new edn 1865–
HLQ	Huntington Library Quarterly
Holmes CBFL	Cabeen D C, Critical Bibliography of French Literature, vol 1 (the Medieval Period), ed U T Holmes jr, Syracuse N Y 1949
HSCL	Harvard Studies in Comparative Literature
HSNPL	Harvard Studies and Notes in Philology and Literature, Boston 1892–
HudR	Hudson Review
IER	Irish Ecclesiastical Review
IS	Italian Studies
Isis	Isis
Ital	Italica
JAAC	Journal of Aesthetics and Art Criticism
JBL	Journal of Biblical Literature
JCS	Journal of Celtic Studies
JEGGP	Jahresbericht über die Erscheinungen auf dem Gebiete der germanischen Philologie
JEGP	Journal of English and Germanic Philology
JEH	Journal of Ecclesiastical History
JfRESL	Jahrbuch für romanische und englische Sprache und Literatur
JGP	Journal of Germanic Philology
JHI	Journal of the History of Ideas
JPhilol	Journal of Philology
JPhilos	Journal of Philosophy
JRLB	Bulletin of the John Rylands Library, Manchester
Kane	Kane G, Middle English Literature: A Critical Study of the Romances, the Religious Lyrics, Piers Plowman, London 1951
Kennedy BWEL	Kennedy A G, A Bibliography of Writings on the English Language from the Beginning of Printing to the End of 1922, Cambridge Mass and New Haven 1927

Kild Ged	Heuser W, Die Kildare-Gedichte, Bonn 1904 (BBA 14)
Körting	Körting G, Grundriss der Geschichte der englischen Literatur von ihren Anfängen bis zur Gegenwart, 5th edn, Münster 1910
KR	Kenyon Review
Krit Jahresber	Vollmüller K, Kritischer Jahresbericht über die Fortschritte der romanischen Philologie, München und Leipzig 1892–1915 (Zweiter Teil, 13 vols in 12)
KSEP	Kieler Studien zur englischen Philologie
Lang	Language
LB	Leuvensche Bijdragen, Periodical for Modern Philology
LC	Library Chronicle
Leeds SE	Leeds Studies in English and Kindred Languages, School of English Literature in the University of Leeds
Legouis	Legouis E, Chaucer, Engl trans by Lailvoix, London 1913
Legouis HEL	Legouis E and L Cazamian, trans H D Irvine and W D MacInnes, A History of English Literature, new edn, N Y 1929
LfGRP	Literaturblatt für germanische und romanische Philologie
Libr	The Library
Litteris	Litteris: An International Critical Review of the Humanities, New Society of Letters
LMS	London Medieval Studies
Loomis ALMA	Loomis R S, Arthurian Literature in the Middle Ages, A Collaborative History, Oxford 1959
LP	Literature and Psychology
LQ	Library Quarterly
Lund SE	Lund Studies in English
LZ	Literarisches Zentralblatt
MÆ	Medium ævum
Manly CT	Manly J M, Canterbury Tales by Geoffrey Chaucer,

	with an Introduction, Notes, and a Glossary, N Y 1928
Manly Spec	Manly J M, Specimens of the Pre-Shakespearean Drama, vol 1, 2nd edn, Boston 1900
Manly & Rickert	Manly J M and E Rickert, The Text of the Canterbury Tales Studied on the Basis of All Known Manuscripts, 8 vols, Chicago 1940
MBREP	Münchener Beiträge zur romanischen und englischen Philologie
MED	Kurath H and S M Kuhn, Middle English Dictionary, Ann Arbor 1952– (M S Ogden, C E Palmer, and R L McKelvey, Bibliography [of ME texts], 1954, p 15)
MH	Medievalia et humanistica
MHRA	MHRA, Bulletin of the Modern Humanities Research Association
Migne PL	Migne, Pastrologiae Latinae cursus completus
Minor Poems	Skeat W W, Chaucer: The Minor Poems, 2nd edn, Oxford 1896
MKAW	Mededeelingen van de Koninklijke akademie van wetenschappen, afdeling letterkunde
ML	Music and Letters
MLF	Modern Language Forum
MLJ	Modern Language Journal
MLN	Modern Language Notes
MLQ (Lon)	Modern Language Quarterly (London)
MLQ (Wash)	Modern Language Quarterly (Seattle, Washington)
MLR	Modern Language Review
Monat	Monatschefte
Moore Meech and Whitehall	Moore S, S B Meech and H Whitehall, Middle English Dialect Characterictics and Dialect Boundaries, University of Michigan Essays and Studies in Language and Literature 13, Ann Arbor 1935
Morley	Morley H, English Writers, vols 3–6, London 1890

Morris Spec	Morris R (ed part 1), R Morris and W W Skeat (ed part 2), Specimens of Early English, part 1, 2nd edn, Oxford 1887; part 2, 4th edn, Oxford 1898
MP	Modern Philology
MS	Mediaeval Studies
MSEP	Marburger Studien zur englischen Philologie, 13 vols, Marburg 1901–11
MUPES	Manchester University Publications, English Series
NA	Neuer Anzeiger
Neophil	Neophilologus, A Modern Language Quarterly
NEQ	New England Quarterly
NLB	Newberry Library Bulletin
NM	Neuphilologische Mitteilungen: Bulletin de la Société neophilologique de Helsinki
NMQ	New Mexico Quarterly
NNAC	Norfolk and Norwich Archaeological Society
N&Q	Notes and Queries
NRFH	Nueva revista de filologia hispánica
NS	Die neueren Sprachen, Zeitschrift für de neusprachlichen Unterrecht
O'Dell CLPF	O'Dell S, A Chronological List of Prose Fiction in English Printed in England and Other Countries, Cambridge Mass 1954
OMETexts	Morsbach L and F Holthausen, Old and Middle English Texts, 11 vols, Heidelberg 1901–26
Oxf Ch	Skeat W W, The Works of Geoffrey Chaucer, Oxford 1894–1900 (6 vols; extra 7th vol of Chaucerian Poems)
Palaes	Palaestra, Untersuchungen und Texte
PAPS	Proceedings of the American Philosophical Society
Paris Litt Franç	Paris G P B, La littérature française au moyen âge, 4th edn, Paris 1909
Patterson	Patterson F A, The Middle English Penitential Lyric, N Y 1911

Paul Grundriss	Paul H, Grundriss der germanischen Philologie, 3 vols, 1st edn, Strassburg 1891–1900; 2nd edn 1900–
PBBeitr	Paul H and W Braune, Beiträge zur Geschichte der deutschen Sprache und Literatur, Halle 1874–
PBSA	Papers of the Bibliographical Society of America
PBSUV	Papers of the Bibliographical Society, Univ of Virginia
PFMS	Furnivall F J and J W Hales, The Percy Folio MS, 4 vols, London 1867–69; re-ed I Gollancz, 4 vols, London 1905–10 (the earlier edn is referred to, unless otherwise indicated)
Philo	Philologus
PMLA	Publications of the Modern Language Association of America
PMRS	Progress of Medieval and Renaissance Studies in the United States and Canada
Pollard 15CPV	Pollard A W, Fifteenth Century Prose and Verse, Westminster 1903
PP	Past and Present
PPR	Philosophy and Phenomenological Research
PPS	Publications of the Percy Society
PQ	Philological Quarterly
PR	Partisan Review
PS	Pacific Spectator
PSTS	Publications of the Scottish Text Society, Edinburgh 1884–
PULC	Princeton University Library Chronicle
QF	Quellen und Forschungen zur Sprach- und Culturgeschichte der germanischen Völker
QQ	Queen's Quarterly
RAA	Revue anglo-américaine
RadMon	Radcliffe College Monographs, Boston 1891–
RB	Revue britannique
RC	Revue celtique

RCHL	Revue critique d'histoire et de littérature
REH	The Review of Ecclesiastical History
Rel Ant	Wright T and J O Halliwell, Reliquiae antiquae, 2 vols, London 1845
Ren	Renascence
Renwick-Orton	Renwick W L and H Orton, The Beginnings of English Literature to Skelton 1509, London 1939; rvsd edn 1952
RES	Review of English Studies
RevP	Revue de philologie
RF	Romanische Forschungen
RFE	Revista de filología espanola
RFH	Revista de filología hispánica
RG	Revue germanique
RHL	Revue d'histoire littéraire de la France
Rickert RofFr, RofL	Rickert E, Early English Romances in Verse: Romances of Friendship (vol 1), Romances of Love (vol 2), London 1908
Ringler BEV	Ringler W, A Bibliography and First-Line Index of English Verse Printed through 1500, PBSA 49.153
Ritson AEMR	Ritson J, Ancient English Metrical Romances, 3 vols, London 1802, rvsd E Goldsmid, Edinburg 1884 (earlier edn referred to, unless otherwise indicated)
Ritson APP	Ritson J, Ancient Popular Poetry, 2nd edn, London 1833
Ritson AS	Ritson J, Ancient Songs from the Time of Henry III, 2 vols, London 1790, new edn 1829; rvsd W C Hazlitt, Ancient Songs and Ballads, 1 vol, London 1877 (last edn referred to, unless otherwise indicated)
RLC	Revue de littérature comparée
RLR	Revue des langues romanes
RN	Renaissance News

Robbins-Cutler	Supplement to Brown-Robbins, Lexington Ky 1965
Robbins-HP	Robbins R H, Secular Lyrics of the 14th and 15th Centuries, Oxford 1959
Robbins SL	Robbins R H, Secular Lyrics of the 14th and 15th Centuries, 2nd edn, Oxford 1955
Robson	Robson J, Three Early English Metrical Romances, London (Camden Society) 1842
Rolls Series	Rerum Britannicarum medii aevi scriptores, Published by Authority of the Lords Commissioners of Her Majesty's Treasury, under the Direction of the Master of the Rolls, London 1857–91
Rom	Romania
RomP	Romance Philology
RomR	Romanic Review
Root	Root R K, The Poetry of Chaucer, Boston 1906
Rot	Rotulus, A Bulletin for MS Collectors
Roxb Club	Publications of the Roxburghe Club, London 1814–
RSLC	Record Society of Lancashire and Cheshire
RUL	Revue de l'Université laval
SA	The Scottish Antiquary, or Northern Notes and Queries
SAQ	South Atlantic Quarterly
SATF	Publications de la Société des anciens textes français, Paris 1875–
SB	Studies in Bibliography: Papers of the Bibliographical Society of the University of Virginia
SBB	Studies in Bibliography and Booklore
ScanSt	Scandinavian Studies
Schipper	Schipper J, Englische Metrik, 2 vols, Bonn 1881–88
Schofield	Schofield W H, English Literature from the Norman Conquest to Chaucer, N Y 1906
SciS	Science and Society
Scrut	Scrutiny
SE	Studies in English

SEER	Slavonic and East European Review
SEP	Studien zur englischen Philologie
ShJ	Jahrbuch der deutschen Shakespeare-Gesellschaft
SHR	Scottish Historical Review
Skeat Spec	Skeat W W, Specimens of English Literature 1394–1579, 6th edn, Oxford
SL	Studies in Lingustics
SN	Studia neophilologica: A Journal of Germanic and Romanic Philology
SP	Studies in Philology
Spec	Speculum: A Journal of Mediaeval Studies
SR	Sewanee Review
SRL	Saturday Review of Literature
SSL	Studies in Scottish Literature
STC	Pollard A W and G R Redgrave, A Short-Title Catalogue of Books Printed in England, Scotland, and Ireland and of English Books Printed Abroad 1475–1640, London 1926
StVL	Studien zur vergleichenden Literaturgeschichte
Summary Cat	Madan F and H H E Craster, A Summary Catalogue of Western Manuscripts Which Have Not Hitherto Been Catalogued in the Quarto Series, Oxford 1895–1953
SUVSL	Skriften utgivna av Vetenskaps-societeten i Lund
SWR	Southwest Review
Sym	Symposium
Ten Brink	Ten Brink B A K, Early English Literature, English Literature, trans Kennedy et al, vol 1, vol 2 (parts 1–2), London and N Y 1887–92 (referred to as vols 1–3)
Texas SE	Texas Studies in English
Thompson Mot Ind	Thompson S, Motif Index of Folk-Literature, 6 vols, Helsinki 1932–36
Thoms	Thomas W J, A Collection of Early Prose Romances,

	London 1828; part ed Morley, Carlsbrooke Library, whole rvsd edn, London (Routledge); new edn, Edinburgh 1904
TLCAS	Transactions of Lancashire and Cheshire Antiquarian Society
TLS	[London] Times Literary Supplement
TNTL	Tijdschrift voor nederlandse taal- en letterkunde
TPSL	Transactions of the Philological Society of London
Trad	Traditio, Studies in Ancient and Medieval History, Thought, and Religion
TRSL	Transactions of the Royal Society of Literature
TTL	Tijdschrift voor taal en letteren
Tucker-Benham	Tucker L L and A R Benham, A Bibliography of Fifteenth-Century Literature, Seattle 1928
UKCR	University of Kansas City Review
UQ	Ukrainian Quarterly
Utley CR	Utley F L, The Crooked Rib: An Analytical Index to the Argument about Women in English and Scots Literature to the End of the Year 1568, Columbus O 1944
UTM	University of Toronto Monthly
UTQ	University of Toronto Quarterly
VMKVA	Verslagen en mededeelingen der Koninklijke vlaamsche academie
VQR	Virginia Quarterly Review
Ward	Ward H L D, Catalogue of Romances in the Department of MSS of the British Museum, 2 vols, London 1883–93 (see Herbert for vol 3)
Ward Hist	Ward A W, A History of English Dramatic Literature to the Death of Queen Anne, 3 vols, new edn, London 1899
Wehrle	Wehrle W O, The Macaronic Hymn Tradition in Medieval English Literature, Washington 1933
WBEP	Wiener Beiträge zur englischen Philologie

Weber MR	Weber H W, Metrical Romances of the 13th, 14th, and 15th Centuries, 3 vols, Edinburgh 1810
Wessex	Wessex
WHR	Western Humanities Review
Wilson EMEL	Wilson R M, Early Middle English Literature, London 1939
° WMQ	William and Mary Quarterly
WR	Western Review
Wright AnecLit	Wright T, Anecdota literaria, London 1844
Wright PPS	Wright T, Political Poems and Songs from the Accession of Edward III to That of Richard III, 2 vols, London (Rolls Series) 1859–61
Wright PS	Wright T, Political Songs of England from the Reign of John to That of Edward III, Camden Society, London 1839 (this edn referred to, unless otherwise indicated); 4 vols, rvsd, privately printed, Goldsmid, Edinburgh 1884
Wright SLP	Wright T, Specimens of Lyric Poety Composed in England in the Reign of Edward I, Percy Society, 2 vols, London 1896
Wülcker	Wülcker R P, Geschichte der englischen Literatur, 2 vols, Leipzig 1896
YCGL	Yearbook of Comparative and General Literature
YFS	Yale French Studies, New Haven 1948–
Yksh Wr	Horstmann C, Yorkshire Writers, Library of Early English Writers, 2 vols, London 1895–96
YR	Yale Review
YSCS	Yorkshire Society for Celtic Studies
YSE	Yale Studies in English, N Y 1898–
YWES	Year's Work in English Studies
YWMLS	Year's Work in Modern Language Studies
ZfCP	Zeitschrift für celtische Philologie (Tübingen)
ZfDA	Zeitschrift für deutsches Alterthum und deutsche Litteratur

ZfDP	Zeitschrift für deutsche Philologie
ZfFSL	Zeitschrift für französische Sprache und Literatur
ZföG	Zeitschrift für die österreichischen Gymnasien
ZfRP	Zeitschrift für romanische Philologie
ZfVL	Zeitschrift für vergleichende Litteraturgeschichte, Berlin

Other Commonly Used Abbreviations

ae	altenglische	AN	Anglo-Norman	OF	Old French
af	altfranzösische	c	copyright	ON	Old Norse
engl	englische	ca	circa	pt	part
f	für	crit	criticized by	re-ed	re-edited by
me	mittelenglische	f, ff	folio, folios	rptd	reprinted
u	und	ME	Middle English	rvsd	revised
z	zu	n d	no date	unptd	unprinted

X. MIDDLE SCOTS WRITERS

by

Florence H. Ridley

1. JAMES I

GENERAL.

Language. Jamieson J, An Etymological Dictionary of the Scottish Language, 2 vols, Edinburgh 1808; rvsd J Longmuir and D Donaldson, 4 vols with suppl, Paisley 1879–82; new edn J Longmuir, London and Edinburgh 1885; another edn with introd by W M Metcalfe, Paisley 1912.

Murray J A H, A New English Dictionary on Historical Principles (The Oxford English Dictionary, ed J A H Murray, H Bradley, W A Craigie, C T Onions), Oxford 1884–1933.

Mackay C, A Dictionary of Lowland Scotch, Boston 1888.

Wright J, The English Dialect Dictionary, 8 vols, London 1896–1905.

Grant W and D D Murison, The Scottish National Dictionary, Edinburgh 1931—(crit Wittig, SSL 1.275).

Craigie W A and A J Aitken, eds., A Dictionary of the Older Scottish Tongue from the Twelfth Century to the End of the Seventeenth Founded on the Collections of Sir William A Craigie, Chicago and London 1931—.

MED.

Woolley J S, Bibliography for Scottish Linguistic Studies, Edinburgh 1954.

Murison D, A Survey of Scottish Language Studies, Forum Mod Lang Stud 3.276.

Authorship. Percy T, Reliques of Ancient English Poetry, London 1765 (numerous subsequent edns); ed H B Wheatley, London 1910, 2.67.

Dalrymple D, A Specimen of Notes on the Statute Law of Scotland, n p 1768, p 6.

Callander J, Two Ancient Scottish Poems The Gaberlunzie-man and Christ's Kirk on the Green, Edinburgh 1782, p 99.

Donaldson G, Statistical Account of Kenethmont, The Statistical Account of Scotland, ed J Sinclair, Edinburgh 1794, 13.77.

Ritson J, A Historical Essay on Scotish Song, Scotish Song, London 1794, 1.xxx, xxxvi.

Sibbald J, Chronicle of Scottish Poetry from the 13th Century to the Union of the Crowns, 4 vols, Edinburgh and London 1802, 1.55, 121, 137.

Irving D, The Lives of the Scotish Poets, 2 vols, Edinburgh 1804; 2nd edn improved London 1810, 1.304, 316.

Chalmers G, The Poetic Remains of Some of the Scotish Kings, London 1824, pp 105, 126.

Percy T, Letters from Thomas Percy . . . to George Paton, Edinburgh 1830, pp 19, 21.

Tytler P F, Lives of Scottish Worthies, London 1833, 3.68, 74.

Dauney W, Preliminary Dissertation, Ancient Scotish Melodies, Edinburgh 1838, p 165 and passim (possibility of James's being a composer).

Morley H, Shorter English Poems, London 1876, p 64.

Craik G L, A Compendious History of English Literature and of the English Language from the Norman Conquest, N Y 1877, 1.408.

Veitch J, History and Poetry of the Scottish Border, Edinburgh 1878; new and enlarged edn Edinburgh 1893, 2.54.

[Robertson J L] Haliburton H, For Puir Auld Scotland's Sake, Edinburgh and London 1887, p 36.

Eyre-Todd G, Mediæval Scottish Poetry, Abbotsford Series of the Scottish Poets, Glasgow 1892, p 21.

Major J, A History of Greater Britain, ed and trans A Constable, Edinburgh 1892, p 366.

Oxf Ch, 1.48.

Liddell M, The Authorship of a Spurious Chaucer Poem, Athen Dec 28 1895, p 902.

Brown J T T, The Bannatyne Manuscript a Sixteenth Century Poetical Miscellany, SHR 1.154.

Gibson A, New Light on Allan Ramsay, Edinburgh 1927, pp 108, 121.

Other Scholarly Problems. Tytler W, Dissertation on Scottish Music, Poetical Remains, Edinburgh 1783, p 195 (James as composer and musician); rptd Trans Soc of Antiquaries of Scotland, Edinburgh 1792, 1.471; rptd Perth 1827, p 249.

Macneill H, The Links O' Forth or a Parting Peep at the Carse O' Stirling a Plaint, Edinburgh 1799, stanza 36, note D (unpaged; James as composer).

Irving D, The Lives of the Scotish Poets, 2nd edn London 1810, 1.325 (lost works).

T J, James the First, Lives of Scottish Poets, ed J Robertson, London 1822, 1.23 (James as composer).

Chalmers G, The Poetic Remains of Some of the Scotish Kings, London 1824, pp v, 205 (documents in James' hand).

Tytler P F, Lives of Scottish Worthies, London 1833, 3.74 (contributions to Scottish music).

Laing D, The Poems of William Dunbar, 2 vols, Edinburgh 1834, 1.41 (paginated separately from text of poems; omission by Dunbar of reference to James).

Irving D, The History of Scotish Poetry, ed J A Carlyle, Edinburgh 1861, pp 152, 158 (lost poems; James as composer).

Morley H, Shorter English Poems, London 1876, p 64 (occasion).

Henderson T F, Scottish Vernacular Literature, Edinburgh 1898; 2nd edn rvsd 1900; 3rd edn rvsd 1910, p 103 (lost poems).

Whiting B J, Proverbs and Proverbial Sayings from Scottish Writings before 1600, MS 11.123; 13.87 (draws on works of James as well as other Scottish material).

Kinghorn A M, Scots Literature and Scottish Antiquarians 1750–1800, SE 33.46 (development of antiquarians' interest).

Whiting B J, Proverbs Sentences and Proverbial Phrases, Cambridge Mass 1968.

Bibliography. Bale J, Illustrium majoris Britanniae scriptorum, Ipswich 1548, f 194ᵇ; Scriptorum illustrium maioris Brytanniæ posterio pars, Basile 1559, p 217.

Thynne F, A generall catalog of the writers of Scotland, The Second volume of Chronicles . . . by Raphaell Holinshed, London 1586, p 461 (vague, brief reference).

Tanner T, Bibliotheca Britannico-Hibernica, ed D Wilkins, London 1748, p 426.

Walpole H, A Catalogue of the Royal and Noble Authors, Strawberry Hill 1758; 2nd edn London 1759; new edn Edinburgh 1796; London 1806, 5.3, 11.

Warton T, History of English Poetry from the 12th to the Close of the 16th Century, London 1774–81; ed W C Hazlitt, London 1871, 3.120.

Pinkerton J, Ancient Scotish Poems, 2 vols, London and Edinburgh 1786, l.lxxxviii.

Irving D, The Lives of the Scotish Poets, 2nd edn, London 1810, 1.298.

Brydges E and J Haslewood, The British Bibliographer, London 1814, 4.306.

Dempster T, Historia ecclesiastica gentis scotorum: sive de scriptoribus scotis, 2 vols, Bannatyne Club Publ no 21, Edinburgh 1829, 2.381.

Lowndes W T, The Bibliographer's Manual of English Literature, London 1834; new edn rvsd corrected and enlarged by H G Bohn, London (1871?), 2.1179.

G W, The Poet-King of Scotland, Fraser's Magazine ns 10.380; rptd Littell's Living Age 5s 123.234.

Craik G L, A Compendious History of English Literature, N Y 1877, 1.406 (brief).

Morley, 6.173; Körting, p 197.

Black G F, A List of Works Relating to Scotland, BNYPL Jan-Dec 1914; rptd N Y 1916, pp 492, 830.

Northup C S, J Q Adams and A Keogh, A Register of Bibliographies of the English Language and Literature, New Haven London and Oxford 1925, p 214.

Tucker-Benham, pp 13, 114.

Bronson B H, Ritson's Bibliographia Scotica, PMLA 52.149.

CBEL, 1.254; 5.147.

[1] THE KINGIS QUAIR.

MS. Bodl 3354 (Arch Selden B 24), ff 192ᵃ–211ᵃ (late 15 cent).

Skeat, edn, p xxxvii.

Brown J T T, The Authorship of The Kingis Quair A New Criticism, Glasgow and N Y 1896, pp 5, 70 (crit SRL 82.55; Arch 99.167; EStn 24.84; MLN 12.115; AnglB 7.98); rptd Trans Glasgow Archæological Soc ns 3.96, 145.

Hammond, p 341.

Lawson, edn, pp lxxvii, 126.

Summary Cat, no 3354.

Simon, edn, p 13.

Editions. Tytler W, Poetical Remains of James the First King of Scotland, Edinburgh 1783, p 55 (MS; crit Skeat, edn, p xliii); rptd W Lang, The Works of James the First King of Scotland, Glasgow 1825 (crit Skeat, edn, p li); rptd The Works of James the First King of Scotland, Perth 1827.

Morison R, The Works of James I King of Scotland, Perth 1786, p 1 (notes at end of text; crit Skeat, edn, p xlvi).

Sibbald J, Chronicle of Scottish Poetry from the 13th Century to the Union of the Crowns, 4 vols, Edinburgh and London 1802, 1.14 (160 stanzas; introductory note; crit Skeat, edn, p xlvii).

Thomson E, The King's Quair A Poem by James the First King of Scots with Explanatory Notes A Glossary &c, Air 1815 (Tytler, edn); 2nd edn Ayr 1824 (crit Skeat, edn, p 1); rptd J Thomson, Glasgow 1877 (printed); 1883 (published; crit Skeat, edn, p lii).

Chalmers G, The Poetic Remains of Some of the Scotish Kings, London 1824, p 23 (glossings at foot of page; MS; Tytler, edn; crit Skeat, edn, p xlviii).

Rogers C, The Poetical Remains of King James the First of Scotland with a Memoir and an Introduction to His Poetry, Trans Royal Hist Soc ns, London 1873, 2.321 (a few glossings and notes at foot of page; collation of Chalmers, edn, and Tytler, edn; crit Skeat, edn, p lii).

Ross J, The Book of Scottish Poems, Paisley 1882, 1.73 (brief introductory note).

Skeat W W, The Kingis Quair together with a Ballad of Good Counsel, PSTS 1, Edinburgh and London 1884; 2nd rvsd edn, PSTS ns 1, Edinburgh and London 1911, pp 1, 57 (MS; notes at end of text).

Eyre-Todd G, Mediæval Scottish Poetry, Abbotsford Series of the Scottish Poets, Glasgow 1892, p 25 (glossings in margin; Skeat, edn).

Steele R, Heirefter Followis the Quair Maid be King Iames of Scotland the First Callit the Kingis Quair and Maid Quhen His Maiestie Wes in Ingland, London 1903.

Lawson A, The Kingis Quair and The Quare of Jelusy, St Andrews Univ Publ no 8, London 1910, pp 3, 129 (notes at end of text; MS; crit M M Gray, SHR 8.305).

The King's Quair, London 1914.

Neilson W A and K G T Webster, Chief British Poets of the 14th and 15th Centuries, Boston N Y etc 1916, pp 347, 433 (notes at end of text, glossings at foot of page; Skeat, edn).

Mackenzie W M, The Kingis Quair, London 1939 (notes at end of text; MS; crit TLS Mar 2 1940, p 115).

Rossi S, I Chauceriani Scozzesi, Napoli 1964, p 76 (notes at foot of page).

Simon J R, Le Livre Du Roi (The Kingis Quair) attribué à Jacques Ier D'Ecosse, Paris 1967 (notes at end of text; MS; crit M D Legge, MLR 64.420; M P McDiarmid, SHR 49.195).

Selections. Ellis G, Specimens of the Early English Poets, 5 edns, London 1790, 1801, 1803, 1811, 1845 (5th edn corrected), 1.244 (spelling, occasional wording modernized; glossings at foot of page).

Campbell T, Specimens of the British Poets, London 1819, 2.73 (glossings at foot of page).

Tytler P F, Lives of Scottish Worthies, London 1833, 3.52 (Tytler, edn).

Craik G L, Sketches of the History of Literature and of Learning in England, London 1844, 1.189 (Chalmers, edn).

Aytoun W E, The Ballads of Scotland, Edinburgh and London 1858; 2nd edn rvsd and augmented, Edinburgh and London 1859, 1.lx (brief; illustrative of critical discussion).

Gilfillan G, Specimens with Memoirs of the Less-Known Poets, Edinburgh and London 1860, 1.41 (glossings at foot of page).

Irving D, The History of Scotish Poetry, ed J A Carlyle, Edinburgh 1861, p 136 (brief excerpts; Tytler, edn).

Bonar A R, The Poets and Poetry of Scotland, Edinburgh 1864; 2nd edn 1866, p 37 (spelling partially modernized).

Clarke C C, Specimens with Memoirs of the Less-Known British Poets, Edinburgh 1868, 1.39.

Masson R O, Three Centuries of English Poetry Being Selections from Chaucer to Herrick, London 1876, p 109 (spelling modernized; glossings at foot of page).

Wilson J G, The Poets and Poetry of Scotland, N Y 1876, 1.15.

Craik G L, A Compendious History of English Literature and of the English Language from the Norman Conquest, N Y 1877, 1.406 (Chalmers edn).

Ward T H, James the First of Scotland, The English Poets, London and N Y 1880; (numerous subsequent edns) N Y 1924, 1.132 (glossings at foot of page).

Collier W F, A History of English Literature, London 1886; new edn rvsd R B Johnson, London 1910, p 57.

Fitzgibbon H M, Early English Poetry Selected and Edited with a Critical Introd and Notes, The Canterbury Poets, ed W Sharp, London N Y and Melbourne 1887; another edn Early English and Scottish Poetry 1250–1600 Selected and Edited with a Critical Introd and Notes, London N Y and Melbourne 1888, pp 80, 430 (spelling modernized; notes at end of text).

Veitch J, The Feeling for Nature in Scottish Poetry, Edinburgh and London 1887, 1.187 (brief quotes interspersed with criticism; glossings in side notes; crit C Patmore, Out-of-door Poetry, St James's Gazette July 9 1887; rptd in Courage in Politics, London 1921, p 32).

Kaye W J, The Leading Poets of Scotland, London 1891, p 182.

Skeat Spec, pp 41, 381 (notes at end of text; MS; brief crit Skeat, edn, p lii).

Browne W H, Selections from the Early Scottish Poets, Baltimore 1896, pp 28, 179 (notes at end of text; Skeat, edn).

Harvey W, The Harp of Stirlingshire, Paisley 1897, p 19.

Quiller-Couch A, The Oxford Book of English Verse 1250–1900, Oxford 1900; new edn Oxford 1939, p 19 (glossings at foot of page).

Brown P H, The Kingis Quair and James I, Chambers' Cyclopædia of English Literature, ed D Patrick, Phila and N Y 1901–03; rvsd J L Geddie, Phila and N Y 1938, 1. 184.

Dixon W M, The Edinburgh Book of Scottish Verse 1300–1900, London 1910, p 7 (glossings at foot of page).

Douglas G, The Book of Scottish Poetry, London and Leipsic 1911, p 64 (glossings at foot of page; Skeat, edn).

Zupitza J, Alt- und mittelenglisches Übungsbuch, 10th edn, Vienna and Leipzig 1912, p 199 (variants at foot of page).

Brougham E M, Corn from Olde Fieldes, London 1918; rptd London 1922, p 146 (7 lines; spelling modernized).

Le Gallienne R, The Le Gallienne Book of English Verse, N Y 1923, p 7 (spelling modernized; brief).

Buchan J, The Northern Muse An Anthology of Scots Vernacular Poetry, London 1924, pp 13, 456 (glossings at foot of page; brief note at end of text).

Squire J C, The Cambridge Book of Lesser Poets, Cambridge 1927, p 29.

Patterson R F, Six Centuries of English Literature, London and Glasgow 1933, 1.83.

Mackie R L, A Book of Scottish Verse, The World's Classics no 417, London 1934, p 5 (glossings at foot of page); 2nd edn, London Glasgow N Y 1967, p 6.

Douglas R M, The Scots Book, London 1935, p 18 (14 lines; spelling modernized).

Gray M M, Scottish Poetry from Barbour to James VI, N Y 1935, p 21 (crit J Speirs, Scrut 6.83; W M Mackenzie, The Scottish Bookman 1, no 4, p 133).

[Grieve C M] MacDiarmid H, The Golden Treasury of Scottish Poetry, London 1940, p 128 (crit L MacNeice, The New Statesman and Nation 21.66; TLS Feb 15 1941, pp 78, 84); rptd in The Golden Treasury Series, London 1948, p 128.

Abramowitz I, Prince and Poet James I of Scotland The Coming of Love, The Great Prisoners, N Y 1946, p 65 (glossings at foot of page).

Fergusson J, The Green Garden, London and Edinburgh 1946, p 3 (spelling modernized).

Mackenzie A M, Scottish Pageant, Edinburgh 1946; 2nd edn 1952, 1.47, 50 (brief glossings at end of 2nd selection).

Oliver J W and J C Smith, A Scots Anthology from the 13th to the 20th Century, Edinburgh and London 1949, p 7 (spelling modernized; glossings at foot of page).

Auden W H and N H Pearson, Poets of the English Language, N Y 1950, p 276 (glossings at foot of page).

MacQueen J and T Scott, The Oxford Book of Scottish Verse, Oxford 1966, p 22 (glossings at foot of page; Mackenzie, edn; crit J Craigie, Engl 16.235).

Scott T, Late Medieval Scots Poetry, London 1967, pp 37, 183 (notes at end of text; Mackenzie, edn; crit A M F Gunn, SSL 5.137).

Kinghorn A M, The Middle Scots Poets, London 1970, p 53 (notes at foot of page; Skeat, edn; Mackenzie, edn).

MacQueen J, Ballattis of Luve, Edinburgh 1970, p 7 (Mackenzie, edn; glossings at foot of page).

Scott T, The Penguin Book of Scottish Verse, London 1970, p 63 (glossings at foot of page).

Sisam C and K Sisam, The Oxford Book of Medieval English Verse, Oxford 1970, p 409 (glossings at foot of page; MS).

Modernizations. Tytler P F, Lives of Scottish Worthies, London 1833, 3.53, 57, 65, 67.

Mackean W, The Kingis Quair by King James I of Scotland, London 1886; rptd Paisley 1908, p 1.

Smith R M, Two Scottish Chaucerians Being Modern Versions of The King's Quair and The Testament of Cresseid, Wesleyan Univ, Middletown Conn 1936, p 3 (based on Skeat, edn).

Loomis R S and R Willard, The King's Quair, Medieval English Verse and Prose, N Y 1948, pp 357, 555 (notes at end of text).

Textual Matters. Irving D, The Lives of the Scotish Poets, 2 vols, Edinburgh 1804; 2nd edn improved, London 1810, 1.299.

Chalmers, edn, p iii.

Tytler, edn, 1825, p 61.

Irving D, The History of Scotish Poetry, ed J A Carlyle, Edinburgh 1861, p 135.

G W, The Poet-King of Scotland, Fraser's Magazine ns 10.380; rptd Littell's Living Age 5s 123.234.

Skeat, edn, pp xv, xxxiv (includes description of edns).

Wischmann W, Untersuchungen über das Kingis Quair Jakobs I von Schottland, Berlin 1887, p 41 (explanation of obscurities in text and notes).

Eyre-Todd, edn, p 19 (brief).

Parker A F, The Kingis Quair, Athen Aug 15 1896, p 225.

Neilson G, The Scribe of the Kingis Quair, Athen Dec 16 1899, p 835.

Millar A H, The Scribe of The Kingis Quair, Athen Dec 30 1899, p 898.

Lawson, edn, pp lxxvii, 126.

Macdonald A, Notes on The Kingis Quair, MLR 34.569.

Mackenzie, edn, pp 11, 41, 127.

Craigie W A, The Language of the Kingis Quair, E&S 25.22.

Cronin G, Two Bibliographical Notes on The Kingis Quair, N&Q 181.341.

Wilson K G, The Lay of Sorrow and The Lufaris Complaynt An Edition, Spec 29.708 (discussion of MS).

Renoir A, A Note on Stanza 107 of The Kingis Quair, Arch 197.15.

Bain C· E, The Kingis Quair Two Emendations, N&Q 206(ns 8).168.

Bessai F, A Crux in The Kingis Quair, N&Q 207(ns 9).48.

Language. Sibbald, edn, vol. 4 [unpaged] (glossary).

Thomson, edn, p [95] (glossary).

Tytler, edn, 1825, Remarks on the Scots Language and its Intimate Connexion with the Other Northern Dialects, p 182 (generally applicable).

Irving D, The History of Scotish Poetry, Edinburgh 1861, p 595 (glossary).

Bonar A R, The Poets and Poetry of Scotland, Edinburgh 1864; 2nd edn 1866, p 397 (glossary).

Murray J A H, The Dialect of the Southern Counties of Scotland, London 1873.

Thomson J, The King's Quair, Glasgow 1877 (printed), 1883 (published), p [74] (glossary).

Skeat, edn, pp xxiv, xxxiii, lix, 102, 122 (introductory discussion; glossary; additions to Jamieson's dictionary).

Hahn O, Zur Verbal- und Nominalflexion bei den schottischen Dichtern, Berlin 1887–89 (generally applicable).

Wischmann W, Untersuchungen über das Kingis Quair, Berlin 1887, pp 2, 41.

Bearder J W, Über den Gebrauch der Praepositionen in der Altschottischen Poesie, Halle 1894 (examples from James; crit J E Wülfing, EStn 19.410).

Brown J T T, The Authorship of The Kingis Quair A New Criticism, Glasgow and N Y 1896, pp 21, 64, 81 (crit C J C, Literary Iconoclasm, SRL 82.55; A Brandl, Arch 99.167; M Kaluza, EStn 24.84; W H Browne, MLN 12.115; F Holthausen, AnglB 7.98); rptd Trans Glasgow Archæological Soc ns 3.93.

Browne W H, Selections from the Early Scottish Poets, Baltimore 1896, pp 1, 197 (discussion in introd; glossary).

Rait R S, The Kingis Quair and the New Criticism, Scottish Notes and Queries 11.155, 171, 183.

Browne W H, The Taill of Rauf Coilyear, Baltimore 1903, pp 10, 35, 139 (general discussion of Middle Scots; glossary).

Millar J H, A Literary History of Scotland, London 1903, p 687 (glossary).

Rodeffer J D, The Inflection of the English Present Plural Indicative, Baltimore 1903, pp 1, 23, 38 (results of language study apply to Kingis Quair, no specific study of it).

CHEL, 2.101, 506 (generally applicable).

Dixon W M, The Edinburgh Book of Scottish Verse, London 1910, p 897 (glossary).

Lawson, edn, pp xliii, xlix, lviii, lxxxiii, lxxxvi, 156 (glossary at end of text; discussion).

Skeat W W, The Author of Lancelot of the Laik, SHR 8.1 (brief references comparing phonology with that of Quair of Jelousy and Lancelot of the Laik).

Gray M M, Introd, Lancelot of the Laik, PSTS ns 2, Edinburgh and London 1912, 2.xviii.

Zupitza J, Wörterbuch, Alt- und mittelenglisches Übungsbuch, 10th edn, Vienna and

Leipzig 1912, p 208 (glossary, definitions in German).

The King's Quair, London 1914, p 68 (glossary).

MacLean C M, Alexander Scott, Montgomerie and Drummond of Hawthornden as Lyric Poets, Cambridge 1915, p 1 (brief).

Taylor R, Some Notes on the Use of Can and Couth as Preteritive Auxiliaries in Early and Middle Scottish Poetry, JEGP 16.573.

Watt L M, Language and Influences, Douglas's Aeneid, Cambridge 1920, p 149 (generally applicable; crit C R Baskerville, MP 18.171; J W Bright, MLN 35.508; O L Jiriczek, LfGRP 42.379; G D Willcock, MLR 15.432; TLS Apr 1 1920, p 210).

Ritchie R L G, Early Instances of French Loan-Words in Scots and English, EStn 63.41 (1 example from James).

Wood H H, The Poems and Fables of Robert Henryson, Edinburgh 1933; 2nd edn rvsd, Edinburgh 1958; rptd 1965, 1968, p xxxi (generally applicable).

Douglas R M, The Scots Book, London 1935, pp 162, 338 (discussion of Scots language; glossary).

Patrick D, Scottish Literature, Chambers's Cyclopædia of English Literature, rvsd J L Geddie, Phila and N Y 1938, 1.164.

Mackenzie, edn, pp 29, 39, 128, 138 (discussion; glossary).

Craigie W A, The Language of the Kingis Quair, E&S 25.22.

[Grieve C M] MacDiarmid H, The Golden Treasury, London 1948, p 392 (glossary).

Fergusson J, The Green Garden, London and Edinburgh 1946, p 228 (glossary).

Oliver J W and J C Smith, A Scots Anthology, Edinburgh and London 1949, p 497 (glossaries).

Renwick-Orton, p 117.

Rossi, edn, p 261 (discussion, glossary).

Scott T, Dunbar A Critical Exposition of the Poems, Edinburgh and London 1966, p 351; Late Medieval Scots Poetry, London 1967, pp 21, 189 (discussion, glossary).

Simon, edn, pp 26, 35, 345 (discussion, glossary).

Kinghorn A M, The Middle Scots Poets, London 1970, pp 45, 164 (a note on Middle Scots; glossary).

Versification. Schipper, passim (crit E Einenkel, Angl 5.139).

Skeat, edn, pp xxxi, 120 (includes Rime Index).

Mackean W, The Kingis Quair, London 1886; rptd Paisley 1908, p xiii.

Bulloch J M, French Metres in Early Scottish Poetry, Scottish Notes and Queries 2.114, 130.

Brandl, 2¹.713, 1070.

Browne W H, Selections from the Early Scottish Poets, Baltimore 1896, p 11 (very brief).

Saintsbury G, History of English Prosody from the 12th Century to the Present Day, London 1908 (crit W P Ker, SHR 4.214); 2nd edn, London 1923, 1.270.

Lawson, edn, pp lxix, lxxii.

Saintsbury G, Historical Manual of English Prosody, London 1910; rptd London 1914, 1.56, 163.

Watt L M, Scottish Life and Poetry, London 1912, p 81.

Hammond E P, English Verse between Chaucer and Surrey, Durham N C and London 1927, p 25 (brief).

Hamer E, The Metres of English Poetry, N Y 1930, p 153 (brief).

Renwick-Orton, p 412 (brief).

Southworth J G, Verses of Cadence, Oxford 1954, p 82.

Scott T, Late Medieval Scots Poetry, London 1967, p 18.

Simon, edn, p 177.

Date. Paterson J, James the Fifth or the Gudeman of Ballangeich His Poetry and Adventures, Edinburgh 1861, p 124.

Craik G L, A Compendious History of English Literature, N Y 1877, 1.405.

Skeat, edn, p lviii.

Wischmann W, Untersuchungen über das Kingis Quair, Berlin 1887, p 33.

Eyre-Todd, edn, p 19.

Millar A H, The Kingis Quair, Athen July 11 1896, p 66; Aug 15 1896, p 225 (date of MS).

Brown J T T, The Kingis Quair, Athen Aug 1 1896,, p 165.

Rait R S, The Kingis Quair and the New Criticism, Scottish Notes and Queries 11.171, 182.

CHEL, 2.277.

Skeat W W, The Author of Lancelot of the Laik, SHR 8.2, 4 (brief).

Craigie J, The Kingis Quair, TLS Apr 20 1940, p 200.

Stock N, Some Notes on Old Scots and Melodic Line in Verse, Shenandoah 6, no 2, p 25.

Bain C E, A Valentine for Queen Joanne, Emory Univ Quarterly 17.234.

Simon, edn, p 14.

Authorship. Paterson J, James the Fifth,

Edinburgh 1861, pp 123, 131, 135.

Skeat, edn, pp xvi, lv.

Brown J T T, The Authorship of The Kingis Quair A New Criticism, Glasgow and N Y 1896 (crit SRL 82.55; Arch 99.167; EStn 24.84; MLN 12.115; AnglB 7.98); rptd Trans Glasgow Archæological Soc ns 3.93.

Jusserand J J, The Romance of a King's Life, trans from the French by M R; rvsd and enlarged London 1896, p 87.

Millar A H, The Kingis Quair, Athen July 11 1896, p 66; Aug 1 1896, p 164; Aug 15 1896, p 225.

C J C, Literary Iconoclasm, SRL 82.55.

Brown J T T, The Kingis Quair, Athen July 25 1896, p 128; Aug 8 1896, p 193; Aug 29 1896, p 291.

Jusserand J J, The Kingis Quair, Athen Aug 15 1896, p 225; Jacques 1er d'Écosse Fut-il Poète? Revue Historique 64.1; rptd Étude sur l'authenticité du Cahier du Roi, Paris 1897 (crit W H Browne, MLN 12.417).

Macintosh W, The King's Quhair, Scottish Notes and Queries 11.36, 53.

Henderson T F, Scottish Vernacular Literature, Edinburgh 1898 (crit G Binz, AnglB 10.291); 2nd edn rvsd, Edinburgh 1900; 3rd edn rvsd, Edinburgh 1910, p 95.

Rait R S, The Kingis Quair and the New Criticism, Scottish Notes and Queries 11.140, 153, 171, 182.

Neilson W A, The Origins and Sources of the Court of Love, Studies and Notes in Philology and Literature 6(1899).155, 235.

Skeat W W, The King's Quair and The Romaunt of the Rose, Athen July 22 1899, p 129.

Neilson G, The Scribe of the Kingis Quair, Athen Dec 16 1899, p 835.

Millar A H, The Scribe of The Kingis Quair, Athen Dec 30 1899, p 898.

Smith G G, The Transition Period, Periods of European Literature, Edinburgh and London 1900, 4.40, 92, 94.

Brown P H, The Kingis Quair and James I, Chambers's Cyclopædia, Phila and N Y 1901–03; rvsd J L Geddie 1938, 1.183.

Millar J H, A Literary History of Scotland, London 1903, p 23.

Lang A, A History of Scotland from the Roman Occupation, 4th edn, Edinburgh and London 1907, 1.314.

Murdoch W G B, The Royal Stewarts in Their Literary Connection with Arts and Letters, Edinburgh 1908, p 30.

Lawson, edn, pp xliii, lxxiii, 126.

Watt L M, Scottish Life and Poetry, London 1912, p 84.

Henderson T F, The Royal Stewarts, Edinburgh and London 1914, p 32.

Buchan J, Homilies and Recreations, London 1926, p 309.

Balfour-Melville E W M, James I at Windsor in 1423, SHR 25.226.

Saintsbury G, The Four Great Scottish Poets, A Short History of English Literature, N Y 1929, p 180.

Balfour-Melville E W M, James I King of Scots, London 1936, p 279 (crit J D Mackie, EHR 52.506; H G Stafford, The American Historical Review 43.363).

Macdonald A, The Kingis Quair, TLS Mar 20 1937, p 222.

Mackenzie, edn, p 16.

Craigie W A, The Language of the Kingis Quair, E&S 25.22.

Bennett OHEL, p 172; Renwick-Orton, p 413 (brief).

Wood H H, Scottish Literature, London 1952, p 13.

Ward A C, Illustrated History of English Literature, London N Y and Toronto 1953, p 40 (brief).

Kinghorn A M, The Mediaeval Makars, Texas Stud Lit and Lang 1.75.

Slabey R M, Art Poetical in The Kingis Quair, N&Q 205(ns 7).208.

Bain C E, A Valentine for Queen Joanne, Emory Univ Quarterly 17.233.

Dickinson W C, Scotland from the Earliest Times to 1603, A New History of Scotland, Edinburgh and London 1961, 1.218.

Kinghorn A M, Warton's History and Early English Poetry, ESts 44.202.

Rossi, edn, pp 26, 31.

Von Hendy A, The Free Thrall a Study of the Kingis Quair, SSL 2.141, 148.

Simon, edn, p 17.

Sources and Literary Relations. Irving D, The Lives of the Scotish Poets, 2nd edn, London 1810, 1.302.

T J, James the First, Lives of Scottish Poets, ed J Robertson, London 1822, 1.8, 20.

Tytler P F, Lives of Scottish Worthies, London 1833, 3.51, 68.

Craik G L, Sketches of the History of Literature and Learning in England, London 1844, 1.187, 192 (brief).

Aytoun W E, The Ballads of Scotland, 2nd edn, Edinburgh and London 1859, 1.lx, lxii.

Gilfillan G, Specimens with Memoirs, Edinburgh and London 1860, 1.39 (brief).

Smith A, William Dunbar Dreamthorp, London 1863; rptd The World's Classics no

200, London 1914; rptd London 1934, pp 60, 64.

Morley H, A First Sketch of English Literature, London 1873; rvsd London 1896, p 177.

Wright T, The History of Scotland from the Earliest Period to the Present Time, London and N Y [1873–74], 1.288.

Craik G L, A Manual of English Literature, Leipzig 1874, 1.226 (brief).

G W, The Poet-King of Scotland, Fraser's Magazine ns 10.382; rptd Littell's Living Age 5s 123.236.

Craik G L, A Compendious History of English Literature, N Y 1877, 1.405, 408.

Ward T H, James the First, The English Poets, N Y 1924, 1.129.

Wood H, Chaucer's Influence upon King James I of Scotland as Poet, Angl 3.223.

Nichol J, A Sketch of Scottish Poetry up to the Time of Sir David Lyndesay, ed J Small; 2nd edn rvsd, EETS 11, London 1883, p xviii.

Ross J M, Scottish History and Literature to the Period of the Reformation, Glasgow 1884, pp 149, 154.

Schipper J, William Dunbar sein Leben und seine Gedichte, Berlin 1884, pp 23, 26, 30. Skeat, edn, pp xxii, liii.

Mackean W, The Kingis Quair, London 1886; rptd Paisley 1908, p xii.

Fitzgibbon H M, Early English and Scottish Poetry, London N Y and Melbourne 1888, p. lvi.

Shairp J C, Sketches in History and Poetry, Edinburgh 1887, pp 204, 249, 252, 266.

Wischmann W, Untersuchungen über das Kingis Quair, Berlin 1887, p 1.

Minto W, Characteristics of English Poets from Chaucer to Shirley, authorized American edn, Boston 1889, p 94.

Bierfreund T, Kong Jakob I af Skotland, The King's Quair, Palemon og Arcite en Literaturhistorisk undersøgelse, Copenhagen 1891, p 26.

Schick J, Introd [and] Notes, Lydgate's Temple of Glas, EETSES 60, London 1891, pp cxxix, 69 (scattered references in Notes). Eyre-Todd, edn, p 20.

Brandl, 2¹.713, 1034; Courthope, passim.

Jusserand J J, Histoire littéraire du peuple Anglais, 2 vols, Paris 1894, 1.523.

Brown J T T, The Authorship of the Kingis Quair A New Criticism, Glasgow and N Y 1896, pp 21, 29, 65, 81 (crit SRL 82.55; Arch 99.167; EStn 24.84; MLN 12.115; AnglB 7.98); rptd Trans Glasgow Archæological Soc ns 3.93.

Turnbull W R, The Heritage of Burns, Haddington 1896, p 240 (brief).

Skeat W W, The Kingis Quair, Athen July 25 1896, p 129.

Brown J T T, The Kingis Quair, Athen Aug 1 1896, p 165.

Millar A H, The Kingis Quair, Athen Aug 1 1896, p 165.

Jusserand J J, The Kingis Quair, Athen Aug 15 1896, p 226.

Gosse E, A Short History of Modern English Literature, N Y 1897; rvsd edn N Y 1906, p 38.

Oxf Ch, 7.lxxv, 540 (brief reference to resemblance to The Court of Love).

Henderson T F, Scottish Vernacular Literature, Edinburgh 1898; 3rd edn rvsd, Edinburgh 1910, p 98.

Rait R S, The Kingis Quair and the New Criticism, Scottish Notes and Queries 11.153, 171, 182.

Neilson W A, The Origins and Sources of the Court of Love, Studies and Notes in Philology and Literature 6.152, 239.

Skeat W W, The King's Quair and The Romaunt of the Rose, Athen July 8 1899, p 66; The Chaucer Canon, Oxford 1900, p 84.

Smith G G, The Transition Period, Periods of European Lit, Edinburgh and London 1900, 4.36, 39, and passim (Chaucer, Romance of the Rose).

Brown P H, The Kingis Quair and James I, Chambers's Cyclopædia, Phila and N Y 1901–03; rvsd J L Geddie 1938, 1.183.

M'Ilwraith W, A Sketch of Scottish Literature from the Earliest Times, Annual Burns Chronicle 10.17.

Ritter O, Quellenstudien zu Robert Burns, Palaes 20.passim.

Mebus F, Studien zu William Dunbar, Breslau 1902, pp 12, 14, 16, 35, 40, 44, 55, 79, 86, 89, 92 (crit R Ackermann, AnglB 14.77; M Weyrauch, EStn 32.126).

Browne W H, The Taill of Rauf Coilyear, Baltimore 1903, p 9.

Ranken T E, The Scottish Reformation and Vernacular Literature, The Month 103.268.

Moorman F W, The Interpretation of Nature in English Poetry from Beowulf to Shakespeare, QF 95.135.

Smeaton O, The Story of Edinburgh, London 1905, p 402 (brief).

Snell F J, The Poets, The Age of Transition, London 1905, 1.64.

Marsh G L, Sources and Analogues of The Flower and the Leaf, MP 4.315, 319.

Mebus F, Beiträge zu William Dunbars

gedicht The Goldin Terge, EStn 39.passim. CHEL, 2.273 and passim.

Steinberger C, Étude sur William Dunbar, Dublin 1908, pp 50, 54 (Chaucer).

Lawson, edn, pp xliii, l, lv, lxxxvii.

Brown J T T, Vidas Achinlek Chevalier, SHR 8.325 (brief).

Enc Brit, 15.139 (brief).

Gray M M, Introd, Lancelot of the Laik, PSTS ns 2, Edinburgh and London 1912, 2. xviii, xxxv.

Watt L M, Scottish Life and Poetry, London 1912, pp 80, 84.

Rhys E, The First Scottish Poets, Lyric Poetry, London Toronto and N Y 1913, p 94.

Mackie R L, Scotland, London 1916, p 248.

Taylor R, Some Notes on the Use of Can and Couth, JEGP 16.588.

Mendenhall J C, Aureate Terms A Study in the Literary Diction of the 15th Century, Lancaster Pa 1919.

Smith G G, Scottish Literature Character and Influence, London 1919, pp 79, 98 (brief references; crit The Spectator 123.279; TLS July 17 1919, p 387).

Knowlton E C, Nature in Middle English, JEGP 20.191, 207.

Barfield O, The Scottish Chaucerians, The New Statesman 17.273.

Golding L, The Scottish Chaucerians, The Saturday Review of Politics Literature Science and Art 134.782.

Quiller-Couch A, Studies in Literature, 2s, N Y and Cambridge Eng 1922, p 264.

Holzknecht K J, Literary Patronage in the Middle Ages, Phila 1923, p 239 (very brief).

Hammond E P, English Verse between Chaucer and Surrey, Durham N C and London 1927, p 25 (brief).

Patch H R, The Goddess Fortuna in Mediaeval Literature, Cambridge Mass 1927, passim.

Ker W P, Form and Style in Poetry, London 1928, p 82 (brief).

Legouis HEL, p 169.

Saintsbury G, The Four Great Scottish Poets, N Y 1929, p 181.

Nichols P H, Lydgate's Influence on the Aureate Terms of the Scottish Chaucerians, PMLA 47.519.

Brown J T T, The Quare of Jelusy, Miscellany Volume, PSTS 3s 4, Edinburgh and London 1933, p 191.

Elton O, The English Muse, London 1933, p 81.

Mackenzie A M, An Historical Survey of Scottish Literature to 1714, London 1933, p 72 (crit The Modern Scot 4.164).

Wood H H, Robert Henryson, Edinburgh Essays on Scots Literature, Edinburgh and London 1933, p 3 (crit The Modern Scot 4.353).

Rait R and G S Pryde, Scotland, N Y 1934; 2nd edn London 1954, pp 308, 314 (brief).

Smith J M, The French Background of Middle Scots Literature, Edinburgh and London 1934, p 97 and passim (crit K Brunner, AnglB 45.265; R L G Ritchie, MÆ 4.44).

Gray M M, Scottish Poetry from Barbour to James VI, N Y 1935, p vii (crit J Speirs, Scrut 6.83; W M Mackenzie, The Scottish Bookman 1, no 4, p 133).

Linklater E, The Question of Culture, The Lion and the Unicorn, London 1935, pp 111, 127 (brief).

Power W, Literature and Oatmeal, London 1935, p 40 (brief; crit K Arns, AnglB 48.151; D Daiches, The Scottish Bookman 1, no 4, p 152).

Smith R M, Two Scottish Chaucerians, Wesleyan Univ, Middletown Conn 1936, p 3 (resemblances particularly to Chaucer pointed out in footnotes).

Patrick D, Scottish Literature, Chambers's Cyclopædia, rvsd J L Geddie, Phila and N Y 1938, 1.166.

Mackenzie, edn, pp 28, 128.

Speirs J, The Scots Literary Tradition, London 1940, p 5 and passim (crit J C Maxwell, Scottish Literature, Scrut 9.193); rvsd 2nd edn London 1962, p 33 and passim.

Grierson H J C and J C Smith, A Critical History of English Poetry, London 1944; 2nd rvsd edn London 1947, p 53 (brief).

Stearns M W, Henryson and Chaucer, MLQ 6.278, 281 (brief).

Abramowitz I, Prince and Poet James I, N Y 1946, p 65.

Bennett OHEL, p 170.

Craig HEL, p 166 (brief).

Renwick-Orton, pp 118, 412 (brief).

Ward A C, Illustrated History of Eng Lit, London N Y and Toronto 1953, pp 31, 40 (brief).

Lewis C S, English Literature in the Sixteenth Century, Oxford 1954, p 236 and passim (brief).

Southworth J G, Verses of Cadence, Oxford 1954, p 82.

Wilson K G, The Lay of Sorrow and The Lufaris Complaynt, Spec 29.709 (brief).

Kinsley J, The Mediaeval Makars, Scottish Poetry A Critical Survey, London 1955, p 11.

Rossi S, Robert Henryson, Milan 1955, p 44.

Sells A L, The Italian Influence in English Poetry, Bloomington Ind 1955, p 62.

Preston J, Fortunys Exiltree A Study of The Kingis Quair, RES ns 7.339, 347.

Schlauch M, English Medieval Literature and Its Social Foundations, Warsaw 1956, p 293.

Bennett J A W, The Parlement of Foules, Oxford 1957, pp 59, 75, 86, 96, 110, 149, 161, 184.

Enkvist N E, The Seasons of the Year Chapters on a Motif from Beowulf to the Shepherd's Calendar, Societas Scientiarum Fennica Commentationes Humanarum Litterarum, Helsingfors 1957, 22⁴.134.

Markland M F, The Structure of the Kingis Quair, Research Studies of the State College of Washington 25.273.

Wittig K, The Scottish Tradition in Literature, Edinburgh 1958, p 34 (crit TLS July 11 1958, p 392).

Kinghorn A M, The Mediaeval Makars, Texas Stud Lit and Lang 1.73.

Rohrberger M, The Kingis Quair An Evaluation, Texas Stud Lit and Lang 2.292, 301.

Slabey R M, Art Poetical in The Kingis Quair, N&Q 205(ns 7).208.

Bain C E, A Valentine for Queen Joanne, Emory Univ Quarterly 17.234, 239, 242.

MacQueen J, Tradition and the Interpretation of the Kingis Quair, RES ns 12.117.

Chew S C, The Pilgrimage of Life, New Haven and London 1962, pp 48, 53.

Elliott C, Robert Henryson Poems, Oxford 1963, p vii (brief); rptd from corrected sheets, Oxford 1966.

Bain C E, The Nightingale and the Dove, Tenn Studies in Lit 9.22.

Maxwell J C, An Echo of Chaucer in The Kingis Quair, N&Q 209(ns 11).172.

Rossi, edn, p 26.

Von Hendy A, The Free Thrall, SSL 2.141.

Bain C E, The Kingis Quair 155:2, ESts 47.420.

Fox D, The Scottish Chaucerians, in Chaucer and Chaucerians, ed D S Brewer, University, Alabama 1966, p 164.

Scott T, Dunbar A Critical Exposition of the Poems, Edinburgh and London 1966, p 354.

MacQueen J, Robert Henryson A Study of the Major Narrative Poems, London 1967, pp 15, 154, 220; Some Aspects of the Early Renaissance in Scotland, Forum Mod Lang Stud 3.204.

Scott T, Late Medieval Scots Poetry, London 1967, pp 7, 13.

Simon, edn, pp 31, 203.

Wood H H, Two Scots Chaucerians, Writers and Their Work no 201, ed G Bullough, London 1967, p 7 (crit D Fox, SSL 7.128).

Bennett J A W, Chaucer's Book of Fame, Oxford 1968, p 170.

Brown I, The Mental Traveller A Study of the Kingis Quair, SSL 5.247.

Lawlor J, Chaucer, London 1968, p 174.

Other Scholarly Problems. Shairp J C, Sketches in History and Poetry, Edinburgh 1887, p 248 (occasion).

Lorne [Marquis of] K T, The Governor's Guide to Windsor Castle, London 1895; rptd 1896, 1897, p 86 (occasion).

Neilson G, The Scribe of the Kingis Quair, Athen Dec 16 1899, p 835 (identity of scribe of MS).

MacCracken H N, King James' Claim to Rhyme Royal, MLN 24.31 (origin of a term).

Kinghorn A M, Scots Literature and Scottish Antiquarians 1750–1800, SE 33.46, 52 (development of antiquarians' interest).

Schlauch M, English Medieval Literature and Its Social Foundations, Warsaw 1956, p 293 (occasion).

Bain C E, A Valentine for Queen Joanne, Emory Univ Quarterly 17.232, 238 (biographical evidence).

Kinghorn A M, Warton's History and Early English Poetry, ESts 44.202.

Whiting B J, Proverbs Sentences and Proverbial Phrases, Cambridge Mass 1968.

Literary Criticism. Walpole H, A Catalogue of the Royal and Noble Authors, Strawberry Hill 1758; 2nd edn London 1759; new edn Edinburgh 1796; London 1806, 5.12 (brief; illustrative quotes).

Henry R, The History of Great Britain, London 1771–85; 6th edn London 1823, 10.214, 216, 218.

Warton T, History of English Poetry from the 12th to the Close of the 16th Century, London 1774–81; ed W C Hazlitt, London 1871, 3.120.

Tytler, edn, p 58.

Morison, edn, p ii.

Pinkerton J, Ancient Scotish Poems, 2 vols, London and Edinburgh 1786, 1.lxxxix.

Irving D, The Lives of the Scotish Poets, 2nd edn, London 1810, 1.316.

don 1810, 1.316.

Irving W, A Royal Poet, Blackwood's Edinburgh Magazine 6.557; rptd The Sketch-Book, The Complete Works of Washington Irving, N Y [19–?], 9.70.

T J, James the First, Lives of Scottish Poets, ed J Robertson, London 1822, 1.7, 18, 27.

Tytler P F, Lives of Scottish Worthies, London 1833, 3.52 (illustrative quotes).

Laing D, The Poems of William Dunbar, 2 vols, Edinburgh 1834, 1.41 (brief; paginated separately from text of poems).

Craik G L, Sketches of the History of Literature, London 1844, 1.188 (brief).

Aytoun W E, The Ballads of Scotland, 2nd edn, Edinburgh and London 1859, 1.lix, lxi.

Gilfillan G, Specimens with Memoirs, Edinburgh and London 1860, 1.39 (brief).

Irving D, The History of Scotish Poetry, ed J A Carlyle, Edinburgh 1861, p 134 (illustrative quotes).

Taylor J, The Imperial Dictionary of Universal Biography, London [1863], 3.12 (very brief).

Morley H, A First Sketch of English Literature, London 1873; rvsd London 1896, p 177.

Rogers, edn, 2.316.

Wright T, The History of Scotland, London and N Y [1873–74], 1.289.

Craik G L, A Manual of English Literature, Leipzig 1874, 1.226 (brief).

G W, The Poet-King of Scotland, Fraser's Magazine ns 10.379; rptd Littell's Living Age 5s 123.234.

Wilson J G, The Poets and Poetry of Scotland, N Y 1876, 1.13 (brief).

Craik G L, A Compendious History of English Literature, N Y 1877, 1.405.

Ward T H, James the First, The English Poets, N Y 1924, 1.129.

Wood H, Chaucer's Influence upon King James I of Scotland as Poet, Angl 3.223, 260.

Nichol J, A Sketch of Scottish Poetry, in J Small, Lyndesay's Monarche, etc, EETS 11, London 1883, p xviii.

Ross J M, Scottish History and Literature, Glasgow 1884, p 148 and passim.

Schipper J, William Dunbar, Berlin 1884, p 26.

Skeat, edn, p xi.

Mackean W, The Kingis Quair, London 1886; rptd Paisley 1908, p xiii.

Fitzgibbon H M, Early English and Scottish Poetry, N Y London and Melbourne 1888, pp lvi, lxvii.

Morley, 6.166.

Scott W B, Essay on the King's Quair, Illustrations to The King's Quair of King James I of Scotland Painted on the Staircase of Penkill Castle, Edinburgh 1887, p 8 (largely paraphrase interspersed with modernized quotes).

Shairp J C, Sketches in History and Poetry, Edinburgh 1887, pp 205, 249.

Skelton J, Maitland of Lethington and the Scotland of Mary Stuart, Edinburgh 1887, 1.106.

Veitch J, The Feeling for Nature in Scottish Poetry, Edinburgh and London 1887, 1.186 (with illustrative quotes).

Minto W, Characteristics of English Poets, authorized American edn, Boston 1889, p 94.

Oliphant [M], Royal Edinburgh, London and N Y 1890, pp 55, 62 (superficial).

Bierfreund T, Kong Jakob I af Skotland, Copenhagen 1891, p 26.

Kaye W J, The Leading Poets of Scotland, London 1891, p 181 (brief).

Eyre-Todd, edn, p 19.

Angellier A, Robert Burns les Oeuvers, Paris 1893, p 43.

Brandl, 2¹.713; Courthope, passim.

Jusserand J J, Histoire littéraire du peuple Anglais, Paris 1894, 1.523.

Maxwell D, Bygone Scotland, Edinburgh Hull and London 1894, p 81 (brief).

Wylie J H, History of England under Henry the Fourth, London 1894, 2.406 (brief).

Callaghan J, The King's Quair, The Scots Magazine ns 14.112.

Jusserand J J, Le Roman d'un Roi d'Écosse, Paris 1895, p 17; trans by M R, The Romance of a King's Life, London 1896, p 24.

Turnbull W R, The Heritage of Burns, Had-

Gosse E, A Short History of Modern English Literature, N Y 1897; rvsd edn N Y 1906, p 38.

Henderson T F, Scottish Vernacular Literature, Edinburgh 1898; 3rd edn rvsd, Edinburgh 1910, p 99.

Neilson W A, The Origins and Sources of the Court of Love, Studies and Notes in Philology and Literature 6.152, 210.

Smith G G, The Transition Period, Periods of European Lit, Edinburgh and London 1900, 4.40 and passim.

Brown P H, The Kingis Quair and James I, Chambers's Cyclopædia, Phila and N Y 1901–03; rvsd J L Geddie 1938, 1.184.

M'Ilwraith W, A Sketch of Scottish Literature, Annual Burns Chronicle 10.17.

Browne W H, The Taill of Rauf Coilyear, Baltimore 1903, p 9.

Millar J H, A Literary History of Scotland,

London 1903, p 23.

Ranken T E, The Scottish Reformation and Vernacular Literature, The Month 103.268.

Moorman F W, The Interpretation of Nature in English Poetry from Beowulf to Shakespeare, QF 95.135.

Snell F J, The Poets, The Age of Transition, London 1905, 1.63 and passim.

Murdoch W G B, The Royal Stewarts, Edinburgh 1908, p 32.

CHEL, 2.273 and passim.

Steinberger C, Étude sur William Dunbar, Dublin 1908, p 50.

Lawson, edn, pp lvi, lx, lxxxvii.

Enc Brit, 15.139 (brief).

Watt L M, Scottish Life and Poetry, London 1912, pp 80, 84, 89.

Rhys E, The First Scottish Poets, Lyric Poetry, London Toronto and N Y 1913, p 94.

Henderson T F, The Royal Stewarts, Edinburgh and London 1914, p 32 (brief).

Mackie R L, Scotland, London 1916, p 248 (brief).

Knowlton E C, Nature in Middle English, JEGP 20.191.

Barfield O, The Scottish Chaucerians, The New Statesman 17.273.

Quiller-Couch A, Studies in Literature, 2s, N Y and Cambridge Eng 1922, p 264.

Golding L, The Scottish Chaucerians, Saturday Review of Politics Literature Science and Art 134.783.

Hammond E P, English Verse between Chaucer and Surrey, Durham N C and London 1927, p 25 (brief).

Ker W P, Form and Style in Poetry, London 1928, p 82 (brief).

Legouis HEL, p 169.

Saintsbury G, The Four Great Scottish Poets, N Y 1929, p 181.

Lewis C S, The Kingis Quair, TLS Apr 18 1929, p 315.

Taylor R A, Dunbar the Poet and His Period, The Poets on the Poets, no 4, London 1931, p 73 (crit J M Reeves, The Criterion 11.331; TLS Mar 17 1932, p 199; D Everett, YWES 13,124); rptd Freeport Long Island N Y 1970.

Nichols P H, Lydgate's Influence on the Aureate Terms of the Scottish Chaucerians, PMLA 47.519.

Elton O, The English Muse, London 1933, p 82.

Mackenzie A M, An Historical Survey of Scottish Literature, London 1933, p 72 (crit The Modern Scot 4.164).

Wood H H, Robert Henryson, Edinburgh Essays on Scots Literature, Edinburgh and London 1933, p 2 (crit The Modern Scot 4.353).

Rait R and G S Pryde, Scotland, N Y 1934; 2nd edn London 1954, p 308 (brief).

Smith J M, The French Background of Middle Scots Literature, Edinburgh and London 1934, p 50 (brief; crit K Brunner AnglB 45.265; R L G Ritchie, MÆ 4.44)

Gray M M, Scottish Poetry, N Y 1935, p vii (crit J Speirs, Scrut 6.83; W M Mackenzie The Scottish Bookman 1, no 4, p 133).

Mackenzie A M, The Rise of the Stewarts London 1935, p 145 (very brief).

Power W, Literature and Oatmeal, London 1935, p 40 (brief; crit K Arns, AnglB 48.151 D Daiches, The Scottish Bookman 1, no 4 p 152).

Grierson H J C, The Problem of the Scottish Poet, E&S 21.105 (very brief).

Lewis C S, The Allegory of Love, London 1936; rptd London 1953, passim.

Mackenzie, edn, pp 26, 37.

Speirs J, The Scots Literary Tradition, London 1940, p 5 and passim (crit J C Maxwell, Scrut 9.193); rvsd edn, London 1962 p 33 and passim.

Cronin G, Two Bibliographical Notes on The Kingis Quair, N&Q 181.342.

Grierson H J C and J C Smith, A Critical History of English Poetry, London 1944 2nd edn rvsd London 1947, p 54 (brief)

Abramowitz I, Prince and Poet James I, N Y 1946, p 65.

Bennett OHEL, p 170; Craig HEL, p 16 (brief); Renwick-Orton, pp 117, 412 (brief)

Wood H H, Scottish Literature, London 1952 p 13.

Ward A C, Illustrated History of Eng Lit London N Y and Toronto 1953, p 4 (brief).

Hyman S E, The Language of Scottish Poetry, KR 16.31 (brief).

Lewis C S, English Literature in the Sixteenth Century, Oxford 1954, p 235 and passim (brief).

Kinsley J, The Mediaeval Makars, London 1955, p 11.

Sells A L, The Italian Influence in English Poetry, Bloomington Ind 1955, p 61.

Stock N, Some Notes on Old Scots and Melodic Line in Verse, Shenandoah 6, no 2, 29.

Preston J, Fortunys Exiltree, RES ns 7.33

Schlauch M, English Medieval Literature an

Its Social Foundations, Warsaw 1956, p 293.

Enkvist N E, The Seasons of the Year Chapters on a Motif from Beowulf to the Shepherd's Calendar, Societas Scientiarum Fennica Commentationes Humanarum Litterarum, Helsingfors 1957, 22⁴.134.

Markland M F, The Structure of the Kingis Quair, Research Studies of the State College of Washington 25.273.

Wittig K, The Scottish Tradition in Literature, Edinburgh 1958, p 34 and passim (crit TLS July 11 1958, p 392).

Kinghorn A M, The Mediaeval Makars, Texas Stud Lit and Lang 1.73.

Rohrberger M, The Kingis Quair An Evaluation, Texas Stud Lit and Lang 2.292.

Slabey R M, Art Poetical in The Kingis Quair, N&Q 205(ns 7).208.

Bain C E, The Kingis Quair Two Emendations, N&Q 206(ns 8).168; A Valentine for Queen Joanne, Emory Univ Quarterly 17.234.

MacQueen J, Tradition and the Interpretation of the Kingis Quair, RES ns 12.117.

Bessai F C, A Crux in The Kingis Quair, N&Q 207(ns 9).48.

Elliott C, Robert Henryson Poems, Oxford 1963, p vii (brief comment).

Bain C E, The Nightingale and the Dove, Tenn Studies in Lit 9.19.

Rossi, edn, p 26.

MacQueen J, As You Like It and Mediaeval Literary Tradition, Forum Mod Lang Stud 1.219.

Von Hendy A, The Free Thrall, SSL 2.141.

Bain C E, The Kingis Quair 155:2, ESts 47.419.

Fox D, The Scottish Chaucerians, Chaucer and Chaucerians, ed D S Brewer, Univ of Alabama 1966, p 164.

MacQueen J, Robert Henryson A Study of the Major Narrative Poems, London 1967, pp 34, 154.

Scott T, Late Medieval Scots Poetry, London 1967, p 9.

Simon, edn, pp 28, 149, 203.

Brown I, The Mental Traveller A Study of the Kingis Quair, SSL 5.246.

Bibliography. Tytler, edn, p 56.

Paterson J, James the Fifth, Edinburgh 1861, p 124.

Rogers, edn, 2.315.

Skeat, edn, pp xxxvii, xliii (description of MS and edns).

DNB, 29.136.

Bearder J W, Über den Gebrauch der Prae-

positionen in der Altschottischen Poesie, Halle 1894, p 7.

Henderson T F, Scottish Vernacular Literature, Edinburgh 1898; 3rd edn rvsd Edinburgh 1910, p 95 (brief footnote).

Brown P H, The Kingis Quair and James I, Chambers's Cyclopædia, Phila and N Y 1901–03; rvsd J L Geddie, 1938, 1.185.

Browne W H, The Taill of Rauf Coilyear, Baltimore 1903, p 66.

CHEL, 2.531; Körting, p 197; Enc Brit, 15.139 (brief).

Geddie W, A Bibliography of Middle Scots Poets, PSTS ns 61, Edinburgh and London 1912, pp 103, 110.

Brown-Robbins, Robbins-Cutler, no 1215; Bennett OHEL, p 287; Renwick-Orton, p 412.

Rossi, edn, p 66.

Scott T, Late Medieval Scots Poetry, London 1967, p 34.

Simon, edn, p 355.

Ridley F H, A Check List 1956–1968 for Study of The Kingis Quair; the Poetry of Robert Henryson, Gawain Douglas, and William Dunbar, SSL 8.30.

[2] GOOD COUNSEL.

MSS. 1, Camb Univ Kk.1.5, Pt VI, f 5ᵃ (1450–1500); 2, Nat Libr Scot 1.1.6 (Bannatyne), p 32, ff 58ᵇ–59ᵃ (1568).

Brown-Robbins, no 3151.

Pinkerton J, Ancient Scotish Poems, London and Edinburgh 1786, 2.471 (MS 2).

Brydges E and J Haslewood, The British Bibliographer, London 1814, 4.183 (MS 2).

Laing D, The Poems of George Bannatyne, Edinburgh 1824, p 3 (MS 2); An Account of the Contents of George Bannatyne's Manuscript, The Bannatyne Club, Edinburgh 1829, 35.43 (MS 2).

Schipper J, The Poems of William Dunbar, pt 1, Denkschriften der kaiserlichen Akademie der Wissenschaften, Philo-Hist Classe, Vienna 1892, 40².9, 17 (MS 2).

Murdoch J B, ed, The Bannatyne Manuscript, 4 vols, Hunterian Club, Glasgow 1896 (MS 2).

Smith G G, Specimens of Middle Scots, Edinburgh and London 1902, pp lxvi, lxxiii (MS 2).

Brown J T T, The Bannatyne Manuscript a Sixteenth Century Poetical Miscellany, SHR 1.136 (MS 2).

Gray M M, Introd, Lancelot of the Laik,

PSTS ns 2, Edinburgh and London 1912, p vii (MS 1).

Ritchie W T, ed, The Bannatyne Manuscript Writtin in Tyme of Pest 1568, 4 vols, PSTS ns 5, 22, 23, 26, Edinburgh 1928–34 (MS 2).

Girvan, edn, p vii (MS 1).

Baxter J W, William Dunbar, Edinburgh and London 1952, p 217 (MS 2).

Editions. Charteris H, Ane Compendious Buik of godlie Psalmes and spiritual Sangis, Edinburgh 1578, p 202 (Huntington Libr [88301]; provisional no 2996.7 in W Jackson's to be published rev of STC; crit Skeat, edn, p liii); rptd D Laing, A Compendious Book of Psalms and Spiritual Songs Commonly Known as The Gude and Godlie Ballates, Edinburgh 1868; rptd A F Mitchell, A Compendious Book of Godly and Spiritual Songs, PSTS 39, Edinburgh and London 1897, p 238.

Smyth R, Ane Compendius Buik of Godly and Spirituall Sangis, Collectit out of sundrie partes of the Scripture, Edinburgh 1600 (unpaged) (STC, no 2997).

Hart A, Ane Compendious Booke of Godly and Spirituall Songs Collectit out of sundrie partes of the Scripture, Edinburgh 1621 (unpaged) (STC, no 2998).

Dalyell J G, Scotish Poems of the Sixteenth Century, Edinburgh and London 1801, 2.216 (Hart edn).

Irving D, The Lives of the Scotish Poets, 2 vols, Edinburgh 1804; 2nd edn improved London 1810, 1.315.

Brydges S E, Censura Literaria, London 1808, 6.34 (ns vol 3; Hart edn).

Irving D, The History of Scotish Poetry, ed J A Carlyle, Edinburgh 1861, p 152 (Hart edn).

Lumby J R, Ratis Raving and Other Moral and Religious Pieces, EETS 43, London 1870, pp 10, 118 (notes at end of text; MS 1; D Laing, A Compendious Book).

Rogers C, The Poetical Remains of King James the First of Scotland, Trans Royal Hist Soc ns, London 1873, 2.391.

Wilson J G, The Poets and Poetry of Scotland, N Y 1876, 1.18.

Ward T H, James the First of Scotland, The English Poets, London and N Y 1880; (numerous subsequent edns) N Y 1924, 1.136 (glossings at foot of page).

Wood H, Chaucer's Influence upon King James I of Scotland as Poet, Angl 3.263 (Rogers edn).

Skeat W W, The Kingis Quair together with a Ballad of Good Counsel, PSTS 1, Edinburgh and London 1884; 2nd rvsd edn, PSTS ns 1, Edinburgh and London 1911, pp 50, 99 (notes at end of text; MSS 1 and 2; D Laing, A Compendious Book; D Irving, edn, The History of Scotish Poetry).

Fitzgibbon H M, Early English Poetry Selected and Edited with a Critical Introd and Notes, The Canterbury Poets, ed W Sharp, London N Y and Melbourne 1887; another edn Early English and Scottish Poetry 1250–1600 Selected and Edited with a Critical Introd and Notes, London N Y and Melbourne 1888, pp 87, 431 (spelling modernized; notes at end of text).

Morley, 6.178 (Skeat edn).

Eyre-Todd G, Mediæval Scottish Poetry, Abbotsford Series of the Scottish Poets, Glasgow 1892, p 75 (rptd from Charteris edn).

Mitchell A F, A Compendious Book of Godly and Spiritual Songs, PSTS 39, Edinburgh and London 1897, p 238 (rptd from Charteris edn).

Brown P H, The Kingis Quair and James I, Chambers's Cyclopædia, Phila and N Y 1901–03; rvsd J L Geddie, 1938, 1.184.

Dixon W M, The Edinburgh Book of Scottish Verse 1300–1900, London 1910, p 8 (glossings at foot of page).

Lawson A, The Kingis Quair and the Quare of Jelusy, St Andrews Univ Publ no 8, London 1910, p 102 (texts based on MS 1 and Charteris edn; crit M M Gray, SHR 8.305).

Cohen H L, The Ballade, CUS 50.296 (Skeat edn).

Neilson W A and K G T Webster, Chief British Poets of the 14th and 15th Centuries, Boston N Y etc 1916, p 366 (glossings at foot of page; Skeat edn).

Leslie S, An Anthology of Catholic Poets, N Y 1925, p 88 (spelling modernized).

Brougham E M, News out of Scotland, London 1926, p 9.

Henderson T F, A Scots Garland An Anthology of Scottish Vernacular Verse, Edinburgh 1931, p 167.

Brown RLxvC, p 290 (MS 1).

Girvan R, Ratis Raving and Other Early Scots Poems on Morals, PSTS 3s 11, Edinburgh and London 1939, p 176 (MS 1).

Modernizations. Bonar A R, The Poets and Poetry of Scotland, Edinburgh 1864; 2nd edn 1866, p 41.

Mackean W, The Kingis Quair by King James I of Scotland, London 1886; rptd Paisley 1908, p 67.

Heard J, Divine Trust by King James I of Scotland, Poet Lore 47, no 1, p 2.

Textual Matters. Lawson, edn, p lxxxiii.

Fox D, Some Scribal Alterations of Dates in the Bannatyne MS, PQ 42.259.

Language. Dalyell, edn, 2.357 (glossary).

Irving D, The History of 'Scotish Poetry, edn, p 595 (glossary).

Laing, edn, p 261 (glossary).

Lumby, edn, pp ix, 131 (largely quoted from J A H Murray, The Dialect of the Southern Counties of Scotland, then unpublished; London 1873; glossary).

Skeat, edn, pp xxxiii, 102 (one brief comment and glossary).

Hahn O, Zur Verbal— und Nominalflexion bei den schottischen Dichtern, Berlin 1887–89 (generally applicable).

Mitchell, edn, p 309 (glossary).

Dixon, edn, p 897 (glossary).

Lawson, edn, pp lxxxiii, 156 (glossary at end of text).

Henderson, edn, p 182 (glossary).

Wood H H, The Poems and Fables of Robert Henryson, Edinburgh 1933; 2nd edn rvsd, Edinburgh 1958; rptd 1965, 1968, p xxxi.

Brown RLxvC, p 352 (glossary).

Girvan, edn, p 195 (glossary).

Scott T, Dunbar A Critical Exposition of the Poems, Edinburgh and London 1966, p 351.

Authorship. Brydges, edn, 6.35.

Skeat, edn, p xxxiii.

Henderson T F, Scottish Vernacular Literature, Edinburgh 1898 (crit G Binz, AnglB

10.291); 2nd edn rvsd, Edinburgh 1900; 3rd edn rvsd, Edinburgh 1910, p 103.

Murdoch W G B, The Royal Stewarts in Their Literary Connection with Arts and Letters, Edinburgh 1908, p 32.

Lawson, edn, p xlii.

Mackenzie W M, The Kingis Quair, London 1939, p 26.

Sources and Literary Relations. Ward, edn, 1.131.

Wood H, Chaucer's Influence upon King James I of Scotland as Poet, Angl 3.263.

Brandl, 2¹.714.

Lawson, edn, p xlii.

Saintsbury G, The Four Great Scottish Poets, N Y 1929, p 182.

Literary Criticism. Ward, edn, 1.131.

Saintsbury, The Four Great Scottish Poets, p 182.

Bibliography. Arber E, A Bibliographical Summary of English Literature in the Reign of Elizabeth 17 November 1558—24 March 1603, A Transcript of the Registers of the Company of Stationers of London, Birmingham 1894, vol 5, no 2434 (Charteris edn).

Mitchell, edn, pp xxxiii, xxxix, lxxx, 297.

Geddie W, A Bibliography of Middle Scots Poets, PSTS ns 61, Edinburgh and London 1912, p 104.

Brown Reg, no 2024; Brown-Robbins, Robbins-Cutler, no 3151; Renwick-Orton, p 413.

2. HENRYSON

GENERAL.

Language. Jamieson J, An Etymological Dictionary of the Scottish Language, 2 vols, Edinburgh 1808; rvsd J Longmuir and D Donaldson, 4 vols with suppl, Paisley 1879–82; new edn J Longmuir, London and Edinburgh 1885; another edn with introd by W M Metcalfe, Paisley 1912.

Murray J A H, A New English Dictionary on Historical Principles (The Oxford English Dictionary, ed J A H Murray, H Bradley, W A Craigie, C T Onions), Oxford 1884–1933.

Mackay C, A Dictionary of Lowland Scotch, Boston 1888.

Wright J, The English Dialect Dictionary, 8 vols, London 1896–1905.

Grant W and D D Murison, The Scottish National Dictionary, Edinburgh 1931–.

Craigie W A and A J Aitken, edd, A Dictionary of the Older Scottish Tongue from the 12th Century to the End of the 17th Founded on the Collections of Sir William A Craigie, Chicago and London 1931–.

Craigie W A, Older Scottish and English A Study in Contrasts, TPSL 1935, p 1.

MED.

Woolley J S, Bibliography for Scottish Linguistic Studies, Edinburgh 1954.

Murison D, A Survey of Scottish Language Studies, Forum Mod Lang Stud 3.276.

Authorship. MacDonald D, Henryson and the Thre Prestis of Peblis, Neophil 51.168 (concerned with Thre Prestis of Peblis only).

Sources and Literary Relations. Gray M M, Introd, Lancelot of the Laik, PSTS ns 2, Edinburgh and London 1912, 2.xviii, xxxv.

Linklater E, The Question of Culture, The Lion and the Unicorn, London 1935, pp 111, 127.

Patrick D, Scottish Literature, Chambers's Cyclopædia of English Literature, Phila and N Y 1901–03; rvsd J L Geddie, Phila and N Y 1938, 1.166.
Other Scholarly Problems. Whiting B J, Proverbs and Proverbial Sayings from Scottish Writings before 1600, MS 11.123; 13.87 (draws on works of Henryson as well as other Scottish material).
Kinghorn A M, Scots Literature and Scottish Antiquarians 1750–1800, SE 33.46.
Whiting B J, Proverbs Sentences and Proverbial Phrases, Cambridge Mass 1968.
Bibliography. Percy T, Reliques of Ancient English Poetry, London 1765; (numerous subsequent edns) ed H B Wheatley, London 1910, 2.79.
H R, Robert Henryson, Lives of Scottish Poets, ed J Robertson, London 1822, 3.2.
Lowndes W T, The Bibliographer's Manual of English Literature, London 1834; new edn rvsd corrected and enlarged by H G Bohn, London (1871?), 2.1045.
Chalmers P, Historical and Statistical Account of Dunfermline, 2 vols, Edinburgh and London 1844–59, 2.312.
Hazlitt W C, Hand-Book to the Popular Poetical and Dramatic Literature of Great Britain, London 1867, p 264.
DNB, 26.131; Morley, 6.257.
Eyre-Todd G, Mediæval Scottish Poetry, Abbotsford Series of Scottish Poets, Glasgow 1892, p 84.
Gray G J, A General Index to Hazlitt's Handbook and His Bibliographical Collections (1867–89), London 1893, p 357.
Smith G G, Specimens of Middle Scots, Edinburgh and London 1902, p lxvi (discussion of MSS).
Browne W H, The Taill of Rauf Coilyear, Baltimore 1903, p 66.
Seccombe T and W R Nicoll, The Scots Poets, The Bookman Illustrated History of English Literature, London 1906, 1.19 (brief).
Körting, p 156; Enc Brit, 13.302 (brief).
Geddie W, A Bibliography of Middle Scots Poets, PSTS ns 61, Edinburgh and London 1912, p 166.
Watt L M, Scottish Life and Poetry, London 1912, p 499 (listing and location of MSS).
Black G F, A List of Works Relating to Scotland, BNYPL Jan-Dec 1914; rptd N Y 1916, p 826.
Forbes-Leith W, Pre-Reformation Scholars in the 16th Century, Their Writings and Their Public Services, with a Bibliography, Glasgow 1915, p 26.

Northrup C S, J Q Adams and A Keogh, A Register of Bibliographies of the English Language and Literature, New Haven London and Oxford 1925, p 197.
Tucker-Benham, p 111.
Wood H H, The Poems and Fables of Robert Henryson, Edinburgh 1933, p xliv.
CBEL, 1.254, 257; 5.147 Bennett OHEL, p 285.
Stearns M W, Robert Henryson, N Y 1949, pp 131, 137 (crit A McIntosh, Spec 24.456); rptd N Y 1966.
Murison D, Selections from the Poems of Robert Henryson, Edinburgh 1952, p 6.
Rossi S, Robert Henryson, Milan 1955, p 100. p 68.
Elliott C, Robert Henryson Poems, Oxford 1963, p xix.
Rossi S, I Chauceriani Scozzesi, Napoli 1964, p 68.
Scott T, Late Medieval Scots Poetry, London 1967, p 34.
Wood H H, Two Scots Chaucerians, Writers and Their Work no 201, ed G Bullough, London 1967, p 45.
Kidd J and R H Carnie, Annual Bibliography of Scottish Literature 1969, Suppl 1, The Bibliotheck, Aberdeen 1970, p 6.
Ridley F H, A Check List, SSL 8.35.

[3] THE FABLES.

MSS. 1, Harley 3865 (The morall fabillis of Esope compylit be maister Robert Henrisoun Scolmaister of Dunfermling), ff 1b–75a (1571); 2, Nat Libr Scot Acc 4233 (Asloan), ff 236a–240a (1513–42; transcribed into Univ of Edinb La.III.450/1, ff 38–45; see MS 5 below); 3, Nat Libr Scot 1.1.6 (Bannatyne), ff 299a–302a, 310b–317b, 326b–342b (1568); 4, Univ of Edinb 205 (Laing 149, Makculloch), ff 2b–3a (MS proper 1477; Henryson insertions 1490–1510); 5, Univ of Edinb La.III.450/1 (formerly Laing 450* [Asloan-Chalmers]), ff 38..45 (1810).
Brown-Robbins, no 3703.
Pinkerton J, Ancient Scotish Poems, 2 vols, London and Edinburgh 1786, 2.471 (MS 3).
Brydges E and J Haslewood, The British Bibliographer, London 1814, 4.183 (MS 3).
Laing D, The Poems of George Bannatyne, Edinburgh 1824, p 3 (MS 3); An Account of the Contents of George Bannatyne's Manuscript, The Bannatyne Club, Edinburgh 1829, 35.43 (MS 3).
Laing, edn, pp 228, 266 (MSS 1 and 4).
Diebler, edn, Angl 9.337, 340, 453 (MS 1 described, rptd).

Schipper J, The Poems of William Dunbar, pt 1, Denkschriften der kaiserlichen Akademie der Wissenchaften, Philo-Hist Classe, Vienna 1892, 40².5, 9, 13, 17 (MSS 2, 3, 4).

Ward H L D, Catalogue of Romances in the Department of Manuscripts in the British Museum, London 1893, 2.354 (MS 1).

Murdoch J B, ed, The Bannatyne Manuscript, 4 vols, Hunterian Club, Glasgow 1896, 4.856, 898, 946 (MS 3).

Smith G G, Specimens of Middle Scots, Edinburgh and London 1902, pp lxvi, lxx, lxxiii (MSS 2, 3, 4).

Brown J T T, The Bannatyne Manuscript, SHR 1.136 (MS 3).

Smith G G, edn, 2.ix, 8 (MSS 1, 2, and 5); 1.3; 2.3 (MS 1, notes in vol 1, alternate pp); 1.3, 2.231 (MS 3, notes in vol 1); 1.3; 2.223 (MS 4, notes in vol 1); 1.5; 2.319 (MSS 2 and 5, notes in vol 1).

Borland C R, A Descriptive Catalogue of the Western Mediaeval Manuscripts in Edinburgh Univ Library, Edinburgh 1916, p 291 (MS 4).

Stevenson G, ed, Pieces from the Makculloch and the Gray MSS, PSTS 65, Edinburgh and London 1918, pp 3, 293 (MS 4, note at end of text).

Craigie W A, ed, The Asloan Manuscript, 2 vols, PSTS ns 14, 16, Edinburgh 1923–25, 2.141, 280 (MS 2, notes at end of text).

Ritchie W T, ed, The Bannatyne Manuscript Writtin in Tyme of Pest, 4 vols, PSTS ns 5, 22, 23, 26, Edinburgh 1928–34, 4.117, 158, 206 (MS 3).

Wood, edn, p xxiii (MSS 1, 4).

Baxter J W, William Dunbar, Edinburgh and London 1952, pp 216, 217 (MSS 2, 3).

Editions. Charteris H, The Morall Fabillis of Esope the Phrygian Compylit in Eloquent and Ornate Scottis Meter be Maister Robert Henrisone Scholemaister of Dunfermeling, Edinburgh 1570 (described in Laing, edn, p 265; R Dickson and J P Edmond, Annals of Scottish Printing from 1507 to the Beginning of the 17th Century, Cambridge 1890, p 240; Wood, edn, p xix) (STC, no 185).

Bassandyne T, The Morall Fabillis of Esope the Phrygian Compylit in Eloquent & Ornate Scottis metir be M Robert henrisone, Edinburgh 1571 (described in Wood, edn, p 217).

Smith R, The Fabulous tales of Esope the Phrygian Compiled moste eloquently in Scottishe Metre by Master Robert Henrison, London 1577 (described in Laing, edn, p 267; Wood, edn, pp xx, 222).

Hart A, The Morall Fables of Esope the Phrygian Compyled into eloquent and ornamentall Meeter by Robert Henrisoun Schoole-master of Dvmfermeling, Edinburgh 1621 (described in Account of an Edition of the Fables of Æsop, The Scots Magazine 75.504; Laing, edn, p 274; Wood, edn, p xxii); rptd D Stewart, The Moral Fables of Robert Henryson, Maitland Club Publication 15, Edinburgh 1832 (STC, no 186).

Laing D, The Poems and Fables of Robert Henryson, Edinburgh 1865, pp 99, 262, 304 (notes at end of text; MSS 2, 3, 4; crit St James Magazine 24.60, rptd North British Review, American edn ns 44.81, British edn ns 44.154).

Diebler A R, Henrisone's Fabeln, Halle 1885 (MS 1); text rptd Angl 9.337, 453; rptd Halle 1886.

Smith G G, The Poems of Robert Henryson, 2 vols, PSTS 55, 64, Edinburgh and London 1906, 1914, vols 1 and 2 (notes in vol 1, text in vol 2; MSS 1, 3, 4, and Charteris edn); rptd N Y 1968.

Metcalfe W M, The Poems of Robert Henryson, Paisley 1917, pp 3, 247 (notes at end of text; MSS 1, 3, 4, and Charteris edn).

Wood H H, The Poems and Fables of Robert Henryson, Edinburgh 1933, pp 3, 225 (variants in footnotes, notes at end of text; Basssandyne edn; crit J Speirs, Scrut 2.296; D Hamer, MLR 29.342; TLS Aug 3 1933, p 523; E Muir, The Spectator 151.290; The Modern Scot 4.163); 2nd edn rvsd Edinburgh 1958; rptd 1965, 1968.

Elliott C, Robert Henryson Poems, Oxford 1963, pp 1, 129 (notes at end of text; Bassandyne edn; crit A J Aitken, SN 36.344; I Ross, SSL 1.268; TLS Apr 9 1964, p 290; D Murison, SHR 43.157; F C DeVries, Neophil 49.191; J MacQueen, RES ns 16.224; D Fox, MÆ 35.82; D Murison, Arch 202.292); rptd from corrected sheets, Oxford 1966 (crit F C DeVries, Neophil 52.467).

Selections. Ramsay A, The Ever Green, 2 vols, Edinburgh 1724, 1.144, 185 (occasional changes in wording, omissions, additions; MS 3); for subsequent edns see B Martin, A Bibliography of the Writings of Allan Ramsay, Records of the Glasgow Biblio Soc, Glasgow 1931, 10.41.

Dalrymple D, Ancient Scottish Poems, Edinburgh 1770, pp 109, 280 (crit O Gilchrist, Ancient Scottish Poems, Censura Literaria, ed Brydges, London 1807, 5.238); rptd Leeds 1815, pp 138, 328 (notes at end of text; MS 3).

Sibbald J, Chronicle of Scottish Poetry, 4

vols, Edinburgh and London 1802, 1.90 (introductory and end notes).

Irving D, The Lives of the Scotish Poets, 2 vols, Edinburgh 1804; 2nd edn improved London 1810, 1.384.

Account of an Edition of the Fables of Æsop, The Scots Magazine 75.504 (Hart edn).

Nott G F, Appendix No VI, The Taill of the uponlandis Mous and the burges Mous, The Works of Sir Thomas Wyatt the Elder, London 1816, 3.451 (MS 1).

Tytler P F, Lives of Scottish Worthies, London 1833, 3.79, 84.

Aytoun W E, The Ballads of Scotland, Edinburgh and London 1858; 2nd edn rvsd and augmented 1859, 1.lxiii (brief; illustrative of critical discussion).

Gilfillan G, Specimens with Memoirs of the Less-Known Poets, Edinburgh and London 1860, 1.53 (glossings at foot of page).

Selections Made Chiefly from Works in the Old Scots Language for the Use of Schools in Scotland, Edinburgh 1867, p 61 (a few glossings at foot of page).

Clarke C C, Specimens with Memoirs of the Less-Known British Poets, Edinburgh 1868, 1.52.

Masson R O, Three Centuries of English Poetry Being Selections from Chaucer to Herrick, London 1876, p 122 (spelling modernized; glossings at foot of page).

Morley H, Shorter English Poems, London 1876, p 77.

Wilson J G, The Poets and Poetry of Scotland, N Y 1876, 1.20.

Henley W E, Robert Henryson, The English Poets, ed T H Ward, London and N Y 1880; (numerous subsequent edns) N Y 1924, 1.141 (glossings at foot of page).

Ross J, The Book of Scottish Poems, Paisley 1882, 1.145 (one brief introductory note).

Gregor W, Introd, The Court of Venus, PSTS 3, Edinburgh and London 1884, p xvi (Laing edn).

Fitzgibbon H M, Early English and Scottish Poetry, London N Y and Melbourne 1888, pp 94, 101, 431 (spelling modernized; notes at end of text).

Veitch J, The Feeling for Nature in Scottish Poetry, Edinburgh and London 1887, 1.213 (brief quotes interspersed with criticism; glossings in side notes).

Eyre-Todd G, Mediæval Scottish Poetry, Abbotsford Series of the Scottish Poets, Glasgow 1892, p 126 (glossings in margin).

Browne W H, Selections from the Early Scottish Poets, Baltimore 1896, pp 45, 181 (notes at end of text; Laing edn).

Chambers R, Chambers's Cyclopædia, Phila and N Y 1901–03; rvsd J L Geddie 1938, 1.190 (brief excerpts).

Smith G G, Specimens of Middle Scots, Edinburgh and London 1902, pp 1, 34, 267, 277 (notes at end of text; MSS 3 and 4; crit Athen Jan 10 1903, p 48; R Ackermann, AnglB 19.378).

Metcalfe W M, Specimens of Scottish Literature 1325–1835, London 1913, pp 42, 156 (notes at end of text).

Neilson W A and K G T Webster, Chief British Poets of the 14th and 15th Centuries, Boston N Y etc 1916, pp 375, 434 (notes at end of text, glossings at foot of page; Smith G G, edn).

Brougham E M, News out of Scotland, London 1926, p 11.

Murray H M R, Selected Fables (Nos 2, 3, 4, 6, and 9), The Testament of Cresseid and Robene and Makyne, London 1930, p 17 (Charteris edn).

Henderson T F, A Scots Garland, An Anthology of Scottish Verse, Edinburgh 1931, p 161.

Patterson R F, Six Centuries of English Literature, London and Glasgow 1933, 1.163.

Mackie R L, A Book of Scottish Verse, The World's Classics no 417, London 1934, p 18 (glossings at foot of page); 2nd edn London Glasgow and N Y 1967, p 19.

Gray M M, Scottish Poetry from Barbour to James VI, N Y 1935, p 98 (crit J Speirs, Scrut 6.83; W M Mackenzie, The Scottish Bookman 1, no 4, p 133).

Fergusson J, The Green Garden, London and Edinburgh 1946, p 8 (spelling modernized).

Oliver J W and J C Smith, A Scots Anthology from the 13th to the 20th Century, Edinburgh and London 1949, p 31 (spelling modernized; glossings at foot of page).

Murison D, Selections from the Poems of Robert Henryson, Edinburgh 1952, p 7 (glossings at foot of page; MS 2; Charteris edn).

McLaren M, The Wisdom of the Scots, London 1961, p 59 (glossings in margin).

Rossi S, I Chauceriani Scozzesi, Napoli 1964, p 143 (notes at foot of page).

MacQueen J and T Scott, The Oxford Book of Scottish Verse, Oxford 1966, p 72 (glossings at foot of page; Wood edn).

Scott T, Late Medieval Scots Poetry, London 1967, p 71 (Wood edn).

Kinghorn A M, The Middle Scots Poets, London 1970, p 78 (notes at foot of page; MS 3).

Scott T, The Penguin Book of Scottish Verse,

London 1970, p 111 (glossings at foot of page).

Sisam C and K Sisam, The Oxford Book of Medieval English Verse, Oxford 1970, p 457 (glossings at foot of page; Charteris edn).

Textual Matters. Account of an Edition of the Fables of Æsop, The Scots Magazine 75.504, 510.

Diebler, edn, Angl 9.340; Smith G G, edn, 2.vii; Metcalfe, edn, p xxi.

Dickins B, Contributions to the Interpretation of Middle Scots Texts, TLS Feb 21 1924, p 112.

Murray H M R, Selected Fables, The Testament of Cresseid and Robene and Makyne, London 1930, pp 5, 14.

Wood, edn, pp xix, xlii, 217.

Elliott C, Sparth, Glebard and Bowranbane, N&Q 207(ns 9).86.

MacQueen J, The Text of Henryson's Morall Fabillis (Two Versions of Henryson's Fabillis,) Innes Review 14.3; Robert Henryson A Study of the Major Narrative Poems, London 1967, p 189 (crit D Young, Forum Mod Lang Stud 3.252; TLS Aug 10 1967, p 726; D Fox, N&Q 212[ns 14].347; M P McDiarmid, SHR 46.159; R D S Jack, Engl 16.234; A C Spearing, SN 39.335; C Elliott, MLR 63.454; C Gullans, Ren Quart 21.214; F H Ridley, JEGP 67.299; F C DeVries, Neophil 53.235; D MacDonald, SSL 6.192; D D Murison, Arch 207.219).

Craik T W, An Emendation in Henryson's Fables, N&Q 214(ns 16).88.

Language. Ramsay A, The Ever Green, Edinburgh 1724, 2.265 (glossary).

Dalrymple D, Ancient Scottish Poems, Edinburgh 1770, p 317 (glossary); rptd Leeds 1815, p 367, [added] Glossary, p 1 [separate pagination].

Sibbald J, Chronicle of Scottish Poetry, Edinburgh and London 1802, vol 4 [unpaged] (glossary).

Irving D, The History of Scotish Poetry, Edinburgh 1861, p 595 (glossary).

Laing, edn, p 309 (glossary).

Murray J A H, The Dialect of the Southern Counties of Scotland, London 1873.

Hahn O, Zur Verbal- und Nominalflexion bei den schottischen Dichtern, Berlin 1887–89 (see especially pt 3, p 14).

Browne W H, Selections from the Early Scottish Poets, Baltimore 1896, pp 4, 197 (discussion; glossary).

Heuser W, Offenes und gescholossenes ee im Schottischen und Nordenglischen, Angl 18.123; 19.340; Die Mittelengl Entwicklung

von U in Offener Silbe, EStn 27.353.

Smith G G, Specimens of Middle Scots, Edinburgh and London 1902, pp xi, 325 (history and philology of Middle Scots; glossary).

Browne W H, The Taill of Rauf Coilyear, Baltimore 1903, pp 35, 139 (general discussion of Middle Scots; glossary).

Millar J H, A Literary History of Scotland, London 1903, p 687 (glossary).

Rodeffer J D, The Inflection of the English Present Plural Indicative, Baltimore 1903, pp 1, 23, 38.

Knopff P, Darstellung der Ablautverhältnisse in der schottischen Schriftsprache, diss Würzburg 1904.

Smith G G, edn, 1.83 (index of words and glossary); CHEL, 2.101, 506.

Gray M M, Introd, Lancelot of the Laik, PSTS ns 2, Edinburgh and London 1912, 2.xviii.

Metcalfe W M, Specimens of Scottish Literature, London 1913, pp 9, 39, 189 (includes glossary); edn, pp xx, 303 (brief discussion, glossary).

Taylor R, Some Notes on the Use of Can and Couth, JEGP 16.573.

Westergaard E, A Few Remarks on the Use and the Significations of the Prepositions in Lowland Scotch, Angl 41.444 (some examples from Henryson); Verbal Forms in Middle-Scotch, Angl 43.95.

Watt L M, Language and Influences, Douglas's Aeneid, Cambridge 1920, p 149 (very generally applicable; crit C R Baskerville, MP 18.171; J W Bright, MLN 35.508; O L Jiriczek, LfGRP 42.379; G D Willcock, MLR 15.432; TLS Apr 1 1920, p 210).

Westergaard E, Studies in Prefixes and Suffixes in Middle Scottish, diss London 1924 (crit C B, MLR 20.497).

Ritchie R L G, Early Instances of French Loan-Words in Scots and English, EStn 63.41 (examples cited from Henryson).

Murray H M R, Selected Fables, The Testament of Cresseid and Robene and Makyne, London 1930, p 12.

Henderson T F, A Scots Garland, Edinburgh 1931, p 182 (glossary).

Wood, edn, pp xxxi, 277 (discussion, glossary).

Patrick D, Scottish Literature, Chambers's Cyclopædia of English Literature, rvsd J L Geddie, Phila and N Y 1938, 1.164.

Fergusson J, The Green Garden, London and Edinburgh 1946, p 228 (glossary).

Murison D, Selections from the Poems of Robert Henryson, Edinburgh 1952, p 4.

Wittig K, The Scottish Tradition in Literature, Edinburgh 1958, p 101 and passim.

Elliott C, Sparth, Glebard and Bowranbane, N&Q 207(ns 9).86; edn, p 165 (glossary).

Rossi S, I Chauceriani Scozzesi, Napoli 1964, p 261 (discussion, glossary).

Aitken A J and P Bratley, An Archive of Older Scottish Texts for Scanning by Computer, SSL 4.45.

Scott T, Dunbar A Critical Exposition of the Poems, Edinburgh and London 1966, p 351.

MacQueen J, Some Aspects of the Early Renaissance in Scotland, Forum Mod Lang Stud 3.209.

Scott T, Late Medieval Scots Poetry, London 1967, pp 21, 189 (discussion, glossary).

Kinghorn A M, The Middle Scots Poets, London 1970, pp 45, 164 (note on Middle Scots, glossary).

Versification. Bulloch J M, French Metres in Early Scottish Poetry, Scottish Notes and Queries 2.115, 130.

Heuser W, Offenes und geschlossenes *ee* im Schottischen und Nordenglischen, Angl 18.123; 19.342.

Smith G G, edn, l.lxxxiii; Elliott, edn, p ix.

Date. Sibbald J, Chronicle of Scottish Poetry, Edinburgh and London 1802, 1.87.

Laing, edn, p xxx; Diebler, edn, Angl 9.337.

Stair-Kerr E, The Poets, Scotland under James IV, Paisley 1911, p 116.

Metcalfe, edn, p xviii.

Stearns M W, Robert Henryson, N Y 1949, p 25 (crit A McIntosh, Spec 24.456).

Crowne D K, A Date for the Composition of Henryson's Fables, JEGP 61.583.

MacQueen J, The Text of Henryson's Morall Fabillis, Innes Review 14.3, 5.

MacDonald D, Henryson and the Thre Prestis of Peblis, Neophil 51.169, 177.

MacQueen J, Robert Henryson A Study of the Major Narrative Poems, London 1967, pp 189, 193.

Fox D, Henryson and Caxton, JEGP 67.586, 592.

Sources and Literary Relations. H R, Robert Henryson, Lives of Scottish Poets, ed J Robertson, London 1822, 3.4.

Aytoun W E, The Ballads of Scotland, 2nd edn, Edinburgh and London 1859, l.lxiii.

Irving D, The History of Scotish Poetry, Edinburgh 1861, p 211.

Laing, edn, pp xxviii, xxxi.

Innes C, Lectures on Scotch Legal Antiquities, Edinburgh 1872, pp 239, 299 (sources in processes and jurisdiction of Consistorial Court).

Wright T, The History of Scotland from the Earliest Period to the Present Time, London and N Y [1873–74], 1.289.

Gregor W, Introd, The Court of Venus, PST 3, Edinburgh and London 1884, p xvi.

Diebler, edn, Halle 1885, p 32.

DNB, 26.131.

Fitzgibbon H M, Early English and Scottis Poetry, N Y London and Melbourne 188 p lix.

Eyre-Todd G, Mediæval Scottish Poetry, At botsford Series, Glasgow 1892, p 88.

Brandl, 2¹.716; Ten Brink, 3.67, 234.

Chambers R, Chambers's Cyclopædia, Phil and N Y 1901–03; rvsd J L Geddie, 193. 1.190.

M'Ilwraith W, A Sketch of Scottish Litera ture, Annual Burns Chronicle 10.19.

Moorman F W, The Interpretation of Natur in English Poetry from Beowulf to Shake speare, QF 95.138.

Dargan E P, Cock and Fox A Critical Stud of the History and Sources of the Medi aeval Fable, MP 4.39.

Plessow M, Geschichte der Fabeldichtung i England bis zu John Gay, diss Berlin 190 p xliv.

Smith G G, edn, l.xxix; CHEL, 2.279.

Tucker S M, Verse Satire in England befor the Renaissance, CUS 2s 3, no 2, pp 27 134 (crit F Brie, LfGRP 31.318).

Marshal L E, Roberto Henryson e la Griseid Borgo San Donnino 1910, p 8.

Enc Brit, 13.302.

Mendenhall J C, Aureate Terms A Study i the Literary Diction of the 15th Century Lancaster Pa 1919.

Knowlton E C, Nature in Middle English JEGP 20.192.

Patch H R, The Goddess Fortuna in Medi aeval Literature, Cambridge Mass 1927, 160 (brief).

Ker W P, Form and Style in Poetry, Londo 1928, p 87 (very brief).

Legouis HEL, p 172 (Chaucer).

Murray H M R, Selected Fables The Testa ment of Cresseid and Robene and Makyne London 1930, p 5.

Smith M E, Æsop a Decayed Celebrity, PMLA 46.226.

Elton O, The English Muse, London 1933, 83.

Wood, edn, p xl.

Bone G, The Source of Henryson's Fox Wol and Cadger, RES 10.319.

Grierson H J C, Robert Henryson, The Mod ern Scot 4.297; rptd Aberdeen Univ Rev 21.206; rptd Robert Henryson, Essays and Addresses, London 1940, p 110.

Smith J M, The French Background of Middle Scots Literature, Edinburgh and London 1934, pp xviii, 62, 78 (crit K Brunner, AnglB 45.265; R L G Ritchie, MÆ 4.44).

Tilgner E, Germanische Studien die Aureate Terms als Stilement bei Lydgate, Berlin 1936; rptd 1967, p 79.

Speirs J, The Scots Literary Tradition, London 1940, p 12 and passim; rvsd edn London 1962, p 37 and passim.

Tillotson G, The Fables of Robert Henryson, Essays in Criticism and Research, Cambridge 1942, p 1.

Grierson H J C and J C Smith, A Critical History of English Poetry, London 1944; 2nd rvsd edn London 1947, p 55 (brief).

Muir E, Robert Henryson, Essays on Literature and Society, London 1949, pp 7, 11; enlarged and rvsd edn London 1965, pp 10, 14.

Stearns M W, Robert Henryson, N Y 1949, p 65.

Murison D, Selections from the Poems of Robert Henryson, Edinburgh 1952, p 3.

Renwick-Orton, p 395 (brief).

Cruttwell P, Two Scots Poets Dunbar and Henryson, The Age of Chaucer, A Guide to English Literature, London 1954; rptd London 1955, 1.183.

Kinsley J, The Mediaeval Makars, Scottish Poetry a Critical Survey, London 1955, pp 16, 18, 20.

Rossi S, Robert Henryson, Milan 1955, pp 15, 41.

Lewis C S, English Literature in the Sixteenth Century, Oxford 1954, p 175.

Schlauch M, English Medieval Literature and Its Social Foundations, Warsaw 1956, p 294.

Bennett J A W, The Parlement of Foules, Oxford 1957, p 149.

Enkvist N E, The Seasons of the Year Chapters on a Motif from Beowulf to the Shepherd's Calendar, Societas Scientiarum Fennica Commentationes Humanarum Litterarum, Helsingfors 1957, 22⁴.134.

Mackie R L, King James IV of Scotland, Edinburgh and London 1958, p 172 (crit J D Mackie, SHR 38.133).

Kinghorn A M, The Mediaeval Makars, Texas Stud Lit and Lang 1.73.

Schirmer W F, John Lydgate Ein Kulturbild aus dem 15 Jahrhundert, Tubingen 1952; trans A E Keep, John Lydgate A Study in the Culture of the 15th Century, Berkeley and Los Angeles 1961, p 23.

Crowne D K, A Date for the Composition of Henryson's Fables, JEGP 61.583.

Fox D, Henryson's Fables, ELH 29.339, 345, 353.

Bauman R, The Folktale and Oral Tradition

in the Fables of Robert Henryson, Fabula 6.108.

Elliott, edn, pp viii, xvii.

MacQueen J, The Text of Henryson's Morall Fabillis, Innes Review 14.4.

Hyde I, Poetic Imagery A Point of Comparison between Henryson and Dunbar, SSL 2.183, 196.

MacDonald D, Narrative Art in Henryson's Fables, SSL 3.101.

Fox D, The Scottish Chaucerians, Chaucer and Chaucerians, ed D S Brewer, University Alabama 1966, p 164 (see especially p 172).

Jamieson I W A, Henryson's Fabillis an Essay towards a Revaluation, Words 2.20.

Jenkins A W, Henryson's The Fox the Wolf and the Cadger Again, SSL 4.107.

Scott T, Dunbar A Critical Exposition of the Poems, Edinburgh and London 1966, pp 36, 113.

Friedman J B, Henryson the Friars and the Confessio Reynardi, JEGP 66.550.

Jamieson I W A, A Further Source for Henryson's Fabillis, N&Q 212(ns 14).403.

MacDonald D, Henryson and Chaucer, Texas Stud Lit and Lang 8.451; Henryson and the Thre Prestis of Peblis, Neophil 51.170.

MacQueen J, Robert Henryson, London 1967, pp 18, 34, 54, 65, 80, 94, 191, 200; Some Aspects of the Early Renaissance in Scotland, Forum Mod Lang Stud 3.205, 209.

Scott T, Late Medieval Scots Poetry, London 1967, pp 7, 13.

Wood H H, Two Scots Chaucerians, Writers and Their Work no 201, ed G Bullough, London 1967, p 16.

Fox D, Henryson and Caxton, JEGP 67.586.

Blake N F, Caxton and His World, London 1969, p 213.

Jamieson I W A, Henryson's Taill of the Wolf and the Wedder, SSL 6.249.

MacDonald D, Chaucer's Influence on Henryson's Fables the Use of Proverbs and Sententiae, MÆ 39.21.

Other Scholarly Problems. Wood, edn, p xli (obscure word).

Stearns M W, Henryson and the Political Scene, SP 40.380 (contemp events; poet's attitude); Robert Henryson and the Socio-Economic Scene, ELH 10.285 (contemp conditions); A Note on Robert Henryson's Allusions to Religion and Law, MLN 59.257, 259 (poet's attitude); Robert Henryson, N Y 1949, pp 15, 106 (contemp conditions).

Rossi S, Robert Henryson, Milan 1955, p 96 (biographical evidence).

Rowlands M, The Fables of Robert Henryson, Dalhousie Rev 39.491 (contemp conditions); Robert Henryson and the Scottish Courts of Law, Aberdeen Univ Rev 39.219 (contemp conditions).

Friedman J B, Henryson the Friars and the Confessio Reynardi, JEGP 66.550 (poet's attitude; contemp conditions).

MacQueen J, Robert Henryson, London 1967, pp 2, 18, 121, 128, 134, 149, 169, 172 (contemp conditions, biographical evidence).

Wood H H, Two Scots Chaucerians, p 10 (biographical evidence).

Shire H M, Song Dance and Poetry of the Court of Scotland under King James VI, Cambridge 1969, p 21 (Reformation influence on editing; brief).

Literary Criticism. Pinkerton J, Ancient Scotish Poems, London and Edinburgh 1786, l.xcix.

Irving D, The Lives of the Scotish Poets, 2 vols, Edinburgh 1804; 2nd edn improved London 1810, 1.383 (illustrative quotes).

H R, Robert Henryson, Lives of Scottish Poets, ed J Robertson, London 1822, 3.3.

Tytler P F, Lives of Scottish Worthies, London 1833, 3.78, 84 (illustrative quotes).

Aytoun W E, The Ballads of Scotland, 2nd edn, Edinburgh and London 1859, l.lxiii.

Irving D, The History of Scotish Poetry, ed J A Carlyle, Edinburgh 1861, p 210.

Taylor J, The Imperial Dictionary of Universal Biography, London [1863], 2.878 (brief).

Laing, edn, pp xxii, xxix.

Morley H, A First Sketch of English Literature, London 1873; rvsd London 1896, p 201.

Wright T, The History of Scotland, London and N Y [1873–74], 1.289.

Wilson J G, The Poets and Poetry of Scotland, N Y 1876, 1.19 (brief).

Henley W E, Robert Henryson, The English Poets, ed T H Ward, London and N Y 1880; (numerous subsequent edns) N Y 1924, 1.137.

Nichol J, A Sketch of Scottish Poetry, ed J Small; 2nd edn rvsd, EETS 11, London 1883, p xxii.

Ross J M, Scottish History and Literature, Glasgow 1884, pp 164, 215.

Diebler, edn, Halle 1885, p 12.

Fitzgibbon H M, Early English and Scottish Poetry, N Y London and Melbourne 1888, p lviii.

Veitch J, The Feeling for Nature in Scottish Poetry, Edinburgh and London 1887, 1.213, 216, 219.

Morley, 6.253 (brief).

Oliphant F R, Robert Henryson, Blackwood's Edinburgh Magazine 148.497, 502, 509; rptd Littell's Living Age 187.537, 541, 546.

Eyre-Todd G, Mediæval Scottish Poetry, Abbotsford Series, Glasgow 1892, p 88.

Brandl, 2¹.716; Courthope, passim; Ten Brink, 3.67.

Jusserand J J, Histoire Littéraire du Peuple Anglais, Paris 1894, 1.526.

Gosse E, A Short History of Modern English Literature, N Y 1897; rvsd edn N Y 1906, p 47 (brief).

Henderson T F, Scottish Vernacular Literature, Edinburgh 1898; 2nd edn rvsd 1900; 3rd edn rvsd 1910, p 125; A Little Book of Scottish Verse, London 1899, p 11.

Smith G G, The Transition Period, Periods of European Lit, Edinburgh and London 1900, 4.46 and passim.

Chambers R, Chambers's Cyclopædia, Phila and N Y 1901–03; rvsd J L Geddie 1938, 1.190.

Millar J H, A Literary History of Scotland, London 1903, p 33.

Moorman F W, The Interpretation of Nature in English Poetry from Beowulf to Shakespeare, QF 95.138.

Snell F J, The Poets, The Age of Transition, London 1905, 1.76.

CHEL, 2.279.

Steinberger C, Étude sur William Dunbar, Dublin 1908, p 35.

Marshal L E, Roberto Henryson e la Griseida, Borgo San Donnino 1910, p 8.

Enc Brit, 13.302.

Stair-Kerr E, The Poets, Scotland under James IV, Paisley 1911, p 116 (brief).

Watt L M, Scottish Life and Poetry, London 1912, p 96.

Rhys E, The First Scottish Poets, London Toronto and N Y 1913, p 97.

Mackie R L, Scotland, London 1916, p 286.

Metcalfe, edn, pp xviii, xxvii.

Knowlton E C, Nature in Middle English, JEGP 20.192.

Quiller-Couch A, Studies in Literature, 2s, N Y and Cambridge Eng 1922, p 267.

Dickins B, Contributions to the Interpretation of Middle Scots Texts, TLS Feb 21 1924, p 112.

Hammond E P, English Verse between Chaucer and Surrey, Durham N C and London 1927, p 25 (brief).

Ker W P, Form and Style in Poetry, London 1928, p 87 (very brief).

Legouis HEL, p 172.

Saintsbury G, The Four Great Scottish Poets,

N Y 1929, p 184 (brief).

Murray H M R, Selected Fables The Testament of Cresseid and Robene and Makyne, London 1930, p 8.

Elton O, The English Muse, London 1933, p 83.

Mackenzie A M, An Historical Survey of Scottish Literature, London 1933, p 78 (crit The Modern Scot 4.164).

Wood, edn, p xiv; Robert Henryson, Edinburgh Essays on Scots Literature, Edinburgh and London 1933, pp 9, 16 (crit The Modern Scot 4.353).

Grierson H J C, Robert Henryson, The Modern Scot 4.297; rptd Aberdeen Univ Rev 21.206; rptd Robert Henryson, Essays and Addresses, London 1940, p 109.

Rait R and G S Pryde, Scotland, N Y 1934; 2nd edn London 1954, p 308 (brief).

Gray M M, Scottish Poetry, N Y 1935, p ix.

Power W, Literature and Oatmeal, London 1935, p 47 (very brief; crit AnglB 48.151; The Scottish Bookman 1, no 4, p 152).

Speirs J, The Scots Literary Tradition, London 1940, p 12 and passim; rvsd edn London 1962, p 37 and passim.

Tillotson G, The Fables of Robert Henryson, Essays in Criticism and Research, Cambridge 1942, p 1.

Grierson H J C and J C Smith, A Critical History of English Poetry, London 1944; 2nd rvsd edn London 1947, p 55 (brief).

Roy J A, Of the Makaris A Causerie, UTQ 16.36.

Bennett OHEL, p 174.

Caird J B, Some Reflections on Scottish Literature, I. Poetry, Scottish Periodical 1.8.

Muir E, Robert Henryson, Essays on Literature and Society, London 1949, p 7; enlarged and rvsd edn London 1965, p 10.

Stearns M W, Robert Henryson, N Y 1949, pp 7, 65, 107.

Craig HEL, p 167 (very brief).

Murison D, Selections from the Poems of Robert Henryson, Edinburgh 1952, p 1.

Renwick-Orton, pp 118, 415 (brief).

Wood H H, Scottish Literature, London 1952, p 15.

Cruttwell P, Two Scots Poets Dunbar and Henryson, The Age of Chaucer, A Guide to Eng Lit, London 1954; rptd London 1955, 1.183.

Kinsley J, The Mediaeval Makars, London 1955, p 16.

Rossi S, Robert Henryson, Milan 1955, pp 8, 30, 71.

Lewis C S, English Literature in the Six-

teenth Century, Oxford 1954, p 174.

Schlauch M, English Medieval Literature and Its Social Foundations, Warsaw 1956, p 294.

Enkvist N E, The Seasons of the Year, Societas Scientiarum Fennica Commentationes Humanarum Litterarum, Helsingfors 1957, $22^4.134$.

Mackie R L, King James IV of Scotland, Edinburgh and London 1958, p 171 (crit J D Mackie, SHR 38.133).

Wittig K, The Scottish Tradition in Literature, Edinburgh 1958, p 39 and passim.

Kinghorn A M, The Mediaeval Makars, Texas Stud Lit and Lang 1.76.

Rowlands M, The Fables of Robert Henryson, Dalhousie Rev 39.491, 497.

Dickinson W C, Scotland from the Earliest Times to 1603, A New Hist of Scotland, Edinburgh and London 1961, 1.280.

Duncan D, Henryson's Testament of Cresseid, EC 11.133, 135.

Harth S, Henryson Reinterpreted, EC 11.480.

McLaren M, The Wisdom of the Scots, London 1961, p 57.

Elliott C, Sparth Glebard and Bowranbane, N&Q 207(ns 9).86.

Fox D, Henryson's Fables, ELH 29.337.

Bauman R, The Folktale and Oral Tradition in the Fables of Henryson, Fabula 6.108, 111, 116, 120.

Elliott, edn, pp viii, x, xxiii.

Rossi S, I Chauceriani Scozzesi, Napoli 1964, p 37.

Hyde I, Poetic Imagery A Point of Comparison Between Henryson and Dunbar, SSL 2.184, 196.

Kinghorn A M, The Minor Poems of Robert Henryson, SSL 3.30, 36, 39.

MacDonald D, Narrative Art in Henryson's Fables, SSL 3.101.

Toliver H E, Robert Henryson from Moralitas to Irony, ESts 46.300.

Fox D, The Scottish Chaucerians, in Chaucer and Chaucerians, ed D S Brewer, Univ of Alabama 1966, p 172.

Jamieson I W A, Henryson's Fabillis, Words 2.20.

Jenkins A W, Henryson's The Fox the Wolf and the Cadger Again, SSL 4.110.

Scott T, Dunbar A Critical Exposition, Edinburgh and London 1966, p 87 and passim.

Friedman J B, Henryson the Friars and the Confessio Reynardi, JEGP 66.550.

Jamieson I W A, A Further Source for Henryson's Fabillis, N&Q 212(ns 14).403.

MacDonald D, Henryson and the Thre Prestis of Peblis, Neophil 51.170.

MacQueen J, Robert Henryson, London 1967,

pp v, 2, 80, 93.
Scott T, Allegorical, TLS Aug 31 1967, p 781 (with response); TLS Sept 14 1967, p 824; Late Medieval Scots Poetry, London 1967, p 33.
Watson E A F, Allegorical, TLS Sept 14 1967, p 824.
Wood H H, Two Scots Chaucerians, Writers and Their Work no 201, ed G Bullough, London 1967, pp 16, 32.
Jamieson I W A, Henryson's Taill of the Wolf and the Wedder, SSL 6.248.
MacDonald D, Chaucer's Influence on Henryson's Fables, MÆ 39.21.
Bibliography. Irving D, The Lives of the Scotish Poets, 2 vols, Edinburgh 1804; 2nd edn improved London 1810, 1.376.
Brydges E and J Haslewood, The British Bibliographer, London 1814, 4.305.
Craik G L, A Compendious History of English Literature, N Y 1877, 1.409 (brief).
Diebler, edn, Angl 9.338.
Arber E, A Bibliographical Summary of English Literature in the Reign of Elizabeth 17 November 1558–24 March 1603, A Transcript of the Registers of the Company of Stationers of London, Birmingham 1894, vol 5, no 1507 (Charteris edn).
Smith G G, edn, 2.vii; CHEL, 2.533.
Metcalfe, edn, p xxi.
Brown Reg, no 2360; Brown-Robbins, Robbins-Cutler, no 3703; Bennett OHEL, p 285; Renwick-Orton, p 415 (brief).

[4] THE TESTAMENT OF CRESSEID.

MSS. 1, Bodl 29640 (Add C.287) (The Sixt & Last Booke of Troilus and Creseid), pp 475–525 (1639; English text and Latin translation, notes at end of text); 2, St John's Camb L.1, II, ff 121ᵇ–128ᵇ (16 cent); 3, Univ of Edinb, Dc.1.43 (Ruthven), f 301ᵇ (1530?–1540?).
Small J, The Poetical Works of Gavin Douglas, Edinburgh and London 1874, l.clxxv (MS 3).
Smith G G, edn, l.xcvii, ciii (MS 1 described, rptd).
James M R, A Descriptive Catalogue of the Manuscripts in the Library of St John's College Cambridge, Cambridge 1913, p 274 (MS 2).
Watt L M, Douglas's Aeneid, Cambridge 1920, p 138 (MS 3).
Summary Cat, no 29640 (MS 1).
Wood, edn, p xxvi (MS 1).
Coldwell D F C, Virgil's Aeneid Translated into Scottish Verse by Gavin Douglas, PSTS

3s 30, Edinburgh and London 1964, 1.98 (MS 3).
Editions. Thynne W, The testament of Creseyde, The workes of Geffray Chaucer newly printed with dyuers workes neuer in print before, London 1532, f 219 (described in Laing, edn, pp 257, 260); ed W Bonham, 1542 (STC, no 5069); Bonham 1545? (STC, no 5071); J Kyngston, 1561 (STC, no 5075); T Speght, 1598 (STC, no 5077); A Islip, 1602 (STC, no 5080); J Urry London 1721; W W Skeat, The Works of Geoffrey Chaucer and Others, Being a Reproduction in Facsimile of the First Collected Edition 1532, London 1905; Smith edn, 1.44; 3.175 (notes in vol 1).
Charteris H, The Testament of Cresseid Compylit be M Robert Henrysone Scule maister in Dunfermeling, Edinburgh 1593 (Brit Mus press mark C.21.c.14; described in Laing, edn, pp 258, 260; R Dickson and J P Edmond, Annals of Scottish Printing from 1507 to the Beginning of the 17th Century, Cambridge 1890, p 368; Skeat edn, p lv); rptd in facsimile, The English Experience, no 92, Amsterdam and N Y 1969; ed G Chalmers, edn; Smith, edn 1.44; 3.3 (notes in vol 1) (STC, no 13165).
[Anderson A], The Testament of Cresseid Compyled by Master Robert Henrison Schoolmaster of Dumfermeling, [Glasgow 1663 (This is Trinity Coll Camb II.12.217; briefly described in, Laing, edn, p 259; Wood, edn, p xxv) (STC, no 1476).
Sibbald J, Chronicle of Scottish Poetry, 4 vols Edinburgh and London 1802, 1.157 (introductory and end notes).
Chalmers A, The Works of the English Poets London 1810, 1.294.
Chalmers G, Robene and Makyne and The Testament of Cresseid, Bannatyne Club Publications 6, Edinburgh 1824, p 1 (separate pagination; Charteris edn).
Laing D, The Poems and Fables of Robert Henryson, Edinburgh 1865, pp 73, 257, 303 (notes at end of text; Charteris edn; crit St James Magazine 24.60; rptd North British Review, American edn ns 44.81, British edn ns 44.154).
Ross J, The Book of Scottish Poems, Paisley 1882, 1.134 (brief introductory note).
Eyre-Todd G, Mediæval Scottish Poetry, Abbotsford Series of the Scottish Poets, Glasgow 1892, p 103 (glossings in margin).
Oxf Ch, 7.327, 520 (notes at end of text; G Chalmers edn).
Arber E, English Songs, Dunbar and Hi

Times 1401–1508, The Dunbar Anthology, British Anthologies, London 1901, 1.156, 297 (spelling modernized, notes at end of text; Charteris edn; crit R Brotanek, AnglB 13.172).

Smith G G, The Poems of Robert Henryson, 3 vols, PSTS 55, 58, 64, Edinburgh and London 1906, 1908, 1914, 1.cv, 44; 3.3, 175 (notes and MS 1 in vol 1; Charteris and Thynne edns in vol 3).

Douglas G, The Book of Scottish Poetry, London and Leipsic 1911, p 73 (glossings at foot of page; Smith edn).

Neilson W A and K G T Webster, Chief British Poets of the 14th and 15th Centuries, Boston N Y etc 1916, pp 367, 434 (brief note at end of text, glossings at foot of page; Smith edn).

Metcalfe W M, The Poems of Robert Henryson, Paisley 1917, pp 143, 280 (notes at end of text; Thynne and Charteris edns).

Dickins B, The Testament of Cresseid, Edinburgh 1925 (Charteris edn).

Attwater A, The Testament of Cresseid, Cambridge 1926 (Laing edn).

Murray H M R, Selected Fables, The Testament of Cresseid and Robene and Makyne, London 1930, p 65 (Charteris edn).

Wood H H, The Poems and Fables of Robert Henryson, Edinburgh 1933, pp 105, 251 (variants in footnotes, notes at end of text; Charteris edn; crit J Speirs, Scrut 2.296; D Hamer, MLR 29.342; TLS Aug 3 1933, p 523; E Muir, The Spectator 151.290; The Modern Scot 4.163); 2nd edn rvsd Edinburgh 1958.

Gordon R K, The Story of Troilus, London 1934, p 351.

Gray M M, Scottish Poetry from Barbour to James VI, N Y 1935, p 58 (crit J Speirs, Scrut 6.83; W M Mackenzie, The Scottish Bookman 1, no 4, p 133).

[Grieve C M] MacDiarmid H, The Golden Treasury of Scottish Poetry, London 1940, p 194 (crit L MacNeice, The New Statesman and Nation, 21.66; TLS Feb 15 1941, pp 78, 84); rptd in The Golden Treasury Series, London 1948, p 128.

Murison D, Selections from the Poems of Robert Henryson, Edinburgh 1952, p 26 (glossings at foot of page; Charteris edn).

Elliott C, Robert Henryson Poems, Oxford 1963, pp 90, 147 (notes at end of text; Charteris edn).

Rossi S, I Chauceriani Scozzesi, Napoli 1964, p 105 (notes at foot of page).

MacQueen J and T Scott, The Oxford Book of Scottish Verse, Oxford 1966, p 50 (glossings at foot of page; Wood edn).

Scott T, Late Medieval Scots Poetry, London 1967, pp 44, 183 (notes at end of text; Wood edn).

Fox D, Testament of Cresseid, London 1968 (notes at end of text; Charteris edn; crit TLS Aug 8 1968, p 852; P Bawcutt, N&Q 213[ns 15].435; M P McDiarmid, MÆ 37.350; S A Khinoy, JEGP 68.166; B Dillon, SSL 6.263; D F C Coldwell, RES ns 20.385; T A Stroud, MP 67.182; F C De Vries, Neophil 53.337; W Weiss, Angl 88.129).

Kinghorn A M, The Middle Scots Poets, London 1970, p 101 (notes at foot of page; Charteris edn).

Scott T, The Penguin Book of Scottish Verse, London 1970, p 85 (glossings at foot of page).

Selections. Anderson R, The Works of the British Poets, London and Edinburgh 1795, 1.409.

Irving D, The Lives of the Scotish Poets, 2 vols, Edinburgh 1804; 2nd edn improved London 1810, 1.378.

Tytler P F, Lives of Scottish Worthies, London 1833, 3. 78, 80.

Masson R O, Three Centuries of English Poetry, London 1876, p 120 (spelling modernized; glossings at foot of page).

Veitch J, The Feeling for Nature in Scottish Poetry, Edinburgh and London 1887, 1. 209, 217 (brief quotes interspersed with criticism; glossings in side notes).

Fitzgibbon H M, Early English and Scottish Poetry, London N Y and Melbourne 1888, pp 99, 431 (spelling modernized; notes at end of text).

Chambers R, Chambers's Cyclopædia, Phila and N Y 1901–03; rvsd J L Geddie, Phila and N Y 1938, 1.190 (brief excerpt).

Brougham E M, News out of Scotland, London 1926, p 12.

Henderson T F, A Scots Garland, An Anthology of Scottish Verse, Edinburgh 1931, p 158.

Mackie R L, A Book of Scottish Verse, The World's Classics no 417, London 1934, p 26 (glossings at foot of page); 2nd edn London Glasgow and N Y 1967, p 27.

Fergusson J, The Green Garden, London and Edinburgh 1946, p 20 (spelling modernized).

Mackenzie A M, Scottish Pageant, Edinburgh 1946; 2nd edn 1952, 1.11 (brief glossings at end of selection).

Oliver J W and J C Smith, A Scots Anthology, Edinburgh and London 1949, p 21 (spelling modernized; glossings at foot of page).

Auden W H and N H Pearson, Poets of the English Language, N Y 1950, p 387.

Davies R T, Medieval English Lyrics A Critical Anthology, London 1963, pp 232, 354 (The Complaint of Cresseid; notes at end of text; Charteris edn).

McLaren M, The Wisdom of the Scots, London 1961, p 66 (glossings in margin).

Modernizations. Smith R M, Two Scottish Chaucerians being Modern Versions of The King's Quair and The Testament of Cresseid, Wesleyan Univ, Middletown Conn 1936, p 72 (based on Charteris edn).

Stearns M W, A Modernization of Robert Henryson's Testament of Cresseid, Bloomington Ind 1945 (based on Charteris edn); The Testament of Cresseid, Medieval English Verse and Prose, ed Loomis and Willard, N Y 1948, pp 461, 557 (notes at end of text).

Cogswell F, The Testament of Cresseid, Toronto 1957 (crit C L Lambertson, Dalhousie Rev 37.204).

Davies R T, Medieval English Lyrics, London 1963, p 232 (The Complaint of Cresseid).

Textual Matters. Skeat, edn, p lv.

Skeat W W, Introd, The Works of Geoffrey Chaucer, London 1905, p xxxi.

Smith, edn, l.xlv; 3.x, xix; Metcalfe, edn, p xxiv.

Dickins B, The Testament of Cresseid, TLS Dec 11 1924, p 850; edn, p 43.

Murray, edn, p 9; Wood, edn, pp xi, xxv.

Elliott C, Two Notes on Henryson's Testament of Cresseid, JEGP 54.243, 247, 253.

Fox, edn, pp 2, 59.

Language. Anderson R, The Works of the British Poets, London and Edinburgh 1795, p 669 (glossary).

Sibbald, edn, vol 4 [unpaged] (glossary).

Irving D, The History of Scotish Poetry, Edinburgh 1861, p 595 (glossary).

Laing, edn, p 309 (glossary).

Murray J A H, The Dialect of the Southern Counties of Scotland, London 1873.

Hahn O, Zur Verbal-und Nominalflexion bei den schottischen Dichtern, Berlin 1887–89 (see especially pt 3, p 14).

Oxf Ch, 7. 555 (glossarial index).

Arber, edn, p 300 (glossary and index).

Browne W H, The Taill of Rauf Coilyear, Baltimore 1903, pp 35, 139 (general discussion of Middle Scots; glossary).

Millar J H, A Literary History of Scotland, London 1903, p 687 (glossary).

Skeat W W, Introd, The Works of Geoffrey Chaucer, London 1905, p xxxi (brief).

Smith G G, edn, 1.83 (index of words and glossary); CHEL, 2.101, 506.

Gray M M, Introd, Lancelot of the Laik PSTS ns 2, Edinburgh and London 1912 2.xviii.

Metcalfe, edn, pp xx, 303 (brief discussion glossary).

Taylor R, Some Notes on the Use of Can and Couth, JEGP 16.573.

Westergaard E, Prepositions in Lowland Scotch Angl 41.444 (some examples from Henryson); Verbal Forms in Middle-Scotch Angl 43.95.

Watt L M, Language and Influences, Douglas's Aeneid, Cambridge 1920, p 149 (very generally applicable).

Westergaard E, Studies in Prefixes and Suffixes in Middle Scottish, London 1924.

Dickins, edn, p 37 (glossary).

Murray H M R, edn, p 12.

Henderson T F, A Scots Garland, Edinburgh 1931, p 182 (glossary).

Wood, edn, pp xxxi, 277 (discussion, glossary).

Gordon R K, edn, p 380 (glossary).

Patrick D, Scottish Literature, Chambers' Cyclopædia of English Literature, Phil and N Y 1901–03; rvsd J L Geddie, Phil and N Y 1938, 1.164.

[Grieve] MacDiarmid, edn, p 398 (glossary).

Fergusson J, The Green Garden, London and Edinburgh 1946, p 228 (glossary).

Murison, edn, p 4.

Stock N, Some Notes on Old Scots, Shenandoah 6, no 2, p 25.

Wittig K, The Scottish Tradition in Literature, Edinburgh 1958, p 101 and passim.

Elliott, edn, p 165 (glossary).

Rossi, edn, p 261 (discussion and glossary).

Aitken A J and P Bratley, An Archive of Older Scottish Texts for Scanning by Computer, SSL 4.45.

Scott T, Dunbar A Critical Exposition of the Poems, Edinburgh and London 1966, p 35.

MacQueen J, Some Aspects of the Early Renaissance in Scotland, Forum Mod Lang Stud 3.209.

Scott T, Late Medieval Scots Poetry, edn, p 21, 189 (discussion, glossary).

Fox, edn, p 141 (glossary).

Kinghorn, edn, pp 45, 164 (note on Middle Scots, glossary).

Versification. Henderson T F, Scottish Vernacular Literature, Edinburgh 1898; 2n edn rvsd 1900; 3rd edn rvsd 1910, p 11.

Smith G G, edn, l.lxxxiii.

Saintsbury G, History of English Prosody from the 12th Century to the Present Day, London 1908; 2nd edn London 1923, 1.271; Historical Manual of English Prosody, London 1910; rptd London 1914, 1.155, 163.

Hamer E, The Metres of English Poetry, N Y 1930, p 153 (brief).

Smith J M, The French Background of Middle Scots Literature, Edinburgh and London 1934, p 162.

Murison, edn, p 5.

Renwick-Orton, p 415 (brief).

Elliott C, Two Notes on Henryson's Testament of Cresseid, JEGP 54.250 (significance of rime and meter in determining form of a word).

Rossi S, Robert Henryson, Milan 1955, p 77.

Wittig K, The Scottish Tradition in Literature, Edinburgh 1958, p 35.

Elliott, edn, p ix.

Scott T, Late Medieval Scots Poetry, edn, p 18.

Date. Metcalfe, edn, p xviii.

Whiting B J, A Probable Allusion to Henryson's Testament of Cresseid, MLR 40.46.

Kinsley J, A Note on Henryson, TLS Nov 14 1952, p 743.

Spearing A C, The Testament of Cresseid and the High Concise Style, Spec 37.212.

Fox, edn, p 17.

Authorship. Kinaston F, Introductory Extracts, The Loves of Troilus and Creseid Written by Chaucer with a Commentary by Sir Francis Kinaston, ed F G Waldron, London 1796, p xxviii.

Lounsbury T R, The Writings of Chaucer, Studies in Chaucer, N Y 1892, 1.457.

Skeat W W, Introd, The Works of Geoffrey Chaucer, London 1905, p xxxi (brief).

Smith G G, edn, 1.xlv.

Hammond, p 457.

Spurgeon C F E, Five Hundred Years of Chaucer Criticism and Allusion, ChS 2s 48¹; rptd corrected and illustrated Cambridge 1925, 1¹.154; 3⁴.35, 37 and passim.

Fox, edn, p 17.

Sources and Literary Relations. Morley H, A First Sketch of English Literature, London 1873; rvsd London 1896, p 201.

Wright T, The History of Scotland, London and N Y [1873–74], 1.290.

Nichol J, A Sketch of Scottish Poetry, ed J Small; 2nd edn rvsd, EETS 11, London 1883, p xxi.

DNB, 26.131.

Fitzgibbon H M, Early English and Scottish Poetry, N Y London and Melbourne 1888, p lix.

Eyre-Todd, edn, p 84.

Brandl, 2¹.716.

Saintsbury G, The Flourishing of Romance and the Rise of Allegory, N Y 1897, p 150.

Neilson W A, Studies and Notes in Philology and Literature 6.159.

M'Ilwraith W, A Sketch of Scottish Literature, Annual Burns Chronicle 10.19.

Browne W H, The Taill of Rauf Coilyear, Baltimore 1903, p 11.

Smith G G, edn, 1.xlviii; CHEL, 2.281.

Marshal L E, Roberto Henryson e la Griseida, Borgo San Donnino 1910, pp 3, 12.

Perrow E C, The Last Will and Testament as a Form of Literature, Trans Wisconsin Acad of Sciences Arts and Letters 7¹.682.

Watt L M, Scottish Life and Poetry, London 1912, p 92.

Lawrence W W, The Love-Story in Troilus and Cressida, Shaksperian Studies, ed B Matthews and A H Thorndike, N Y 1916, p 203.

Rollins H E, The Troilus-Cressida Story, PMLA 32.394.

Mendenhall J C, Aureate Terms A Study in the Literary Diction of the 15th Century, Lancaster Pa 1919.

Smith G G, Scottish Literature Character and Influence, London 1919, p 13 (brief reference).

Knowlton E C, Nature in Middle English, JEGP 20.192.

Golding L, The Scottish Chaucerians, The Saturday Review of Politics Literature Science and Art 134.783.

Quiller-Couch A, Studies in Literature, 2s, N Y and Cambridge Eng 1922, p 265.

Bullet G, The Fortunes of Cressida, The New Statesman 21.361.

Spurgeon C F E, Five Hundred Years of Chaucer Criticism, ChS 2s 48¹; rptd Cambridge 1925, 3⁴.1 and passim.

Huxley A, Chaucer, Essays New and Old, London 1926; rptd N Y 1932, p 271.

Patch H R, The Goddess Fortuna in Mediaeval Literature, Cambridge Mass 1927, p 97 (brief).

Graydon J S, Defense of Criseyde, PMLA 44.142 (brief).

Legouis HEL, p 171.

Murray H M R, edn, p 9.

Mackenzie W M, The Poems of William Dunbar, London 1932; rptd London 1950; ed B Dickins, rptd and rvsd London 1960, p xi; rptd London 1970.

Nichols P H, Lydgate's Influence on the Aureate Terms of the Scottish Chaucerians, PMLA 47.518.

Elton O, The English Muse, London 1933, p 81.

Mackenzie A M, An Historical Survey of Scottish Literature to 1714, London 1933, p 76.

Mackenzie W M, William Dunbar, Edinburgh Essays on Scots Literature, Edinburgh and London 1933, pp 29, 37.

Wood, edn, p xxxix.

Grierson H J C, Robert Henryson, The Modern Scot 4.297; rptd Aberdeen Univ Rev 21.206; rptd Robert Henryson, Essays and Addresses, London 1940, p 111.

Rait R and G S Pryde, Scotland, N Y 1934; 2nd edn London 1954, p 308 (very brief).

Smith J M, The French Background of Middle Scots Literature, Edinburgh and London 1934, pp xviii, 70, 101.

Gray M M, Scottish Poetry from Barbour to James VI, N Y 1935, p ix.

Stearns M W, Robert Henryson and the Fulgentian Horse, MLN 54.239.

Speirs J, The Scots Literary Tradition, London 1940, pp 11, 23 and passim (crit Scrut 9.193); rvsd edn London 1962, pp 37, 45 and passim.

Grierson H J C and J C Smith, A Critical History of English Poetry, London 1944; 2nd rvsd edn London 1947, p 55 (brief).

Stearns M W, Robert Henryson and the Leper Cresseid, MLN 59.265; Robert Henryson and the Aristotelian Tradition of Psychology, SP 41.492; The Planet Portraits of Robert Henryson, PMLA 59.911.

Utley CR, p 63.

Parr J, Cresseid's Leprosy Again, MLN 60.487 (sources of information about leprosy).

Stearns M W, Henryson and Chaucer, MLQ 6.271; A Note on Henryson and Lydgate, MLN 60.101.

Whiting B J, A Probable Allusion to Henryson's Testament of Cresseid, MLR 40.46.

Tillyard E M W, Henryson The Testament of Cresseid, Five Poems 1470–1870, London 1948, p 5; rptd as Henryson; The Testament of Cresseid 1470? Poetry and its Background Illustrated by Five Poems 1470–1870, London 1955, p 5.

Muir E, Robert Henryson, Essays on Literature and Society, London 1949, pp 7, 14, 18; rvsd edn London 1965, pp 10, 17, 21.

Stearns M W, Robert Henryson, N Y 1949, pp 48, 57, 69, 134.

Craig HEL, p 167.

Kinsley J, A Note on Henryson, TLS Nov 14 1952, p 743.

Morgan E, Dunbar and the Language of Poetry, EC 2.142.

Murison, edn, p 3.

Gray J, A Note on Henryson, TLS Mar 13 1953, p 176.

Ward A C, Illustrated History of English Literature, London N Y and Toronto 1953, pp 31, 40 (brief).

Cruttwell P, Two Scots Poets Dunbar and Henryson, The Age of Chaucer, A Guide to Eng Lit, London 1954; rptd London 1955, 1.184.

Elliott C, Two Notes on Henryson's Testament of Cresseid, JEGP 54.249, 253.

Kinsley J, The Mediaeval Makars, Scottish Poetry A Critical Survey, London 1955, p 20.

Rossi S, Robert Henryson, Milan 1955, pp 6, 47.

Sells A L, The Italian Influence in English Poetry, Bloomington Ind 1955, pp 64, 66.

Lewis C S, English Literature in the Sixteenth Century, Oxford 1954, p 175.

Bennett J A W, The Parlement of Foules, Oxford 1957, pp 84, 87.

Mackie R L, King James IV of Scotland, Edinburgh and London 1958, p 173 (crit J D Mackie, SHR 38.133).

Wittig K, The Scottish Tradition in Literature, Edinburgh 1958, p 35.

Kinghorn A M, The Mediaeval Makars, Texas Stud Lit and Lang 1.73.

Moran T, The Testament of Cresseid and the Book of Troylus, Litera 6.18.

Duncan D, Henryson's Testament of Cresseid, EC 11.129.

Harth S, Henryson Reinterpreted, EC 11.472, 475.

Spearing A C, The Testament of Cresseid and the High Concise Style, Spec 37.208.

Elliott, edn, pp vii, xxiv.

Moran T, The Meeting of the Lovers in the Testament of Cresseid, N&Q 208(ns 10).11.

Bullough G, The Lost Troilus and Cressida, E&S 2s 17.35, 39.

Howard E J, Geoffrey Chaucer, N Y 1964, p 193.

Marken R, Chaucer and Henryson a Comparison, Discourse 7.381.

Rossi, edn, p 34.

Spearing A C, Conciseness and The Testament of Cresseid, Criticism and Medieval Poetry, London 1964, p 118 (expanded modified version of Spearing; The Testament of Cresseid and the High Concise Style; crit R M Wilson, Engl 15.107).

Hyde I, Poetic Imagery, SSL 2.184, 189, 195.

Kinghorn A M, The Minor Poems of Robert

Henryson, SSL 3.37.

Fox D, The Scottish Chaucerians, in Chaucer and Chaucerians, ed D S Brewer, University Alabama 1966, p 164 (see especially p 177).

Aswell E D, The Role of Fortune in The Testament of Cresseid, PQ 46.471, 480.

McDermott J J, Henryson's Testament of Cresseid and Heywood's A Woman Killed with Kindness, Ren Quart 20.16.

MacDonald D, Henryson and the Thre Prestis of Peblis, Neophil 51.176.

MacQueen J, Robert Henryson a Study of the Major Narrative Poems, London 1967, pp 18, 26, 46, 62, 65, 140, 145, 157, 165, 169; Some Aspects of the Early Renaissance in Scotland, Forum Mod Lang Stud 3.209.

Scott T, Late Medieval Scots Poetry, edn, p 11.

Wood H H, Two Scots Chaucerians, Writers and Their Work no 201, ed G Bullough, London 1967, pp 11, 28.

Bennett J A W, Chaucer's Book of Fame, Oxford 1968, p 38.

Fox, edn, pp 1, 21, 48.

Lawlor J, Chaucer, London 1968, p 89.

Blake N F, Caxton and His World, London 1969, p 213.

Chessell D, In the Dark Time Henryson's Testament of Cresseid, Critical Rev 12.61.

Scheps W William Wallace and his Buke Some Instances of Their Influence on Subsequent Literature, SSL 6.224.

Shire H M, Song Dance and Poetry of the Court of Scotland under King James VI, Cambridge 1969, p 199.

Other Scholarly Problems. Simpson J Y, Antiquarian Notices of Leprosy and Leper Hospitals in Scotland and England, The Edinburgh Medical and Surgical Journal 57.139, 424 (nature of Cresseid's disease).

Cook A S, Henryson Testament of Cresseid 8–14, MLN 22.62 (astronomical phenomenon).

Stearns M W, Robert Henryson, N Y 1949, p 42 (contemp conditions).

Larkey S V, Leprosy in Medieval Romance A Note on Robert Henryson's Testament of Cresseid, Bull of the History of Medicine 35.77 (nature of Cresseid's disease).

Rowland B, The Seiknes Incurabill in Henryson's Testament of Cresseid, Engl Lang Notes 1.175 (nature of Cresseid's disease).

Wood H H, Two Scots Chaucerians, p 10 (biographical evidence).

Hume K, Leprosy or Syphilis in Henryson's Testament of Cresseid, Engl Lang Notes 6.242.

Literary Criticism. Warton T, History of English Poetry, London 1774–81; ed W C Hazlitt, London 1871, 3.265 (very brief).

Godwin W, Sequel to Troilus and Creseide by Robert Henryson, Life of Geoffrey Chaucer, London 1803; 2nd edn London 1804, 1.487.

Irving D, The Lives of the Scotish Poets, 2 vols, Edinburgh 1804; 2nd edn improved London 1810, 1.378.

H R, Robert Henryson, Lives of Scottish Poets, ed J Robertson, London 1822, 3.3.

Tytler P F, Lives of Scottish Worthies, London 1833, 3.78 (illustrative quotes).

Irving D, The History of Scotish Poetry, ed J A Carlyle, Edinburgh 1861, p 213 (illustrative quotes).

Taylor J, The Imperial Dictionary of Universal Biography, London [1863], 2.878 (brief).

Laing D, edn, p xxv.

Morley H, A First Sketch of English Literature, London 1873; rvsd London 1896, p 201.

Mackintosh J, The History of Civilisation in Scotland, London and Edinburgh 1878–88; new edn partly rewritten Paisley 1892–96, 1.462.

Henley W E, Robert Henryson, The English Poets, ed T H Ward, London and N Y 1880; (numerous subsequent edns) N Y 1924, 1.138.

Nichol J, A Sketch of Scottish Poetry, ed J Small, 2nd edn rvsd, EETS 11, London 1883, p xxi.

Ross J M, Scottish History and Literature, Glasgow 1884, pp 165, 333, 352.

Schipper J, William Dunbar, Berlin 1884, p 37.

DNB, 26.131.

Fitzgibbon H M, Early English and Scottish Poetry, N Y London and Melbourne 1888, p lix.

Skelton J, Maitland of Lethington and the Scotland of Mary Stuart, Edinburgh 1887, 1.107.

Veitch J, The Feeling for Nature in Scottish Poetry, Edinburgh and London 1887, 1.208, 210, 216, 219.

Minto W, Characteristics of English Poets from Chaucer to Shirley, authorized American edn, Boston 1889, p 97 (brief).

Morley, 6.254 (very brief).

Oliphant F R, Robert Henryson, Blackwood's Edinburgh Magazine 148.506; rptd Littell's Living Age 187.544.

Eyre-Todd, edn, p 84.

Brandl, 2¹.716.

Jusserand J J, Histoire littéraire du peuple anglais, Paris 1894, 1.525.

Turnbull W R, The Heritage of Burns, Haddington 1896, p 240 (brief).

Gosse E, A Short History of Modern English Literature, N Y 1897; rvsd edn N Y 1906, p 47 (brief).

Saintsbury G, The Flourishing of Romance and the Rise of Allegory, N Y 1897, p 150 (brief).

Henderson T F, Scottish Vernacular Literature, Edinburgh 1898; 2nd edn rvsd 1900; 3rd edn rvsd 1910, p 123; A Little Book of Scottish Verse, London 1899, p 11.

Neilson W A, Studies and Notes in Philology and Literature 6.159.

Smith G G, The Transition Period, Periods of European Lit, Edinburgh and London 1900, 4.47 and passim.

Chambers R, Chambers's Cyclopædia, Phila and N Y 1901–03; rvsd J L Geddie, 1938, 1.189 (very brief).

M'Ilwraith W, A Sketch of Scottish Literature, Annual Burns Chronicle 10.19.

Browne W H, The Taill of Rauf Coilyear, Baltimore 1903, p 11 (brief).

Millar J H, A Literary History of Scotland, London 1903, p 31.

Moorman F W, The Interpretation of Nature in English Poetry from Beowulf to Shakespeare, QF 95.140.

Skeat W W, Introd, The Works of Geoffrey Chaucer, London 1905, p xxxii (brief).

Snell F J, The Poets, The Age of Transition, London 1905, 1.77.

CHEL, 2.281.

Steinberger C, Étude sur William Dunbar, Dublin 1908, p 35.

Marshal L E, Roberto Henryson e la Griseida, Borgo San Donnino 1910, pp 3, 12.

Enc Brit, 13.302.

Perrow E C, The Last Will and Testament as a Form of Literature, Trans Wisconsin Acad of Sciences Arts and Letters 7¹.718.

Stair-Kerr E, The Poets, Scotland under James IV, Paisley 1911, p 114 (brief).

Watt L M, Scottish Life and Poetry, London 1912, p 92.

Lawrence W W, The Love-Story in Troilus and Cressida, Shaksperian Studies, N Y 1916, p 203.

Mackie R L, Scotland, London 1916, p 286.

Metcalfe, edn, pp xviii, xxvii.

Rollins H E, The Troilus-Cressida Story, PMLA 32.396.

Barfield O, The Scottish Chaucerians, The New Statesman 17.274.

Knowlton E C, Nature in Middle English,

JEGP 20.192.

Golding L, The Scottish Chaucerians, The Saturday Review of Politics Literature Science and Art 134.783.

Quiller-Couch A, Studies in Literature, 2s, N Y and Cambridge Eng 1922, p 265.

Bullet G, The Fortunes of Cressida, The New Statesman 21.362.

Huxley A, Chaucer, Essays New and Old, London 1926; rptd N Y 1932, p 271.

Hammond E P, English Verse between Chaucer and Surrey, Durham N C and London 1927, p 25 (brief).

Ker W P, Form and Style in Poetry, London 1928, p 85.

Legouis HEL, p 171.

Saintsbury G, The Four Great Scottish Poets, N Y 1929, p 183.

Murray H M R, edn, p 10.

Nichols P H, Lydgate's Influence on the Aureate Terms of the Scottish Chaucerians, PMLA 47.518.

Elton O, The English Muse, London 1933, p 81.

Mackenzie A M, An Historical Survey of Scottish Literature, London 1933, p 76 (crit The Modern Scot 4.164).

Mackenzie W M, William Dunbar, Edinburgh Essays on Scots Literature, Edinburgh and London 1933, p 31.

Wood H H, Robert Henryson, Edinburgh Essays on Scots Literature, Edinburgh and London 1933, pp 12, 15, 17 (crit The Modern Scot 4.353).

Grierson H J C, Robert Henryson, The Modern Scot 4.297; rptd Aberdeen Univ Rev 21.206; rptd Robert Henryson, Essays and Addresses, London 1940, p 111.

Power W, Scotland and the Scots, Edinburgh and London 1934, p 190 (brief).

Rait R and G S Pryde, Scotland, N Y 1934; 2nd edn London 1954, p 308 (very brief).

Power W, Literature and Oatmeal, London 1935, p 47 (very brief; crit AnglB 48.151; The Scottish Bookman 1, no 4, p 152).

Muir E, Scottish Literature, Scott and Scotland, London 1936, p 62.

Speirs J, The Scots Literary Tradition, London 1940, pp 11, 23 and passim; rvsd edn London 1962, pp 37, 45 and passim.

Grierson H J C and J C Smith, A Critical History of English Poetry, London 1944; 2nd rvsd edn London 1947, p 55 (brief).

Stearns M W, Robert Henryson and the Leper Cresseid, MLN 59.266; Robert Henryson and the Aristotelian Tradition of Psychology, SP 41.492; The Planet Portraits of Robert Henryson, PMLA 59.911; Henry-

son and Chaucer, MLQ 6.271.
Roy J A, Of the Makaris A Causerie, UTQ 16.30.
Bennett OHEL, p 175.
Caird J B, Some Reflections on Scottish Literature, I. Poetry, Scottish Periodical 1.9.
Tillyard E M W, Henryson The Testament of Cresseid, London 1948; rptd as Henryson The Testament of Cresseid 1470? Poetry and its Background, London 1955, p 5.
Muir E, Robert Henryson, Essays on Literature and Society, London 1949, pp 7, 14; rvsd edn London 1965, pp 10, 17.
Stearns M W, Robert Henryson, N Y 1949, pp 4, 48, 60, 97.
Craig HEL, p 167.
Morgan E, Dunbar and the Language of Poetry, EC 2.142 (brief).
Murison, edn, p 1.
Renwick-Orton, pp 118, 415 (brief).
Wood H H, Scottish Literature, London 1952, p 14.
Ward A C, Illustrated History of Eng Lit, London N Y and Toronto 1953, p 40 (brief).
Cruttwell P, Two Scots Poets Dunbar and Henryson, The Age of Chaucer, A Guide to Eng Lit, London 1954; rptd London 1955, 1.184.
Elliott C, Two Notes on Henryson's Testament of Cresseid, JEGP 54.241.
Kinsley J, The Mediaeval Makars, London 1955, pp 18, 20.
Rossi S, Robert Henryson, Milan 1955, pp 8, 11, 47.
Sells A L, The Italian Influence in English Poetry, Bloomington Ind 1955, p 64.
Lewis C S, English Literature in the Sixteenth Century, Oxford 1954, p 174.
Stock N, Some Notes on Old Scots, Shenandoah 6, no 2, pp 27, 29.
Schlauch M, English Medieval Literature, Warsaw 1956, p 294.
Speirs J, Medieval English Poetry The Non-Chaucerian Tradition, London 1957, p 299 (brief reference).
Mackie R L, King James IV of Scotland, Edinburgh and London 1958, p 173 (crit J D Mackie, SHR 38.133).
Wittig K, The Scottish Tradition in Literature, Edinburgh 1958, p 35 and passim.
Kinghorn A M, The Mediaeval Makars, Texas Stud Lit and Lang 1.76.
Moran T, The Testament of Cresseid and the Book of Troylus, Litera 6.18.
Bayley J, The Characters of Love, N Y 1960, p 122.
Dickinson W C, Scotland from the Earliest Times to 1603, A New History of Scotland, Edinburgh and London 1961, 1.280.
Duncan D, Henryson's Testament of Cresseid, EC 11.128.
Harth S, Henryson Reinterpreted, EC 11.471.
Larkey S V, Leprosy in Medieval Romance, Bull of the History of Medicine 35.77.
McLaren M, The Wisdom of the Scots, London 1961, p 57.
Spearing A C, The Testament of Cresseid and the High Concise Style, Spec 37.208, 214.
Elliott, edn, pp vii, xxiii.
Moran T, The Meeting of the Lovers in the Testament of Cresseid, N&Q 208(ns 10).11.
Marken R, Chaucer and Henryson, Discourse 7.381.
Rossi, edn, p 34.
Spearing A C, Conciseness and the Testament of Cresseid, Criticism and Medieval Poetry, London 1964, pp 118, 125, 128, 130.
Hyde I, Poetic Imagery, SSL 2.184, 189, 195.
Kinghorn A M, The Minor Poems of Robert Henryson, SSL 3.39.
MacQueen J, As You Like It and Mediaeval Literary Tradition, Forum Mod Lang Stud 1.220 (brief).
Toliver H E, Robert Henryson from Moralitas to Irony, ESts 46.300, 305.
Fox D, The Scottish Chaucerians, Chaucer and Chaucerians, ed D S Brewer, University Alabama 1966, p 177.
Scott T, Dunbar A Critical Exposition of the Poems, Edinburgh and London 1966, pp 42, 347 and passim.
Aswell E D, The Role of Fortune in The Testament of Cresseid, PQ 46.471.
MacDonald D, Henryson and the Thre Prestis of Peblis, Neophil 51.176.
MacQueen J, Robert Henryson, London 1967, pp 26, 45, 145, 157.
Scott T, Late Medieval Scots Poetry, edn, pp 11, 33.
Wood H H, Two Scots Chaucerians, Writers and Their Work no 201, ed G Bullough, London 1967, pp 10, 23, 28, 43.
Fox, edn, pp 1, 20.
Chessell D, In the Dark Time, Critical Rev 12.61.
Hume K, Leprosy or Syphilis in Henryson's Testament of Cresseid, Engl Lang Notes 6.242.
Bibliography. Brydges E and J Haslewood, The British Bibliographer, London 1814, 4.305.
Smith G G, edn, 1.xlv; CHEL, 2.534.
Hammond, p 457.
Metcalfe, edn, p xxiv.

Rollins H E, The Troilus-Cressida Story, PMLA 32.395.

Dickins, edn, p 46.

Northrup C S, J Q Adams and A Keogh, A Register of Bibliographies of the English Language and Literature, New Haven London and Oxford 1925, p 197.

Spurgeon C F E, Five Hundred Years of Chaucer Criticism, ChS 2s 48[1]; rptd Cambridge 1925, 1[1].79 and passim.

Utley CR, p 99; Bennett OHEL, p 285; Brown-Robbins, Robbins-Cutler, no 285; Renwick-Orton, p 414 (brief).

Fox, edn, p 133.

[5] ORPHEUS AND EURYDICE.

MSS. 1, Nat Libr Scot Acc 4233 (Asloan), ff 247[a]–256[b] (1513–42; transcribed by Bülbring [Asloan-Bülbring] 1885–1895); 2, Nat Libr Scot 1.1.6 (Bannatyne), ff 317[b]–325[a] (1568). PRINT: 3, Nat Libr Scot 19.1.16 (Porteous of Noblenes and Ten Other Rare Tracts . . . Be W Chepman and A Myllar), pp 149–166 (1508) (STC, no 13166).

Pinkerton J, Ancient Scotish Poems, 2 vols, London and Edinburgh 1786, 2.471 (MS 2).

Brydges E and J Haslewood, The British Bibliographer, London 1814, 4.183 (MS 2).

Laing D, The Poems of George Bannatyne, Edinburgh 1824, p 3 (MS 2); An Account of the Contents of George Bannatyne's Manuscript, The Bannatyne Club, Edinburgh 1829, 35.43 (MS 2); The Knightly Tale of Golagrus and Gawane, Edinburgh 1827, f 2[a] (3 rptd).

Dickinson R and J P Edmond, Annals of Scottish Printing from 1507 to the Beginning of the 17th Century, Cambridge 1890, p 49 (PRINT 3).

Schipper J, The Poems of William Dunbar, pt 1, Denkschriften der kaiserlichen Akademie der Wissenschaften, Philo-Hist Classe, Vienna 1892, 40[2].5, 9, 14, 17 (MSS 1, 2, PRINT 3).

Murdoch J B, ed, The Bannatyne Manuscript, 4 vols, Hunterian Club, Glasgow 1896, 4.922 (MS 2).

Smith G G, Specimens of Middle Scots. Edinburgh and London 1902, pp lxvi, lxx, lxxiii, lxxiv (MSS 1, 2, PRINT 3).

Brown J T T, The Bannatyne Manuscript, SHR 1.136 (MS 2).

Smith G G, edn, l.xlix (Bülbring's Transcription of MS 1); 1.53; 3.27 (MS 1, notes in vol 1, alternate pp); 1.53; 3.66 (MS 2, notes in vol 1); 1.53; 3.26 (PRINT 3, notes in vol 1).

Stevenson G, ed, Pieces from the Makculloch and the Gray MSS, PSTS 65, Edinburgh and London 1918, pp 219, 303 (PRINT 3, note at end of text).

Craigie W A, ed, The Asloan Manuscript, 2 vols, PSTS ns 14, 16, Edinburgh 1923–25, 2.155, 281 (MS 1, notes at end of text).

Ritchie W T, ed, The Bannatyne Manuscript Writtin in Tyme of Pest, 4 vols, PSTS ns 5, 22, 23, 26, Edinburgh 1928–34, 4.182 (MS 2).

Beattie W, The Chepman and Myllar Prints A Facsimile with a Bibliographical Note, Edinburgh Biblio Soc, Oxford 1950, pp viii, 149 (3 described, rptd).

Baxter J W, William Dunbar, Edinburgh and London 1952, pp 178, 216, 217 (MSS 1, 2, PRINT 3).

Editions. Laing D, The Poems and Fables of Robert Henryson, Edinburgh 1865, pp 47, 248, 302 (notes at end of text; MSS 1, 2, PRINT 3; crit St James Magazine 24.60; rptd North British Review, American edn ns 44.81, Brit edn ns 44.154).

Smith G G, The Poems of Robert Henryson, 3 vols, PSTS 55, 58, 64, Edinburgh and London 1906, 1908, 1914, 1.53; 3.26 (notes in vol 1, text in vol 3; MS Asloan-Bülbring and MSS 2 and 3).

Metcalfe W M, The Poems of Robert Henryson, Paisley 1917, pp 171, 286 (notes at end of text; MSS 1, 2, 3).

Wood H H, The Poems and Fables of Robert Henryson, Edinburgh 1933, pp 129, 258 (variants in footnotes, notes at end of text; MS 2; crit J Speirs, Scrut 2.296; D Hamer, MLR 29.342; TLS Aug 3 1933, p 523; E Muir, The Spectator 151.290; The Modern Scot 4.163); 2nd edn rvsd Edinburgh 1958.

Gray M M, Scottish Poetry from Barbour to James VI, N Y 1935, p 75 (crit J Speirs, Scrut 6.83; W M Mackenzie, The Scottish Bookman 1, no 4, p 133).

Kinghorn A M, The Middle Scots Poets, London 1970, p 86 (notes at foot of page; MSS 1, 2, 3).

Selections. Murison D, Selections from the Poems of Robert Henryson, Edinburgh 1952, p 45 (glossings at foot of page; MS 1).

Elliott C, Robert Henryson Poems, Oxford 1963, pp 108, 156 (notes at end of text; MS 1); rptd from corrected sheets, Oxford 1966.

Textual Matters. Smith, edn, l.xlix; 3.x, xix.

Metcalfe, edn, p xxvi.

Isaac F, Walter Chepman and Andrew Myllar, Facsimiles and Illustrations No II, Eng-

lish & Scottish Printing Types 1501–35*
1508–41, printed for Bibliographical Soc,
Oxford 1930 (unpaged; brief discussion and
figure 87).
Wood, edn, p xxvi.
Language. Irving D, The History of Scotish
Poetry, Edinburgh 1861, p 595 (glossary).
Laing, edn, p 309 (glossary).
Murray J A H, The Dialect of the Southern
Counties of Scotland, London 1873.
Hahn O, Zur Verbal- und Nominalflexion
bei den schottischen Dichtern, Berlin 1887–
89 (see especially pt 3, p 14).
Browne W H, The Taill of Rauf Coilyear,
Baltimore 1903, pp 35, 139 (general discus-
sion of Middle Scots; glossary).
Millar J H, A Literary History of Scotland,
London 1903, p 687 (glossary).
Rodeffer J D, The Inflection of the English
Present Plural Indicative, Baltimore 1903,
pp 1, 23, 38.
Smith G G, edn, 1.83 (index of words, glos-
sary); CHEL, 2.101, 506.
Gray M M, Introd, Lancelot of the Laik,
PSTS ns 2, Edinburgh and London 1912,
2.xviii.
Metcalfe, edn, pp xx, 303 (brief discussion,
glossary).
Taylor R, Some Notes on the Use of Can
and Couth, JEGP 16.573.
Westergaard E, Prepositions in Lowland
Scotch, Angl 41.444 (some examples from
Henryson); Verbal Forms in Middle-Scotch,
Angl 43.95.
Watt L M, Language and Influences, Doug-
las's Aeneid, Cambridge 1920, p 149 (very
generally applicable).
Westergaard E, Studies in Prefixes and Suf-
fixes in Middle Scottish, London 1924.
Wood, edn, pp xxxi, 277 (discussion, glossary).
Patrick D, Scottish Literature, Chambers's
Cyclopædia, rvsd J L Geddie, Phila and
N Y 1938, 1.164.
Elliott C, Robert Henryson Poems, p 165
(glossary).
Murison D, Selections from the Poems of
Robert Henryson, Edinburgh 1952, p 4.
Aitken A J and P Bratley, An Archive of
Older Scottish Texts for Scanning by Com-
puter, SSL 4.45.
Scott T, Dunbar A Critical Exposition of the
Poems, Edinburgh and London 1966, p 351.
MacQueen J, Some Aspects of the Early Ren-
aissance in Scotland, Forum Mod Lang
Stud 3.209.
Kinghorn, edn, pp 45, 164 (note on Middle
Scots, glossary).

Versification. Smith G G, edn, 1.lxxxiii.
Saintsbury G, History of English Prosody,
London 1908; 2nd edn London 1923, 1.272.
Murison D, Selections from the Poems of
Robert Henryson, Edinburgh 1952, p 5.
Renwick-Orton, p 415 (brief).
Rossi S, Robert Henryson, Milan 1955, p 77.
Elliott C, Robert Henryson Poems, p x.
Date. Metcalfe, edn, p xviii.
Authorship. Douglas G, Trinity Coll Camb
1184 (Gale 0.3.12), f 9ᵃ (early 16 cent; gloss
to Eneados, book 1, line 12).
Wood, edn, pp xiii, xxvi.
Sources and Literary Relations. Laing D, edn,
p xxiv.
Smith G G, edn, 1.1; CHEL, 2.281.
Marshal L E, Roberto Henryson e la Gris-
eida, Borgo San Donnino 1910, p 11.
Enc Brit, 13.302.
Wirl J, Orpheus in der Englischen Literatur,
Vienna and Leipzig 1913, p 27.
Mendenhall J C, Aureate Terms A Study in
the Literary Diction of the 15th Century,
Lancaster Pa 1919.
Smith G G, Scottish Literature Character and
Influence, London 1919, p 17 (brief refer-
ence).
Patch H R, The Goddess Fortuna in Medi-
aeval Literature, Cambridge Mass 1927, p
167.
Ker W P, Form and Style in Poetry, London
1928, p 84 (brief).
Smith J M, The French Background of Mid-
dle Scots Literature, Edinburgh and Lon-
don 1934, p xviii.
Tilgner E, Germanische Studien die Aureate
Terms, Berlin 1936; rptd 1967, p 79.
Speirs J, The Scots Literary Tradition, Lon-
don 1940, p 30; rvsd 2nd edn London 1962,
p 50.
Rossi S, Robert Henryson, Milan 1955, p 76.
Mackie R L, King James IV of Scotland,
Edinburgh and London 1958, p 171 (crit
J D Mackie, SHR 38.133).
Kinghorn A M, The Mediaeval Makars,
Texas Stud Lit and Lang 1.73.
Hollander J, The Untuning of the Sky,
Princeton 1961, pp 84, 168.
Elliott C, Robert Henryson Poems, Oxford
1963, p x.
McMillan D J, Classical Tale Plus Folk Tale,
AN&Q 1.117.
Hyde I, Poetic Imagery, SSL 2.184.
Kinghorn A M, The Minor Poems of Robert
Henryson, SSL 3.32.
Gros Louis K R R, Robert Henryson's Or-
pheus and Eurydice and the Orpheus Tra-

ditions of the Middle Ages, Spec 41.643.
Scott T, Dunbar A Critical Exposition, Edinburgh and London 1966, p 354.
MacDonald D, Henryson and the Thre Prestis of Peblis, Neophil 51.174.
MacQueen J, Robert Henryson, London 1967, pp 18, 26, 65, 81, 88, 135, 145, 157; Some Aspects of the Early Renaissance in Scotland, Forum Mod Lang Stud 3.216.
Scheps W, William Wallace and His Buke, SSL 6.224.
Friedman J B, Orpheus in the Middle Ages, Cambridge Mass 1970.
Other Scholarly Problems. Stearns M W, A Note on Robert Henryson's Allusions to Religion and Law, MLN 59.258 (poet's attitude); Robert Henryson, N Y 1949, p 25 (contemp conditions).
Rossi S, Robert Henryson, Milan 1955, p 96 (biographical evidence).
Friedman J B, Henryson the Friars and the Confessio Reynardi, JEGP 66.555 (poet's attitude).
Wood H H, Two Scots Chaucerians, in Writers and Their Work no 201, ed G Bullough, London 1967, p 9 (biographical evidence).
Literary Criticism. Irving D, The History of Scotish Poetry, ed J A Carlyle, Edinburgh 1861, p 219 (illustrative quotes).
Laing D, edn, p xxiv.
Nichol J, A Sketch of Scottish Poetry, ed J Small, 2nd edn rvsd, EETS 11, London 1883, p xxi.
Schipper J, William Dunbar, Berlin 1884, p 38.
Eyre-Todd G, Mediæval Scottish Poetry, Glasgow 1892, p 87.
Gosse E, A Short History of Modern English Literature, N Y 1897; rvsd edn N Y 1906, p 47 (brief).
Millar J H, A Literary History of Scotland, London 1903, p 31.
Snell F J, The Poets, The Age of Transition, London 1905, 1.78.
CHEL, 2.281.
Steinberger C, Étude sur William Dunbar, Dublin 1908, p 35.
Marshal L E, Roberto Henryson e la Griseida, Borgo San Donnino 1910, pp 11, 17.
Enc Brit, 13.302.
Watt L M, Scottish Life and Poetry, London 1912, p 96 (brief).
Rhys E, The First Scottish Poets, London Toronto and N Y 1913, p 98.
Wirl J, Orpheus in der Englischen Literatur, Vienna and Leipzig 1913, p 27.

Ker W P, Form and Style in Poetry, London 1928, p 84 (brief).
Saintsbury G, The Fourt Great Scottish Poets, N Y 1929, p 183 (brief).
Mackenzie A M, An Historical Survey of Scottish Literature, London 1933, p 80 (crit The Modern Scot 4.164).
Wood H H, edn, pp xiv, xviii; Robert Henryson, Edinburgh Essays on Scots Literature, Edinburgh and London 1933, p 19 (crit The Modern Scott 4.353).
Gray M M, Scottish Poetry, N Y 1935, p ix.
Speirs J, The Scots Literary Tradition, London 1940, p 30; 2nd edn rvsd London 1962, p 50.
Moore M, Feeling and Precision, SR 52.503 (brief reference).
Stearns M W, Robert Henryson, N Y 1949, p 7.
Craig HEL, p 167 (very brief).
Murison D, Selections from the Poems of Robert Henryson, Edinburgh 1952, p 1.
Ward A C, Illustrated History of English Literature, London N Y and Toronto 1953, p 40 (brief).
Kinsley J, The Mediaeval Makars, London 1955, p 23.
Rossi S, Robert Henryson, Milan 1955, p 76.
Lewis C S, English Literature in the Sixteenth Century, Oxford 1954, p 174.
Mackie R L, King James IV of Scotland, Edinburgh and London 1958, p 171 (crit SHR 38.133).
Wittig K, The Scottish Tradition in Literature, Edinburgh 1958, pp 40, 44.
Kinghorn A M, The Mediaeval Makars, Texas Stud Lit and Lang 1.74, 84.
Harth S, Henryson Reinterpreted, EC 11.480.
Hollander J, The Untuning of the Sky, Princeton 1961, p 85.
McMillan D J, Classical Tale Plus Folk Tale, AN&Q 1.117.
Hyde I, Poetic Imagery, SSL 2.184.
Kinghorn A M, The Minor Poems of Robert Henryson, SSL 3.32, 39.
Fox D, The Scottish Chaucerians, Chaucer and Chaucerians, ed D S Brewer, University Alabama 1966, pp 176, 189.
Gros Louis K R R, Robert Henryson's Orpheus and Eurydice, Spec 41.646.
MacDonald D, Henryson and the Thre Prestis of Peblis, Neophil 51.171, 174.
MacQueen J, Robert Henryson, London 1967, pp 26, 31, 65, 81, 88, 93, 135, 143, 157; Some Aspects of the Early Renaissance in Scotland, Forum Mod Lang Stud 3.216.
Wood H H, Two Scots Chaucerians, London

1967, pp 20, 23.
Friedman J B, Orpheus in the Middle Ages, Cambridge Mass 1970, pp 12, 146, 148, 167, 195, 239.
Bibliography. Smith G G, edn, l.xlix; CHEL, 2.534.
Brown-Robbins, Robbins-Cutler, no 3442; Bennett OHEL, p 285; Renwick-Orton, p 415 (brief).
Beattie W, The Chepman and Myllar Prints, Edinburgh Bibliographical Soc, Oxford 1950, p xiii (crit W A Jackson, SHR 31.89).

[6] ROBENE AND MAKYNE.

MSS. 1, Nat Libr Scot 1.1.6 (Bannatyne), ff 365ᵃ–366ᵇ (1568); 2, BM Addit 30371 (Collection of Ancient Scotish Poems . . . Written Jan 1724 by James Bruce, Alderman), ff 77ᵃ–77ᵇ.
Pinkerton J, Ancient Scotish Poems, 2 vols, London and Edinburgh 1786, 2.471 (MS 1).
Brydges E and J Haslewood, The British Bibliographer, London 1814, 4.183 (MS 1).
Laing D, The Poems of George Bannatyne, Edinburgh 1824, p 3 (MS 1); An Account of the Contents of George Bannatyne's Manuscript, The Bannatyne Club, Edinburgh 1829, 35.43 (MS 1).
Schipper J, The Poems of William Dunbar, pt 1, Denkschriften der kaiserlichen Akademie der Wissenschaften, Philo-Hist Classe, Vienna 1892, 40².9, 17 (MS 1).
Murdoch J B, ed, the Bannatyne Manuscript, 4 vols, Hunterian Club, Glasgow 1896, 4.1050.
Smith G G, Specimens of Middle Scots, edn, pp lxvi, lxxiii (MS 1).
Brown J T T, The Bannatyne Manuscript, SHR 1.136.
Smith G G, The Poems of Robert Henryson, edn, 1.59; 3.90 (notes in vol 1).
Ritchie W T, ed, The Bannatyne Manuscript Written in Tyme of Pest, 4 vols, PSTS ns 5, 22, 23, 26, Edinburgh 1928–34, 4.308.
Baxter J W, William Dunbar, Edinburgh and London 1952, p 217 (MS 1).
Editions. Ramsay A, The Ever Green, 2 vols, Edinburgh 1724, 1.56 (occasional changes in wording, omissions, additions; MS 1); for subsequent edns of Ramsay see B Martin, Records of the Glasgow Biblio Soc 10 (1931).41.
Percy T, Reliques of Ancient English Poetry, London 1765; (numerous subsequent edns); ed H B Wheatley, London 1910, 2.82 (glossings at foot of page; Ramsay edn).

Dalrymple D, Ancient Scottish Poems from the MS of George Bannatyne, Edinburgh 1770, pp 98, 277; rptd Leeds 1815, pp 124, 325 (notes at end of text; MS 1).
The Caledoniad, London 1775, 2.96.
Pinkerton J, Select Scotish Ballads, 2 vols, London 1783, 2.63, 181 (notes at end of text; Dalrymple edn).
Caw G, The Poetical Museum, Hawick 1784, p 271 (glossings at foot of page).
Sibbald J, Chronicle of Scottish Poetry from the 13th Century, 4 vols, Edinburgh and London 1802, 1.115 (introductory and end notes; MS 1).
Campbell T, Specimens of the British Poets, London 1819, 2.77 (glossings at foot of page).
Ritson J, The Caledonian Muse, printed 1785, published London 1821, p 21 (Dalrymple edn).
Chalmers G, Robene and Makyne and The Testament of Cresseid, Bannatyne Club Publications 6, Edinburgh 1824, p 1 (separate pagination; MS 1).
Child F J, English and Scottish Ballads, Boston 1857–59, 4.245 (Sibbald edn).
Laing D, The Poems and Fables of Robert Henryson, Edinburgh 1865, pp 3, 229 (notes at end of text; MS 1; crit St James Magazine 24.60; rptd North British Review, American edn ns 44.81, British edn ns 44.154).
Morley H, Shorter English Poems, London 1876, p 74.
Ross J, The Book of Scottish Poems, Paisley 1882, 1.131.
Eyre-Todd G, Mediæval Scottish Poetry, Abbotsford Series of the Scottish Poets, Glasgow 1892, p 91 (glossings in margin).
Browne W H, Selections from the Early Scottish Poets, Baltimore 1896, pp 39, 181 (notes at end of text; Laing edn).
Henderson T F, A Little Book of Scottish Verse, London 1899; 2nd edn London 1909, p 17 (glossings at foot of page).
Quiller-Couch A, The Oxford Book of English Verse, Oxford 1900; new edn Oxford 1939, p 20 (glossings at foot of page).
Arber E, English Songs, Dunbar and His Times, The Dunbar Anthology, British Anthologies, London 1901, 1.146, 298 (13½ stanzas; spelling modernized, notes at end of text; MS 1).
Smith G G, Specimens of Middle Scots, Edinburgh and London 1902, pp 21, 272 (notes at end of text; MS 1).
Smith G G, The Poems of Robert Henryson,

3 vols, PSTS 55, 58, 64, Edinburgh and London 1906, 1908, 1914, 1.59; 3.90 (notes in vol 1, text in vol 3; MS 1).

Dixon W M, The Edinburgh Book of Scottish Verse, London 1910, p 12 (glossings at foot of page).

Douglas G, The Book of Scottish Poetry, London and Leipsic 1911, p 95 (glossings at foot of page; Smith edn; The Poems of Robert Henryson).

Neilson W A and K G T Webster, Chief British Poets of the 14th and 15th Centuries, Boston N Y etc 1916, pp 383, 434 (brief note at end of text, glossings at foot of page; Smith edn, The Poems of Robert Henryson).

Metcalfe W M, The Poems of Robert Henryson, Paisley 1917, pp 199, 291 (notes at end of text; MS 1).

Lawson Mrs A and A Lawson, A St Andrews Treasury of Scottish Verse, London 1920; 2nd edn London 1933, p 2 (glossings at foot of page).

Buchan J, The Northern Muse, An Anthology of Scots Vernacular Poetry, London 1924, pp 41, 463 (glossings at foot of page, brief note at end of text; MS 1).

Murray H M R, Selected Fables The Testament of Cresseid and Robene and Makyne, London 1930, p 91 (MS 1).

Wood H H, The Poems and Fables of Robert Henryson, Edinburgh 1933, pp 151, 266 (notes at end of text; MS 1; crit J Speirs, Scrut 2.296; D Hamer, MLR 29.342; TLS Aug 3 1933, p 523; E Muir, The Spectator 151.290; The Modern Scot 4.163); 2nd edn rvsd Edinburgh 1958.

Mackie R L, A Book of Scottish Verse, The World's Classics no 417, London 1934, p 11 (glossings at foot of page); 2nd edn London Glasgow N Y 1967, p 12.

Gray M M, Scottish Poetry from Barbour to James VI, N Y 1935, p 87 (crit J Speirs, Scrut 6.83; W M Mackenzie, The Scottish Bookman 1, no 4, p 133).

[Grieve C M] MacDiarmid H, The Golden Treasury of Scottish Poetry, London 1940 (crit L MacNeice, The New Statesman and Nation 21.66; TLS Feb 15 1941, pp 78, 84); rptd in The Golden Treasury Series, London 1948, p 147.

Oliver J W and J C Smith, A Scots Anthology from the 13th to the 20th Century, Edinburgh and London 1949, p 27 (spelling modernized; glossings at foot of page).

Auden W H and N H Pearson, Poets of the English Language, N Y 1950, p 296 (glossings at foot of page).

Murison D, Selections from the Poems of Robert Henryson, Edinburgh 1952, p 47 (glossings at foot of page; MS 1).

Elliott C, Robert Henryson Poems, Oxford 1963, pp 125, 161 (notes at end of text; MS 1); rptd from corrected sheets, Oxford 1966.

Rossi S, I Chauceriani Scozzesi, Napoli 1964, p 164 (notes at foot of page).

Scott T, Late Medieval Scots Poetry, London 1967, p 66 (Wood edn).

Kinghorn A M, The Middle Scots Poets, London 1970, p 66 (notes at foot of page; MS 1).

MacQueen J, Ballattis of Luve, Edinburgh 1970, p 11 (MS 1; glossings at foot of page).

Scott T, The Penguin Book of Scottish Verse, London 1970, p 107 (glossings at foot of page).

Selections. Poems in the Scottish Dialect by Several Celebrated Poets, Glasgow 1748, p 33.

Masson R O, Three Centuries of English Poetry Being Selections from Chaucer to Herrick, London 1876, p 118 (spelling modernized; glossings at foot of page).

Chambers R, Chambers's Cyclopædia, Phila and N Y 1901–03; rvsd J L Geddie, Phila and N Y 1938, 1.189 (brief excerpts).

Textual Matters. Percy, edn, 2.81.

Smith G G, The Poems of Robert Henryson, edn, l.lv, lvii; 3.x, xix.

Murray, edn, p 11; Wood, edn, p xxvii.

Language. Ramsay A, edn, 2.265 (glossary).

Percy, edn, 3.377 (glossary).

Dalrymple, edn, p 317 (glossary); rptd Leeds 1815, p 367, [added] Glossary, p 1 [separate pagination].

Pinkerton, edn, 1.154; 2.193 (glossaries).

Sibbald, edn, vol 4 [unpaged] (glossary).

Laing, edn, p 309 (glossary).

Murray J A H, The Dialect of the Southern Counties of Scotland, London 1873.

Hahn O, Zur Verbal- und Nominalflexion bei den schottischen Dictern, Berlin 1887–89 (see especially pt 3, p 14).

Browne, edn, pp 1, 197 (discussion in introd; glossary).

Arber, edn, p 300 (glossary and index).

Smith G G, Specimens of Middle Scots, edn, pp xi, 325 (history and philology of Middle Scots; glossary).

Browne W H, The Taill of Rauf Coilyear, Baltimore 1903, pp 35, 139 (general discussion of Middle Scots; glossary).

Millar J H, A Literary History of Scotland, London 1903, p 687 (glossary).

Rodeffer J D, The Inflection of the English Present Plural Indicative, Baltimore 1903, pp 1, 23, 38.

Smith G G, The Poems of Robert Henryson, edn, 1.83 (index of words, glossary); CHEL, 2.101, 506.

Dixon, edn, p 897 (glossary).

Gray M M, Introd, Lancelot of the Laik, PSTS ns 2, Edinburgh and London 1912, 2.xviii.

Metcalfe, edn, pp xx, 303 (brief discussion, glossary).

Westergaard E, Prepositions in Lowland Scotch, Angl 41.444 (some examples from Henryson); Verbal Forms in Middle-Scotch, Angl 43.95.

Lawson Mrs A and A Lawson, edn, p 263 (glossary).

Watt L M, Language and Influences, Douglas's Aeneid, Cambridge 1920, p 149 (very generally applicable).

Westergaard E, Studies in Prefixes and Suffixes in Middle Scottish, London 1924.

Murray H M R, edn, p 12.

Wood H H, edn, pp xxxi, 277 (discussion, glossary).

Patrick D, Scottish Literature, Chambers's Cyclopædia of English Literature, rvsd J L Geddie, Phila and N Y 1938, 1.164.

[Grieve] MacDiarmid, edn, p 393 (glossary).

Oliver and Smith, edn, p 497 (glossaries).

Murison, edn, p 4.

Elliott, edn, p 165 (glossary).

Rossi, edn, p 261 (discussion and glossary).

Scott T, Dunbar A Critical Exposition, Edinburgh and London 1966, p 351; Late Medieval Scots Poetry, edn, pp 21, 189 (discussion, glossary).

Kinghorn, edn, pp 45, 164 (note on Middle Scots, glossary).

Versification. Guest E, A History of English Rhythms, 2 vols, London 1838; ed W W Skeat, new edn [in 1 vol] London 1882, p 594 (brief reference).

Bulloch J M, French Metres in Early Scottish Poetry, Scottish Notes and Queries 2.115.

Henderson T F, Scottish Vernacular Literature, Edinburgh 1898; 2nd edn rvsd 1900; 3rd edn rvsd 1910, p 117.

Smith G G, The Poems of Robert Henryson, edn, 1.lxxxiii.

Saintsbury G, History of English Prosody, London 1908; 2nd edn London 1923, 1.271; Historical Manual of English Prosody,

London 1910; rptd London 1914, 1.56.

Smith J M, The French Background of Middle Scots Literature, Edinburgh and London 1934, p 161.

Murison, edn, p 5.

Renwick-Orton, p 415 (brief).

Elliott, edn, p ix.

Scott T, Late Medieval Scots Poetry, edn, pp 18, 20.

Date. Metcalfe, edn, p xviii.

Authorship. Wood, edn, p xxvii.

Sources and Literary Relations. Saintsbury G, The Flourishing of Romance and the Rise of Allegory, N Y 1897, p 271.

Smith G G, The Transition Period, Periods of European Lit, Edinburgh and London 1900, 4.47.

Chambers R, Chambers's Cyclopaedia, Phila and N Y 1901–03; rvsd J L Geddie, Phila and N Y 1938, 1.189.

Seccombe T and W R Nicoll, The Scots Poets, The Bookman Illustrated History of Eng Lit, London 1906, 1.19.

Smith G G, The Poems of Robert Henryson, edn, 1.lvi; CHEL, 2.283.

Marshal L E, Roberto Henryson e la Griseida, Borgo San Donnino 1910, p 9.

Enc Brit, 13.302.

Mendenhall J C, Aureate Terms A Study in the Literary Diction of the 15th Century, Lancaster Pa 1919.

Smith G G, Scottish Literature Character and Influence, London 1919, p 98 (brief reference).

Legouis HEL, p 173.

Murray H M R, edn, p 11.

Jones W P, The Pastourelle, Cambridge Mass 1931, pp 24, 168 (brief); A Source for Henryson's Robene and Makyne? MLN 46.457.

Smith J M, The French Background of Middle Scots Literature, Edinburgh and London 1934, pp xviii, xxviii, 42, 101.

Grierson H J C and J C Smith, A Critical History of English Poetry, London 1944; 2nd rvsd edn London 1947, p 55 (brief).

Moore A K, Robene and Makyne, MLR 43.400; The Secular Lyric in Middle English, Lexington Ky 1951, p 189.

Renwick-Orton, p 415 (brief).

Kinsley J, The Mediaeval Makars, Scottish Poetry A Critical Survey, London 1955, p 23.

Rossi S, Robert Henryson, Milan 1955, p 71.

Lewis C S, English Literature in the Sixteenth Century, Oxford 1954, p 175.

Schlauch M, English Medieval Literature,

Warsaw 1956, p 295.
Enkvist N E, The Seasons of the Year, Societas Scientiarum Fennica Commentationes Humanarum Litterarum, Helsingfors 1957, p 156.
Mackie R L, King James IV of Scotland, Edinburgh and London 1958, p 173 (crit J D Mackie, SHR 38.133).
Elliott, edn, pp viii, xxiv.
Maclaine A H, The Christis Kirk Tradition, SSL 2.16.
Kinghorn A M, The Minor Poems of Robert Henryson, SSL 3.30.
Wood H H, Two Scots Chaucerians, Writers and Their Work no 201, ed G Bullough, London 1967, p 38.
Mustanoja T F, The Suggestive Use of Christian Names in Middle English Poetry, Medieval Literature and Folklore Studies Essays in Honor of Francis Lee Utley, ed J Mandel and B A Rosenberg, New Brunswick N J 1970, pp 63, 71.
Literary Criticism. Warton T, History of English Poetry, London 1774–81; ed W C Hazlitt, London 1871, 3.265.
Irving D, The Lives of the Scotish Poets, 2nd edn, London 1810, 1.388.
H R, Robert Henryson, Lives of Scottish Poets, ed J Robertson, London 1822, 3.10.
Laing D, edn, 1.43 (very brief; paginated separately from text of poems).
Gilfillan G, Specimens with Memoirs, Edinburgh and London 1860, 1.53 (brief).
Irving D, The History of Scotish Poetry, ed J A Carlyle, Edinburgh 1861, p 224 (illustrative quotes).
Taylor J, The Imperial Dictionary of Universal Biography, London [1863], 2.878 (very brief).
Morley H, A First Sketch of English Literature, London 1873; rvsd London 1896, p 201.
Wright T, The History of Scotland, London and N Y [1873–74], 1.290.
Wilson J G, The Poets and Poetry of Scotland, N Y 1876, 1.19 (brief).
Henley W E, Robert Henryson, The English Poets, ed T H Ward, London and N Y 1880; (numerous subsequent edns) N Y 1924, 1.138.
Nichol J, A Sketch of Scottish Poetry, ed J Small; 2nd edn rvsd EETS 11, London 1883, p xxii.
Ross J M, Scottish History and Literature, Glasgow 1884, p 163.
Schipper J, William Dunbar, Berlin 1884, p 39.

Fitzgibbon H M, Early English and Scottish Poetry, N Y London and Melbourne 1888, p lix.
Morley, 6.254.
Oliphant F R, Robert Henryson, Blackwood's Edinburgh Magazine 148.504; rptd Littell's Living Age 187.543.
Eyre-Todd, edn, p 90; Brandl, 2^1.716.
Jusserand J J, Histoire littéraire du peuple anglais, Paris 1894, 1.525.
Gosse E, A Short History of Modern English Literature, N Y 1897; rvsd edn N Y 1906, p 47 (brief).
Saintsbury G, The Flourishing of Romance and the Rise of Allegory, N Y 1897, p 272.
Henderson T F, Scottish Vernacular Literature, Edinburgh 1898; 2nd edn rvsd; 3rd edn rvsd Edinburgh 1910, pp 118, 125; edn, pp xv, 11, 17.
Smith G G, The Transition Period, Periods of European Lit, Edinburgh and London 1900, 4.47 and passim.
Chambers R, Chambers's Cyclopædia, Phila and N Y 1901–03; rvsd J L Geddie 1938, 1.189.
M'Ilwraith W, A Sketch of Scottish Literature, Annual Burns Chronicle 10.20.
Millar J H, A Literary History of Scotland, London 1903, p 29.
Moorman F W, The Interpretation of Nature in English Poetry from Beowulf to Shakespeare, QF 95.138, 141.
Snell F J, The Poets, The Age of Transition, London 1905, 1.78.
Seccombe T and W R Nicoll, The Scots Poets, The Bookman Illustrated Hist of Eng Lit, London 1906, 1.19 (very brief).
CHEL, 2.283.
Steinberger C, Étude sur William Dunbar, Dublin 1908, p 35.
Marshal L E, Roberto Henryson e la Griseida, Borgo San Donnino 1910, p 9.
Enc Brit, 13.302.
Stair-Kerr E, The Poets, Scotland under James IV, Paisley 1911, p 115 (brief).
Watt L M, Scottish Life and Poetry, London 1912, p 93.
Metcalfe, edn, pp xviii, xxvii.
Golding L, The Scottish Chaucerians, The Saturday Review of Politics Literature Science and Art 134.783.
Quiller-Couch A, Studies in Literature, 2s, N Y and Cambridge Eng 1922, p 268.
Legouis HEL, p 173.
Saintsbury G, The Four Great Scottish Poets, N Y 1929, p 184.
Murray H M R, edn, p 11.

Mackenzie A M, An Historical Survey of Scottish Literature, London 1933, p 80 (crit The Modern Scot 4.164).

Wood H H, edn, pp 15, 20.

Grierson H J C, Robert Henryson, The Modern Scot 4.297; rptd Aberdeen Univ Review 21.206; rptd Robert Henryson, Essays and Addresses, London 1940, p 116.

Rait R and G S Pryde, Scotland, N Y 1934; 2nd edn London 1954, p 308 (brief).

Grierson H J C and J C Smith, A Critical History of English Poetry, London 1944; 2nd rvsd edn London 1947, p 55 (brief).

Bennett OHEL, p 175.

Caird J B, Some Reflections on Scottish Literture, I. Poetry, Scottish Periodical 1.10.

Stearns M W, Robert Henryson, N Y 1949, p 7.

Craig HEL, p 167 (brief).

Moore A K, The Secular Lyric in Middle English, Lexington Ky 1951, p 188.

Murison, edn, p 1.

Renwick-Orton, pp 118, 415 (brief).

Hyman S E, The Language of Scottish Poetry, KR 16.31 (brief).

Kinsley J, The Mediaeval Makars, London 1955, p 23.

Rossi S, Robert Henryson, Milan 1955, pp 10, 71, 94.

Lewis C S, English Literature in the Sixteenth Century, Oxford 1954, p 175.

Schlauch M, English Medieval Literature, Warsaw 1956, p 295.

Enkvist N E, The Seasons of the Year, Societas Scientiarum Fennica Commentationes Humanarum Litterarum, Helsingfors 1957, p 156.

Mackie R L, King James IV of Scotland, Edinburgh and London, 1958, pp 171, 173.

Wittig K, The Scottish Tradition in Literature, Edinburgh 1958, pp 36, 44.

Harth S, Henryson Reinterpreted, EC 11.480.

Elliott, edn, pp viii, xxiv.

Maclaine A H, The Christis Kirk Tradition, SSL 2.16.

Rossi, edn, p 41.

Kinghorn A M, The Minor Poems of Robert Henryson, SSL 3.30, 39.

Fox D, The Scottish Chaucerians, Chaucer and Chaucerians, ed D S Brewer, University Alabama 1966, p 178.

Wood H H, Two Scots Chaucerians, Writers and Their Work no 201, ed Bullough, London 1967, pp 20, 23, 38.

Bibliography. Craik G L, A Compendious History of English Literature, N Y 1877, 1.409 (brief).

Smith G G, The Poems of Robert Henryson, edn, l.lv, lvii.

Brown-Robbins, Robbins-Cutler, no 2831; Bennett OHEL, p 285; Renwick-Orton, p 415 (brief).

[7] THE BLUDY SERK.

MS. Nat Libr Scot 1.1.6 (Bannatyne), ff 325ᵃ–326ᵇ (1568).

Pinkerton J, Ancient Scotish Poems, 2 vols, London and Edinburgh 1786, 2.471.

Brydges E and J Haslewood, The British Bibliographer, London 1814, 4.183.

Laing D, The Poems of George Bannatyne, Edinburgh 1824, p 3; An Account of the Contents of George Bannatyne's Manuscript, The Bannatyne Club, Edinburgh 1829, 35.43.

Schipper J, The Poems of William Dunbar, pt 1, Denkschriften der kaiserlichen Akademie der Wissenschaften, Philo-Hist Classe, Vienna 1892, 40ᵃ.9, 17.

Murdoch J B, ed, The Bannatyne Manuscript, 4 vols, Hunterian Club, Glasgow 1896, 4.942.

Smith G G, Specimens of Middle Scots, Edinburgh and London 1902, pp lxvi, lxxiii.

Brown J T T, The Bannatyne Manuscript, SHR 1.136.

Smith G G, edn, 1.61; 3.96 (notes in vol 1).

Ritchie W T, ed, The Bannatyne Manuscript Written in Tyme of Pest, 4 vols, PSTS ns 5, 22, 23, 26, Edinburgh 1928–34, 4.202.

Baxter J W, William Dunbar, Edinburgh and London 1952, p 217.

Editions. Pinkerton J, Scotish Poems Reprinted from Scarce Editions, 3 vols, London 1792, 3.189.

Sibbald J, Chronicle of Scottish Poetry from the 13th Century, 4 vols, Edinburgh and London 1802, 1.178 (introductory and end notes).

Laing D, Select Remains of the Ancient Popular Poetry of Scotland, Edinburgh 1822; rptd Edinburgh 1884; edited with additions and corrections J Small, Edinburgh and London 1885, p 199.

Child F J, English and Scottish Ballads, Boston 1857–59, 8.147.

Aytoun W E, The Ballads of Scotland, Edinburgh and London 1858; 2nd edn rvsd and augmented, Edinburgh and London 1859, 1.86.

Laing D, The Poems and Fables of Robert Henryson, Edinburgh 1865, pp 10, 238 (notes at end of text; crit St James Magazine 24.60, rptd North British Review,

American edn ns 44.81, Brit edn ns 44.154).

Arber E, English Songs, Dunbar and His Times, The Dunbar Anthology, British Anthologies, London 1901, 1.151, 299 (spelling modernized, note at end of text).

Quiller-Couch A, The Oxford Book of English Verse, Oxford 1900; new edn 1939, p 16 (glossings at foot of page).

Smith G G, The Poems of Robert Henryson, 3 vols, PSTS 55, 58, 64, Edinburgh and London 1906, 1908, 1914, 1.61; 3.96 (notes in vol 1, text in vol 3).

Dixon W M, The Edinburgh Book of Scottish Verse, London 1910, p 17 (glossings at foot of page).

Metcalfe W M, The Poems of Robert Henryson, Paisley 1917, pp 204, 291 (notes at end of text).

Carver G, The Catholic Tradition in English Literature, N Y 1926, p 30 (glossings at foot of page).

Wood H H, The Poems and Fables of Robert Henryson, Edinburgh 1933; 2nd edn rvsd Edinburgh 1958, pp 173, 271 (notes at end of text; crit J Speirs, Scrut 2.296; D Hamer, MLR 29.342; TLS Aug 3 1933, p 523; E Muir, The Spectator 151.290; The Modern Scot 4.163).

Gray M M, Scottish Poetry from Barbour to James VI, N Y 1935, p 90 (crit J Speirs, Scrut 6.83; W M Mackenzie, The Scottish Bookman 1, no 4, p 133).

Cecil D, The Oxford Book of Christian Verse, Oxford 1940, p 19.

Elliott C, Robert Henryson Poems, Oxford 1963, pp 115, 158 (notes at end of text); rptd from corrected sheets, Oxford 1966.

Selection. Irving D, The Lives of the Scotish Poets, 2 vols, Edinburgh 1804; 2nd edn improved London 1810, 1.387.

Textual Matters. Smith G G, edn, 1.lviii; 3.x, xix; Wood, edn, p xxviii.

Language. Pinkerton, edn, 3.227 (glossary).

Sibbald, edn, vol 4 [unpaged] (glossary).

Irving D, The History of Scotish Poetry, Edinburgh 1861, p 595 (glossary).

Laing, Poems and Fables, edn, p 309 (glossary).

Murray J A H, The Dialect of the Southern Counties of Scotland, London 1873.

Hahn O, Zur Verbal- und Nominalflexion bei den schottischen Dichtern, Berlin 1887–89 (see especially pt 3, p 14).

Arber, edn, p 300 (glossary and index).

Millar J H, A Literary History of Scotland, London 1903, p 687 (glossary).

Browne W H, The Taill of Rauf Coilyear, Baltimore 1903, pp 35, 139 (general discussion of Middle Scots; glossary).

Rodeffer J D, The Inflection of the English Present Plural Indicative, Baltimore 1903, pp 1, 23, 38.

Smith G G, edn, 1.83 (index of words and glossary); CHEL, 2.101, 506.

Dixon, edn, p 897 (glossary).

Gray M M, Introd, Lancelot of the Laik, PSTS ns 2, Edinburgh and London 1912, 2.xviii.

Metcalfe, edn, pp xx, 303 (brief discussion, glossary).

Westergaard E, Prepositions in Lowland Scotch, Angl 41.444 (some examples from Henryson); Verbal Forms in Middle-Scotch, Angl 43.95.

Watt L M, Language and Influences, Douglas's Aeneid, Cambridge 1920, p 149 (very generally applicable).

Westergaard E, Studies in Prefixes and Suffixes in Middle Scottish, London 1924.

Wood, edn, pp xxxi, 277 (discussion, glossary).

Patrick D, Scottish Literature, Chambers's Cyclopædia of English Literature, rvsd J L Geddie, Phila and N Y 1938, 1.164.

Elliott, edn, p 165 (glossary).

Scott T, Dunbar A Critical Exposition of the Poems, Edinburgh and London 1966, p 351.

Versification. Brandl, 2¹.716.

Henderson T F, Scottish Vernacular Literature, Edinburgh 1898; 2nd edn rvsd Edinburgh 1900; 3rd edn rvsd Edinburgh 1910, p 117.

Smith G G, edn, 1.lxxxiii.

Smith J M, The French Background of Middle Scots Literature, Edinburgh and London 1934, p 161.

Renwick-Orton, p 415 (brief); Elliott, edn, p ix.

Date. Metcalfe, edn, p xviii.

Sources and Literary Relations. Irving D, The History of Scotish Poetry, Edinburgh 1861, p 222.

Nichol J, A Sketch of Scottish Poetry, ed J Small; 2nd edn rvsd, EETS 11, London 1883, p xxii.

Smith G G, edn, 1.lix.

Mendenhall J C, Aureate Terms A Study in the Literary Diction of the 15th Century, Lancaster Pa 1919.

Smith J M, The French Background of Middle Scots Literature, p 101.

Renwick-Orton, p 415 (brief).

Rossi S, Robert Henryson, Milan 1955, p 88.

Kinghorn A M, The Minor Poems of Robert Henryson, SSL 3.32, 39.
Literary Criticism. Irving D, The Lives of the Scotish Poets, 2nd edn, London 1810, 1.386.
H R, Robert Henryson, Lives of Scottish Poets, ed J Robertson, London 1822, 3.8.
Irving D, The History of Scotish Poetry, ed J A Carlyle, Edinburgh 1861, p 221 (illustrative quotes).
Morley H, A First Sketch of English Literature, London 1873; rvsd London 1896, p 201.
Ross J M, Scottish History and Literature, Glasgow 1884, p 162.
Schipper J, William Dunbar, Berlin 1884, p 39.
Morley, 6.256 (very brief).
Oliphant F R, Robert Henryson, Blackwood's Edinburgh Magazine 148.504; rptd Littell's Living Age 187.543.
Eyre-Todd G, Mediæval Scottish Poetry, Abbotsford Series, Glasgow 1892, p 89.
Brandl, 2¹.716.
Henderson T F, Scottish Vernacular Literature, Edinburgh 1898; 2nd edn rvsd 1900; 3rd edn rvsd Edinburgh 1910, p 120.
Chambers R, Chambers's Cyclopædia, Phila and N Y 1901–03; rvsd J L Geddie, Phila and N Y 1938, 1.190 (brief).
Millar J H, A Literary History of Scotland, London 1903, p 30.
Snell F J, The Poets, The Age of Transition, London 1905, 1.79.
Stair-Kerr E, The Poets, Scotland under James IV, Paisley 1911, p 115 (brief).
Watt L M, Scottish Life and Poetry, London 1912, p 95.
Quiller-Couch A, Studies in Literature, 2s, N Y and Cambridge Eng 1922, p 268 (very brief).
Saintsbury G, The Four Great Scottish Poets, N Y 1929, p 185 (brief).
Wood H H, edn, p 25.
Rait R and G S Pryde, Scotland, N Y 1934; 2nd edn London 1954, p 308 (brief).
Craig HEL, p 167 (brief).
Renwick-Orton, p 415 (brief).
Kinsley J, The Mediaeval Makars, London 1955, p 23 (very brief).
Rossi S, Robert Henryson, Milan 1955, pp 11, 83, 86.
Elliott, edn, p ix.
Hyde I, Poetic Imagery, SSL 2.185.
Kinghorn A M, The Minor Poems of Robert Henryson, SSL 3.32, 39.

Wood H H, Two Scots Chaucerians, Writers and Their Work, no 201, ed Bullough, London 1967, p 23.
Bibliography. Smith G G, edn, 1.lviii.
Brown Reg, no 2318; Brown-Robbins, Robbins-Cutler, no 3599.

[8] THE GARMONT OF GUD LADEIS.

MS. Nat Libr Scot 1.1.6 (Bannatyne), ff 215ª–215ᵇ (1568).
Pinkerton J, Ancient Scottish Poems, 2 vols, London and Edinburgh 1786, 2.471.
Brydges E and J Haslewood, The British Bibliographer, London 1814, 4.183.
Laing D, The Poems of George Bannatyne, Edinburgh 1824, p 3; An Account of the Contents of George Bannatyne's Manuscript, The Bannatyne Club, Edinburgh 1829, 35.43.
Schipper J, The Poems of William Dunbar, pt 1, Denkschriften der kaiserlichen Akademie der Wissenschaften, Philo-Hist Classe, Vienna 1892, 40².9, 17.
Murdoch J B, ed, The Bannatyne Manuscript, 4 vols, Hunterian Club, Glasgow 1896, 3.611.
Smith G G, Specimens of Middle Scots, Edinburgh and London 1902, pp lxvi, lxxiii.
Brown J T T, The Bannatyne Manuscript, SHR 1.136.
Smith G G, edn, 1.63; 3.102 (notes in vol 1).
Ritchie W T, ed, The Bannatyne Manuscript Written in Tyme of Pest, 4 vols, PSTS ns 5, 22, 23, 26, Edinburgh 1928–34, 3.252.
Baxter J W, William Dunbar, Edinburgh and London 1952, p 217.
Editions. Ramsay A, The Ever Green, 2 vols, Edinburgh 1724, 1.234 (occasional changes in wording, omissions, additions); for subsequent edns of Ramsay see B Martin, Records of the Glasgow Biblio Soc, 10 (1931).41.
Ruddiman W, Choice Collection of Scots Poems, Edinburgh 1766, p 134.
Dalrymple D, Ancient Scottish Poems, from the MS of George Bannatyne, Edinburgh 1770, pp 103, 279 (crit O Gilchrist, Ancient Scottish Poems, Censura Literaria, ed Brydges, London 1807, 5.238); rptd Leeds 1815, pp 130, 327 (notes at end of text).
Ellis G, Specimens of the Early English Poets, 5 edns, London 1790, 1801, 1803, 1811, 1845 (5th edn corrected), 1.294 (spelling, occasional wording modernized; glossings at foot of page; Dalrymple edn).
Fairholt F W, Satirical Songs and Poems on Costume from the 13th to the 19th Cen-

tury, Percy Soc 27, London 1849, p 59 (glossings at foot of page; Dalrymple edn).

Gilfillan G, Specimens with Memoirs of the Less-Known Poets, Edinburgh and London 1860, 1.57 (glossings at foot of page).

Irving D, The History of Scotish Poetry, ed J A Carlyle, Edinburgh 1861, p 223 (Dalrymple edn).

Laing D, The Poems and Fables of Robert Henryson, Edinburgh 1865, pp 8, 238 (notes at end of text; crit St James Magazine 24.60, rptd North British Review, American edn ns 44.81, Brit edn ns 44.154).

Clarke C C, Specimens with Memoirs of the Less-Known British Poets, Edinburgh 1868, 1.57.

Henderson E, The Annals of Dunfermline, Glasgow 1879, p 722 (Laing edn).

Henley W E, Robert Henryson, The English Poets, ed T H Ward, London and N Y 1880; (numerous subsequent edns) N Y 1924, 1.140 (glossings at foot of page).

Fitzgibbon H M, Early English and Scottish Poetry, London ·N Y and Melbourne 1888 pp 90, 431 (spelling modernized; notes at end of text).

Eyre-Todd G, Mediæval Scottish Poetry, Abbotsford Series of the Scottish Poets, Glasgow 1892, p 96 (glossings in margin).

Browne W H, Selections from the Early Scottish Poets, Baltimore 1896, p 43 (Laing edn).

Smith G G, The Poems of Robert Henryson, 3 vols, PSTS 55, 58, 64, Edinburgh and London 1906, 1908, 1914, 1.63; 3.102 (notes in vol 1, text in vol 3).

Dixon W M, The Edinburgh Book of Scottish Verse, London 1910, p 22 (glossings at foot of page).

Neilson W A and K G T Webster, Chief British Poets of the 14th and 15th Centuries, Boston N Y etc 1916, pp 384, 434 (brief note at end of text, glossings at foot of page; Smith edn).

Metcalfe W M, The Poems of Robert Henryson, Paisley 1917, pp 209, 292 (notes at end of text).

Brougham E M, Corn from Olde Fieldes, London 1918; rptd 1922, p 63 (spelling modernized).

Buchan J, The Northern Muse, An Anthology of Scots Vernacular Poetry, London 1924, pp 82, 473 (glossings at foot of page, brief note at end of text).

Wood H H, The Poems and Fables of Robert Henryson, Edinburgh 1933, 2nd edn rvsd 1958, pp 169, 270 (notes at end of text; crit

J Speirs, Scrut 2.296; D Hamer, MLR 29.342; TLS Aug 3 1933, p 523; E Muir, The Spectator 151.290; The Modern Scot 4.163).

Gray M M, Scottish Poetry from Barbour to James VI, N Y 1935, p 94 (crit J Speirs, Scrut 6.83; W M Mackenzie, The Scottish Bookman 1, no 4, p 133).

[Grieve C M] MacDiarmid H, The Golden Treasury of Scottish Poetry, London 1940, p 152 (crit L MacNeice, The New Statesman and Nation, 21.66; TLS Feb 15 1941, pp 78, 84); rptd in The Golden Treasury Series, London 1948, p 152.

Fergusson J, The Green Garden, London and Edinburgh 1946, p 7 (spelling modernized).

Oliver J W and J C Smith, A Scots Anthology from the 13th to the 20th Century, Edinburgh and London 1949, p 26 (spelling modernized; glossings at foot of page).

Murison D, Selections from the Poems of Robert Henryson, Edinburgh 1952, p 57 (glossings at foot of page).

Elliott C, Robert Henryson Poems, Oxford 1963, pp 110, 157 (notes at end of text); rptd from corrected sheets, Oxford 1966.

Selections. Oliphant F R, Robert Henryson, Blackwood's Edinburgh Magazine 148.506; rptd Littell's Living Age 187.544.

Chambers R, Chambers's Cyclopædia, Phila and N Y 1901–03; rvsd J L Geddie 1938, 1.190 (brief excerpts).

Leslie S, An Anthology of Catholic Poets, N Y 1925, p 90 (spelling modernized).

Textual Matters. Smith, edn, 1.lxiv; 3.x, xix.

Wood, edn, p xxvii.

Language. Ramsay, edn, 2.265 (glossary).

Dalrymple, edn, p 317 (glossary); rptd Leeds 1815, p 367, [added] Glossary, p 1 [separate pagination].

Laing, edn, p 309 (glossary).

Murray J A H, The Dialect of the Southern Counties of Scotland, London 1873.

Hahn O, Zur Verbal- und Nominalflexion bei den schottischen Dichtern, Berlin 1887–89 (see especially pt 3, p 14).

Browne, edn, pp 1, 197 (discussion; glossary).

Smith G G, edn, 1.83 (index of words; glossary); CHEL, 2.101, 506.

Dixon, edn, p 897 (glossary).

Gray M M, Introd, Lancelot of the Laik, PSTS ns 2, Edinburgh and London 1912, 2.xviii.

Metcalfe, edn, pp xx, 303 (brief discussion, glossary).

Westergaard E, Prepositions in Lowland Scotch, Angl 41.444 (some examples from

Henryson); Verbal Forms in Middle-Scotch, Angl 43.95.

Watt L M, Language and Influences, Douglas's Aeneid, Cambridge 1920, p 149 (very generally applicable).

Westergaard E, Studies in Prefixes and Suffixes in Middle Scottish, London 1924.

Wood H H, edn, pp xxxi, 277 (discussion, glossary).

Patrick D, Scottish Literature, Chambers's Cyclopædia of English Literature, rvsd J L Geddie, Phila and N Y 1938, 1.164.

[Grieve] MacDiarmid, edn, p 389 (glossary).

Fergusson, edn, p 228 (glossary).

Oliver and Smith, edn, p 497 (glossaries).

Murison, edn, p 4.

Elliott, edn, p 165 (glossary).

Scott T, Dunbar A Critical Exposition, Edinburgh and London 1966, p 351.

Versification. Henderson T F, Scottish Vernacular Literature, Edinburgh 1898; 2nd edn rvsd Edinburgh 1900; 3rd edn rvsd Edinburgh 1910, p 117.

Smith G G, edn, 1.lxxxiii.

Saintsbury G, History of English Prosody, London 1908; 2nd edn London 1923, 1.272. p 272.

Renwick-Orton, p 415 (brief).

Elliott, edn, p ix.

Date. Metcalfe, edn, p xviii.

Sources and Literary Relations. Fairholt, edn, p 59 (brief comment).

Neilson W A, Studies and Notes in Philology and Literature 6.93 (very brief).

Hentsch A A, De la littérature didactique du moyen age, Halle 1903, pp 6, 179.

Snell F J, The Poets, The Age of Transition, London 1905, 1.79.

Smith, edn, 1.lxiv.

Mendenhall J C, Aureate Terms A Study in the Literary Diction of the 15th Century, Lancaster Pa 1919.

Ker W P, Form and Style in Poetry, London 1928, p 84 (very brief).

Wood H H, Robert Henryson, Edinburgh Essays on Scots Literature, Edinburgh and London 1933, p 24.

Smith J M, The French Background of Middle Scots Literature, Edinburgh and London 1934, p 101.

Utley CR, pp 63, 314.

Morgan E, Dunbar and the Language of Poetry, EC 2.142.

Renwick-Orton, p 415 (brief).

Rossi S, Robert Henryson, Milan 1955, p 85.

Kinghorn A M, The Minor Poems of Robert Henryson, SSL 3.37.

Literary Criticism. H R, Robert Henryson, Lives of Scottish Poets, ed J Robertson, London 1822, 3.10.

Gilfillan, edn, p 53 (brief).

Henley, edn, p 138.

Nichol J, A Sketch of Scottish Poetry, ed J Small; 2nd edn rvsd, EETS 11, London 1883, p xxii.

Schipper J, William Dunbar, Berlin 1884, p 39.

Fitzgibbon, edn, p lix.

Oliphant F R, Robert Henryson, Blackwood's Edinburgh Magazine 148.506; rptd Littell's Living Age 187.544.

Eyre-Todd, edn, p 89.

Henderson T F, Scottish Vernacular Literature, Edinburgh 1898; 2nd edn rvsd 1900; 3rd edn rvsd Edinburgh 1910, p 119.

Chambers R, Chambers's Cyclopædia, Phila and N Y 1901–03; rvsd J L Geddie 1938, 1.189 (very brief).

Hentsch A A, De la littérature didactique, Halle 1903, pp 6, 179.

Watt L M Scottish Life and Poetry, London 1912, p 94.

Ker W P, Form and Style in Poetry, London 1928, p 84 (very brief).

Saintsbury G, The Four Great Scottish Poets, N Y 1929, p 185 (brief).

Wood H H, Robert Henryson, Edinburgh Essays on Scots Literature, Edinburgh and London 1933, p 24 (crit The Modern Scot 4.353).

Grierson H J C, Robert Henryson, The Modern Scot 4.297; rptd Aberdeen Univ Rev 21.206; rptd Robert Henryson, Essays and Addresses, London 1940, p 116.

Craig HEL, p 167 (brief).

Morgan E, Dunbar and the Language of Poetry, EC 2.142 (brief).

Renwick-Orton, p 415 (brief).

Kinsley J, The Mediaeval Makars, London 1955, p 23 (very brief).

Rossi S, Robert Henryson, Milan 1955, p 85.

Schlauch M, English Medieval Literature, Warsaw 1956, p 295.

Elliott, edn, p ix.

Kinghorn A M, The Minor Poems, SSL 3.36, 39.

Bibliography. Smith, edn, 1.lxiv.

Brown Reg, no 2681; Brown-Robbins, Robbins-Cutler, no 4237; Utley CR, p 313.

[9] THE PRAIS OF AIGE.

MSS. 1, Nat Libr Scot 1.1.6 (Bannatyne), p 44, ff 57ᵃ–57ᵇ (1568); 2, Univ of Edinb 205 (Laing 149, Makculloch), f 87ᵃ (MS proper

1477, Henryson insertions 1490–1510). PRINT: 3, Nat Libr Scot 19.1.16 (Chepman and Myllar), pp 144–145 (1508) (STC, no 20120).

Pinkerton J, Ancient Scotish Poems, 2 vols, London and Edinburgh 1786, 2.471 (MS 1).

Brydges E and J Haslewood, The British Bibliographer, London 1814, 4.183 (MS 1).

Laing D, The Poems of George Bannatyne, Edinburgh 1824, p 3 (MS 1); An Account of the Contents of George Bannatyne's Manuscript, The Bannatyne Club, Edinburgh 1829, 35.43 (MS 1).

Laing D, The Knightly Tale of Golagrus and Gawane, Edinburgh 1827, f 10ᵇ (PRINT 3 rptd).

Laing, edn, p 228 (MS 2).

Dickson R and J P Edmond, Annals of Scottish Printing from 1507 to the Beginning of the 17th Century, Cambridge 1890, p 49 (PRINT 3).

Schipper J, The Poems of William Dunbar, pt 1, Denkschriften der kaiserlichen Akadamie der Wissenschaften, Philo-Hist Classe, Vienna 1892, 40².9, 13, 14, 17 (MSS 1, 2, PRINT 3).

Murdoch J B, ed, The Bannatyne Manuscript, 4 vols, Hunterian Club, Glasgow 1896, 2.155 (MS 1).

Smith G G, Specimens of Middle Scots, Edinburgh and London 1902, pp lxvi, lxxiii, lxxiv (MSS 1, 2, PRINT 3 rptd).

Brown J T T, The Bannatyne Manuscript, SHR 1.136 (MS 1).

Smith G G, edn 1.64; 2.108 (MS 1, notes in vol 1); 1.64; 3.106 (MS 2, notes in vol 1); 1.64; 3.107 (PRINT 3, notes in vol 1).

Borland C R, A Descriptive Catalogue of the Western Mediaeval Manuscripts in Edinburgh University Library, Edinburgh 1916, p 291 (MS 2).

Stevenson G, ed, Pieces from The Makculloch and the Gray MSS, PSTS 65, Edinburgh and London 1918, pp 15, 295 (MS 2, note at end of text); 216, 302 (PRINT 3, note at end of text).

Ritchie W T, ed, The Bannatyne Manuscript Written in Tyme of Pest, 4 vols, PSTS ns 5, 22, 23, 26, Edinburgh 1928–34, 1.73; 2.141 (MS 1).

Wood, edn, p xxiii (MS 2).

Beattie W, The Chepman and Myllar Prints A Facsimile with a Bibliographical Note, Edinburgh Biblio Soc, Oxford 1950, pp viii 144 (PRINT 3 described, rptd).

Baxter J W, William Dunbar, Edinburgh and London 1952, pp 178, 216, 217 (MS 1,

PRINT 3).

Editions. Dalrymple D, Ancient Scottish Poems from the MS of George Bannatyne, Edinburgh 1770, p 107 (crit O Gilchrist, Ancient Scottish Poems, Censura Literaria, ed Brydges, London 1807, 5.238); rptd Leeds 1815, p 136 (MS 1).

Pinkerton J, Scotish Poems Reprinted from Scarce Editions, London 1792, 3.128.

Laing D, The Poems and Fables of Robert Henryson, Edinburgh 1865, pp 21, 242 (notes at end of text; MS 2; crit St James Magazine 24.60, rptd North British Review, American edn ns 44.81, British edn ns 44.154.)

Selections Made Chiefly from Works in the Old Scots Language for the Use of Schools in Scotland, Edinburgh 1867, p 46 (glossings at foot of page).

Fitzgibbon H M, Early English and Scottish Poetry, London N Y and Melbourne 1888, pp 104, 431 (spelling modernized; note at end of text).

Oliphant F R, Robert Henryson, Blackwood's Edinburgh Magazine 148.503; rptd Littell's Living Age 187.542.

Eyre-Todd G, Mediæval Scottish Poetry, Abbotsford Series of the Scottish Poets, Glasgow 1892, p 101 (glossings in margin).

Smith G G, The Poems of Robert Henryson, 3 vols, PSTS 55, 58, 64, Edinburgh and London 1906, 1908, 1914, 1.64; 3.106 (notes in vol 1, text in vol 3; MSS 1, 2; PRINT 3).

Metcalfe W M, The Poems of Robert Henryson, Paisley 1917, pp 211, 292 (notes at end of text; MSS 1, 2).

Brougham E M, News out of Scotland, London 1926, p 13.

Wood H H, The Poems and Fables of Robert Henryson, Edinburgh 1933, 2nd edn rvsd 1958, pp 185, 273 (variants in footnotes, notes at end of text; MS 1, PRINT 3; crit J Speirs, Scrut 2.296; D Hamer, MLR 29.342; TLS Aug 3 1933, p 523; E Muir, The Spectator 151.290; The Modern Scot 4.163).

Mackie R L, A Book of Scottish Verse, The World's Classics no 417, London 1934, p 38 (glossings at foot of page); 2nd edn London Glasgow and N Y 1967, p 39.

Elliott C, Robert Henryson Poems, Oxford 1963, pp 121, 160 (notes at end of text; MS 2); rptd from corrected sheets, Oxford 1966.

Scott T, Late Medieval Scots Poetry, London 1967, p 70 (Wood edn).

Selection. Tytler P F, Lives of Scottish Worthies, London 1833, 3.83.

Modernization. Tytler, Lives of Scottish Worthies, 3.84 (excerpt).
Textual Matters. Brown J T T, The Bannatyne Manuscript, SHR 1.141.
Smith, edn, 1.lxv; 3.x, xix; Wood, edn, p xxviii.
Language. Dalrymple, edn, p 317 (glossary); rptd Leeds 1815, p 367, [added] Glossary, p 1 [separate pagination].
Murray J A H, The Dialect of the Southern Counties of Scotland, London 1873.
Browne W H, The Taill of Rauf Coilyear, Baltimore 1903, pp 35, 139 (general discussion of Middle Scots; glossary).
Smith G G, edn, 1.83 (index of words, glossary); CHEL, 2.101, 506.
Gray M M, Introd, Lancelot of the Laik, PSTS ns 2, Edinburgh and London 1912, 2.xviii.
Metcalfe, edn, pp xx, 303 (brief discussion, glossary).
Westergaard E, Prepositions in Lowland Scotch, Angl 41.444 (some examples from Henryson); Verbal Forms in Middle-Scotch, Angl 43.95.
Watt L M, Language and Influences, Douglas's Aeneid, Cambridge 1920, p 149 (very generally applicable).
Westergaard E, Studies in Prefixes and Suffixes in Middle Scottish, London 1924.
Wood, edn, pp xxxi, 277 (discussion, glossary).
Patrick D, Scottish Literature, Chambers's Cyclopædia of English Literature, rvsd J L Geddie, Phila and N Y 1938, 1.164.
Elliott, edn, p 165 (glossary).
Scott T, Dunbar A Critical Exposition, Edinburgh and London 1966, p 351; edn, pp 21, 189 (discussion, glossary).
Versification. Smith, edn, 1.lxxxiii; Elliot, edn, p ix; Scott, edn, p 18.
Date. Metcalfe, edn, p xviii.
Authorship. Smith, edn, 1.lxv.
Sources and Literary Relations. Laing D, The Poems of William Dunbar, 2 vols, Edinburgh 1834, 2.445 (relation to poem of Kennedy; brief reference).
Sandison H E, The Chanson D'Aventure in Middle English, Bryn Mawr Pa 1913, p 143.
Mendenhall J C, Aureate Terms A Study in the Literary Diction of the 15th Century, Lancaster Pa 1919.
Elliott, edn, p ix.
MacDonald D, Henryson and the Thre Prestis of Peblis, Neophil 51.171.
Literary Criticism. H R, Robert Henryson, Lives of Scottish Poets, ed J Robertson, London 1822, 3.10 (brief).

Tytler P F, Lives of Scottish Worthies, London 1833, 3.83 (illustrative quote).
Taylor J, The Imperial Dictionary of Universal Biography, London [1863], 2.878 (very brief).
Ross J M, Scottish History and Literature, Glasgow 1884, p 161.
Minto W, Characteristics of English Poets, authorized American edn, Boston 1889, p 97 (brief; illustrative quote).
Oliphant F R, Robert Henryson, Blackwood's Edinburgh Magazine 148.503; rptd Littell's Living Age 187.542.
Henderson T F, Scottish Vernacular Literature Edinburgh 1898; 2nd edn rvsd 1900; 3rd edn rvsd Edinburgh 1910, p 120.
M'Ilwraith W, A Sketch of Scottish Literature, Annual Burns Chronicle 10.20.
Watt L M, Scottish Life and Poetry, London 1912, p 95 (brief).
Rait R and G S Pryde, Scotland, N Y 1934; 2nd edn London 1954, p 308 (very brief).
Renwick-Orton, p 416 (very brief).
Rossi S, Robert Henryson, Milan 1955, pp 9, 89.
Stock N, Some Notes on Old Scots, Shenandoah 6, no 2, p 29.
Kinghorn A M, The Minor Poems, SSL 3.35, 39.
Scott T, Dunbar A Critical Exposition, Edinburgh and London 1966, pp 246 and passim.
MacDonald D, Neophil 51.171.
Bibliography. Smith, edn, 1.lxv.
Beattie W, The Chepman and Myllar Prints, Edinburgh Biblio Soc, Oxford 1950, p xiii.
Brown-Robbins, Robbins-Cutler, no 1598.

[10] THE RESSONING BETUIX AIGE AND YOWTH.

MSS. 1, Magdalene Coll Camb 2553 (Pepysian Libr, Maitland Folio), pp 176–178 (1570–71); 2, Nat Libr Scot 1.1.6 (Bannatyne), pp 42–43, ff 55ᵃ–56ᵃ (1568); 3, Univ of Edinb 205 (Laing 149, Makculloch), f 181ᵇ (MS proper 1477, Henryson insertions 1490–1510).
Pinkerton J, Ancient Scotish Poems, 2 vols, London and Edinburgh 1786, 1.v; 2.437, 471 (MSS 1, 2).
Brydges E and J Haslewood, The British Bibliographer, London 1814, 4.183 (MS 2).
Laing D, The Poems of George Bannatyne, Edinburgh 1824, p 3 (MS 2); An Account of the Contents of George Bannatyne's Manuscript, The Bannatyne Club, Edinburgh 1829, 35.43 (MS 2).

Laing, edn, p 228 (MS 3).

Small J, The Poetical Works of Gavin Douglas, Edinburgh and London 1874, l.clxxi (MS 1).

Schipper J, The Poems of William Dunbar, pt 1, Denkschriften der kaiserlichen Akademie der Wissenschaften, Philo-Hist Classe, Vienna 1892, 40².9, 11, 13, 17 (MSS 1, 2, 3).

Murdoch J B, ed, The Bannatyne Manuscript, 4 vols, Hunterian Club, Glasgow 1896, 2.149 (MS 2).

Smith G G, Specimens of Middle Scots, Edinburgh and London 1902, pp lxvi, lxxiii (MSS 1, 2, 3).

Brown J T T, The Bannatyne Manuscript, SHR 1.136 (MS 2).

Smith G G, edn, 1.64; 3.121 (MS 1, notes in vol 1); 1.64; 3.115 (MS 2, notes in vol 1); 1.64; 3.114 (MS 3, notes in vol 1).

Borland C R, A Descriptive Catalogue of the Western Mediaeval Manuscripts in Edinburgh University Library, Edinburgh 1916, p 291 (MS 3).

Stevenson G, ed, Pieces from The Makculloch and the Gray MSS, PSTS 65, Edinburgh and London 1918, pp 22, 295 (MS 3, notes at end of text).

Craigie W A, ed, The Maitland Folio Manuscript, 2 vols, PSTS ns 7, 20, Edinburgh and London 1919–27, 1.200; 2.101 (MS 1, notes in vol 2).

Ritchie W T, ed, The Bannatyne Manuscript Written in Tyme of Pest, 4 vols, PSTS ns 5, 22, 23, 26, Edinburgh 1928–34, 1.68; 2.137 (MS 2).

Wood, edn, p xxiii (MS 3).

Baxter J W, William Dunbar, Edinburgh and London 1952, p 217 (MSS 1, 2).

Bawcutt P, The Shorter Poems of Gavin Douglas, PSTS 4s 3, Edinburgh and London 1967, p lv (MS 1).

Editions. Dalrymple D, Ancient Scottish Poems from the MS of George Bannatyne, Edinburgh 1770, pp 131, 283 (crit O Gilchrist, Ancient Scottish Poems, Censura Literaria, ed Brydges, London 1807, 5.238); rptd Leeds 1815, pp 167, 332 (notes at end of text; MS 2).

Sibbald J, Chronicle of Scottish Poetry, 4 vols, Edinburgh and London 1802, 1.186 (introductory and end notes).

Laing D, The Poems and Fables of Robert Henryson, Edinburgh 1865, pp 23, 243 (notes at end of text; MSS 2, 3; crit St James Magazine 24.60, rptd North British Review, American edn ns 44.81, British edn

ns 44.154).

Henderson T F, A Little Book of Scottish Verse, London 1899; 2nd edn London 1909, p 14 (glossings at foot of page).

Smith G G, The Poems of Robert Henryson, 3 vols, PSTS 55, 58, 64, Edinburgh and London 1906, 1908, 1914, 1.64; 3.114 (notes in vol 1, text in vol 3; MSS 1, 2, 3).

Metcalfe W M, The Poems of Robert Henryson, Paisley 1917, pp 213, 293 (notes at end of text; MSS 1, 2, 3).

Wood H H, The Poems and Fables of Robert Henryson, Edinburgh 1933, pp 179, 272 (variants in footnotes, notes at end of text; MS 2; crit J Speirs, Scrut 2.296; D Hamer, MLR 29.342; TLS Aug 3 1933, p 523; E Muir, The Spectator 151.290; The Modern Scot 4.163).

Gray M M, Scottish Poetry from Barbour to James VI, N Y 1935, p 95 (crit J Speirs, Scrut 6.83; W M Mackenzie, The Scottish Bookman 1, no 4, p 133).

Fergusson J, The Green Garden, London and Edinburgh 1946, p 18 (spelling modernized).

Murison D, Selections from the Poems of Robert Henryson, Edinburgh 1952, p 54 (glossings at foot of page; MSS 1, 3).

Textual Matters. Smith, edn, l.lxvi; 3.x, xvi, xix.

Wood, edn, p xxviii.

Language. Dalrymple, edn, p 317 (glossary); rptd Leeds 1815, p 367, [added] Glossary, p 1 [separate pagination].

Sibbald, edn, vol 4 [unpaged] (glossary).

Laing, edn, p 309 (glossary).

Murray J A H, The Dialect of the Southern Counties of Scotland, London 1873.

Hahn O, Zur Verbal- und Nominalflexion bei den schottischen Dichtern, Berlin 1887–89 (see especially pt 3, p 14).

Browne W H, The Taill of Rauf Coilyear, Baltimore 1903, pp 35, 139 (general discussion of Middle Scots; glossary).

Millar J H, A Literary History of Scotland, London 1903, p 687 (glossary).

Smith G G, edn, 1.83 (index of words, glossary); CHEL, 2.101, 506.

Gray M M, Introd, Lancelot of the Laik, PSTS ns 2, Edinburgh and London 1912, 2.xviii.

Metcalfe, edn, pp xx, 303 (brief discussion; glossary).

Westergaard E, Prepositions in Lowland Scotch, Angl 41.444 (some examples from Henryson); Verbal Forms in Middle-Scotch,

Angl 43.95.
Craigie W A, The Maitland Folio, 2 vols, PSTS ns 7, 20, Edinburgh and London 1919–27, 2.135 (glossary).
Watt L M, Language and Influences, Douglas's Aeneid, Cambridge 1920, p 149 (very generally applicable).
Westergaard E, Studies in Préfixes and Suffixes in Middle Scottish, London 1924.
Wood, edn, pp xxxi, 277 (discussion; glossary).
Patrick D, Scottish Literature, Chambers's Cyclopædia of English Literature, rvsd J L Geddie, Phila and N Y 1938, 1.164.
Fergusson, edn, p 228 (glossary).
Murison, edn, p 4.
Scott T, Dunbar A Critical Exposition, Edinburgh and London 1966, p 351.
Versification. Smith G G, edn, l.lxxxiii.
Saintsbury G, History of English Prosody, London 1908; 2nd edn London 1923, 1.271.
Date. Metcalfe, edn, p xviii.
Sources and Literary Relations. Smith, edn, l.lxvii.
Sandison H E, The Chanson D'Aventure in Middle English, Bryn Mawr Pa 1913, p 143.
Mendenhall J C, Aureate Terms A Study in the Literary Diction of the 15th Century, Lancaster Pa 1919.
Smith J M, The French Background of Middle Scots Literature, Edinburgh and London 1934, p 49.
MacDonald D, Henryson and the Thre Prestis of Peblis, Neophil 51.174.
Woolf R, The English Religious Lyric in the Middle Ages, Oxford 1968, p 332.
Literary Criticism. H R, Robert Henryson, Lives of Scottish Poets, ed J Robertson, London 1822, 3.10 (brief).
Henley W E, Robert Henryson, The English Poets, ed T H Ward, London and N Y 1880; (numerous subsequent edns) N Y 1924, 1.138.
Oliphant F R, Robert Henryson, Blackwood's Edinburgh Magazine 148.503; rptd Littell's Living Age 187.541.
Brandl, 2¹.717.
Henderson T F, Scottish Vernacular Literature, Edinburgh 1898; 2nd edn rvsd 1900; 3rd edn rvsd 1910, p 122; edn, p 11.
Marshal L E, Roberto Henryson e la Griseida, Borgo San Donnino 1910, p 10.
Watt L M, Scottish Life and Poetry, London 1912, p 96 (brief).
Rossi S, Robert Henryson, Milan 1955, p 88.
Schlauch M, English Medieval Literature, Warsaw 1956, p 295.

Elliott C, Robert Henryson Poems, Oxford 1963, p xxi (brief comment); rptd from corrected sheets, Oxford 1966.
Kinghorn A M, The Minor Poems, SSL 3.34, 39.
MacDonald D, Neophil 51.174.
Woolf R, The English Religious Lyric, p 333.
Bibliography. Smith, edn, l.lxvi.
Brown Reg, no 2524; Brown-Robbins, Robbins-Cutler, no 3942.

[11] THE ABBAY WALK.

MSS. 1, Magdalene Coll Camb 2553 (Pepysian Libr, Maitland Folio), pp 297, 310 (1570–71); 2, Nat Libr Scot 1.1.6 (Bannatyne), pp 30–31, ff 46ᵇ–47ᵃ (1568).
Pinkerton J, Ancient Scotish Poems, 2 vols, London and Edinburgh 1786, 1.v; 2.437, 471 (MSS 1, 2).
Brydges E and J Haslewood, The British Bibliographer, London 1814, 4.183 (MS 2).
Laing D, The Poems of George Bannatyne, Edinburgh 1824, p 3 (MS 2); An Account of the Contents of George Bannatyne's Manuscript, The Bannatyne Club, Edinburgh 1829, 35.43 (MS 2).
Small J, The Poetical Works of Gavin Douglas, Edinburgh and London 1874, l.clxxi (MS 1).
Schipper J, The Poems of William Dunbar, pt 1, Denkschriften der kaiserlichen Akademie der Wissenschaften, Philo-Hist Classe, Vienna 1892, 40².9, 11, 17 (MSS 1, 2).
Murdoch J B, ed, The Bannatyne Manuscript, 4 vols, Hunterian Club, Glasgow 1896, 2.125 (MS 2).
Smith G G, Specimens of Middle Scots, Edinburgh and London 1902, pp lxvi, lxxiii (MSS 1, 2).
Brown J T T, The Bannatyne Manuscript, SHR 1.136 (MS 2).
Smith G G, edn, 1.68; 3.130 (MS 1, notes in vol 1); 1.68; 3.126 (MS 2, notes in vol 1).
Craigie W A, ed, The Maitland Folio, 2 vols, PSTS ns 7, 20, Edinburgh and London 1919–27, 1.351; 2.119 (MS 1, notes in vol 2).
Ritchie W T, ed, The Bannatyne Manuscript Written in Tyme of Pest, 4 vols, PSTS ns 5, 22, 23, 26, Edinburgh 1928–34, 1.50; 2.116 (MS 2).
Baxter J W, William Dunbar, Edinburgh and London 1952, p 217 (MSS 1, 2).
Editions. Dalrymple D, Ancient Scottish Poems from the MS of George Bannatyne, Edinburgh 1770, pp 105, 279 (crit O Gilchrist, Ancient Scottish Poems, Censura Literaria, ed Brydges, London 1807, 5.238);

rptd Leeds 1815, pp 133, 327 (notes at end of text; MS 2).

Ellis G, Specimens of the Early English Poets, 5 edns, London 1790, 1801, 1803, 1811, 1845 (5th edn corrected), p 297 (spelling, occasional wording modernized; glossings at foot of page; Dalrymple edn).

Sibbald J, Chronicle of Scottish Poetry, 4 vols, Edinburgh and London 1802, 1.183 (introductory note; MS 2).

Mercer A, The History of Dunfermline from the Earliest Records down to the Present Time, Dunfermline 1828, p 66.

Chalmers P, Historical and Statistical Account of Dunfermline, 2 vols, Edinburgh and London 1844–59, 1.531 (one stanza omitted).

Aytoun W E, The Ballads of Scotland, Edinburgh and London 1858; 2nd edn rvsd and augmented, Edinburgh and London, 1859, 1.lxv (illustrative of critical discussion).

Laing D, The Poems and Fables of Robert Henryson, Edinburgh 1865, pp 15, 240 (notes at end of text; MS 2; crit St James Magazine 24.60, rptd North British Review, American edn ns 44.81, British edn ns 44.154).

Selections Made Chiefly from Works in the Old Scots Language for the Use of Schools in Scotland, Edinburgh 1867, p 56 (glossings at foot of page).

Morley H, Shorter English Poems, London 1876, p 76.

Henderson E, The Annals of Dunfermline, Glasgow 1879, p 721 (Laing edn).

Fitzgibbon H M, Early English and Scottish Poetry, London N Y and Melbourne 1888, pp 88, 431 (spelling modernized; notes at end of text).

Eyre-Todd G, Mediæval Scottish Poetry, Abbotsford Series of the Scottish Poets, Glasgow 1892, p 98 (glossings in margin).

Henderson T F, A Little Book of Scottish Verse, London 1899; 2nd edn London 1909, p 11 (glossings at foot of page).

Smith G G, The Poems of Robert Henryson, 3 vols, PSTS 55, 58, 64, Edinburgh and London 1906, 1908, 1914, 1.68; 3.126 (notes in vol 1, text in vol 3; MSS 1, 2).

Metcalfe W M, Specimens of Scottish Literature, London 1913, pp 48, 161 (notes at end of text).

Metcalfe W M, The Poems of Robert Henryson, Paisley 1917, pp 217, 293 (notes at end of text; MSS 1, 2).

Buchan J, The Northern Muse, An Anthology of Scots Vernacular Poetry, London 1924, pp 442, 533 (glossings at foot of page, brief note at end of text; MS 2).

Wood H H, The Poems and Fables of Robert Henryson, Edinburgh 1933, 2nd edn rvsd 1958, pp 195, 274 (variants in footnotes, notes at end of text; MS 2; crit J Speirs, Scrut 2.296; D Hamer, MLR 29.342; TLS Aug 3 1933, p 523; E Muir, The Spectator 151.290; The Modern Scot 4.163).

Mackie R L, A Book of Scottish Verse, The World's Classics no 417, London 1934, p 16 (glossings at foot of page); 2nd edn, London Glasgow N Y 1967, p 17.

Scott T, Late Medieval Scots Poetry, London 1967, pp 64, 183 (notes at end of text; Wood edn); The Penguin Book of Scottish Verse, London 1970, p 83 (glossings at foot of page).

Textual Matters. Smith, edn, 1.lxvii; 3.x, xix. Wood, edn, p xxviii.

Language. Dalrymple, edn, p 317 (glossary); rptd Leeds 1815, p 367, [added] Glossary, p 1 [separate pagination].

Sibbald, edn, vol 4 [unpaged] (glossary).

Irving D, The History of Scotish Poetry, Edinburgh 1861, p 595 (glossary).

Laing, edn, p 309 (glossary).

Murray J A H, The Dialect of the Southern Counties of Scotland, London 1873.

Hahn O, Zur Verbal- und Nominalflexion bei den schottischen Dichtern, Berlin 1887–89 (see especially pt 3, p 14).

Browne W H, The Taill of Rauf Coilyear, Baltimore 1903, pp 35, 139 (general discussion of Middle Scots; glossary).

Smith G G, edn, 1.83 (index of words and glossary); CHEL, 2.101, 506.

Gray M M, Introd, Lancelot of the Laik, PSTS ns 2, Edinburgh and London 1912, 2.xviii.

Metcalfe, Specimens of Scottish Literature, edn, pp 9, 39, 189 (includes glossary); The Poems of Robert Henryson, edn, pp xx, 303 (brief discussion; glossary).

Westergaard E, Prepositions in Lowland Scotch, Angl 41.444 (some examples from Henryson); Verbal Forms in Middle-Scotch, Angl 43.95.

Craigie W A, The Maitland Folio, 2 vols, PSTS ns 7, 20, Edinburgh and London 1919–27, 2.135 (glossary).

Watt L M, Language and Influences, Douglas's Aeneid, Cambridge 1920, p 149 (very generally applicable).

Westergaard E, Studies in Prefixes and Suffixes in Middle Scottish, London 1924.

Patrick D, Scottish Literature, Chambers's Cyclopædia of English Literature, rvsd J L Geddie, Phila and N Y 1938, 1.164.

Wood, edn, pp xxxi, 277 (discussion, glossary).

Scott T, Dunbar A Critical Exposition, Edinburgh and London 1966, p 351; Late Medieval Scots Poetry, edn, pp 21, 189 (discussion, glossary).

Versification. Guest E, A History of English Rhythms, 2 vols, London 1838; ed W W Skeat, new edn [in 1 vol] London 1882, p 594 (brief reference).

Smith G G, edn, 1.lxxxiii.

Saintsbury G, History of English Prosody, London 1908; 2nd edn London 1923, 1.271.

Renwick-Orton, p 415 (brief).

Scott T, Late Medieval Scots Poetry, edn, p 18.

Date. Metcalfe, The Poems of Robert Henryson, edn, p xviii.

Authorship. Smith, edn, 1.lxvii.

Wood, edn, p xxviii.

Sources and Literary Relations. Irving D, The Lives of the Scotish Poets, 2 vols, Edinburgh 1804; 2nd edn improved London 1810, 1.385.

Varnhagen H, Die kleineren Gedichte der Vernon- und Simeon-handschrift, Angl 7.306 (possible original).

Snell F J, The Poets, The Age of Transition, London 1905, 1.79.

Smith, edn, 1.lxviii.

Sandison H E, The Chanson D'Aventure in Middle English, Bryn Mawr Pa 1913, p 141.

Mendenhall J C, Aureate Terms A Study in the Literary Diction of the 15th Century, Lancaster Pa 1919.

Wood, edn, p xxix.

Smith J M, The French Background of Middle Scots Literature, Edinburgh and London 1934, p 49.

Rossi S, Robert Henryson, Milan 1955, p 92.

Elliott C, Robert Henryson Poems, Oxford 1963, p xxiv; rptd from corrected sheets, Oxford 1966.

Kinghorn A M, The Minor Poems of Robert Henryson, SSL 3.35.

MacDonald D, Henryson and the Thre Prestis of Peblis, Neophil 51.174, 177.

Other Scholarly Problems. Henderson E, The Annals of Dunfermline, edn, p 722 (occasion; location).

Stair-Kerr E, The Poets, Scotland under James IV, Paisley 1911, p 115 (location; brief).

Rossi, Robert Henryson, pp 91, 96 (title; biographical evidence).

Literary Criticism. Irving D, The Lives of the Scotish Poets, 2nd edn, London 1810, 1.385.

H R, Robert Henryson, Lives of Scottish Poets, ed J Robertson, London 1822, 3.10 (brief).

Irving D, The History of Scotish Poetry, ed J A Carlyle, Edinburgh 1861, p 222 (very brief statement of theme).

Taylor J, The Imperial Dictionary of Universal Biography, London [1863], 2.878 (very brief).

Henley W E, Robert Henryson, The English Poets, ed T H Ward, London and N Y 1880; (numerous subsequent edns) N Y 1924, 1.138.

Ross J M, Scottish History and Literature, Glasgow 1884, p 161.

Fitzgibbon, edn, p lix.

Oliphant F R, Robert Henryson, Blackwood's Edinburgh Magazine 148.504; rptd Littell's Living Age 187.542.

Brandl, 2¹.716.

Henderson T F, Scottish Vernacular Literature, Edinburgh 1898; 2nd edn rvsd 1900; 3rd edn rvsd 1910, p 120; edn, p 11.

M'Ilwraith W, A Sketch of Scottish Literature, Annual Burns Chronicle 10.20.

Snell F J, The Poets, The Age of Transition, London 1905, 1.79.

Watt L M, Scottish Life and Poetry, London 1912, p 95 (brief).

Saintsbury G, The Four Great Scottish Poets, N Y 1929, p 185 (brief).

Rait R and G S Pryde, Scotland, N Y 1934; 2nd edn London 1954, p 308 (very brief).

Craig HEL, p 167 (brief).

Renwick-Orton, pp 118, 415 (brief).

Rossi, Robert Henryson, pp 9, 83, 91.

Elliott C, Robert Henryson Poems, Oxford 1963, pp xxi, xxiv (brief comments); rptd from corrected sheets, Oxford 1966.

Kinghorn A M, The Minor Poems of Robert Henryson, SSL 3.35, 39.

MacDonald D, Henryson and the Thre Prestis of Peblis, Neophil 51.174, 177.

Bibliography. Smith, edn, 1.lxvii.

Brown Reg, no 171; Brown-Robbins, Robbins-Cutler, no 265; Renwick-Orton, p 415 (brief).

[12] THE RESSONING BETWIXT DETH AND MAN.

MS. Nat Libr Scot 1.1.6 (Bannatyne), pp 43–44, ff 56ᵃ–57ᵃ (1568).

Pinkerton J, Ancient Scotish Poems, 2 vols, London and Edinburgh 1786, 2.471.

Brydges E and J Haslewood, The British Bibliographer, London 1814, 4.183.

Laing D, The Poems of George Bannatyne, Edinburgh 1824, p 3; An Account of the Contents of George Bannatyne's Manuscript, The Bannatyne Club, Edinburgh 1829, 35.43.

Schipper J, The Poems of William Dunbar, pt 1, Denkschriften der kaiserlichen Akademie der Wissenschaften, Philo-Hist Classe, Vienna 1892, 40².9, 17.

Murdoch J B, ed, The Bannatyne Manuscript, 4 vols, Hunterian Club, Glasgow, 1896, 2.153.

Smith G G, Specimens of Middle Scots, Edinburgh and London 1902, pp lxvi, lxxiii.

Brown J T T, The Bannatyne Manuscript, SHR 1.136.

Smith G G, edn, 1.69; 3.134 (notes in vol 1).

Ritchie W T, ed, The Bannatyne Manuscript Writtin in Tyme of Pest, 4 vols, PSTS ns 5, 22, 23, 26, Edinburgh 1928–34, 1.71; 2.139.

Baxter J W, William Dunbar, Edinburgh and London 1952, p 217.

Editions. Dalrymple D, Ancient Scottish Poems from the MS of George Bannatyne, Edinburgh 1770, pp 134, 285 (crit O Gilchrist, Ancient Scottish Poems, Censura Literaria, ed Brydges, London 1807, 5.238); rptd Leeds 1815, pp 171, 333 (notes at end of text).

The Reasoning betwixt Deth and Man, The Scottish Journal 2.96 (Dalrymple edn).

Laing D, The Poems and Fables of Robert Henryson, Edinburgh 1865, pp 27, 245 (notes at end of text; crit St James Magazine 24.60; rptd North British Review, American edn ns 44.81, British edn ns 44.154).

Smith G G, The Poems of Robert Henryson, 3 vols, PSTS 55, 58, 64, Edinburgh and London 1906, 1908, 1914, 1.69; 3.134 (notes in vol 1, text in vol 3).

Metcalfe W M, The Poems of Robert Henryson, Paisley 1917, pp 220, 294 (notes at end of text).

Wood H H, The Poems and Fables of Robert Henryson, Edinburgh 1933, 2nd edn rvsd 1958, pp 211, 276 (variants in footnotes, notes at end of text; crit J Speirs, Scrut 2.296; D Hamer, MLR 29.342; TLS Aug 3 1933, p 523; E Muir, The Spectator 151.290; The Modern Scot 4.163).

Selection. Henderson E, The Annals of Dunfermline, Glasgow 1879, p 722 (Laing edn).

Textual Matters. Smith, edn, 1.lxxi; 3.x, xix.

Wood, edn, p xxx.

Language. Dalrymple, edn, p 317 (glossary); rptd Leeds 1815, p 367, [added] Glossary, p 1 [separate pagination].

Laing, edn, p 309 (glossary).

Murray J A H, The Dialect of the Southern Counties of Scotland, London 1873.

Hahn O, Zur Verbal- und Nominalflexion bei den schottischen Dichtern, Berlin 1887–89 (see especially pt 3, p 14).

Browne W H, The Taill of Rauf Coilyear, Baltimore 1903, pp 35, 139 (general discussion of Middle Scots; glossary).

Smith G G, edn, 1.83 (index of words and glossary); CHEL, 2.101, 506.

Gray M M, Introd, Lancelot of the Laik, PSTS ns 2, Edinburgh and London 1912, 2.xviii.

Metcalfe, edn, pp xx, 303 (brief discussion; glossary).

Westergaard E, Prepositions in Lowland Scotch, Angl 41.444 (some examples from Henryson); Verbal Forms in Middle-Scotch, Angl 43.95.

Watt L M, Language and Influences, Douglas's Aeneid, Cambridge 1920, p 149 (very generally applicable).

Westergaard E, Studies in Prefixes and Suffixes in Middle Scottish, London 1924.

Wood, edn, pp xxxi, 277 (discussion, glossary).

Patrick D, Scottish Literature, Chambers's Cyclopædia of English Literature, rvsd J L Geddie, Phila and N Y 1938, 1.164.

Scott T, Dunbar A Critical Exposition of the Poems, Edinburgh and London 1966, p 351.

Versification. Smith G G, edn, 1.lxxxiii.

Date. Metcalfe, edn, p xviii.

Sources and Literary Relations. Smith, edn, 1.lxxi.

Mendenhall J C, Aureate Terms A Study in Literary Diction, Lancaster Pa 1919.

Gray D, Two Songs of Death, NM 64.56 (brief).

Hyde I, Poetic Imagery, SSL 2.195.

Kinghorn A M, The Minor Poems of Robert Henryson, SSL 3.34.

Literary Criticism. H R, Robert Henryson, Lives of Scottish Poets, ed J Robertson, London 1822, 3.10 (brief).

Taylor J, The Imperial Dictionary of Universal Biography, London [1863], 2.878 (very brief).

Ross J M, Scottish History and Literature, Glasgow 1884, p 161.

Watt L M, Scottish Life and Poetry, London 1912, p 96 (brief).

Elliott C, Robert Henryson Poems, Oxford

1963, p xxi (brief comment); rptd from corrected sheets, Oxford 1966.
Hyde I, SSL 2.195.
Kinghorn, SSL 3.34, 39.
Bibliography. Smith edn, 1.lxxi.
Brown Reg, no 1548; Brown-Robbins, Robbins-Cutler, no 2520.

[13] AGANIS HAISTY CREDENCE OF TITLARIS.

MSS. 1, Magdalene Coll Camb 2553 (Pepysian Libr, Maitland Folio), pp 309–310 (1570–71); 2, Nat Libr Scot 1.1.6 (Bannatyne), ff 67ᵇ–68ᵃ (1568).
Pinkerton J, Ancient Scotish Poems, 2 vols, London and Edinburgh 1786, 1.v; 2.437, 471 (MSS 1, 2).
Brydges E and J Haslewood, The British Bibliographer, London 1814, 4.183 (MS 2).
Laing D, The Poems of George Bannatyne, Edinburgh 1824, p 3 (MS 2); An Account of the Contents of George Bannatyne's Manuscript, The Bannatyne Club, Edinburgh 1829, 35.43 (MS 2).
Small J, The Poetical Works of Gavin Douglas, Edinburgh and London 1874, 1.clxxi (MS 1).
Schipper J, The Poems of William Dunbar, pt 1, Denkschriften der kaiserlichen Akademie, Philo-Hist Classe, Vienna 1892, 40².9, 11, 17 (MSS 1, 2).
Murdoch J B, ed, The Bannatyne Manuscript, 4 vols, Hunterian Club, Glasgow 1896, 2.182 (MS 2).
Smith G G, Specimens of Middle Scots, Edinburgh and London 1902, pp lxvi, lxxiii (MSS 1, 2).
Brown J T T, The Bannatyne Manuscript, SHR 1.136 (MS 2).
Smith G G, edn, 1.70; 3.142 (MS 1, notes in vol 1); 1.70; 3.140 (MS 2, notes in vol 1).
Craigie W A, ed, The Maitland Folio, 2 vols, PSTS ns 7, 20, Edinburgh and London 1919–27, 1.348; 2.119 (MS 1, notes in vol 2).
Ritchie W T, ed, The Bannatyne Manuscript Writtin in Tyme of Pest, 4 vols, PSTS ns 5, 22, 23, 26, Edinburgh 1928–34, 2.165 (MS 2).
Baxter J W, William Dunbar, Edinburgh and London 1952, p 217 (MSS 1, 2).
Editions. Dalrymple D, Ancient Scottish Poems from the MS of George Bannatyne, Edinburgh 1770, p 136 (crit O Gilchrist, Ancient Scottish Poems, Censura Literaria, ed Brydges, London 1807, 5.238); rptd Leeds 1815, p 174 (MS 2).

Laing D, The Poems and Fables of Robert Henryson, Edinburgh 1865, pp 18, 242 (notes at end of text; MSS 1, 2; crit St James Magazine 24.60, rptd North British Review, American edn ns 44.81, British edn ns 44.154).
Smith G G, The Poems of Robert Henryson, 3 vols, PSTS 55, 58, 64, Edinburgh and London 1906, 1908, 1914, 1.70; 3.140 (notes in vol 1, text in vol 3; MSS 1, 2).
Metcalfe W M, The Poems of Robert Henryson, Paisley 1917, pp 223, 294 (notes at end of text; MSS 1, 2).
Wood H H, The Poems and Fables of Robert Henryson, Edinburgh 1933, 2nd edn rvsd 1958, pp 215, 276 (variants in footnotes, notes at end of text; MS 2; crit J Speirs, Scrut 2.296; D Hamer, MLR 29.342; TLS Aug 3 1933, p 523; E Muir, The Spectator 151.290; The Modern Scot 4.163).
Textual Matters. Smith, edn, 1.lxxi; 3.xvi, xix.
Wood, edn, p xxxi.
Language. Dalrymple, edn, p 317 (glossary); rptd Leeds 1815, p 367, [added] Glossary, p 1 [separate pagination].
Laing, edn, p 309 (glossary).
Murray J A H, The Dialect of the Southern Counties of Scotland, London 1873.
Hahn O, Zur Verbal- und Nominalflexion bei den schottischen Dichtern, Berlin 1887–89 (see especially pt 3, p 14).
Browne W H, The Taill of Rauf Coilyear, Baltimore 1903, pp 35, 139 (general discussion of Middle Scots; glossary).
Smith G G, edn, 1.83 (index of words and glossary); CHEL, 2.101, 506.
Gray M M, Introd, Lancelot of the Laik, PSTS ns 2, Edinburgh and London 1912, 2.xviii.
Metcalfe, edn, pp xx, 303 (brief discussion; glossary).
Westergaard E, Prepositions in Lowland Scotch, Angl 41.444 (some examples from Henryson); Verbal Forms in Middle-Scotch, Angl 43.95.
Craigie W A, The Maitland Folio, 2 vols, PSTS ns 7, 20, Edinburgh and London 1919–27, 2.135 (glossary).
Watt L M, Language and Influences, Douglas's Aeneid, Cambridge 1920, p 149 (very generally applicable).
Westergaard E, Studies in Prefixes and Suffixes in Middle Scottish, London 1924.
Wood, edn, pp xxxi, 277 (discussion, glossary).
Patrick D, Scottish Literature, Chambers's Cyclopædia of English Literature, rvsd J L Geddie, Phila and N Y 1938, 1.164.

Scott T, Dunbar A Critical Exposition of the Poems, Edinburgh and London 1966, p 351.
Versification. Smith G G, edn, l.lxxxiii.
Date. Metcalfe, edn, p xviii.
Sources and Literary Relations. Smith G G, edn, l.lxxii.
Mendenhall J C, Aureate Terms A Study in Literary Diction, Lancaster Pa 1919.
Rossi S, Robert Henryson, Milan 1955, p 93.
Wittig K, The Scottish Tradition in Literature, Edinburgh 1958, p 76.
Hyde I, Poetic Imagery, SSL 2.188.
MacDonald D, Henryson and the Thre Prestis of Peblis, Neophil 51.174.
Literary Criticism. Rossi, Robert Henryson, p 93.
Elliott C, Robert Henryson Poems, Oxford 1963, p xxi (brief comment); rptd from corrected sheets, Oxford 1966.
Hyde, SSL 2.188.
Kinghorn A M, The Minor Poems, SSL 3.35, 39.
MacDonald D, Neophil 51.174.
Bibliography. Smith G G, edn, l.lxxi.
Brown Reg, no 499; Brown-Robbins, Robbins-Cutler, no 758.

[14] THE ANNUNCIATION.

MS. Nat Libr Scot 34.7.3 (Gray), ff 70ᵃ–71ᵇ (1490–1510?).
Smith G G, Specimens of Middle Scots, edn, p lxix; The Poems of Robert Henryson, edn, 1.70; 3.146 (notes in vol 1).
Stevenson G, ed, Pieces from The Makculloch and the Gray MSS, PSTS 65, Edinburgh and London 1918, pp 43, 298 (note at end of text).
Editions. Laing D, The Poems and Fables of Robert Henryson, Edinburgh 1865, pp 33, 246 (notes at end of text; crit St James Magazine 24.60, rptd North British Review, American edn ns 44.81, British edn ns 44.154).
Smith G G, Specimens of Middle Scots, Edinburgh and London 1902, pp 8, 269 (notes at end of text).
Smith G G, The Poems of Robert Henryson, 3 vols, PSTS 55, 58, 64, Edinburgh and London 1906, 1908, 1914, 1.70; 3.145 (notes in vol 1, text in vol 3).
Metcalfe W M, The Poems of Robert Henryson, Paisley 1917, pp 226, 294 (notes at end of text).
Wood H H, The Poems and Fables of Robert Henryson, Edinburgh 1933, 2nd edn rvsd 1958, pp 199, 274 (variants in footnotes, notes at end of text; crit J Speirs, Scrut

2.296; D Hamer, MLR 29.342; TLS Aug 3 1933, p 523; E Muir, The Spectator 151.290; The Modern Scot 4.163).
Murison D, Selections from the Poems of Robert Henryson, Edinburgh 1952, p 51 (glossings at foot of page).
Rossi S, L'Annunciazione di Robert Henryson, Aevum 29.73 (Wood edn).
Elliott C, Robert Henryson Poems, Oxford 1963, pp 112, 157 (notes at end of text); rptd from corrected sheets, Oxford 1966.
Selections. Leslie S, An Anthology of Catholic Poets, N Y 1925, p 89 (spelling modernized).
Walsh T, The Catholic Anthology, N Y 1927; rvsd N Y 1932, p 110.
Modernization. Rossi, edn, p 73 (in Italian).
Textual Matters. Smith G G, The Poems of Robert Henryson, edn, l.lxxii; 3.x, xix.
Wood, edn, p xxix.
Language. Laing, edn, p 309 (glossary).
Murray J A H, The Dialect of the Southern Counties of Scotland, London 1873.
Hahn O, Zur Verbal- und Nominalflexion bei den schottischen Dichtern, Berlin 1887–89 (see especially pt 3, p 14).
Smith G G, Specimens of Middle Scots, edn, pp xi, 325 (history and philology of Middle Scots; glossary).
Browne W H, The Taill of Rauf Coilyear, Baltimore 1903, pp 35, 139 (general discussion of Middle Scots; glossary).
Smith G G, The Poems of Robert Henryson, edn, 1.83 (index of words and glossary); CHEL, 2.101, 506.
Gray M M, Introd, Lancelot of the Laik, PSTS ns 2, Edinburgh and London 1912, 2.xviii.
Metcalfe, edn, pp xx, 303 (brief discussion; glossary).
Westergaard E, Prepositions in Lowland Scotch, Angl 41.444 (some examples from Henryson); Verbal Forms in Middle-Scotch, Angl 43.95.
Watt L M, Language and Influences, Douglas's Aeneid, Cambridge 1920, p 149 (very generally applicable).
Westergaard E, Studies in Prefixes and Suffixes in Middle Scottish, London 1924.
Wood, edn, pp xxxi, 277 (discussion, glossary).
Patrick D, Scottish Literature, Chambers's Cyclopædia of English Literature, rvsd J L Geddie, Phila and N Y 1938, 1.164.
Murison, edn, p 4.
Elliott, edn, p 165 (glossary).
Scott T, Dunbar A Critical Exposition of the Poems, Edinburgh and London 1966, p 351.
Versification. Henderson T F, Scottish Ver-

nacular Literature, Edinburgh 1898; 2nd edn rvsd 1900; 3rd edn rvsd 1910, p 117.
Smith G G, The Poems of Robert Henryson, edn, 1.lxxxiii.
Rossi, edn, p 77.
Elliott, edn, p x.
Date. Metcalfe, edn, p xviii.
Authorship. Smith G G, The Poems of Robert Henryson, edn, 1.lxxiii.
Sources and Literary Relations. Smith G G, The Poems of Robert Henryson, edn, 1.lxxiii.
Mendenhall J C, Aureate Terms A Study in Literary Diction, Lancaster Pa 1919.
Rossi, edn, pp 72, 76; Robert Henryson, Milan 1955, p 93.
MacDonald D, Henryson and the Thre Prestis of Peblis, Neophil 51.174.
Stephens J, Devotion and Wit in Henryson's The Annunciation, ESts 51.323.
Other Scholarly Problems. Rossi, edn, p 70 (poet's attitude).
Literary Criticism. Ross J M, Scottish History and Literature, Glasgow 1884, p 162.
Oliphant F R, Robert Henryson, Blackwood's Edinburgh Magazine 148.504; rptd Littell's Living Age 187.542.
Rossi, edn, p 77; Robert Henryson, Milan 1955, pp 11, 83, 93.
Elliott, edn, p x.
Kinghorn A M, The Minor Poems of Robert Henryson, SSL 3.36, 39.
MacDonald D, Neophil 51.175.
Stephens J, ESts 51.323.
Bibliography. Smith G G, The Poems of Robert Henryson, edn, 1.lxxii.
Brown Reg, no 534; Brown-Robbins, Robbins-Cutler, no 856.

[15] SUM PRACTYSIS OF MEDECYNE.

MS. Nat Libr Scot 1.1.6 (Bannatyne), ff 141ᵇ–142ᵇ (1568).
Pinkerton J, Ancient Scotish Poems, 2 vols, London and Edinburgh 1786, 2.471.
Brydges E and J Haslewood, The British Bibliographer, London 1814, 4.183.
Laing D, The Poems of George Bannatyne, Edinburgh 1824, p 3; An Account of the Contents of George Bannatyne's Manuscript, The Bannatyne Club, Edinburgh 1829, 35.43.
Schipper J, The Poems of William Dunbar, pt 1, Denkschriften der kaiserlichen Akadamie der Wissenshaften, Philo-Hist Classe, Vienna 1892, 40².9, 17.
Murdoch J B, ed, The Bannatyne Manuscript, 4 vols, Hunterian Club, Glasgow

1896, 3.401.
Smith G G, Specimens of Middle Scots, Edinburgh and London 1902, pp lxvi, lxxiii.
Brown J T T, The Bannatyne Manuscript, SHR 1.136.
Smith G G, edn, 1.72; 3.150 (notes in vol 1).
Ritchie W T, ed, The Bannatyne Manuscript Writtin in Tyme of Pest, 4 vols, PSTS ns 5, 22, 23, 26, Edinburgh 1928–34, 3.28.
Baxter J W, William Dunbar, Edinburgh and London 1952, p 217.
Editions. Laing D, The Poems and Fables of Robert Henryson, Edinburgh 1865, pp 43, 248, 302 (notes at end of text; crit St James Magazine 24.60, rptd North British Review, American edn ns 44.81, British edn ns 44.154).
Smith G G, The Poems of Robert Henryson, 3 vols, PSTS 55, 58, 64, Edinburgh and London 1906, 1908, 1914, 1.72; 3.150 (notes in vol 1, text in vol 3).
Metcalfe W M, The Poems of Robert Henryson, Paisley 1917, pp 229, 295 (notes at end of text).
Wood H H, The Poems and Fables of Robert Henryson, Edinburgh 1933, 2nd edn rvsd 1958, pp 157, 268 (notes at end of text; crit J Speirs, Scrut 2.296; D Hamer, MLR 29.342; TLS Aug 3 1933, p 523; E Muir, The Spectator 151.290; The Modern Scot 4.163).
Kinghorn A M, The Middle Scots Poets, London 1970, p 74 (notes at foot of page).
Textual Matters. Smith, edn, 1.lxxiii; 3.x.
Wood, edn, p xxvii.
Language. Laing, edn, p 309 (glossary).
Murray J A H, The Dialect of the Southern Counties of Scotland, London 1873.
Hahn O, Zur Verbal- und Nominalflexion bei den schottischen Dichtern, Berlin 1887–89 (see especially pt 3, p 14).
Browne W H, The Taill of Rauf Coilyear, Baltimore 1903, pp 35, 139 (general discussion of Middle Scots; glossary).
Millar J H, A Literary History of Scotland, London 1903, p 687 (glossary).
Smith G G, edn, 1.83 (index of words and glossary); CHEL, 2.101, 506.
Gray M M, Introd, Lancelot of the Laik, PSTS ns 2, Edinburgh and London 1912, 2.xviii.
Metcalfe, edn, pp xx, 303 (brief discussion; glossary).
Westergaard E, Prepositions in Lowland Scotch, Angl 41.444 (some examples from Henryson); Verbal Forms in Middle-Scotch, Angl 43.95.
Watt L M, Language and Influences, Doug-

las's Aeneid, Cambridge 1920, p 149 (very generally applicable).

Westergaard E, Studies in Prefixes and Suffixes in Middle Scottish, London 1924.

Wood, edn, pp xxxi, 277 (discussion, glossary).

Patrick D, Scottish Literature, Chambers's Cyclopædia of English Literature, rvsd J L Geddie, Phila and N Y 1938, 1.164.

Scott T, Dunbar A Critical Exposition of the Poems, Edinburgh and London 1966, p 351.

Kinghorn, edn, pp 45, 164 (note on Middle Scots, glossary).

Versification. Amours F J, Scottish Alliterative Poems in Riming Stanzas, PSTS 27, 38, Edinburgh and London 1897, p lxxxii.

Smith G G, edn, l.lxxxiii.

Henderson T F, Scottish Vernacular Literature, Edinburgh 1898; 2nd edn rvsd 1900; 3rd edn rvsd 1910, p 117.

Craigie W, The Scottish Alliterative Poems, Proc of the British Acad 28.217.

Date. Metcalfe, edn, p xviii.

Authorship. Brown J T T, The Bannatyne Manuscript, SHR 1.151.

Smith, edn, l.lxxiv.

Enc Brit, 13.302 (brief); CHEL, 2.283.

Sources and Literary Relations. Smith, edn, l.lxxiv.

Enc Brit, 13.302 (brief); CHEL, 2.283.

Mendenhall J C, Aureate Terms A Study in Literary Diction, Lancaster Pa 1919.

Speirs J, The Scots Literary Tradition, London 1940, p 12; rvsd 2nd edn London 1962, p 38.

Craigie W, The Scottish Alliterative Poems, Proc of the British Acad 28.217.

Renwick-Orton, p 414 (very brief).

Rossi S, Robert Henryson, Milan 1955, p 83.

Wittig K, The Scottish Tradition in Literature, Edinburgh 1958, p 76.

Kinghorn A M, The Minor Poems of Robert Henryson, SSL 3.37.

Literary Criticism. Millar J H, A Literary History of Scotland, London 1903, p 31.

Smith, edn, l.lxxiv, lxxxvii.

CHEL, 2.283; Enc Brit, 13.302 (brief).

Saintsbury G, The Four Great Scottish Poets, N Y 1929, p 185 (brief).

Speirs J, The Scots Literary Tradition, London 1940, p 12 (crit Scrut 9.193); rvsd 2nd edn London 1962, p 38.

Craigie W, The Scottish Alliterative Poems, Proc of the British Acad 28.230.

Stearns M W, Robert Henryson, N Y 1949, p 8.

Craig HEL, p 167 (very brief).

Renwick-Orton, pp 414, 416 (brief).

Lewis C S, English Literature in the Sixteenth Century, Oxford 1954, p 175.

Rossi, Robert Henryson, p 83.

Elliott C, Robert Henryson Poems, Oxford 1963, p xxi (brief comment); rpt from corrected sheets, Oxford 1966.

Kinghorn A M, Minor Poems, SSL 3.37; Dunbar and Villon A Comparison and a Contrast, MLR 62.205.

Bibliography. Smith, edn, l.lxxiii.

Brown-Robbins, Robbins-Cutler, no 1021.

[16] THE THRE DEID POLLIS.

MSS. 1, Magdalene Coll Camb 2553 (Pepysian Libr, Maitland Folio), pp 327–328 (1570–71); 2, Nat Libr Scot 1.1.6 (Bannatyne), ff 57^b–58^b (1568).

Pinkerton J, Ancient Scotish Poems, 2 vols, London and Edinburgh 1786, 1.v; 2.437, 471 (MSS 1, 2).

Brydges E and J Haslewood, The British Bibliographer, London 1814, 4.183 (MS 2).

Laing D, The Poems of George Bannatyne, Edinburgh 1824, p 3 (MS 2); An Account of the Contents of George Bannatyne's Manuscript, The Bannatyne Club, Edinburgh 1829, 35.43 (MS 2).

Small J, The Poetical Works of Gavin Douglas, Edinburgh and London 1874, 1.clxxi (MS 1).

Schipper J, The Poems of William Dunbar, pt 1, Denkschriften der kaiserlichen Akadamie der Wissenschaften, Philo-Hist Classe, Vienna 1892, 40².9, 11, 17 (MSS 1, 2).

Murdoch J B, ed, The Bannatyne Manuscript, 4 vols, Hunterian Club, Glasgow 1896, 2.157 (MS 2).

Smith G G, Specimens of Middle Scots, Edinburgh and London 1902, pp lxvi, lxxiii (MSS 1, 2).

Brown J T T, The Bannatyne Manuscript, SHR 1.136 (MS 2).

Smith G G, edn, 1.75; 3.158 (MS 1, notes in vol 1); 1.75; 3.156 (MS 2, notes in vol 1).

Craigie W A, ed, The Maitland Folio, 2 vols, PSTS ns 7, 20, Edinburgh and London 1919–27, 1.394; 2.124 (MS 1, notes in vol 2).

Ritchie W T, ed, The Bannatyne Manuscript Writtin in Tyme of Pest, 4 vols, PSTS ns 5, 22, 23, 26, Edinburgh 1928–34, 2.142 MS 2); rptd from corrected sheets, Oxford 1966.

Baxter J W, William Dunbar, Edinburgh and London 1952, p 217 (MSS 1, 2).

Editions. Dalrymple D, Ancient Scottish Poems Published from the MS of George

Bannatyne, Edinburgh 1770, pp 139, 285 (crit O Gilchrist, Ancient Scottish Poems, Censura Literaria, ed Brydges, London 1807, 5.238); rptd Leeds 1815, pp 177, 334 (notes at end of text; MS 2).

Ellis G, Specimens of the Early English Poets, 5 edns, London 1790, 1801, 1803, 1811, 1845 (5th edn corrected), 1.300 (4 stanzas; spelling, occasional wording modernized; glossings at foot of page; Dalrymple edn).

Sibbald J, Chronicle of Scottish Poetry, 4 vols, Edinburgh and London 1802, 1.191 (introductory and end notes; MS 2).

Laing D, The Poems and Fables of Robert Henryson, Edinburgh 1865, pp 30, 246, 301 (notes at end of text; MSS 1, 2; crit St James Magazine 24.60, rptd North British Review, American edn ns 44.81, British edn ns 44.154).

Fitzgibbon H M, Early English and Scottish Poetry, London N Y and Melbourne 1888, pp 92, 431 (spelling modernized; notes at end of text).

Smith G G, The Poems of Robert Henryson, 3 vols, PSTS 55, 58, 64, Edinburgh and London 1906, 1908, 1914, 1.75; 3.156 (notes in vol 1, text in vol 3; MSS 1, 2).

Metcalfe W M, The Poems of Robert Henryson, Paisley 1917, pp 233, 297 (notes at end of text; MSS 1, 2).

Wood H H, The Poems and Fables of Robert Henryson, Edinburgh 1933, 2nd edn rvsd 1958, pp 205, 275 (variants in footnotes, notes at end of text; MS 2; crit J Speirs, Scrut 2.296; D Hamer, MLR 29.342; TLS Aug 3 1933, p 523; E Muir, The Spectator 151.290; The Modern Scot 4.163).

Gray M M, Scottish Poetry from Barbour to James VI, N Y 1935, p 96 (crit J Speirs, Scrut 6.83; W M Mackenzie, The Scottish Bookman 1, no 4, p 133).

Fergusson J, The Green Garden, London and Edinburgh 1946, p 5 (spelling modernized).

Elliott C, Robert Henryson Poems, Oxford 1963, pp 119, 159 (notes at end of text; MS 2); rptd from corrected sheets, Oxford 1966.

Kinghorn A M, The Middle Scots Poets, London 1970, p 71 (notes at foot of page; MSS 1, 2).

Textual Matters. Smith, edn, 1.lxxv; 3.x, xix.
Wood, edn, p xxx.
Language. Dalrymple, edn, p 317 (glossary); rptd Leeds 1815, p 367, [added] Glossary, p 1 [separate pagination].
Laing, edn, p 309 (glossary).
Murray J A H, The Dialect of the Southern

Counties of Scotland, London 1873.

Hahn O, Zur Verbal- und Nominalflexion bei den schottischen Dichtern, Berlin 1887–89 (see especially pt 3, p 14).

Browne W H, The Taill of Rauf Coilyear, Baltimore 1903, pp 35, 139 (general discussion of Middle Scots; glossary).

Smith, edn, 1.83 (index of words and glossary); CHEL, 2.101, 506.

Gray, M M, Introd, Lancelot of the Laik, PSTS ns 2, Edinburgh and London 1912, 2.xviii.

Metcalfe, edn, pp xx, 303 (brief discussion; glossary).

Westergaard E, Prepositions in Lowland Scotch, Angl 41.444 (some examples from Henryson); Verbal Forms in Middle-Scotch, Angl 43.95.

Craigie W A, The Maitland Folio, 2 vols, PSTS ns 7, 20, Edinburgh and London 1919–27, 2.135 (glossary).

Watt L M, Language and Influences, Douglas's Aeneid, Cambridge 1920, p 149 (very generally applicable).

Westergaard E, Studies in Prefixes and Suffixes in Middle Scottish, London 1924.

Wood, edn, pp xxxi, 277 (discussion, glossary).

Patrick D, Scottish Literature, Chambers's Cyclopædia of English Literature, rvsd J L Geddie, Phila and N Y 1938, 1.164.

Fergusson, edn, p 228 (glossary).
Elliott, edn, p 165 (glossary).
Scott T, Dunbar A Critical Exposition of the Poems, Edinburgh and London 1966, p 351.
Kinghorn, edn, pp 45, 164 (note on Middle Scots, glossary).

Versification. Smith, edn, 1.lxxxiii.
Elliott, edn, p ix.
Date. Metcalfe, edn, p xviii.
Authorship. Smith, edn, 1.lxxv.
Wood, edn, p xxx.
Rossi S, Robert Henryson, Milan 1955, p 93.
Elliott, edn, p xix.
Sources and Literary Relations. Mendenhall J C, Aureate Terms A Study in Literary Diction, Lancaster Pa 1919.

Smith J M, The French Background of Middle Scots Literature, Edinburgh and London 1934, p 71.

Clark J M, The Dance of Death in the Middle Ages and the Renaissance, Glasgow Univ Publ 86, Glasgow 1950, p 20.

Rossi, Robert Henryson, p 94.
Kinghorn A M, The Mediæval Makars, Texas Stud Lit and Lang 1.73.
Elliott, edn, p viii.
Hyde I, Poetic Imagery, SSL 2.193, 195.

MacDonald D, Henryson and the Thre Prestis of Peblis, Neophil 51.175.
Woolf R, The English Religious Lyric in the Middle Ages, Oxford 1968, p 319.
Literary Criticism. Henley W E, Robert Henryson, The English Poets, ed T H Ward, London and N Y 1880; (numerous subsequent edns) N Y 1924, 1.138.
Snell F J, The Poets, The Age of Transition, London 1905, 1.79.
Miller F, The Poets of Dumfriesshire, Glasgow 1910, p 11 (brief).
Saintsbury G, The Four Great Scottish Poets, N Y 1929, p 185 (brief).
Craig HEL, p 167 (brief).
Renwick-Orton, p 416 (brief).
Rossi, Robert Henryson, p 93.
Kinghorn, Texas Stud Lit and Lang 1.80.
Elliott, edn, p viii.
Hyde, SSL 2.185, 193, 195.
Kinghorn A M, Minor Poems of Robert Henryson, SSL 3.33, 39.
MacDonald, Neophil 51.175.
Woolf R, English Religious Lyric, Oxford 1968, p 320.
Bibliography. Smith, edn, l.lxxv.
Brown Reg, no 1567; Brown-Robbins, Robbins-Cutler, no 2551.

[17] ANE PRAYER FOR THE PEST.

MS. Nat Libr Scot 1.1.6 (Bannatyne), pp 20–21, ff 24ᵃ–25ᵇ (1568).
Pinkerton J, Ancient Scotish Poems, 2 vols, London and Edinburgh 1786, 2.471.
Brydges E and J Haslewood, The British Bibliographer, London 1814, 4.183.
Laing D, The Poems of George Bannatyne, Edinburgh 1824, p 3; An Account of the Contents of George Bannatyne's Manuscript, The Bannatyne Club, Edinburgh 1829, 35.43.
Schipper J, The Poems of William Dunbar, pt 1, Denkschriften der kaiserlichen Akademie der Wissenschaften, Philo-Hist Classe, Vienna 1892, 40².9, 17.
Murdoch J B, ed, The Bannatyne Manuscript, 4 vols, Hunterian Club, Glasgow 1896, 2.61.
Smith G G, Specimens of Middle Scots, Edinburgh and London 1902, pp lxvi, lxxiii.
Brown J T T, The Bannatyne Manuscript, SHR 1.136.
Smith G G, edn, 1.77; 3.162 (notes in vol 1).
Ritchie W T, ed, the Bannatyne Manuscript Writtin in Tyme of Pest, 4 vols, PSTS ns 5, 22, 23, 26, Edinburgh 1928–34, 1.33; 2.58.

Baxter J W, William Dunbar, Edinburgh and London 1952, p 217.
Editions. Laing D, The Poems and Fables of Robert Henryson, Edinburgh 1865, pp 39, 247 (notes at end of text; crit St James Magazine 24.60, rptd North British Review, American edn ns 44.81, British edn ns 44.154).
Smith G G, The Poems of Robert Henryson, 3 vols, PSTS 55, 58, 64, Edinburgh and London 1906, 1908, 1914, 1.77; 3.162 (notes in vol 1, text in vol 3).
Metcalfe W M, The Poems of Robert Henryson, Paisley 1917, pp 236, 298 (notes at end of text).
Wood H H, The Poems and Fables of Robert Henryson, Edinburgh 1933, 2nd edn rvsd 1958, pp 163, 269 (variants in footnotes, notes at end of text; crit J Speirs, Scrut 2.296; D Hamer, MLR 29.342; TLS Aug 3 1933, p 523; E Muir, The Spectator 151.290; The Modern Scot 4.163).
Elliott C, Robert Henryson Poems, Oxford 1963, pp 122, 160 (notes at end of text); rptd from corrected sheets, Oxford 1966.
Selection. Henderson E, The Annals of Dunfermline, Glasgow 1879, p 722 (Laing edn).
Textual Matters. Smith, edn, l.lxxvi; 3.x, xix. Wood, edn, p xxvii.
Language. Laing, edn, p 309 (glossary).
Murray J A H, The Dialect of the Southern Counties of Scotland, London 1873.
Hahn O, Zur Verbal- und Nominalflexion bei den schottischen Dichtern, Berlin 1887–89 (see especially pt 3, p 14).
Browne W H, The Taill of Rauf Coilyear, Baltimore 1903, pp 35, 139 (general discussion of Middle Scots; glossary).
Smith, edn, 1.83 (index of words, glossary).
Gray M M, Introd, Lancelot of the Laik, PSTS ns 2, Edinburgh and London 1912, 2.xviii.
Metcalfe, edn, pp xx, 303 (brief discussion, glossary).
Wood, edn, pp xxxi, 277 (discussion, glossary).
Patrick D, Scottish Literature, Chambers's Cyclopædia of English Literature, rvsd J L Geddie, Phila and N Y 1938, 1.164.
Elliott, edn, p 165 (glossary).
Scott T, Dunbar A Critical Exposition of the Poems, Edinburgh and London 1966, p 351.
Versification. Smith, edn, l.lxxxiii.
Elliott, edn, p x.
Date. Henderson E, The Annals of Dunfermline, Glasgow 1879, p 175.
Metcalfe, edn, p xviii.

Authorship. Smith, edn, l.lxxvi.
Wood, edn, p xxvii.
Sources and Literary Relations. Mendenhall J C, Aureate Terms A Study in Literary Diction, Lancaster Pa 1919.
Smith G G, Scottish Literature Character and Influence, London 1919, p 14 (brief reference).
Nichols P H, Lydgate's Influence on the Aureate Terms of the Scottish Chaucerians, PMLA 47.517.
Tilgner E, Germanische Studien die Aureate Terms als Stilement bei Lydgate, Berlin 1936; rptd 1967, p 79.
Elliott, edn, pp viii, x.
Scott T, Dunbar A Critical Exposition, p 4.
MacDonald D, Henryson and the Thre Prestis of Peblis, Neophil 51.174.
Other Scholarly Problems. Henderson E, The Annals of Dunfermline, p 175 (occasion).
Literary Criticism. Nichols, Lydgate's Influence, PMLA 47.517.
Wood H H, Robert Henryson, Edinburgh Essays on Scots Literature, Edinburgh and London 1933, p 22 (crit The Modern Scot 4.353).
Rossi S, Robert Henryson, Milan 1955, p 84.
Schlauch M, English Medieval Literature and Its Social Foundations, Warsaw 1956, p 295.
Duncan D, Henryson's Testament of Cresseid, EC 11.133.
Elliott, edn, p viii.
Kinghorn A M, The Minor Poems of Robert Henryson, SSL 3.36, 39.
MacDonald D, Neophil 51.174.
Wood H H, Two Scots Chaucerians, Writers and Their Work, no 201, ed G Bullough, London 1967, p 20.
Bibliography. Smith, edn, l.lxxvi.
Brown Reg, no 1488; Brown-Robbins, Robbins-Cutler, no 2420.

[18] THE WANT OF WYSE MEN.

MS. 1, Nat Libr Scot 1.1.6 (Bannatyne), ff 78ᵃ–78ᵇ (1568). PRINT: 2, Nat Libr Scot 19.1.16 (Chepman and Myllar), pp 166–168 (1508) (STC, no 20120).
Pinkerton J, Ancient Scotish Poems, 2 vols, London and Edinburgh 1786, 2.471 (MS 1).
Brydges E and J Haslewood, The British Bibliographer, London 1814, 4.183 (MS 1).
Laing D, The Poems of George Bannatyne, Edinburgh 1824, p 3 (MS 1); An Account of the Contents of George Bannatyne's
Manuscript, The Bannatyne Club, Edinburgh 1829, 35.43 (MS 1).
Laing D, The Knightly Tale of Golagrus and Gawane, Edinburgh 1827, f 11ᵇ (2 rptd).
Dickson R and J P Edmond, Annals of Scottish Printing from 1507 to the Beginning of the 17th Century, Cambridge 1890, p 49 (PRINT 2).
Schipper J, The Poems of William Dunbar, pt 1, Denkschriften der kaiserlichen Akademie der Wissenschaften, Philo-Hist Classe, Vienna 1892, 40².9, 14, 17 (MS 1, PRINT 2).
Murdoch J B, ed, The Bannatyne Manuscript, 4 vols, Hunterian Club, Glasgow 1896, 2.213 (MS 1).
Smith G G, Specimens of Middle Scots, Edinburgh and London 1902, pp lxvi, lxxiii, lxxiv (MS 1, PRINT 2).
Brown J T T, The Bannatyne Manuscript, SHR 1.136 (MS 1).
Smith G G, edn, 1.78; 3.172 (MS 1, notes in vol 1); 1.78; 3.170 (2 rptd, notes in vol 1).
Stevenson G, ed, Pieces from The Makculloch and the Gray MSS, PSTS 65, Edinburgh and London 1918, pp 236, 303 (notes at end of text; PRINT 2).
Ritchie W T, ed, The Bannatyne Manuscript Writtin in Tyme of Pest, 4 vols, PSTS ns 5, 22, 23, 26, Edinburgh 1928–34, 2.195 (MS 1).
Beattie W, The Chepman and Myllar Prints, Edinburgh Biblio Soc, Oxford 1950, p viii, 166 (2 described, rptd).
Baxter J W, William Dunbar, Edinburgh and London 1952, pp 178, 216, 217 (MS 1, PRINT 2).
Editions. Sibbald J, Chronicle of Scottish Poetry, 4 vols, London and Edinburgh 1802, 1.199 (PRINT 2).
Laing D, The Poems and Fables of Robert Henryson, Edinburgh 1865, pp 36, 247, 302 (notes at end of text; MS 1, PRINT 2; crit St James Magazine 24.60, rptd North British Review, American edn ns 44.81, British edn ns 44.154).
Smith G G, The Poems of Robert Henryson, 3 vols, PSTS 55, 58, 64, Edinburgh and London 1906, 1908, 1914, 1.78; 3.170 (notes in vol 1, text in vol 3; MS 1, PRINT 2).
Metcalfe W M, The Poems of Robert Henryson, Paisley 1917, pp 240, 299 (notes at end of text; MS 1, PRINT 2).
Wood H H, The Poems and Fables of Robert Henryson, Edinburgh 1933, 2nd edn rvsd 1958, pp 189, 273 (variants in footnotes, notes at end of text; MS 1, PRINT 2; crit J Speirs, Scrut 2.296; D Hamer, MLR

29.342; TLS Aug 3 1933, p 523; E Muir, The Spectator 151.290; The Modern Scot 4.163).

Modernization. Mudge E L, A Fifteenth-Century Critic, CE 5.155.

Textual Matters. Brown J T T, The Bannatyne Manuscript, SHR 1.142.

Smith, edn, 1.lxxvi; 3.x, xvi, xix.

Wood, edn, p xxviii.

Language. Laing, edn, p 309 (glossary).

Murray J A H, The Dialect of the Southern Counties of Scotland, London 1873.

Hahn O, Zur Verbal- und Nominalflexion bei den schottischen Dichtern, Berlin 1887–89 (see especially pt 3, p 14).

Browne W H, The Taill of Rauf Coilyear, Baltimore 1903, pp 35, 139 (general discussion of Middle Scots; glossary).

Millar J H, A Literary History of Scotland, London 1903, p 687 (glossary).

Smith, edn, 1.83 (index of words, glossary); CHEL, 2.101, 506.

Gray M M, Introd, Lancelot of the Laik, PSTS ns 2, Edinburgh and London 1912, 2.xviii.

Metcalfe, edn, pp xx, 303 (brief discussion; glossary).

Westergaard E, Prepositions in Lowland Scotch, Angl 41.444 (some examples from Henryson); Verbal Forms in Middle-Scotch, Angl 43.95.

Watt L M, Language and Influences, Douglas's Aeneid, Cambridge 1920, p 149 (very generally applicable).

Westergaard E, Studies in Prefixes and Suffixes in Middle Scottish, London 1924.

Wood, edn, pp xxxi, 277 (discussion, glossary).

Patrick D, Scottish Literature, Chambers's Cyclopædia of English Literature, rvsd J L Geddie, Phila and N Y 1938, 1.164.

Scott T, Dunbar A Critical Exposition of the Poems, Edinburgh and London 1966, p 351.

Versification. Smith, edn, 1.lxxxiii.

Date. Smith, edn, 1.lxxvii.

Metcalfe, edn, p xviii.

Authorship. Brown J T T, The Bannatyne Manuscript, SHR 1.150.

Smith, edn, 1.lxxvii.

Sources and Literary Relations. Mendenhall J C, Aureate Terms A Study in Literary Diction, Lancaster Pa 1919.

Rossi S, Robert Henryson, Milan 1955, p 89.

MacDonald D, Henryson and the Thre Prestis of Peblis, Neophil 51.172.

Literary Criticism. Oliphant F R, Robert Henryson, Blackwood's Edinburgh Magazine 148.504; rptd Littell's Living Age 187.542.

Mudge E L, A Fifteenth-Century Critic, CE 5.154.

Rossi, Robert Henryson, p 89.

Elliott C, Robert Henryson Poems, Oxford 1963, p xxi (brief comment); rptd from corrected sheets, Oxford 1966.

Kinghorn A M, The Minor Poems of Robert Henryson, SSL 3.35, 39.

MacDonald D, Neophil 51.172.

Wood H H, Two Scots Chaucerians, Writers and Their Work no 201, ed G Bullough, London 1967, p 23.

Bibliography. Smith, edn, 1.lxxvi.

Brown-Robbins, Robbins-Cutler, no 2139.

Beattie W, The Chepman and Myllar Prints, Edinburgh Biblio Soc, Oxford 1950, p xiv.

3. DOUGLAS

GENERAL.

Language. Jamieson J, An Etymological Dictionary of the Scottish Language, 2 vols, Edinburgh 1808; rvsd J Longmuir and D Donaldson, 4 vols with supplement, Paisley 1879–82; new edn J Longmuir, London and Edinburgh 1885; another edn with introd by W M Metcalfe, Paisley 1912.

Murray J A H, A New English Dictionary on Historical Principles (The Oxford English Dictionary, ed J A H Murray, H Bradley, W A Craigie, C T Onions), Oxford 1884–1933.

Mackay C, A Dictionary of Lowland Scotch, Boston 1888.

Wright J, The English Dialect Dictionary, 8 vols, London 1896–1905.

Grant W and D D Murison, The Scottish National Dictionary, Edinburgh 1931—(crit Wittig, SSL 1.275).

Craigie W A and A J Aitken, edd, A Dictionary of the Older Scottish Tongue from the Twelfth Century to the End of the Seventeenth Founded on the Collections of Sir William A Craigie, Chicago and London 1931—.

Craigie W A, Older Scottish and English A Study in Contrasts, TPSL 1935, p 1.

MED.
Woolley J S, Bibliography for Scottish Linguistic Studies, Edinburgh 1954.
Murison D, A Survey of Scottish Language Studies, Forum Mod Lang Stud 3.276.
Authorship. Gunn C B, The Three Tales of the Three Priests of Peebles, Selkirk 1894, p 94 (here attributed to Douglas).
Sources and Literary Relations. Mackay Æ J G, A Life of the Author, in John Major, A History of Greater Britain, Edinburgh 1892, p xxxi (relation between Douglas, Major, Polydore Vergil).
Gray M M, Introd, Lancelot of the Laik, PSTS ns 2, Edinburgh and London 1912, 2.xviii, xxxv.
Wood H H, Robert Henryson, Edinburgh Essays on Scots Literature, Edinburgh and London 1933, p 1 (crit The Modern Scot 4.353).
Linklater E, The Question of Culture, The Lion and the Unicorn, London 1935, pp 111, 127 (brief).
Other Scholarly Problems. Irving D, The Lives of the Scotish Poets, 2 vols, Edinburgh 1804; 2nd edn improved London 1810, 2.66 (lost works).
Irving D, The History of Scotish Poetry, ed J A Carlyle, Edinburgh 1861, p 287 (lost works).
Whiting B J, Proverbs and Proverbial Sayings from Scottish Writings Before 1600, MS 11.123; 13.87 (draws on works of Douglas as well as other Scottish material).
Kinghorn A M, Scots Literature and Scottish Antiquarians 1750–1800, SE 33.46 (development of antiquarians' interest).
Whiting B J, Proverbs Sentences and Proverbial Phrases, Cambridge Mass 1968.
Bibliography. Bale J, Illustrium majoris Britanniæ scriptorum, Ipswich 1548, f 254ᵇ (brief reference); Scriptorum illustrium maioris Brytanniæ posterio pars, Basile 1559, p 218.
Thynne F, A generall catalog of the writers of Scotland, The Second volume of Chronicles . . . by Raphaell Holinshed, London 1586, p 462.
Ruddiman T, Virgil's Æneis translated into Scottish verse, Edinburgh 1710, p 14.
Mackenzie G, The Lives and Characters of the Most Eminent Writers of the Scots Nation, Edinburgh 1711, 2.296, 301, 308 (lists early commentators, works extant and lost).
Tanner T, Bibliotheca Britannico-Hibernica, ed D Wilkins, London 1748, p 232.

Pinkerton J, Ancient Scotish Poems, 2 vols, London and Edinburgh 1786, 1.xcv.
The Scottish Register, Edinburgh 1794, 1.193.
Dempster T, Historia Ecclesiastica Gentis Scotorum: sive De Scriptoribus Scotis, 2 vols, Bannatyne Club Publ no 21, Edinburgh 1829, 1.221.
Hunter W, An Anglo-Saxon Grammar and Derivatives and an Analysis of the Style of Chaucer Douglas and Spenser, London Edinburgh and Glasgow 1832, p 70 (listing of both works extant and lost).
Charters L, Catalogues of Scotish Writers, ed J Maidment, Edinburgh 1833, p 84.
Lowndes W T, The Bibliographer's Manual of English Literature, London 1834; new edn rvsd corrected and enlarged by H G Bohn, London [1871?], 1.663.
Gray G J, A General Index to Hazlitt's Handbook and His Bibliographical Collections (1867–89), London 1893, p 229.
Bale J, Index Britanniæ Scriptorum, ff 57ᵇ, 215; ed R L Poole and M Bateson, Oxford 1902, p 83.
Browne W H, The Taill of Rauf Coilyear, Baltimore 1903, p 68.
Körting, p 199; Enc Brit, 8.445.
Watt L M, Scottish Life and Poetry, London 1912, p 499 (listing and location of MSS).
Black G F, A List of Works Relating to Scotland, BNYPL Jan-Dec 1914; rptd N Y 1916, pp 815, 817, 854.
Northup C S, J Q Adams and A Keogh, A Register of Bibliographies of the English Language and Literature, New Haven London and Oxford 1925, p 121.
Tucker-Benham, pp 148, 151, 153.
Baxter J H and C J Fordyce, Books Published Abroad by Scotsmen before 1700, Records of the Glasgow Biblio Soc, Glasgow 1933, 11.27.
Bronson B H, Ritson's Bibliographia Scotica, PMLA 52.130.
CBEL, 1.254, 259; 5.147.
Lewis C S, English Literature in the Sixteenth Century, Oxford 1954, pp 80, 640.
Smith S G, Gavin Douglas A Selection from His Poetry, Edinburgh 1959, pp 12, 14.
Rossi S, I Chauceriani Scozzesi, Napoli 1964, p 70.
Scott T, Late Medieval Scots Poetry, London 1967, p 34.
Kidd J and R H Carnie, Annual Bibliography of Scottish Literature 1969, Suppl 1, The Bibliotheck, Aberdeen 1970, p 5.
Ridley F H, A Check List, SSL 8.41.

[19] ENEADOS.

MSS. 1, Trinity Coll Camb 1184 (Gale 0.3.12), ff 1–328ᵇ (early 16 cent); 2, Nat Libr Scot 1.1.6 (Bannatyne), pp 77–82, 149–150, 637–644, ff 9ª–11ᵇ, 45ª–45ᵇ, 291ª–294ᵇ (1568); 3, Univ of Edinb, Dc.1.43 (Ruthven), ff 2–300 (1530?–1540?); 4, Univ of Edinb, Dk.7.49 (Elphystoun), ff 1–367 (early 16 cent); 5, Univ of Edinb, La II 655, 3 leaves (fragments; 16 cent); 6, Libr Arbp of Cantb (Lambeth 117), unfoliated (1545); 7, Libr Marquis of Bath (Longleat 252a), ff 3ª–360ᵇ (1547).

Pinkerton J, Ancient Scotish Poems, 2 vols, London and Edinburgh 1786, 2.471 (MS 2).

Brydges E and J Haslewood, The British Bibliographer, London 1814, 4.183 (MS 2).

Laing D, The Poems of George Bannatyne, Edinburgh 1824, p 3 (MS 2); An Account of the Contents of George Bannatyne's Manuscript, The Bannatyne Club, Edinburgh 1829, 35.43 (MS 2).

Dundas, edn (MS 1 rptd).

Schipper J, The Poems of William Dunbar, pt 1, Denkschriften der kaiserlichen Akademie der Wissenschaften, Philo-Hist Classe, Vienna 1892, 40².9, 17 (MS 2).

Murdoch J B, ed, The Bannatyne Manuscript, Hunterian Club, Glasgow 1896, 2.21, 122; 4.844 (MS 2 rptd).

Small, edn, 1.clxxii, clxxiii, clxxv, clxxvi, clxxvii (MSS 1, 4, 3, 6, 7).

James M R, The Western Manuscripts in the Library of Trinity College Cambridge, Cambridge 1902, 3.195 (MS 1).

Smith G G, Specimens of Middle Scots, Edinburgh and London 1902, pp lxvi, lxxiii (MS 2).

Brown J T T, The Bannatyne Manuscript, SHR 1.136 (MS 2).

Watt L M, Douglas's Aeneid, Cambridge 1920, pp 130, 135, 138, 139, 140 (MSS 1, 4, 3, 6, 7; crit C R Baskerville, MP 18.171; J W Bright, MLN 35.508; O L Jiriczek, LFGRP 42.379; G D Willcock, MLR 15.432; TLS Apr 1 1920, p 210).

Ritchie W T, ed, The Bannatyne Manuscript Writtin in Tyme of Pest, 4 vols, PSTS ns 5, 22, 23, 26, Edinburgh 1928–34, 2.20, 113; 4.108 (MS 2 rptd).

James M R and C Jenkins, A Descriptive Catalogue of the Manuscripts in the Library of Lambeth Palace, Cambridge 1930, pt 2, p 192 (MS 6).

Baxter J W, William Dunbar, Edinburgh and London 1952, p 217 (MS 2).

Coldwell, edn, 1.96 (MSS 1, 3, 4, 5, 6, 7 described; MS 1 rptd).

Editions. The xiii Bukes of Eneados, London 1553 (described in Ruddiman edn; S E Brydges, Censura Literaria, London 1808, 8.37; Small, edn, 1.clxxviii; L M Watt, Douglas's Aeneid, Cambridge 1920, p 140; described and variants listed in Coldwell, edn, 1.101; 4.196) (STC, no 24797).

Ruddiman T, Virgil's Æneis translated into Scottish verse, Edinburgh 1710 (based upon W Copland, The Palis of Honoure, London 1553?; described in Small, edn, 1.clxxx; O L Jiriczek, Specimens of Tudor Translations from the Classics, Heidelberg 1923, p 2; Coldwell, edn, 1.103).

Dundas G, The Æneid of Virgil Translated into Scottish Verse, 2 vols, Bannatyne Club Publications 64, Edinburgh 1839 (MS 1; briefly described in Coldwell, edn, 1.104).

Small J, The Poetical Works of Gavin Douglas, Edinburgh and London 1874, vols 2–4 (based primarily upon MS 4; described in Coldwell, edn, 1.104).

Coldwell D F C, Virgil's Aeneid Translated into Scottish Verse by Gavin Douglas, 4 vols, PSTS 3s 25, 27, 28, 30, Edinburgh and London 1957, 1959, 1960, 1964 (MS 1; notes in vol 1; crit H Käsmann, Angl 78.375; TLS Dec 30 1960, p 844; J A W Bennett, RES ns 14.73; L R N Ashley, BHR 28.802; R G Austin, MÆ 35.154; D Murison, SHR 46.66; vol 1 crit J A W Bennett, RES ns 18.310).

Selections. Fawkes F, A Description of May, London 1752, p 290 (prologue 12; Ruddiman edn); 3rd edn corrected London 1752; rptd A Description of May [and] A Description of Winter, Original Poems and Translations, London 1761, p 236; A Chalmers, The Works of the English Poets, 16.266; Aungervyle Soc Rpts 3s, nos 9–10, Edinburgh 1885, p 290.

Fawkes F, A Description of Winter, London 1754, p 270 (prologue 7; Ruddiman edn); rptd A Description of May [and] A Description of Winter, Original Poems and Translations, p 266; rptd A Chalmers, The Works of the English Poets, 16.270.

Warton T, History of English Poetry from the 12th to the Close of the 16th Century, London 1774–81; ed W C Hazlitt, London 1871, 3.220 (from prologue 12; glossings at foot of page).

Morison R, Select Works of Gawin Douglas Bishop of Dunkeld Containing Memoirs of the Author The Palice of Honour Prologues to the Æneid and A Glossary of Obsolete Words, The Scotish Poets, Perth 1787, 2. 89 (prologues 4, 7, 8, 12, 13; Ruddiman edn; briefly described in Coldwell, edn, 1.103).

T[owers J], Biographia Britannica, ed A Kippis, London 1789; 2nd edn with corrections enlargements and the addition of new lives, London 1793, 5.340 (major portion of prologue 12).

Ellis G, Specimens of the Early English Poets, 5 edns, London 1790, 1801, 1803, 1811, 1845 (5th edn corrected), 1. 317, 320 (from prologues 7, 1, 12; spelling, occasional wording modernized; glossings at foot of page).

Sibbald J, Chronicle of Scotish Poetry, 4 vols, Edinburgh and London 1802, 1.427 (from Heir followys the tyme, space and dait of the translatioun of this buke, Heir the translatar direkkis hys buk and excusis hym self, prologue 7, prologue 12, from prologues 13 and 4, prologue 8 from bk 6, prologue 1, Ane exclamatioun aganyst detractouris; introductory and end notes).

Irving D, The Lives of the Scotish Poets, 2 vols, Edinburgh 1804; 2nd edn improved London 1810, 2.62, 66 (brief excerpts).

Chalmers A, The Works of the English Poets, London 1810, 16.266 (Fawkes, edns, p 236).

Ritson J, The Caledonian Muse, printed 1785; published London 1821, p 219 (prologue 7; Ruddiman edn).

Tytler P F, Lives of Scottish Worthies, London 1833, 3.171.

Aytoun W E, The Ballads of Scotland, Edinburgh and London 1858; 2nd edn rvsd and augmented, Edinburgh and London 1859, l.lxxii, lxxiv (brief excerpt from prologue 13; illustrative of critical discussion).

Gilfillan G, Specimens with Memoirs of the Less-Known Poets, Edinburgh and London 1860, 1.72 (from prologue 12; glossings at foot of page).

Irving D, The History of Scotish Poetry, ed J A Carlyle, Edinburgh 1861, p 286 (brief excerpts).

Selections Made Chiefly from Works in the Old Scots Language for the Use of Schools in Scotland, Edinburgh 1867, p 11 (from bks 1, 2, prologue 2; glossings at foot of page).

Clarke C C, Specimens with Memoirs of the Less-Known British Poets, Edinburgh 1868, 1.72 (from prologue 12).

Innes C, XIV. Two Pages from Gavin Douglas's Virgil, Facsimiles of National MSS of Scotland, Southampton 1871, vol 3 (unpaged; from bk 1; MS 1).

Masson R O, Three Centuries of English Poetry, London 1876, p 156 (from prologues 4, 7, 12, bk 13; spelling modernized; glossings at foot of page; Small edn).

Lang A, Gawain Douglas, The English Poets, ed T H Ward, London and N Y 1880; (numerous subsequent edns) N Y 1924, 1.164, 168 (from prologues 7, 5, bks 2, 4; glossings at foot of page).

Ross J, The Book of Scottish Poems, Paisley 1882, 1.261 (from The Dyrectioun of His Buik, The Conclusioune of This Buik of Eneados, bk 6, prologue 13; brief introductory notes).

Fitzgibbon H M, Early English and Scottish Poetry, London N Y and Melbourne 1888, pp 173, 433 (from prologues 4, 5, 12, bk 4; spelling modernized; notes at end of text).

Veitch J, The Feeling for Nature in Scottish Poetry, Edinburgh and London 1887, 1.243, 252, 259, 274 (Colophon [To knaw the naym of the translatour] from prologues 1, 12, 13, 3, 7; brief quotes interspersed with criticism; glossings in side notes; crit C Patmore, Out-of-door Poetry, St James's Gazette July 9 1887; rptd in Courage in Politics, London 1921, p 23).

Eyre-Todd G, Mediæval Scottish Poetry, Abbotsford Series of the Scottish Poets, Glasgow 1892, p 244 (from bk 4, prologue 13; prologues 7 and 12 complete; glossings in margin).

Skeat Spec, pp 127, 415 (prologue 12; notes at end of text; MS 1).

Flügel NL, p 426 (from bks 1 and 2; Small edn).

Browne W H, Selections from the Early Scottish Poets, Baltimore 1896, pp 154, 191 (excerpts from prologues 7, 12; notes at end of text; Small edn).

Chambers R, Chambers's Cyclopædia, Phila and N Y 1901–03; rvsd J L Geddie, Phila and N Y 1938, 1.202 (brief excerpts from bks 1, 6, prologues 1, 7, 12).

Smith G G, Specimens of Middle Scots, Edinburgh and London 1902, pp 107, 295 (prologues 1, 7; notes at end of text; MS 4; crit Athen Jan 10 1903, p 48; R Ackerman, AnglB 19.378).

Dixon W M, The Edinburgh Book of Scottish Verse, London 1910, p 76 (from prologue 7; glossings at foot of page).

Douglas G, The Book of Scottish Poetry, London and Leipsic 1911, p 132 (from prologue 7; glossings at foot of page; Small edn).

Metcalfe W M, Specimens of Scottish Literature 1325–1835, London 1913, pp 58, 163 (from prologue 1; notes at end of text).

Neilson W A and K G T Webster, Chief British Poets of the 14th and 15th Centuries, Boston N Y etc 1916, pp 400, 435 (from prologue 1, bk 2, prologue 12 complete; notes at end of text; glossings at foot of page; Small edn).

Jiriczek O L, Specimens of Tudor Translations from the Classics, Heidelberg 1923, p 5 (bk 4; Copland, The Palis of Honoure, with lines 330–354 from Ruddiman edn; variants from Dundas' edn of MS 1 and Small's edn of MS 4 in footnotes).

Buchan J, The Northern Muse, An Anthology of Scots Vernacular Poetry, London 1924, pp 254, 283, 288, 500, 504 (from bk 6, prologues 7, 13; glossings at foot of page; notes at end of text).

Leslie S, An Anthology of Catholic Poets, N Y 1925, p 105 (from prologue 12; spelling modernized).

Brinton A C, Maphaeus Vegius and His Thirteenth Book of the Aeneid, Stanford Univ Calif 1930, p 93 (Small edn).

Patterson R F, Six Centuries of English Literature, London and Glasgow 1933, 1.204 (from bk 6, prologue 7).

Mackie R L, A Book of Scottish Verse, The World's Classics no 417, London 1934, p 68 (from prologues 13, 7, bk 6; glossings at foot of page); 2nd edn London Glasgow N Y 1967, p 69.

Pound E, A B C of Reading, London 1934; New Classics Series 30, Norfolk Conn 1951, p 115 (with brief critical ftnts).

Gray M M, Scottish Poetry from Barbour to James VI, N Y 1935, p 171 (from prologues 1, 7, 12, 13, bks 1, 4, 5, 6, 9; crit Scrut 6.83; The Scottish Bookman 1, no 4, p 133).

Cecil D, The Oxford Book of Christian Verse, Oxford 1940, p 37.

[Grieve C M] MacDiarmid H, The Golden Treasury of Scottish Poetry, London 1940 (crit L MacNiece, The New Statesman 21.66; TLS Feb 15 1941, pp 78, 84); rptd Golden Treasury Series, London 1948, pp 303, 331.

Fergusson J, The Green Garden, London and Edinburgh 1946, p 53 (prologue 7, from prologues 10, 12, 13; spelling modernized).

Mackenzie A M, Scottish Pageant, Edinburgh 1946; 2nd edn 1952, 1.5, 41, 255 (from prologues 12, 13, 7, bk 6, Ane exclamatioun, Conclusio; glossings at end of 4th and 5th selections).

Oliver J W and J C Smith, A Scots Anthology, Edinburgh and London 1949, p 51 (from prologue 7; spelling modernized; glossings at foot of page).

Smith S G, Gavin Douglas A Selection from His Poetry, Edinburgh 1959, p 25 (from prologues 1, 3, 4, 6, 7, 8, 10, 11, 12, 13, bks 1–11, Ane Exclamatioun, Colophon [To knaw the naym of the translatour]; glossings and notes at foot of page; Small edn; G G Smith, Specimens of Middle Scots).

McLaren M, The Wisdom of the Scots, London 1961, p 80 (glossings in margin).

Coldwell D F C, Selections from Gavin Douglas, Oxford 1964, pp 1, 116 (notes at end of text; MS 1; crit TLS July 16 1964, p 632; A M Kinghorn, SSL 2.130; R G Austin, MÆ 34.159; D Fox, N&Q 210[ns 12].69; A M L Knuth, Neophil 49.278; H Plett, Angl 83.356; M Pollet, EA 18.302; A J Aitken, SN 38.152).

Rossi S, I Chauceriani Scozzesi, Napoli 1964, p 237 (notes at foot of page).

MacQueen J and T Scott, The Oxford Book of Scottish Verse, Oxford 1966, p 158 (glossings at foot of page; Coldwell edn).

Scott T, Late Medieval Scots Poetry, London 1967, pp 128, 186 (notes at end of text; S G Smith, Gavin Douglas A Selection; D F C Coldwell, Selections from Gavin Douglas).

Kinghorn A M, The Middle Scots Poets, London 1970, p 155 (notes at foot of page; MS 2).

Scott T, The Penguin Book of Scottish Verse, London 1970, p 159 (glossings at foot of page).

Modernizations. Fawkes F, A Description of May, London 1752; 3rd edn corrected London 1752, p 291.

Fawkes F, A Description of Winter, London 1754, p 270.

Stone J, Description of a May Morning, The Scots Magazine 17.294 (prologue 12).

Warton T, History of English Poetry, London 1774–81; ed W C Hazlitt, London 1871, 3.225 (from prologues 12, 7).

Wall A, Gawain Douglas Bishop of Dunkeld, The Western ns 3.736 (brief excerpt; Fawkes, A Description of May).

Ross J, The Book of Scottish Poems, Paisley 1882, 1.260 (brief excerpt).

Textual Matters. Ruddiman, edn, p [i], f Aaª.

Small, edn, l.clxxii; 2.299; 3.353; 4.235 (includes notes and some variant readings from MSS and early edns).

Smith G G, Specimens of Middle Scots, Edinburgh and London 1902, p 295 (notes to prologues 1, 7).

Watt L M, Douglas's Aeneid, Cambridge 1920 pp 9, 18, 124, 179 (discussion of early edns, MSS; variant readings given in appendices).

Jiriczek O L, Specimens of Tudor Translations, Heidelberg 1923, p 1 (discussion of early printed texts and all MSS).

Isaac F, William Copland, Facsimiles and Illustrations No III, English and Scottish Printing Types 1535–58* 1552–58, ptd for the Bibliographical Soc, Oxford 1932 (unpaged; brief discussion and figure 105).

Bennett J A W, The Early Fame of Gavin Douglas's Eneados, MLN 61.84.

Coldwell D F C, Selections from Gavin Douglas, Oxford 1964, p xxii; edn, 1.96.

Language. Lisle W, Divers Ancient Monuments in the Saxon Tongue, London 1638 (unpaged; brief reference to Eneados as aid in understanding Anglo-Saxon).

Ruddiman, edn, ff A_1, B_2 (rules for understanding the language of Douglas's translation, glossary).

Fawkes F, A Description of May, Aungervyle Soc Rpts 3s, nos 9–10, Edinburgh 1885, p 308 (glossary).

Fawkes F, A Description of May [and] A Description of Winter, Original Poems and Translations, London 1761 (unpaged; glossary); rptd A Chalmers, The Works of the English Poets, 16.273.

Tooke J H, Diversions of Purley, London 1786; rvsd and corrected by R Taylor, London 1860, p 706 (discussion of Douglas' language illustrated by passages from Eneados).

Morison R, Select Works of Gawin Douglass, The Scotish Poets, Perth 1787, 2.139 (glossary).

Sibbald J, Chronicle of Scottish Poetry, Edinburgh and London 1802, vol 4 [unpaged] and 4.xlv (brief discussion; glossary).

Hunter W, An Anglo-Saxon Grammar and an Analysis of the Style of Chaucer Douglas and Spencer, London Edinburgh and Glasgow 1832, p 70 and passim.

Aytoun W E, The Ballads of Scotland, 2nd edn Edinburgh and London 1859, p lxxi (difficulty of his dialect).

Irving D, The History of Scotish Poetry, ed J A Carlyle, Edinburgh 1861, p 595 (glossary).

Murray J A H, The Dialect of the Southern Counties of Scotland, London 1873.

Small, edn, 1.clxii; 4.249 (discussion in vol 1, glossary in vol 4).

Wall A, Gawain Douglas Bishop of Dunkeld, The Western ns 3.735 (brief).

Hahn O, Zur Verbal- und Nominalflexion bei den schottischen Dichtern, Berlin 1887–89 (see especially pt 3, p 19).

Veitch J, The Feeling for Nature in Scottish Poetry, Edinburgh and London 1887, 1.250.

Minto W, Characteristics of English Poets, authorized American edn, Boston 1889, p 109.

Merlin M, Douglas' Virgil, Scottish Notes and Queries 7.27 (meaning of obscure words).

Moir J, Douglas' Virgil, Scottish Notes and Queries 7.48 (answers Merlin).

Bremner G St J, Douglas' Virgil, Scottish Notes and Queries 7.61 (second answer to Merlin).

Curtis F J, An Investigation of the Rimes and Phonology of the Middle-Scotch Romance Clariodus, Angl 16.387; 17.1, 125.

Browne W H, Selections from the Early Scottish Poets, Baltimore 1896, pp 1, 197 (discussion; glossary).

Heuser W, Die Dehnung vor -*nd* im Mittelschottischen, Die Dehnung -*end*, Angl 19.401 (very brief); Offenes und gescholossenes *ee* im Schottischen und Nordenglischen, Angl 19.334; Der Ursprung des unorganischen *I* in der mittelschottischen Schreibung, Angl 19.409 (brief).

Gerken H, Die Sprache des Bischofs Douglas von Dunkeld, Strassburg 1898, passim.

Flom G T, Scandinavian Influence on Southern Lowland Scotch, diss Columbia 1900.

Heuser W, Die mittelengl Entwicklung von U in offener Silbe, EStn 27.353.

Smith G G, Specimens of Middle Scots, Edinburgh and London 1902, pp xi, 325 (history and philology of Middle Scots; glossary).

Browne W H, The Taill of Rauf Coilyear, Baltimore 1903, pp 15, 35, 139 (general discussion of Middle Scots; glossary).

Luick K, Studien zur englischen Lautgeschichte, WBEP, 17.104.

Millar J H, A Literary History of Scotland, London 1903, p 687 (glossary).

Rodeffer J D, The Inflection of the English Present Plural Indicative, Baltimore 1903, pp 1, 23, 38.

Knopff P, Darstellung der Ablautverhältnisse in der schottischen Schriftsprache, diss Würzburg 1904.

Larue J L, Das Pronomen in den Werken des schottischen Bischop Gavin Douglas, diss Strassburg 1908 (crit O Ritter, EStn 44.101).

CHEL, 2.101, 301, 506.

Dixon W M, The Edinburgh Book of Scottish

Verse, London 1910, p 897 (glossary).

Gray M M, Introd, Lancelot of the Laik, PSTS ns 2, Edinburgh and London 1912, 2.xviii.

Ritter O, Wortkundliches zu Gavin Douglas, Arch 129.220.

Lenz K, Zur Lautlehre der französischen Elemente in den schottischen Dichtungen von 1500–1550, diss Marburg 1913 (examples taken from Douglas, Dunbar, Lyndesay, Clariodus).

Metcalfe W M, Specimens of Scottish Literature, London 1913, pp 9, 39, 189 (discussion of origin, development, grammatical forms of Early and Middle Scots; glossary).

Thornton R H, Words in Bishop Douglas's Eneados, N&Q 11s 12.156, 177, 215, 235, 255.

Taylor R, Some Notes on the Use of Can and Couth, JEGP 16.573.

Westergaard E, Remarks on the Use of Prepositions in Lowland Scotch, Angl 41.444 (some examples from Douglas); Verbal Forms in Middle-Scotch, Angl 43.95.

Watt L M, Language and Influences, Douglas's Aeneid, Cambridge 1920, pp 32, 149.

Jiriczek O L, Specimens of Tudor Translations, Heidelberg 1923, p 169 (glossary for bk 4 and other Tudor translations).

Westergaard E, Studies in Prefixes and Suffixes in Middle Scottish, diss London 1924 (crit C B, MLR 20.497).

Hofmann J, Die nordischen Lehnwörter bei Gavin Douglas, diss München 1925 (crit E Ekwall, AnglB 37.165).

Westergaard E, Plural Forms in Lowland Scottish, Angl 51.77.

Bald M A, The Pioneers of Anglicised Speech in Scotland, SHR 24.179 (brief).

Hartig P, Die Edinburger Dialektgruppe, Palaes 161.90 (cites Douglas among others to illustrate development of Scots dialect).

Ritchie R L G, Early Instances of French Loan-Words in Scots and English, EStn 63.41 (examples from Douglas).

Mackenzie A M, An Historical Survey of Scottish Literature, London 1933, p 104.

Wood H H, The Poems and Fables of Robert Henryson, Edinburgh 1933; 2nd edn rvsd Edinburgh 1958, p xxxi (discussion in introd; glossary at end of commentary).

Gray M M, Surrey's Vocabulary, TLS Oct 3 1936, p 791.

Patrick D, Scottish Literature, Chambers's Cyclopædia of English Literature, rvsd J L Geddie, Phila and N Y 1938, 1.164.

[Grieve C M] MacDiarmid H, The Golden

Treasury, London 1940; rptd Golden Treasury Series, London 1948, p 403 (glossary).

Fergusson J, The Green Garden, London and Edinburgh 1946, p 228 (glossary).

Oliver J W and J C Smith, A Scots Anthology, Edinburgh and London 1949, p 497 (glossaries).

Morgan E, Dunbar and the Language of Poetry, EC 2.143 (diction of prologues 1, 7).

Mackenzie A M, The Renaissance Poets Scots and English, Scottish Poetry A Critical Survey, ed J Kinsley, London 1955, p 35.

Wittig K, The Scottish Tradition in Literature, Edinburgh 1958, p 101.

Preston P, Did Gavin Douglas Write King Hart?, MÆ 28.40.

Bawcutt P, Gavin Douglas Some Additions to OED and DOST, N&Q 208(ns 10).289.

Coldwell D F C, Selections from Gavin Douglas, Oxford 1964, p 143 (glossary); edn, 1.111, 265 (discussion, glossary).

Rossi S, I Chauceriani Scozzesi, Napoli 1964, p 261 (discussion, glossary).

Scott T, Dunbar A Critical Exposition of the Poems, Edinburgh and London 1966, p 351.

Bawcutt P, The Shorter Poems of Gavin Douglas, PSTS 4s 3, Edinburgh and London 1967, p lxxvii (brief).

Scott T, Late Medieval Scots Poetry, London 1967, pp 21, 189 (discussion, glossary).

Kinghorn A M, The Middle Scots Poets, London 1970, pp 45, 164 (a note on Middle Scots, glossary).

Versification. Sibbald J, Chronicle of Scottish Poetry, Edinburgh and London 1802, 4.xlvi.

Irving D, The Lives of the Scotish Poets, 2 vols, Edinburgh 1804; 2nd edn improved London 1810, 2.27.

Guest E, A History of English Rhythms, 2 vols, London 1838; ed W W Skeat, new edn [in 1 vol] London 1882, passim.

Gray T, Metrum, Observations on English Metre, The Works of Thomas Gray, ed J Mitford, London 1843, vol 5, passim (brief references).

Irving D, The History of Scotish Poetry, ed J A Carlyle, Edinburgh 1861, p 267.

Schipper, passim; Brandl, 2¹.1015; Ten Brink, 3.85.

Curtis F J, An Investigation of the Rimes and Phonology of Clariodus, Angl 16.387; 17.1, 125.

Amours F J, Scottish Alliterative Poems, PSTS 27, 38, Edinburgh and London 1897,

p lxxxii (prologue 8).
Heuser W, Offenes und geschlossenes *ee* im Schottischen und Nordenglischen, Angl 19. 334.
Henderson T F, Scottish Vernacular Literature, Edinburgh 1898; 2nd edn rvsd Edinburgh 1900; 3rd edn rvsd Edinburgh 1910, p 201 (brief).
Schneider A, Die mittelenglische Stabzeile im 15 und 16 Jahrhundert, BBA 12.103.
Browne W H, The Taill of Rauf Coilyear, Baltimore 1903, p 57.
Saintsbury G, History of English Prosody, London 1908; 2nd edn London 1923, 1.275.
Schmidt E, Die schottische Aeneisübersetzung von Gavin Douglas, diss Leipzig 1910, pp 13, 18.
Watt L M, Douglas's Aeneid, Cambridge 1920, pp 102, 104, 109, 111.
Saintsbury G, The Four Great Scottish Poets, A Short History of Eng Lit, N Y 1929, p 191.
Oakden J P, Alliterative Poetry in Middle English, Manchester 1930, p 217 (crit K Brunner, AnglB 42.334).
Smith J M, The French Background of Middle Scots Literature, Edinburgh and London 1934, pp 161, 166.
Craigie W, The Scottish Alliterative Poems, Proc of the British Acad 28.217.
Stock N, Some Notes on Old Scots, Shenandoah 6, no 2, p 27.
Wittig K, The Scottish Tradition in Literature, Edinburgh 1958, p 111.
Ridley F H, The Aeneid of Henry Howard Earl of Surrey, Berkeley and Los Angeles 1963, p 33 (crit L V Ryan, Seventeenth Century News 21[Autumn 1963].55; A H Elliott, RES ns 16.106).
Coldwell, edn, 1.70.
Thompson J, The Founding of English Metre, London and N Y 1966, p 30.
Scott T, Late Medieval Scots Poetry, London 1967, p 18.
Date. Utley CR, p 309 (prologue 4, no 381).
Lewis C S, English Literature in the Sixteenth Century, Oxford 1954, p 80.
Ridley, The Aeneid of Surrey, p 14.
Authorship. Ridley F H, Did Gawin Douglas Write King Hart? Spec 34.402.
Sources and Literary Relations. Irving D, The Lives of the Scotish Poets, London 1810, 2.27, 60.
Nott G F, The Works of Henry Howard Earl of Surrey and of Sir Thomas Wyatt the Elder, London 1816, 1.cciii, 225*, 225**.

D, On Gawin Douglas's Translation of Virgil's Æneid, The Edinburgh Magazine 4.100.
Remarks on the Different Translations of Virgil, The Edinburgh Magazine 4.214.
On Gawin Douglas's Translation of Virgil's Æneid, The Edinburgh Magazine 6.41.
McN F, Gavin Douglas, Lives of Scottish Poets, ed J Robertson, London 1822, 1.160 (brief).
Tytler P F, Lives of Scottish Worthies, London 1833, 3.169.
Craik G L, Sketches of the History of Literature and Learning in England, London 1844, 1.257 (brief).
Bell R, A Translation of the Second and Fourth Books of Virgil's Æneid, Poetical Works of Henry Howard Earl of Surrey, Minor Contemporaneous Poets and Thomas Sackville Lord Buckhurst, London 1854, p 142 (relation to Surrey).
Irving D, The History of Scotish Poetry, ed J A Carlyle, Edinburgh 1861, p 284 (relation to Surrey).
Small, edn, 1.cxlv.
Craik G L, A Compendious History of English Literature, N Y 1877, 1.456.
Lang A, Gawain Douglas, The English Poets, ed T H Ward, London and N Y 1880; (numerous subsequent edns) N Y 1924, 1.161.
Lange P, Chaucer's Einfluss auf die Originaldichtungen des schotten Gavin Douglas, diss Halle 1882; rptd Angl 6.90.
Nichol J, A Sketch of Scottish Poetry, ed J Small; 2nd edn rvsd, EETS 11, London 1883, p xxiv.
Ross J M, Scottish History and Literature, Glasgow 1884, pp 317, 353, 364, 367.
Fitzgibbon H M, Early English and Scottish Poetry, N Y London and Melbourne 1888, p lxvii.
Schmidt H, Richard Stanyhursts Übersetzung von Vergils Aeneide, I-IV Ihr Verhältnis zum Original, Stil und Wortschatz, Breslau 1887, pp 4, 44 (relation to Stanyhurst).
Shairp J C, Sketches in History and Poetry, Edinburgh 1887, p 212 (brief).
Eyre-Todd G, Mediæval Scottish Poetry, Glasgow 1892, p 233.
Courthope, passim.
Molenaar H, Robert Burns' Beziehungen zur Litteratur, Erlangen and Leipzig 1899, p 5 (brief).
Ritter O, Quellenstudien zu Robert Burns, Palaes 20.161, 180, 218.
Dittes R, Zu Surrey's Aeneisübertragung,

Beiträge Zur Neueren Philologie, July 19
1902, p 181 (relation to Surrey).

Lawson A, The Poems of Alexander Hume,
PSTS 48, Edinburgh and London 1902, pp
1,227.

Mebus F, Studien zu William Dunbar, Breslau 1902, passim (resemblances of wording
scattered throughout notes to Dunbar's
poems).

Fest O, Über Surrey's Virgilübersetzung nebst
Neuausgabe des vierten Buches, Palaes
34.47 (collation of similar passages from
translations of bk 2; relation to Surrey,
Octavien de St Gelais; crit R Ackerman
AnglB 19.377; J Delcourt, EStn 35.296).

Imelmann R, Zu den Anfängen des Blank-
verses Surreys Aeneis IV in ursprünglicher
Gestalt, Jahrbuch der Deutschen Shakespeare-Gesellschaft 41.81 (relation to Surrey).

Moorman F W, The Interpretation of Nature
in English Poetry from Beowulf to Shakespeare, QF 95.147, 150.

Mebus F, Beiträge zu William Dunbars
Gedicht The Goldin Terge, EStn 39.passim.

CHEL, 2.294, 298.

Imelmann R, Der Britwell-Surrey, Jahrbuch
der Deutschen Shakespeare-Gesellschaft 45.
204 (relation to Surrey).

Schmidt E, Die schottische Aeneisübersetzung,
diss Leipzig 1910, pp 12, 19, 103 (relation
to Servius, Virgil, Surrey, Octavien de St
Gelais, Chaucer).

Schumacher A, Des Bischofs Gavin Douglas
Übersetzung der Aeneis Vergils, diss Strass-
burgh 1910, p 9 (relation to Virgil, Chaucer,
Surrey, Badius Ascensius, Octavien de St
Gelais, Maffeo Vegio).

Scholderer V, Introd, List of English Editions
and Translations of Greek and Latin Classics Printed before 1641 by Henrietta R
Palmer, London 1911, p xxx (brief).

Watt L M, Scottish Life and Poetry, London
1912, p 117 (relation to Surrey).

Mendenhall J C, Aureate Terms A Study in
the Literary Diction of the 15th Century,
Lancaster Pa 1919.

Nitchie E, Vergil and the English Poets, CUS
66.86 (relation to Surrey).

Smith G G, Scottish Literature Character
and Influence, London 1919, pp 66, 92, 100
(brief references).

Willcock G D, A Hitherto Uncollated Version of Surrey's Translation, MLR 14.163;
15.113; 17.131 (relation to Surrey; see especially 17.135).

Berdan J M, Studies in Tudor Literature,
Early Tudor Poetry, N Y 1920, p 534.

Padelford F M, The Poems of Surrey, Univ
of Wash Publ in Lang and Lit 1, Seattle
1920; rvsd edn Seattle 1928, 5.233 (relation
to Surrey).

Watt L M, Douglas's Aeneid, Cambridge
1920, pp 28, 40.

Knowlton E C, Nature in Middle English,
JEGP 20.192 (brief).

Jiriczek O L, Specimens of Tudor Translations, Heidelberg 1923, pp 3, 34 (question
of Virgilian text; relation to Surrey).

Hofmann J, Die nordischen Lehnwörter bei
Gavin Douglas, diss München 1925, p 2
(crit E Ekwall, AnglB 37.165).

Hammond E P, English Verse between
Chaucer and Surrey, Durham N C and
London 1927, p 25 (brief).

Patch H R, The Goddess Fortuna in Medieval Literature, Cambridge Mass 1927, p
54 (brief).

Saintsbury G, The Four Great Scottish Poets,
N Y 1929, p 191 (brief).

Mackenzie W M, The Poems of William
Dunbar, London 1932, rptd London 1950;
ed B Dickins, rptd and rvsd London 1960,
rptd London 1970, pp xii, xxviii.

Nichols P H, Lydgate's Influence on the
Aureate Terms of the Scottish Chaucerians,
PMLA 47.518.

Elton O, The English Muse, London 1933, p
84.

Hartman H, Introd, Surrey's Fourth Boke of
Virgill, London and N Y 1933, p xxiii (relation to Surrey).

Lathrop H B, Translations from the Classics into English from Caxton to Chapman,
Univ of Wis Stud in Lang and Lit, Madison 1933, 35.100 (relation to Surrey).

Mackenzie W M, William Dunbar, Edinburgh Essays on Scots Literature, Edinburgh and London 1933, p 36.

Power W, Scotland and the Scots, Edinburgh
and London 1934, p 188.

Smith J M, The French Background of Middle Scots Literature, Edinburgh and London 1934, p 106.

Gray M M, Surrey's Vocabulary, TLS Oct 3
1936, p 791 (Surrey's borrowing).

Bannister E, Surrey's Vocabulary, TLS Oct
24 1936, p 863 (Surrey's borrowing).

Gordan I A, Variations on a Theme of Maro,
Essays in Literature, ed J Murray, Edinburgh and London 1936, p 27.

Tilgner E, Germanische Studien die Aureate

Terms als Stilement bei Lydgate, Berlin 1936; rptd 1967, p 79.

Patrick D, Scottish Literature, Chambers's Cyclopædia of English Literature, rvsd J L Geddie, Phila and N Y 1938, 1.166.

Speirs J, The Scots Literary Tradition, London 1940, p 56 (crit Scrut 9.193); rvsd edn London 1962, p 69.

Rubel V L, Poetic Diction in the English Renaissance from Skelton through Spenser, London 1941, pp 68, 81, 84, 132, 169, 198, 224, 227, 237, 263.

Craigie W, The Scottish Alliterative Poems, Proc of the British Acad 28.217 (prologue 8).

Utley CR, p 308 (no 381, prologue 4).

Bennett J A W, The Early Fame of Gavin Douglas's Eneados, MLN 61.84.

Russell P, Gavin Douglas and His Eneados, Nine 2.300.

Morgan E, Dunbar and the Language of Poetry, EC 2.138.

Renwick-Orton, p 120 (brief).

Day R A, Marvell's Glew, PQ 32.344.

Ward A C, Illustrated Hist of Eng Lit, London N Y and Toronto 1953, pp 32, 41 (brief).

Lewis C S, English Literature in the Sixteenth Century, Oxford 1954, pp 234, 516.

Tillyard E M W, The English Epic and Its Background, London 1954, pp 14, 338, 347.

Howe T P, The Zeitgeist as Translator, Aeneid IV.1–5, CJ 50.243 (relation to Surrey).

Mackenzie A M, The Renaissance Poets, ed J Kinsley, London 1955, p 37.

Sells A L, The Italian Influence in English Poetry, Bloomington Ind 1955, p 78.

Schlauch M, English Medieval Literature, Warsaw 1956, pp 330, 340 (brief).

Bennett J A W, The Parlement of Foules, Oxford 1957, pp 75, 147, 184, 191.

Enkvist N E, The Seasons of the Year Chapters on a Motif from Beowulf to the Shepherd's Calendar, Societas Scientiarum Fennica Commentationes Humanarum Litterarum, Helsingfors 1957, 22⁴.137.

Speirs J, Medieval English Poetry The Non-Chaucerian Tradition, London 1957, p 30 (brief reference).

Wittig K, The Scottish Tradition in Literature, Edinburgh 1958, p 79.

Kinghorn A M, The Mediaeval Makars, Texas Stud Lit and Lang 1.73.

Mason H A, Humanism and Poetry in the Early Tudor Period, London 1959, p 250.

Preston P, Did Gavin Douglas Write King Hart? MÆ 28.31, 36, 41.

Ridley F H, Did Gawin Douglas Write King Hart? Spec 34.403.

Smith S G, Gavin Douglas A Selection from His Poetry, Edinburgh 1959, p 9 (very brief).

Hall L B, An Aspect of the Renaissance in Gavin Douglas' Eneados, Studies in the Renaissance 7.184; Caxton's Eneydos and the Redactions of Vergil, MS 22.136.

Renoir A, John Lydgate Poet of the Transition, English Miscellany 11.11.

Lewis R W B, On Translating the Aeneid Yif That I Can, YCGL 10.7.

Ridley F H, Surrey's Debt to Gawin Douglas, PMLA 76.25; The Aeneid of Surrey, Berkeley and Los Angeles 1963, p 1.

Coldwell D F C, Selections from Gavin Douglas, Oxford 1964, pp vii, xix, xxiv, xxix; edn, 1.19, 78, 116.

Fulton R, Douglas and Virgil, SSL 2.125.

Rossi S, I Chauceriani Scozzesi, Napoli 1964, p 57; Il tredicesimo libro dell'Eneide nella versione di Gavin Douglas, Studi di letteratura storia e filosofia in onore de Bruno Revel, Biblioteca dell'archivum romanicum, Firenze 1965, ls 74.521, 526.

Fox D, The Scottish Chaucerians, Chaucer and Chaucerians, ed D S Brewer, University Alabama 1966, pp 164 (see especially pp 188, 200).

Scott T, Dunbar A Critical Exposition, Edinburgh and London 1966, p 354.

MacQueen J, Some Aspects of the Early Renaissance in Scotland, Forum Mod Lang Stud 3.214 and passim.

Renoir A, The Poetry of John Lydgate, Cambridge Mass 1967, pp 36, 67.

Scott T, Late Medieval Scots Poetry, London 1967, pp 7, 20.

Bawcutt P, The Source of Gavin Douglas's Eneados IV Prologue 92–9, N&Q 214[ns 16] .366.

Scheps W, William Wallace and His Buke, SSL 6.227.

Bawcutt P, Gavin Douglas and Chaucer, RES ns 21.401.

Blyth C R, Gavin Douglas' Prologues of Natural Description, PQ 49.175.

Other Scholarly Problems. Blake N F, Caxton and His World, London 1969, pp 195, 200 (reason for attack on Caxton's Eneydos).

Kinghorn A M, Warton's History and Early English Poetry, ESts 44.202 (literary history).

Shire H M, Song Dance and Poetry of the Court of Scotland under King James VI, Cambridge 1969, pp 13, 16, 20 (attitude toward courtly love).

Literary Criticism. Leslie J, De origine moribus & rebus gestis Scotorum, Rome 1578, p 378 (brief).

Hume D, The History of the Houses of Douglas and Angus, Edinburgh 1644, p 220.

Dunton J, The Athenian Mercury 12, no 1 (Oct 24 1693; brief, early reference [unpaged]).

Nicolson W, The Scottish Historical Library, London 1702, p 99 (brief).

Hickes G, Linguarum veterum septentrionalium thesaurus grammatico criticus et archaeologicus, Oxford 1703, 1.128 (very brief reference to wording).

Ruddiman T, The Judgment and Testimonies of Learned Men Concerning Gawin Douglas and his Works, Virgil's Æneis translated into Scottish Verse, Edinburgh 1710, p i.

Mackenzie G, The Lives and Characters of the Most Eminent Writers of the Scots Nation, Edinburgh 1711, 2.298 (brief).

Campbell J, The Polite Correspondence or Rational Amusement, London 1741; reissued as The Rational Amusement Comprehending a Collection of Letters on a Great Variety of Subjects, London 1754, p 301 (brief comment).

Farmer R, An Essay on the Learning of Shakespeare, 2nd edn, Cambridge 1767, p 43 (doctrine of purgatory).

Henry R, The History of Great Britain, London 1771–85; 6th edn, London 1823, 12.295.

Warton T, History of English Poetry from the 12th to the 16th Century, London 1774–81; ed W C Hazlitt, London 1871, 3.220, 225.

Pinkerton J, Ancient Scotish Poems, 2 vols, London and Edinburgh 1786, 1.xcvii.

Ellis G, Specimens of the Early English Poets, 5 edns, London 1790, 1801, 1803, 1811, 1845 (5th edn corrected), 1. 317 (brief; interspersed with excerpts).

Irving D, The Lives of the Scotish Poets, 2nd edn, London 1810, 2.27, 36, 60.

D, On Gawin Douglas's Translation of Virgil's Æneid, The Edinburgh Magazine 4.100.

Remarks on the Different Translations of Virgil, The Edinburgh Magazine 4.214.

On Gawin Douglas's Translation of Virgil's Æneid, The Edinburgh Magazine 6.41.

McN F, Gavin Douglas, Lives of Scottish Poets, ed J Robertson, London 1822, 1.60.

Junius F, Letter CXLVI, Haegh 3 Feb 1668, The Life Diary and Correspondence of Sir William Dugdale, ed W Hamper, London 1827, p 383 (Douglas as an aid in reading Chaucer; his misunderstanding of Virgil).

Tytler P F, Lives of Scottish Worthies, London 1833, 3.169.

Guest E, A History of English Rhythms, 2 vols, London 1838; ed W W Skeat, new edn [in 1 vol] London 1882, p 463 (prologue 8).

Nicholls N, Reminiscences of Gray by His Intimate Friend the Rev Norton Nicholls Nov 18 1805, The Correspondence of Thomas Gray and the Rev Norton Nicholls, The Works of Thomas Gray, ed J Mitford, London 1843, 5.36 (brief reference).

Aytoun W E, The Ballads of Scotland, Edinburgh and London 1859, 1.lxxi, lxxiv.

Gilfillan G, Specimens with Memoirs, Edinburgh and London 1860, 1.70 (brief).

Irving D, The History of Scotish Poetry, ed J A Carlyle, Edinburgh 1861, pp 267, 282, 286 (illustrative quotes).

Taylor J, The Imperial Dictionary of Universal Biography, London [1863], 2.137 (brief).

Chambers R, A Biographical Dictionary of Eminent Scotsmen, new edn rvsd T Thomson, London Glasgow Edinburgh 1872, 1.455 (excerpts from prologues 7 and 12).

Morley H, A First Sketch of English Literature, London 1873; rvsd London 1896, p 259.

Small, edn, l.cxliv, cxlviii.

Wilson J G, The Poets and Poetry of Scotland, N Y 1876, 1.29 (brief).

Craik G L, A Compendious History of English Literature, N Y 1877, 1.456.

Wall A, Gawain Douglas Bishop of Dunkeld, The Western ns 3.735.

Mackintosh J, The History of Civilisation in Scotland, London and Edinburgh 1878–88; new edn partly rewritten Paisley 1892–96, 2.313 (illustrative quotes).

Lang A, Gawain Douglas, The English Poets, ed T H Ward, London and N Y 1880; (numerous subsequent edns) N Y 1924, 1.161.

Nichol J, A Sketch of Scottish Poetry, ed J Small; 2nd edn rvsd, EETS 11, London 1883, p xxiv.

Ross J M, Scottish History and Literature, Glasgow 1884, pp 317, 352.

Schipper J. William Dunbar, Berlin 1884, p 55.

DNB, 15.294.

Fitzgibbon H M, Early English and Scottish

Poetry, N Y London and Melbourne 1888, p lxiii.

Shairp J C, Sketches in History and Poetry, Edinburgh 1887, p 209.

Veitch J, The Feeling for Nature in Scottish Poetry, Edinburgh and London 1887, 1.248, 259 (with illustrative quotes).

Minto W, Characteristics of English Poets, authorized American edn, Boston 1889, p 107.

Kaye W J, The Leading Poets of Scotland, London 1891, p 139 (brief).

Morley, 7.161.

Eyre-Todd G, Mediæval Scottish Poetry, Glasgow 1892, p 232.

Horneber F, Über King Hart und Testament of the Papyngo, Straubing 1893, pp 12, 15 (crit P Lange, AnglB 4.328).

Courthope, passim; Ten Brink, 3.84.

Gosse E, Modern English Literature A Short History, N Y 1897; rvsd edn N Y 1906, p 59 (brief).

Henderson T F, Scottish Vernacular Literature, Edinburgh 1898; 3rd edn rvsd Edinburgh 1910, pp 193, 199.

Smith G G, The Transition Period, Periods of European Lit, Edinburgh and London 1900, 4.58, 76.

Power W, Literature and Oatmeal, London 1935, p 47 (brief; crit AnglB 48.151; Scottish Bookman 1, no 4, p 152).

Chambers R, Chambers's Cyclopædia, Phila and N Y 1901–03; rvsd J L Geddie, Phila and N Y 1938, 1.202 (brief).

M'Ilwraith W, A Sketch of Scottish Literature, Annual Burns Chronicle 10.25.

Dittes R, Zu Surrey's Aeneisübertragung, Beiträge Zur Neueren Philologie July 19 1902, p 181 (Douglas' style compared to Surrey's).

Browne W H, The Taill of Rauf Coilyear, Baltimore 1903, p 19.

Millar J H, A Literary History of Scotland, London 1903, p 81.

Lowell J R, Spenser, Among My Books, The Complete Writings of James Russell Lowell, Boston 1904, 4.228.

Moorman F W, The Interpretation of Nature in English Poetry from Beowulf to Shakespeare, QF 95.147.

Snell F J, The Poets, The Age of Transition, London 1905, 1.97.

Seccombe T and W R Nicoll, The Scots Poets, The Bookman Illustrated History of Eng Lit, London 1906, 1.21.

CHEL, 2.294, 298.

Schmidt E, Die schottische Aeneisübersetzung, diss Leipzig 1910, p 13.

Schumacher A, Des Bischofs Gavin Douglas Übersetzung, diss Strassburgh 1910, p 7 (style; influence of Chaucer, Surrey, Badius Ascensius, Octavien de St Gelais, Maffeo Vegio).

Enc Brit, 8.445.

Stair-Kerr E, The Poets, Scotland under James IV, Paisley 1911, p 130.

Watt L M, Scottish Life and Poetry, London 1912, pp 112, 116, 264.

Mackie R L, Scotland, London 1916, pp 285, 532 (brief).

Nitchie E, Vergil and the English Poets, CUS 66.passim.

Smith G G, Scottish Literature Character and Influence, London 1919, pp 11, 16, 66, 92, 100 (brief references).

Amos F R, Early Theories of Translation, N Y 1920, p 107.

Watt L M, Douglas's Aeneid, Cambridge 1920, pp 6, 11, 20, 35, 53, 57, 59, 74, 80, 91.

Golding L, The Scottish Chaucerians, The Saturday Review of Politics Literature Science and Art 134.783.

Quiller-Couch A, Studies in Literature, 2s, N Y and Cambridge Eng 1922, p 273 (brief).

Hammond E P, English Verse between Chaucer and Surrey, Durham N C and London 1927, p 25 (brief).

Legouis HEL, pp 178, 232.

Saintsbury G, The Four Great Scottish Poets, N Y 1929, p 189.

Brinton A C, Maphaeus Vegius and His Thirteenth Book of the Aeneid, Stanford Univ Calif 1930, p 33.

Pound E, How to Read, London 1931, p 45.

Taylor R A, Dunbar the Poet, The Poets on the Poets no 4, London 1931, pp 73, 77 (crit The Criterion 11.331; TLS Mar 17 1932, p 199; YWES 13.124).

Nichols P H, Lydgate's Influence on the Aureate Terms of the Scottish Chaucerians, PMLA 47.518.

Elton O, The English Muse, London 1933, pp 87, 104.

Lathrop H B, Univ of Wis Stud in Lang and Lit, Madison Wis 1933, 35.100 (Douglas' style compared to Surrey's).

Mackenzie A M, An Historical Survey of Scottish Literature, London 1933, p 101 (crit The Modern Scot 4.164).

Mackenzie W M, William Dunbar, Edinburgh Essays on Scots Literature, Edinburgh and London 1933, p 36.

Power W, Scotland and the Scots, Edinburgh

and London 1934, p 190.

Rait R and G S Pryde, Scotland, N Y 1934; 2nd edn London 1954, p 309 (very brief).

Smith J M, The French Background of Middle Scots Literature, Edinburgh and London 1934, pp xxviii, 106 (crit AnglB 45.265; MÆ 4.44).

Gordan I A, Variations on a Theme of Maro, Essays in Literature, ed J Murray, Edinburgh and London 1936, pp 28, 31.

Speirs J, The Scots Literary Tradition, London 1940, p 56 (crit Scrut 9.193); rvsd 2nd edn London 1962, pp 69, 165.

Rubel V L, Poetic Diction in the English Renaissance, London 1941, p 72.

Craigie W, The Scottish Alliterative Poems, Proc of the British Acad 28.230.

Grierson H J C and J C Smith, A Critical History of English Poetry, London 1944; 2nd rvsd edn London 1947, p 58 (brief).

Utley CR, pp 65, 309 (no 381, prologue 4; primarily summary).

Bennett J A W, The Early Fame of Gavin Douglas's Eneados, MLN 61.83.

Mackenzie A M, Scottish Pageant, Edinburgh 1946; 2nd edn 1952, 1.5 (brief critical comment; illustrative excerpts).

Caird J B, Some Reflections on Scottish Literature, I. Poetry, Scottish Periodical 1.12.

Smith S G, The Aeneid of Gawin Douglas, Life and Letters 55.112 (extravagant praise).

Craig HEL, p 169 (brief).

Russell P, Gavin Douglas and His Eneados, Nine 2.300.

Dearing B, Gavin Douglas' Eneados A Reinterpretation, PMLA 67.845.

Morgan E, Dunbar and the Language of Poetry, EC 2.144.

Renwick-Orton, pp 120, 419 (brief).

Wood H H, Scottish Literature, London 1952, p 18.

Hyman S E, The Language of Scottish Poetry, KR 16.30 (brief).

Lewis C S, English Literature in the Sixteenth Century, Oxford 1954, p 81.

Tillyard E M W, The English Epic and Its Background, London 1954, pp 14, 338, 347.

Howe T P, The Zeitgeist as Translator, Aeneid IV.1–5, CJ 50.243.

Mackenzie A M, The Renaissance Poets, ed J Kinsley, London 1955, p 37.

Sells A L, The Italian Influence in English Poetry, Bloomington Ind 1955, p 78.

Stock N, Some Notes on Old Scots, Shenandoah 6, no 2, p 29.

Schlauch M, English Medieval Literature, Warsaw 1956, p 330.

Bennett J A W, The Parlement of Foules, Oxford 1957, p 191.

Enkvist N E, The Seasons of the Year, Societas Scientiarum Fennica Commentationes Humanarum Litterarum, Helsingfors 1957, 22⁴.137.

Speirs J, Medieval English Poetry The Non-Chaucerian Tradition, London 1957, p 30 (brief reference).

Mackie R L, King James IV of Scotland, Edinburgh and London 1958, p 183 (crit J D Mackie, SHR 38.133).

Morrison W S, Some Makars and Makers of St Andrews and Dundee, Edinburgh and London 1958, p 5.

Wittig K, The Scottish Tradition in Literature, Edinburgh 1958, p 77 and passim.

Kinghorn A M, The Mediaeval Makars, Texas Stud Lit and Lang 1.82.

Mason H A, Humanism and Poetry in the Early Tudor Period, London 1959, p 251.

Preston P, Did Gavin Douglas Write King Hart? MÆ 28.31, 36.

Ridley F H, Did Gawin Douglas Write King Hart? Spec 34.403.

Smith S G, Gavin Douglas A Selection from His Poetry, Edinburgh 1959, p 9.

Hall L B, An Aspect of the Renaissance in Gavin Douglas' Eneados, Studies in the Renaissance 7.184, 188.

Renoir A, John Lydgate Poet of Transition, English Miscellany 11.10.

Lewis R W B, On Translating the Aeneid Yif That I Can, YCGL 10.10.

McLaren M, The Wisdom of the Scots, London 1961, pp 79, 85.

Ridley F H, Surrey's Debt to Gawin Douglas, PMLA 76.25; The Aeneid of Surrey, Berkeley and Los Angeles 1963, pp 33, 36.

Kinghorn A M, Warton's History and Early English Poetry, ESts 44.202.

Coldwell D F C, Selections from Gavin Douglas, Oxford 1964, pp viii, xviii, xxiv; edn, 1.19, 32, 87, 116, 122.

Fulton R, Douglas and Virgil, SSL 2.125.

Käsmann H, Gavin Douglas' Aeneis-Übersetzung, Festschrift für Walter Hübner, Berlin 1964, p 164.

Rossi S, I Chauceriani Scozzesi, Napoli 1964, p 57; Il tredicesimo libro dell'Eneide, Studi di letteratura storia e filosofia 74.521, 525.

Fox D, The Scottish Chaucerians, Chaucer and Chaucerians, ed D S Brewer, Univer-

sity Alabama 1966, pp 188, 200.
Scott T, Dunbar A Critical Exposition, Edinburgh and London 1966, pp 35, 354, 357.
Renoir A, The Poetry of Lydgate, Cambridge Mass 1967, p 36.
Scott T, Late Medieval Scots Poetry, London 1967, p 24.
Bennett J A W, Chaucer's Book of Fame, Oxford 1968, p 57.
Blyth C R, Gavin Douglas' Prologues of Natural Description, PQ 49.164.
Bibliography. Warton T, History of English Poetry, London 1774–81; ed W C Hazlitt, London 1871, 3.219.
Irving D, The Lives of the Scotish Poets, 2nd edn, London 1810, 2.24.
Brydges S E, Censura Literaria, London 1807, 1808, 3.286; 8.37 (ns 5).
Ames J, Typographical Antiquities, London 1816, 3.135.
Laing D, Gawin Douglas, Bannatyne Club Publ 115, Edinbugh 1867, p 20 (brief).
Small, edn, l.clxxii.
Arber E, A Bibliographical Summary of English Literature in the Reign of Mary 6 July 1553–17 November 1558, A Transcript of the Registers of the Company of Stationers of London, Birmingham 1894, vol 5, no 95 (The xiii Bukes of Eneados).
Henderson T F, Scottish Vernacular Literature, Edinburgh 1898; 2nd edn rvsd Edinburgh 1900; 3rd edn rvsd Edinburgh 1910, p 192 (lists MSS and edns in footnote).
Schneider A, Die mittelenglische Stabzeile im 15 und 16 Jahrhundert, BBA 12.107 (brief).
Seccombe T and W R Nicoll, The Scots Poets, The Bookman Illustrated History of Eng Lit, London 1906, 1.22.
CHEL, 2.537.
Geddie W, A Bibliography of Middle Scots Poets, PSTS ns 61, Edinburgh and London 1912, pp 223, 226.
Duff E G, Bibliotheca Pepysiana, A Descriptive Catalogue of the Library of Samuel Pepys, pt 2, London 1914, p 70 (1 reference).
Forbes-Leith W, Pre-Reformation Scholars in the 16th Century, Glasgow 1915, p 45.
Watt L M, Douglas's Aeneid, Cambridge 1920, pp 9, 18 (discussion of early edns and selections).
Jiriczek O L, Specimens of Tudor Translations, Heidelberg 1923, p 1 (listing and brief description of MSS and early edns; brief list of commentaries).

Utley CR, p 308 (no 381, prologue 4).
Renwick-Orton, p 419 (brief); Robbins-Cutler, no 1842.5.

[20] THE PALICE OF HONOUR.

MSS. No MS extant.
Editions. Davidson T, The Palyce of Honour, Edinburgh 1530?–1540? (Univ of Edinb De.6.123) (fragments; described D Laing, Gawin Douglas Bishop of Dunkeld, Adversaria Notices, Bannatyne Club Publ 115, Edinburgh 1867, p 19; R Dickson and J P Edmond, Annals of Scottish Printing from 1507 to the Beginning of the 17th Century, Cambridge 1890, p 133; J F K Johnstone and A W Robertson, Bibliographia Aberdonensis, Aberdeen 1929, 1.34; W Beattie, Fragments of The Palyce of Honour of Gawin Douglas printed by Thomas Davidson at Edinburgh ca 1540, Edinburgh Bibl Soc Trans 3¹.31; Bawcutt, edn, p xv); rptd Beattie, Fragments, Edinburgh Bibl Soc Trans 3¹.31; Bawcutt, edn, p 2.
Copland W, The Palis of Honoure Compyled by Gawayne Dowglas Bysschope of Dunkyll, London 1553? (described E Brydges and J Haslewood, The British Bibliographer, London 1814, 2.420; Small, edn, l.clxviii; Bawcutt, edn, pp xvi, xx, 245); rptd in facsimile, The English Experience no 89, Amsterdam and N Y 1969; ed Bawcutt, edn, pp 8, 173 (alternate pages) (STC, no 7073).
Ros J, Heir beginnis ane Treatise Callit the Palice of Honovr Compylit be M. Gawine Dowglas Bischop of Dunkeld, Edinburgh 1579 (described Small, edn, l.clxix; R Dickson and J P Edmond, Annals of Scottish Printing, Cambridge 1890, p 340; W Beattie, Gavin Douglas's Palice of Honour, TLS Feb 23 1946, p 91; Bawcutt, edn, pp xviii, xx, 244); rptd Morison, edn, 2.1; Pinkerton, edn, 1.51; Kinnear, edn; Bawcutt, edn, pp 7, 173 (STC, no 7074).
Morison R, Select Works of Gawih Douglass Bishop of Dunkeld Containing Memoirs of the Author The Palice of Honour Prologues to the Æneid and A Glossary of Obsolete Words, The Scotish Poets, vol 2, Perth 1787, p 1 (Ros edn).
Pinkerton J, Scotish Poems Reprinted from Scarce Editions, 3 vols, London 1792, 1.51 (Ros edn).
Kinnear J G, The Palice of Honour, Bannatyne Club Publ 17, Edinburgh 1827 (Ros edn).

Small J, The Poetical Works of Gavin Douglas, 4 vols, Edinburgh and London 1874, 1.1.

Bawcutt P, The Shorter Poems of Gavin Douglas, PSTS 4s 3, Edinburgh and London 1967, pp 7, 173 (notes at end of text; Ros edn, Copland edn; crit L R N Ashley, BHR 30.439; J Norton-Smith, MÆ 37.353; TLS Oct 3 1968, p 1134; M P McDiarmid, SHR 48.180; K Wittig, Angl 87.454; P J Frankis, RES ns 21.75).

Selections. Sibbald J, Chronicle of Scottish Poetry, 4 vols, Edinburgh and London 1802, 1.385 (introductory and end notes).

Irving D, The Lives of the Scotish Poets, 2 vols, Edinburgh 1804; 2nd edn improved London 1810, 2.37, 40, 46, 51 (brief excerpts).

Brydges E and J Haslewood, The British Bibliographer, London 1814, 2.422 (Copland edn).

Tytler P F, Lives of Scottish Worthies, London 1833, 3.153, 158, 164.

Irving D, The History of Scotish Poetry, ed J A Carlyle, Edinburgh 1861, p 270 (brief excerpts).

Masson R O, Three Centuries of English Poetry, London 1876, p 156 (spelling modernized, glossings at foot of page; Small edn).

Morley H, Shorter English Poems, London 1876, p 128 (3 stanzas).

Wilson J G, The Poets and Poetry of Scotland, N Y 1876, 1.31 (1 stanza).

Lang A, Gawain Douglas, The English Poets, ed T H Ward, London and N Y 1880; (numerous subsequent edns) N Y 1924, 1.163, 166 (glossings at foot of page).

Ross J, The Book of Scottish Poems, Paisley 1882, 1.254 (4 stanzas).

Fitzgibbon H M, Early English and Scottish Poetry, London N Y and Melbourne 1888, pp 181, 433 (spelling modernized; notes at end of text).

Veitch J, The Feeling for Nature in Scottish Poetry, Edinburgh and London 1887, 1.254 (brief quotes interspersed with criticism; glossings in side notes).

Eyre-Todd G, Mediæval Scottish Poetry, Abbotsford Series of the Scottish Poets, Glasgow 1892, p 235 (3 stanzas; glossings in margin).

Chambers R, Chambers's Cyclopædia, Phila and N Y 1901–03! rvsd J L Geddie, Phila and N Y 1938, 1.203 (brief excerpt).

Cohen H L, The Ballade, CUS 50.296 (3 stanzas; Kinnear edn).

Neilson W A and K G T Webster, Chief British Poets of the 14th and 15th Centuries, Boston N Y etc 1916, pp 408, 435 (3 stanzas, brief note at end of text, glossings at foot of page; Small edn).

Auden W H and N H Pearson, Poets of the English Language, N Y 1950, p 323 (glossings at foot of page).

Smith S G, Gavin Douglas A Selection from His Poetry, Edinburgh 1959, p 17 (glossings and notes at foot of page; Small edn).

Coldwell D F C, Selections from Gavin Douglas, Oxford 1964, pp 107, 138 (notes at end of text; Ros edn, with occasional readings from Copland edn).

Scott T, Late Medieval Scots Poetry, London 1967, p 128 (S G Smith, Gavin Douglas).

MacQueen J, Ballattis of Luve, Edinburgh 1970, p 40 (Copland edn; glossings at foot of page).

Modernizations. Tytler P F, Lives of Scottish Worthies, London 1833, 3.154, 160, 167.

Bonar A R, The Poets and Poetry of Scotland, Edinburgh 1864; 2nd edn 1866, p 45 (selections).

Ross J, The Book of Scottish Poems, Paisley 1882, 1.254 (brief excerpts).

Textual Matters. Kinnear, Collations of the Earlier Editions of the Palice of Honour, edn, p ix (Copland edn and Ros edn).

Small, edn, 1.clxviii, 125 (includes notes and some variant readings from early edns).

Isaac F, William Copland, Facsimiles and Illustrations No III, English & Scottish Printing Types 1535–58* 1552–58, ptd for the Bibliographical Soc, Oxford 1932 (unpaged; brief reference).

Beattie W, Gavin Douglas's Palice of Honour, TLS Feb 23 1946, p 91.

Coldwell D F C, Selections from Gavin Douglas, p xxiii.

Bawcutt, edn, pp xv, lxxxvii, 244.

Language. Morison, edn, p 139 (glossary).

Pinkerton, edn, 3.227 (glossary).

Sibbald J, Chronicle of Scottish Poetry, Edinburgh and London 1802, vol 4 [unpaged] and 4.xlv (brief discussion, glossary).

Irving D, The History of Scotish Poetry, ed J A Carlyle, Edinburgh 1861, p 595 (glossary).

Murray J A H, The Dialect of the Southern Counties of Scotland, London 1873.

Small, edn, 1.clxii; 4.249 (discussion in vol 1; glossary in vol 4).

Hahn O, Zur Verbal- und Nominalflexion bei den schottischen Dichtern, Berlin 1887–89 (see especially pt 3, p 19).

Veitch J, The Feeling for Nature in Scottish Poetry, Edinburgh and London 1887, 1.250.

Curtis F J, An Investigation of the Rimes and Phonology of the Middle-Scotch Romance Clariodus, Angl 16.387; 17.1, 125.

Heuser W, Offenes und gescholossenes *ee* im Schottischen und Nordenglischen, Angl 19.334.

Gerken H, Die Sprache des Bischofs Douglas, Strassburg 1898, passim.

Flom G T, Scandinavian Influence on Southern Lowland Scotch, diss Columbia 1900.

Browne W H, The Taill of Rauf Coilyear, Baltimore 1903, pp 15, 35, 139 (general discussion of Middle Scots; glossary).

Millar J H, A Literary History of Scotland, London 1903, p 687 (glossary).

Knopff P, Darstellung der Ablautverhältnisse in der schottischen Schriftsprache, diss Würzburg 1904.

Larue J L, Das Pronomen in den Werken des Douglas, diss Strassburg 1908 (crit O Ritter, EStn 44.101).

CHEL, 2.101, 506.

Gray M M, Introd, Lancelot of the Laik, PSTS ns 2, Edinburgh and London 1912, 2.xviii.

Ritter O, Wortkundliches zu Gavin Douglas, Arch 129.220 (etymology of one word).

Lenz K, Zur Lautlehre der französischen Elemente in den schottischen Dichtungen von 1500–1550, diss Marburg 1913 (examples taken from Douglas, Dunbar, Lyndesay, Clariodus).

Taylor R, Some Notes on the Use of Can and Couth, JEGP 16.573.

Westergaard E, Prepositions in Lowland Scotch, Angl 41.444 (some examples from Douglas); Verbal Forms in Middle-Scotch, Angl 43.95; Plural Forms in Lowland Scottish, Angl 51.77.

Bald M A, The Pioneers of Anglicised Speech in Scotland, SHR 24.179 (brief).

Hartig P, Die Edinburger Dialektgruppe, Palaes 161.90 (cites Douglas among others to illustrate development of Scots dialect).

Ritchie R L G, Early Instances of French Loan-Words in Scots and English, EStn 63.41 (cites one example).

Wood H H, The Poems and Fables of Robert Henryson, Edinburgh 1933; 2nd edn rvsd Edinburgh 1958, p xxxi (discussion in introd).

Patrick D, Scottish Literature, Chambers's Cyclopædia of English Literature, rvsd J L Geddie, Phila and N Y 1938, 1.164.

Preston P, Did Gavin Douglas Write King Hart? MÆ 28.40.

Bawcutt P, Gavin Douglas Some Additions

to OED and DOST, N&Q 208(ns 10).289.

Coldwell D F C, Selections from Gavin Douglas, Oxford 1964, p 143 (glossary).

Scott T, Dunbar A Critical Exposition, Edinburgh and London 1966, p 351.

Bawcutt, edn, pp xxviii, xlviii, lxxvii, 247 (discussion, glossary).

Scott T, Late Medieval Scots Poetry, London 1967, pp 21, 189 (discussion, glossary).

Versification. Guest E, A History of English Rhythms, 2 vols, London 1838; ed W W Skeat, new edn [in 1 vol] London 1882, pp 643, 652.

Gray T, Metrum Observations on English Metre, The Works of Thomas Gray, ed J Mitford, London 1843, 5.248 (brief references).

Schipper, 1.518.

Bulloch J M, French Metres in Early Scottish Poetry, Scottish Notes and Queries 2.114, 130.

Curtis F J, An Investigation of the Rimes and Phonology of Clariodus, Angl 16.387; 17.1, 125.

Saintsbury G, History of English Prosody, London 1908; 2nd edn London 1923, 1.276.

Smith J C, Some Characteristics of Scots Literature, Oxford 1912, p 5 (brief).

Watt L M, Douglas's Aeneid, Cambridge 1920, pp 105, 112.

Smith J M, The French Background of Middle Scots Literature, Edinburgh and London 1934, p 162.

Renwick-Orton, p 418 (very brief).

Lewis C S, English Literature in the Sixteenth Century, Oxford 1954, p 79.

Ridley F H, Did Gawin Douglas Write King Hart? Spec 34.406, 409.

Fox D, The Scottish Chaucerians, Chaucer and Chaucerians, ed D S Brewer, University Alabama 1966, p 196.

Bawcutt, edn, p *l.*

Scott T, Late Medieval Scots Poetry, p 18.

Date. Murray J A H, Introd, The Complaynt of Scotlande, EETSES 17–18, London 1872; rptd 1891, 1906, p lxxx.

Snell F J, The Poets, The Age of Transition, London 1905, 1.94.

Lewis C S, English Literature in the Sixteenth Century, p 80.

Bawcutt P, Gavin Douglas Some Additions to OED and DOST, N&Q 208(ns 10).289; edn, p xxvii.

Authorship. Ridley F H, Spec 34.402.

Bawcutt, edn, p xxviii.

Sources and Literary Relations. Ellis G, Specimens of the Early English Poets, 5 edns,

London 1790, 1801, 1803, 1811, 1845 (5th edn corrected), 1. 316 (very brief).

Irving D, The Lives of the Scotish Poets, 2nd edn, London 1810, 2.59.

Tytler P F, Lives of Scottish Worthies, London 1833, 3. 151.

Laing D, Preface, The Seven Sages in Scotish Metre by John Rolland, Bannatyne Club Publ 57, Edinburgh 1837, p xix.

Craik G L, Sketches of the History of Literature and Learning in England, London 1844, 1.257 (brief).

Irving D, The History of Scotish Poetry, ed J A Carlyle, Edinburgh 1861, p 277. Small, edn, l.cxxxvii.

Craik G L, A Compendious History of English Literature, N Y 1877, 1. 456.

Lang A, Gawain Douglas, The English Poets, ed T H Ward, London and N Y 1880; (numerous subsequent edns) N Y 1924, 1.160.

Lange P, Chaucer's Einfluss, diss Halle 1882; rptd Angl 6.50 (relation to Chaucer and Octavien de St Gelais).

Nichol J, A Sketch of Scottish Poetry, ed J Small; 2nd edn rvsd, EETS 11, London 1883, p xxvi.

Gregor W, Introd, The Court of Venus, PSTS 3, Edinburgh and London, p xx.

Ross J M, Scottish History and Literature, Glasgow 1884, pp 321, 331, 352.

Jusserand J J, Histoire littéraire du peuple Anglais, Paris 1894, 1.528.

Ten Brink, 3.82 (Chaucer).

Turnbull W R, The Heritage of Burns, Haddington 1896, p 241 (brief).

Neilson W A, Studies and Notes in Philology and Literature 6.160 and passim.

Smith G G, The Transition Period, Periods of European Lit, Edinburgh and London 1900, 4.59.

M'Ilwraith W, A Sketch of Scottish Literature, Annual Burns Chronicle 10.24.

Lawson A, The Poems of Alexander Hume, PSTS 48, Edinburgh and London 1902, p 228.

Mebus F, Studien zu William Dunbar, Breslau 1902, passim (resemblances of wording scattered throughout notes to Dunbar's poems).

Moorman F W, The Interpretation of Nature in English Poetry from Beowulf to Shakespeare, QF 95.151 (brief).

Snell F J, The Poets, The Age of Transition, London 1905, p 95.

Marsh G L, Sources and Analogues of The Flower and the Leaf, MP 4.318.

Mebus F, Beiträge zu William Dunbars

Gedicht The Golden Terge, EStn 39.passim. CHEL, 2.295, 297.

Schmidt E, Die schottische Aeneisübersetzung, diss Leipzig 1910, p 107 (relation to Octavien de St Gelais, Chaucer).

Enc Brit, 8.445.

Watt L M, Scottish Life and Poetry, London 1912, p 130 (relation to Lyndsay).

Mendenhall J C, Aureate Terms A Study in the Literary Diction of the 15th Century, Lancaster Pa 1919.

Smith G G, Scottish Literature Character and Influence, London 1919, p 11 (brief reference).

Schofield W H, Mythical Bards and the Life of William Wallace, HSCL, Cambridge Mass and London 1920, 5.63, 76.

Knowlton E C, Nature in Middle English, JEGP 20.192 (brief).

Patch H R, The Goddess Fortuna in Medieval Literature, Cambridge Mass 1927, p 55 (brief).

Legouis HEL, p 176.

Saintsbury G, The Four Great Scottish Poets, N Y 1929, p 190 (brief).

Cornelius R D, The Castell of Pleasure, EETS 179, London 1930, p 19 (brief).

Mackenzie A M, An Historical Survey of Scottish Literature, London 1933, p 101 (crit The Modern Scot 4.164).

Smith J M, The French Background of Middle Scots Literature, Edinburgh and London 1934, p 109.

Patrick D, Scottish Literature, Chambers's Cyclopædia of English Literature, Phila and N Y 1901–03; rvsd J L Geddie, Phila and N Y 1938, 1.166.

Lewis C S, The Allegory of Love, London 1936; rptd London 1953, pp 80, 292.

Grierson H J C and J C Smith, A Critical History of English Poetry, London 1944; 2nd edn rvsd London 1947, p 58 (brief).

McPeek J A S, Keats and the Palice of Honour, PQ 27.273.

Craig HEL, p 169 (very brief); Renwick-Orton, p 418 (brief).

Ward A C, Illustrated Hist of Eng Lit, London N Y and Toronto 1953, pp 32, 41 (brief).

Lewis C S, English Literature in the Sixteenth Century, Oxford 1954, p 77.

Mackenzie A M, The Renaissance Poets, ed J Kinsley, London 1955, p 35.

Stock N, Some Notes on Old Scots, Shenandoah 6, no 2, p 26.

Bennett J A W, The Parlement of Foules, Oxford 1957, p 103.

Enkvist N E, The Seasons of the Year, Societas Scientiarum Fennica Commentationes Humanarum Litterarum, Helsingfors 1957, 22⁴.137.

Mackie R L, King James IV of Scotland, Edinburgh and London 1958, pp 168, 184 (crit J D Mackie, SHR ˙38.133).

Kinghorn A M, The Mediaeval Makars, Texas Stud Lit and Lang 1.73.

Preston P, Did Gavin Douglas Write King Hart? MÆ 28.31, 36.

Ridley F H, Did Gawin Douglas Write King Hart? Spec 34.403.

Smith S G, Gavin Douglas A Selection from His Poetry, Edinburgh 1959, p 9 (brief).

Fox D, Dunbar's The Golden Targe, ELH 26.329.

Hollander J, The Untuning of the Sky, Princeton 1961, p 81.

Price H T, Russet Mantle in Gavin Douglas and Shakespeare, N&Q 207(ns 9).205.

Coldwell D F C, Selections from Gavin Douglas, Oxford 1964, p xvii (brief reference); Virgil's Aeneid Translated into Scottish Verse, 4 vols, PSTS 3s 25, 27, 28, 30, Edinburgh and London 1964, 1.78.

Fox D, The Scottish Chaucerians, Chaucer and Chaucerians, ed D S Brewer, University Alabama 1966, p 164 (see especially pp 188, 193).

Bawcutt, edn, pp xxix, xxxix.

MacQueen J, Some Aspects of the Early Renaissance in Scotland, Forum Mod Lang Stud 3.214 and passim.

Scott T, Late Medieval Scots Poetry, London 1967, pp 7, 13, 20.

Bennett J A W, Chaucer's Book of Fame, Oxford 1968, pp 48, 58, 177.

Kinneavy G B, The Poet in The Palice of Honour, Chaucer Rev 3.281, 292, 295.

Other Scholarly Problems. Pinkerton J, The History of Scotland from the Accession of the House of Stuart, London 1797, pp 425, 428 (contemp conditions).

Literary Criticism. Warton T, History of English Poetry, London 1774–81; ed W C Hazlitt, London 1871, 3.228.

Ellis G, Specimens of the Early English Poets, 5 edns, London 1790, 1801, 1803, 1811, 1845 (5th edn corrected), 1. 316 (very brief).

Irving D, The Lives of the Scotish Poets, 2nd edn London 1810, 2.37.

McN F, Gavin Douglas, Lives of Scottish Poets, ed J Robertson, London 1822, 1.61.

Hunter W, An Anglo-Saxon Grammar and an Analysis of the Style of Chaucer Douglas and Spenser, London Edinburgh and Glasgow 1832, p 70.

Tytler P F, Lives of Scottish Worthies, London 1833, 3.150, 167.

Gilfillan G, Specimens with Memoirs, Edinburgh and London 1860, 1.71 (brief).

Irving D, The History of Scotish Poetry, ed J A Carlyle, Edinburgh 1861, p 268 (illustrative quotes).

Taylor J, The Imperial Dictionary of Universal Biography, London [1863], 2.137 (brief).

Chambers R, A Biographical Dictionary, new edn rvsd T Thomson, London Glasgow and Edinburgh 1872, p 455.

Morley H, A First Sketch of English Literature, London 1873; rvsd London 1896, p 215.

Small, edn, 1.cxxix.

Wilson J G, The Poets and Poetry of Scotland, N Y 1876, 1.30 (brief).

Craik G L, A Compendious History of English Literature, N Y 1877, 1.456.

Wall A, Gawain Douglas Bishop of Dunkeld, The Western ns 3.733, 736.

Mackintosh J, The History of Civilisation in Scotland, London and Edinburgh 1878–88; new edn partly rewritten, Paisley 1892–96, 2.311 (very brief).

Lang A, Gawain Douglas, The English Poets, ed T H Ward, London and N Y 1880; (numerous subsequent edns) N Y 1924, 1.160.

Nichol J, A Sketch of Scottish Poetry, ed J Small; 2nd edn rvsd, EETS 11, London 1883, p xxvi.

Ross J M, Scottish History and Literature, Glasgow 1884, p 318.

Schipper J, William Dunbar, Berlin 1884, p 51 (brief).

DNB, 15.294.

Skelton J, Maitland of Lethington, Edinburgh 1887, 1.94, 103, 111.

Fitzgibbon H M, Early English and Scottish Poetry, N Y London and Melbourne 1888, p lxii.

Veitch J, The Feeling for Nature in Scottish Poetry, Edinburgh and London 1887, 1.254 (with illustrative quotes).

Minto W, Characteristics of English Poets, Boston 1889, p 107 (brief).

Kaye W J, The Leading Poets of Scotland, London 1891, p 139 (brief).

Morley, 7.159.

Eyre-Todd G, Mediæval Scottish Poetry, Glasgow 1892, p 231.

Horneber F, Über King Hart und Testament of the Papyngo, Straubing 1893, pp 11, 14, 16 (crit AnglB 4.328).

Courthope, passim; Ten Brink, 3.80.

Turnbull W R, The Heritage of Burns, Haddington 1896, p 241 (brief reference).

Gosse E, Modern English Literature A Short History, N Y 1897; rvsd edn N Y 1906, p 59.

Smeaton O, A Quartette of Court Singers Four Centuries Ago, Westminster Review 148.187 (brief; fictionalized).

Henderson T F, Scottish Vernacular Literature, Edinburgh 1898; 3rd edn rvsd Edinburgh 1910, p 192.

Neilson W A, Studies and Notes in Philology and Literature 6.161.

Smith G G, The Transition Period, Periods of European Lit, Edinburgh and London 1900, 4.59.

Chambers R, Chambers's Cyclopædia, Phila and N Y 1901–03; rvsd J L Geddie, Phila and N Y 1938, 1.202 (brief).

M'Ilwraith W, A Sketch of Scottish Literature, Annual Burns Chronicle 10.24.

Browne W H, The Taill of Rauf Coilyear, Baltimore 1903, p 19.

Millar J H, A Literary History of Scotland, London 1903, p 73.

Moorman F W, The Interpretation of Nature in English Poetry from Beowulf to Shakespeare, QF 95.147, 150 (brief).

Snell F J, The Poets, The Age of Transition, London 1905, 1.94.

CHEL, 2.295; Enc Brit, 8.445.

Stair-Kerr E, The Poets, Scotland under James IV, Paisley 1911, p 129 (brief).

Smith J C, Some Characteristics of Scots Literature, Oxford 1912, p 5 (brief).

Watt L M, Scottish Life and Poetry, London 1912, p 112.

Rhys E, The First Scottish Poets, London N Y and Toronto 1913, p 101.

Smith G G, Scottish Literature Character and Influence, London 1919, pp 11, 17 (brief references).

Golding L, The Scottish Chaucerians, The Saturday Review of Politics Literature Science and Art 134.783.

Legouis HEL, p 176.

Saintsbury G, The Four Great Scottish Poets, N Y 1929, p 190.

Elton O, The English Muse, London 1933, pp 84, 87.

Mackenzie A M, An Historical Survey of Scottish Literature, London 1933, p 100.

Smith J M, The French Background of Middle Scots Literature, Edinburgh and London 1934, p 109 (crit AnglB 45.265; MÆ 4.44).

Lewis C S, The Allegory of Love, London 1936; rptd London 1953, pp 244, 290.

Grierson H J C and J C Smith, A Critical History of English Poetry, London 1944; 2nd edn rvsd London 1947, p 58 (brief).

Beattie W, Gavin Douglas's Palice of Honour, TLS Feb 23 1946, p 91.

Russell P, Gavin Douglas and His Eneados, Nine 2.298.

Cazamian L, The Development of English Humor, Durham N C 1952, pt 1, p 94 (very brief).

Renwick-Orton, pp 120, 418 (brief).

Ward A C, Illustrated History of English Literature, London N Y and Toronto 1953, p 41 (brief).

Lewis C S, English Literature in the Sixteenth Century, Oxford 1954, p 76.

Mackenzie A M, The Renaissance Poets, ed J Kinsley, London 1955, p 35.

Stock N, Some Notes on Old Scots, Shenandoah 6, no 2, p 26.

Enkvist N E, The Seasons of the Year, Societas Scientiarum Fennica Commentationes Humanarum Litterarum, Helsingfors 1957, 22⁴.137.

Mackie R L, King James IV of Scotland, Edinburgh and London 1958, p 183.

Wittig K, The Scottish Tradition in Literature, Edinburgh 1958, pp 78, 81.

Fox D, Dunbar's The Golden Targe, ELH 26.324.

Kinghorn A M, The Mediaeval Makars, Texas Stud Lit and Lang 1.81.

Preston P, Did Gavin Douglas Write King Hart? MÆ 28.31, 36.

Ridley F H, Did Gawin Douglas Write King Hart? Spec 34.403.

Hollander J, The Untuning of the Sky, Princeton 1961, p 81.

Coldwell D F C, Selections from Gavin Douglas, Oxford 1964, p xvii; edn, 1.65, 81.

Käsmann H, Gavin Douglas' Aeneis-Übersetzung, Festschrift für Walter Hübner, Berlin 1964, p 167.

Rossi S, I Chauceriani Scozzesi, Napoli 1964, p 56; Il tredicesimo libro dell'Eneide, Studi di letteratura storia e filosofia 74.524.

Fox D, The Scottish Chaucerians, Chaucer and Chaucerians, ed D S Brewer, University Alabama 1966, p 193.

Bawcutt, edn, pp xxix, lxxvi, lxxix.

Scott T, Late Medieval Scots Poetry, London 1967, p 13.

Kinneavy G B, The Poet in The Palice of Honour, Chaucer Rev 3.280.

Bibliography. Beattie W, Fragments, Edinburgh Bibl Soc Trans 3¹.31.

Warton T, History of English Poetry, London 1774–81; ed W C Hazlitt, London 1871, 3.228.

Irving D, The Lives of the Scotish Poets, 2nd edn London 1810, 2.23.

Brydges S E, Censura Literaria, London 1807, 1808, 3.288.

Brydges E and J Haslewood, The British Bibliographer, London 1814, 2.420 (includes full description of Copland edn and excerpt).

Ames J, Topographical Antiquities, London 1816, 3.136.

McN F, Gavin Douglas, Lives of Scottish Poets, ed J Robertson, London 1822, 1.61 (brief).

Hazlitt W C, Hand-Book to the Popular Poetical and Dramatic Literature of Great Britain, London 1867, p 162.

Laing D, Gawin Douglas, Bannatyne Club Publ 115, Edinburgh 1867, p 19 (brief).

Small, edn, l.clxviii.

Hazlitt W C, Collections and Notes 1867–1876, ls, London 1876, p 132.

DNB, 15.294.

Eyre-Todd G, Mediæval Scottish Poetry, Abbotsford Series, Glasgow 1892, p 231.

Arber E, A Bibliographical Summary of English Literature in the Reign of Mary 6 July 1553–17 November 1558, A Transcript of the Registers of the Company of Stationers of London, Birmingham 1894, vol 5, no 43 (Copland edn).

Henderson T F, Scottish Vernacular Literature, Edinburgh 1898; 2nd edn rvsd Edinburgh 1900; 3rd edn rvsd Edinburgh 1910, p 192 (lists edns in footnote).

CHEL, 2.536.

Geddie W, A Bibliography of Middle Scots Poets, PSTS ns 61, Edinburgh and London 1912, pp 223, 227.

Forbes-Leith W, Pre-Reformation Scholars in the 16th Century, Glasgow 1915, p 45.

Renwick-Orton, p 418 (brief); Robbins-Cutler, no 4002.5.

[21] KING HART.

MS. Magdalene Coll Camb 2553 (Pepysian Libr, Maitland Folio), pp 226–256 (1570–71).

Pinkerton, edn, l.v; 2.437.

Small, edn, l.clxxi.

Schipper J, The Poems of William Dunbar, pt 1, Denkschriften der kaiserlichen Akademie der Wissenschaften, Philo-Hist Classe, Vienna 1892, 40².11, 17.

Smith G G, Specimens of Middle Scots, Edinburgh and London 1902, pp lxvi, lxxiii.

Craigie W A, ed, The Maitland Folio, 2 vols, PSTS ns 7, 20, Edinburgh and London 1919–27, 1.254; 2.107 (notes in vol 2).

Baxter J W, William Dunbar, Edinburgh and London 1952, p 217.

Bawcutt, edn, pp lv, 141, 216 (MS described, rptd; notes at end of text).

Editions. Pinkerton J, Ancient Scotish Poems, 2 vols, London and Edinburgh 1786, 1.3; 2.365 (notes in vol 2; MS; crit W A Craigie, The Maitland Folio, 2.11, 13, 30); preface rptd Craigie, The Maitland Folio, 2.12.

Small J, The Poetical Works of Gavin Douglas, Edinburgh and London 1874, 1.85.

Morley H, Shorter English Poems, London 1876, p 116 (a few lines omitted).

Ross J, The Book of Scottish Poems, Paisley 1882, 1.234 (brief introductory notes).

Arber E, Selections from the English Poets, The Surrey and Wyatt Anthology, British Anthologies, London 1901, 2.212 (MS; some words supplied from Pinkerton edn; glossings of obscure words also taken from Pinkerton).

Bawcutt P, The Shorter Poems of Gavin Douglas, PSTS 4s 3, Edinburgh and London 1967, pp 141, 216 (notes at end of text; MS).

Selections. Irving D, The Lives of the Scotish Poets, 2 vols, Edinburgh 1804; 2nd edn improved London 1810, 2.28.

Tytler P F, Lives of Scottish Worthies, London 1833, 3.143.

Irving D, The History of Scotish Poetry, ed J A Carlyle, Edinburgh 1861, p 278 (brief excerpts).

Wilson J G, The Poets and Poetry of Scotland, N Y 1876, 1.30.

Kaye W J, The Leading Poets of Scotland, London 1891, p 141 (3 stanzas).

Eyre-Todd G, Mediæval Scottish Poetry, Abbotsford Series, Glasgow 1892, p 237 (glossings in margin).

Smith G G, Specimens of Middle Scots, Edinburgh and London 1902, pp 49, 282 (canto 1; notes at end of text; MS).

Neilson W A and K G T Webster, Chief British Poets of the 14th and 15th Centuries, Boston N Y etc 1916, pp 406, 435 (brief note at end of text, glossings at foot of page; Small edn).

Fergusson J, The Green Garden, London and Edinburgh 1946, p 47 (spelling modernized).

Auden W H and N H Pearson, Poets of the

English Language, N Y 1950, p 322.
Smith S G, Gavin Douglas A Selection from His Poetry, Edinburgh 1959, p 19 (glossings and notes at foot of page; G G Smith, Specimens of Middle Scots).
Modernizations. Tytler P F, Lives of Scottish Worthies, London 1833, 3.143.
Bonar A R, The Poets and Poetry of Scotland, Edinburgh 1864; 2nd edn 1866, p 44 (selection).
Textual Matters. Small, edn, l.clxxi, 145 (includes notes).
Smith G G, Specimens of Middle Scots, Edinburgh and London 1902, p 282 (notes).
Bawcutt, edn, pp lv, lxxxvii.
Language. Pinkerton, edn, l.cxliii; 2.520 (synorthographic and symphonious words, glossary).
Irving D, The History of Scotish Poetry, ed J A Carlyle, Edinburgh 1861, p 595 (glossary).
Murray J A H, The Dialect of the Southern Counties of Scotland, London 1873.
Small, edn, l.clxii; 4.249 (discussion in vol 1; glossary in vol 4).
Hahn O, Zur Verbal- und Nominalflexion bei den schottischen Dichtern, Berlin 1887–89 (see especially pt 3, p 19).
Horneber F, Über King Hart und Testament of the Papyngo, Straubing 1893, pp 13, 18 (crit P Lange, AnglB 4.328).
Curtis F J, An Investigation of the Rimes and Phonology of the Middle-Scotch Romance Clariodus, Angl 16.387; 17.1, 125.
Heuser W, Offenes und gescholossenes *ee* im Schottischen und Nordenglischen, Angl 19.334.
Gerken H, Die Sprache des Bischofs Douglas, Strassburg 1898, pp 62 and passim.
Flom G T, Scandinavian Influence on Southern Lowland Scotch, diss Columbia 1900.
Heuser W, Die mittelengl Entwicklung von *ū* in offener Silbe, EStn 27.353.
Smith G G, Specimens of Middle Scots, Edinburgh and London 1902, pp xi, 325 (history and philology of Middle Scots; glossary).
Browne W H, The Taill of Rauf Coilyear, Baltimore 1903, pp 15, 35, 139 (general discussion of Middle Scots; glossary).
Knopff P, Darstellung der Ablautverhältnisse in der schottischen Schriftsprache, diss Würzburg 1904.
Larue J L, Das Pronomen in den Werken des Douglas, diss Strassburg 1908 (crit O Ritter, EStn 44.101).
CHEL, 2.101, 506.

Gray M M, Introd, Lancelot of the Laik, PSTS ns 2, Edinburgh and London 1912, 2.xviii.
Lenz K, Zur Lautlehre der französischen Elemente in den schottischen Dichtungen von 1500–1550, diss Marburg 1913 (examples taken from Douglas, Dunbar, Lyndesay, Clariodus).
Taylor R, Some Notes on the Use of Can and Couth, JEGP 16.573.
Westergaard E, Prepositions in Lowland Scotch, Angl 41.444 (some examples from Douglas); Verbal Forms in Middle-Scotch, Angl 43.95.
Craigie W A, The Maitland Folio, 2 vols, PSTS ns 7, 20, Edinburgh and London 1919–27, 2.135 (glossary).
Hartig P, Die Edinburger Dialektgruppe, Palaes 161.90 (cites Douglas among others to illustrate development of Scots dialect).
Westergaard E, Plural Forms in Lowland Scottish, Angl 51.77.
Wood H H, The Poems and Fables of Robert Henryson, Edinburgh 1933; 2nd edn rvsd Edinburgh 1958, p xxxi (discussion in introd).
Patrick D, Scottish Literature, Chambers's Cyclopædia of English Literature, rvsd J L Geddie, Phila and N Y 1938, 1.164.
Fergusson J, The Green Garden, London and Edinburgh 1946, p 228 (glossary).
Preston P, Did Gavin Douglas Write King Hart? MÆ 28.40.
Ridley F H, Did Gawin Douglas Write King Hart? Spec 34.411.
Bawcutt P, Gavin Douglas Some Additions to OED and DOST, N&Q 208(ns 10).289.
Scott T, Dunbar A Critical Exposition, Edinburgh and London 1966, p 351.
Bawcutt, edn, pp lxxv, 247 (discussion, glossary).
Versification. Horneber F, Über King Hart und Testament of the Papyngo, Straubing 1893, p 5.
Courthope, p 377; Ten Brink, 3.90.
Saintsbury G, History of English Prosody, London 1908; 2nd edn London 1923, 1.276.
Renwick-Orton, p 418 (very brief).
Curtis F J, An Investigation of the Rimes and Phonology of Clariodus, Angl 16.387; 17.1, 125.
Ridley F H, Spec 34.409.
Bawcutt, edn, p lxx.
Date. Pinkerton, edn, l.ix, xcv, xcvii.
McN F, Gavin Douglas, Lives of Scottish Poets, ed J Robertson, London 1822, 1.62.
Small, edn, l.cxxxix.

Schipper J, William Dunbar, Berlin 1884, p 52.

Horneber F, Über King Hart, pp 6, 12, 20, 24.

Snell F J, The Poets, The Age of Transition, London 1905, 1.94.

Ridley F H, Spec 34.403, 412.

Bawcutt P, N&Q 208(ns 10).289; edn, p lxxviii.

Authorship. Horneber F, Über King Hart, p 5.

Gerken H, Die Sprache des Bischofs Douglas, Strassburg 1898, p 62.

Larue J L, Das Pronomen in den Werken des Douglas, diss Strassburg 1908 (crit EStn 44.101).

Lewis C S, English Literature in the Sixteenth Century, Oxford 1954, p 80.

Preston P, Did Gavin Douglas Write King Hart? MÆ 28.31.

Ridley F H, Spec 34.402.

Coldwell D F C, Selections from Gavin Douglas, Oxford 1964, p xxi (brief reference).

Bawcutt, edn, p lxxii.

Sources and Literary Relations. Irving D, The Lives of the Scotish Poets, 2nd edn, London 1810, 2.35.

Craik G L, Sketches of the History of Literature and Learning in England, London 1844, 1.257 (brief).

Small, edn, l.cxlii.

Craik G L, A Compendious History of English Literature, N Y 1877, 1. 456.

Lang A, Gawain Douglas, The English Poets, ed T H Ward, London and N Y 1880; (numerous subsequent edns) N Y 1924, 1.160.

Lange P, Chaucer's Einfluss, diss Halle 1882; rptd Angl 6.86.

Nichol J, A Sketch of Scottish Poetry, ed J Small; 2nd edn rvsd, EETS 11, London 1883, p xxvi.

Ross J M, Scottish History and Literature, Glasgow 1884, pp 336, 350.

Horneber F, Über King Hart, p 23 (relation to other poems of Douglas, Dunbar, Villon, Langland).

Courthope, passim; Ten Brink, 3.89.

Neilson W A, Studies and Notes in Philology and Literature 6.102, 163.

Smith G G, The Transition Period, Periods of European Lit, Edinburgh and London 1900, 4.59.

M'Ilwraith W, A Sketch of Scottish Literature, Annual Burns Chronicle 10.24.

Lawson A, The Poems of Alexander Hume, PSTS 48, Edinburgh and London 1902, p 228.

Mebus F, Studien zu William Dunbar, Breslau 1902, passim (resemblances of wording scattered throughout notes to Dunbar's poems).

CHEL, 2.297.

Perrow E C, Trans Wis Acad of Sciences Arts and Letters 7, no 1, p 682.

Knowlton E C, Nature in Middle English, JEGP 20.192 (brief).

Patch H R, The Goddess Fortuna in Medieval Literature, Cambridge Mass 1927, p 53 (brief).

Legouis HEL, p 177.

Saintsbury G, The Four Great Scottish Poets, N Y 1929, p 190 (brief).

Cornelius R D, The Castell of Pleasure, EETS 179, London 1930, p 19 (brief); The Figurative Castle, Bryn Mawr Pa 1930, pp 9, 34.

Mackenzie A M, An Historical Survey of Scottish Literature, London 1933, p 101 (crit The Modern Scot 4.164).

Smith J M, The French Background of Middle Scots Literature, Edinburgh and London 1934, p 117.

Patrick D, Scottish Literature, Chambers's Cyclopædia of English Literature, rvsd J L Geddie, Phila and N Y 1938, 1.166.

Lewis C S, The Allegory of Love, London 1936; rptd London 1953, p 287.

Grierson H J C and J C Smith, A Critical History of English Poetry, London 1944; 2nd rvsd edn London 1947, p 58 (brief).

Craig HEL, p 169 (brief); Renwick-Orton, p 418 (brief).

Ward A C, Illustrated History of Eng Lit, London N Y and Toronto 1953, pp 32, 41 (brief).

Fox D, Dunbar's The Golden Targe, ELH 26.328.

Kinghorn A M, The Mediaeval Makars, Texas Stud Lit and Lang 1.73.

Preston P, Did Gavin Douglas Write King Hart? MÆ 28.31.

Ridley F H, Did Gawin Douglas Write King Hart? Spec 34.403.

Smith S G, Gavin Douglas A Selection from His Poetry, Edinburgh 1959, p 9 (very brief).

Bawcutt, edn, p lvii.

Literary Criticism. Ellis G, Specimens of the Early English Poets, 5 edns, London 1790, 1801, 1803, 1811, 1845 (5th edn corrected), 1. 316 (very brief).

Irving D, The Lives of the Scotish Poets, 2nd edn London 1810, 2.28.

McN F, Gavin Douglas, Lives of Scottish Poets, ed J Robertson, London 1822, 1.62.

Tytler P F, Lives of Scottish Worthies, London 1833, 3.141.

Gilfillan G, Specimens with Memoirs, Edinburgh and London 1860, 1.71 (brief).

Irving D, The History of Scotish Poetry, ed J A Carlyle, Edinburgh 1861, p 277.

Taylor J, The Imperial Dictionary of Universal Biography, London [1863], 2.137 (brief).

Morley H, A First Sketch of English Literature, London 1873; rvsd London 1896, p 215.

Small, edn, 1.cxxxix.

Wilson J G, The Poets and Poetry of Scotland, N Y 1876, 1.30 (brief).

Craik G L, A Compendious History of English Literature, N Y 1877, 1.456.

Wall A, Gawain Douglas Bishop of Dunkeld, The Western ns 3.734.

Mackintosh J, The History of Civilisation in Scotland, London and Edinburgh 1878–88; new edn partly rewritten Paisley 1892–96, 2.311.

Lang A, Gawain Douglas, The English Poets, ed T H Ward, London and N Y 1880; (numerous subsequent edns) N Y 1924, 1.160.

Nichol J, A Sketch of Scottish Poetry, ed J Small; 2nd edn rvsd, EETS 11, London 1883; p xxvi.

Ross J M, Scottish History and Literature, Glasgow 1884, pp 318, 334.

Schipper J, William Dunbar, Berlin 1884, p 53.

DNB, 15.294.

Fitzgibbon H M, Early English and Scottish Poetry, N Y London and Melbourne 1888, p lxii.

Minto W, Characteristics of English Poets, authorized American edn, Boston 1889, p 107 (brief).

Kaye W J, The Leading Poets of Scotland, London 1891, p 140 (brief).

Morley, 7.160.

Eyre-Todd G, Mediæval Scottish Poetry, Glasgow 1892, p 232.

Horneber F, Über King Hart, Straubing 1893, pp 5, 19, 25, 35 (crit AnglB 4.328).

Courthope, passim; Ten Brink, 3.88.

Gosse E, Modern English Literature A Short History, N Y 1897; rvsd edn N Y 1906, p 59 (brief).

Henderson T F, Scottish Vernacular Literature, Edinburgh 1898; 3rd edn rvsd Edinburgh 1910, pp 192, 197.

Neilson W A, Studies and Notes in Philology and Literature 6.163.

Smith G G, The Transition Period, Periods of European Lit, Edinburgh and London 1900, 4.59.

Chambers R, Chambers's Cyclopædia, Phila and N Y 1901–03; rvsd J L Geddie, Phila and N Y 1938, 1.202 (very brief).

M'Ilwraith W, A Sketch of Scottish Literature, Annual Burns Chronicle 10.24.

Browne W H, The Taill of Rauf Coilyear, Baltimore 1903, p 19.

Millar J H, A Literary History of Scotland, London 1903, p 81 (brief).

Moorman F W, The Interpretation of Nature in English Poetry from Beowulf to Shakespeare, QF 95.147 (brief).

Snell F J, The Poets, The Age of Transition, London 1905, 1.94.

CHEL, 2.297; Enc Brit, 8.445.

Perrow E C, Trans Wis Acad of Sciences Arts and Letters 7, no 1, p 721.

Stair-Kerr E, The Poets, Scotland under James IV, Paisley 1911, p 129 (brief).

Watt L M, Scottish Life and Poetry, London 1912, pp 112, 115.

Legouis HEL, p 177.

Saintsbury G, The Four Great Scottish Poets, N Y 1929, p 190 (brief).

Elton O, The English Muse, London 1933, p 87.

Mackenzie A M, An Historical Survey of Scottish Literature, London 1933, p 100.

Smith J M, The French Background of Middle Scots Literature, Edinburgh and London 1934, p 117 (crit AnglB 45.265; MÆ 4.44).

Lewis C S, The Allegory of Love, London 1936; rptd London 1953, p 287.

Grierson H J C and J C Smith, A Critical History of English Poetry, London 1944; 2nd rvsd edn London 1947, p 58 (brief).

Craig HEL, p 169 (brief).

Russell P, Gavin Douglas and His Eneados, Nine 2.298.

Cazamian L, The Development of English Humor, Durham N C 1952, pt 1, p 94 (very brief).

Renwick-Orton, pp 120, 418 (brief).

Ward A C, Illustrated History of English Literature, London N Y and Toronto 1953, p 41 (brief).

Lewis C S, English Literature in the Sixteenth Century, Oxford 1954, p 80.

Mackenzie A M, The Renaissance Poets, ed J Kinsley, London 1955, p 36.

Mackie R L, King James IV of Scotland, Edinburgh and London 1958, p 184.

Kinghorn A M, The Mediaeval Makars, Texas Stud Lit and Lang 1.81.

Preston P, Did Gavin Douglas Write King Hart? MÆ 28.31, 39.

Ridley F H, Did Gawin Douglas Write King Hart? Spec 34.403, 408.

Rossi S, Il tredicesimo libro dell'Eneide, Studi di letteratura storia e filosofia 74.524.

Bawcutt, edn, pp lvii, lxxiv.

Bibliography. Small, edn, l.clxxi.

CHEL, 2.536.

Geddie W, A Bibliography of Middle Scots Poets, PSTS ns 61, Edinburgh and London 1912, p 226.

Forbes-Leith W, Pre-Reformation Scholars in the 16th Century, Glasgow 1915, p 45.

Renwick-Orton, p 418 (brief).

Robbins-Cutler, no 1820.5.

[22] CONSCIENCE.

MS. Magdalene Coll Camb 2553 (Pepysian Libr, Maitland Folio), pp 192–193 (1570–71).

Pinkerton J, Ancient Scotish Poems, 2 vols, London and Edinburgh 1786, 1.v; 2.437.

Small, edn, l.clxxi.

Schipper J, The Poems of William Dunbar, pt 1, Denkschriften der kaiserlichen Akademie der Wissenschaften, Philo-Hist Classe, Vienna 1892, 40².11, 17.

Smith G G, Specimens of Middle Scots, Edinburgh and London 1902, pp lxvi, lxxiii.

Craigie W A, ed, The Maitland Folio, 2 vols, PSTS ns 7, 20, Edinburgh and London 1919–27, 1.217; 2.102 (notes in vol 2).

Baxter J W, William Dunbar, Edinburgh and London 1952, p 217.

Bawcutt, edn, pp lv, 137, 215 (notes at end of text; MS described, rptd).

Editions. Small, edn, J, The Poetical Works of Gavin Douglas, 4 vols, Edinburgh and London 1874, 1.121 [mispaged for 122].

Kaye W J, The Leading Poets of Scotland, London 1891, p 140 (omits 1 line).

Bawcutt P, The Shorter Poems of Gavin Douglas, PSTS 4s 3, Edinburgh and London 1967, pp 137, 215 (notes at end of text; MS).

Textual Matters. Small, edn, l.clxxi, 154 (includes one note).

Bawcutt, edn, pp lv, lxxxvii.

Language. Murray J A H, The Dialect of the Southern Counties of Scotland, London 1873.

Small, edn, l.clxii; 4.249 (discussion in vol 1; glossary in vol 4).

Hahn O, Zur Verbal- und Nominalflexion bei den schottischen Dichtern, Berlin 1887–

89 (see especially pt 3, p 19).

Curtis F J, An Investigation of the Rimes and Phonology of the Middle-Scotch Romance Clariodus, Angl 16.387; 17.1, 125.

Gerken H, Die Sprache des Bischofs Douglas, Strassburg 1898, passim.

Flom G T, Scandinavian Influence on Southern Lowland Scotch, diss Columbia 1900.

Browne W H, The Taill of Rauf Coilyear, Baltimore 1903, pp 15, 35, 139 (general discussion of Middle Scots; glossary).

Knopff P, Darstellung der Ablautverhältnisse in der schottischen Schriftsprache, diss Würzburg 1904.

CHEL, 2.101, 506.

Gray M M, Introd, Lancelot of the Laik, PSTS ns 2, Edinburgh and London 1912, 2.xviii.

Lenz K, Zur Lautlehre der französischen Elemente in den schottischen Dichtungen von 1500–1550, diss Marburg 1913 (examples taken from Douglas, Dunbar, Lyndesay, Clariodus).

Taylor R, Some Notes on the Use of Can and Couth, JEGP 16.573.

Westergaard E, Prepositions in Lowland Scotch, Angl 41.444 (some examples from Douglas); Verbal Forms in Middle-Scotch, Angl 43.95.

Craigie W A, The Maitland Folio, 2 vols, PSTS ns 7, 20, Edinburgh and London 1919–27, 2.135 (glossary).

Hartig P, Die Edinburger Dialektgruppe, Palaes 161.90 (cites Douglas among others to illustrate development of Scots dialect).

Westergaard E, Plural Forms in Lowland Scottish, Angl 51.77.

Wood H H, The Poems and Fables of Robert Henryson, Edinburgh 1933; 2nd edn rvsd Edinburgh 1958, p xxxi (discussion in introd).

Patrick D, Scottish Literature, Chambers's Cyclopædia of English Literature, rvsd J L Geddie, Phila and N Y 1938, 1.164.

Scott T, Dunbar A Critical Exposition, Edinburgh and London 1966, p 351.

Bawcutt, edn, p 247 (glossary).

Versification. Curtis F J, An Investigation of the Rimes and Phonology of Clariodus, Angl 16.387; 17.1, 125.

Renwick-Orton, p 418 (very brief).

Date. Bawcutt, edn, p liii.

Authorship. Bawcutt, edn, p liii.

Sources and Literary Relations. Small, edn, l.cxliii.

Patrick D, Scottish Literature, Chambers's Cyclopædia, 1.166.

Bawcutt, edn, p liii.
Other Scholarly Problems. Bawcutt, edn, p liv (contemp conditions).
Literary Criticism. Lang A, Gawain Douglas, The English Poets, ed T H Ward, London and N Y 1880; (numerous subsequent edns) N Y 1924, 1.160.
Morley, 7.161.
Smith G G, The Transition Period, Periods of European Lit, Edinburgh and London 1900, 4.60.
Snell F J, The Poets, The Age of Transition,

London 1905, 1.95.
CHEL, 2.298; Enc Brit, 8.445.
Coldwell D F C, Selections from Gavin Douglas, Oxford 1964, p xxi (brief reference).
Bawcutt, edn, p liii.
Bibliography. CHEL, 2.537.
Geddie W, A Bibliography of Middle Scots Poets, PSTS ns 61, Edinburgh and London 1912, p 228.
Renwick-Orton, p 419 (brief); Robbins-Cutler, no 3954.5.

4. DUNBAR

GENERAL.

Language. Jamieson J, An Etymological Dictionary of the Scottish Language, 2 vols, Edinburgh 1808; rvsd J Longmuir and D Donaldson, 4 vols with supplement, Paisley 1879–82; new edn J Longmuir, London and Edinburgh 1885; another edn with introd by W M Metcalfe, Paisley 1912.
Murray J A H, A New English Dictionary on Historical Principles (The Oxford English Dictionary, ed J A H Murray, H Bradley, W A Craigie, C T Onions), Oxford 1884–1933.
Mackay C, A Dictionary of Lowland Scotch, Boston 1888.
Wright J, The English Dialect Dictionary, 8 vols, London 1896–1905.
Grant W and D D Murison, The Scottish National Dictionary, Edinburgh 1931– (crit K Wittig, SSL 1.275).
Craigie W A and A J Aitken, edd, A Dictionary of the Older Scottish Tongue from the Twelfth Century to the End of the Seventeenth Founded on the Collections of Sir William A Craigie, Chicago and London 1931–.
Craigie W A, Older Scottish and English A Study in Contrasts, TPSL 1935, p 1.
MED.
Woolley J S, Bibliography for Scottish Linguistic Studies, Edinburgh 1954.
Murison D, A Survey of Scottish Language Studies, Forum Mod Lang Stud 3.276.
Authorship. Henderson T F, A Little Book of Scottish Verse, London 1899, pp 41, 74 (suggests authorship of Why sowld nocht Allane honorit be? and When Tayis Bank).
Sources and Literary Relations. Gray M M, Introd, Lancelot of the Laik, PSTS ns 2, Edinburgh and London 1912, pp xviii, xxxv.

Wood H H, Robert Henryson, Edinburgh Essays on Scots Literature, Edinburgh and London 1933, pp 1, 8 (crit The Modern Scot 4.353).
Linklater E, The Question of Culture, The Lion and the Unicorn, London 1935, pp 111, 118, 120, 127.
Other Scholarly Problems. [Grieve C M] MacDiarmid H, Not Burns—Dunbar! The Spectator 144.893 (contemp reputation).
Whiting B J, Proverbs and Proverbial Sayings from Scottish Writings before 1600, MS 11.123; 13.87 (draws on works of Dunbar as well as other Scottish material).
Kinghorn A M, Scots Literature and Scottish Antiquarians 1750–1800, SE 33.46 (development of antiquarians' interest).
Whiting B J, Proverbs Sentences and Proverbial Phrases, Cambridge Mass 1968.
Bibliography. Warton T, History of English Poetry from the 12th to the Close of the 16th Century, London 1774–81; ed W C Hazlitt, London 1871, 3.219 (brief).
Brydges E and J Haslewood, The British Bibliographer, London 1814, 4.304.
Lowndes W T, The Bibliographer's Manual of English Literature, London 1834; new edn rvsd corrected and enlarged by H G Bohn, London (1871?), 1.694.
Paterson J, The Works of William Dunbar Including His Life 1465–1536, Edinburgh 1863, p 3.
Hazlitt W C, Hand-Book to the Popular Poetical and Dramatic Literature of Great Britain, London 1867, p 172.
Kaufmann J, Traité de la langue du poète ecossais William Dunbar, Bonn 1873, p 11 (discussion of MSS and early edns).
Schipper J, William Dunbar sein Leben und seine Gedichte, Berlin 1884, p 60.
DNB, 16.156.

Mackay Æ J G and W Gregor, Bibliography
of Dunbar, Appendix to Introd, The
Poems of William Dunbar, ed J Small,
PSTS 2, 4, 16, 21, 29, 3 vols, Edinburgh
1884–1893, l.cxciv (MSS sources and early
edns identified).
Robertson J L] Haliburton H, Our Earlier
Burns, In Scottish Fields, London 1890, p
210 (brief discussion of MSS and edns).
Morley, 7.123.
Eyre-Todd G, Mediæval Scottish Poetry, Ab-
botsford Series of Scottish Poets, Glasgow
1892, p 148.
Schipper J, The Poems of William Dunbar,
pt 1, Denkschriften der kaiserlichen Akad-
emie der Wissenschaften, Philo-Hist Classe,
Vienna 1892–93, 40².1 (discussion of early
edns and MSS Nat Libr Scot Acc 4233
[Asloan], Nat Libr Scot 1.1.6, Magdalene
Coll Camb 2553 [Pepysian Libr, Maitland
Folio], Camb Univ L1.5.10, Laing 149, Cot-
ton Vitell A XVI, Royal Appendix 58,
Arundel 285, Aberdeen Minute Book of
Sasines, Nat Libr Scot 19.1.16; see also
headnotes to each poem).
Gray G J, A General Index to Hazlitt's
Handbook and His Bibliographical Collec-
tions, London 1893, p 237.
Oliphant F R, William Dunbar, Blackwood's
Edinburgh Magazine 154.424.
Bearder J W, Über den Gebrauch der
Praepositionen in der altschottischen Poe-
sie, Halle 1894, p 8.
Chambers R, Chambers's Cyclopædia, Phila
and N Y 1901–03; rvsd J L Geddie 1938,
1.200.
Browne W H, The Taill of Rauf Coilyear,
Baltimore 1903, p 67.
Seccombe T and W R Nicoll, The Scots
Poets, The Bookman Illustrated History
of English Literature, London 1906, 1.21.
Baildon H B, The Poems of William Dun-
bar, Cambridge 1907, p xii (briefly identi-
fies MSS and early edns).
Steinberger C, Étude sur William Dunbar,
Dublin 1908, p 177.
Körting, p 199; CHEL, 2.535; Enc Brit, 8.669.
Watt L M, Scottish Life and Poetry, Lon-
don 1912, p 499 (listing and location of
MSS).

Black G F, A List of Works Relating to Scot-
land, BNYPL Jan-Dec 1914; rptd N Y 1916,
p 817.
Forbes-Leith W, Pre-Reformation Scholars
in the 16th Century, Their Writings and
Their Public Services, with a Bibliography,
Glasgow 1915, p 27.
Northup C S, J Q Adams and A Keogh, A
Register of Bibliographies of the English
Language and Literature, New Haven Lon-
don and Oxford 1925, p 148.
Tucker-Benham, pp 147, 149, 153.
Bronson B H, Ritson's Bibliographia Scotica,
PMLA 52.141 (brief comment on early
edns).
Baxter J W, William Dunbar, Edinburgh
and London 1952, p 240 (lists MSS, records
relevant to and studies of Dunbar).
Renwick-Orton, p 416; CBEL, 1.254, 258; 5.147.
Lewis C S, English Literature in the Six-
teenth Century, Oxford 1954, p 642.
McClure N E, Sixteenth-century English Po-
etry, The Harper English Literature Series,
ed K J Holzknecht, N Y 1954, p 20 (brief).
Kinsley J, William Dunbar Poems, Oxford
1958, p xx (crit TLS Apr 18 1958, p 208;
N MacC, Saltire Review 5.65; J A Michie,
Aberdeen Univ Rev 37.387; D Young, SHR
38.10; E Morgan, RES ns 11.71; J Wordsworth, MÆ 30.128).
Rossi S, I Chauceriani Scozzesi, Napoli 1964,
p 70.
Scott T, Dunbar a Critical Exposition of the
Poems, Edinburgh and London 1966, p
360 (crit QR 304.351; TLS July 21 1966,
p 636; J B Caird, Library Review, no
159.507; J A Burrow, The New Statesman
73.233; M P McDiarmid, SHR 46.65; R D S
Jack, Scottish Studies 11.113; D Pirie, EC
17.356; D Young, Forum Mod Lang Stud
3.253; A J Smith, MLQ [Wash] 29.341).
Scott T, Late Medieval Scots Poetry, London
1967, p 34.
Wood H H, Two Scots Chaucerians, Writers
and Their Work, no 201, ed G Bullough,
London 1967, pp 45, 47.
Kidd J and R H Carnie, Annual Bibliography of Scottish Literature, 1969, Suppl 1,
The Bibliotheck, Aberdeen 1970, p 6.
Ridley F H, A Check List, SSL 8.44.

I. Personal

(Note: Folios for items [23–32] are listed by MS number, as appropriate, after each title. See under *MSS* below for full listing and information. Titles are from Mackenzie edn.)

[23] TO THE KING.

3, ff 113ᵇ–114ᵃ.

[24] ANE HIS AWIN ENNEMY.

2, pp 212–213; 3, ff 115ᵇ–116ᵃ.

[25] ON HIS HEID-AKE.

1, f 6ᵃ.

[26] HOW DUMBAR WES DESYRD TO BE ANE FREIR.

1, ff 42ᵃ–42ᵇ; 2, pp 333–334; 3, ff 115ᵃ–115ᵇ.

[27] COMPLAINT TO THE KING AGANIS MURE.

1, f 11ᵃ; 2, pp 10–11.

[28] THE FLYTING OF DUNBAR AND KENNEDIE.

1, ff 58ᵃ–65ᵃ; 2, pp 53–54, 59–63, 69–72, 77–80; 3, ff 147ᵃ–154ᵃ; 4, pp 137–144.

[29] LAMENT FOR THE MAKARIS.

2, pp 189–192; 3, ff 109ᵃ–110ᵃ; 4, pp 189–192.

[30] OF DEMING.

2, pp 168–170; 3, ff 63ᵇ–64ᵃ.

[31] HOW SALL I GOVERNE ME?.

1, ff 38ᵃ–38ᵇ; 2, pp 323–324; 3, ff 66ᵃ–66ᵇ.

[32] MEDITATIOUN IN WYNTIR.

1, f 1ᵃ; 2, p 3.

MSS. 1, Camb Univ L1.5.10 (Reidpeth or Moore), ff 1ᵃ, 6ᵃ, 11ᵃ, 38ᵃ–38ᵇ, 42ᵃ–42ᵇ, 58ᵃ–65ᵃ (1623; contains lines 1–22 of item [32], and items [25], [27], [31], [26], [28]); 2, Magdalene Coll Camb 2553 (Pepysian Libr, Maitland Folio), pp 3, 10–11, 53–54, 59–63, 69–72, 77–80, 168–170, 189–192, 212–213, 313–314, 318–319, 323–324, 333–334 (1570–71; items [32], [27], [28], [30], [29], [24], [31], [26]); 3, Nat Libr Scot 1.1.6 (Bannatyne), ff 63ᵇ–64ᵃ, 66ᵃ–66ᵇ, 109ᵃ–110ᵃ, 113ᵇ–114ᵃ, 115ᵃ–116ᵃ, 147ᵃ–154ᵃ (1568; items [30], [31], [29],

[23], [26], [24], [28]). PRINT: 4, Nat Libr Scot 19.1.16 (Chepman and Myllar), pp 137–144, 189–192 (1508; contains lines 316–552 of item [28], and item [29]) (STC, n° 7348).

Pinkerton J, Ancient Scotish Poems, 2 vols London and Edinburgh 1786, l.v; 2.437 471 (MSS 2, 3).

Brydges E and J Haslewood, The British Bibliographer, London 1814, 4.183 (MS 3).

Laing D, The Poems of George Bannatyne Edinburgh 1824, p 3 (MS 3); The Knightly Tale of Golagrus and Gawane, Edinburgh 1827, f 2ᵃ (PRINT 4 rptd); An Account of the Contents of George Bannatyne' Manuscript, The Bannatyne Club, Edinburgh 1829, 35.43 (MS 3).

A Catalogue of the Manuscripts Preserved in The Library of The University of Cambridge, Cambridge 1861, 4.94 (MS 1).

Small J, The Poetical Works of Gavin Douglas, Edinburgh and London 1874, l.clxxi (MS 2).

Dickson R and J P Edmond, Annals of Scottish Printing from 1507 to the Beginning of the 17th Century, Cambridge 1890, p 49 (MS 4).

Schipper, edn, pt 1, 40².9 (MSS 1, 2, 3 PRINT 4).

Murdoch J B, ed, The Bannatyne Manuscript, 4 vols, Hunterian Club, Glasgow 1896, 2.171, 178, 308, 322, 327; 3.420 (MS 3 rptd).

Smith G G, Specimens of Middle Scots, Edinburgh and London 1902, pp lxvi, lxxiii lxxiv (MSS 2, 3, PRINT 4).

Brown J T T, The Bannatyne Manuscript, SHR 1.136 (MS 3).

Stevenson G, ed, Pieces from The Makculloch and the Gray MSS, PSTS 65, Edinburgh and London 1918, pp 207, 259, 302 (PRINT 4 rptd, notes at end of text).

Craigie W A, ed, The Maitland Folio, PSTS ns 7, 20, 2 vols, Edinburgh and London 1919–27, 2.34, 53 (MS 1); 1.1, 10, 71, 191 214, 239, 372, 380, 388, 404; 2.34, 37, 69, 99, 102, 105, 121, 126 (MS 2 rptd, notes in vol 2); variants between MSS 1 and 2 listed in 2.69, 121.

Ritchie W T, ed, The Bannatyne Manuscript Writtin in Tyme of Pest, PSTS ns 5, 22, 23, 26, 4 vols, Edinburgh 1928–34, 2.156, 162, 287, 301, 306; 3.44 (MS 3 rptd).

Beattie W, The Chepman and Myllar Prints, Edinburgh Biblio Soc, Oxford 1950, pp viii, 137, 189 (PRINT 4 described, rptd).

Baxter J W, William Dunbar, Edinburgh and London 1952, p 216 (MSS 1, 2, 3, PRINT 4).

Bawcutt P, The Shorter Poems of Gavin Douglas, PSTS 4s 3, Edinburgh and London 1967, p lv (MS 2).

Editions. Laing D, The Poems of William Dunbar, 2 vols, Edinburgh 1834, 1.28, 107, 117, 128, 157, 181, 211, 253, 315; 2.63, 231, 293, 300, 310, 331, 341, 352, 370, 417 (notes in vol 2 and Supplement; MSS 1 and 3; PRINT 4; Memoirs of William Dunbar preceding text of poems in vol 1 is paginated (separately); Supplement, Edinburgh 1865, pp 261ff (continuation of vol 1, with which it was intended to be bound).

Paterson J, The Life and Poems of William Dunbar, Edinburgh 1860 (crit Athen July 14 1860, p 49); reissued The Works of William Dunbar Including His Life 1465–1536, Edinburgh 1863, pp 91, 160, 173, 184, 203, 222, 245, 313 (glossings in footnotes).

Small J, Æ J G Mackay, G P McNeill, W Gregor, The Poems of William Dunbar, PSTS 2, 4, 16, 21, 29, 3 vols, Edinburgh 1884–93, 2.11, 48, 92, 129, 210, 233, 254; 3.36, 90, 162, 208, 292, 315, 339 (notes in vol 3; MSS 1, 2, 3; PRINT 4).

Schipper J, The Poems of William Dunbar, pts 2–4, Denkschriften der kaiserlichen Akademie der Wissenschaften Philo-Hist Classe, Vienna 1892–93, 40⁴.50; 41⁴.28, 34, 38, 86; 42⁴.1, 26 (MS sources and variants given in headnotes and ftnts to each poem; MSS 1, 2, 3; crit E Kölbing, EStn 20.439).

Baildon H B, The Poems of William Dunbar, Cambridge 1907, pp 71, 109, 112, 115, 146, 156, 168, 254, 265, 275, 278, 283 (notes at end of text; sources vary, selects reading which seems to him most likely to be correct; crit J H Millar, The Bookman 32.207).

Mackenzie W M, The Poems of William Dunbar, London 1932, p 1 (notes at end of text; MSS 1, 2, 3; PRINT 4; crit B Dickins, MLR 28.506; TLS Jan 26 1933, p 55; The Modern Scot 4.63); rptd London 1950; ed B Dickins, rptd and rvsd London 1960 (crit A Macdonald, ESts 43.219); rptd 1970.

Selections. Ramsay A, The Ever Green, Edinburgh 1724, 1.129, 204; 2.47, 90 ([29] omits 1 stanza and adds 3 stanza postscript, [24], [28] omits 1 stanza, [30] omits 1 stanza; oc-

casional changes in wording; MS 3); The Poetical Works of Allan Ramsay, ed C Mackay, London and N Y n d, pp 252, 267, 274, 276 ([24], [28], [30]).

Dalrymple D, Ancient Scottish Poems from the MS of George Bannatyne, Edinburgh 1770, pp 25, 53, 60, 68, 74, 261, 263, 267 (crit O Gilchrist, Ancient Scottish Poems, Censura literaria, ed Brydges, London 1807, 5.238); rptd Leeds 1815, pp 29, 66, 76, 87, 94, 310, 312, 316, 318 ([26], [24], [31], [30], [23], [29]; notes at end of text; MS 3).

The Caledoniad, London 1775, 2.102 ([29]).

Pinkerton J, Select Scotish Ballads, 2 vols, London 1783, 2.55 ([24]; Dalrymple, Ancient Scottish Poems).

Pinkerton J, Ancient Scotish Poems, 2 vols, London and Edinburgh 1786, 1.107, 125; 2.413, 416 ([27], [32]; notes in vol 2; MS 2).

Morison R, Select Poems of Wil Dunbar Part First from the MS of George Bannatyne, Perth 1788, pp 31, 59, 65, 73, 78 ([26], [24], [31], [30], [23], [29]; MS 3).

Ellis G, Specimens of the Early English Poets, 5th edn corrected London 1845, 1.306 ([32]; spelling modernized, glossings at foot of page; Pinkerton, Ancient Scotish Poems).

Sibbald J, Chronicle of Scottish Poetry, 4 vols, Edinburgh and London 1802, 1.240, 280, 325, 345, 350; 2.2, 11 ([26], [23], [29], [24], from [28], from [30], from [31], [32]; introductory and end notes; sources not always indicated but include MSS 2 and 3, PRINT 4).

Irving D, The Lives of the Scotish Poets, 2nd edn, London 1810, 1.394, 430, 440 ([28], [32], [26]; some brief excerpts).

Tytler P F, Lives of Scottish Worthies, London 1833, 3.90, 113, 133 (from [26], [28], [29]; brief excerpts; Laing edn).

Ancient Scotish Poetry No I Dunbar, Blackwood's Edinburgh Magazine 37.307 ([25], [32]).

William Dunbar, The Scottish Journal 1.132 ([29]; Laing edn).

Irving D, The History of Scotish Poetry, ed J A Carlyle, Edinburgh 1861, pp 227, 253 ([28]; brief excerpts).

Kaufmann J, Traité de la langue, Bonn 1873, p 43 ([29]; Laing edn).

Morley H, Shorter English Poems, London 1876, p 109 ([29]).

Nichol J, William Dunbar, The English Poets, ed T H Ward, London and N Y 1880 (numerous subsequent edns), N Y 1924, 1.157 ([29]; glossings at foot of page;

Laing edn, with variations for metrical improvement).

Schipper, 1.514 ([26]).

Ross J, The Book of Scottish Poems, Paisley 1882, 1.186, 193 ([32], [29]).

Schipper J, William Dunbar sein Leben und seine Gedichte, Berlin 1884, pp 72, 245, 253, 296, 311 (in German; [26], [27], from [24], [31], [30], [32]; crit E Kölbing, EStn 10.128; M Trautmann, Angl 7.146; The Nation 40.144).

Fitzgibbon H M, Early English and Scottish Poetry, London N Y and Melbourne 1888, pp 119, 123, 149, 432 ([32], from [29], from [31]; spelling modernized, notes at end of text).

Veitch J, The Feeling for Nature in Scottish Poetry, Edinburgh and London 1887, 1.234 ([32], [29]; brief quotes interspersed with criticism, glossings in side notes; crit C Patmore, Out-of-door Poetry, St James Gazette July 9 1887; rptd in Courage in Politics, London 1921, p 32).

Eyre-Todd G, Mediæval Scottish Poetry, Abbotsford Series, Glasgow 1892, pp 187, 213 ([29], [32]; glossings in margin).

Skeat Spec, pp 116, 412 ([26]; notes at end of text; Laing edn).

Browne W H, Selections from the Early Scottish Poets, Baltimore 1896, pp 121, 131, 189 ([26], [32]; notes at end of text; Small edn).

Ten Brink, 3.71 ([26]).

Henley W E, English Lyrics Chaucer to Poe 1340–1809, London 1897, pp 5, 372 ([29], [32]; spelling modernized, notes at end of text; Small edn).

Henderson T F, A Little Book of Scottish Verse, London 1899; 2nd edn, London 1909, pp 44, 64 ([29], [32]; glossings at foot of page).

Quiller-Couch A, The Oxford Book of English Verse, Oxford 1900; new edn Oxford 1939, p 30 ([29]; glossings at foot of page).

Arber E, English Songs, The Dunbar Anthology, British Anthologies, London 1901, 1.23, 298 ([29], [26]; spelling and some words modernized, identification of sources in notes; Small edn; crit R Brotanek, AnglB 13.172).

Chambers R, Chambers's Cyclopædia, Phila and N Y 1901–03; rvsd J L Geddie, Phila and N Y 1938, 1.196 (from [29]).

Dixon W M, The Edinburgh Book of Scottish Verse, London 1910, pp 24, 45 ([29], [32]; glossings at foot of page).

Douglas G, The Book of Scottish Poetry, London and Leipsic 1911, p 110 ([29]; glossings at foot of page; Small edn).

Zupitza J, Alt- und mittelenglisches Übungsbuch, 10th edn Vienna and Leipzig 1912, p 203 ([26]; variants at foot of page).

Neilson W A and K G T Webster, Chief British Poets of the 14th and 15th Centuries, Boston N Y etc 1916, pp 392, 398, 434 ([29], [26]; brief note at end of text, glossings at foot of page; Small edn).

Lawson Mrs A and A Lawson, A St Andrews Treasury of Scottish Verse, London 1920; 2nd edn London 1933, p 6 (from [32]; glossings at foot of page).

Buchan J, The Northern Muse, London 1924, pp 3, 245, 454, 500 (from [32], [29]; glossings at foot of page, brief notes at end of text; Small edn).

Leslie S, An Anthology of Catholic Poets, N Y 1925, p 102 (from [29]; spelling modernized).

Henderson T F, A Scots Garland, Edinburgh 1931, p 168 (from [29]).

Patterson R F, Six Centuries of English Literature, London and Glasgow 1933, 1.188 ([29]).

Mackie R L, A Book of Scottish Verse, The World's Classics, no 417, London 1934, p 59 ([32], [29]; glossings at foot of page); 2nd edn 1967, p 58.

Gray M M, Scottish Poetry from Barbour to James VI, N Y 1935, pp 160, 165 ([32], [29]; crit J Speirs, Scrut 6.83; W M Mackenzie, The Scottish Bookman 1, no 4, p 133).

[Grieve C M] MacDiarmid H, The Golden Treasury of Scottish Poetry, London 1940 (crit L MacNeice, The New Statesman and Nation, 21.66; TLS Feb 15 1941, pp 78, 84); rptd in The Golden Treasury Series, London 1948, p 21 ([29]).

Fergusson J, The Green Garden, London and Edinburgh 1946, pp 28, 42 (from [28], [29]; spelling modernized).

Oliver J W and J C Smith, A Scots Anthology from the 13th to the 20th Century, Edinburgh and London 1949, p 46 ([32], [29]; spelling modernized, glossings at foot of page).

Auden W H and N H Pearson, Poets of the English Language, N Y 1950, p 302 ([29]).

[Grieve C M] MacDiarmid H, Selections from the Poems of William Dunbar, The Saltire Classics, Edinburgh 1952, pp 17, 39, 45 ([32], [24], from [28], [29]; glossings in footnotes; Mackenzie edn).

McClure N E, Sixteenth-century English Poetry, N Y 1954, p 28 ([29]; glossings at foot of page; PRINT 4).

Grieve] MacDiarmid, Selected Poems of William Dunbar, Glasgow 1955, pp 24, 55 ([24], [29]).

Kinsley J, William Dunbar Poems, Oxford 1958, pp 43, 59, 79, 118, 123, 128 ([26], [24], [25], [29], [32], [28]; notes at end of text; MSS 1, 2, 3, PRINT 4; crit TLS Apr 18 1958, p 208; D Young, SHR 38.10; E Morgan, RES ns 11.71; J Wordsworth, MÆ 30.128).

McLaren M, The Wisdom of the Scots, London 1961, p 70 ([31]; glossings in margin).

Davies R T, Medieval English Lyrics A Critical Anthology, London 1963, pp 250, 348 (lines 1–52, 81–100 of [29]; glossings at foot of page, notes at end of text; MS 3).

Rossi S, I Chauceriani Scozzesi, Napoli 1964, p 204 ([29]; notes at foot of page).

MacQueen J and T Scott, The Oxford Book of Scottish Verse, Oxford 1966, p 101 ([32], [29]; glossings at foot of page; Mackenzie edn).

Scott T, Late Medieval Scots Poetry, London 1967, pp 107, 117, 184 ([23], [25], [32], [29]; notes at end of text; Mackenzie edn).

Ridley F [H], Selected Poems of William Dunbar, Los Angeles 1969, pp 7, 13 ([25], [32]; glossings in margin; MSS 1, 2).

Kinghorn A M, The Middle Scots Poets, London 1970, p 123 ([29]; notes at foot of page; PRINT 4).

Scott T, The Penguin Book of Scottish Verse, London 1970, pp 128, 148 ([32], [29], [25]; glossings at foot of page).

Modernization. [Robertson J L] Haliburton H, Dunbar Being a Selection from the Poems of an Old Makar Adapted for Modern Readers, London 1895, pp 11, 26, 34, 42, 103 ([24], [25], from [29], from [32], from [28]; essentially modernized paraphrase, abbreviated, extremely free; crit R Brotanek, AnglB 6.71).

Textual Matters. Irving D, The Lives of the Scotish Poets, 2nd edn, London 1810, 1.393 ([28]).

Laing, edn, 2.293, 301, 341, 370, 417 ([24], [27], [30], [32], [28]).

Schipper, edn, pt 1, 40².4, 16, 19, 25; pt 2, 40⁴.53; pt 4, 42⁴.27 ([28], [29], [32]; see also introductory and ftnts to individual poems).

Brown J T T, The Bannatyne Manuscript, SHR 1.147 ([29]).

Dickins B, Contributions to the Interpretation of Middle Scots Texts, TLS Feb 21 1924, p 112 ([28]).

Isaac F, Walter Chepman and Andrew Myllar, Facsimiles and Illustrations No II, English and Scottish Printing Types, printed for Bibliographical Soc, Oxford 1930 (unpaged; [28]; brief discussion and figure 86).

Mackenzie, edn, pp 197ff ([23–32]).

Dickins B, The Flyting of Dunbar and Kennedy, TLS Dec 14 1935, p 859; Jan 20 1945, p 31.

Baxter J W, William Dunbar, Edinburgh and London 1952, pp 65, 126, 128, 133, 136, 143, 178, 192, 235 ([28], [26], [27], [29], [32], [24], [31], [30]; crit M P McDiarmid, SHR 33.46; M Lindsay, Saltire Review 1.84).

Language. Ramsay A, The Ever Green, Edinburgh 1724, 2.265 ([29], [24], [28], [30]; glossary).

Dalrymple D, Ancient Scottish Poems, Edinburgh 1770, p 317 (glossary); rptd Leeds 1815, p 367, [added] Glossary, p 1 [separate pagination] ([26], [24], [31], [30], [23], [29]).

Pinkerton J, Select Scottish Ballads, London 1783, 1.154; 2.193 ([24]; glossaries).

Pinkerton J, Ancient Scotish Poems, London and Edinburgh 1786, 1.cxliii; 2.520 ([27], [32]; synorthographic and symphonious words, glossary).

Sibbald J, Chronicle of Scottish Poetry, Edinburgh and London 1802, vol 4 [unpaged] (glossary; [26], [23], [29], [24], [28], [30–32]).

Irving D, The History of Scotish Poetry, ed J A Carlyle, Edinburgh 1861, p 595 (glossary; [28]).

Murray J A H, The Dialect of the Southern Counties of Scotland, London 1873 (group as a whole).

Kaufmann J, Traité de la langue, Bonn 1873, p 47 (group as a whole).

Hahn O, Zur Verbal- und Nominalflexion bei den schottischen Dichtern, Berlin 1887–89 (see especially pt 3, p 17; group as a whole).

Schipper, edn, pt 1, 40².18 (group as a whole).

Gregor W, Glossary, Small edn, 3.401 (group as a whole).

Curtis F J, An Investigation of the Rimes and Phonology of Clariodus, Angl 16.387; 17.1, 125 (group as a whole).

Bearder J W, Über den Gebrauch der Praepositionen in der altschottischen Poesie, Halle 1894 ([28], [26]; examples from Dunbar; crit J E Wülfing, EStn 19.410).

Browne W H, Selections from the Early Scottish Poets, Baltimore 1896, pp 4, 197 ([26], [32]; discussion in introd, glossary).

Heuser W, Die Dehnung vor -nd im Mittelschottischen, Die Dehnung -*end,* Angl 19.401 (brief; group as a whole).

Baildon H B, On the Rimes in the Authentic Poems of William Dunbar, Trans Royal Soc Edinburgh 39³.629; issued separately Edinburgh 1899 (group as a whole).

Flom G T, Scandinavian Influence on Southern Lowland Scotch, diss Columbia 1900 (group as a whole).

Arber E, English Songs, The Dunbar Anthology, British Anthologies, London 1901, 1.300 ([29], [26]; glossary, index).

Millar J H, A Literary History of Scotland, London 1903, p 687 (glossary; [26], [28–29]).

Browne W H, The Taill of Rauf Coilyear, Baltimore 1903, pp 15, 35, 139 (general discussion of Middle Scots, glossary; group as a whole).

Knopff P, Darstellung der Ablautverhältnisse in der schottischen Schriftsprache, diss Würzburg 1904 (group as a whole).

Baildon, edn, pp xxvi, 299 (discussion, glossary; group as a whole).

CHEL, 2.101, 506 (group as a whole).

Dixon W M, The Edinburgh Book of Scottish Verse, London 1910, p 897 (glossary; [29], [32]).

Zupitza J, Alt- und mittelenglisches Übungsbuch, 10th edn Vienna and Leipzig 1912, p 208 ([26]; glossary, definitions in German).

Gray M M, Introd, Lancelot of the Laik, PSTS ns 2, Edinburgh and London 1912, 2.xviii (group as a whole).

Lenz K, Zur Lautlehre der französischen Elemente in den schottischen Dichtungen, diss Marburg 1913 (examples taken from Douglas, Dunbar, Lyndesay, Clariodus; group as a whole).

Westergaard E, Prepositions in Lowland Scotch, Angl 41.444 (some examples from Dunbar; group as a whole); Verbal Forms in Middle-Scotch, Angl 43.95 (group as a whole).

Craigie W A, ed, The Maitland Folio, PSTS ns 7, 20, 2 vols, Edinburgh and London 1919–27, 2.135 (glossary; [32], [27–28], [30], [29], [24], [31], [26]).

Watt L M, Language and Influences, Douglas's Aeneid, Cambridge 1920, p 149 (very generally applicable; group as a whole; crit C R Baskerville, MP 18.171; J W Bright, MLN 35.508; O L Jiriczek, LfGRP 42.379; G D Willcock, MLR 15.432; TLS Apr 1 1920, p 210).

Westergaard E, Studies in Prefixes and Suffixes in Middle Scottish, diss London 1924 (group as a whole).

Wilson J, The Spelling of Scotch before 1600, The Dialects of Central Scotland, London 1926, p 168 (group as a whole; attempts to determine pronunciation from spelling, rimes, modern Lothian pronunciation).

Westergaard E, Plural Forms in Lowland Scottish, Angl 51.77 (group as a whole).

Lawson Mrs A and A Lawson, A St Andrews Treasury of Scottish Verse, 2nd edn London 1933, p 263 (glossary; [32]).

Ritchie R L G, Early Instances of French Loan-Words in Scots and English, EStn 63.41 ([29], [28]; examples from Dunbar).

Henderson T F, A Scots Garland, Edinburgh 1931, p 182 (glossary; [29]).

Mackenzie, edn, pp xii, xxxvii, 245 ([23–32]; discussion, glossary).

Wood H H, The Poems and Fables of Robert Henryson, Edinburgh 1933; 2nd edn rvsd, Edinburgh 1958; rptd 1965, 1968, p xxxi.

Patrick D, Scottish Literature, Chambers's Cyclopædia, rvsd J L Geddie, Phila and N Y 1938, 1.164 (group as a whole).

[Grieve C M] MacDiarmid H, The Golden Treasury of Scottish Poetry, London 1940; rptd in The Golden Treasury Series, London 1948, p 389 (glossary; [29]).

Fergusson J, The Green Garden, London and Edinburgh 1946, p 228 (glossary; [28–29]).

Oliver J W and J C Smith, A Scots Anthology, Edinburgh and London 1949, p 497 (glossaries; [29], [32]).

[Grieve C M] MacDiarmid H, Selections from the Poems of William Dunbar, The Saltire Classics, Edinburgh 1952, pp 5, 49 ([32], [24], [28], [29]; brief note, glossary); Selected Poems of William Dunbar, Glasgow 1955, p 60 ([24], [29]; glossary).

Kinsley J, William Dunbar Poems, Oxford 1958, p 139 (glossary; [26], [24–25], [29], [32], [28]).

Wittig K, The Scottish Tradition in Literature, Edinburgh 1958, pp 62, 101 and passim ([28]; general reference to group as a whole).

Rossi S, I Chauceriani Scozzesi, Napoli 1964, p 261 ([29]; discussion and glossary).

Scott T, Dunbar A Critical Exposition of the Poems, Edinburgh and London 1966, pp 346, 351; Late Medieval Scots Poetry, London 1967, pp 21, 189 ([32], [23], [25], [29]; discussion and glossary).

Conley J, William Dunbar Additions to and Corrections of OED and DOST, N&Q 213 (ns 15). 169 ([26], [28], [23]).

Hope A D, A Midsummer Eve's Dream, N Y 1970, p 319 ([29]; glossary).

Kinghorn A M, The Middle Scots Poets, London 1970, pp 45, 164 ([29]).

Versification. Guest E, A History of English Rhythms, 2 vols, London 1838; ed W W Skeat, new edn [in 1 vol] London 1882, pp 464, 649 ([29], [32]).

Schipper, passim ([26], [29], [25]).

Bulloch J M, French Metres in Early Scottish Poetry, Scottish Notes and Queries 2.115, 130 ([28], [26], [29]).

McNeill G P, Note on the Versification and Metres of Dunbar, Small edn, 1.clxxix ([26], [32], [25], [28–31], [23–24], [27]).

Schipper, edn, pt 2, 40⁴.51 ([28]; discussion in headnote to poem).

Brandl, 2¹.1062, 1067 ([29], [25]).

Curtis F J, An Investigation of the Rimes and Phonology of Clariodus, Angl 16.387; 17.1, 125 (group as a whole).

Baildon H B, Burns and Dunbar, Scottish Art and Letters 2.167 ([28]).

Henderson T F, Scottish Vernacular Literature, Edinburgh 1898; 1900; 3rd edn rvsd, Edinburgh 1910, p 155 ([28–29], [25]).

Baildon H B, Rimes in the Authentic Poems of Dunbar, Trans Royal Soc Edinburgh 39³.629 (group as a whole).

Saintsbury G, History of English Prosody, London 1908, 2nd edn 1923, 1.273 ([29]).

Legouis HEL, p 176 ([29]).

Smith J M, The French Background of Middle Scots Literature, Edinburgh and London 1934, pp 56, 159 ([28], [29]; crit AnglB 45.265; MÆ 4.44).

Moore A K, The Secular Lyric in Middle English, Lexington Ky 1951, p 199 ([27]).

Baxter J W, William Dunbar, Edinburgh and London 1952, p 69 ([28]).

Morgan E, Dunbar and the Language of Poetry, EC 2.147 ([28]).

McClure N E, Sixteenth Century English Poetry, The Harper Eng Lit Series, ed K J Holzknecht, N Y 1954, p 19 ([29]).

Wittig K, The Scottish Tradition in Literature, Edinburgh 1958, pp 58 and passim ([29], [24]).

Leyerle J, The Two Voices of William Dunbar, UTQ 31.336 ([28]).

Scott T, Dunbar A Critical Exposition of the Poems, pp 141, 306, 311, 313 ([30], [27], [26], [32], [25], [28], [29], [24], [31], [23]); Late Medieval Scots Poetry, p 19 ([29]).

Date. Laing, edn, 1.13, 29 (Memoirs); 2.232, 331, 352, 371, 420, 437, 452 ([28], [29], [26], [23], [32]).

Paterson, edn, pp 19, 21, 29, 106, 187, 205, 224, 248 ([28], [29], [24], [26], [23], [31], [32]).

Schipper J, William Dunbar sein Leben und seine Gedichte, Berlin 1884, pp 245, 254, 290, 296, 298, 310 ([27], [26], [29], [31], [30], [32]).

Mackay Æ J G, Introd [and] Appendix to Introd, Small edn, 1.xl, cxii, cxxxi, cxxxiii, clxiii, clxv, clxvii ([29], [28], [32], [30], [31], [26], [25], [27], [23], [24]).

Morley, 7.140 ([28]).

Schipper, edn, pt 2, 40⁴.52, 56; pt 3, 41⁴.28, 34, 38, 40, 86; pt 4, 42⁴.1, 4, 27 ([28], [27], [23], [25], [24], [26], [29], [31], [30], [32]).

Steinberger C, Étude sur William Dunbar, Dublin 1908, p 106 ([28]).

Baxter J W, William Dunbar, Edinburgh and London 1952, pp 60, 74, 126, 133 ([23], [28], [26], [29]).

Lewis C S, English Literature in the Sixteenth Century, Oxford 1954, 3.91 ([28], [29]).

Fox D, The Chronology of William Dunbar, PQ 39.418 ([23], [25], [26], [27], [28], [29], [30], [31], [32]).

Elliott C, Robert Henryson Poems, Oxford 1963, p xvii ([29]); rptd from corrected sheets, Oxford 1966.

Scott T, Dunbar A Critical Exposition of the Poems, p 362 ([28]).

Kinghorn A M, Dunbar and Villon A Comparison and a Contrast, MLR 62.196 ([29]).

MacQueen J, Some Aspects of the Early Renaissance in Scotland, Forum Mod Lang Stud 3.203 ([29]).

Authorship. Baxter J W, William Dunbar, p 193 ([30], [31]).

Sources and Literary Relations. Irving D, The Lives of the Scotish Poets, 2nd edn London 1810, 1.440 ([26]).

Laing, edn, 1.315, 319; 2.232, 331, 361, 417 ([29], [28], [26], [23]).

Paterson, edn, pp 252, 340, 342 ([29], [28]).

Irving D, The History of Scotish Poetry, ed J A Carlyle, Edinburgh 1861, p 250 ([28]).

Schipper J, William Dunbar sein Leben und seine Gedichte, Berlin 1884, pp 64, 206, 250 ([28], [23]).

Cranstoun J, The Poems of Alexander Montgomerie, PSTS 9, 10, 11, Edinburgh and London 1887, pp xxxiii, 308, 318, 320, 326, 337, 345, 354 ([28; brief discussion and scattered references in notes).

Mackay Æ J G, Introd, Small edn, 1.xxiii, xl,

cix, cxxii, cxxix, cxxxi ([26], [29], [28], [27]).
Morley, 7.140 ([28]).
Schipper, edn, pt 2, 40⁴.51 ([28]).
Horneber F, Über King Hart und Testament of the Papyngo, Straubing 1893, p 23 ([25]; crit AnglB 4.328).
[Robertson J L] Haliburton H, Dunbar in Burns, Furth in Field, London 1894, p 280 ([32]).
Brotanek R, Untersuchungen über das Leben und die Dichtungen Alexander Montgomeries, WBEP 3.95 and passim ([28]; crit O Hoffmann, EStn 24.436).
Turnbull W R, The Heritage of Burns, Haddington 1896, pp 238, 251 ([29]; brief references).
Henderson T F, Scottish Vernacular Literature, Edinburgh 1898, 1900; 3rd edn rvsd Edinburgh 1910, p 181 ([29]).
Wollmann F, Über politisch-satirische Gedichte aus der schottischen Reformationszeit, WBEP 8.43 ([31], [30]; brief).
Smith G G, The Transition Period, Periods of European Lit, Edinburgh and London 1900, 4.36, 39, 42, and passim ([28]).
Chambers R, Chambers's Cyclopædia, Phila and N Y 1901–03; rvsd J L Geddie, Phila and N Y 1938, 1.195, 199 ([29], [28]).
Gummere F B, The Beginnings of Poetry, N Y 1901, p 150 ([29]; brief).
CHEL, 2.289, 291 ([26], [28], [29]).
Steinberger C, Étude sur William Dunbar, Dublin 1908, pp 105, 123 ([28], [29]; Poggo, Pulci, Matteo Franco, Villon).
Tucker S M, Verse Satire in England, CUS 3, no 2, pp 57, 137, 141 ([28], [26]).
Patterson F A, The Middle English Penitential Lyric, N Y 1911, p 23 ([29]; brief).
Sandison H E, The Chanson D'Aventure in Middle English, Bryn Mawr Pa 1913, p 147 ([30]).
Ayres H M, Theodulus in Scots, MP 15.539 ([28]).
Taylor A, Notes on the Wandering Jew, MLN 33.394 ([28]).
Mendenhall J C, Aureate Terms A Study in the Literary Diction of the 15th Century, Lancaster Pa 1919 (group as a whole).
Jacobi J B, William Dunbar—an Appreciation, The American Catholic Quarterly Review 44.314 ([29]).
Schofield W H, Mythical Bards, HSCL 5.passim ([29]).
Knowlton E C, Nature in Middle English, JEGP 20.191 ([32]).
Patch H R, The Goddess Fortuna in Mediæval Lit, Cambridge Mass 1927, p 115 ([32]; brief).

Ker W P, Form and Style in Poetry, London 1928, p 88 ([28]).
Saintsbury G, The Four Great Scottish Poets, A Short History of Eng Lit, N Y 1929, p 187 ([28], [29]).
Nichols P H, William Dunbar as a Scottish Lydgatian, PMLA 46.215 ([29], [30], [31]).
Mackenzie, edn, p xxxii ([28]); William Dunbar, Edinburgh Essays on Scots Literature, Edinburgh and London 1933, p 41 ([28]).
Smith J M, The French Background of Middle Scots Literature, Edinburgh and London 1934, pp 40, 49, 51, 69 ([30], [28], [29], [32]; crit AnglB 45.265; MÆ 4.44).
Patrick D, Scottish Literature, Chambers's Cyclopædia, rvsd J L Geddie, Phila and N Y 1938, 1.166 (group as a whole).
Clark J M, The Dance of Death in the Middle Ages, Glasgow Univ Publ 86, Glasgow 1950, p 20 ([29]).
Moore A K, The Secular Lyric in Middle English, Lexington Ky 1951, pp 206, 209, 215 ([25], [32], [29]).
Baxter J W, William Dunbar, Edinburgh and London 1952, pp 65, 134 ([28], [29]).
Morgan E, Dunbar and the Language of Poetry, EC 2.151 ([29]).
Kinsley J, The Mediaeval Makars, Scottish Poetry, A Critical Survey, London 1955, pp 26, 31 ([28], [29]); William Dunbar Poems, Oxford 1958, pp xvi, xxvi ([29], [26]).
Mackie R L, King James IV of Scotland, Edinburgh and London 1958, p 181 ([29]; brief; crit SHR 38.133).
Kinghorn A M, The Mediaeval Makars, Texas Stud Lit and Lang 1.73 ([28], [29], [32]).
Schirmer W F, John Lydgate ein Kulturbild aus dem 15 Jahrhundert, Tubingen 1952; trans A E Keep, John Lydgate A Study in the Culture of the XVth Century, Berkeley and Los Angeles 1961, p 204 ([29]).
Leyerle J, The Two Voices of William Dunbar, UTQ 31.334 ([28]).
Gray D, Two Songs of Death, NM 64.58, 63 ([29]).
Rigg A G, William Dunbar The Fenyeit Freir, RES ns 14.270 ([26]).
Maclaine A H, The Christis Kirk Tradition Its Evolution in Scots Poetry to Burns, SSL 2.16 ([25]).
Fox D, The Scottish Chaucerians, Chaucer and Chaucerians, ed D S Brewer, University Alabama 1966, p 164 (see especially p 181; [28]).
Scott T, Dunbar A Critical Exposition of the Poems, Edinburgh and London 1966,

pp 2, 37, 175, 246, 250, 270, 318, 335, 337, 345 and passim ([28], [32], [29], [26], [25]).

Kinghorn A M, Dunbar and Villon, MLR 62.196, 204, 208 ([29], [32], [28], [31]).

Scott T, Late Medieval Scots Poetry, London 1967, p 19 ([29]).

Swetnam F T Jr, Lattimore's Witness to Death, Expl 25.59 ([29]).

Bennett J A W, Chaucer's Book of Fame, Oxford 1968, p 169 ([29]).

Woolf R, The English Religious Lyric in the Middle Ages, Oxford 1968, p 335 ([29]).

Scheps W, William Wallace and His Buke Some Instances of Their Influence on Subsequent Literature, SSL 6.224 ([28]).

Other Scholarly Problems. Pinkerton J, Ancient Scotish Poems, London and Edinburgh 1786, 1.xcii ([28], [26]; biographical evidence).

The Scottish Register, Edinburgh 1794, 2.195 ([26]; biographical evidence).

Irving D, The Lives of the Scotish Poets, 2nd edn London 1810, 1.392 ([28], [26]; biographical evidence, attitude).

Tytler P F, Lives of Scottish Worthies, London 1833, 3. 89 ([26]; biographical evidence, illustrative quote).

Laing, edn, 1.10, 13, 15, 58 (Memoirs); 2.300, 355, 417, 420, 426, 458 ([26], [28], [27], [29]; biographical evidence, questionable morality of writings, identity of subjects).

Ancient Scotish Poetry No I Dunbar, Blackwood's Edinburgh Magazine 37.290 ([26], [28]; biographical evidence).

Wright T, On the Scottish Poet Dunbar, Essays on Subjects Connected with the Literature Popular Superstitions and History of England in the Middle Ages, London 1846, 2.293 ([26]; biographical evidence).

The Ballads and Songs of Ayrshire, Edinburgh 1847, p 85 ([28]; attitude, identity of subject).

William Dunbar, The Scottish Journal 1.129 ([26], [28]; biographical evidence).

Paterson, edn, pp 174, 247, 253, 340 ([27], [32], [29], [28]; identity of subjects, occasion, biographical evidence).

Irving D, The History of Scotish Poetry, ed J A Carlyle, Edinburgh 1861, p 253 ([28]; identity of subject).

Kaufmann J, Traité de la langue, Bonn 1873, pp 2, 16 ([28], [26]; biographical evidence, occasion).

Veitch J, History and Poetry of the Scottish Border, Edinburgh 1878; new and enlarged edn Edinburgh 1893, 2.83 ([29]; identity of subject).

Nichol J, A Sketch of Scottish Poetry, ed J Small, 2nd edn rvsd EETS 11, London 1883, p xxvi ([26]; biographical evidence).

Schipper J, William Dunbar sein Leben und seine Gedichte, Berlin 1884, pp 66, 73, 76, 86, 94 ([28], [25], [29]; biographical evidence; crit EStn 10.128; Angl 7.146; The Nation 40.144).

DNB, 16.154 ([26], [28]; biographical evidence).

Mackay Æ J G, Introd, Small edn, 1.xli ([29]; identity of subject).

Minto W, Characteristics of English Poets, authorized American edn, Boston 1899, p 99 ([26]; biographical evidence).

[Robertson J L] Haliburton H, Our Earlier Burns, In Scottish Fields, London 1890, pp 215, 218, 221 ([28], [26]; biographical evidence, occasion).

Morley, 7.139, 142 ([28], [29]; identity of subjects).

Schipper, edn, pt 3, 41⁴.28, 39 ([27], [26]; identity of subject, biographical evidence).

Oliphant F R, William Dunbar, Blackwood's Edinburgh Magazine 154.417, 433 ([28], [26], [23], [29]; biographical evidence, occasion).

Henderson T F, Scottish Vernacular Literature, Edinburgh 1898; 3rd edn rvsd Edinburgh 1910, p 142 ([28]; identity of subject, attitude).

Smeaton O, William Dunbar, N Y (1898?), pp 24, 34, 38, 52, 54, 58, 98, 105, 152 ([28], [26], [25], [29], [31]; biographical evidence; crit J W Baxter, William Dunbar, Edinburgh and London 1952, passim; The Scottish Antiquary 13.95).

Brown J T T, The Wallace and The Bruce Restudied, BBA 6.62 ([29]; identity of subject).

Rait R S, An Outline of the Relations between England and Scotland, London 1901, p xxxiv ([28]; attitude, brief).

Schipper J, The Poems of Walter Kennedy, Denkschriften der kaiserlichen Akademie der Wissenschaften, Philo-Hist Classe, Vienna 1902, 48¹.1 ([28]; attitude, biographical evidence).

Millar J H, A Literary History of Scotland, London 1903, p 9 ([29]; identity of subject).

Teichert O P, Schottische Zustände unter Jacob IV nach den Dichtungen von William Dunbar, Görlitz 1903, pp 8, 14, 19, 27, 30 ([26], [31], [30], [28]; contemp conditions; crit O Glöde, EStn 36.267).

CHEL, 2.285 ([26]; biographical evidence).

Brown J T T, Vidas Achinlek Chevalier, SHR 8.325 ([29]; identity of subject).

Gray M, Vidas Achinlek Chevalier, SHR

8.321 ([29]; identity of subject).

Lawson A, Vidas Achinlek Chevalier, SHR 8.324 ([29]; identity of subject).

Skeat W W, Vidas Achinlek Chevalier, SHR 8.324 ([29]; identity of subject).

Stair-Kerr E, The Poets, Scotland under James IV, Paisley 1911, p 122 ([29]; identity of subject).

Ayres H M, Theodulus in Scots, MP 15.539 ([28]; chronology, purpose, obscure passage).

Dickins B, Middle Scots Texts, TLS July 10 1924, p 436 ([28]; obscure word).

Moore A K, The Secular Lyric in Middle English, Lexington Ky 1951, p 196 ([26]; biographical evidence).

Baxter J W, William Dunbar, Edinburgh and London 1952, pp 62, 192, 229 ([28], [31], [29]; identity of subjects, occasion).

[Grieve C M] MacDiarmid H, Selections from the Poems of William Dunbar, The Saltire Classics, Edinburgh 1952, p 39 ([28]; identity of subject).

Renwick-Orton, p 416 ([26]; biographical evidence).

Milner I, Some Aspects of Satire in the Poetry of Dunbar, Philologica (cizojazyčná priloha Casopisu pro moderní filologii) 8.33, 41 ([26], [28], [29], [32]; contemp conditions; attitude).

Mackie R L, King James IV of Scotland, Edinburgh and London 1958, p 175 ([28], [26]; biographical evidence; crit SHR 38.133).

Fox D, The Chronology of William Dunbar, PQ 39.414 ([28]; biographical evidence).

Rigg A G, William Dunbar The Fenyeit Freir, RES ns 14.269, 272 ([26], [28]; biographical evidence).

Scott T, Dunbar A Critical Exposition, Edinburgh and London 1966, pp 10, 134, 138, 143, 269, ([23], [30], [25], [31], [26], [28]; contemp conditions, occasion, biographical evidence).

Wood H H, Two Scots Chaucerians, Writers and Their Work, no 201, ed G Bullough, London 1967, pp 23, 39 ([28], [26], [30]; biographical evidence).

Kinghorn A M, Dunbar and Villon, MLR 62.199 ([30], [32]; biographical evidence).

Scott T, Late Medieval Scots Poetry, London 1967, p 31 ([23], [25]; contemp conditions, occasion).

Dorsch T S, Of Discretioun in Asking Dunbar's Petitionary Poems, Chaucer und Seine Zeit Symposion für Walter F Schirmer, ed A Esch, Tübingen 1968, p 288 ([23]; attitude).

Literary Criticism. Irving D, The Lives of the Scotish Poets, 2nd edn London 1810, 1.395, 430, 440 ([28], [32], [26]).

Tytler P F, Lives of Scottish Worthies, London 1833, 3. 112 ([28]).

Laing, edn, 1.14, 58 (Memoirs); 2.310, 331, 343, 352, 370 ([28], [25], [23], [31], [29], [32]).

Ancient Scotish Poetry No I Dunbar, Blackwood's Edinburgh Magazine 37.307 ([25], [32]).

The Ballads and Songs of Ayrshire, Edinburgh 1847, p 84 ([28]).

Paterson, edn, pp 16, 25, 92, 224, 247, 252, 340 ([28], [29], [24], [31], [32]).

Irving D, The History of Scotish Poetry, ed J A Carlyle, Edinburgh 1861, pp 240, 250, 253 ([32], [28]).

Smith A, William Dunbar Dreamthorp, London 1863; rptd no 200 The World's Classics, London 1914; rptd London 1934, p 72 ([28]).

Taylor J, The Imperial Dictionary of Universal Biography, London [1863], 2.170 ([32], [28]; brief).

Kaufmann J, Traité de la langue, Bonn 1873, p 17 ([28]).

Morley H, A First Sketch of English Literature, London 1873; rvsd London 1896, p 213 [28–29].

Wright T, The History of Scotland, London and N Y [1873–74], 1.291 ([29]; brief).

Mackintosh J, The History of Civilisation in Scotland, London and Edinburgh 1878–88; new edn partly rewritten Paisley 1892–96, 2.309 ([28]).

Veitch J, History and Poetry of the Scottish Border, Edinburgh 1878; new and enlarged edn Edinburgh 1893, 2.82 ([29]).

Nichol J, William Dunbar, The English Poets, ed T H Ward, London and N Y 1880 (numerous subsequent edns), N Y 1924, 1.150 ([32]; very brief); A Sketch of Scottish Poetry, ed J Small, 2nd edn rvsd EETS 11, London 1883, p xxvii ([26]).

Ross J M, Scottish History and Literature, Glasgow 1884, pp 206, 210 ([28], [29], [30], [31], [26], [23]).

Schipper J, William Dunbar sein Leben und seine Gedichte, Berlin 1884, pp 64, 206, 249, 253, 296, 310, 352 ([28], [23], [24], [26], [31], [32]).

DNB, 16.155 ([28–29]).

Fitzgibbon H M, Early English and Scottish Poetry, London N Y and Melbourne 1888, p lxi ([29]).

Shairp J C, Sketches in History and Poetry, Edinburgh 1887, p 209 ([29]; brief).

Veitch J, The Feeling for Nature in Scottish

Poetry, Edinburgh and London 1887, 1.234 ([32], [29]; with illustrative quotes).

Mackay Æ J G, Introd, Small edn, l.xl, cviii, cxxii, cxxix, cxxxvi ([29], [28], [27], [26], [32], [30–31]).

Minto W, Characteristics of English Poets, authorized American edn, Boston 1899, p 105 ([28]).

[Robertson J L] Haliburton H, Our Earlier Burns, In Scottish Fields, London 1890, pp 221, 238 ([28–29], [25], [32]).

Eyre-Todd G, Mediæval Scottish Poetry, Abbotsford Series, Glasgow 1892, p 154 ([28–29]).

Schipper, edn, pt 2, 40⁴.50; pt 3, 41⁴.28, 34, 38, 86; pt 4, 42⁴.1, 4, 26 ([28], [27], [23], [24], [29], [31], [30], [32]).

Oliphant F R, William Dunbar, Blackwood's Edinburgh Magazine 154.417, 433, 436 ([28–29]).

Ten Brink, 3.67, 71, 75 ([28], [26], [29]).

Turnbull W R, The Heritage of Burns, Haddington 1896, p 238 ([29]; brief).

Gosse E, A Short History of Modern English Literature, N Y 1897; rvsd edn, N Y 1906, p 48 ([29]).

Smeaton O, A Quartette of Court Singers Four Centuries Ago, Westminster Review 148.183 ([28], [29]; brief, extravagant, fictionalized).

Henderson T F, Scottish Vernacular Literature, Edinburgh 1898; 3rd edn rvsd Edinburgh 1910, pp 144, 153, 180 ([28–29]).

Smeaton O, William Dunbar, N Y (1898?), pp 59, 98, 134, 146 ([28–29], [31]).

Smith G G, The Transition Period, Periods of European Lit, Edinburgh and London 1900, 4.50 and passim ([28]).

Chambers R, Chambers's Cyclopædia, Phila and N Y 1901–03; rvsd J L Geddie, Phila and N Y 1938, 1.196, 199 ([29], [26], [28]).

Gummere F B, The Beginnings of Poetry, N Y 1901, p 150 ([29]; brief).

M'Ilwraith W, A Sketch of Scottish Literature, Annual Burns Chronicle 10.21 ([29]).

Baildon H, Burns and Dunbar, Scottish Art and Letters 2.263 ([29]).

Browne W H, The Taill of Rauf Coilyear, Baltimore 1903, p 17 ([28–29]).

Millar J H, A Literary History of Scotland, London 1903, p 60 ([28–29]).

Ranken T E, The Scottish Reformation and Vernacular Literature, The Month 103.269 ([29]).

Moorman F W, The Interpretation of Nature in English Poetry from Beowulf to Shakespeare, QF 95.150 ([32]; brief).

Smeaton O, The Story of Edinburgh, London 1905, p 403 ([29]; brief).

Snell F J, The Poets, The Age of Transition, London 1905, 1.87 ([28]).

Wülker R, Geschichte der englischen Literatur, Leipzig and Wien 1906–07, 1.208 ([28–29]; brief comment).

CHEL, 2.289, 291 ([26], [28–29]).

Steinberger C, Étude sur William Dunbar, Dublin 1908, pp 104, 121, 127 ([28–29], [32], [30–31]).

Tucker S M, Verse Satire in England, CUS 3, no 2, pp 137, 141 ([26], [28]).

Enc Brit, 8.669 ([28–29]).

Stair-Kerr E, The Poets, Scotland under James IV, Paisley 1911, p 122 ([29]; brief).

Watt L M, Scottish Life and Poetry, London 1912, p 104 ([28]).

Rhys E, The First Scottish Poets, Lyric Poetry, London Toronto and N Y 1913, p 101 ([28]).

Mackie R L, Scotland, London 1916, p 290 ([32], [29]).

Jacobi J B, William Dunbar—an Appreciation, The American Catholic Quarterly Rev 44.314 ([29]).

Smith G G, Scottish Literature Character and Influence, London 1919, p 14 ([28]; brief).

Barfield O, The Scottish Chaucerians, The New Statesman 17.274 ([29]).

Knowlton E C, Nature in Middle English, JEGP 20.191 ([32]).

Golding L, The Scottish Chaucerians, The Saturday Review of Politics Literature Science and Art 134.783 ([29]).

Quiller-Couch A, Studies in Literature, 2s, N Y and Cambridge Eng 1922, p 273 ([28]).

Powys L, William Dunbar, The Freeman 7.516 ([28–29]).

Ker W P, Form and Style in Poetry, London 1928, p 88 ([28]).

Jacob V, James IV and His Poet, Scots Magazine 10.280 ([28–29]).

Legouis HEL, p 176 ([29]).

Saintsbury G, The Four Great Scottish Poets, A Short Hist of Eng Lit, N Y 1929, p 187 ([28–29]; brief).

William Dunbar, TLS Apr 10 1930, p 306 ([29], [32]).

Taylor R A, Dunbar the Poet, The Poets on the Poets, no 4, London 1931, pp 62, 66, 68, 80 ([26], [28–29]; crit J M Reeves, The Criterion 11.331; TLS Mar 17 1932, p 199; D Everett, YWES 13.124); rptd Freeport Long Island N Y 1970.

Craigie W, The Northern Element in English Literature, Chicago 1933, pp 36, 52, 95 ([28–29]; crit The Modern Scot 4.163).

Mackenzie A M, An Historical Survey of Scottish Literature to 1714, London 1933, pp 94, 98 ([28–29]; crit The Modern Scot 4.164).

Elton O, The English Muse, London 1933, p 86 ([29]).

Mackenzie W M, William Dunbar, Edinburgh Essays on Scots Lit, Edinburgh and London 1933, p 41 ([28]).

Rait R and G S Pryde, Scotland, N Y 1934; 2nd edn London 1954, p 308 ([28–29]; brief).

Smith J M, The French Background of Middle Scots Literature, Edinburgh and London 1934, pp xxviii, 51, 65, 69, 72 ([28–29]).

Speirs J, William Dunbar, Scrut 7.64, 67 ([28], [32]).

Kerr J, An Almost Forgotten Scottish Poet, Poetry Review 29.374 ([29], [26]).

Speirs J, The Scots Literary Tradition, London 1940, pp 36, 49, 53 ([28], [32]; crit Scrut 9.193); 2nd edn rvsd London 1962, pp 55, 63.

Grierson H J C and J C Smith, A Critical History of English Poetry, London 1944; 2nd rvsd edn London 1947, p 56 ([32], [28]; brief).

Caird J B, Some Reflections on Scottish Literature, I. Poetry, Scottish Periodical 1.10 ([28], [32], [29]).

Craig HEL, p 168 ([28–29]; brief).

Moore A K, The Secular Lyric in ME, Lexington Ky 1951, pp 197, 199, 205, 215 ([32], [25], [28]).

Baxter J W, William Dunbar, Edinburgh and London 1952, pp 28, 60, 65, 81, 134 ([26], [23], [28–29], [32]).

Morgan E, Dunbar and the Language of Poetry, EC 2.148, 151 ([28–29]).

Renwick-Orton, p 416 ([28], [29]; brief).

Cunningham J V, Logic and Lyric, MP 51.33; rptd Tradition and Poetic Structure, Denver 1960, p 40 ([29]).

Ward A C, Illustrated Hist of Eng Lit, London N Y and Toronto 1953, p 41 ([28–29]; brief).

Hyman S E, The Language of Scottish Poetry, KR 16.32 ([29]; brief).

Lewis C S, English Literature in the Sixteenth Century, Oxford 1954, p 93 ([28–29], [26], [32]).

Towne F, Logic Lyric and Drama, MP 51.265 ([29]).

Kinsley J, The Mediaeval Makars, Scottish Poetry A Critical Survey, London 1955, pp 26, 31 ([32], [28–29]).

Milner I, Some Aspects of Satire in the Po-

etry of Dunbar, Philologica (cizojazyčná prioloha Časopisu pro moderní filologii) 8.33, 41 ([26], [28–29], [32]).

Peter J, Complaint and Satire in Early English Literature, Oxford 1956, pp 11, 51 ([28], [29]; brief reference).

Schlauch M, English Medieval Literature, Warsaw 1956, p 295 ([26], [29]).

Kinsley J, William Dunbar Poems, Oxford 1958, pp xvi, xix ([28], [29]).

Mackie R L, King James IV of Scotland, Edinburgh and London 1958, p 181 ([29]; brief comment).

Wittig K, The Scottish Tradition in Literature, Edinburgh 1958, pp 56, 58, 60 ([29], [24], [26–27]).

Fox D, Dunbar's The Golden Targe, ELH 26.311 ([29]).

Kinghorn A M, The Mediaeval Makars, Texas Stud Lit and Lang 1.78 ([25], [28], [29], [32]).

McLaren M, The Wisdom of the Scots, London 1961, p 68 ([31]).

Schirmer W F, John Lydgate ein Kulturbild aus dem 15 Jahrhundert, Tubingen 1952, trans A E Keep, John Lydgate A Study in the Culture of the XVth Century, Berkeley and Los Angeles 1961, p 204 ([29]).

Leyerle J, The Two Voices of William Dunbar, UTQ 31.334 ([28], [29]).

Rossi S, I Chauceriani Scozzesi, Napoli 1964, pp 50, 52 ([29], [28]).

Hyde I, Poetic Imagery A Comparison between Henryson and Dunbar, SSL 2.195 ([32]).

Fox D, The Scottish Chaucerians, Chaucer and Chaucerians, ed D S Brewer, University Alabama 1966, pp 180, 184 ([28], [29]).

Scott T, Dunbar A Critical Exposition, Edinburgh and London 1966, pp 2, 63, 93, 120, 134, 137, 164, 169, 183, 226, 239, 244, 256, 269, 285, 298, 304, 318, 333, 342, 345, 359 and passim ([28], [26], [23], [27], [25], [30], [31], [29], [32]).

Kinghorn A M, Dunbar and Villon, MLR 62.196, 204, 208 ([29], [32], [28], [31]).

MacQueen J, Some Aspects of the Early Renaissance in Scotland, Forum Mod Lang Stud 3.220 ([29]).

Scott T, Late Medieval Scots Poetry, London 1967, p 33 ([29]).

Wood H H, Two Scots Chaucerians, Writers and Their Work, no 201, ed G Bullough, London 1967, p 38 ([25], [27], [28]).

Woolf R, The English Religious Lyric in the Middle Ages, Oxford 1968, p 335 ([29]).

Bibliography. Geddie W, A Bibliography of

Middle Scots Poets, PSTS ns 61, Edinburgh
and London 1912, p 194 ([28]).
Beattie W, The Chepman and Myllar Prints
A Facsimile, Edinburgh Biblio Soc, Oxford
1950, pp xiii, xv ([28–29]; crit W A Jackson,

SHR 31.89).
Robbins-Cutler, nos 1148.5 ([24]), 1264.5 ([31]),
1370.5 ([29]), 1599.5 ([32]), 2226.5 ([30]),
2244.3 ([25]), 3051.5 ([23]), 3117.5 ([27]),
3117.8 ([28]), 3634.3 ([26]).

II. Petitions

(Note: Folios for items [33–46] are listed
by MS number, as appropriate, after each
title. See under *MSS* below for full listing
and information. Titles are from Mackenzie
edn.)

[33] QUHONE MONY BENEFICES
VAKIT.

1, ff 9ᵇ–10ᵃ; 2, pp 7–8, 316.

[34] TO THE KING—OFF BENEFICE
SCHIR.

1, ff 10ᵃ–10ᵇ; 2, pp 8–9, 321–322.

[35] OF THE WARLDIS INSTABILITIE.

1, ff 27ᵃ–28ᵇ; 2, pp 178–181.

[36] OF DISCRETIOUN IN ASKING.

1, ff 21ᵃ–21ᵇ; 2, pp 259–260; 3, pp 45–46, ff
61ᵃ–61ᵇ.

[37] OF DISCRETIOUN IN GEVING.

1, ff 22ᵃ–22ᵇ; 2, pp 260–261; 3, p 46, ff 61ᵇ–
62ᵇ.

[38] OF DISCRETIOUN IN TAKING.

1, ff 22ᵇ–23ᵃ; 2, pp 261–262; 3, ff 62ᵇ–63ᵃ.

[39] REMONSTRANCE TO THE KING.

2, pp 196–198.

[40] THAT THE KING WAR JOHNE
THOMSOUNIS MAN.

2, pp 194–195.

[41] COMPLAINT TO THE KING.

1, ff 13ᵃ–14ᵃ; 2, pp 16–18.

[42] TO THE KING—SCHIR YIT
REMEMBIR.

1, f 34ᵃ; 2, pp 295–309; 3, ff 94ᵇ–95ᵃ.

[43] NONE MAY ASSURE IN THIS
WARLD.

1, ff 40ᵇ–42ᵃ; 2, pp 331–333; 3, ff 84ᵃ–85ᵃ.

[44] THE PETITION OF THE GRAY
HORSE AULD DUNBAR.

1, ff 1ᵃ–1ᵇ, 14ᵃ–14ᵇ; 2, p 18.

[45] WELCOME TO THE LORD TREAS-
URER.

1, ff 5ᵇ–6ᵃ.

[46] TO THE LORDIS OF THE KINGIS
CHALKER.

1, ff 6ᵃ–6ᵇ.

MSS. 1, Camb Univ L1.5.10 (Reidpeth or
Moore), ff 1ᵃ–1ᵇ, 5ᵇ–6ᵇ, 9ᵇ–10ᵇ, 13ᵃ–14ᵇ, 21ᵃ–
23ᵃ, 27ᵃ–28ᵇ, 34ᵃ, 40ᵇ–42ᵃ (1623; contains
lines 1–24, 55–74 of item [44], and items
[45], [46], [33], [34], [41], lines 25–53 of item
[44], and items [36–38], [35], lines 76–85 of
item [42], and item [43]); 2, Magdalene
Coll Camb 2553 (Pepysian Libr, Maitland
Folio), pp 7–9, 16–18, 178–181, 194–198,
259–262, 295–296, 309, 316, 321–322, 331–
333 (1570–71; contains items [33–34], [41],
lines 23–52 of item [44], [35], [40], [39],
lines 1–15, 21–45 of item [36], lines 1–30,
36–60 of item [37], [38], [42–43]); 3, Nat
Libr Scot 1.1.6 (Bannatyne), pp 45–46, ff
61ᵃ–63ᵃ, 84ᵃ–85ᵃ, 94ᵇ–95ᵇ (1568; contains
items [36], lines 1–33 of [37], [38], [43],
[42]).
Pinkerton J, Ancient Scotish Poems, 2 vols,
London and Edinburgh 1786, 1.v; 2.437
(MSS 2, 3).
Brydges E and J Haslewood, The British
Bibliographer, London 1814, 4.183 (MS 3).
Laing D, The Poems of George Bannatyne,
Edinburgh 1824, p 3 (MS 3); An Account
of the Contents of George Bannatyne's
Manuscript, The Bannatyne Club, Edin-
burgh 1829, 35.43 (MS 3).
A Catalogue of the Manuscripts Preserved

in The Library of The University of Cambridge, Cambridge 1861, 4.94 (MS 1).

Small J, The Poetical Works of Gavin Douglas, Edinburgh and London 1874, l.clxxi (MS 2).

Schipper, edn, pt 1, 40².9ff (MSS 1, 2, 3).

Murdoch J B, ed, The Bannatyne Manuscript, 4 vols, Hunterian Club, Glasgow 1896, 2.165, 234, 271 (MS 3 rptd).

Smith G G, Specimens of Middle Scots, Edinburgh and London 1902, pp lxvi, lxxiii (MSS 2, 3).

Brown J T T, The Bannatyne Manuscript, SHR 1.136 (MS 3).

Craigie W A, ed, The Maitland Folio, PSTS ns 7, 20, 2 vols, Edinburgh and London 1919–27, 2.40, 51 (MS 1); 1.6, 17, 202, 220, 289, 346, 376, 385, 401; 2.36, 39, 101, 103, 110, 118, 122, 125 (MS 2 rptd, notes in vol 2); variants between MSS 1 and 2 listed in 2.101, 110, 125.

Ritchie W T, ed, The Bannatyne Manuscript Writtin in Tyme of Pest, PSTS ns 5, 22, 23, 26, 4 vols, Edinburgh 1928–34, 1.76; 2.150, 215, 251 (MS 3 rptd).

Baxter J W, William Dunbar, Edinburgh and London 1952, pp 217ff (MSS 1, 2, 3).

Editions. Laing D, The Poems of William Dunbar, 2 vols, Edinburgh 1834, 1.105, 109, 113, 142, 156, 159, 195, 204; 2.292, 297, 322, 330, 346, 350 (notes in vol 2; MSS 1 and 2; Memoirs of William Dunbar preceding text of poems in vol 1 is paginated separately).

Paterson J, The Life and Poems of William Dunbar, Edinburgh 1860 (crit Athen July 14 1860, p 49); reissued The Works of William Dunbar Including His Life, Edinburgh 1863, pp 56, 179, 202, 224, 238, 261, 275 (glossings in footnotes).

Small J, Æ J G Mackay, G P McNeill, W Gregor, The Poems of William Dunbar, PSTS 2, 4, 16, 21, 29, 3 vols, Edinburgh 1884–1893, 2.84, 100, 205, 208, 212, 226, 255, 264; 3.152, 172, 288, 292, 308, 340, 354 (notes in vol 3; MSS 1, 2, 3).

Schipper J, The Poems of William Dunbar, pt 3, Denkschriften der kaiserlichen Akademie der Wissenschaften, Philo-Hist Classe, Vienna 1892–93, 41⁴.30, 36, 49, 81 (MS sources and variants given in headnotes and footnotes to each poem; MSS 1, 2, 3; crit E Kölbing, EStn 20.439).

Baildon H B, The Poems of William Dunbar, Cambridge 1907, pp 110, 113, 121, 266 (notes at end of text; sources vary, selects reading which seems to him most likely

to be correct; crit J H Millar, The Bookman 32.307).

Mackenzie W M, The Poems of William Dunbar, London 1932, p 27 (notes at end of text; MSS 1, 2, 3; crit B Dickins, MLR 28.506; TLS Jan 26 1933, p 55; The Modern Scot 4.63); rptd London 1950; ed B Dickins, rptd and rvsd London 1960 (crit A Macdonald, ESts 43.219); rptd 1970.

Selections. Ramsay A, The Ever Green, Edinburgh 1724, 2.82 ([36], [37], [38]; occasional changes in wording; adds 1 stanza to [38]; MS 3); The Poetical Works of Allan Ramsay, ed C Mackay, London and N Y n d, p 274 ([36], [38]).

Dalrymple D, Ancient Scottish Poems, Edinburgh 1770, pp 46, 64, 70, 259, 265; rptd Leeds 1815, pp 56, 82, 89, 308, 314 ([36], [37], [38], [42], [43]; notes at end of text; MS 3).

Pinkerton J, Ancient Scotish Poems, 2 vols, London and Edinburgh 1786, 1.101, 104, 109, 115; 2.411 ([33], [34], [41], from [44], [35], [40]; notes in vol 2; MS 2).

Morison R, Select Poems of Wil Dunbar Part First from the MS of George Bannatyne, Perth 1788, pp 52, 69, 75 ([36], [37], [38], [42], [43]; MS 3).

Sibbald J, Chronicle of Scottish Poetry, 4 vols, Edinburgh and London 1802, 1.315, 333; 2.7, 14 (from [34], [40], [35], from [44], from [41], from [36], from [37], [38], [43]; introductory and end notes; sources not always indicated but include MSS 2, 3).

Irving D, The Lives of the Scotish Poets, 2nd edn London 1810, 1.399 ([33], [40]; some are brief excerpts).

Chalmers G, The Poetic Remains of Some of the Scotish Kings, London 1824, p 119 (Respontio Regis from [44]).

Tytler P F, Lives of Scottish Worthies, London 1833, 3.91, 93, 99, 111 ([46], from [39], [41], [44]; Laing edn).

Ancient Scotish Poetry No I Dunbar, Blackwood's Edinburgh Magazine 37.304, 310 ([44], [39]).

Irving D, The History of Scotish Poetry, ed J A Carlyle, Edinburgh 1861, p 229 ([40]; brief excerpt).

Masson R O, Three Centuries of English Poetry Being Selections from Chaucer to Herrick, London 1876, pp 134, 138 ([44], from [35]; spelling modernized, glossings at foot of page; Laing edn).

Ross J, The Book of Scottish Poems, Paisley 1882, 1.192 ([44]).

Schipper J, William Dunbar sein Leben und

seine Gedichte, Berlin 1884, pp 249, 251, 263, 278, 284 (poems in German scattered through text of discussion; [46], [40], [33], [34], [42], from [35], from [41], [44], [43]; crit E Kölbing, EStn 10.128; M Trautmann, Angl 7.146; The Nation 40.144).

Fitzgibbon H M, Early English and Scottish Poetry, London N Y and Melbourne 1888, p 121 (from [35]; spelling modernized).

Eyre-Todd G, Mediæval Scottish Poetry, Abbotsford Series, Glasgow 1892, p 206 ([36], [44]; glossings in margin).

Henderson T F, A Little Book of Scottish Verse, London 1899; 2nd edn 1909, p 54 ([43]; glossings at foot of page).

Dixon W M, The Edinburgh Book of Scottish Verse, London 1910, p 73 ([44]; glossings at foot of page).

Neilson W A and K G T Webster, Chief British Poets of the 14th and 15th Centuries, Boston N Y etc 1916, pp 395, 434 ([44]; brief note at end of text, glossings at foot of page; Small edn).

Gray M M, Scottish Poetry from Barbour to James VI, N Y 1935, pp 142, 162, 168 ([38], [44], from [43]; crit J Speirs, Scrut 6.83; W M Mackenzie, The Scottish Bookman 1, no 4, p 133).

Fergusson J, The Green Garden, London and Edinburgh 1946, p 31 ([46]; spelling modernized).

[Grieve C M] MacDiarmid H, Selected Poems of Dunbar, Glasgow 1955, p 36 ([44]).

Kinsley J, William Dunbar Poems, Oxford 1958, pp 88, 132 ([39], [40], lines 1–5, 46–85 of [42], [44]; notes at end of text; MSS 2, 3; crit TLS Apr 18 1958, p 208; D Young, William Dunbar, SHR 38.10; E Morgan, RES ns 11.71; J Wordsworth, MÆ 30.128).

McLaren M, The Wisdom of the Scots, London 1961, p 72 ([36]; glossings in margin).

MacQueen J and T Scott, The Oxford Book of Scottish Verse, Oxford 1966, p 112 ([39], [44]; glossings at foot of page; Mackenzie edn).

Scott T, Late Medieval Scots Poetry, London 1967, pp 109, 113, 184 ([39], [44]; notes at end of text; Mackenzie edn).

Ridley F [H], Selected Poems of William Dunbar, Los Angeles 1969, pp 3, 16 ([44], [45], [43]; glossings in margin; MSS 1, 2, 3).

Scott T, The Penguin Book of Scottish Verse, London 1970, p 140 ([44], [39]; glossings at foot of page).

Modernizations. Tytler P F, Lives of Scottish Worthies, London 1833, 3.91 ([46]).

Wright T, On the Scottish Poet Dunbar, Essays on Subjects Connected with the Literature Popular Superstitions and History of England in the Middle Ages, London 1846, 2.296 ([40]).

Green M A E, Lives of the Princesses of England, London 1852, 4.120 ([40]; Laing edn).

[Robertson J L] Haliburton H, Dunbar Being a Selection from the Poems of an Old Makar Adapted for Modern Readers, London 1895, pp 28, 37, 58, 62, 105 (from [34], from [43], [46], from [40], from [36], from [45]; essentially modernized paraphrase, abbreviated, extremely free; crit R Brotanek, AnglB 6.71).

Textual Matters. Laing, edn, 2.297, 323, 326, 328, 335, 346 ([40], [41], [44], [42], [36], [37], [38], [43]).

Schipper, edn, pt 3, 41⁴.57, 76 ([33], [34], [44]; see also introd and ftnts to individual poems).

Mackenzie, edn, pp 203ff ([33–46]).

Baxter J W, William Dunbar, Edinburgh and London 1952, pp 95, 127, 144 ([46], [36–38], [33], [34], [42], [35], [41], [39], [43], [44]).

Scott T, Dunbar a Critical Exposition, Edinburgh and London 1966, p 115 ([44]).

Language. Ramsay A, The Ever Green, Edinburgh 1724, 2.265 ([36], [37], [38]; glossary).

Dalrymple D, Ancient Scottish Poems, Edinburgh 1770, p 317 (glossary); rptd Leeds 1815, p 367, [added] Glossary, p 1 [separate pagination] ([36–38], [42], [43]).

Pinkerton J, Ancient Scotish Poems, London and Edinburgh 1786, 1.cxliii; 2.520 (synorthographic and symphonious words, glossary; [33], [34], [41], from [44], [35], [40]).

Sibbald J, Chronicle of Scottish Poetry, Edinburgh and London 1802, vol 4 [unpaged] (glossary; [34], [40], [35], [44], [41], [36–38], [43]).

Murray J A H, The Dialect of the Southern Counties of Scotland, London 1873 (group as a whole).

Kaufmann J, Traité de la langue, Bonn 1873, p 47 (group as a whole).

Hahn O, Zur Verbal- und Nominalflexion bei den schottischen Dichtern, Berlin 1887–89 (see especially pt 3, p 17; group as a whole).

Schipper, edn, pt 1, 40².18 (group as a whole).

Gregor W, Glossary, Small edn, 3.401 (group as a whole).

Curtis F J, An Investigation of the Rimes

and Phonology of Clariodus, Angl 16.387; 17.1, 125 (group as a whole).

Bearder J W, Über den Gebrauch der Praepositionen in der altschottischen Poesie, Halle 1894 ([41]; examples from Dunbar; crit EStn 19.410).

Heuser W, Die Dehnung vor -nd im Mittelschottischen, Die Dehnung -end, Angl 19.401 (brief; group as a whole).

Baildon H B, On the Rimes in the Authentic Poems of William Dunbar, Trans Royal Soc Edinburgh 39³.629; issued separately Edinburgh 1899 (group as a whole).

Flom G T, Scandinavian Influence on Southern Lowland Scotch, diss Columbia 1900 (group as a whole).

Browne W H, The Taill of Rauf Coilyear, Baltimore 1903, pp 15, 35, 139 (general discussion of Middle Scots, glossary; group as a whole).

Luick K, Studien zur englischen Lautgeschichte, WBEP 17.109 ([43]).

Knopff P, Darstellung der Ablautverhältnisse in der schottischen Schriftsprache, diss Würzburg 1904 (group as a whole).

Baildon, edn, pp xxvi, 299 (discussion, glossary; group as a whole).

CHEL, 2.101, 506 (group as a whole).

Gray M M, Introd, Lancelot of the Laik, PSTS ns 2, Edinburgh and London 1912, 2.xviii (group as a whole).

Lenz K, Zur Lautlehre der französischen Element in den schottischen Dichtungen, diss Marburg 1913 (examples taken from Douglas, Dunbar, Lyndesay, Clariodus; group as a whole).

Westergaard E, Prepositions in Lowland Scotch, Angl 41.444 (some examples from Dunbar; group as a whole); Verbal Forms in Middle-Scotch, Angl 43.95 (group as a whole).

Craigie W A, ed, The Maitland Folio, PSTS ns 7,. 20, 2 vols, Edinburgh and London 1919–27, 2.135 (glossary; [33], [34], [41], [44], [35], [40], [39], [36–38], [42], [43]).

Watt L M, Language and Influences, Douglas's Aeneid, Cambridge 1920, p 149 (very generally applicable; group as a whole).

Westergaard E, Studies in Prefixes and Suffixes, London 1924 (group as a whole).

Wilson J, The Spelling of Scotch before 1600, The Dialects of Central Scotland, London 1926, p 168 (group as a whole; attempts to determine pronunciation from spelling, rimes, modern Lothian pronunciation).

Westergaard E, Plural Forms in Lowland Scottish, Angl 51.77 (group as a whole).

Mackenzie, edn, pp xii, xxxvii, 245 ([33–46]; discussion, glossary).

Wood H H, The Poems and Fables of Robert Henryson, Edinburgh 1933; 2nd edn rvsd 1958; rptd 1965, 1968, p xxxi.

Patrick D, Scottish Literature, Chambers's Cyclopædia, rvsd J L Geddie, Phila and N Y 1938, 1.164 (group as a whole).

Fergusson J, The Green Garden, London and Edinburgh 1946, p 228 (glossary; [46]).

[Grieve C M] MacDiarmid H, Selected Poems of William Dunbar, Glasgow 1955, p 60 ([44]; glossary).

Kinsley J, William Dunbar Poems, Oxford 1958, p 139 (glossary; [39], [40], [42], [44]).

Wittig K, The Scottish Tradition in Literature, Edinburgh 1958, pp 62, 101 and passim ([42]; general reference to group as a whole).

Scott T, Dunbar A Critical Exposition, Edinburgh and London 1966, pp 346, 351; Late Medieval Scots Poetry, London 1967, pp 21, 189 ([39], [44]; discussion and glossary).

Conley J, William Dunbar Additions and Corrections of OED and DOST, N&Q 213 (ns 15).169 ([37], [39], [42–44]).

Versification. Guest E, A History of English Rhythms, 2 vols, London 1838; ed W W Skeat, new edn [in 1 vol] London 1882, p 649 ([42]).

Schipper, 1.510 and passim ([39], [45], [44]).

Bulloch J M, French Metres in Early Scottish Poetry, Scottish Notes and Queries 2.131 ([42]).

McNeill G P, Note on the Versification and Metres of Dunbar, Small edn, 1.clxxxiv, clxxxviii ([41], [39], [44], [33], [46], [35], [40], [45], [43], [42], [37], [38], [36], [34]).

Schipper, edn, pt 3, 41⁴.76 ([44]; discussion in headnote to poem).

Brandl, 2¹.1066 ([44]).

Curtis F J, The Rimes and Phonology of Clariodus, Angl 16.387; 17.1, 125 (group as a whole).

Henderson T F, Scottish Vernacular Literature, Edinburgh 1898; 3rd edn rvsd Edinburgh 1910, pp 154, 158 ([41], [39], [44]).

Baildon H B, Rimes in the Authentic Poems of Dunbar, Trans Royal Soc Edinburgh 39³.629 (group as a whole).

Steinberger C, Étude sur William Dunbar, Dublin 1908, p 156 ([41]).

Smith J M, The French Background of Middle Scots Literature, Edinburgh and London 1934, p 161 ([44]; crit AnglB 45.265; MÆ 4.44).

Wittig K, The Scottish Tradition in Literature, p 59 and passim ([40]).

Scott T, Dunbar A Critical Exposition, pp 311, 318, 325 ([44], [41], [39], [33], [46], [35], [40], [45], [36], [37], [38], [43], [42], [34]).

Date. Laing, edn, 2.292, 323, 332 ([45], [39], [34]).

Paterson, edn, pp 60, 182, 203, 277, 287 ([43], [45], [46], [33], [34], [42], [40], [44]).

Schipper J, William Dunbar sein Leben und seine Gedichte, Berlin 1884, pp 248, 277, 282, 285 ([45], [39], [41], [44], [43]).

Mackay Æ J G, Introd [and] Appendix to Introd, Small edn, l.cxxxvi, clxvi, clxx ([35], [40], [33], [34], [42], [41], [39], [44], [36], [37], [38], [45], [46], [43]).

Schipper, edn, pt 3, 41⁴.32, 37, 49, 57, 60, 64, 69, 72, 76, 81 ([46], [40], [36], [37], [38], [33], [42], [35], [41], [39], [44], [43]).

Fox D, The Chronology of William Dunbar, PQ 39.419 ([33–46]).

Dorsch T S, Of Discretioun in Asking Dunbar's Petitionary Poems, Chaucer und seine Zeit Symposion fur Walter F Schirmer, ed A Esch, Tubingen 1968, p 287 ([39], [35], [42], [37], [36], [34], [43], [41], [40], [44]).

Authorship. Laing, edn, 1.25 (Memoirs); 2.328, 343 ([44]).

Paterson, edn, p 286 ([44]).

Schipper J, William Dunbar seine Leben und seine Gedichte, Berlin 1884, p 281 ([44]).

Mackay Æ J G, Introd, Small edn, l.xxxix, lxviii ([44]).

Schipper J, Anonymous Early Scottish Poems, pt 5, Denkschriften der kaiserlichen Akademie der Wissenschaften, Philo-Hist Classe, Vienna 1893, 43¹.54 ([44]).

Brown J T T, The Bannatyne Manuscript, SHR 1.149 ([36], [37], [38]).

Baxter J W, William Dunbar, Edinburgh and London 1952, pp 126, 151, 225 ([36], [37], [38], [44]).

Wood H H, Two Scots Chaucerians, Writers and Their Work, no 201, ed G Bullough, London 1967, p 26 ([44]).

Sources and Literary Relations. Laing, edn, 2.297 ([40]).

Child F J, The English and Scottish Popular Ballads, Boston and N Y 1882–98, 5.8 ([40]; brief).

Mackay Æ J G, Introd, Small edn, l.cxxii ([33], [34], [39], [40], [41], [42], [44], [45], [46]).

[Robertson J L] Haliburton H, Dunbar in Burns, Furth in Field, London 1894, p 277 ([44], [39], [42]).

Smith G G, The Transition Period, Periods of European Lit, Edinburgh and London 1900, 4.36, 39, 42 and passim ([41] and

group as a whole).

Chambers R, Chambers's Cyclopædia, Phila and N Y 1901–03; rvsd Phila and N Y 1938, 1.195 ([35]).

CHEL 2.293 ([41]).

Ross A S C, Jólaköttur, Yuillis Yald and Similar Expressions, Viking Society for Northern Research, Saga Book, 12.1 ([44]).

Mendenhall J C, Aureate Terms A Study in the Literary Diction of the 15th Century, Lancaster Pa 1919 (group as a whole).

Patch H R, The Goddess Fortuna in Mediæval Lit, Cambridge Mass 1927, pp 57, 84 ([43], [36]; brief).

Nichols P H, William Dunbar as a Scottish Lydgatian, PMLA 46.215 ([36], [37], [38]).

Smith J M, The French Background of Middle Scots Literature, Edinburgh and London 1934, p 74 ([35]; crit AnglB 45.265; MÆ 4.44).

Patrick D, Scottish Literature, Chambers's Cyclopaedia, rvsd J L Geddie, Phila and N Y 1938, 1.166 (group as a whole).

Craig HEL, p 169 ([35]; brief).

Moore A K, The Secular Lyric in Middle English, Lexington Ky 1951, pp 211, 216 ([44]).

Renwick-Orton, p 417 ([35]; brief).

Hyde I, Primary Sources and Associations of Dunbar's Aureate Imagery, MLR 51.488 ([34]).

Leyerle J, The Two Voices of William Dunbar, UTQ 31.325, 331, 334 ([41]).

Hyde I, Poetic Imagery, SSL 2.184 ([35]).

Scott T, Dunbar A Critical Exposition, Edinburgh and London 1966, pp 46, 100, 113, 117, 311, 334 and passim ([33], [44], [42], [36], [41], [39]).

Kinghorn A M, Dunbar and Villon, MLR 62.198, 207 ([43], [44]).

Other Scholarly Problems. Irving D, The Lives of the Scotish Poets, 2nd edn London 1810, 1.399 ([40]; biographical evidence).

Tytler P F, Lives of Scottish Worthies, London 1833, 3. 90, 93 ([46], [39]; biographical evidence, contemp conditions).

Laing, edn, 2. 292, 333 ([45], [42]; identity of subjects).

Ancient Scotish Poetry No I Dunbar, Blackwood's Edinburgh Magazine 37.304 ([44]; obscure phrase).

Wright T, On the Scottish Poet Dunbar, Essays on Subjects Connected with the Literature Popular Superstitions and History of England in the Middle Ages, London 1846, 2.295 ([33], [40], group as a whole; occasion).

William Dunbar, The Scottish Journal 1.131

([44]; biographical evidence).

Strickland A, Lives of the Queens of Scotland and English Princesses, N Y 1851, 1.54 ([44]; occasion).

Green M A E, Lives of the Princesses of England, London 1852, 4.119 ([40]; occasion).

Paterson, edn, pp 107, 180, 244, 282, 286 ([39], [45], [36], [37], [38], [40], [44]; contemp conditions, subject, purpose, occasion).

Ross J M, Scottish History and Literature, Glasgow 1884, p 179 ([39]; contemp conditions).

Schipper J, William Dunbar sein Leben und seine Gedichte, Berlin 1884, pp 88, 92 ([35]; biographical evidence).

[Robertson J L] Haliburton H, Our Earlier Burns, In Scottish Fields, London 1890, pp 227, 233 ([40], [45], group as a whole; biographical evidence).

Schipper, edn, pt 3, 41⁴.30, 36, 49 ([45], [40], [36], [37]; identity of subject, purpose).

Smeaton O, William Dunbar, N Y (1898?), pp 50, 55, 68, 92, 107, 152 ([45], [33], [34], [41], [42], [35], [44], [39], [43], group as a whole; biographical evidence, contemp conditions; crit J W Baxter, William Dunbar, Edinburgh and London 1952, passim; The Scottish Antiquary 13.95).

Teichert O P, Schottische Zustände unter Jacob IV nach den Dichtungen von William Dunbar, Görlitz 1903, pp 6, 12, 21 ([39], [44], [42], [43], [36], [37], [38], [41], [34], [33]; contemp conditions; crit O Glöde, EStn 36.267).

Snell F J, The Poets, The Age of Transition, London 1905, 1.89 ([44]; occasion).

Murdoch W G B, The Royal Stewarts in Their Literary Connection with Arts and Letters, Edinburgh 1908, p 59 ([44], [39]; occasion).

Taylor I A, The Life of James IV, London 1913, p 181 ([40]; occasion, brief).

Holzknecht K J, Literary Patronage in the Middle Ages, Phila 1923, p 208 and passim ([42], [35], [39], [33], [34], [45], [46], [40], [44], group as a whole; occasion).

Mackenzie W M, William Dunbar, Edinburgh Essays on Scots Literature, Edinburgh and London 1933, p 46 ([40]; occasion).

Roy J A, Of the Makaris A Causerie, UTQ 16.33, 36 (contemp conditions; [39], [40]).

Baxter J W, William Dunbar, Edinburgh and London 1952, pp 95, 122, 150, 182 ([46], [40], [44], [45]; occasion).

Milner I, Some Aspects of Satire in the Poetry of Dunbar, Philologica (cizojazyčná prioloha Časopisu pro moderní filologii) 8.33 ([38], [34], [39], [35], [41], [44], [43]; contemp conditions).

Scott T, Dunbar A Critical Exposition, Edinburgh and London 1966, pp 1, 5, 8, 10, 56, 136, 149, 157, 174, 268, 274, 341, 344 (group as a whole, [38], [39], [33], [34], [35], [37], [40], [41], [43], [44], [46], [42]; occasion, contemp conditions, relation between poems, biographical evidence); Late Medieval Scots Poetry, London 1967, p 31 ([39], [44]; contemp conditions, occasion).

Wood H H, Two Scots Chaucerians, Writers and Their Work, no 201, ed G Bullough, London 1967, pp 24, 37 ([41], [35], [44], [40]; biographical evidence).

Dorsch T S, Of Discretioun in Asking Dunbar's Petitionary Poems, Chaucer und seine Zeit Symposion fur Walter F Schirmer, ed A Esch, Tubingen 1968, p 285 ([39], [35], [42], [37], [36], [34], [43], [41], [40], [44]; attitude, biographical evidence).

Shire H M, Song Dance and Poetry of the Court of Scotland, Cambridge 1969, p 21 ([34]; mention of lost works).

Literary Criticism. Irving D, The Lives of the Scotish Poets, 2nd edn London 1810, 1.398 ([33], [40]).

Laing, edn, 2.322, 325, 347, 350 ([41], [39], [44], [43], [35]).

Ancient Scotish Poetry No I Dunbar, Blackwood's Edinburgh Magazine 37.303, 309 ([42], [35], [44], [41], [39]).

William Dunbar, Littell's Living Age 1.383 ([35]).

Paterson, edn, pp 60, 227, 266 ([43], [41], [35]).

Nichol J, A Sketch of Scottish Poetry, ed J Small, 2nd edn rvsd EETS 11, London 1883, p xxvii (group as a whole).

Ross J M, Scottish History and Literature, Glasgow 1884, pp 179, 206, 210, 213 ([39], [41], [34], [42], [36–38], [43]).

Schipper J, William Dunbar sein Leben und seine Gedichte, Berlin 1884, pp 247, 259, 268, 285 ([45], [46], [40], [36–38], [33], [34], [42], [35], [41], [39], [44], [43]).

DNB, 16.156 (group as a whole).

Mackay Æ J G, Introd, Small edn, l.cxxi, cxxx, cxxxvi ([33], [34], [39], [40], [41], [42], [44], [45], [46], [35], [36–38]).

Oliphant [M], Royal Edinburgh, London and N Y 1890, p 191 ([40], [44], [45]; superficial).

[Robertson J L] Haliburton H, Our Earlier Burns, In Scottish Fields, London 1890, pp 227, 240 ([44]; group as a whole).

Schipper, edn, pt 3, 41⁴.30, 52, 54, 57, 60, 64,

68, 72, 76, 81 ([45], [46], [37–38], [33], [34], [42], [35], [41], [39], [44], [43]).
Oliphant F R, William Dunbar, Blackwood's Edinburgh Magazine 154.418, 434 ([42], [46], [40]).
Ten Brink, 3.73 ([39]).
Henderson T F, Scottish Vernacular Literature, Edinburgh 1898; 3rd edn rvsd Edinburgh 1910, pp 172, 178 ([43], [44]).
Smith G G, The Transition Period, Periods of European Lit, Edinburgh and London 1900, 4.50 and passim ([41], group as a whole).
Millar J H, A Literary History of Scotland, London 1903, p 50 (group as a whole; brief comment).
CHEL, 2.293 ([41]).
Steinberger C, Étude sur William Dunbar, Dublin 1908, pp 110, 123, 154 ([40], [44], [35]).
William Dunbar, TLS Apr 10 1930, p 306 (group as a whole).
Taylor R A, Dunbar the Poet, The Poets on the Poets, no 4, London 1931, p 64 ([44], [40], [35], [39], group as a whole).
Speirs J, William Dunbar, Scrut 7.65 ([41], [38], [43], [35]); The Scots Literary Tradition, London 1940, p 51 ([38], [43], [35]); 2nd rvsd edn London 1962, p 65.
Craig HEL, p 169 ([35]; brief).
Moore A K, The Secular Lyric in ME, Lexington Ky 1951, pp 197, 209, 216 ([44]).
Morgan E, Dunbar and the Language of Poetry, EC 2.149 ([39], [41], [43]).
Renwick-Orton, p 417 ([35]; brief).
Lewis C S, English Literature in the Sixteenth Century, Oxford 1954, pp 93, 96 ([46], [40], [41], [39], [43]).
Kinsley J, The Mediaeval Makars, Scottish Poetry A Critical Survey, London 1955, p 27 ([35], [39], [44]).
Hyde I, Primary Sources and Associations of Dunbar's Aureate Imagery, MLR 51.488 ([34]).

Milner I, Some Aspects of Satire in the Poetry of Dunbar, Philologica (cizojazyčná prioloha Casopisu pro moderní filologii) 8.33 ([38], [34], [39], [35], [41], [44], [43]).
Peter J, Complaint and Satire in Early English Literature, Oxford 1956, p 51 ([35], [43]; brief reference).
Mackie R L, King James IV of Scotland, Edinburgh and London 1958, p 181 ([43]; brief comment).
McLaren M, The Wisdom of the Scots, London 1961, p 69 ([36]).
Leyerle J, The Two Voices of William Dunbar, UTQ 31.322, 331 ([41]).
Hyde I, Poetic Imagery, SSL 2.184 ([35]).
Kinghorn A M, The Minor Poems of Robert Henryson, SSL 3.30, 35, 39 ([44], group in general).
Fox D, The Scottish Chaucerians, Chaucer and Chaucerians, ed D S Brewer, University Alabama 1966, p 183 ([43]).
Scott T, Dunbar A Critical Exposition, Edinburgh and London 1966, pp 51, 94, 136, 145, 156, 183, 212, 214, 255, 268, 275, 283, 333, 342, 346, 371 and passim ([39], [43], [41], [33], [34], [35], [44], [42], [45], [46], [36], [37], [38], [40]).
Kinghorn A M, Dunbar and Villon, MLR 62.198 ([43]).
Wood H H, Two Scots Chaucerians, Writers and Their Work, no 201, ed G Bullough, London 1967, p 26 ([44]).
Dorsch T S, Of Discretioun in Asking, Chaucer und seine Zeit Symposion für Walter F Schirmer, ed A Esch, Tübingen 1968, p 285 ([39], [35], [42], [37], [36], [34], [43], [41], [40], [44]).
Bibliography. Robbins-Cutler, nos 121.5 ([38]), 649.8 ([41]), 1373.5 ([45]), 2258.5 ([46]), 2349.5 ([44]), 2619.8 ([34]), 2621.5 ([36]), 3116.5 ([33]), 3117.3 ([40]), 3118.6 ([39]), 3118.8 ([42]), 3646.3 ([35]), 3768.3 ([37]), 4116.5 ([43]).

III. Court Life

(Note: Folios for items [47–62] are listed by MS number, as appropriate, after each title. See under *MSS* below for full listing and information. Titles are from Mackenzie edn.)

[47] A NEW YEAR'S GIFT TO THE KING.

1, ff 2ᵇ–3ᵃ.

[48] THE WOWING OF THE KING QUHEN HE WAS IN DUNFERMLINE.

1, f 58ᵃ; 2, pp 335–337; 4, ff 116ᵃ–116ᵇ.

[49] IN SECREIT PLACE.

1, ff 34ᵇ–35ᵃ; 2, pp 308–311; 4, ff 103ᵇ–104ᵃ.

[50] AGANIS THE SOLISTARIS IN COURT.

1, f 10ª; 2, pp 8, 316.

[51] THE DREGY OF DUNBAR.

1, ff 55ᵇ–56ᵇ; 2, pp 290–292; 4, ff 102ª–103ᵇ.

[52] TO THE QUENE.

1, ff 46ª–46ᵇ; 2, p 342.

[53] OF A DANCE IN THE QUENIS CHALMER.

1, ff 45ª–45ᵇ; 2, pp 340–341.

[54] OF JAMES DOG KEPAR OF THE QUENIS WARDROP.

1, ff 44ª–44ᵇ; 2, p 339.

[55] OF THE SAID JAMES QUHEN HE HAD PLESETT HIM.

1, ff 44ᵇ–45ª; 2, pp 339–340.

[56] OF SIR THOMAS NORNY.

1, ff 8ª–8ᵇ; 2, pp 3–5.

[57] EPITAPHE FOR DONALD OWRE.

1, ff 11ª–11ᵇ; 2, pp 11–12; 4, pp 53–54.

[58] OF ANE BLAK-MOIR.

1, ff 45ᵇ–46ª; 2, pp 341–342.

[59] THE FENYEIT FREIR OF TUNGLAND.

3, ff 211ᵇ–212ᵇ; 4, ff 117ª–118ᵇ.

[60] THE BIRTH OF ANTICHRIST.

1, ff 42ᵇ–43ª; 2, pp 334–335; 4, ff 133ª–134ª.

[61] THE TESTAMENT OF MR ANDRO KENNEDY.

1, ff 24ᵇ–26ª; 2, pp 135–138; 4, ff 154ª–155ᵇ; 5, pp 193–196.

[62] REWL OF ANIS SELF.

4, ff 68ª–69ª.

MSS. 1, Camb Univ L1.5.10 (Reidpeth or Moore), ff 2ᵇ–3ª, 8ª–8ᵇ, 10ª, 11ª–11ᵇ, 24ᵇ–26ª, 34ᵇ–35ª, 42ᵇ–43ª, 44ª–46ᵇ, 55ᵇ–56ᵇ, 58ª (1623; contains items [47], [56], [50], [57], [61], [49], [60], [54–55], [53], [58], [52], [51],

and lines 1–14 of item [48]); 2, Magdalene Coll Camb 2553 (Pepysian Libr, Maitland Folio), pp 3–5, 8, 11–12, 135–138, 290–292, 308–311, 316, 334–337, 339–342 (1570–71; items [56], [50], [57], [61], [51], [49], [60], [48], [54–55], [53], [58], [52]); 3, Nat Libr Scot Acc 4233 (Asloan), ff 211ᵇ–212ᵇ (1513–42; item [59]); 4, Nat Libr Scot 1.1.6 (Bannatyne), pp 53–54, ff 68ª–69ª, 102ª–104ª, 116ª–118ᵇ, 133ª–134ª, 154ª–155ᵇ (1568; items [57], [62], [51], [49], [48], [59–61]). PRINT: 5, Nat Libr Scot 19.1.16 (Chepman and Myllar), pp 193–196 (1508; item [61]).

Pinkerton J, Ancient Scotish Poems, 2 vols, London and Edinburgh 1786, 1.v; 2.437, 471 (MSS 2, 4).

Brydges E and J Haslewood, The British Bibliographer, London 1814, 4.183 (MS 4).

Laing D, The Poems of George Bannatyne, Edinburgh 1824, p 3 (MS 4); The Knightly Tale of Golagrus and Gawane, Edinburgh 1827, f 11ª (PRINT 5 rptd); An Account of the Contents of George Bannatyne's Manuscript, The Bannatyne Club, Edinburgh 1829, 35.43 (MS 4).

A Catalogue of the Manuscripts Preserved in The Library of The University of Cambridge, Cambridge 1861, 4.94 (MS 1).

Small J, The Poetical Works of Gavin Douglas, Edinburgh and London 1874, 1.clxxi (MS 2).

Dickson R and J P Edmond, Annals of Scottish Printing from 1507 to the Beginning of the 17th Century, Cambridge 1890, p 49 (PRINT 5).

Schipper, edn, pt 1, 40².5ff (MSS 1, 2, 3, 4, PRINT 5).

Murdoch J B, ed, The Bannatyne Manuscript, 4 vols, Hunterian Club, Glasgow 1896, 2.184, 292, 330; 3.375, 438; 4.1094 (MS 4 rptd).

Smith G G, Specimens of Middle Scots, Edinburgh and London 1902, pp lxvi, lxx, lxxiii, lxxiv (MSS 2, 3, 4, PRINT 5).

Brown J T T, The Bannatyne Manuscript, SHR 1.136 (MS 4).

Stevenson G, ed, Pieces from The Makculloch and the Gray MSS, PSTS 65, Edinburgh and London 1918, pp 263, 303 (PRINT 5 rptd, notes at end of text).

Craigie W A, ed, The Maitland Folio, PSTS ns 7, 20, 2 vols, Edinburgh and London 1919–27, 2.44 (MS 1); 1.2, 7, 11, 155, 337, 368, 377, 405, 413; 2.35, 96, 116, 121, 126 (MS 2 rptd, notes in vol 2); variants between MSS 1 and 2 listed in 2.35, 96, 116, 121; The Asloan Manuscript, PSTS ns 14,

16, 2 vols, Edinburgh 1923–25, 2.92, 280 (MS 3 rptd, notes at end of text).

Ritchie W T, ed, The Bannatyne Manuscript Writtin in Tyme of Pest, PSTS ns 5, 22, 23, 26, 4 vols, Edinburgh 1928–34, 1.87; 2.167, 271, 309; 3.4, 62 (MS 4 rptd).

Beattie W, ed, The Chepman and Myllar Prints, Edinburgh Biblio Soc, Oxford 1950, pp viii, 193 (PRINT 5 described, rptd).

Baxter J W, William Dunbar, Edinburgh and London 1952, pp 216ff (MSS 1, 2, 3, 4, PRINT 5).

Editions. Laing D, The Poems of William Dunbar, 2 vols, Edinburgh 1834, 1.36, 83, 101, 110, 115, 119, 123, 135, 179; 2.28, 235, 278, 287, 295, 299, 315, 340, 406 (notes in vol 2; MSS 1 and 4; Memoirs of William Dunbar preceding text of poems in vol 1 is paginated separately).

Small J, Æ J G Mackay, G P McNeill, W Gregor, The Poems of William Dunbar, PSTS 2, 4, 16, 21, 29, 3 vols, Edinburgh 1884–93, 2.54, 98, 112, 136, 149, 190, 206, 247, 256; 3.99, 167, 187, 215, 236, 277, 290, 334, 342 (notes in vol 3; MSS 1, 2, 4, PRINT 5).

Schipper J, The Poems of William Dunbar, pts 1–4, Denkschriften der kaiserlichen Akademie der Wissenschaften, Philo-Hist Classe, Vienna 1892–93, 40².33; 40⁴.33; 41⁴.1; 42⁴.23 (MS sources and variants given in headnotes and ftnts to each poem; MSS 1, 2, 4, PRINT 5; crit E Kölbing, EStn 20.439).

Baildon H B, The Poems of William Dunbar, Cambridge 1907, pp 1, 60, 94, 166, 239, 251, 262, 282 (notes at end of text; sources vary, selects reading which seems to him most likely to be correct; crit J H Millar, The Bookman 32.207).

Mackenzie W M, The Poems of William Dunbar, London 1932, p 51 (notes at end of text; MSS 1, 2, 4, PRINT 5; crit B Dickins, MLR 28.506; TLS Jan 26 1933, p 55; The Modern Scot 4.63); rptd London 1950; ed B Dickins, rptd and rvsd London 1960 (crit A Macdonald, ESts 43.219); rptd 1970.

Selections. Ramsay A, The Ever Green, Edinburgh 1724, 1.91, 200; 2.18, 41, 76, 209 ([59], [48], [49], [51], [61], [57]; occasional changes in wording; MS 4); The Poetical Works of Allan Ramsay, ed C Mackay, London and N Y n d, p 266 ([51]).

Poems in the Scottish Dialect by Several Celebrated Poets, Glasgow 1748, p 18 ([61]).

Dalrymple D, Ancient Scottish Poems, Edinburgh 1770, pp 19, 35, 96, 228, 243, 276;

rptd Leeds 1815, pp 20, 42, 121, 280, 294, 324 ([59], [60], [61], [62]; notes at end of text; MS 4).

Pinkerton J, Ancient Scotish Poems, 2 vols, London and Edinburgh 1786, 1.90, 102; 2.359, 408 ([54], [55], [53], [58], [52], [50], [56]; notes in vol 2; MS 2).

Morison R, Select Poems of Wil Dunbar Part First from the MS of George Bannatyne, Perth 1788, pp 23, 41 ([59], [60], [61]; MS 4).

Sibbald J, Chronicle of Scottish Poetry, 4 vols, Edinburgh and London 1802, 1.234, 243, 274, 296, 370 ([51], [48], [50], [53], [54], [55], [61], [59], [60], from [49]; introductory and end notes; sources not always indicated but include MS 4).

Irving D, The Lives of the Scotish Poets, 2nd edn London 1810, 1.397, 407 (from [53], from [61]).

Gilchrist O, Censura Literaria, ed S E Brydges, London 1807, 5.244 (from [61]; Dalrymple, Ancient Scottish Poems).

[Sandys W] Specimens of Macaronic Poetry, London 1831, p 28 ([61]; Dalrymple, Ancient Scottish Poems).

Tytler P F, Lives of Scottish Worthies, London 1833, 3.109, 114 ([55], [53]; Laing edn).

Ancient Scotish Poetry No I Dunbar, Blackwood's Edinburgh Magazine 37.306, 312 ([54], [55], [51]).

Paterson J, The Works of William Dunbar, Edinburgh 1863 pp 133, 143, 150, 164, 170, 175, 187, 273 ([50], [47], [61], [57], [51], [53], [56], [54], [55], [60], [59], [58]; glossings in ftnts).

Irving D, The History of Scotish Poetry, ed J A Carlyle, Edinburgh 1861, pp 228, 247, 252 (brief excerpts from [53], from [59], from [60], from [61]).

Kaufmann J, Traité de la langue, Bonn 1873, p 40 ([48]; Laing edn).

Ross J, The Book of Scottish Poems, Paisley 1882, 1.191 ([54], [55]).

Schipper J, William Dunbar sein Leben und seine Gedichte, Berlin 1884, pp 117, 125, 217, 228, 237 (in German; [47–48], [51], [50], [54–55], [61], [60], [59]; crit E Kölbing, EStn 10.128; M Trautmann, Angl 7.146; The Nation 40.144).

Eyre-Todd G, Mediæval Scottish Poetry, Abbotsford Series, Glasgow 1892, p 199 ([59]; glossings in margin).

Browne W H, Selections from the Early Scottish Poets, Baltimore 1896, pp 123, 190 (from [59], [62]; a few notes at end of text; Small edn).

Harvey W, The Harp of Stirlingshire, Paisley 1897, p 458 ([51]).

Henderson T F, A Little Book of Scottish Verse, London 1899; 2nd edn 1909, pp 50, 58 ([61], [57]; brief introductory notes, glossings at foot of page).

Chambers R, Chambers's Cyclopædia, Phila and N Y 1901–03; rvsd Phila and N Y 1938, p 199 ([61]; brief excerpt).

Dixon W M, The Edinburgh Book of Scottish Verse, London 1910, pp 37, 48 ([59], [47]; glossings at foot of page).

Zupitza J, Alt- und mittelenglisches Übungsbuch, 10th edn Vienna and Leipzig 1912, p 205 ([54], [55]; variants at foot of page).

Neilson W A and K G T Webster, Chief British Poets of the 14th and 15th Centuries, Boston N Y etc 1916, pp 396, 399, 434 ([51], [47]; brief note at end of text; glossings at foot of page; Small edn).

Buchan J, The Northern Muse, London 1924, pp 219, 495 ([54]; glossings at foot of page, brief note at end of text; Small edn).

Brougham E M, News out of Scotland, London 1926, p 35 ([47]).

A New Year's Gift to the King, World Review 1.213 ([47]).

Patterson R F, Six Centuries of English Literature, London and Glasgow 1933, 1.195 ([61]).

Douglas R M, The Scots Book, London 1935, p 37 ([47]).

Gray M M, Scottish Poetry from Barbour to James VI, N Y 1935, p 130 ([47]; crit J Speirs, Scrut 6.83; W M Mackenzie, The Scottish Bookman 1, no 4, p 133).

Fergusson J, The Green Garden, London and Edinburgh 1946, pp 32, 36 ([53], from [51]; spelling modernized).

Mackenzie A M, Scottish Pageant, Edinburgh 1946; 2nd edn 1952, 1.14, 33 (from [51], [59]; glossings at end of 2nd selection).

Sitwell E, A Poet's Notebook, London 1943; rptd Boston 1950, p 241 (from [49]).

[Grieve C M] MacDiarmid H, Selections from the Poems of William Dunbar, The Saltire Classics, Edinburgh 1952, pp 22, 26, 43 ([49], [53], [58], [59], [47]; glossings in footnotes; Mackenzie edn).

Robbins R H, Secular Lyrics of the XIV and XV Centuries, Oxford 1952, 2nd edn 1955, p 91 ([47]; MS 1).

[Grieve] MacDiarmid, Selected Poems of William Dunbar, Glasgow 1955, pp 14, 39, 45, 53 ([58], [49], [53], [54], [48], [57]).

Kinsley J, William Dunbar Poems, Oxford 1958, pp 20, 40, 44, 83, 96, 112, 118, 130,

135 ([58], [49], [59], [60], [53], [56], [54–55], [61], [51]; notes at end of text; MSS 2, 4; PRINT 5; crit TLS Apr 18 1958, p 208; D Young, William Dunbar, SHR 38.10; E Morgan, RES ns 11.71; J Wordsworth, MÆ 30.128).

Davies R T, Medieval English Lyrics, London 1963, pp 248, 358 ([49]; glossings at foot of page, notes at end of text; MSS 2, 4).

Smith Rowland, The Poetry of William Dunbar, Theoria 22.80, 82 (from [49], [54], [55]).

MacQueen J and T Scott, The Oxford Book of Scottish Verse, Oxford 1966, p 153 ([61]; glossings at foot of page; Mackenzie edn).

Scott T, Late Medieval Scots Poetry, London 1967, pp 90, 111, 184 ([49], [53]; notes at end of text; Mackenzie edn).

Ridley F [H], Selected Poems of William Dunbar, Los Angeles 1969, p 8 ([49]; glossings in margin; MS 2).

Scott T, The Penguin Book of Scottish Verse, London 1970, p 146 ([54] with 1 stanza omitted, [55]; glossings at foot of page).

Modernizations. [Robertson J L] Haliburton H, Dunbar Being a Selection from the Poems of an Old Makar Adapted for Modern Readers, London 1895, pp 22, 30 ([53], [62]; paraphrase, abbreviated, extremely free; crit R Brotanek, AnglB 6.71).

Linklater E, A Bawdy Revival, New Saltire, no 9, Sept 1963, p 25 ([53]).

Textual Matters. Laing, edn, 1.314, 319; 2.237, 278, 287, 295, 300, 305, 307, 316 ([51], [49], [59], [48], [50], [54], [55], [52], [53], [56], [57], [61]).

Schipper, edn, pt 1, 40².19, 21, 26, 37, 44 ([61], [49], [50]; see also introd and ftnts to individual poems).

Mackenzie, edn, pp 208ff ([47–62]).

Baxter J W, William Dunbar, Edinburgh and London 1952, pp 51, 58, 60, 120, 129, 141, 160, 166, 168, 170, 178, 194 ([48], [51], [50], [54], [55], [56], [61], [57], [53], [58], [60], [59], [62]).

Scott T, Dunbar A Critical Exposition, Edinburgh and London 1966, pp 135, 163 ([47], [52]).

Language. Ramsay A, The Ever Green, Edinburgh 1724, 2.265 ([59], [48], [49], [51], [61], [57]; glossary).

Dalrymple D, Ancient Scottish Poems, Edinburgh 1770, p 317 (glossary); rptd Leeds 1815, p 367, [added] glossary, p 1 [separate pagination] ([59], [60], [61], [62]).

Pinkerton J, Ancient Scotish Poems, London and Edinburgh 1786, 1.cxliii; 2.520 (synorthographic and symphonious words, glos-

sary; [54], [55], [53], [58], [52], [50], [56]).
ibbald J, Chronicle of Scottish Poetry, Edinburgh and London 1802, vol 4 [unpaged] (glossary; [51], [48], [50], [53], [54], [55], [61], [59], [60], [49]).
rving D, The History of Scotish Poetry, ed J A Carlyle, Edinburgh 1861, p 595 (glossary; [53], [59], [60], [61]).
Murray J A H, The Dialect of the Southern Counties of Scotland, London 1873 (group) as a whole).
Kaufmann J, Traité de la langue, Bonn 1873, p 47 (group as a whole).
Iahn O, Zur Verbal- und Nominalflexion bei den schottischen Dichtern, Berlin 1887–89 (see especially pt 3, p 17; group as a whole).
chipper, edn, pt 1, 40².18 (group as a whole).
Gregor W, Glossary, Small edn, 3.401 (group as a whole).
Curtis F J, An Investigation of the Rimes and Phonology of Clariodus, Angl 16.387; 17.1, 125 (group as a whole).
Bearder J W, Über den Gebrauch der Praepositionen in der altschottischen Poesie, Halle 1894 ([47], [48], [49], [51], [50]; examples from Dunbar; crit EStn 19.410).
Browne W H, Selections from the Early Scottish Poets, Baltimore 1896, pp 3, 197 ([59], [62]; discussion in introd, glossary).
Ieuser W, Die Dehnung vor -nd im Mittelschottischen, Die Dehnung - end, Angl 19.401 (brief; group as a whole).
Baildon H B, On the Rimes in the Authentic Poems of William Dunbar, Trans Royal Soc Edinburgh 39³.629; issued separately Edinburgh 1899 (group as a whole).
Flom G T, Scandinavian Influence on Southern Lowland Scotch, diss Columbia 1900 (group as a whole).
Browne W H, The Taill of Rauf Coilyear, Baltimore 1903, pp 15, 35, 139 (general discussion of Middle Scots, glossary; group as a whole).
Millar J H, A Literary History of Scotland, London 1903, p 687 (glossary; [61], [57], [51]).
Luick K, Studien zur englischen Lautgeschichte, WBEP 17.109 ([59], [51], [48], [60]).
Knopf P, Darstellung der Ablautverhältnisse in der schottischen Schriftsprache, diss Würzburg 1904 (group as a whole).
Baildon, edn, pp xxvi, 299 (discussion, glossary; group as a whole).
CHEL, 2.101, 506 (group as a whole).
Dixon W M, The Edinburgh Book of Scottish Verse, London 1910, p 897 (glossary; [59], [47]).
Zupitza J, Alt- und mittelenglisches Übungsbuch, 10th edn Vienna and Leipzig 1912, p 208 ([54], [55]; glossary, definitions in German).
Gray M M, Introd, Lancelot of the Laik, PSTS ns 2, Edinburgh and London 1912, 2.xviii (group as a whole).
Lenz K, Zur Lautlehre der französischen Elemente in den schottischen Dichtungen, diss Marburg 1913 (examples taken from Douglas, Dunbar, Lyndesay, Clariodus; group as a whole).
Westergaard E, Prepositions in Lowland Scotch, Angl 41.444 (some examples from Dunbar; group as a whole); Verbal Forms in Middle-Scotch, Angl 43.95 (group as a whole).
Craigie W A, ed, The Maitland Folio, PSTS ns 7, 20, 2 vols, Edinburgh and London 1919–27, 2.135 (glossary; [56], [50], [57], [61], [51], [49], [60], [48], [54], [55], [53], [58], [52]).
Watt L M, Language and Influences, Douglas's Aeneid, Cambridge 1920, p 149 (very generally applicable).
Westergaard E, Studies in Prefixes and Suffixes, London 1924 (group as a whole).
Wilson J, The Spelling of Scotch before 1600, The Dialects of Central Scotland, London 1926, p 168 (group as a whole; attempts to determine pronunciation from spelling, rimes, modern Lothian pronunciation).
Westergaard E, Plural Forms in Lowland Scottish, Angl 51.77 (group as a whole).
Mackenzie, edn, pp xii, xxxvii, 245 ([47–62]; discussion, glossary).
Wood H H, The Poems and Fables of Robert Henryson, Edinburgh 1933; 2nd edn rvsd 1958; rptd 1965, 1968, p xxxi.
Douglas R M, The Scots Book, London 1935, pp 162, 338 ([47]; discussion, glossary).
Patrick D, Scottish Literature, Chambers's Cyclopædia, rvsd J L Geddie, Phila and N Y 1938, 1.164 (group as a whole).
Fergusson J, The Green Garden, London and Edinburgh 1946, p 228 (glossary; [53], [51]).
[Grieve C M] MacDiarmid H, Selections from the Poems of William Dunbar, The Saltire Classics, Edinburgh 1952, pp 5, 49 ([49], [53], [58], [59], [47]; brief note, glossary); Selected Poems of William Dunbar, Glasgow 1955, p 60 ([58], [49], [53], [54], [48], [57]).
Kinsley J, William Dunbar Poems, Oxford

1958, p 139 (glossary; [58], [49], [59], [60], [53], [56], [54], [55], [61], [51]).

Scott T, What Did Dunbar Mean, TLS Jan 20 1966, p 48 ([52]); Dunbar A Critical Exposition, Edinburgh and London 1966, pp 346, 351; Late Medieval Scots Poetry, London 1967, pp 21, 189 ([49], [53]; discussion and glossary).

Conley J, William Dunbar Additions to and Corrections of OED and DOST, N&Q 213 (ns 15).170, 172 ([59], [49], [52], [57]).

Hope A D, A Midsummer Eve's Dream, N Y 1970, p 319 ([53]; glossary).

Versification. Schipper, 1.510 and passim ([59], [57], [51], [60]).

Schipper J, William Dunbar sein Leben und seine Gedichte, Berlin 1884, p 225 ([61]).

Bulloch J M, French Metres in Early Scottish Poetry, Scottish Notes and Queries 2.130 ([48], [53]).

Mackay Æ J G, Introd, Small edn, l.xcvi, cxvii ([51], [57]).

McNeill G P, Note on the Versification and Metres of Dunbar, Small edn, l.clxxvii, clxxxiv ([51], [50], [60], [61], [54], [55], [47], [52], [58], [49], [53], [62], [56], [59], [57]).

Schipper, edn, pt 1, 40².33, 35, 41; pt 3, 41⁴.5, 10, 12, 22 ([47], [48], [51], [56], [57], [61], [59]; discussion in headnotes to poems).

Brandl, 2¹.1064 ([59]).

Curtis F J, The Rimes and Phonology of Clariodus, Angl 16.387; 17.1, 125 (group as a whole).

Henderson T F, Scottish Vernacular Literature, Edinburgh 1898; 3rd edn rvsd Edinburgh 1910, pp 154, 157, 160 ([57], [51], [50], [54], [58], [53], [61], [56], [59]).

Baildon H B, Rimes in the Authentic Poems of Dunbar, Trans Royal Soc Edinburgh 39³.629 (group as a whole).

Steinberger C, Étude sur William Dunbar, Dublin 1908, p 156 ([59]).

Tucker S M, Verse Satire in England, CUS 3, no 2, p 138 ([57]).

Taylor R A, Dunbar the Poet, The Poets on the Poets, no 4, London 1931, p 83 ([51]).

Smith J M, The French Background of Middle Scots Literature, Edinburgh and London 1934, p 164 ([51]; crit AnglB 45.265; MÆ 4.44).

Morgan E, Dunbar and the Language of Poetry, EC 2.147 ([53], [59]).

Wittig K, The Scottish Tradition in Literature, Edinburgh 1958, p 59 and passim ([57], [56]).

Scott T, Dunbar A Critical Exposition, Edinburgh and London 1966, pp 124, 311, 313,

317 ([59], [51], [50], [60], [61], [54], [55], [47], [52], [58], [48], [49], [53], [62], [57], [56]).

Date. Laing, edn, 2.235 ([60]).

Paterson J, The Works of William Dunbar, Edinburgh 1863, p 189 ([60]).

Schipper J, William Dunbar sein Leben und seine Gedichte, Berlin 1884, pp 116, 122, 129, 194, 222, 310 ([47], [48], [49], [51], [50], [53], [56], [62]).

Mackay Æ J G, Introd [and] Appendix to Introd, Small edn, l.xlvii, xcvi, cxiv, cxvii, cxix, cxxviii, cxxxi, cxxxiv, clviii, clxi, clxviii ([59], [60], [51], [61], [49], [53], [52], [57], [50], [62], [47], [58], [54], [55], [56]).

Morley, 7.128, 137 ([48], [51], [49], [47], [50], [59]).

Schipper, edn, pt 1, 40².33, 41, 44; pt 2, 40⁴.33, 35; pt 3, 41⁴.9; pt 4, 42⁴.23 ([47], [48], [51], [50], [53], [52], [57], [62]).

Steinberger C, Étude sur William Dunbar, Dublin 1908, p 103 ([53], [52]).

Utley CR, pp 178, 186 ([58], [52]).

Baxter J W, William Dunbar, Edinburgh and London 1952, pp 50, 130, 141, 194 ([47], [48], [56], [57], [62]).

Lewis C S, English Literature in the Sixteenth Century, Oxford 1954, p 90 ([57], [59], [60], [58], [61]).

Fox D, The Chronology of William Dunbar, PQ 39.418 ([56], [57], [58], [59], [60], [47], [48], [49], [51], [52], [53], [54], [55], [61], [62]).

Scott T, Dunbar A Critical Exposition, p 135 ([47]).

Dorsch T S, Of Discretioun in Asking Dunbar's Petitionary Poems, Chaucer und seine Zeit Symposion fur Walter F Schirmer, ed A Esch, Tubingen 1968, p 292 ([47]).

Authorship. Laing, edn, 2.406 ([49]).

Schipper J, William Dunbar sein Leben und seine Gedichte, Berlin 1884, p 122 ([49]).

Mackay Æ J G, Introd, Small edn, l.xcix ([49]).

Schipper, edn, pt 1, 40².37 ([49]).

Baxter J W, William Dunbar, p 130 ([61]).

Sources and Literary Relations. Keith R, A Large New Catalogue of the Bishops of the Several Sees within the Kingdom of Scotland down to the Year 1688, Edinburgh 1755, p 245 ([59], [60]; very brief).

Irving D, The Lives of the Scotish Poets, 2nd edn London 1810, 1.406 ([61]).

[Sandys W] Specimens of Macaronic Poetry, London 1831, p i ([61]; general discussion of the genre).

Laing, edn, 2.246, 281, 316, 340, 407 ([59], [47], [57], [61], [62], [49]).

Wright T, On the Scottish Poet Dunbar, Essays on Subjects Connected with the Literature Popular Superstitions and History of England in the Middle Ages, London 1846, 2.304 ([61]).

Irving D, The History of Scotish Poetry, ed J A Carlyle, Edinburgh 1861, p 250 ([61]).

Schipper J, William Dunbar sein Leben und seine Gedichte, Berlin 1884, pp 119, 308 ([48], [62]).

Mackay Æ J G, Introd, Small edn, l.xcv, cxiv, cxxxiv ([51], [61], [57], [62]).

Schipper, edn, pt 1, 40^2.35; pt 4, 42^4.24 ([48], [62]).

Robertson J L] Haliburton H, Dunbar in Burns, Furth in Field, London 1894, p 274 ([62], [59], [57]).

Turnbull W R, The Heritage of Burns, Haddington 1896, pp 251, 256 ([61], [59], [51]; brief references).

Henderson T F, Scottish Vernacular Literature, Edinburgh 1898; 2nd edn 1900; 3rd edn rvsd Edinburgh 1910, p 173 ([61]).

Neilson W A, The Origins and Sources of the Court of Love, Studies and Notes in Philology and Literature, Boston 1899, 6.224 ([51]).

Smith G G, The Transition Period, Periods of European Lit, Edinburgh and London 1900, 4.36, 39, 42 and passim ([51], [57], [58], [59]).

Chambers R, Chambers's Cyclopædia, Phila and N Y 1901–03; rvsd Phila and N Y 1938, 1.198 ([51], [59], [61]).

Ritter O, Quellenstudien zu Robert Burns, Palaes 20.146 ([62]).

Moorman F W, The Interpretation of Nature in English Poetry from Beowulf to Shakespeare, QF 95.144 ([48]; brief).

Plessow M, Geschichte der Fabeldichtung in England bis zu John Gay, diss Berlin 1906, p xlix ([48]).

CHEL, 2.289, 291 ([59], [60], [57], [61]).

Steinberger C, Étude sur William Dunbar, Dublin 1908, p 128 ([62]; Shakespeare, Lydgate).

Tucker S M, Verse Satire in England, CUS 3, no 2, pp 137, 141 ([59], [57], [50], [51]).

Snyder F B, Sir Thomas Norray and Sir Thopas, MLN 25.78 ([56]).

Perrow E C, The Last Will and Testament as a Form of Literature, Trans Wisconsin Acad of Sciences Arts and Letters 7^1.682 ([61]).

Sandison H E, The Chanson D'Aventure in Middle English, Bryn Mawr Pa 1913, p 132 ([49]).

Jacobi J B, William Dunbar—an Appreciation, The American Catholic Quarterly Rev 44.306 ([51]; brief).

Mendenhall J C, Aureate Terms A Study in the Literary Diction of the 15th Century, Lancaster Pa 1919 (group as a whole).

Patch H R, The Goddess Fortuna in Mediæval Lit, Cambridge Mass 1927, pp 40, 74, 83, 102 ([62], [59], [60]; brief).

Kitchin G, A Survey of Burlesque and Parody in English, Edinburgh and London 1931, p 23 ([51], [61], [56], [58]).

Nichols P H, William Dunbar as a Scottish Lydgatian, PMLA 46.214 ([61], [54]).

Mackenzie W M, William Dunbar, Edinburgh Essays on Scots Literature, Edinburgh and London 1933, p 40 ([61]).

Smith J M, The French Background of Middle Scots Literature, Edinburgh and London 1934, pp 40, 47, 65, 164 ([49], [47], [61], [51]; crit AnglB 45.265; MÆ 4.44).

Patrick D, Scottish Literature, Chambers's Cyclopædia, rvsd J L Geddie, Phila and N Y 1938, 1.166 (group as a whole).

Speirs J, William Dunbar, Scrut 7.62 ([51], [61]).

Utley C R, pp 65, 178, 186 ([58], [52]).

Baxter J W, William Dunbar, Edinburgh and London 1952, pp 52, 58, 132 ([48], [51], [61]).

Morgan E, Dunbar and the Language of Poetry, EC 2.150 ([61], [51]).

Kinsley J, The tretis of the tua mariit wemen and the wedo, MÆ 23.31 ([56], [61], [51], [59], [49]; The Mediaeval Makars, Scottish Poetry, A Critical Survey, London 1955, p 29 ([48], [51], [59], [56], [58], [49]; brief); William Dunbar Poems, Oxford 1958, pp xv, xxvi ([49], [61], [58], [51], [56], [53]).

Schlauch M, English Medieval Literature, Warsaw 1956, p 296 ([49]).

Bennett J A W, Dunbar's Birth of Antichrist, MÆ 26.196 ([60]).

Leyerle J, The Two Voices of William Dunbar, UTQ 31.319, 330 ([61], [60]).

Smith Rowland, The Poetry of William Dunbar, Theoria 22.79 ([49]).

Hyde I, Poetic Imagery, SSL 2.184, 190 ([59], [54], [53]).

Scott T, Dunbar A Critical Exposition, Edinburgh and London 1966, pp 36, 63, 131, 212, 311, 318, 326, 329, 337 and passim ([48], [61], [49], [60], [56], [51], [50], [59], [57]).

Wood H H, Two Scots Chaucerians, Writers and Their Work, no 201, ed G Bullough, London 1967, p 38 ([49]).

Hope A D, A Midsummer Eve's Dream, N Y 1970, p 173 ([53]).

Other Scholarly Problems. Irving D, The Lives of the Scotish Poets, 2nd edn London 1810, 1.396 ([61]; attitude).

Laing, edn, 1.57 (Memoirs); 2.237, 279, 295, 299, 315, 321 ([52], [53], [59], [48], [51], [47], [54], [55], [58], [56], [57], [61]; identity of subjects, questionable morality of writings, occasion).

Ancient Scotish Poetry No I Dunbar, Blackwood's Edinburgh Magazine 37.306, 311 ([54], [59]; occasion, identity of subject).

Wright T, On the Scottish Poet Dunbar, Essays on Subjects Connected with the Literature Popular Superstitions and History of England in the Middle Ages, London 1846, 2.298 ([53]; occasion, brief).

Green M A E, Lives of the Princesses of England, London 1852, 4.110, 126 ([54], [55], [58], [51]; occasion).

Paterson J, The Works of William Dunbar, Edinburgh 1863, pp 135, 149, 152, 157, 167, 173, 178, 189, 197, 274 ([47], [61], [57], [51], [53], [56], [54], [55], [60], [59], [58]; occasion, identity of subjects).

Irving D, The History of Scotish Poetry, ed J A Carlyle, Edinburgh 1861, p 247 ([59], [60]; identity of subject, occasion).

Campbell J F, Popular Tales of the West Highlands, Edinburgh 1862, 4.57 ([61]; contemp conditions).

Michel F X, Les Écossais en France les Français en Écosse, London 1862, 1.331 ([59]; identity of subject).

Wright T, The History of Scotland from the Earliest Period to the Present Time, London and N Y [1873–74], 1.290 ([48], [51], [59], [60]; occasion, identity of subject).

Ross J M, Scottish History and Literature, Glasgow 1884, p 198 ([59]; occasion).

Schipper J, William Dunbar sein Leben und seine Gedichte, Berlin 1884, pp 216, 220, 223, 226, 234, 244 ([54], [56], [58], [57], [61], [60], [59]; identity of subject, occasion).

Mackay Æ J G, Introd, Small edn, l.xlvi, xc, xcvi, ci, cxiv ([59], [60], [53], [61], [56], [58], [57]; identity of subject, occasion).

[Robertson J L] Haliburton H, Our Earlier Burns, In Scottish Fields, London 1890, p 230 ([51], [59], [61]; biographical evidence).

Morley, 7.138 ([59]; identity of subject, occasion).

Eyre-Todd G, Mediæval Scottish Poetry, Abbotsford Series, Glasgow 1892, p 155 ([59]; occasion).

Schipper, edn, pt 3, 41⁴.1, 3, 7, 12, 18, 21 ([54],

[55], [56], [58], [57], [61], [60], [59]; occasion, purpose, identity of subject).

Oliphant F R, William Dunbar, Blackwood's Edinburgh Magazine 154.433 ([55], [59]; occasion).

Smeaton O, William Dunbar, N Y (1898?), pp 48, 50, 71, 82, 106, 152, 156 ([60], [59], [51], [47], [54], [52], [53], [62], [61]; biographical evidence, occasion).

Paul J B, Preface, Accounts of the Lord High Treasurer of Scotland, Edinburgh 1901, 3.xlix ([58]; occasion, identity of subject).

Rait R S, An Outline of the Relations between England and Scotland, London 1901, p xxxv ([57]; attitude, brief).

Teichert O P, Schottische Zustände unter Jacob IV nach den Dichtungen von William Dunbar, Görlitz 1903, pp 6, 11, 18, 20, 26, 30 ([59], [60], [48], [51], [53], [50], [58], [56], [52], [61], [49]; contemp conditions; crit O Glöde, EStn 36.267).

Snell F J, The Poets, The Age of Transition, London 1905, 1.88 ([60], [59]; occasion).

Steinberger C, Étude sur William Dunbar, Dublin 1908, p 75 ([53]; identity of subject).

Stair-Kerr E, The Poets, Scotland under James IV, Paisley 1911, p 127 ([51]; biographical evidence, brief).

Taylor I A, The Life of James IV, London 1913, p 183 ([51]; occasion, brief).

Mackie R L, Scotland, London 1916, p 271 ([59]; occasion, brief).

Powys L, William Dunbar, The Freeman 7.516 ([53]; biographical evidence).

Jacob V, James IV and His Poet, Scots Magazine 10.279 ([59]; occasion).

Mackenzie W M, William Dunbar, Edinburgh Essays on Scots Literature, Edinburgh and London 1933, pp 44, 47, 49 ([59], [60], [54], [55], [51]; occasion).

Roy J A, Of the Makaris A Causerie, UTQ 16.33, 36 (contemp conditions; [59], [53]).

Baxter J W, William Dunbar, Edinburgh and London 1952, pp 58, 120, 129, 140, 161 ([51], [54], [55], [56], [61], [57], [53], [52], [58], [60], [59]; occasion, identity of subjects).

Milner I, Some Aspects of Satire in the Poetry of Dunbar, Philologica (cizojazyčná prioloha Časopisu pro moderní filologii) 8.37, 41 ([57], [49]; contemp conditions).

Leyerle J, The Two Voices of William Dunbar, UTQ 31.329 ([59], [60]; identity of subject).

Scott T, Dunbar A Critical Exposition, Edinburgh and London 1966, pp 1, 8, 12, 60, 68, 125, 155, 159, 261, 286, 344 (group a a whole, [50], [59], [48], [53], [54], [56], [58], [60], [62], [55], [57], [52]; occasion, contemp conditions, biographical evidence, identity of subjects, classification of poem).

Kinghorn A M, Dunbar. and Villon, MLR 62.199 ([60]; biographical evidence).

Scott T, Late Medieval Scots Poetry, London 1967, p 31 ([53]; occasion).

Dorsch T S, Of Discretioun in Asking Dunbar's Petitionary Poems, Chaucer und seine Zeit Symposion fur Walter F Schirmer, ed A Esch, Tubingen 1968, pp 287, 291 ([59], [47]; attitude).

Literary Criticism. The Scottish Register, Edinburgh 1794, 2.203 ([61]).

Irving D, The Lives of the Scotish Poets, 2nd edn London 1810, 1.396, 406 ([61], [53]).

Gilchrist O, Censura Literaria, ed S E Brydges, London 1807, 5.244 ([61]; brief).

[Sandys W] Specimens of Macaronic Poetry, London 1831, pp iii, xix ([61]).

Laing, edn, 2.279, 296, 299, 306, 316, 407, 458 ([51], [55], [52], [58], [61], [49], [53]).

Ancient Scotish Poetry No I Dunbar, Blackwood's Edinburgh Magazine 37.305, 311 ([53], [59], [51]).

Wright T, On the Scottish Poet Dunbar, Essays on Subjects Connected with the Literature Popular Superstitions and History of England in the Middle Ages, London 1846, 2.303 ([61]).

Green M A E, Lives of the Princesses of England, London 1852, 4.129 ([51]; brief comment).

Paterson J, The Works of William Dunbar, Edinburgh 1860; reissued Edinburgh 1863, pp 148, 157, 166, 197 ([61], [51], [53], [59]).

Irving D, The History of Scotish Poetry, ed J A Carlyle, Edinburgh 1861, pp 247, 251 ([59], [60], [61]; brief).

Ross J M, Scottish History and Literature, Glasgow 1884, pp 198, 206, 210 ([59], [61], [62]).

Schipper J, William Dunbar sein Leben und seine Gedichte, Berlin 1884, pp 117, 122, 190, 216, 221, 223, 234, 239, 307 ([47], [48], [49], [51], [52], [53], [54], [55], [56], [58], [57], [61], [60], [59], [62]).

Mackay Æ J G, Introd, Small edn, l.xlvii, xlix, liii, xc, xciii, xcix, cviii, cxiv, cxvii, cxxviii, cxxx, cxxxiv, cxxxvii ([60], [48], [53], [52], [62], [49], [51], [61], [56], [54], [55], [57], [59], [50]).

Minto W, Characteristics of English Poets, authorized American edn, Boston 1899, p 105 ([61], [59]).

Oliphant [M], Royal Edinburgh, London and N Y 1890, p 190 ([51]; superficial).

[Robertson J L] Haliburton H, Our Earlier Burns, In Scottish Fields, London 1890, pp 230, 239 (group as a whole and [61], [51], [59]).

Morley, 7.128 ([51]).

Schipper, edn, pt 1, 40².33, 37, 40, 44; pt 2, 40⁴.35; pt 3, 41⁴.5, 10 ([47], [48], [49], [51], [50], [52], [56], [57], [61]).

Brandl, 2¹.718 ([47], [48], [51]).

Oliphant F R, William Dunbar, Blackwood's Edinburgh Magazine 154.432, 434 ([61], [47], [51], group as a whole).

Ten Brink, 3.67, 74 ([48], [51], [61]).

Smeaton O, A Quartette of Court Singers Four Centuries Ago, Westminster Rev 148.183 ([59]; brief, extravagant, fictionalized).

Gosse E, A Short History of Modern English Literature, N Y 1898; rvsd edn N Y 1906, p 50 ([61]; brief).

Henderson T F, Scottish Vernacular Literature, Edinburgh 1898; 3rd edn rvsd Edinburgh 1910, pp 154, 174 ([57], [59], [47], [51]).

Smeaton O, William Dunbar, N Y (1898?), p 133 ([54], [58], [61], [53], [57], [59], [60]).

Neilson W A, The Origins and Sources of the Court of Love, Studies and Notes in Philology and Literature, Boston 1899, 6.224 ([51]).

Smith G G, The Transition Period, Periods of European Lit, Edinburgh and London 1900, 4.50 and passim ([51], [57], [58], [59]).

Chambers R, Chambers's Cyclopædia, Phila and N Y 1901–03; rvsd J L Geddie, Phila and N Y 1938, 1.198 ([51], [61]).

Browne W H, The Taill of Rauf Coilyear, Baltimore 1903, p 17 ([59]).

Millar J H, A Literary History of Scotland, London 1903, p 65 ([61]).

Moorman F W, The Interpretation of Nature in English Poetry from Beowulf to Shakespeare, QF 95.144 ([48]; brief).

Snell F J, The Poets, The Age of Transition, London 1905, 1.88 ([60], [59]).

Wülker R, Geschichte der englischen Literatur, Leipzig und Wien 1906–07, 1.207 ([52], [53], [59]; brief comment).

CHEL, 2.289 ([59], [60], [57], [58], [61]).

Steinberger C, Étude sur William Dunbar, Dublin 1908, pp 41, 100, 128 ([48], [49], [51], [50], [61], [60], [57], [62]).

Tucker S M, Verse Satire in England, CUS 3, no 2, pp 137, 141 ([59], [57], [50], [51]).

Enc Brit, 8.669 ([57], [61]).

Perrow E C, The Last Will and Testament

as a Form of Literature, Trans Wisconsin Acad of Sciences Arts and Letters 7¹.720 ([61]).

Stair-Kerr E, The Poets, Scotland under James IV, Paisley 1911, p 124 ([58], [59]; brief).

Watt L M, Scottish Life and Poetry, London 1912, p 105 ([59]).

Jacobi J B, William Dunbar—an Appreciation, The American Catholic Quarterly Rev 44.306 ([51]; brief).

Saintsbury G, The Four Great Scottish Poets, A Short Hist of Eng Lit, N Y 1929, p 188 ([61], [53], [58]; brief).

Kitchin G, A Survey of Burlesque and Parody in English, Edinburgh and London 1931, p 23 ([51], [61], [56], [58]).

Taylor R A, Dunbar the Poet, The Poets on the Poets, no 4, London 1931, pp 51, 54, 58, 60, 70, 79, 83 ([48], [49], [51], [53], [52], [57], [58], [60], [59], [54], [55], [61]).

Mackenzie A M, An Historical Survey of Scottish Literature, London 1933, pp 88, 95 ([59], [51]).

Mackenzie W M, William Dunbar, Edinburgh Essays on Scots Lit, Edinburgh and London 1933, pp 40, 45, 49 ([61], [59], [51]).

Rait R and G S Pryde, Scotland, N Y 1934; 2nd edn London 1954, p 309 ([61]; very brief).

Smith J M, The French Background of Middle Scots Literature, Edinburgh and London 1934, pp 47, 65, 164 ([49], [61], [51]).

Speirs J, William Dunbar, Scrut 7.62 ([51], [61]);The Scots Literary Tradition, London 1940, p 46 ([51], [61]); 2nd rvsd edn 1962, p 62.

Utley CR, pp 65, 178, 186 ([58], [52]; mainly summary with occasional brief comment).

Craig HEL, p 168 ([61]; brief).

Sitwell E, A Poet's Notebook, London 1943; rptd Boston 1950, p 240 ([49]).

Moore A K, The Secular Lyric in ME, Lexington Ky 1951, p 205 ([58], [53], [48], [49]).

Baxter J W, William Dunbar, Edinburgh and London 1952, pp 52, 58, 129, 131, 141, 160, 168 ([49], [51], [50], [56], [61], [57], [53], [60]).

Morgan E, Dunbar and the Language of Poetry, EC 2.147, 150 ([53], [59], [61], [51]).

Renwick-Orton, p 416 ([61], [53]; brief).

Kinsley J, The tretis of the tua mariit wemen and the wedo, MÆ 23.31 ([56], [61], [51], [59], [49]).

Lewis C S, English Literature in the Sixteenth Century, Oxford 1954, p 93 ([60], [58], [61], [50], [48]).

Kinsley J, The Mediaeval Makars, Scottish Poetry A Critical Survey, London 1955, p 29 ([48], [51], [59], [56], [58], [49]).

Milner I, Some Aspects of Satire in the Poetry of Dunbar, Philologica (cizojazyčná prioloha Casopisu pro moderní filologii) 8.37, 39, 41 ([57], [61], [49]).

Schlauch M, English Medieval Literature, Warsaw 1956, p 296 ([49]).

Kinsley J, William Dunbar Poems, Oxford 1958, pp xv, xix ([59], [49], [61], [58], [51], [56]).

Mackie R L, King James IV of Scotland, Edinburgh and London 1958, p 180 ([49], [60]; brief comments).

Wittig K, The Scottish Tradition in Literature, Edinburgh 1958, p 57 ([51]).

Kinghorn A M, The Mediaeval Makars, Texas Stud Lit and Lang 1.78 ([53], [56], [61]).

Leyerle J, The Two Voices of William Dunbar, UTQ 31.319, 324, 329, 333, 337 ([61], [51], [59], [60], [48], [53]).

Davies R T, Medieval English Lyrics, London 1963, p 26 ([49]; brief reference).

Smith Rowland, The Poetry of William Dunbar, Theoria 22.79, 82 ([53], [49], [54], [55], [58]).

Hyde I, Poetic Imagery, SSL 2.184, 189, 197 ([59], [54], [53], [61]).

Fox D, The Scottish Chaucerians, Chaucer and Chaucerians, ed D S Brewer, University Alabama 1966, p 182 ([57], [61]).

Rattray R F, What Did Dunbar Mean? TLS Jan 27 1966, p 63 ([52]).

Meier H H, What Dunbar Meant, TLS Feb 24 1966, p 148 ([52]).

Scott T, Dunbar A Critical Exposition, Edinburgh and London 1966, pp 63, 67, 92, 121, 154, 158, 188, 212, 244, 251, 261, 333, 344, 346, 366 and passim ([49], [58], [50], [59], [60], [47], [62], [54], [55], [53], [52], [48], [56], [51], [61], [57], general).

Wood H H, Two Scots Chaucerians, Writers and Their Work, no 201, ed G Bullough, London 1967, pp 36, 38 ([51], [48], [53]).

Bibliography. Brown-Robbins, Robbins-Cutler, nos 566 ([50]), 1527 ([49]), 2267 ([47]), 3598 ([48]), 3870 ([51]); Robbins-Cutler, nos 417.5 ([59]), 1330.5 ([61]), 1587.3 ([57]), 1934.5 ([58]), 2018.5 ([60]), 2032.5 ([52]), 2349.3 ([56]), 2457.5 ([55]), 3117.7 ([53]), 3496.3 ([54]), 3751.5 ([62]).

Utley CR, pp 178, 186 ([58], [52]).

Beattie W, The Chepman and Myllar Prints, A Facsimile, Edinburgh Biblio Soc, Oxford 1950, p xiv (PRINT 5 of [61]).

IV. Town Life

(Note: Folios for items [63–65] are listed by MS number, as appropriate, after each title. See under *MSS* below for full listing and information. Titles are from Mackenzie edn.)

[63] THE DEVILLIS INQUEST.

1, ff 18ᵇ–19ª; 2, pp 55–57; 3, ff 132ᵇ–133ª.

[64] TYDINGIS FRA THE SESSIOUN.

1, ff 37ª–38ª; 2, pp 314–315; 3, ff 59ª–59ᵇ.

[65] TO THE MERCHANTIS OF EDINBURGH.

1, ff 1ᵇ–2ᵇ.

MSS. 1, Camb Univ L1.5.10 (Reidpeth or Moore), ff 1ᵇ–2ᵇ, 18ᵇ–19ª, 37ª–38ª (1623; items [65], lines 21–55, 71–75, 81–105 of [63], [64]); 2, Magdalene Coll Camb 2553 (Pepysian Libr, Maitland Folio), pp 55–57, 314–315 (1570–71; lines 21–55, 71–75, 81–105 of item [63]; item [64]); 3, Nat Libr Scot 1.1.6 (Bannatyne), ff 59ª–59ᵇ, 132ᵇ–133ª (1568; items [64], [63]).

Pinkerton J, Ancient Scotish Poems, London and Edinburgh 1786, 1.v; 2.437, 471 (MSS 2, 3).

Brydges E and J Haslewood, The British Bibliographer, London 1814, 4.183 (MS 3).

Laing D, The Poems of George Bannatyne, Edinburgh 1824, p 3 (MS 3); An Account of the Contents of George Bannatyne's Manuscript, The Bannatyne Club, Edinburgh 1829, 35.43 (MS 3).

A Catalogue of the Manuscripts Preserved in the Library of the University of Cambridge, Cambridge 1861, 4.94 (MS 1).

Small J, The Poetical Works of Gavin Douglas, Edinburgh and London 1874, 1.clxxi (MS 2).

Schipper, edn, pt 1, 40².9ff (MSS 1, 2, 3).

Murdoch J B, ed, The Bannatyne Manuscript, 4 vols, Hunterian Club, Glasgow 1896, 2.160; 3.372 (MS 3 rptd).

Smith G G, Specimens of Middle Scots, Edinburgh and London 1902, pp lxvi, lxxiii (MSS 2, 3).

Brown J T T, The Bannatyne Manuscript, SHR 1.136 (MS 3).

Craigie W A, ed, The Maitland Folio, PSTS ns 7, 20, 2 vols, Edinburgh and London 1919–27, 2.41 (MS 1); 1.62, 374; 2.64, 121 MS 2 rptd, notes in vol 2); variants between MSS 1 and 2 listed in 2.64, 121.

Ritchie W T, ed, The Bannatyne Manuscript Writtin in Tyme of Pest, PSTS ns 5, 22, 23, 26, 4 vols, Edinburgh 1928–34, 2.145; 3.1 (MS 3 rptd).

Baxter J W, William Dunbar, Edinburgh and London 1952, pp 217ff (MSS 1, 2, 3).

Editions. Laing D, The Poems of William Dunbar, 2 vols, Edinburgh 1834, 1.45, 97, 102; 2.248, 283, 290 (notes in vol 2; MSS 3, 2, 1; Memoirs of William Dunbar preceding text of poems in vol 1 is paginated separately).

Paterson J, The Life and Poems of William Dunbar, Edinburgh 1860 (crit Athen July 14 1860, p 49); reissued The Works of William Dunbar Including His Life 1465–1536, Edinburgh 1863, pp 95, 127, 140 (glossings in ftnts).

Small J, Æ J G Mackay, G P McNeill, W Gregor, The Poems of William Dunbar, PSTS 2, 4, 16, 21, 29, 3 vols, Edinburgh 1884–93, 2.78, 144, 261; 3.132, 226, 348 (notes in vol 3; MSS 1, 3).

Schipper J, The Poems of William Dunbar, pt 1, Denkschriften der kaiserlichen Akademie der Wissenschaften, Philo-Hist Classe, Vienna 1892–93, 40².78 (MS sources and variants given in headnotes and ftnts to each poem; MSS 1, 3; crit E Kölbing, EStn 20.439).

Baildon H B, The Poems of William Dunbar, Cambridge 1907, pp 29, 245 (notes at end of text; sources vary, selects reading which seems to him most likely to be correct; crit J H Millar, The Bookman 32.207).

Mackenzie W M, The Poems of William Dunbar, London 1932, p 76 (notes at end of text; MSS 1, 2, 3; crit B Dickins, MLR 28.506; TLS Jan 26 1933, p 55; The Modern Scot 4.63); rptd London 1950; ed B Dickins, rptd and rvsd London 1960 (crit A Macdonald, ESts 43.219); rptd 1970.

Selections. Ramsay A, The Ever Green, Edinburgh 1724, 1.98, 171 ([64], [63]); occasional changes in wording, adds 2 stanzas to [64]; MS 3); The Poetical Works of Allan Ramsay, ed C Mackay, London and N Y n d, pp 234, 247 ([64], [63]).

Ruddiman W, Choice Collection of Scots Poems, Edinburgh 1766, p 89 ([64]).

Dalrymple D, Ancient Scottish Poems, Edinburgh 1770, pp 31, 40, 240, 247; rptd Leeds 1815, pp 37, 48, 291, 297 ([63], [64]; notes at end of text; MS 3).

The Caledoniad, London 1775, 3.52 ([64]; adds 2 stanzas at end).

Morison R, Select Poems of Wil Dunbar Part First from the MS of George Bannatyne, Perth 1788, pp 38, 46 ([63], [64]; MS 3).

Sibbald J, Chronicle of Scottish Poetry, 4 vols, Edinburgh and London 1802, 1.247, 290 ([64], from [63]; introductory and end notes; sources not always indicated but include MSS 2, 3).

Tytler P F, Lives of Scottish Worthies, London 1833, 3.115 (from [65]; Laing edn).

Ancient Scotish Poetry No I Dunbar, Blackwood's Edinburgh Magazine 37.314 ([65]).

William Dunbar, The Scottish Journal 1.131 ([65]; Laing edn).

Irving D, The History of Scotish Poetry, ed J A Carlyle, Edinburgh 1861, p 249 (from [63]).

Masson R O, Three Centuries of English Poetry Being Selections from Chaucer to Herrick, London 1876, p 136 ([65]; spelling modernized, glossings at foot of page; Laing edn).

Ross J, The Book of Scottish Poems, Paisley 1882, 1.189 ([65]).

Schipper J, William Dunbar sein Leben und seine Gedichte, Berlin 1884, pp 152, 155 (in German; from [64], from [63], [65]; crit E Kölbing, EStn 10.128; M Trautmann, Angl 7.146; The Nation 40.144).

Fitzgibbon H M, Early English and Scottish Poetry, London N Y and Melbourne 1888, pp 142, 433 (from [63]; spelling modernized, notes at end of text).

Brown P H, Scotland Before 1700 from Contemporary Documents, Edinburgh 1893, p 109 ([65]).

Chambers R, Chambers's Cyclopædia, Phila and N Y 1901–03; rvsd Phila and N Y 1938, 1.198 ([63], [64], [65]; brief excerpts).

Gray M M, Scottish Poetry from Barbour to James VI, N Y 1935, p 158 ([65]; crit J Speirs, Scrut 6.83; W M Mackenzie, The Scottish Bookman 1, no 4, p 133).

[Grieve C M] MacDiarmid H, Selections from the Poems of William Dunbar, The Saltire Classics, Edinburgh 1952, p 37 ([65]; glossings in ftnts; Mackenzie edn).

Kinsley J, William Dunbar Poems, Oxford 1958, pp 73, 126 ([64], [65]; notes at end of text; MSS 1, 3; crit TLS Apr 18 1958, p 208; D Young, William Dunbar, SHR 38.10; E Morgan, RES ns 11.71; J Wordsworth, MÆ 30.121).

MacQueen J and T Scott, The Oxford Book of Scottish Verse, Oxford 1966, p 118 ([65];

glossings at foot of page; Mackenzie edn).

Scott T, Late Medieval Scots Poetry, London 1967, pp 123, 186 ([65]; notes at end of text; Mackenzie edn).

Textual Matters. Laing, edn, 2.248 ([63]).

Schipper, edn, pt 1, 40².78, 81 ([64], [63]; see also introductory and ftnts to individual poems).

Mebus F, Studien zu William Dunbar, Breslau 1902, p 60 ([65]; explanation of obscure words and phrases, discussion of references).

Mackenzie, edn, pp 214, 238 ([63–65]).

Baxter J W, William Dunbar, Edinburgh and London 1952, pp 110, 238 ([65], [63]).

Language. Ramsay A, The Ever Green, Edinburgh 1724, 2.265 ([64], [63]; glossary).

Dalrymple D, Ancient Scottish Poems, Edinburgh 1770, p 317 (glossary); rptd Leeds 1815, p 367, [added] Glossary, p 1 [separate pagination] ([63], [64]).

Sibbald J, Chronicle of Scottish Poetry, Edinburgh and London 1802, vol 4 [unpaged] (glossary; [64], [63]).

Murray J A H, The Dialect of the Southern Counties of Scotland, London 1873 (group as a whole).

Kaufmann J, Traité de la langue, Bonn 1873, p 47 (group as a whole).

Hahn O, Zur Verbal- und Nominalflexion bei den schottischen Dichtern, Berlin 1887–89 (see especially pt 3, p 17; group as a whole).

Schipper, edn, pt 1, 40².18 (group as a whole).

Gregor W, Glossary, Small edn, 3.401 (group as a whole).

Curtis F J, An Investigation of the Rime and Phonology of Clariodus, Angl 16.387, 17.1, 125 (group as a whole).

Bearder J W, Über den Gebrauch der Praepositionen in der altschottischen Poesie, Halle 1894 ([64], [63], [65]; examples from Dunbar; crit EStn 19.410).

Heuser W, Die Dehnung vor -nd im Mittelschottischen, Die Dehnung -end, Ang 19.401 (brief; group as a whole).

Baildon H B, On the Rimes in the Authentic Poems of William Dunbar, Trans Roya Soc Edinburgh 39³.629; issued separately Edinburgh 1899 (group as a whole).

Flom G T, Scandinavian Influence on Southern Lowland Scotch, diss Columbia 1900 (group as a whole).

Browne W H, The Taill of Rauf Coilyear Baltimore 1903, pp 15, 35, 139 (general discussion of Middle Scots, glossary; group a a whole).

Millar J H, A Literary History of Scotland

London 1903, p 687 (glossary; [65], [64]).

Knopff P, Darstellung der Ablautverhältnisse in der schottischen Schriftsprache, diss Würzburg 1904 (group as a whole).

Baildon, edn, pp xxvi, 299 (discussion, glossary; group as a whole).

CHEL, 2.101, 506 (group as a whole).

Gray M M, Introd, Lancelot of the Laik, PSTS ns 2, Edinburgh and London 1912, 2.xviii (group as a whole).

Lenz K, Zur Lautlehre der französischen Elemente in den schottischen Dichtungen, diss Marburg 1913 (examples taken from Douglas, Dunbar, Lyndesay, Clariodus; group as a whole).

Westergaard E, Prepositions in Lowland Scotch, Angl 41.444 (some examples from Dunbar; group as a whole); Verbal Forms in Middle-Scotch, Angl 43.95 (group as a whole).

Craigie W A, ed, The Maitland Folio, PSTS ns 7, 20, 2 vols, Edinburgh and London 1919–27, 2.135 (glossary; [63], [65], [64]).

Watt L M, Language and Influences, Douglas's Aeneid, Cambridge 1920, p 149 (very generally applicable; group as a whole).

Westergaard E, Studies in Prefixes and Suffixes, London 1924, (group as a whole).

Wilson J, The Spelling of Scotch before 1600, The Dialects of Central Scotland, London 1926, p 168 (group as a whole; attempts to determine pronunciation from spelling, rimes, modern Lothian pronunciation).

Westergaard E, Plural Forms in Lowland Scottish, Angl 51.77 (group as a whole).

Mackenzie, edn, pp xii, xxxvii, 245 ([63–65]; discussion, glossary).

Wood H H, The Poems and Fables of Robert Henryson, Edinburgh 1933; 2nd edn rvsd 1958; rptd 1965, 1968, p xxxi.

Patrick D, Scottish Literature, Chambers's Cyclopaedia, rvsd J L Geddie, Phila and N Y 1938, 1.164 (group as a whole).

[Grieve C M] MacDiarmid H, Selections from the Poems of William Dunbar, The Saltire Classics, Edinburgh 1952, pp 5, 49 ([65]; brief note, glossary).

Kinsley J, William Dunbar Poems, Oxford 1958, p 139 (glossary; [64], [65]).

Scott T, Dunbar A Critical Exposition, Edinburgh and London 1966, pp 346, 351; Late Medieval Scots Poetry, London 1967, pp 21, 189 ([65]; discussion, glossary).

Versification. Guest E, A History of English Rhythms, 2 vols, London 1838; ed W W Skeat, new edn [in 1 vol] London 1882, p 650 ([64]).

Schipper, passim ([63], [65]).

McNeill G P, Note on the Versification and Metres of Dunbar, Small edn, l.clxxix, clxxxvi, cxciii ([63], [64], [65]).

Schipper, edn, pt 1, 40².85 ([65]; discussion in headnote to poem).

Brandl, 2¹.1067 ([63]).

Curtis F J, The Rimes and Phonology of Clariodus, Angl 16.387; 17.1, 125 (group as a whole).

Henderson T F, Scottish Vernacular Literature, Edinburgh 1898; 3rd edn rvsd Edinburgh 1910, p 159 ([65]).

Baildon H B, Rimes in the Authentic Poems of Dunbar, Trans Royal Soc Edinburgh 39³.629 (group as a whole).

Tucker S M, Verse Satire in England, CUS 3, no 2, p 138 ([64]).

Scott T, Dunbar A Critical Exposition, pp 81, 318, 322, 326, 329 ([65], [64]).

Date. Laing, edn, 2.284, 290 ([65], [64]).

Paterson, edn, pp 106, 132, 142 ([63], [65], [64]).

Schipper J, William Dunbar sein Leben und seine Gedichte, Berlin 1884, p 116 ([64], [63], [65]).

Mackay Æ J G, Appendix to Introd, Small edn, l.clxi ([64], [65], [63]).

Morley, 7.129 ([64], [65], [63]).

Schipper, edn, pt 1, 40².78, 81, 85 ([64], [63], [65]).

Brown P H, Scotland before 1700 from Contemporary Documents, Edinburgh 1893, pp 109, 111 ([65]).

Mebus F, Studien zu William Dunbar, Breslau 1902, p 59 ([65]).

Baxter J W, William Dunbar, Edinburgh and London 1952, p 106 ([64]).

Authorship. Mackenzie, edn, p 238 ([63]).

Sources and Literary Relations. Nichol J, William Dunbar, The English Poets, ed T H Ward, London and N Y 1880 (numerous subsequent edns); N Y 1924, 1.150 ([63]).

[Robertson J L] Haliburton H, Dunbar in Burns, Furth in Field, London 1894, p 276 ([63]).

Smith G G, The Transition Period, Periods of European Lit, Edinburgh and London 1900, 4.36, 39, 42, and passim ([63–65]).

Chambers R, Chambers's Cyclopædia, Phila and N Y 1938, 1.198 ([63]).

Mebus F, Studien zu William Dunbar, p 60 ([65]; brief similarities to works of other writers in wording or reference).

CHEL, 2.289 ([64], [65]).

Mendenhall J C, Aureate Terms A Study in

the Literary Diction of the 15th Century, Lancaster Pa 1919 (group as a whole).

Patrick D, Scottish Literature, Chambers's Cyclopædia, rvsd J L Geddie, Phila and N Y 1938, 1.166 (group as a whole).

Tucker S M, Verse Satire in England, CUS 3, no 2, p 137 ([64], [65]).

Craig HEL, p 169 ([63]; brief).

Maclaine A H, The Christis Kirk Tradition, SSL 2.16 ([63]).

Scott T, Dunbar A Critical Exposition, Edinburg and London 1966, pp 79, 326, 329 and passim ([65], [63]).

Other Scholarly Problems. Laing, edn, 2.283, 290 ([65], [64]; setting, identity of subject).

Paterson, edn, pp 98, 131, 142 ([63], [65], [64]; identity of subject, obscure passages, occasion).

Irving D, The History of Scotish Poetry, ed J A Carlyle, Edinburgh 1861, p 248 ([63]; contemp conditions).

Mackay Æ J G, Introd, Small edn, l.xlix, cxxiv ([65], [64], [63]; occasion, identity of subject, contemp conditions).

Smeaton O, William Dunbar, N Y (1898?), pp 71, 85, 152 ([65], [64], [63]; biographical evidence, contemp conditions).

Teichert O P, Schottische Zustände unter Jacob IV nach den Dichtungen von William Dunbar, Görlitz 1903, pp 20, 25, 31, 36 ([64], [63], [65]; contemp conditions; crit O Glöde, EStn 36.267).

Smeaton O, The Story of Edinburgh, London 1905, p 59 ([64]; occasion, brief).

Stair-Kerr E, The Poets, Scotland under James IV, Paisley 1911, p 126 ([65]; attitude, brief).

Baxter J W, William Dunbar, Edinburgh and London 1952, pp 106, 110 ([64], [65], [63]; occasion).

Scott T, Dunbar A Critical Exposition, pp 6, 14 ([65], [63], [64]; contemp conditions); Late Medieval Scots Poetry, London 1967, p 28 ([65]; contemp conditions).

Literary Criticism. Irving D, The Lives of the Scotish Poets, 2nd edn London 1810, 1.426 ([63]).

Tytler P F, Lives of Scottish Worthies, London 1833, 3.114 ([65]; brief comment).

Laing, edn, 1.31 (Memoirs; [65]).

Ancient Scotish Poetry No I Dunbar, Blackwood's Edinburgh Magazine 37.313 ([65]; brief comment).

Paterson, edn, p 132 ([65]).

Irving D, The History of Scotish Poetry, ed J A Carlyle, Edinburgh 1861, p 248 ([63]).

Smith A, William Dunbar Dreamthorp,

London 1863; rptd no 200 The World's Classics, London 1914; rptd London 1934, p 76 ([63]).

Ross J M, Scottish History and Literature, Glasgow 1884, p 204 ([63–65]).

Schipper J, William Dunbar sein Leben und seine Gedichte, Berlin 1884, pp 151, 158 ([64], [63], [65]).

Mackay Æ J G, Introd, Small edn, l.cxxiii ([64], [63], [65]).

Oliphant [M], Royal Edinburgh, London and N Y 1890, p 189 ([65]; brief, superficial).

[Robertson J L] Haliburton H, Our Earlier Burns, In Scottish Fields, London 1890, p 240 ([65]).

Schipper, edn, pt 1, 40².81, 85 ([63], [65]).

Oliphant F R, William Dunbar, Blackwood's Edinburgh Magazine 154.430 ([63]).

Ten Brink, 3.67, 74 ([64], [63]).

Smeaton O, A Quartette of Court Singers Four Centuries Ago, Westminster Rev 148.183 ([64], [63]; brief, extravagant, fictionalized).

Henderson T F, Scottish Vernacular Literature, Edinburgh 1898; 3rd edn rvsd Edinburgh 1910, p 173 ([65]).

Smeaton O, William Dunbar, N Y (1898?), pp 134, 139 ([65], [63]).

Smith G G, The Transition Period, Periods of European Lit, Edinburgh and London 1900, 4.50 and passim ([63], [64], [65]).

Chambers R, Chambers's Cyclopædia, Phila and N Y 1901–03; rvsd J L Geddie, Phila and N Y 1938, 1.198 ([63–65]).

Millar J H, A Literary History of Scotland, London 1903, p 64 ([64]).

CHEL, 2.289 ([64–65]).

Steinberger C, Étude sur William Dunbar, Dublin 1908, p 94 ([64], [65], [63]).

Tucker S M, Verse Satire in England, CUS 3, no 2, p 137 ([64–65]).

Enc Brit, 8.669 ([65]).

Smith G G, Scottish Literature Character and Influence, London 1919, p 14 ([64]; brief reference).

William Dunbar, TLS Apr 10 1930, p 305 ([65]).

Taylor R A, Dunbar the Poet, The Poets on the Poets, no 4, London 1931, p 62 ([64–65]).

Mackenzie, edn, p 238 ([63]).

Speirs J, William Dunbar, Scrut 7.63, 66 ([65], [64]); The Scots Literary Tradition, London 1940, pp 36, 48, 51 ([65], [64]); rvsd 2nd edn 1962, pp 55, 63, 65.

Baxter J W, William Dunbar, Edinburgh and London 1952, pp 107, 111 ([64], [63]).

Renwick-Orton, p 416 ([63]; brief).

Ward A C, Illustrated Hist of Eng Lit, London N Y and Toronto 1953, p 42 ([65]; brief).

Milner I, Some Aspects of Satire in the Poetry of Dunbar, Philologica (cizojazyčná prioloha Časopisu pro moderní filologii) 8.33, 38 ([65]).

Schlauch M, English Medieval Literature, Warsaw 1956, p 296 ([65]).

Leyerle J, The Two Voices of William Dunbar, UTQ 31.337 ([65]).

Scott T, Dunbar A Critical Exposition, Edinburgh and London 1966, pp 73, 167, 190, 236, 333 and passim ([64], [65], [63]).

Wood H H, Two Scots Chaucerians, Writers and Their Work, no 201, ed G Bullough, London 1967, p 36 ([65]).

Bibliography. Robbins-Cutler, nos 293.5 ([64]), 3634.6 ([63]), 4165.5 ([65]).

V. Of Women

(Note: Folios for items [66–73] are listed by MS number, as appropriate, after each title. See under *MSS* below for full listing and information. Titles are from Mackenzie edn.)

[66] IN PRAIS OF WEMEN.

2, pp 294–295; 3, f 278ᵇ.

[67] THE TWA CUMMERIS.

1, f 19ᵇ; 2, pp 57–58; 3, f 137ᵃ; 4, unpaged.

[68] THE TRETIS OF THE TUA MARIIT WEMEN AND THE WEDO.

2, pp 81–96; 5, pp 177–189.

[69] OF THE LADYIS SOLISTARIS AT COURT.

1, ff 38ᵇ–39ᵃ; 2, pp 324–325; 3, ff 261ᵃ–261ᵇ.

[70] TO A LADYE.

2, p 320.

[71] QUHONE HE LIST TO FEYNE.

2, pp 322–323.

[72] INCONSTANCY OF LUVE.

3, f 281ᵃ.

[73] OF LUVE ERDLY AND DIVINE.

3, ff 284ᵇ–285ᵇ.

MSS. 1, Camb Univ L1.5.10 (Reidpeth or Moore), ff 19ᵇ, 38ᵇ–39ᵃ (1623; items [67], [69]); 2, Magdalene Coll Camb 2553 (Pepysian Libr, Maitland Folio), pp 57–58, 81–96, 294–295, 320, 322–325 (1570–71; items [67–68], [66], [70–71], [69]); 3, Nat Libr Scot 1.1.6 (Bannatyne), ff 137ᵃ, 261ᵃ–261ᵇ, 278ᵇ,

281ᵃ, 284ᵇ–285ᵇ (1568; items [67], [69], [66], [72–73]); 4, Aberdeen Town Clerk's Office, Aberdeen Minute Book of Sasines, vol 2, unpaged (1503–04; item [67]). PRINT: 5, Nat Libr Scot 19.1.16 (Chepman and Myllar), pp 177–189 (1508; lines 104–530 of item [68]) (STC, no 7350).

Pinkerton J, Ancient Scotish Poems, 2 vols, London and Edinburgh 1786, 1.v; 2.437, 471 (MSS 2, 3).

Brydges E and J Haslewood, The British Bibliographer, London 1814, 4.183 (MS 3).

Laing D, The Poems of George Bannatyne, Edinburgh 1824, p 3 (MS 3); The Knightly Tale of Golagrus and Gawane, Edinburgh 1827, f 2ᵃ (PRINT 5 rptd); An Account of the Contents of George Bannatyne's Manuscript, The Bannatyne Club, Edinburgh 1829, 35.43 (MS 3); The Poems of William Dunbar, edn, 1.303 (in Supplement; MS 4).

A Catalogue of the Manuscripts Preserved in The Library of The University of Cambridge, Cambridge 1861, 4.94 (MS 1).

Small J, The Poetical Works of Gavin Douglas, Edinburgh and London 1874, 1.clxxi (MS 2).

Dickson R and J P Edmond, Annals of Scottish Printing from 1507 to the Beginning of the 17th Century, Cambridge 1890, p 49 (PRINT 5).

Schipper, edn, pt 1, 40².9ff (MSS 1, 2, 3, 4, PRINT 5).

Murdoch J B; ed, The Bannatyne Manuscript, 4 vols, Hunterian Club, Glasgow 1896, 3.386; 4.762, 809, 816, 826 (MS 3 rptd).

Smith G G, Specimens of Middle Scots, Edinburgh and London 1902, pp lxvi, lxxiii, lxxiv (MSS 2, 3, PRINT 5).

Brown J T T, The Bannatyne Manuscript, SHR 1.136 (MS 3).

Stevenson G, ed, Pieces from The Makculloch and the Gray MSS, PSTS 65, Edinburgh and London 1918, pp 245, 303 PRINT 5 rptd, notes at end of text).

Craigie W A, ed, The Maitland Folio, PSTS ns 7, 20, 2 vols, Edinburgh and London 1919–27, 1.64, 98, 345, 383, 386, 390; 2.65, 71, 118, 122 (MS 2 rptd, notes in vol 2).

Ritchie W T, ed, The Bannatyne Manuscript Writtin in Tyme of Pest, PSTS ns 5, 22, 23, 26, 4 vols, Edinburgh 1928–34, 3.14; 4.30, 75, 81, 91 (MS 3 rptd).

Baxter J W, TLS Apr 8 1939, p 208 (MS 4).

Beattie W, The Chepman and Myllar Prints, Edinburgh Biblio Soc, Oxford 1950, pp viii, 177 (PRINT 5 described, rptd).

Baxter J W, William Dunbar, Edinburgh and London 1952, pp 216ff (MSS 1, 2, 3, 4, PRINT 5).

Editions. Laing D, The Poems of William Dunbar, 2 vols, Edinburgh 1834, 1.27, 61, 92, 121, 172, 221; 2.230, 267, 282, 305, 338, 363 (notes in vol 2; MSS 2, 3, PRINT 5; Memoirs of William Dunbar preceding text of poems in vol 1 is paginated separately).

Paterson J, The Life and Poems of William Dunbar, Edinburgh 1860 (crit Athen July 14 1860, p 49); reissued The Works of William Dunbar Including His Life 1465–1536, Edinburgh 1863, pp 6, 42, 90, 93, 136, 182, 303 (glossings in footnotes).

Small J, Æ J G Mackay, G P McNeill, W Gregor, The Poems of William Dunbar, PSTS 2, 4, 16, 21, 29, 3 vols, Edinburgh 1884–93, 2.30, 160, 168, 179, 223, 245; 3.69, 249, 259, 266, 306, 331 (notes in vol 3; MSS 2, 3, PRINT 5).

Schipper J, The Poems of William Dunbar, pts 1, 2, 4, Denkschriften der kaiserlichen Akademie der Wissenschaften, Philo-Hist Classe, Vienna 1892–93, 40².45, 72; 40⁴.26; 42⁴.49 (MS sources and variants given in headnotes and footnotes to each poem; MSS 2, 3, PRINT 5; crit E Kölbing, EStn 20.439).

Baildon H B, The Poems of William Dunbar, Cambridge 1907, pp 10, 25, 56, 182, 241, 250, 288 (notes at end of text; sources vary, selects reading which seems to him most likely to be correct; crit J H Millar, The Bookman 32.207).

Mackenzie W M, The Poems of William Dunbar, London 1932, p 83 (notes at end of text; MSS 3, 2; crit B Dickins, MLR 28.506; TLS Jan 26 1933, p 55; The Modern Scot 4.63); rptd London 1950; ed B Dickins, rptd and rvsd London 1960 (crit A Macdonald, ESts 43.219); rptd 1970.

Selections. Ramsay A, The Ever Green, Edinburgh 1724, 1.206 ([69]; minor changes in wording; MS 3); The Poetical Works of Allan Ramsay, ed C Mackay, London and N Y n d, p 253 ([69]).

Dalrymple D, Ancient Scottish Poems, Edinburgh 1770, pp 79, 275; rptd Leeds 1815, pp 100, 323 ([73]; notes at end of text; MS 3).

Pinkerton J, Ancient Scotish Poems, 2 vols, London and Edinburgh 1786, 1.44, 89, 113; 2.380, 407, 414 ([68], [70], [67]; notes in vol 2; MS 2).

Morison R, Select Poems of Wil Dunbar Part First from the MS of George Bannatyne, Perth 1788, p 83 ([73]; MS 3).

Sibbald J, Chronicle of Scottish Poetry, 4 vols, Edinburgh 1802, 1.210, 251; 2.20 ([68], [67], [69], [73], [70]; introductory and end notes; sources not always indicated but include MSS 2, 3).

Irving D, The Lives of the Scotish Poets, 2nd edn London 1810, 1.415, 428 (from [68], [70]).

Brydges E and J Haslewood, The British Bibliographer, London 1814, 4.192 ([72]).

Irving D, The History of Scotish Poetry, ed J A Carlyle, Edinburgh 1861, pp 240, 244 ([70], [68]).

Masson R O, Three Centuries of English Poetry Being Selections from Chaucer to Herrick, London 1876, p 129 ([67]; spelling modernized, glossings at foot of page; Laing edn).

Ross J, The Book of Scottish Poems, Paisley 1882, 1.188, 193 ([73], [70]).

Schipper J, William Dunbar sein Leben und seine Gedichte, Berlin 1884, pp 135, 146, 187, 330 (poems in German scattered through text of discussion; from [68], [67], [69], [66], [70], [73]; crit E Kölbing, EStn 10.128; M Trautmann, Angl 7.146; The Nation 40.144).

Fitzgibbon H M, Early English and Scottish Poetry, London N Y and Melbourne 1888, pp 114, 432 ([70]; spelling modernized, notes at end of text).

Veitch J, The Feeling for Nature in Scottish Poetry, Edinburgh and London 1887, 1.233, 235 (brief quotes interspersed with criticism; from [68], from [70]; glossings in side notes).

Eyre-Todd G, Mediæval Scottish Poetry, Abbotsford Series, Glasgow 1892, pp 186, 204 ([70], [69]; glossings in margin).

Browne W H, Selections from the Early Scottish Poets, Baltimore 1896, p 129 (from [68]; notes at end of text; Small edn).

Quiller-Couch A, The Oxford Book of English Verse, Oxford 1900; new edn Oxford 1939, p 25 ([70]; glossings at foot of page).

Arber E, English Songs, The Dunbar Anthology, British Anthologies, London 1901, 1.46, 298 ([73]; spelling and some words modernized, identification of source in notes; Small edn).

Chambers R, Chambers's Cyclopædia, Phila and N Y 1901–03; rvsd Phila and N Y 1938, 1.198 (from [68]).

Smith G G, Specimens of Middle Scots, Edinburgh and London 1902, pp 47, 281 (from [68]; notes at end of text; MS 2).

Steinberger C, Étude sur William Dunbar, Dublin 1908, p 132 ([72]; Small edn).

Dixon W M, The Edinburgh Book of Scottish Verse, London 1910, p 42 ([70]; glossings at foot of page).

Douglas G, The Book of Scottish Poetry, London and Leipsic 1911, p 109 ([70]; glossings at foot of page; Small edn).

Buchan J, The Northern Muse, London 1924, pp 22, 459 ([70]; glossing at foot of page, brief note at end of text; Small edn).

Mackie R L, A Book of Scottish Verse, The World's Classics, no 417, London 1934, pp 39, 52 (from [68], [70]; glossings at foot of page); 2nd edn London Glasgow N Y 1967, pp 40, 52.

Gray M M, Scottish Poetry from Barbour to James VI, N Y 1935, pp 132, 140, 149 ([70], [71], from [68]; crit J Speirs, Scrut 6.83; W M Mackenzie, The Scottish Bookman 1, no 4, p 133).

[Grieve C M] MacDiarmid H, The Golden Treasury of Scottish Poetry, London 1940 (crit L MacNeice, The New Statesman and Nation, 21.66; TLS Feb 15 1941, pp 78, 84); rptd in The Golden Treasury Series, London 1948, p 167 ([68]).

Fergusson J, The Green Garden, London and Edinburgh 1946, p 33 (from [68]; spelling modernized).

Mackenzie A M, Scottish Pageant, Edinburgh 1946; 2nd edn 1952, 1.51 ([70]).

Gierasch W, Dunbar's To a Ladye, Expl 6, item 21.

Oliver J W and J C Smith, A Scots Anthology from the 13th to the 20th Century, Edinburgh and London 1949, p 44 (from [68]; spelling modernized, glossings at foot of page).

Auden W H and N H Pearson, Poets of the English Language, N Y 1950, p 306 (from [68]).

[Grieve C M] MacDiarmid H, Selections from the Poems of William Dunbar, The Saltire

Classics, Edinburgh 1952, pp 21, 24, 42 ([67], from [68], [70]; glossings in ftnts; Mackenzie edn); Selected Poems of William Dunbar, Glasgow 1955, pp 13, 51 ([67], [72], [66]).

Kinsley J, William Dunbar Poems, Oxford 1958, pp 21, 33, 68, 77, 116, 125, 128 ([70], lines 1–75, 89–93, 98–112, 239–316, 413–483, 489–530 of [68], lines 1–30, 73–90 of [73], [67]; notes at end of text; MSS 2, 3, PRINT 5).

McLaren M, The Wisdom of the Scots, London 1961, p 73 ([73]; glossings in margin).

Davies R T, Medieval English Lyrics, London 1963, pp 246, 357 ([70]; glossings at foot of page, notes at end of text; MS 2).

Rossi S, I Chauceriani Scozzesi, Napoli 1964, p 215 (from [68]; notes at foot of page).

Smith Rowland, The Poetry of William Dunbar, Theoria 22.81 ([70]).

MacQueen J and T Scott, The Oxford Book of Scottish Verse, Oxford 1966, pp 100, 130 ([70], [68]; glossings at foot of page; Mackenzie edn).

Scott T, Dunbar A Critical Exposition, Edinburgh and London 1966, p 58 ([70]; Mackenzie edn); Late Medieval Scots Poetry, London 1967, pp 92, 116, 184 ([68], [70]; notes at end of text; Mackenzie edn).

Ridley F [H], Selected Poems of William Dunbar, Los Angeles 1969, p 10 ([69]; glossings in margin; MSS 3, 2).

Hope A D, A Midsummer Eve's Dream, N Y 1970, pp 202, 270 ([69], [68]; Mackenzie edn).

Kinghorn A M, The Middle Scots Poets, London 1970, p 138 ([68]; notes at foot of page; PRINT 5).

MacQueen J, Ballattis of Luve, Edinburgh 1970, p 35 ([70], [71]; MS 2; glossings at foot of page).

Scott T, The Penguin Book of Scottish Verse, London 1970, p 134 ([70], from [68]; glossings at foot of page).

Modernizations. Tytler P F, Lives of Scottish Worthies, London 1833, 3.118 (from [68]; Laing edn).

Dunbar's Two Married Women and The Widow Translated into English* Verse, Edinburgh 1840 (Laing edn).

Bonar A R, The Poets and Poetry of Scotland, Edinburgh 1864; 2nd edn 1866, p 55 (from [68]).

[Robertson J L] Haliburton H, Dunbar Being a Selection from the Poems of an Old Makar Adapted for Modern Readers, London 1895, pp 54, 87 ([70], [67]; paraphrase, abbreviated, extremely free; crit R Brotanek, AnglB 6.71).

Linklater E, A Bawdy Revival, New Saltire, no 9 Sept 1963, p 7 ([68]).

Hope A D, A Midsummer Eve's Dream, p 271 ([68]).

Textual Matters. Laing, edn, 1.311; 2.267, 277, 282 ([67], [68], [69]).

Schipper, edn, pt 1, 40².17, 19, 24, 72 ([68], [67]; see also introductory and ftnts to individual poems).

Mebus F, Studien zu William Dunbar, Breslau 1902, p 34 ([70], [71], [72]; explanation of obscure words and phrases, discussion of references).

Isaac F, Walter Chepman and Andrew Myllar, Facsimiles and Illustrations No II English and Scottish Printing Types, printed for Biblio Soc, Oxford 1930 [unpaged] ([68]; brief discussion and figure 90).

Mackenzie, edn, pp 215 ff ([66–73]).

Baxter J W, William Dunbar, Edinburgh and London 1952, pp 52, 56, 121, 136, 178, 195 ([68], [67], [66], [71], [70], [72], [73]).

Dobson E J and P Ingham, Three Notes on Dunbar's Tua Mariit Wemen and the Wedo, MÆ 36.38 ([68]).

Language. Ramsay A, The Ever Green, Edinburgh 1724, 2.265 ([69]; glossary).

Dalrymple D, Ancient Scottish Poems, Edinburgh 1770, p 317 (glossary); rptd Leeds 1815, p 367, [added] glossary, p 1 [separate pagination] ([73]).

Pinkerton J, Ancient Scotish Poems, London and Edinburgh 1786, 1.cxliii; 2.520 (synorthographic and symphonious words, glossary; [68], [70], [67]).

Sibbald J, Chronicle of Scottish Poetry, Edinburgh and London 1802, vol 4 [unpaged] (glossary; [68], [67], [69], [73], [70]).

Laing, edn, 2.372 ([68]).

Irving D, The History of Scotish Poetry, ed J A Carlyle, Edinburgh 1861, p 595 (glossary; [70], [68]).

Murray J A H, The Dialect of the Southern Counties of Scotland, London 1873 (group as a whole).

Kaufmann J, Traité de la langue, Bonn 1873, p 47 (group as a whole).

Hahn O, Zur Verbal- und Nominalflexion bei den schottischen Dichtern, Berlin 1887–89 (see especially pt 3, p 17; group as a whole).

Schipper, edn, pt 1, 40².18 (group as a whole).

Gregor W, Glossary, Small edn, 3.401 (group as a whole).

Curtis F J, An Investigation of the Rimes and Phonology of Clariodus, Angl 16.387;

17.1, 125 (group as a whole).

Bearder J W, Über den Gebrauch der Praepositionen in der altschottischen Poesie, Halle 1894 ([68], [67], [69], [66]; examples from Dunbar; crit EStn 19.410).

Browne W H, Selections from the Early Scottish Poets, Baltimore 1896, pp 3, 197 ([68]; discussion in introd, glossary).

Heuser W, Die Dehnung vor -nd im Mittelschottischen, Die Dehnung -end, Angl 19.401 (brief; group as a whole).

Baildon H B, On the Rimes in the Authentic Poems of William Dunbar, Trans Royal Soc Edinburgh 39³.629; issued separately Edinburgh 1899 (group as a whole).

Flom G T, Scandinavian Influence on Southern Lowland Scotch, diss Columbia 1900 (group as a whole).

Arber E, English Songs, The Dunbar Anthology, British Anthologies, London 1901, 1.300 ([73]; glossary, index).

Smith G G, Specimens of Middle Scots, Edinburgh and London 1902, pp xi, 325 ([68]; history and philology of Middle Scots, glossary).

Millar J H, A Literary History of Scotland, London 1903, p 687 (glossary; [68]).

Rodeffer J D, The Inflection of the English Present Plural Indicative, Baltimore 1903, pp 1, 23, 38 ([68]).

Browne W H, The Taill of Rauf Coilyear, Baltimore 1903, pp 15, 35, 139 (general discussion of Middle Scots, glossary; group as a whole).

Knopff P, Darstellung der Ablautverhältnisse in der schottischen Schriftsprache, diss Würzburg 1904 (group as a whole).

Baildon, edn, pp xxvi, 299 (discussion, glossary; group as a whole).

CHEL, 2.101, 506 (group as a whole).

Dixon W M, The Edinburgh Book of Scottish Verse, London 1910, p 897 (glossary; [70]).

Gray M M, Introd, Lancelot of the Laik, PSTS ns 2, Edinburgh and London 1912, 2.xviii (group as a whole).

Lenz K, Zur Lautlehre der französischen Elemente in den schottischen Dichtungen, diss Marburg 1913 (examples taken from Douglas, Dunbar, Lyndesay, Clariodus; group as a whole).

Westergaard E, Prepositions in Lowland Scotch, Angl 41.444 (some examples from Dunbar; group as a whole); Verbal Forms in Middle-Scotch, Angl 43.95 (group as a whole).

Craigie W A, ed, The Maitland Folio, PSTS

ns 7, 20, 2 vols, Edinburgh and London 1919–27, 2.135 (glossary; [67], [68], [66], [70], [71], [69]). °

Watt L M, Language and Influences, Douglas's Aeneid, Cambridge 1920, p 149 (very generally applicable).

Westergaard E, Studies in Prefixes and Suffixes, London 1924 (group as a whole).

Wilson J, The Spelling of Scotch before 1600, The Dialects of Central Scotland, London 1926, p 168 (group as a whole; attempts to determine pronunciation from spelling, rimes, modern Lothian pronunciation).

Westergaard E, Plural Forms in Lowland Scottish, Angl 51.77 (group as a whole).

Mackenzie, edn, pp xii, xxxvii, 245 ([66–73]; discussion, glossary).

Wood H H, The Poems and Fables of Robert Henryson, Edinburgh 1933; 2nd edn rvsd 1958; rptd 1965, 1968, p xxxi.

Patrick D, Scottish Literature, Chambers's Cyclopædia, rvsd J L Geddie, Phila and N Y 1938, 1.164 (group as a whole).

[Grieve C M] MacDiarmid H, The Golden Treasury of Scottish Poetry, London 1940; rptd in The Golden Treasury Series, London 1948, p 394 (glossary; [68]).

Fergusson J, The Green Garden, London and Edinburgh 1946, p 228 (glossary; [68]).

Oliver J W and J C Smith, A Scots Anthology, Edinburgh and London 1949, p 497 (glossaries; [68]).

[Grieve C M] MacDiarmid H, Selections from the Poems of William Dunbar, The Saltire Classics, Edinburgh 1952, pp 5, 49 ([67], [68], [70]; brief note, glossary); Selected Poems of William Dunbar, Glasgow 1955, p 60 (glossary; [67], [72], [66]).

Kinsley J, William Dunbar Poems, Oxford 1958, p 139 (glossary; [70], [68], [73], [67]).

Rossi S, I Chauceriani Scozzesi, Napoli 1964, p 261 (discussion and glossary).

Scott T, Dunbar A Critical Exposition, Edinburgh and London 1966, pp 346, 351; Late Medieval Scots Poetry, London 1967, pp 21, 189 ([68], [70]; discussion and glossary).

Conley J, William Dunbar Additions to and Corrections of OED and DOST, N&Q 213(ns 15).170 ([68], [69]).

Hope A D, A Midsummer Eve's Dream, N Y 1970, p 319 ([69], [68]; glossary).

Kinghorn A M, The Middle Scots Poets, London 1970, pp 45, 164 (note on Middle Scots, glossary; [68]).

Versification. Irving D, The Lives of the Scotish Poets, 2nd edn London 1810, 1.409,

413 ([68]).

Conybeare J J, On the Derivation of the Later English Alliterative Metres, Introductory Essay on the Metre of Anglo-Saxon Poetry, Illustrations of Anglo-Saxon Poetry, London 1826, p lxv ([68]).

Laing, edn, 2.269 ([68]).

Guest E, A History of English Rhythms, 2 vols, London 1838; ed W W Skeat, new edn [in 1 vol] London 1882, passim ([68]).

Paterson, edn, pp 5, 8 ([68]).

Irving D, The History of Scotish Poetry, ed J A Carlyle, Edinburgh 1861, p 243 ([68]).

Schipper, 1.510 and passim ([66], [68], [69], [73]).

Schipper J, William Dunbar sein Leben und seine Gedichte, Berlin 1884, pp 133, 188 ([68], [72]).

Luick K, Die englische Stabreimzeile im XIV, XV und XVI Jahrhundert, Angl 11.602, 614 ([68]).

Mackay Æ J G, Introd, Small edn, 1.lxxxviii ([68]).

McNeill G P, Note on the Versification and Metres of Dunbar, Small edn, 1.clxxiii, clxxix, clxxxiv, clxxxviii ([68], [66], [70], [71], [67], [73], [72], [69]).

Morley, 7.129 ([68]).

Eyre-Todd G, Mediæval Scottish Poetry, Abbotsford Series, Glasgow 1892, p 151 ([68]).

Schipper, edn, pt 1, 40².45, 72, 74, 77; pt 2, 40⁴.27, 30 ([68], [67], [69], [66], [70], [71], [72]; discussion in headnotes to poems).

Brandl, 2¹.1013, 1029, 1065 ([68], [69], [72], [73]).

Curtis F J, The Rimes and Phonology of Clariodus, Angl 16.387; 17.1, 125 (group as a whole).

Baildon H B, Burns and Dunbar, Scottish Art and Letters 2.167 ([68]).

Browne W H, Selections from the Early Scottish Poets, Baltimore 1896, p 11 ([68]; very brief).

Henderson T F, Scottish Vernacular Literature, Edinburgh 1898; 3rd edn rvsd Edinburgh 1910, pp 154, 158, 163 ([66], [73], [72], [69]).

Baildon H B, Rimes in the Authentic Poems of Dunbar, Trans Royal Soc Edinburgh 39³.629 (group as a whole).

Schneider A, Die mittelenglische Stabzeile im 15 und 16 Jahrhundert, BBA 12.103 ([68]).

Browne W H, The Taill of Rauf Coilyear, Baltimore 1903, p 56 ([68]).

Saintsbury G, History of English Prosody, London 1908; 2nd edn 1923, 1.273 ([68]).

Steinberger C, Étude sur William Dunbar,

Dublin 1908, pp 132, 155 ([72], [68]).

Saintsbury G, Historical Manual of English Prosody, London 1910; rptd London 1914, 1. 56 ([68]).

Legouis HEL, p 176 ([68]; very brief).

Oakden J P, Alliterative Poetry in Middle English, Manchester 1930, p 153 and passim ([68]; crit K Brunner, AnglB 42.334).

Mackenzie, edn, p xiv ([68]).

Smith J M, The French Background of Middle Scots Literature, Edinburgh and London 1934, pp 158, 161 ([69], [73]; crit AnglB 45.265; MÆ 4.44).

Craigie W, The Scottish Alliterative Poems, Proc of the British Acad 28.217 ([68]).

Morgan E, Dunbar and the Language of Poetry, EC 2.153 ([68]).

Kinsley J, The tretis of the tua mariit wemen and the wedo, MAE 23.35; The Mediaeval Makars, Scottish Poetry A Critical Survey, London 1955, p 31 ([68]).

Wittig K, The Scottish Tradition in Literature, Edinburgh 1958, p 59 and passim ([68], [69], [72]).

Kinsley J, William Dunbar Poems, Oxford 1958, p xvii ([68]).

Kinghorn A M, The Mediaeval Makars, Texas Stud Lit and Lang 1.78 ([68]).

Scott T, Dunbar A Critical Exposition, Edinburgh and London 1966, pp 72, 179, 204, 278, 307, 313, 318, 325, 345 ([69], [68], [73], [66], [70], [67], [72]); Late Medieval Scots Poetry, London 1967, p 18 ([68]).

Date. Pinkerton J, Ancient Scotish Poems, 2 vols, London and Edinburgh 1786, l.x, xciii ([68]).

Paterson, edn, pp 43, 106, 184, 303, 306 ([70], [72], [67], [71], [73]).

Schipper J, William Dunbar sein Leben und seine Gedichte, Berlin 1884, p 116 ([68], [67], [69], [66]).

Mackay Æ J G, Introd [and] Appendix to Introd, Small edn, l.xci, cxxxix, clviii, clxi, clxiv, clxix ([70], [71], [73], [68], [67], [69], [72], [66]).

Morley, 7.129 ([69], [68]).

Schipper, edn, pt 1, 40².45, 74, 76; pt 2, 40⁴.26; pt 4, 42⁴.49 ([68], [69], [66], [70], [73]).

Steinberger C, Étude sur William Dunbar, Dublin 1908, pp 115, 144 ([68], [73]).

Utley CR, pp 200, 209, 227, 260, 282, 304 ([71], [73], [66], [67], [69], [68], [72]).

Baxter J W, William Dunbar, Edinburgh and London 1952, pp 55, 195 ([68], [69], [73]).

Lewis C S, English Literature in the Six-

teenth Century, Oxford 1954, p 91 ([68]).

Fox D, The Chronology of William Dunbar, PQ 39.419 ([68], [67]).

Authorship. Laing, edn, 2.283 ([66]).

Paterson, edn, p 140 ([66]).

Morley, 7.129 ([68]).

Utley CR, p 210 ([66]).

Baxter J W, William Dunbar, p 57 ([66]).

Sources and Literary Relations. Laing, edn, 2.269, 373 ([68]).

Schipper J, William Dunbar sein Leben und seine Gedichte, Berlin 1884, p 144 ([68]).

Cranstoun J, The Poems of Alexander Montgomerie, PSTS 9, 10, 11, Edinburgh and London 1887, pp 318, 322, 326, 370 ([68]; scattered references in notes).

Mackay Æ J G, Introd, Small edn, l.lxxxvi ([68]).

[Robertson J L] Haliburton H, Our Earlier Burns, In Scottish Fields, London 1890, p 238 ([68]).

Schipper, edn, pt 1, 40².46 ([68]).

[Robertson J L] Haliburton H, Dunbar in Burns, Furth in Field, London 1894, p 276 ([71]).

Wollmann F, Über politisch-satirische Gedichte aus der schottischen Reformationszeit, WBEP 8.63 ([68]; brief).

Smith G G, The Transition Period, Periods of European Lit, Edinburgh and London 1900, 4.36, 39, 42 and passim ([68], [70]).

Chambers R, Chambers's Cyclopædia, Phila and N Y 1901–03; rvsd Phila and N Y 1938, 1.194, 197 ([71], [68]).

M'Ilwraith W, A Sketch of Scottish Literature from the Earliest Times, Annual Burns Chronicle 10.22 ([68]).

Ritter O, Quellenstudien zu Robert Burns, Palaes 20.23, 51 ([71], [66]).

Mebus F, Studien zu William Dunbar, Breslau 1902, p 34 ([70], [71], [72]; brief similarities to Chaucer, The Kingis Quair, Lydgate, Shakespeare, of wording or reference).

Moorman F W, The Interpretation of Nature in English Poetry from Beowulf to Shakespeare, QF 95.146 ([68]).

Marsh G L, Sources and Analogues of The Flower and the Leaf, MP 4.318 ([68]).

CHEL, 2.288 ([68]).

Steinberger C, Étude sur William Dunbar, Dublin 1908, p 116 ([68]; Chaucer).

Tucker S M, Verse Satire in England, CUS 3, no 2, pp 137, 139, 177 ([68]).

Sandison H E, The Chanson D'Aventure in Middle English, Bryn Mawr Pa 1913, pp 53, 135 and passim ([68]).

Mendenhall J C, Aureate Terms A Study in

the Literary Diction of the 15th Century, Lancaster Pa 1919 (group as a whole).

Saintsbury G, The Four Great Scottish Poets, A Short Hist of Eng Lit, N Y 1929, p 186 ([68]).

William Dunbar, TLS Apr 10 1930, p 305 ([68]).

Nichols P H, William Dunbar as a Scottish Lydgatian, PMLA 46.219 ([73]).

Taylor R A, Dunbar the Poet, The Poets on the Poets, no 4, London 1931, p 49 ([68]; crit The Criterion 11.331; TLS Mar 17 1932, p 199; YWES 13.124).

Mackenzie W M, William Dunbar, Edinburgh Essays on Scots Literature, Edinburgh and London 1933, p 41 ([67]; very brief).

Smith J M, The French Background of Middle Scots Literature, Edinburgh and London 1934, pp xviii, xxviii, 38, 62, 66 ([68], [70]; crit AnglB 45.265; MÆ 4.44).

Patrick D, Scottish Literature, Chambers's Cyclopædia, rvsd J L Geddie, Phila and N Y 1938, 1.166 (group as a whole).

Speirs J, William Dunbar, Scrut 7.57, 59, 68 ([68], [70]); The Scots Literary Tradition, London 1940, p 42 ([68]; crit Scrut 9.193); rvsd 2nd edn 1962, p 58.

Craigie W, The Scottish Alliterative Poems, Proc of the British Acad 28.217 ([68]).

Utley CR, pp 4, 65, 200, 209, 226, 260, 282, 304 ([68], [67], [71], [73], [66], [69] [72]).

Moore A K, The Secular Lyric in Middle English, Lexington Ky 1951, pp 201, 215 ([70], [71], [67]); The Setting of The Tua Mariit Wemen and the Wedo, ESts 32.56.

Baxter J W, William Dunbar, Edinburgh and London 1952, p 54 ([68]).

Morgan E, Dunbar and the Language of Poetry, EC 2.153 ([68]).

Cruttwell P, Two Scots Poets Dunbar and Henryson, The Age of Chaucer, A Guide to Eng Lit, London 1954; rptd London 1955, 1.177 ([68]).

Kinsley J, The tretis of the tua mariit wemen and the wedo, MÆ 23.31.

Lewis C S, English Literature in the Sixteenth Century, Oxford 1954, p 94 ([68]).

Kinsley J, The Mediaeval Makars, Scottish Poetry, A Critical Survey, London 1955, p 30 ([68]).

Schlauch M, English Medieval Literature, Warsaw 1956, p 296 ([68]).

Bennett J A W, The Parlement of Foules, Oxford 1957, p 212 ([68]).

Kinsley J, William Dunbar Poems, Oxford, 1958, p xvi ([68]).

Fox D, Dunbar's The Golden Targe, ELH 26.328 ([68]).

Kinghorn A M, The Mediaeval Makars, Texas Stud Lit and Lang 1.73 ([68]).

Leyerle J, The Two Voices of William Dunbar, UTQ 31.331 ([68]).

Bawcutt P, Dunbar's Tretis of the Tua Mariit Wemen and the Wedo 185–187 and Chaucer's Parson's Tale, N&Q 209(ns 11) .332 ([68]).

Hope A D, The two mariit wemen and the wedo Protest or Satire? Australasian Univ Lang and Lit Assoc Proc, 9th Congress, Melbourne Aug 1964, p 48 ([68]).

Hyde I, Poetic Imagery, SSL 2.190 ([68]).

Fox D, The Scottish Chaucerians, Chaucer and Chaucerians, ed D S Brewer, University Alabama 1966, pp 164ff (see especially p 187; ([68]).

Rogers K M, The Troublesome Helpmate A History of Misogyny in Literature, Seattle 1966, p 86 ([68]).

Scott T, Dunbar A Critical Exposition, Edinburgh and London 1966, pp 36, 58, 61, 65, 179, 195, 198, 205, 209, 275, 326, 329, 337 and passim (group as a whole, [68], [67], [69], [73], [70], [71], [72]); Dunbar Translated, TLS Aug 11 1966, p 730 ([68]).

Kinghorn A M, Dunbar and Villon, MLR 62.201 ([68], [72], [73]).

Scott T, Late Medieval Scots Poetry, London 1967, p 13 ([68]).

Wood H H, Two Scots Chaucerians, Writers and Their Work, no 201, ed G Bullough, London 1967, pp 28, 40 ([68]).

Scheps W, William Wallace and his Buke, SSL 6.223 ([66]).

Hope A D, A Midsummer Eve's Dream, N Y 1970, p 1 ([68–69]).

Other Scholarly Problems. Pinkerton J, The History of Scotland from the Accession of the House of Stuart, London 1797, 2.413, 417, 432 ([68]; contemp conditions).

Laing, edn, 2.231 ([70]; identity of subject).

Paterson, edn, p 42 ([70]; identity of subject).

Ross J M, Scottish History and Literature, Glasgow 1884, p 179 ([68]; contemp conditions).

Schipper J, William Dunbar sein Leben und seine Gedichte, Berlin 1884, p 186 ([70]; identity of subject).

Mackay Æ J G, Introd, Small edn, 1.xci ([70], [71]; identity of subject).

Morley, 7.132 ([68]; contemp conditions).

Schipper, edn, pt 2, 40⁴.26 ([70]; identity of subject).

Smeaton O, William Dunbar, N Y (1898?), pp

96, 141 ([71]; biographical evidence).

Mebus F, Studien zu William Dunbar, Breslau 1902, pp 34, 37, 46 ([70]; Dunbar's relation to Mrs. Musgrave, [71]; purpose).

Baildon H B, Burns and Dunbar, Scottish Art and Letters 2.259 ([70], [71]; occasion, identity of subject).

Teichert O P, Schottische Zustände unter Jacob IV nach den Dichtungen von William Dunbar, Görlitz 1903, pp 25, 28, 37 ([69], [67], [68]; contemp conditions).

Smeaton O, The Story of Edinburgh, London 1905, p 59 ([69]; occasion, brief).

Steinberger C, Étude sur William Dunbar, Dublin 1908, p 76 ([70], [71], [73]; identity of subject).

Stair-Kerr E, The Poets, Scotland under James IV, Paisley 1911, p 123 ([70]; identity of subject, brief).

Roy J A, Of the Makaris A Causerie, UTQ 16.33, 36 (contemp conditions; [68]).

Baxter J W, William Dunbar, Edinburgh and London 1952, p 121 ([70]; identity of subject, occasion).

Milner I, Some Aspects of Satire in the Poetry of Dunbar, Philologica (cizojazyčná prioloha Casopisu pro moderní filologii) 8.39 ([68]; contemp conditions).

Scott T, Dunbar A Critical Exposition, Edinburgh and London 1966, pp 17, 40, 169, 277, 363, ([69], [68], [66], [73]; contemp conditions, attitude, occasion, biographical evidence, classification of poems).

Kinghorn A M, Dunbar and Villon, MLR 62.199 ([68]; biographical evidence).

Scott T, Late Medieval Scots Poetry, London 1967, p 31 ([68]; occasion).

Shire H M, Song Dance and Poetry of the Court of Scotland, Cambridge 1969, p 21 ([66]; Reformation influence on editing).

Literary Criticism. Percy T, Reliques of Ancient English Poetry, London 1765 (numerous subsequent edns); ed H B Wheatley, London 1910, 2.391 ([68]).

Pinkerton J, Ancient Scotish Poems, London and Edinburgh 1786, 1.ix ([68]).

Ellis G, Specimens of the Early English Poets, 5 edns, London 1790, 1801, 1803, 1811, 1845 (5th edn corrected), 1.315 ([68]; very brief).

Irving D, The Lives of the Scotish Poets, 2nd edn London 1810, 1.409, 415, 428 ([68], [70]).

Tytler P F, Lives of Scottish Worthies, London 1833, 3.117, 120 ([68]).

Laing, edn, 1.56 (Memoirs); 2.268, 283, 305, 338, 363, 372 ([66], [68], [71–73]).

William Dunbar, Littell's Living Age 1.383

([68]).

Wright T, On the Scottish Poet Dunbar, Essays on Subjects Connected with the Literature Popular Superstitions and History of England, London 1846, 2.298 ([68]).

Gilfillan G, Specimens with Memoirs of the Less-Known Poets, Edinburgh and London 1860, 1.60 ([68]; brief).

Paterson, edn, pp 5, 8, 42, 95 ([68], [70], [67]).

Irving D, The History of Scotish Poetry, ed J A Carlyle, Edinburgh 1861, p 243 ([68]; illustrative quotes).

Smith A, William Dunbar Dreamthorp, London 1863; rptd no 200 The World's Classics, London 1914; rptd London 1934, pp 72, 79 ([68], [70]).

Kaufmann J, Traité de la langue, Bonn 1873, pp 15, 17 ([70], [68], [67]).

Wilson J G, The Poets and Poetry of Scotland, N Y 1876, 1.25 ([68]; very brief).

Nichol J, William Dunbar, The English Poets, ed T H Ward, London and N Y 1880, (numerous subsequent edns); N Y 1924, 1.149 ([68]; A Sketch of Scottish Poetry, ed J Small, 2nd edn rvsd EETS 11, London 1883, p xxx ([68]).

Ross J M, Scottish History and Literature, Glasgow 1884, p 202 ([68]).

Schipper J, William Dunbar sein Leben und seine Gedichte, Berlin 1884, pp 133, 145, 149, 187, 330 ([68], [67], [66], [71], [72], [73]).

Skelton J, Maitland of Lethington and the Scotland of Mary Stuart, Edinburgh 1887, 1.109 ([68]).

Veitch J, The Feeling for Nature in Scottish Poetry, Edinburgh and London 1887, 1.233 ([68], [70]).

Mackay Æ J G, Introd, Small edn, 1.1, lviii, lxxxvi, xci, xciii, xcviii, cviii, cxx, cxxiii, cxxviii, cxxxvii ([68], [70], [71], [67], [66], [69], [73]).

Minto W, Characteristics of English Poets, Boston 1899, p 106 ([68]).

[Robertson J L] Haliburton H, Our Earlier Burns, In Scottish Fields, London 1890, pp 238, 240 ([68], [67]).

Morley, 7.129 ([68]).

Eyre-Todd G, Mediæval Scottish Poetry, Abbotsford Series, Glasgow 1892, p 151 ([68]).

Schipper, edn, pt 1, 40².45, 72, 76; pt 2, 40⁴.27, 30; pt 4, 42⁴.49 ([68], [67], [66], [71], [72], [73]).

Oliphant F R, William Dunbar, Blackwood's Edinburgh Magazine 154.416, 432 ([68]).

Ten Brink, 3.74 ([68]).

Smeaton O, A Quartette of Court Singers Four Centuries Ago, Westminster Rev

148.183 ([67]; brief, extravagant, fictionalized).

Henderson T F, Scottish Vernacular Literature, Edinburgh 1898; 3rd edn rvsd Edinburgh 1910, pp 152, 167 ([68], [67]).

Smeaton O, William Dunbar, N Y (1898?), pp 134, 143, 153 ([66], [68], [70], [71], [72], [73]).

Smith G G, The Transition Period, Periods of European Lit, Edinburgh and London 1900, 4.50 and passim ([68] [70]).

Chambers R, Chambers's Cyclopaedia, Phila and N Y 1901–03; rvsd J L Geddie, Phila and N Y 1938, 1.197 ([68]).

M'Ilwraith W, A Sketch of Scottish Literature, Annual Burns Chronicle 10.21 ([68]).

Mebus F, Studien zu William Dunbar, Breslau 1902, p 48 ([72]; brief).

Baildon H, Burns and Dunbar, Scottish Art and Letters 2.167, 259 ([68], [70]).

Millar J H, A Literary History of Scotland, London 1903, p 59 ([68]).

Moorman F W, The Interpretation of Nature in English Poetry from Beowulf to Shakespeare, QF 95.146 ([68]).

Seccombe T and W R Nicoll, The Scots Poets, The Bookman Illustrated Hist of Eng Lit, London 1906, 1.21 ([68], [67]).

Wülker R, Geschichte der Englischen Literatur, Leipzig and Wien 1906–07, 1.205 ([66]; brief comment).

CHEL, 2.288 ([68]).

Steinberger C, Étude sur William Dunbar, Dublin 1908, pp 41, 100, 114, 131, 144 ([67], [69], [68], [72], [73]).

Tucker S M, Verse Satire in England, CUS 3, no 2, pp 137, 139, 177 ([68]).

Stair-Kerr E, The Poets, Scotland under James IV, Paisley 1911, p 123 ([70]; brief).

Watt L M, Scottish Life and Poetry, London 1912, p 104 ([68]).

Smith G G, Scottish Literature Character and Influence, London 1919, p 14 ([68]); brief reference).

Golding L, The Scottish Chaucerians, The Saturday Review of Politics Literature Science and Art 134.783 ([68]).

Legouis HEL, p 176 ([68]).

Saintsbury G, The Four Great Scottish Poets, A Short Hist of Eng Lit, N Y 1929, p 186 ([68]).

William Dunbar, TLS Apr 10 1930, p 305 ([68]).

Taylor R A, Dunbar the Poet, The Poet on the Poets, no 4, London 1931, p 49 ([68]).

Mackenzie, edn, p xxxi ([68]).

Elton O, The English Muse, London 1933, p 86 ([68]).

Mackenzie A M, An Historical Survey of Scottish Literature, London 1933, p 85 ([67–68]).

Mackenzie W M, William Dunbar, Edinburgh Essays on Scots Lit, Edinburgh and London 1933, pp 35, 42 ([68]).

Rait R and G S Pryde, Scotland, N Y 1934; 2nd edn, London 1954, p 309 ([68]; very brief).

Smith J M, The French Background of Middle Scots Literature, Edinburgh and London 1934, pp xviii, xxviii, 38, 62, 65 ([68], [70]).

Power W, Literature and Oatmeal, London 1935, p 43 ([68]; brief; crit AnglB 48.151; The Scottish Bookman 1, no 4, p 152).

Speirs J, William Dunbar, Scrut 7.56, 59, 68 ([68], [70]); The Scots Literary Tradition, London 1940, pp 36, 40 ([68], [70]; crit Scrut 9.193); rvsd 2nd edn London 1962, pp 55, 57.

Craigie W, The Scottish Alliterative Poems, Proc of the British Acad 28.222 ([68]).

Grierson H J C and J C Smith, A Critical History of English Poetry, London 1944; 2nd rvsd edn London 1947, p 57 ([68]; brief).

Utley C R, pp 65, 200, 209, 211, 227, 260, 282, 304 ([67–68], [66], [71], [73], [72], [69]; mainly summary with occasional brief comment).

Roy J A, Of the Makaris A Causerie, UTQ 16.39 ([68]).

Caird J B, Some Reflections on Scottish Literature, I. Poetry, Scottish Periodical 1.11 ([68]).

Gierasch W, Dunbar's To a Ladye, Explicator 6, item 21.

Craig HEL, p 169 ([68]; brief).

Moore A K, The Secular Lyric in ME, Lexington Ky 1951, pp 195, 197, 200, 215 ([68], [70], [73], [71], [67], [69]).

Moore A K, The Setting of The Tua Mariit Wemen and the Wedo, ESts 32.56 ([68]).

Baxter J W, William Dunbar, Edinburgh and London 1952, pp 52, 121 ([66–71]).

Morgan E, Dunbar and the Language of Poetry, EC 2.153 ([68]).

Renwick-Orton, p 416 ([68]; brief).

Ward A C, Illustrated Hist of Eng Lit, London N Y and Toronto 1953, p 42 ([68]; brief).

Cruttwell P, Two Scots Poets A Guide to Eng Lit, London 1954; rptd London 1955, 1.176 ([68]).

Kinsley J, The tretis of the tua mariit wemen and the wedo, MÆ 23.31 ([68]).

Lewis C S, English Literature in the Sixteenth Century, Oxford 1954, p 92 ([68], [70]).

Kinsley J, The Mediaeval Makars, Scottish Poetry A Critical Survey, London 1955, p 30 ([68]).

Hyde I, Primary Sources and Associations of Dunbar's Aureate Imagery, MLR 51.482 ([68]).

Milner I, Some Aspects of Satire in the Poetry of Dunbar, Philologica (cizojazyčná prioloha Casupisu pro moderní filologii) 8.32, 39 ([68]).

Schlauch M, English Medieval Literature, Warsaw 1956, p 296 ([68]).

Peter J, Complaint and Satire in Early English Literature, Oxford 1956, pp 10, 87, 90 ([68], [66]; brief reference).

Enkvist N E, The Seasons of the Year, Societas Scientiarum Fennica Commentationes Humanarum Litterarum, Helsingfors 1957, 22⁴.143 ([68]).

Speirs J, Medieval English Poetry, London 1957, p 239 ([68]; brief reference).

Kinsley J, William Dunbar Poems, Oxford 1958, pp xv, xxvi ([68], [70]).

Mackie R L, King James IV of Scotland, Edinburgh and London 1958, p 179 ([68], [66], [71]; brief comments).

Morrison W S, Some Makars and Makers of St Andrews and Dundee, Edinburgh and London 1958, pp 7, 15 ([68]).

Fox D, Dunbar's The Golden Targe, ELH 26.311 ([68]).

Kinghorn A M, The Mediaeval Makars, Texas Stud Lit and Lang, 1.78 ([68]).

McLaren M, The Wisdom of the Scots, London 1961, p 69 ([73]).

Leyerle J, The Two Voices of William Dunbar, UTQ 31.331, 337 ([68]).

Davies R T, Medieval English Lyrics, London 1963, p 44 ([70]; brief reference).

Linklater E, A Bawdy Revival, New Saltire, no 9, Sept 1963, p 6 ([68]).

Hope A D, The two mariit wemen and the wedo, Australasian Univ Lang and Lit Assoc Proc, 9th Congress, Melbourne Aug 1964, p 48 ([68]).

Rossi S, I Chauceriani Scozzesi, Napoli 1964, pp 45, 50 ([68]).

Smith Rowland, The Poetry of William Dunbar, Theoria 22.79, 81 ([68], [70]).

Hyde I, Poetic Imagery, SSL 2.189 ([68]).

Fox D, The Scottish Chaucerians, Chaucer and Chaucerians, ed D S Brewer, University Alabama 1966, p 184 ([72]).

Meier H H, What Dunbar Meant, TLS Feb 24 1966, p 148 ([68]).

Rogers K M, The Troublesome Helpmate, Seattle 1966, p 86 ([68]).

Scott T, Dunbar A Critical Exposition, Edinburgh and London 1966, pp 38, 40, 56, 65, 70, 88, 169, 179, 244, 275, 283, 298, 333, 337, 342, 359, 362, 366 and passim (group as a whole); Dunbar Translated, TLS Aug 11 1966, p 730 ([68]).

Kinghorn A M, Dunbar and Villon, MLR 62.201 ([68], [72–73]).

Scott T, Late Medieval Scots Poetry, London 1967, p 13 ([68]).

Wood H H, Two Scots Chaucerians, Writers and Their Work, no 201, ed G Bullough, London 1967, pp 28, 39 ([67–68]).

Shire H M, Song Dance and Poetry of the Court of Scotland, Cambridge 1969, p 16 ([71]).

Hope A D, A Midsummer Eve's Dream, N Y 1970, pp 1, 61, 69, 124, 148, 164, 196, 200, 256 ([68–69]).

Bibliography. Geddie W, A Bibliography of Middle Scots Poets, PSTS ns 61, Edinburgh and London 1912, pp 195, 206 ([68]).

Utley CR, pp 200, 209, 226, 260, 282, 304 ([71], [73], [66], [67], [69] [68], [72]).

Beattie W, The Chepman and Myllar Prints A Facsimile, Edinburgh Biblio Soc, Oxford 1950, p xiv ([68]).

Robbins-Cutler, nos 2247.5 ([71]), 2306.5 ([73]), 2354.3 ([66]), 2821.3 ([67]), 3243.3 ([70]), 3556.5 ([69]), 3845.5 ([68]), 4112.5 ([72]).

VI. Allegories and Addresses

(Note: Folios for items [74–86] are listed by MS number, as appropriate, after each title. See under *MSS* below for full listing and information. Titles are from Mackenzie edn.)

[74] DUNBAR AT OXINFURDE.
1, f 10ᵇ; 2, pp 9–10, 317–318.

[75] BEWTY AND THE PRESONEIR.
1, f 8ᵃ; 4, ff 214ᵃ–215ᵃ.

[76] THE THRISSIL AND THE ROIS.

4, ff 342ᵇ–345ᵃ.

[77] THE GOLDYN TARGE.

2, pp 64–81; 4, ff 345ᵃ–348ᵇ; 5, pp 89–100.

[78] THE DANCE OF THE SEVIN DEIDLY SYNNIS.

1, ff 11ᵇ–13ᵃ; 2, pp 12–16, 161–162; 4, ff 110ᵃ–111ᵃ.

[79] THE SOWTAR AND TAILYOURIS WAR.

2, pp 162–165; 3, ff 210ᵃ–211ᵇ; 4, ff 111ᵃ–112ᵇ.

[80] AMENDS TO THE TELYOURIS AND SOWTARIS.

2, p 317; 4, ff 112ᵇ–113ᵃ.

[81] THE DREAM.

1, ff 3ᵇ–5ᵃ.

[82] THE BALLADE OF LORD BERNARD STEWART.

5, pp 169–174.

[83] ELEGY ON THE DEATH OF LORD BERNARD STEWART.

1, ff 6ᵇ–7ᵃ.

[84] THE MERLE AND THE NYCHTINGAILL.

2, pp 165–168; 4, ff 283ᵃ–284ᵇ.

[85] TO ABERDEIN.

1, ff 7ᵃ–7ᵇ.

[86] QUHEN THE GOVERNOUR PAST IN FRANCE.

1, ff 28ᵇ–29ᵃ; 2, pp 186–187.

MSS. 1, Camb Univ L1.5.10 (Reidpeth or Moore), ff 3ᵇ–5ᵃ, 6ᵇ–8ᵃ, 10ᵇ, 11ᵇ–13ᵃ, 28ᵇ–29ᵃ (1623; items [81], [83], [85], lines 1–16 of [75], [74], [78], [86]); 2, Magdalene Coll Camb 2553 (Pepysian Libr, Maitland Folio), pp 9–10, 12–16, 64–81, 161–168, 186–187, 317–318 (1570–71; items [74], [78], [77], [79], lines 1–16, 33–120 of [84], [86], [80], [74]); 3, Nat Libr Scot Acc 4233 (Asloan), ff 210ᵃ–211ᵇ (1513–1542; item [79]); 4, Nat Libr Scot 1.1.6 (Bannatyne), ff 110ᵃ–113ᵃ, 214ᵃ–215ᵃ, 283ᵃ–284ᵇ, 342ᵇ–348ᵇ (1568; items

[78–80], [75], [84], [76–77]). PRINT: 5, Nat Libr Scot 19.1.16 (Chepman and Myllar), pp 89–100, 169–174 (1508; items [77], [82]) (STC, nos 7347, 7349).

Pinkerton J, Ancient Scotish Poems, 2 vols, London and Edinburgh 1786, l.v; 2.437, 471 (MSS 2, 4).

Brydges E and J Haslewood, The British Bibliographer, London 1814, 4.183 (MS 4).

Laing D, The Poems of George Bannatyne, Edinburgh 1824, p 3 (MS 4); The Knightly Tale of Golagrus and Gawane, Edinburgh 1827, f 2ᵃ (PRINT 5 rptd); An Account of the Contents of George Bannatyne's Manuscript, The Bannatyne Club, Edinburgh 1829, 35.43 (MS 4).

A Catalogue of the Manuscripts Preserved in The Library of The University of Cambridge, Cambridge 1861, 4.94 (MS 1).

Small J, The Poetical Works of Gavin Douglas, Edinburgh and London 1874, l.clxxi (MS 2).

Dickson R and J P Edmond, Annals of Scottish Printing from 1507 to the Beginning of the 17th Century, Cambridge 1890, p 49 (PRINT 5).

Schipper, edn, pt 1, 40².5ff (MSS 1, 2, 3, 4, PRINT 5).

Murdoch J B, ed, The Bannatyne Manuscript, 4 vols, Hunterian Club, Glasgow 1896, 2.312; 3.607; 4.822, 988 (MS 4 rptd).

Smith G G, Specimens of Middle Scots, Edinburgh and London 1902, pp lxvi, lxx, lxxiii, lxxiv (MSS 2, 3, 4, PRINT 5).

Brown J T T, The Bannatyne Manuscript, SHR 1.136 (MS 4).

Stevenson G, ed, Pieces from The Makculloch and the Gray MSS, PSTS 65, Edinburgh and London 1918, pp 157, 239, 302 (PRINT 5 rptd, notes at end of text).

Craigie W A, ed, The Maitland Folio, PSTS ns 7, 20, 2 vols, Edinburgh and London 1919–27, 2.46, 54 (MS 1); 1.9, 12, 89, 183, 210, 378; 2.37, 70, 98, 102, 122 (MS 2 rptd, notes in vol 2); The Asloan Manuscript, PSTS ns 14, 16, 2 vols, Edinburgh 1923–25, 2.89, 280 (MS 3 rptd, notes at end of text).

Ritchie W T, ed, The Bannatyne Manuscript Writtin in Tyme of Pest, PSTS ns 5, 22, 23, 26, 4 vols, Edinburgh 1928–34, 2.291; 3.249; 4.87, 246 (MS 4 rptd).

Beattie W, The Chepman and Myllar Prints, Edinburgh Biblio Soc, Oxford 1950, pp viii, 89, 169 (PRINT 5 described, rptd).

Baxter J W, William Dunbar, Edinburgh and London 1952, pp 216ff (MSS 1, 2, 3, 4, PRINT 5).

Editions. The Thistle and The Rose, A Poem in Honour of Margaret Daughter to Henry VII of England Queen to James IV King of Scots, Glasgow 1750.

Laing D, The Poems of William Dunbar, 2 vols, Edinburgh 1834, 1.3, 31, 49, 129, 153, 199, 216, 251; 2.211, 234, 265, 311, 328, 347, 363, 368 (notes in vol 2; MSS 1, 4; PRINT 5; Memoirs of William Dunbar preceding text of poems in vol 1 is paginated separately).

Paterson J, The Life and Poems of William Dunbar, Edinburgh 1860 (crit Athen July 14 1860, p 49); reissued The Works of William Dunbar Including His Life, Edinburgh 1863, pp 29, 43, 100, 118, 159, 206, 214, 220, 233, 266, 288, 299 (glossings in footnotes).

Small J, Æ J G Mackay, G P McNeill, W Gregor, The Poems of William Dunbar, PSTS 2, 4, 16, 21, 29, 3 vols, Edinburgh 1884–93, 2.1, 59, 117, 164, 174, 183, 224, 235, 251, 257; 3.9, 117, 192, 253, 263, 269, 307, 318, 334, 344 (notes in vol 3; MSS 1, 2, 4; PRINT 5).

Schipper J, The Poems of William Dunbar, pts 2–4, Denkschriften der kaiserlichen Akademie der Wissenschaften, Philo-Hist Classe, Vienna 1892–93, 40⁴.2, 37; 41⁴.43, 93; 42⁴.19, 43, 79 (MS sources and variants given in headnotes and ftnts to each poem; MSS 1, 2, 3, 4; PRINT 5; crit E Kölbing, EStn 20.439).

Baildon H B, The Poems of William Dunbar, Cambridge 1907, pp 39, 63, 117, 150, 165, 178, 204, 247, 252, 268, 277, 282, 287, 292 (notes at end of text; sources vary, selects reading which seems to him most likely to be correct; crit J H Millar, The Bookman 32.207).

Frazier R D, The Thrissill and The Rois, Houston Texas 1931.

Mackenzie W M, The Poems of William Dunbar, London 1932, p 104 (notes at end of text; MSS 1, 2, 4; PRINT 5; crit B Dickins, MLR 28.506; TLS Jan 26 1933, p 55; The Modern Scot 4.63); rptd London 1950; ed B Dickins, rptd and rvsd London 1960 (crit A Macdonald, ESts 43.219); rptd 1970.

Selections. Ramsay A, The Ever Green, Edinburgh 1724, 1.15, 240; 2.22 ([76], [78], [79], [80] omits 1 stanza, [77] adds 1 line to stanza 7; occasional changes in wording; MS 4); The Poetical Works of Allan Ramsay, ed C Mackay, London and N Y n d, pp 220, 255, 263 ([76], [78], [77]).

Ruddiman W, Choice Collection of Scots Poems, Edinburgh 1766, pp 99, 125, 151 ([79], [80], [77], [76]).

Dalrymple D, Ancient Scottish Poems, Edinburgh 1770, pp 1, 27, 89, 223, 234, 276; rptd Leeds 1815, pp 1, 32, 112, 275, 286, 324 ([76], [77], [78], [84]; notes at end of text; MS 4).

The Caledoniad, London 1775, 2.50, 74 ([76], [77]).

Pinkerton J, Ancient Scotish Poems, 2 vols, London and Edinburgh 1786, 1.106, 128; 2.412, 417 ([74], [86]; notes in vol 2; MS 2).

Morison R, Select Poems of Wil Dunbar Part First from the MS of George Bannatyne, Perth 1788, pp 1, 13, 33, 93 ([77], [76], [78], [84]; MS 4).

Ellis G, Specimens of the Early English Poets, 5 edns, London 1790, 1801, 1803, 1811, 1845 (5th edn corrected), 1.305, 313 ([74], from [76]; spelling modernized, glossings at foot of page; Pinkerton, Ancient Scotish Poems; Dalrymple, Ancient Scottish Poems).

Sibbald J, Chronicle of Scottish Poetry, 4 vols, Edinburgh and London 1802, 1.253, 282; 2.25 ([77], [76], [78], [86]; introductory and end notes; sources not always indicated but include MS 4).

Irving D, The Lives of the Scotish Poets, 2nd edn London 1810, 1.409, 429, 434 ([78], [74], [77], [76]).

Gilchrist O, Ancient Scottish Poems, Censura Literaria, ed S E Brydges, London 1807, 5.242 (from [78]; Dalrymple, Ancient Scottish Poems).

Brydges E, Restituta, London 1815, 2.508 ([76]).

Campbell T, Specimens of the British Poets, London 1819, 2.85 ([78]; some omissions; glossings at foot of page).

Ritson J, The Caledonian Muse, printed 1785, published London 1821, p 12 ([76]; Dalrymple, Ancient Scottish Poems).

Drake N, Chaucer Dunbar and Burns Compared, Mornings in Spring, London 1828, 2.17 (from [77], from [76]).

Tytler P F, Lives of Scottish Worthies, London 1833, 3.100, 116, 128 (from [76], [81], [77]; Laing edn).

Ancient Scotish Poetry No I Dunbar, Blackwood's Edinburgh Magazine 37.294, 299, 316 ([76], [84], extracts from [77]).

William Dunbar, Littell's Living Age 1.383 ([84]).

Fairholt F W, Satirical Songs and Poems on Costume from the 13th to the 19th Century, Percy Soc 27, London 1849, p 62 ([80]; Laing edn).

The Book of Celebrated Poems, London 1854, p 38 ([84]; spelling partially modernized).

Aytoun W E, The Ballads of Scotland, Edinburgh and London 1858; 2nd edn rvsd and augmented, Edinburgh and London 1859, l.lxviii (from [77], from [76]; brief, illustrative of critical discussion).

Gilfillan G, Specimens with Memoirs of the Less-Known Poets, Edinburgh and London 1860, 1.61 ([78], [84]; glossings at foot of page).

Irving D, The History of Scotish Poetry, ed J A Carlyle, Edinburgh 1861, p 232 ([76], [77], [78]; brief excerpts).

Clarke C C, Specimens with Memoirs of the Less-Known British Poets, Edinburgh 1868, 1.61 (from [78], [84]).

Kaufmann J, Traité de la langue, Bonn 1873, p 23 ([76–78]; Laing edn).

Masson R O, Three Centuries of English Poetry Being Selections from Chaucer to Herrick, London 1876, pp 127, 130 (from [76], from [77], from [78]; spelling modernized, glossings at foot of page; Laing edn).

Morley H, Shorter English Poems, London 1876, p 113 ([78]).

Wilson J G, The Poets and Poetry of Scotland, N Y 1876, 1.26 ([76]).

Nichol J, William Dunbar, The English Poets, ed T H Ward, London and N Y 1880 (numerous subsequent edns); N Y 1924, 1.151 (from [76], [77], [78]; glossings at foot of page; Laing edn, with variations for metrical improvement).

Ross J, The Book of Scottish Poems, Paisley 1882, 1.177, 195 ([74], [76–78]).

Schipper J, William Dunbar sein Leben und seine Gedichte, Berlin 1884, pp 169, 178, 182, 197, 205, 255, 326, 347 (poems in German scattered through text of discussion; [76], from [77], from [78], [80], [81], [84], [86]; crit E Kölbing, EStn 10.128; M Trautmann, Angl 7.146; The Nation 40.144).

Fitzgibbon H M, Early English and Scottish Poetry, London N Y and Melbourne 1888, pp 107, 127, 138, 147, 431 ([84], from [77], from [76], from [78], from [80]; spelling modernized, notes at end of text).

Veitch J, The Feeling for Nature in Scottish Poetry, Edinburgh and London 1887, 1.222 ([76], [77]; brief quotes interspersed with criticism, glossings in side notes; crit C Patmore, St James Gazette July 9 1887; rptd in Courage in Politics, London 1921, p 32).

Kaye W J, The Leading Poets of Scotland, London 1891, p 145 (from [76]).

Eyre-Todd G, Mediæval Scottish Poetry, Abbotsford Series, Glasgow 1892, pp 159, 192 ([75–78], [80]; glossings in margin).

Skeat Spec, pp 109, 410 ([76]; notes at end of text; MS 4).

Browne W H, Selections from the Early Scottish Poets, Baltimore 1896, pp 114, 188 ([76]; a few notes at end of text; Small edn).

Warner C D, A Library of the World's Best Literature, N Y 1897, 12.5066; ed J W Cunliffe and A H Thorndike, The World's Best Literature, The Warner Library, N Y 1917, 8.5066 (from [76], from [77]; spelling partially modernized).

Henderson T F, A Little Book of Scottish Verse, London 1899; 2nd edn 1909, p 60 ([80]; glossings at foot of page).

Smeaton O, English Satires, London 1899; London 1924; London [1925], p 14 ([78]).

Smith G G, The Days of James iiii, Scottish History by Contemporary Writers, London 1900, p 119 (from [85]; Small edn).

Arber E, English Songs, The Dunbar Anthology, British Anthologies, London 1901, 1.1, 34, 297 ([75–78], [84]; spelling and some words modernized, identification of sources in notes; Small edn).

Chambers R, Chambers's Cyclopædia, Phila and N Y 1901–03; rvsd Phila and N Y 1938, 1.193 ([76], [77], [84], [78]; brief excerpts).

Smith G G, Specimens of Middle Scots, Edinburgh and London 1902, pp 27, 275 ([76]; notes at end of text; MS 4).

Steinberger C, Étude sur William Dunbar, Dublin 1908, pp 57, 86, 133 ([76], from [77], [78], [84]; Small edn).

Dixon W M, The Edinburgh Book of Scottish Verse, London 1910, pp 32, 55, 885 ([78], [77], [76]; glossings at foot of page, brief note at end of text).

Douglas G, The Book of Scottish Poetry, London and Leipsic 1911, pp 105, 114 ([78], [76], [77]; glossings at foot of page; Small edn).

Neilson W A and K G T Webster, Chief British Poets of the 14th and 15th Centuries, Boston N Y etc 1916, pp 386, 394, 434 ([77], [76], [78]; brief note at end of text, glossings at foot of page; Small edn).

Le Gallienne R, The Le Gallienne Book of English Verse, N Y 1923, p 8 (from [77]; spelling modernized, brief).

Buchan J, The Northern Muse, London 1924,

pp 8, 244, 410, 444, 455, 527, 533 (from [76], from [77], from [83], [84]; glossings at foot of page, brief notes at end of text; Small edn).

Brougham E M, News out of Scotland, London 1926, p 40 (from [83]).

Carver G, The Catholic Tradition in English Literature, N Y 1926, p 34 ([84]; glossings at foot of page).

Musser B F, The Chaucer of Scotland, Franciscan Poets, N Y 1933, p 7 (from [78]).

Patterson R F, Six Centuries of English Literature, London and Glasgow 1933, 1.198 ([78]).

Mackie R L, A Book of Scottish Verse, The World's Classics, no 417, London 1934, p 43 ([77], [78], [80]; glossings at foot of page); 2nd edn London Glasgow N Y 1967, p 42.

Gray M M, Scottish Poetry from Barbour to James VI, N Y 1935, pp 115, 124, 143, 156 ([77], [76], [78], [80], [85]; crit J Speirs, Scrut 6.83; W M Mackenzie, The Scottish Bookman 1, no 4, p 133).

[Grieve C M] MacDiarmid H, The Golden Treasury of Scottish Poetry, London 1940 (crit L MacNeice, The New Statesman and Nation 21.66; TLS Feb 15 1941, pp 78, 84); rptd in The Golden Treasury Series, London 1948, p 311 ([78]).

Fergusson J, The Green Garden, London and Edinburgh 1946, pp 29, 40 (from [77], [83]; spelling modernized).

Mackenzie A M, Scottish Pageant, Edinburgh 1946; 2nd edn 1952, 1.9 (from [77]; glossings at end of selection).

Oliver J W and J C Smith, A Scots Anthology from the 13th to the 20th Century, Edinburgh and London 1949, p 39 ([78]; spelling modernized, glossings at foot of page).

Auden W H and N H Pearson, Poets of the English Language, N Y 1950, p 310 (from [77]).

[Grieve C M] MacDiarmid H, Selections from the Poems of William Dunbar, The Saltire Classics, Edinburgh 1952, pp 13, 33, 40, 44 ([84], [78], [85], [83]; glossings in ftnts; Mackenzie edn).

McClure N E, Sixteenth-century English Poetry, N Y 1954, p 21 ([77]; glossings at foot of page; PRINT 5).

[Grieve C M] MacDiarmid H, Selected Poems of William Dunbar, Glasgow 1955, pp 20, 44, 47 ([78], [77], [74], [84]).

Kinsley J, William Dunbar Poems, Oxford 1958, pp 10, 21, 50, 69, 109, 120, 125 ([74–80], [82], [85]; notes at end of text; MSS

4, 1, 2; PRINT 5; crit TLS Apr 18 1958, p 208; D Young, William Dunbar, SHR 38.10; E Morgan, RES ns 11.71; J Wordsworth, MÆ 30.128).

McLaren M, The Wisdom of the Scots, London 1961, p 76 ([74]; glossings in margin).

Shire H M, The Thrissil the Rois and the Flour-de-lys, Cambridge Eng 1962, p 9 ([83]; Mackenzie edn).

Rossi S, I Chauceriani Scozzesi, Napoli 1964, p 174 ([76–78]; notes at foot of page).

Smith Rowland, The Poetry of William Dunbar, Theoria 22.76 (from [77]).

MacQueen J and T Scott, The Oxford Book of Scottish Verse, Oxford 1966, pp 120, 149 ([77], [78]; glossings at foot of page; Mackenzie edn).

Richmond V B, Laments for the Dead in Medieval Narrative, Duquesne Studies, Philological Series 8, Pittsburgh 1966, p 135 ([83]; Mackenzie edn).

Scott T, Late Medieval Scots Poetry, London 1967, pp 81, 183, ([77]; notes at end of text; Mackenzie edn).

Kinghorn A M, The Middle Scots Poets, London 1970, p 128 ([77]; notes at foot of page; PRINT 5).

Scott T, The Penguin Book of Scottish Verse, London 1970, p 130 ([78]; last 12 lines of MS 4 text omitted; glossings at foot of page).

Modernizations. The Union or Select Scots and English Poems, Edinburgh 1753; 2nd edn London 1759; 3rd edn London 1766; new edn Oxford 1796, p 1 ([76]; A Ramsay, The Ever Green).

Tytler P F, Lives of Scottish Worthies, London 1833, 3.101, 129 (from [76], [77]; Laing edn).

Green M A E, Lives of the Princesses of England, London 1852, 4.140 ([85]; Laing edn).

[Robertson J L] Haliburton H, Dunbar Being a Selection from the Poems of an Old Makar Adapted for Modern Readers, London 1895, p 72 (from [76], [81]; paraphrase, abbreviated, extremely free).

Markham E, The Book of Poetry, N Y 1927, 4.901 ([78]; text slightly altered).

Frazier, edn ([76]).

Linklater E, A Bawdy Revival, New Saltire, no 9, Sept 1963, p 22 ([78]).

Textual Matters. Laing, edn, 2.218, 220, 226, 256, 262, 265, 311, 330, 363, 456 ([75–80], [82], [84–85]).

Schipper, edn, pt 1, 40².4, 15, 19, 27; pt 2, 40⁴.43 ([77], [82], [79]; see also introductory and ftnts to individual poems).

Mebus F, Studien zu William Dunbar, Breslau 1902, pp 12, 83 ([75], [84]; obscure words and phrases, discussion of references).

Mackenzie, edn, pp 217ff ([74–86]).

Baxter J W, William Dunbar, Edinburgh and London 1952, pp 105, 125, 143, 153, 159, 178, 204 ([75], [84], [81], [78], [79], [80], [77], [82], [86]).

Scott T, Dunbar A Critical Exposition, Edinburgh and London 1966, pp 151, 231 ([78–81]).

Language. Ramsay A, The Ever Green, Edinburgh 1724, 2.265 ([76], [78], [79], [80], [77]; glossary).

Dalrymple D, Ancient Scottish Poems, Edinburgh 1770, p 317 (glossary); rptd Leeds 1815, p 367, [added] Glossary, p 1 [separate pagination] ([76], [77], [78], [84]).

Pinkerton J, Ancient Scottish Poems, London and Edinburgh 1786, 1.cxliii; 2.520 (synorthographic and symphonious words, glossary; [74], [86]).

Sibbald J, Chronicle of Scottish Poetry, Edinburgh and London 1802, vol 4 [unpaged] (glossary; [77], [76], [78], [86]).

Irving D, The History of Scotish Poetry, ed J A Carlyle, Edinburgh 1861, p 595 (glossary; [76–78]).

Murray J A H, The Dialect of the Southern Counties of Scotland, London 1873 (group as a whole).

Kaufmann J, Traité de la langue, Bonn 1873, p 47 (group as a whole).

Mackay C, The Poetry and Humour of the Scottish Language, London 1882, p 9 ([76]; brief).

Hahn O, Zur Verbal- und Nominalflexion bei den schottischen Dichtern, Berlin 1887–89 (see especially pt 3, p 17; group as a whole).

Schipper, edn, pt 1, 40^2.18 (group as a whole).

Gregor W, Glossary, Small edn, 3.401 (group as a whole).

Curtis F J, An Investigation of the Rimes and Phonology of Clariodus, Angl 16.387; 17.1, 125 (group as a whole).

Bearder J W, Über den Gebrauch der Praepositionen in der altschottischen Poesie, Halle 1894 ([76], [77], [80]; examples from Dunbar; crit EStn 19.410).

Browne W H, Selections from the Early Scottish Poets, Baltimore 1896, pp 3, 197 ([76]; discussion in introd, glossary).

Heuser W, Die Dehnung vor -nd im Mittelschottischen, Die Dehnung *-end*, Angl 19.401 (brief; group as a whole).

Baildon H B, On the Rimes in the Authentic Poems of William Dunbar, Trans Royal Soc Edinburgh 39^3.629; issued separately Edinburgh 1899 (group as a whole).

Flom G T, Scandinavian Influence on Southern Lowland Scotch, diss Columbia 1900 (group as a whole).

Arber E, English Songs, The Dunbar Anthology, British Anthologies, London 1901, 1.300 ([84], [77], [75], [76], [78]; glossary, index).

Smith G G, Specimens of Middle Scots, Edinburgh and London 1902, pp xi, 325 ([76]; history and philology of Middle Scots, glossary).

Millar J H, A Literary History of Scotland, London 1903, p 687 (glossary; [76], [85], [77], [78]).

Luick K, Studien zur englischen Lautgeschichte, WBEP, 17.109 ([76], [77], [78]).

Browne W H, The Taill of Rauf Coilyear, Baltimore 1903, pp 15, 35, 139 (general discussion of Middle Scots, glossary; group as a whole).

Knopff P, Darstellung der Ablautverhältnisse in der schottischen Schriftsprache, diss Würzburg 1904 (group as a whole).

Baildon, edn, pp xxvi, 299 (discussion, glossary; group as a whole).

CHEL, 2.101, 506 (group as a whole).

Dixon W M, The Edinburgh Book of Scottish Verse, London 1910, p 897 (glossary; [78], [77], [76]).

Gray M M, Introd, Lancelot of the Laik, PSTS ns 2, Edinburgh and London 1912, 2.xviii (group as a whole).

Lenz K, Zur Lautlehre der französischen Elemente in den schottischen Dichtungen, diss Marburg 1913 (examples taken from Douglas, Dunbar, Lyndesay, Clariodus; group as a whole).

Westergaard E, Prepositions in Lowland Scotch, Angl 41.444 (some examples from Dunbar; group as a whole); Verbal Forms in Middle-Scotch, Angl 43.95 (group as a whole).

Watt L M, Language and Influences, Douglas's Aeneid, Cambridge 1920, p 149 (very generally applicable; group as a whole).

Westergaard E, Studies in Prefixes and Suffixes, London 1924 (group as a whole).

Wilson J, The Spelling of Scotch before 1600, The Dialects of Central Scotland, London 1926, p 168 (group as a whole; attempts to determine pronunciation from spelling, rimes, modern Lothian pronunciation).

Craigie W A, ed, The Maitland Folio, PSTS ns 7, 20, 2 vols, Edinburgh and London

1919–27, 2.135 (glossary; [74], [78], [77], [79], [84], [86], [80]).

Westergaard E, Plural Forms in Lowland Scottish, Angl 51.77 (group as a whole).

Ritchie R L G, Early Instances of French Loan-Words in Scots and English, EStn 63.41 ([79]; 1 example from Dunbar).

Mackenzie, edn, pp xii, xxxvii, 245 ([74–86]; discussion, glossary).

Wood H, H, The Poems and Fables of Robert Henryson, Edinburgh 1933; 2nd edn rvsd 1958; rptd 1965, 1968, p xxxi.

Grierson H J C, The Problem of the Scottish Poet, E&S 21.105 ([77]).

Patrick D, Scottish Literature, Chambers's Cyclopædia, Phila and N Y 1901–03; rvsd J L Geddie, Phila and N Y 1938, 1.164 (group as a whole).

[Grieve C M] MacDiarmid H, The Golden Treasury of Scottish Poetry, London 1940; rptd in The Golden Treasury Series, London 1948, p 402 (glossary; [78]).

Fergusson J, The Green Garden, London and Edinburgh 1946, p 228 (glossary; [77], [83]).

Oliver J W and J C Smith, A Scots Anthology, Edinburgh and London 1949, p 497 (glossaries; [78]).

[Grieve C M] MacDiarmid H, Selections from the Poems of William Dunbar, The Saltire Classics, Edinburgh 1952, pp 5, 49 ([84], [78], [85], [83]; brief note, glossary); Selected Poems of William Dunbar, Glasgow 1955, p 60 (glossary; [78], [77], [74], [84]).

Stock N, Some Notes on Old Scots, Shenandoah 6, no 2, p 25 ([77]).

Kinsley J, William Dunbar Poems, Oxford 1958, p 139 (glossary; [76], [85], [82], [75], [77], [78], [79], [80], [74]).

Wittig K, The Scottish Tradition in Literature, Edinburgh 1958, pp 62, 101 and passim ([77]; general reference to group as a whole).

Rossi S, I Chauceriani Scozzesi, Napoli 1964, p 261 ([76–78]; discussion and glossary).

Scott T, Dunbar A Critical Exposition, Edinburgh and London 1966, pp 346, 351; Late Medieval Scots Poetry, London 1967, pp 21, 189 ([77]; discussion, glossary).

Conley J, William Dunbar Additions to and Corrections of OED and DOST, N&Q 213 (ns 15).169 ([78], [77], [86], [82], [75], [81]).

Hope A D, A Midsummer Eve's Dream, N Y 1970, p 319 ([77], [85], [78]; glossary).

Kinghorn A M, Middle Scots Poets, London 1970, pp 45, 164 (note on Middle Scots, glossary; [77]).

Versification. Guest E, A History of English Rhythms, 2 vols, London 1838; ed W W Skeat, new edn [in 1 vol] London 1882, p 643 ([77]).

Morley H, A First Sketch of English Literature, London 1873; rvsd London 1896, p 212 ([77]).

Schipper, 1.512 and passim ([77], [76], [78], [79], [84]).

Schipper J, William Dunbar sein Leben und seine Gedichte, Berlin 1884, p 177 ([77]).

Bulloch J M, French Metres in Early Scottish Poetry, Scottish Notes and Queries 2.130 ([76]).

McNeill G P, Note on Versification and Metres of Dunbar, Small edn, l.clxxix, clxxxiv, clxxxvii ([74–85]).

Minto W, Characteristics of English Poets from Chaucer to Shirley, authorized American edn, Boston 1889, p 99 ([78]).

Morley, 7.120 ([76]).

Schipper, edn, pt 2, 40⁴.3, 11, 23, 37; pt 3, 41⁴.93, 100 ([76], [77], [75], [78], [82], [85]; discussion in headnotes to poems).

Brandl, 2¹.1035, 1036, 1062, 1072 ([76–77]).

Curtis F J, The Rimes and Phonology of Clariodus, Angl 16.387; 17.1, 125 (group as a whole).

Henderson T F, Scottish Vernacular Literature, Edinburgh 1898; 3rd edn rvsd Edinburgh 1910, pp 156, 159, 162 ([83], [85], [82], [75], [80], [76], [77], [78], [79]).

Baildon H B, Rimes in the Authentic Poems of Dunbar, Trans Royal Soc Edinburgh 39³.629 (group as a whole).

Saintsbury G, History of English Prosody, London 1908, 2nd edn 1923, 1.273 ([76–78]).

Steinberger C, Étude sur William Dunbar, Dublin 1908, p 156 ([81], [78], [79]).

Mackenzie A M, An Historical Survey of Scottish Literature, London 1933, p 90 ([78], [76]).

Smith J M, The French Background of Middle Scots Literature, Edinburgh and London 1934, pp 162, 164, 166 ([77]; crit AnglB 45.265; MÆ 4.44).

Renwick-Orton, p 397 ([77], [76], [75]; very brief).

Kinsley J, William Dunbar Poems, Oxford 1958, p xix ([78]; brief).

Wittig K, The Scottish Tradition in Literature, Edinburgh 1958, p 58 and passim ([76–78]).

Fox D, Dunbar's The Golden Targe, ELH 26.320 ([77]).

Scott T, Dunbar A Critical Exposition, Edinburgh and London 1966, pp 46, 154, 167,

204, 237, 313, 316, 323 ([76], [81], [85], [77], [78], [79], [80], [84], [82], [83], [75]); Late Medieval Scots Poetry, p 18 ([77]).

Date. Pinkerton J, Ancient Scotish Poems, 2 vols, London and Edinburgh 1786, l.xciii ([76]).

Laing, edn, 1.21 (Memoirs); 2.211, 234, 254, 347, 368, 373, 415 ([76], [81], [78], [74], [86]).

Paterson, edn, pp 25, 29, 40, 47, 106, 126, 160, 212, 301 ([76], [77], [84], [75], [74], [78], [86]).

Morley H, A First Sketch of English Literature, London 1873; rvsd London 1896, p 205 ([77]).

Schipper J, William Dunbar sein Leben und seine Gedichte, Berlin 1884, pp 176, 195, 291, 293, 346 ([77], [78], [82], [85], [86]).

Mackay Æ J G, Introd [and] Appendix to Introd, Small edn, l.xlv, lxvii, lxix, lxxx, cxxxix, clix, clxii, clxviii, clxx ([82], [86], [84], [77], [75], [74], [76], [81], [78], [79], [80], [83], [85]).

Morley, 7.136 ([78]).

Schipper, edn, pt 2, 40^4.3, 11, 23, 37; pt 3, 41^4.44, 93, 99; pt 4, 42^4.19, 43, 79 ([76], [77], [75], [78], [81], [82], [85], [74], [84], [86]).

Mebus F, Studien zu William Dunbar, Breslau 1902, p 8 ([75]).

Steinberger C F, Étude sur William Dunbar, Dublin 1908, p 141 ([84]).

Bühler C F, London Thow Art the Flowre of Cytes All, RES 13.6 ([76]).

Utley CR, p 166 ([84]).

Baxter J W, William Dunbar, Edinburgh and London 1952, pp 84, 114, 126, 154, 205 ([74], [76], [84], [78], [79], [80], [86]).

Lewis C S, English Literature in the Sixteenth Century, Oxford 1954, p 90 ([74], [76], [77], [82], [83], [85], [86]).

Fox D, The Chronology of William Dunbar, PQ 39.418 ([76], [82], [83], [86], [85], [77], [78], [79], [81]).

Scott T, Dunbar A Critical Exposition, Edinburgh and London 1966, pp 41, 229, 264, 267 ([77], [78], [86], [74]).

Authorship. Laing, edn, 1.292; 2.226 ([86], [75]).

Schipper, edn, pt 2, 40^4.23 ([75]).

Baxter J W, William Dunbar, pp 105, 204, 224 ([75], [86], [85]).

Fox D, The Chronology of Dunbar, PQ 39.422 ([86]).

Sources and Literary Relations. Laing, edn, 1.310; 2.213, 222, 225, 227, 265, 315, 363, 369 ([78], [76], [77], [75], [79], [83], [84], [86]).

Aytoun W E, The Ballads of Scotland, Edinburgh and London 1858; 2nd edn rvsd and augmented 1859, 1.lxiv ([77]).

Paterson, edn, pp 40, 104, 212 [77], [75], [78]).

Morley H, A First Sketch of English Literature, London 1873; rvsd London 1896, p 211 ([77], [76]).

Nichol J, William Dunbar, The English Poets, ed T H Ward, London and N Y 1880 (numerous subsequent edns); N Y 1924, 1.148 ([77], [76], [78], [79]).

McElroy J G R, The Thrissill and the Rois, The Penn Monthly 12.535.

Nichol J, A Sketch of Scottish Poetry, ed J Small, 2nd edn rvsd, EETS 11, London 1883, p xxviii ([77]).

Schipper J, William Dunbar sein Leben und seine Gedichte, Berlin 1884, pp 168, 176, 183 ([76], [77]).

Fitzgibbon H M, Early English and Scottish Poetry, N Y London and Melbourne 1888, p lx ([76], [78]).

Shairp J C, Sketches in History and Poetry, Edinburgh 1887, p 208 ([76], [77], [78]; brief).

Mackay Æ J G, Introd, Small edn, l.lxxxii, cx, cxxvii ([75], [77], [76], [79], [78]).

Minto W, Characteristics of English Poets, authorized American edn, Boston 1889, p 101 ([77], [84]).

[Robertson J L] Haliburton H, Our Earlier Burns, In Scottish Fields, London 1890, p 238 ([76], [77]).

Morley, 7.122 ([77]).

Schipper, edn, pt 2, 40^4.11 ([77]).

Horneber F, Über King Hart und Testament of the Papyngo, Straubing 1893, p 23 ([75]; crit AnglB 4.328).

Oliphant F R, William Dunbar, Blackwood's Edinburgh Magazine 154.427 ([76], [77]).

Jusserand J J, Histoire Littéraire du Peuple Anglais, 2 vols, Paris 1894, 1.528 ([77], [76]).

Ten Brink, 3.67, 70, 83 ([76], [77]).

Turnbull W R, The Heritage of Burns, Haddington 1896, pp 228, 241, 256 ([78], [76]; brief references).

Neilson W A, Studies and Notes in Philology and Literature 6.163, 220, 227 ([77], [76], [75]).

Smith G G, The Transition Period, Periods of European Lit, Edinburgh and London 1900, 4.36, 39, 42 and passim ([76], [77], [78], [79], [80]).

Chambers R, Chambers's Cyclopædia, Phila and N Y 1901–03; rvsd Phila and N Y 1938, 1.192, 197 ([76], [77], [78]).

M'Ilwraith W, A Sketch of Scottish Literature from the Earliest Times, Annual Burns Chronicle 10.21 ([77]).

Ritter O, Quellenstudien zu Robert Burns, Palaes 20.72 ([76]).

Mebus F, Studien zu William Dunbar, Breslau 1902, pp 9, 83 ([75], [84]; wording and references of Dunbar compared with other poets; brief).

Baildon H B, Burns and Dunbar, Scottish Art and Letters 2.263 ([78]).

Moorman F W, The Interpretation of Nature in English Poetry from Beowulf to Shakespeare, QF 95.143 ([77], [76], [84]).

Snell F J, The Poets, The Age of Transition, London 1905, 1.84 ([76], [77]).

Marsh G L, Sources and Analogues of The Flower and the Leaf, MP 4.318, 323 ([77], [76]).

Seccombe T and W R Nicoll, The Scots Poets, The Bookman Illustrated History of Eng Lit, London 1906, 1.20 ([77], [78]).

Mebus F, Beiträge zu William Dunbars Gedicht The Goldin Terge, EStn 39.40 ([77]).

CHEL, 2.287 ([77], [75], [76], [78]).

Steinberger C, Étude sur William Dunbar, Dublin 1908, pp 47, 54, 140, 143 ([76], [84]).

Tucker S M, Verse Satire in England, CUS 3, no 2, pp 136, 137, 140 ([76], [77], [79], [78]).

Lawson A, The Kingis Quair and the Quare of Jelusy, St Andrews Univ Publ no 8, London 1910, p lxxv ([77]).

Enc Brit, 8.668 (group in general).

Gray M, Vidas Achinlek Chevalier, SHR 8.323 ([77], [76]).

Sandison H E, The Chanson D'Aventure in Middle English, Bryn Mawr Pa 1913, pp 76, 138 ([84]).

Mendenhall J C, Aureate Terms A Study in Literary Diction of the 15th Century, Lancaster Pa 1919 (group as a whole).

Knowlton E C, Nature in Middle English, JEGP 20.189 ([76], [84], [77]).

Golding L, The Scottish Chaucerians, Saturday Review of Politics Literature Science and Art 134.782 ([77]).

Patch H R, The Goddess Fortuna in Mediæval Lit, Cambridge Mass 1927, p 117 ([83]; brief).

Saintsbury G, The Four Great Scottish Poets, A Short Hist of Eng Lit, N Y 1929, p 187 ([77]; brief).

Cornelius R D, The Castell of Pleasure, EETS 179, London 1930, p 20 ([77]; brief).

William Dunbar, TLS Apr 10 1930, p 305 ([76], [77]).

Nichols P H, William Dunbar as a Scottish Lydgatian, PMLA 46.214, 218 ([79], [82], [83], [85], [86]).

Elton O, The English Muse, London 1933, pp 81, 84 ([77], [76]).

Taylor R A, Dunbar the Poet, The Poets on the Poets, no 4, London 1931, p 40 ([76]; crit The Criterion 11.331; TLS Mar 17 1932, p 199; YWES 13.124).

Nichols P H, Lydgate's Influence on the Aureate Terms of the Scottish Chaucerians, PMLA 47.520 ([77]).

Musser B F, The Chaucer of Scotland, Franciscan Poets, N Y 1933, pp 2, 5, 10 ([77], [78]).

Mackenzie A M, An Historical Survey of Scottish Literature, London 1933, p 63 ([77]).

Mackenzie W M, William Dunbar, Edinburgh Essays on Scots Literature, Edinburgh and London 1933, p 41 ([84]).

Power W, Scotland and the Scots, Edinburgh and London 1934, p 189 ([77]).

Smith J M, The French Background of Middle Scots Literature, Edinburgh and London 1934, pp 40, 48, 62, 69, 164 ([84], [76], [77], [81], [75], [82], [83], [85], [78]; crit AnglB 45.265; MÆ 4.44).

Rait R and G S Pryde, Scotland, N Y 1934; 2nd edn London 1954, pp 308, 314 (group as a whole).

Power W, Literature and Oatmeal, London 1935, p 42 ([78]; very brief; crit AnglB 48.151; The Scottish Bookman 1, no 4, p 152).

Tilgner E, Germanische Studien die Aureate Terms als Stilement bei Lydgate, Berlin 1936; rptd 1967, p 79 ([77]).

Patrick D, Scottish Literature, Chambers's Cyclopædia, rvsd J L Geddie, Phila and N Y 1938, 1.166 (group as a whole).

Speirs J, William Dunbar, Scrut 7.56, 61 ([77], [76], [78]).

Utley CR, pp 65, 166 ([84]).

Chambers OHEL, p 138 ([77]).

Craig HEL, p 168 ([76], [75], [77], [79]; brief).

Moore A K, The Secular Lyric in Middle English, Lexington Ky 1951, p 200 ([77]).

Baxter J W, William Dunbar, Edinburgh and London 1952, pp 103, 114, 153, 158 ([77], [75], [76], [78], [79], [80]).

Bloomfield M W, The Seven Deadly Sins, [East Lansing] 1952, passim ([78]).

Renwick-Orton, p 416 ([77], [84]; brief).

Ward A C, Illustrated Hist of Eng Lit, London N Y and Toronto 1953, pp 32, 41 ([76], [77]).

Brewer D S, The Ideal of Feminine Beauty in Medieval Literature Especially Harley Lyrics Chaucer and Some Elizabethans, MLR 50.257 ([77]).

Kinsley J, The Mediaeval Makars, Scottish

Poetry A Critical Survey, London 1955, pp 30, 32 ([78], [77]).

Stock N, Some Notes on Old Scots, Shenandoah 6, no 2, p 25 ([77]).

Hyde I, Primary Sources and Associations of Dunbar's Aureate Imagery, MLR 51.486, 490 ([83], [77], [85]).

Peter J, Complaint and Satire in Early English Literature, Oxford 1956, p 47 ([78]; brief reference).

Schlauch M, English Medieval Literature, Warsaw 1956, p 296 ([79]).

Bennett J A W, The Parlement of Foules, Oxford 1957, pp 84, 147, 150, 152, 185, 212 ([77], [76], [82], [84]).

Enkvist N E, The Seasons of the Year, Societas Scientiarum Fennica Commentationes Humanarum Litterarum, Helsingfors 1957, 22⁴. 143 ([77], [76]).

Speirs J, Medieval English Poetry, London 1957, pp 140, 368 ([77], [78]; brief references).

Kinsley J, William Dunbar Poems, Oxford 1958, p xiii ([77], [76], [79], [78]).

Wittig K, The Scottish Tradition in Literature, Edinburgh 1958, p 65 ([77]; crit TLS July 11 1958, p 392).

Fox D, Dunbar's The Golden Targe, ELH 26.311, 331 ([77]).

Wenzel S, The Sin of Sloth Acedia in Medieval Thought and Literature, Chapel Hill N C 1960, pp 106, 236 ([78]).

Chew S C, The Pilgrimage of Life, New Haven and London 1962, pp 85, 104, 108 ([78]).

Leyerle J, The Two Voices of William Dunbar, UTQ 31.318, 325 ([77]).

Shire H M, The Thrissil the Rois and the Flour-de-lys, Cambridge Eng 1962, p 25 ([83]).

Davies R T, Medieval English Lyrics, London 1963, p 26 ([77]; brief reference).

Maclaine A H, The Christis Kirk Tradition, SSL 2.3, 111, 163, 234 ([79], [80]).

Smith Rowland, The Poetry of William Dunbar, Theoria 22.77 ([77]).

Hyde I, Poetic Imagery, SSL 2.186 ([76]).

Fox D, The Scottish Chaucerians, Chaucer and Chaucerians, ed D S Brewer, University Alabama 1966, p 164 (see especially p 187; [77]).

Richmond V B, Laments for the Dead in Medieval Narrative, Duquesne Studies, Philological Series 8, Pittsburgh 1966, p 13 ([83]).

Scott T, Dunbar A Critical Exposition, Edinburgh and London 1966, pp 36, 40, 51, 117, 232, 280, 317, 326, 338, 345 and passim ([76], [78], [74], [77], [75], [84], [79], [83], [86], [81]).

Bawcutt P, The Shorter Poems of Gavin Douglas, PSTS 4s 3, Edinburgh and London 1967, p lx ([77], [75]).

Kinghorn A M, Dunbar and Villon, MLR 62.201, 206 ([84], [83], [76]).

MacQueen J, Robert Henryson A Study of the Major Narrative Poems, London 1967, p 86 ([84]); Some Aspects of the Early Renaissance in Scotland, Forum Mod Lang Stud 3.208 ([76]).

Scott T, Late Medieval Scots Poetry, London 1967, pp 7, 14 ([77], [76]).

Wood H H, Two Scots Chaucerians, Writers and Their Work, no 201, ed G Bullough, London 1967, pp 7, 29, 31 ([77], [76]).

Brookhouse C, Deschamps and Dunbar Two Elegies, SSL 7.123 ([82]).

Hope A D, A Midsummer Eve's Dream, N Y 1970, pp 11, 259 ([77], [85], [78]).

Scheps W, William Wallace and his Buke, SSL 6.224 ([77], [78]).

Other Scholarly Problems. Warton T, History of English Poetry from the 12th to the Close of the 16th Century, London 1774–81; ed W C Hazlitt, London 1871, 3.204 ([76]; occasion).

Pinkerton J, Ancient Scotish Poems, London and Edinburgh 1786, l.xciii ([76]; biographical evidence).

Ellis G, Specimens of the Early English Poets, 5 edns, London 1790, 1801, 1811, 1845 (5th edn corrected), 1.311 ([76]; occasion).

Irving D, The Lives of the Scotish Poets, 2nd edn London 1810, 1.394 ([74]; biographical evidence).

Tytler P F, Lives of Scottish Worthies, London 1833, 3.99, 106 ([76]; occasion).

Laing, edn, 1.21, 31 (Memoirs), 275; 2.211, 311, 328, 369, 373 ([76], [85], [82], [83], [86]; occasion, identity of subject).

Ancient Scotish Poetry No I Dunbar, Blackwood's Edinburgh Magazine 37.292 ([76]; occasion).

Green M A E, Lives of the Princesses of England, London 1852, 4.139 ([85]; occasion).

Paterson, edn, pp 117, 160, 218, 237, 270, 291, 301 ([76], [74], [79], [81], [82], [83], [85], [86]; occasion, setting).

Irving D, The History of Scotish Poetry, ed J A Carlyle, Edinburgh 1861, p 232 ([76]; occasion).

Campbell J F, Popular Tales of the West Highlands, Edinburgh 1862, 4.54 ([78]; brief; contemp conditions).

Kaufmann J, Traité de la langue, Bonn 1873, pp 7, 15 ([76], [85]; occasion).

Morley H, A First Sketch of English Literature, London 1873; rvsd London 1896, p
210 ([76]; occasion).

Wright T, The History of Scotland from the
Earliest Period, London and N Y [1873–74],
1.290 ([76]; occasion).

McElroy J G R, The Thrissill and the Rois,
The Penn Monthly 12.533 ([76]; occasion).

Schipper J, William Dunbar sein Leben und
seine Gedichte, Berlin 1884, pp 84, 290, 305
([76], [82], [83], [85], [74]; occasion, identity
of subject, place written).

Walker W, The Bards of Bon-Accord, Aberdeen 1887, p 19 ([85]; occasion, illustrative
quotes).

Mackay Æ J G, Introd, Small edn, l.xxxv,
xlv, xlviii, lvii, lxvii, lxxix, cviii, cxv ([76],
[82], [85], [78], [86], [75]; occasion, identity
of subject, attitude, contemp conditions).

[Robertson J L] Haliburton H, Our Earlier
Burns, In Scottish Fields, London 1890, pp
216, 231, 236 ([74], [76], [85], [86]; occasion,
biographical evidence).

Morley, 7.114, 120 ([76]; occasion).

Schipper, edn, pt 2, 40⁴.2, 37, 43, 49; pt 3,
41⁴.93, 99 ([76], [78], [79], [80], [82], [85];
occasion, identity of subject).

Oliphant F R, William Dunbar, Blackwood's
Edinburgh Magazine 154.422 ([85]; occasion).

Maxwell D, Bygone Scotland, Edinburgh
Hull and London 1894, p 153 ([85]; occasion).

Smeaton O, William Dunbar, N Y (1898?), pp
32, 78, 103, 117, 120, 152 ([74], [76], [85],
[86], [79]; biographical evidence, occasion,
contemp conditions; crit J W Baxter, William Dunbar, passim; The Scottish Antiquary 13.95).

Smith G G, The Days of James iiii, Scottish
History by Contemporary Writers, London
1900, p 119 ([85]; occasion, illustrative
quote).

Rait R S, An Outline of the Relations between England and Scotland, London 1901,
pp xxxv, 102 ([78], [76]; attitude, occasion,
brief).

Baildon H B, Burns and Dunbar, Scottish
Art and Letters 2.259 ([75]; occasion).

Millar J H, A Literary History of Scotland,
London 1903, p 51 ([76], [85]; occasion).

Teichert O P, Schottische Zustände unter
Jacob IV nach den Dichtungen von William Dunbar, Görlitz 1903, pp 10, 21, 26,
30, 34, 39 ([79], [81], [78], [76], [82], [85],
[77], [80]; contemp conditions, occasion;
crit O Glöde, EStn 36.267).

Smeaton O, The Story of Edinburgh, London
1905, pp 51, 403 ([76]; occasion, brief).

Steinberger C, Étude sur William Dunbar,
Dublin 1908, p 75 ([77], [84]; identity of
subject).

Stair-Kerr E, The Poets, Scotland under
James IV, Paisley 1911, pp 119, 126 ([76],
[85]; occasion, contemp conditions).

Taylor I A, The Life of James IV, London
1913, p 161 ([76]; occasion, brief).

Mackenzie W M, William Dunbar, Edinburgh Essays on Scots Literature, Edinburgh and London 1933, p 43 ([76]; occasion.)

Bühler C F, London Thow Art the Flowre of
Cytes All, RES 13.6 ([76]; occasion).

Roy J A, Of the Makaris A Causerie, UTQ
16.33, 36 ([76]; contemp conditions).

Baxter J W, William Dunbar, Edinburgh
and London 1952, pp 22, 113, 154, 159, 173,
184, 203 ([74], [76], [78], [80], [82], [83], [85],
[86]; occasion, identity of subject).

[Grieve C M] MacDiarmid H, Selections from
the Poems of William Dunbar, The Saltire
Classics, Edinburgh 1952, p 44 ([83]; identity of subject).

Milner I, Some Aspects of Satire in the Poetry of Dunbar, Philologica (cizojazyčná
prioloha Casopisu pro moderní filologii)
8.37, 41 ([80], [78]; contemp conditions).

Dickinson W C, Scotland from the Earliest
Times to 1603, A New History of Scotland,
Edinburgh and London 1961, 1.281 ([76],
[85]; occasion).

Shire H M, The Thrissil the Rois and the
Flour-de-lys, Cambridge Eng 1962, p 25
([82], [83], [86]; occasion).

Kinghorn A M, Warton's History and Early
English Poetry, ESts 44.202 (literary history; brief).

Coldwell D F C, Virgil's Aeneid Translated
into Scottish Verse by Gavin Douglas, PSTS
3s 30, Edinburgh and London 1964, 1.14
([86]; occasion).

Scott T, Dunbar A Critical Exposition, Edinburgh and London 1966, pp 1, 16, 40, 49,
56, 153, 280 ([76], [85], [86], [77], [81], [84];
occasion, contemp conditions, attitude, biographical evidence, classification of poems).

Literary Criticism. Henry R, The History of
Great Britain, London 1771–85; 6th edn
London 1823, 12.293 ([76], [77]; brief).

Warton T, History of English Poetry, London 1774–81; ed W C Hazlitt, London 1871,
3.205 ([76], [77], [78]; paraphrase with illustrative quotes).

Pinkerton J, Ancient Scotish Poems, London

and Edinburgh 1786, 1.xi, xciii ([77], [76]).
Ellis G, Specimens of the Early English Poets, 5 edns, London 1790, 1801, 1803, 1811, 1845 (5th edn corrected), 1. 311, 314 ([76], [77]).
The Scottish Register, Edinburgh 1794, 2.195 ([76], [77], [78]).
Irving D, The Lives of the Scotish Poets, 2nd edn London 1810, 1.405, 408, 432 ([79], [78], [76], [77]).
Gilchrist O, Censura Literaria, ed S E Brydges, London 1807, 5.242 ([78]).
Drake N, Chaucer Dunbar and Burns Compared, Mornings in Spring, London 1828, 2.7, 11, 22 ([77], [76]; illustrative excerpts).
Tytler P F, Lives of Scottish Worthies, London 1833, 3.100, 115, 128 ([76], [81], [77]).
Laing, edn, 1.21, 58 (Memoirs); 2.212, 216, 221, 225, 253, 265, 347, 374, 458 ([76], [79], [77], [78], [74]).
Ancient Scotish Poetry No I Dunbar, Blackwood's Edinburgh Magazine 37.292, 298, 314 ([76], [77], [78], [79], [84]).
William Dunbar, Littell's Living Age 1.382 ([76], [78], [77], [84], [79]).
Wright T, On the Scottish Poet Dunbar, Essays on Subjects Connected with the Literature Popular Superstitions and History of England, London 1846, 2.299 ([76], [77], [84], [78], [79], [80]).
Strickland A, Lives of the Queens of Scotland, N Y 1851, 1.53 ([76]).
Aytoun W E, The Ballads of Scotland, Edinburgh and London 1858; 2nd edn rvsd and augmented 1859, 1.lxiv ([77], [76]).
Gilfillan G, Specimens with Memoirs of the Less-Known Poets, Edinburgh and London 1860, 1.59 ([78], [84]; brief).
Paterson, edn, pp 40, 47, 126, 211, 218 ([77], [84], [76], [78], [79]).
Irving D, The History of Scotish Poetry, ed J A Carlyle, Edinburgh 1861, p 231 ([77], [76], [74] brief statement, [78]).
Smith A, William Dunbar Dreamthorp, London 1863; rptd no 200 The World's Classics, London 1914; rptd London 1934, p 72 ([77], [76], [78], [84]).
Taylor J, The Imperial Dictionary of Universal Biography, London [1863], 2.170 ([76], [77], [78], [79]; brief).
Kaufmann J, Traité de la langue, Bonn 1873, p 14 ([77], [76] [75], [81], [82], [83], [78], [79], [80]).
Morley H, A First Sketch of English Literature, London 1873; rvsd London 1896, p 212 ([77], [76], [78], [79], [80]).
Wilson J G, The Poets and Poetry of Scotland, N Y 1876, 1.24 ([76], [77], [78], [79]; brief).

Mackintosh J, The History of Civilisation in Scotland, London and Edinburgh 1878–88; new edn partly rewritten, Paisley 1892–96, 2.307 ([77], [76], [78], [79]).
Nichol J, William Dunbar, The English Poets, ed T H Ward, London and N Y 1880 (numerous subsequent edns); N Y 1924, 1.148 ([77], [76], [78], [79], [84]).
McElroy J G R, The Thrissill and the Rois, The Penn Monthly 12.534 ([76]).
Nichol J, A Sketch of Scottish Poetry, ed J Small, 2nd edn rvsd EETS 11, London 1883, p xxviii ([77], [76], [78], [79]).
Ross J M, Scottish History and Literature, Glasgow 1884, pp 189, 199, 214 ([76], [77], [79], [80], [78]).
Schipper J, William Dunbar sein Leben und seine Gedichte, Berlin 1884, pp 166, 169, 175, 183, 196, 254, 291, 306, 325 ([76], [77], [75], [78], [79], [80], [81], [82], [83], [85], [74], [84]).
DNB, 16.155 ([76], [77], [85], [78]).
Fitzgibbon H M, Early English and Scottish Poetry, London N Y and Melbourne 1888, p lx ([76], [77], [84], [78]).
Shairp J C, Sketches in History and Poetry, Edinburgh 1887, p 208 ([76], [77], [78]; brief).
Veitch J, The Feeling for Nature in Scottish Poetry, Edinburgh and London 1887, 1.222 ([76], [77]; with illustrative quotes).
Mackay Æ J G, Introd, Small edn, 1.xxxv, lviii, lxvii, lxx, lxxviii, lxxxii, c, cviii, cxxiii, cxxxvii ([76], [77], [84], [86], [75], [79], [80], [85], [82], [78]).
Minto W, Characteristics of English Poets, authorized American edn, Boston 1889, p 100 ([77], [76], [84], [78], [79]).
[Robertson J L] Haliburton H, Our Earlier Burns, In Scottish Fields, London 1890, pp 238, 240 ([76], [77], [80], [85], [82], [81]).
Morley, 7.120, 136 ([76], [77], [78]).
Eyre-Todd G, Mediæval Scottish Poetry, Abbotsford Series, Glasgow 1892, pp 149, 153 ([77], [76], [75], [78], [79]).
Schipper, edn, pt 2, 40⁴.2, 10, 43; pt 3, 41⁴.43, 97; pt 4, 42⁴.20, 44 ([76], [77], [79], [81], [83], [74], [84]).
Oliphant F R, William Dunbar, Blackwood's Edinburgh Magazine 154.420, 426, 437 ([76], [77], [78], [79], [80], [84]).
Jusserand J J, Histoire Littéraire, 2 vols, Paris 1894, 1.529 ([77], [76]).
Courthope, passim ([77] [76], [75], [78]).
Ten Brink, 3.68, 73, 77 ([76], [77], [79], [78], [84]).

Turnbull W R, The Heritage of Burns, Haddington 1896, pp 228, 240 ([78], [76]; brief references).

Gosse E, A Short History of Modern English Literature, N Y 1897; rvsd edn N Y 1906, p 50 ([78]; brief).

Smeaton O, A Quartette of Court Singers Four Centuries Ago, Westminster Rev 148.183 ([77], [76], [79], [78]; brief, extravagant, fictionalized).

Warner C D, A Library of the World's Best Literature, N Y 1897, 12.5064; ed J W Cunliffe and A H Thorndike, The World's Best Literature, The Warner Library, N Y 1917, 8.5064 ([76], [77], [78]).

Henderson T F, Scottish Vernacular Literature, Edinburgh 1898; 3rd edn rvsd Edinburgh 1910, pp 164, 171 ([77], [76], [78], [79], [85], [82]).

Smeaton O, William Dunbar, N Y (1898?), pp 127, 147 ([76], [77], [84], [79], [78], [83]); English Satires, London 1899, 1924, [1925], p xxiv ([78]; brief).

Smith G G, The Transition Period, Periods of European Lit, Edinburgh and London 1900, 4.50 and passim ([76], [77], [78], [79], [80]).

Neilson W A, Studies and Notes in Philology and Literature 6.163, 220, 227 ([77], [76], [75]).

Chambers R, Chambers's Cyclopædia, Phila and N Y 1901–03; rvsd J L Geddie, Phila and N Y 1938, 1.192 ([76], [77], [78], [84], [79], [80]).

M'Ilwraith W, A Sketch of Scottish Literature, Annual Burns Chronicle 10.21 ([77], [76]).

Mebus F, Studien zu William Dunbar, Breslau 1902, pp 8, 83 ([75], [84]).

Baildon H, Burns and Dunbar, Scottish Art and Letters 2.168, 257, 263 ([76], [77], [75], [78]).

Browne W H, The Taill of Rauf Coilyear, Baltimore 1903, p 16 ([77], [76], [78]).

Millar J H, A Literary History of Scotland, London 1903, pp 57, 64 ([77], [78]).

Lowell J R, Spenser, Among My Books, The Complete Writings of James Russell Lowell, Boston 1904, 4.224 ([84], [78]).

Moorman F W, The Interpretation of Nature in English Poetry from Beowulf to Shakespeare, QF 95.143 ([77], [76], [84]).

Snell F J, The Poets, The Age of Transition, London 1905, 1.84 ([76], [77]).

Seccombe T and W R Nicoll, The Scots Poets, The Bookman Illustrated Hist of Eng Lit, London 1906, 1.20 ([76], [77], [78]).

Wülker R, Geschichte der englischen Literatur, Liepzig and Wein 1906–07, 1.205 ([76], [77], [78], [84]; some illustrative quotes and summary, brief comment).

CHEL, 2.287 ([77], [75], [76], [78], [79]).

Steinberger C, Étude sur William Dunbar, Dublin 1908, pp 54, 68, 74, 79, 83, 104, 133, 140, 154, 167 ([76], [77], [75], [78], [79], [84]).

Tucker S M, Verse Satire in England, CUS 3, no 2, pp 136, 137, 140 ([76], [77], [79], [78]).

Enc Brit, 8.668 ([77], [76], [75], [78]).

Stair-Kerr E, The Poets, Scotland under James IV, Paisley 1911, p 119 ([76], [77]; brief).

Smith J C, Some Characteristics of Scots Literature, Oxford 1912, pp 6, 10 ([78], [77]; brief).

Watt L M, Scottish Life and Poetry, London 1912, p 101 ([77], [78], [76]).

Rhys E, The First Scottish Poets, Lyric Poetry, London Toronto and N Y 1913, p 99 ([78]).

Sandison H E, The Chanson D'Aventure in Middle English, Bryn Mawr Pa 1913, p 76 ([84]).

Mackie R L, Scotland, London 1916, pp 275, 288 ([76], [78]; brief).

Jacobi J B, William Dunbar—an Appreciation, The American Catholic Quarterly Rev 44.307, 313 ([76], [77], [78], [84]; brief).

Smith G G, Scottish Literature Character and Influence, London 1919, pp 10, 14, 90 ([84], [77], [78], [79], [76]; brief references).

Knowlton E C, Nature in Middle English, JEGP 20.189 ([76], [84], [77]).

Golding L, The Scottish Chaucerians, The Saturday Review of Politics Literature Science and Art 134.783 ([77], [78]).

Quiller-Couch A, Studies in Literature, 2s, N Y and Cambridge Eng 1922, p 272 ([77]).

Powys L, William Dunbar, The Freeman 7.517 ([78]).

Markham E, The Book of Poetry, N Y 1927, 4.901 ([78]; brief).

Jacob V, James IV and His Poet, Scots Magazine 10.279, 281 ([85], [76]).

Legouis HEL, p 174 ([76], [77], [78]).

Saintsbury G, The Four Great Scottish Poets, A Short Hist of Eng Lit, N Y 1929, p 187 ([77], [78], [76]; brief).

William Dunbar, TLS Apr 10 1930, p 305 ([78], [80], [76], [77]).

Frazier, edn, [unpaged] ([76]; brief).

Kitchin G, A Survey of Burlesque and Parody, Edinburgh and London 1931, p 24 ([79]).

Taylor R A, Dunbar the Poet, The Poets on the Poets, no 4, London 1931, pp 35, 39, 46, 52, 55, 59, 79 ([76], [84], [77], [85], [78], [82] [79]).

Elton O, The English Muse, London 1933, p 84 ([77], [76], [84], [78]).

Mackenzie A M, An Historical Survey of Scottish Literature, London 1933, pp 87, 90, 97 ([78], [76], [77], [83], [84]).

Mackenzie W M, William Dunbar, Edinburgh Essays on Scots Lit, Edinburgh and London 1933, pp 41, 48 ([84], [77], [76], [78]).

Musser B F, The Chaucer of Scotland, Franciscan Poets, N Y 1933, pp 7, 9 ([78], [77]).

Power W, Scotland and the Scots, Edinburgh and London 1934, p 189 ([77]).

Rait R and G S Pryde, Scotland, N Y 1934; 2nd edn London 1954, p 309 ([76], [77], [78]; very brief).

Smith J M, The French Background of Middle Scots Literature, Edinburgh and London 1934, pp xxviii, 48, 62, 69 ([78], [84], [76], [77], [81], [75], [82], [83], [85]).

Lewis C S, The Allegory of Love, London 1936; rptd London 1953, pp 251, 258 ([76], [77]).

Muir E, Scottish Literature, Scott and Scotland, London 1936, pp 44, 106 ([77], [78]).

Grierson H J C, The Problem of the Scottish Poet, E&S 21.105 ([77]).

Speirs J, William Dunbar, Scrut 7.56, 61 ([77], [76], [78]).

Kerr J, An Almost Forgotten Scottish Poet, Poetry Rev 29.374 ([76], [84], [78]).

Speirs J, The Scots Literary Tradition, London 1940, pp 33, 36, 44, 60 ([77], [78], [76]); rvsd 2nd edn 1962, pp 52, 55.

Grierson H J C and J C Smith, A Critical History of English Poetry, London 1944; 2nd rvsd edn London 1947, p 56 ([76], [84], [78]; brief).

Utley CR, p 166 ([84]; summary).

Chambers OHEL, p 138 ([77]; very brief).

Caird J B, Some Reflections on Scottish Literature, I. Poetry, Scottish Periodical 1.10, 18 ([77], [76]).

Craig HEL, p 168 ([76], [75], [77], [79], [84], [78]; brief).

Moore A K, The Secular Lyric in ME, Lexington Ky 1951, pp 195, 200 ([76], [77]).

Baxter J W, William Dunbar, Edinburgh and London 1952, pp 21, 103, 113, 125, 143,

156, 174 ([77], [75], [76], [84], [81], [78], [79], [80], [82], [83]).

Bloomfield M W, The Seven Deadly Sins, [East Lansing] 1952, p 236 ([78]).

Morgan E, Dunbar and the Language of Poetry, EC 2.147 ([78]).

Renwick-Orton, p 416 ([77], [76], [75], [79], [80], [78], [84]; brief).

Ward A C, Illustrated Hist of Eng Lit, London N Y and Toronto 1953, p 42 ([76], [77], [78]; brief).

Cruttwell P, Two Scots Poets Dunbar and Henryson, The Age of Chaucer, A Guide to Eng Lit, London 1954; rptd London 1955, 1.175 ([77], [76]).

Lewis C S, English Literature in the Sixteenth Century, Oxford 1954, p 91 ([76], [77], [75], [84], [78], [74]).

Kinsley J, The Mediaeval Makars, Scottish Poetry, A Critical Survey, London 1955, p 30 ([78]).

Stock N, Some Notes on Old Scots, Shenandoah 6, no 2, p 29 ([77]).

Hyde I, Primary Sources and Associations of Dunbar's Aureate Imagery, MLR 51.481, 486 ([77], [76], [83]).

Milner I, Some Aspects of Satire in the Poetry of Dunbar, Philologica (cizojazyčná prioloha Časopisu pro moderní filologii) 8.33, 35, 37, 41 ([78], [84], [80]).

Peter J, Complaint and Satire in Early English Literature, Oxford 1956, p 227 ([78]; brief reference).

Schlauch M, English Medieval Literature, Warsaw 1956, p 295 ([76], [84], [81], [77], [79]).

Enkvist N E, The Seasons of the Year, Societas Scientiarum Fennica Commentationes Humanarum Litterarum, Helsingfors 1957, 22⁴.143 ([77], [76]).

Kinsley J, William Dunbar Poems, Oxford 1958, pp xv, xix, xxiii ([76], [77], [79], [78]).

Mackie R L, King James IV of Scotland, Edinburgh and London 1958, p 179 ([77], [78], [79], [80]; brief comments).

Wittig K, The Scottish Tradition in Literature, Edinburgh 1958, p 65 ([77], [76]).

Kinghorn A M, The Mediaeval Makars, Texas Stud Lit and Lang 1.73, 78 ([84], [79], [77], [76], [85]).

Fox D, Dunbar's The Golden Targe, ELH 26.311 ([77], [84], [76]); The Chronology of William Dunbar, PQ 39.421 ([86]).

McLaren M, The Wisdom of the Scots, London 1961, p 69 ([74]).

Leyerle J, The Two Voices of William Dunbar, UTQ 31.318, 333, 337 ([77], [76], [85]).

Shire H M, The Thrissil the Rois and the Flour-de-lys, Cambridge Eng 1962, p 25 ([83], [86]).

Maclaine A H, The Christis Kirk Tradition, SSL 2.16 ([79]).

Rossi S, I Chauceriani Scozzesi, Napoli 1964, pp 45, 50 ([77], [76], [78]).

Smith Rowland, The Poetry of William Dunbar, Theoria 22.76, 84 ([77], [79]).

Hyde I, Poetic Imagery, SSL 2.186, 190, 195 ([76], [77], [83]).

Fox D, The Scottish Chaucerians, Chaucer and Chaucerians, ed D S Brewer, University Alabama 1966, p 182 ([77], [84], [74]).

Richmond V B, Laments for the Dead in Medieval Narrative, Duquesne Studies, Philological Series 8, Pittsburgh 1966, p 26 ([83]).

Scott T, Dunbar A Critical Exposition, Edinburgh and London 1966, pp 16, 40, 55, 117, 151, 165, 169, 196, 203, 212, 229, 244, 260, 264, 276, 278, 332, 338, 345, 359, 366, 371 and passim ([85], [77], [76], [75], [84], [81], [78], [79], [80], [82], [83], [74], [86], group as a whole).

Kinghorn A M, Dunbar and Villon, MLR 62.201, 206 ([84], [83], [76]).

MacQueen J, Some Aspects of the Early Renaissance in Scotland, Forum Mod Lang Stud 3.210 ([76]).

Scott T, Late Medieval Scots Poetry, London 1967, pp 10, 14, 33 ([77], [76]).

Wood H H, Two Scots Chaucerians, Writers and Their Work, no 201, ed G Bullough, London 1967, pp 29, 37 ([77], [76], [75], [78], [80], [81], [85], [82], [83], [86]).

Shire H M, Song Dance and Poetry of the Court of Scotland, Cambridge 1969, p 15 ([76], [84]).

Hope A D, A Midsummer Eve's Dream, N Y 1970, p 259 ([78]).

Bibliography. Geddie W, A Bibliography of Middle Scots Poets, PSTS ns 61, Edinburgh and London 1912, p 193 ([77], [82], [76]).

Utley C R, p 166 ([84]).

Beattie W, The Chepman and Myllar Prints A Facsimile, Edinburgh Biblio Soc, Oxford 1950, pp xi, xiv ([77], [82]; crit W A Jackson, SHR 31.89).

Robbins-Cutler, nos 515.5 ([80]), 541.5 ([85]), 1444.5 ([83]), 1503.5 ([84]), 2289.8 ([79]), 2623.3 ([78]), 2811.5 ([82]), 2820.5 ([77]), 3140.5 ([75]), 3595.3 ([81]), 3694.6 ([86]), 3768.6 ([74]), 3990.5 ([76]).

VII. Moralizings

(Note: Folios for items [87–98] are listed by MS number, as appropriate, after each title. See under *MSS* below for full listing and information. Titles are from Mackenzie edn.)

[87] OF THE CHANGES OF LIFE.

1, ff 8ᵇ–9ᵃ; 2, pp 5–6, 315.

[88] OF COVETYCE.

1, ff 9ᵃ–9ᵇ; 2, pp 6–7; 3, ff 64ᵇ–65ᵃ.

[89] GUDE COUNSALE.

3, f 212ᵇ.

[90] BEST TO BE BLYTH.

1, ff 43ᵃ–43ᵇ; 2, p 337; 3, ff 98ᵇ, 115ᵇ.

[91] OF CONTENT.

1, ff 5ᵃ–5ᵇ; 2, p 307.

[92] ALL ERDLY JOY RETURNIS IN PANE.

2, pp 319–320; 3, f 48ᵇ.

[93] ADVICE TO SPEND ANIS AWIN GUDE.

2, pp 225–226; 3, ff 136ᵃ–136ᵇ.

[94] NO TRESSOUR AVAILIS WITHOUT GLAIDNES.

2, pp 221–222; 3, ff 97ᵇ–98ᵇ; 4, unpaged.

[95] OF MANIS MORTALITIE.

2, pp 193–194; 3, ff 47ᵃ–47ᵇ.

[96] OF THE WARLDIS VANITIE.

2, pp 195–196.

[97] OF LYFE.

2, p 310; 3, f 75ᵇ.

[98] A GENERAL SATYRE.

2, pp 187–189; 3, pp 47–48, ff 60ᵃ–61ᵃ.

MSS. 1, Camb Univ L1.5.10 (Reidpeth or Moore), ff 5ᵃ–5ᵇ, 8ᵇ–9ᵇ, 43ᵃ–43ᵇ (1623; items

[91], [87], [88], [90] with lines 16–20 omitted); 2, Magdalene Coll Camb 2553 (Pepysian Libr, Maitland Folio), pp 5–7, 187–189, 193–196, 221–222, 225–226, 307, 310, 315, 319–320, 337 (1570–71; items [87–88], [98], [95–96], [94], [93], [91], [97], [92], and [90] with lines 16–20 omitted); 3, Nat Libr Scot 1.1.6 (Bannatyne), pp 47–48, ff 47ᵃ–47ᵇ, 48ᵇ, 60ᵃ–61ᵃ, 64ᵇ–65ᵃ, 75ᵇ, 97ᵇ–98ᵇ, 115ᵇ, 136ᵃ–136ᵇ, 212ᵇ (1568; items [95], [92], [98], [88], [97], [94], [90], [93], [89]); 4, Aberdeen Town Clerk's Office, Aberdeen Minute Book of Sasines, vol 3, unpaged (1510–11; item [94]).

Pinkerton J, Ancient Scotish Poems, 2 vols, London and Edinburgh 1786, 1.v; 2.437, 471 (MSS 2, 3).

Brydges E and J Haslewood, The British Bibliographer, London 1814, 4.183 (MS 3).

Laing D, The Poems of George Bannatyne, Edinburgh 1824, p 3 (MS 3); An Account of the Contents of George Bannatyne's Manuscript, The Bannatyne Club, Edinburgh 1829, 35.43 (MS 3); The Poems of William Dunbar, edn, 1.303 (in Supplement; MS 4).

A Catalogue of the Manuscripts Preserved in The Library of The University of Cambridge, Cambridge 1861, 4.94 (MS 1).

Small J, The Poetical Works of Gavin Douglas, Edinburgh and London 1874, 1.clxxi (MS 2).

Schipper, edn, pt 1, 40².9ff (MSS 1, 2, 3, 4).

Murdoch J B, ed, The Bannatyne Manuscript, 4 vols, Hunterian Club, Glasgow 1896, 2.127, 131, 162, 175, 204, 279, 329; 3.383, 602 (MS 3 rptd).

Smith G G, Specimens of Middle Scots, Edinburgh and London 1902, pp lxvi, lxxiii (MSS 2, 3).

Brown J T T, The Bannatyne Manuscript, SHR 1.136 (MS 3).

Craigie W A, ed, The Maitland Folio, PSTS ns 7, 20, 2 vols, Edinburgh and London 1919–27, 2.50 (MS 1); 1.4, 211, 218, 221, 249, 253, 350, 366, 376, 382 410; 2.36, 102, 106, 119, 122, 126 (MS 2 rptd, notes in vol 2).

Ritchie W T, ed, The Bannatyne Manuscript Writtin in Tyme of Pest, PSTS ns 5, 22, 23, 26, 4 vols, Edinburgh 1928–34, 1.79; 2.117, 121, 147, 159, 186, 259, 308; 3.11, 244 (MS 3 rptd).

Baxter J W, TLS Apr 8 1939, p 208 (MS 4); William Dunbar, Edinburgh and London 1952, pp 216ff (MSS 1, 2, 3, 4).

Editions. Laing D, The Poems of William Dunbar, 2 vols, Edinburgh 1834, 1.175, 187, 201, 209, 235, 249; 2.24, 339, 344, 349, 352,

366, 390 (notes in vol 2; MSS 2, 3; Memoirs of William Dunbar preceding text of poems in vol 1 is paginated separately).

Small J, Æ J G Mackay, G P McNeill, W Gregor, The Poems of William Dunbar, PSTS 2, 4, 16, 21, 29, 3 vols, Edinburgh 1884–93, 2.74, 81, 108, 152, 158, 162, 230, 244, 250; 3.125, 137, 181, 239, 246, 252, 312, 329, 334 (notes in vol 3; MSS 2, 3).

Schipper J, The Poems of William Dunbar, pts 3–4, Denkschriften der kaiserlichen Akademie der Wissenschaften, Philo-Hist Classe, Vienna 1892–93, 41⁴.85; 42⁴.7, 21, 29, 81 (MS sources and variants given in headnotes and ftnts to each poem; MSS 2, 3, 1; crit E Kölbing, EStn 20.439).

Baildon H B, The Poems of William Dunbar, Cambridge 1907, pp 145, 160, 170, 206, 275, 279, 292 (notes at end of text; sources vary, selects reading which seems to him most likely to be correct; crit J H Millar, The Bookman 32.207).

Mackenzie W M, The Poems of William Dunbar, London 1932, p 140 (notes at end of text; MSS 2, 3; crit B Dickins, MLR 28.506; TLS Jan 26 1933, p 55; The Modern Scot 4.63); rptd London 1950; ed B Dickins, rptd and rvsd London 1960 (crit A Macdonald, ESts 43.219); rptd 1970.

Selections. Ramsay A, The Ever Green, Edinburgh 1724, 1.64, 102; 2.95 ([93], [98], [88]; occasional changes in wording; MS 3); The Poetical Works of Allan Ramsay, ed C Mackay, London and N Y n d, pp 229, 235, 277 ([93], [98], [88]).

Poems in the Scottish Dialect by Several Celebrated Poets, Glasgow 1748, p 28 ([88]).

Ruddiman W, Choice Collection of Scots Poems, Edinburgh 1766, pp 141, 158 ([93], [98]).

Dalrymple D, Ancient Scottish Poems, Edinburgh 1770, pp 42, 54, 87, 94, 168, 249, 262, 297; rptd Leeds 1815, pp 51, 68, 109, 118, 212, 299, 311, 346 ([98], [94], [93], [90], [92], [95], [88]; notes at end of text; MS 3).

The Caledoniad, London 1775, 3.23 ([98]).

Pinkerton J, Select Scotish Ballads, 2 vols, London 1783, 2.57 ([93], [90]; Dalrymple, Ancient Scottish Poems); Ancient Scotish Poems, 2 vols, London and Edinburgh 1786, 1.122; 2.416 ([91], [87]; notes in vol 2; MS 2).

London and Edinburgh 1786, 1.122; 2.416 ([91], [87]; notes in vol 2; MS 2).

Morison R, Select Poems of Wil Dunbar Part First from the MS of George Bannatyne, Perth 1788, pp 49, 60, 91, 98 ([98], [94], [93], [90], [92], [95]; MS 3).

Ellis G, Specimens of the Early English Poets, 5 edns, London 1790, 1801, 1803, 1811, 1845 (5th edn corrected), 1.309 ([94]; spelling modernized, glossings at foot of page; Dalrymple, Ancient Scottish Poems).

Sibbald J, Chronicle of Scottish Poetry, 4 vols, Edinburgh and London 1802, 1.342, 373; 2.13, 17 ([93], [98], [87], [88]; introductory and end notes; sources not always indicated but include MS 3).

A Curious Collection of Scottish Poems, Aberdeen 1821, p 59 ([93]; spelling partially modernized).

Ancient Scotish Poetry No I Dunbar, Blackwood's Edinburgh Magazine 37.308 ([94], [90]).

William Dunbar, The Scottish Journal 1.132 ([87]; Laing edn).

Paterson J, The Works of William Dunbar, Edinburgh 1863, pp 48, 60, 87, 291, 311 ([90], [91], [94], [93], [92], [96], [87], [95], [97], [89], [98]; glossings in ftnts).

Selections Made Chiefly from Works in the Old Scots Language for the Use of Schools in Scotland, Edinburgh 1867, p 67 ([91]; glossings at foot of page).

Morley H, Shorter English Poems, London 1876, p 112 ([87], [94]).

Wilson J G, The Poets and Poetry of Scotland, N Y 1876, 1.28 (from [92]).

Ross J, The Book of Scottish Poems, Paisley 1882, 1.187, 193 ([94], [87]).

Schipper J, William Dunbar sein Leben und seine Gedichte, Berlin 1884, pp 289, 301, 312, 350 (poems in German interspersed through text of discussion; [87], [88], [92], [91], [90], [93], [94], [97], [96]; crit E Kölbing, EStn 10.128; M Trautmann, Angl 7.146; The Nation 40.144).

Fitzgibbon H M, Early English and Scottish Poetry, London N Y and Melbourne 1888, pp 116, 136, 146, 432 ([87], [94], [91], [97]; spelling modernized, note at end of text).

Veitch J, The Feeling for Nature in Scottish Poetry, Edinburgh and London 1887, 1.235 ([87]; brief quote interspersed with criticism, glossings in side notes; crit C Patmore, Out-of-door Poetry, St James Gazette July 9 1887; rptd in Courage in Politics, London 1921, p 32).

Eyre-Todd G, Mediæval Scottish Poetry, Abbotsford Series, Glasgow 1892, pp 185, 211 ([89], [90]; glossings in margin).

Henley W E, English Lyrics Chaucer to Poe, London 1897, pp 8, 373 ([96]; spelling modernized, notes at end of text; Small edn).

Warner C D, A Library of the World's Best Literature Ancient and Modern, N Y 1897, 12.5068; ed J W Cunliffe and A H Thorndike, The World's Best Literature, The Warner Library, N Y 1917, 8.5068 ([94]; spelling partially modernized).

Henderson T F, A Little Book of Scottish Verse, London 1899; 2nd edn 1909, p 61 ([94], [87]; brief introductory note, glossings at foot of page).

Steinberger C, Étude sur William Dunbar, Dublin 1908, p 151 ([97]; Small edn).

Dixon W M, The Edinburgh Book of Scottish Verse, London 1910, pp 30, 43, 47 ([94], [91], [87], [97]; glossings at foot of page).

Zupitza J, Alt- und mittelenglisches Übungsbuch, 10th edn Vienna and Leipzig 1912, p 207 ([96]; variants at foot of page).

Metcalfe W M, Specimens of Scottish Literature, London 1913, pp 55, 162 ([94], [87]; notes at end of text).

Patterson R F, Six Centuries of English Literature, London and Glasgow 1933, 1.191 ([95]).

Mackie R L, A Book of Scottish Verse, The World's Classics, no 417, London 1934, p 64 ([96]; glossings at foot of page); 2nd edn London Glasgow N Y 1967, p 63.

Gray M M, Scottish Poetry from Barbour to James VI, N Y 1935, pp 131, 133, 139, 143, 161, 164 ([94], [91], [92], [87], [96], [97]; crit J Speirs, Scrut 6.83; W M Mackenzie, The Scottish Bookman 1, no 4, p 133).

Fergusson J, The Green Garden, London and Edinburgh 1946, pp 31, 41 ([87], [97]; spelling modernized).

Mackenzie A M, Scottish Pageant, Edinburgh 1946; 2nd edn 1952, 1.36 ([87]).

Oliver J W and J C Smith, A Scots Anthology from the 13th to the 20th Century, Edinburgh and London 1949, p 38 ([87]; spelling modernized).

Baxter J W, William Dunbar, Edinburgh and London 1952, p 220 ([94]; MS 4; crit M P McDiarmid, SHR 33.46).

[Grieve C M] MacDiarmid H, Selections from the Poems of William Dunbar, The Saltire Classics, Edinburgh 1952, p 18 ([87]; glossings in ftnts; MacKenzie edn); Selected Poems of William Dunbar, Glasgow 1955, p 52 ([87]).

Kinsley J, William Dunbar Poems, Oxford 1958, pp 60, 66, 70, 125 ([87], [90], [97], [98]; notes at end of text, MSS 2, 3; crit TLS Apr 18 1958, p 208; D Young, SHR 38.10; E Morgan, RES ns 11.71; J Wordsworth, MÆ 30.128).

McLaren M, The Wisdom of the Scots, London 1961, p 77 ([87], [91]; glossings in margin).

Smith Rowland, The Poetry of William Dunbar, Theoria 22.82 (from [90]).

Scott T, Dunbar A Critical Exposition, Edinburgh and London 1966, p 239 ([97]; Mackenzie edn).

Ridley F [H], Selected Poems of William Dunbar, Los Angeles 1969, pp 12, 15 ([87], [97]; glossings in margin; MSS 2, 1).

Modernization. [Robertson J L] Haliburton H, Dunbar Being a Selection from the Poems of an Old Makar Adapted for Modern Readers, London 1895, pp 13, 45, 56, 60, 69 (from [93], [94], [90], from [92], from [91], [87], from [88]; essentially modernized paraphrase, abbreviated, extremely free; crit R Brotanek, AnglB 6.71).

Textual Matters. Laing, edn, 2.339, 344, 352, 368, 406 ([88], [90], [91], [92], [95], [98]).

Schipper, edn, pt 3, 41⁴.85; pt 4, 42⁴.9, 31, 35 ([87], [98], [91], [93]; see also introductory and ftnts to individual poems).

Mackenzie, edn, pp 222ff [87–98].

Baxter J W, William Dunbar, Edinburgh and London 1952, pp 136, 195, 206, 219 ([92], [87], [95], [97], [89], [94], [93], [91], [90], [88], [98]).

Fox D, Some Scribal Alterations of Dates in the Bannatyne MS, PQ 42.260 ([94]).

Language. Ramsay A, The Ever Green, Edinburgh 1724, 2.265 ([93], [98], [88]; glossary).

Dalrymple D, Ancient Scottish Poems, Edinburgh 1770, p 317 (glossary); rptd Leeds 1815, p 367, [added] Glossary, p 1 [separate pagination] ([98], [94], [93], [90], [92], [95], [88]).

Pinkerton J, Select Scotish Ballads, London 1783, 1.154; 2.193 ([93], [90]; glossaries); Ancient Scotish Poems, London and Edinburgh 1786, 1.cxliii; 2.520 (synorthographic and symphonious words, glossary; [91], [87]).

Sibbald J, Chronicle of Scottish Poetry, Edinburgh and London 1802, vol 4 [unpaged] (glossary; [93], [98], [87], [88]).

Murray J A H, The Dialect of the Southern Counties of Scotland, London 1873 (group as a whole).

Kaufmann J, Traité de la langue, Bonn 1873, p 47 (group as a whole).

Hahn O, Zur Verbal- und Nominalflexion bei den schottischen Dichtern, Berlin 1887–89 (see especially pt 3, p 17; group as a whole).

Schipper, edn, pt 1, 40².18 (group as a whole).

Gregor W, Glossary, Small edn, 3.401 (group as a whole).

Curtis F J, An Investigation of the Rimes and Phonology of Clariodus, Angl 16.387; 17.1, 125 (group as a whole).

Heuser W, Die Dehnung vor -nd im Mittelschottischen, Die Dehnung *- end,* Angl 19.401 (brief; group as a whole).

Baildon H B, On the Rimes in the Authentic Poems of William Dunbar, Trans Royal Soc Edinburgh 39³.629; issued separately Edinburgh 1899 (group as a whole).

Flom G T, Scandinavian Influence on Southern Lowland Scotch, diss Columbia 1900 (group as a whole).

Browne W H, The Taill of Rauf Coilyear, Baltimore 1903, pp 15, 35, 139 (general discussion of Middle Scots, glossary; group as a whole).

Knopff P, Darstellung der Ablautverhältnisse in der schottischen Schriftsprache, diss Würzburg 1904 (group as a whole).

Baildon, edn, pp xxvi, 299 (discussion, glossary; group as a whole).

CHEL, 2.101, 506 (group as a whole).

Dixon W M, The Edinburgh Book of Scottish Verse, London 1910, p 897 (glossary; [94], [91], [87], [97]).

Zupitza J, Alt- und mittelenglisches Übungsbuch, 10th edn Vienna and Leipzig 1912, p 208 ([96]; glossary, definitions in German).

Gray M M, Introd, Lancelot of the Laik, PSTS ns 2, Edinburgh and London 1912, 2.xviii (group as a whole).

Lenz K, Zur Lautlehre der französischen Elemente in den schottischen Dichtungen, diss Marburg 1913 (examples taken from Douglas, Dunbar, Lyndesay, Clariodus; group as a whole).

Metcalfe W M, Specimens of Scottish Literature, London 1913, pp 9, 39, 189 ([94], [87]).

Westergaard E, Prepositions in Lowland Scotch, Angl 41.444 (some examples from Dunbar; group as a whole); Verbal Forms in Middle-Scotch,, Angl 43.95 (group as a whole).

Watt L M, Language and Influences, Douglas's Aeneid, Cambridge 1920, p 149 (very generally applicable; group as a whole).

Westergaard E, Studies in Prefixes and Suffixes, London 1924 (group as a whole).

Wilson J, The Spelling of Scotch before 1600, The Dialects of Central Scotland, London 1926, p 168 (group as a whole; attempts to determine pronunciation from spelling, rimes, modern Lothian pronunciation).

Westergaard E, Plural Forms in Lowland Scottish, Angl 51.77 (group as a whole).

Craigie W A, ed, The Maitland Folio, PSTS ns 7, 20, 2 vols, Edinburgh and London 1919–27, 2.135 (glossary; [87], [88], [98], [95], [96], [94], [93], [97], [91], [92], [90]).

Ritchie R L G, Early Instances of French Loan-Words in Scots and English, EStn 63.41 ([98]; 2 examples from Dunbar).

Mackenzie, edn, pp xii, xxxvii, 245 ([87–98]; discussion, glossary).

Wood H H, The Poems and Fables of Robert Henryson, Edinburgh 1933; 2nd edn rvsd 1958; rptd 1965, 1968, p xxxi.

Patrick D, Scottish Literature, Chambers's Cyclopædia, rvsd J L Geddie, Phila and N Y 1938, 1.164 (group as a whole).

Fergusson J, The Green Garden, London and Edinburgh 1946, p 228 (glossary; [87], [97]).

Oliver J W and J C Smith, A Scots Anthology, Edinburgh and London 1949, p 497 (glossaries; [87]).

[Grieve C M] MacDiarmid H, Selections from the Poems of William Dunbar, The Saltire Classics, Edinburgh 1952, pp 5, 49 ([87]; brief note, glossary); Selected Poems of William Dunbar, Glasgow 1955, p 60 (glossary; [87]).

Kinsley J, William Dunbar Poems, Oxford 1958, p 139 (glossary; [87], [90], [97], [98]).

Wittig K, The Scottish Tradition in Literature, Edinburgh 1958, pp 62, 101 and passim (general reference to group as a whole).

Scott T, Dunbar A Critical Exposition, Edinburgh and London 1966, pp 346, 351.

Conley J, William Dunbar Additions to and Corrections of OED and DOST, N&Q 213 (ns 15).169 ([98], [92]).

Versification. Schipper J, William Dunbar sein Leben und seine Gedichte, Berlin 1884, p 303 ([98]).

McNeill G P, Note on the Versification and Metres of Dunbar, Small edn, l.clxxix, clxxxiv ([87], [97], [88], [92], [93], [90], [91], [98], [95], [94], [96], [89]).

Schipper, edn, pt 4, $42^4.10$ ([98]; discussion in headnote to poem).

Curtis F J, The Rimes and Phonology of Clariodus, Angl 16.387; 17.1, 125 (group as a whole).

Henderson T F, Scottish Vernacular Literature, Edinburgh 1898; 3rd edn rvsd Edinburgh 1910, p 156 ([94]).

Baildon H B, Rimes in the Authentic Poems of Dunbar, Trans Royal Soc Edinburgh $39^3.629$ (group as a whole).

Scott T, Dunbar A Critical Exposition, Edinburgh and London 1966, pp 86, 313, 316, 318 ([98], [87], [97], [88], [92], [93], [90], [91], [94], [89], [96], [95]).

Date. Laing, edn, 2.390, 402 ([98]).

Paterson J, The Works of William Dunbar, Edinburgh 1863, pp 51, 106, 296 ([91], [94], [93], [90], [98]).

Schipper J, William Dunbar sein Leben und seine Gedichte, Berlin 1884, pp 288, 296, 300, 304, 314, 319 ([87], [88], [98], [91], [90], [93], [94]).

Mackay Æ J G, Introd [and] Appendix to Introd, Small edn, l.lxix, xci, cxx, cxxxi, cxxxviii, clxii, clxiv, clxvii, clxxii ([88], [87], [96], [97], [89], [98], [92], [90], [94], [91], [93], [95]).

Schipper, edn, pt 3, $41^4.85$; pt 4, $42^4.7$, 22, 29, 31, 33, 35, 38, 82 ([87], [88], [89], [92], [91], [90], [93], [94], [95], [97], [96]).

Steinberger C, Étude sur William Dunbar, Dublin 1908, p 144 ([92]).

Baxter J W, William Dunbar, Edinburgh and London 1952, pp 136, 194, 206, 208 ([92], [89], [94], [93], [91], [90], [88], [98]).

Shire H M and A Fenton, The Sweepings of Parnassus, Aberdeen Univ Rev 36.53 ([94]).

Fox D, The Chronology of William Dunbar, PQ 39.419 ([94], [88], [98]).

Authorship. Laing, edn, 2.390 ([98]).

Paterson J, The Works of William Dunbar, Edinburgh 1863, pp 87, 296, 311 ([97], [98]).

Schipper J, William Dunbar sein Leben und seine Gedichte, p 302 ([98]).

Mackay Æ J G, Introd, Small edn, l.cxx ([98]).

Schipper, edn, pt 4, $42^4.9$, 35 ([98], [93]).

Brown J T T, The Bannatyne Manuscript, SHR 1.149 ([88]).

Baxter J W, William Dunbar, pp 137, 206 ([95], [88], [98]).

Scott T, Dunbar A Critical Exposition, Edinburgh and London 1966, p 260 ([93]).

Sources and Literary Relations. Laing, edn, 2.339, 349 ([88], [96]).

Schipper J, William Dunbar sein Leben und seine Gedichte, p 289 ([87]).

Mackay Æ J G, Introd, Small edn, l.cxx, cxxxv ([98], [94], [90]).

Ten Brink, 3.78 ([94]).

Turnbull W R, The Heritage of Burns, Haddington 1896, pp 228, 256 ([94]; brief scattered references).

Neilson W A, Studies and Notes in Philology and Literature 6.212 ([89]).

Smith G G, The Transition Period, Periods of European Literature, Edinburgh and London 1900, 4.36, 39, 42 and passim ([92],

[96], [90]).

Chambers R, Chambers's Cyclopædia, Phila and N Y 1901–03; rvsd Phila and N Y 1938, 1.195 ([87]).

Tucker S M, Verse Satire in England, CUS 3, no 2, p 139 ([98]).

Mendenhall J C, Aureate Terms A Study in the Literary Diction of the 15th Century, Lancaster Pa 1919 (group as a whole).

Jacobi J B, William Dunbar—an Appreciation, The American Catholic Quarterly Rev 44.311 ([95]; brief).

Smith J M, The French Background of Middle Scots Literature, Edinburgh and London 1934, p 74 ([95], [92]; crit AnglB 45.265; MÆ 4.44).

Patrick D, Scottish Literature, Chambers's Cyclopædia, Phila and N Y 1901–03; rvsd J L Geddie Phila and N Y 1938, 1.166 (group as a whole).

Hyde I, Primary Sources and Associations of Dunbar's Aureate Imagery, MLR 51.483 ([90], [95], [96], [92]).

Peter J, Complaint and Satire in Early English Literature, Oxford 1956, p 190 ([98]; brief reference).

Kinghorn A M, The Mediaeval Makars, Texas Stud Lit and Lang 1.73 ([95], [97]).

Wordsworth J, Dunbar's Quod Cinis Es A Note and a Reply, MLR 54.223 ([95]).

Hyde I, Dunbar's Quod Cinis Es A Note and a Reply, MLR 54.223 ([95]).

Maclaine A H, The Christis Kirk Tradition, SSL 2.16 ([98]).

Hyde I, Poetic Imagery, SSL 2.184, 193 ([95], [92], [96]).

Scott T, Dunbar A Critical Exposition, Edinburgh and London 1966, pp 240, 243, 338 and passim ([96], [95], [92], [90], [94]).

Kinghorn A M, Dunbar and Villon, MLR 62.197, 201, 203 ([94]), [90], [89], [95]).

Other Scholarly Problems. Laing, edn, 2.391 ([98]; identity of subject).

Paterson J, The Works of William Dunbar, Edinburgh 1863, p 56 ([93]; obscure line).

Ross J M, Scottish History and Literature, Glasgow 1884, p 208 ([88]; contemp conditions).

Schipper J, William Dunbar sein Leben und seine Gedichte, Berlin 1884, p 302 ([98]; identity of author).

Mackay Æ J G, Introd, Small edn, l.xci ([89]; identity of subject).

Smeaton O, William Dunbar, N Y (1898?), p 106 ([91]; biographical evidence).

Teichert O P, Schottische Zustände unter Jacob IV nach den Dichtungen von Wil-

liam Dunbar, Görlitz 1903, pp 11, 17, 24, 27, 30, 38 ([98], [88]; contemp conditions; crit O Glöde, EStn 36.267).

Milner I, Some Aspects of Satire in the Poetry of Dunbar, Philologica (cizojazyčná prioloha Casopisu pro moderní filologii) 8.34, 38 ([98]; contemp conditions).

Fox D, The Chronology of William Dunbar, PQ 39.419 ([88]; contemp conditions).

Scott T, Dunbar A Critical Exposition, Edinburgh and London 1966, pp 17, 258 ([98], [88], [93]; contemp conditions, biographical evidence).

Shire H M, Song Dance and Poetry of the Court of Scotland, Cambridge 1969, p 21 ([98]; Reformation influence on editing).

Literary Criticism. Laing, edn, 2.344, 349, 366 ([91], [94], [87], [97]).

Ancient Scotish Poetry No I Dunbar, Blackwood's Edinburgh Magazine 37.308 ([94], [90]).

William Dunbar, Littell's Living Age 1.383 ([90], [93], [94]).

Paterson J, The Works of William Dunbar, Edinburgh 1863, pp 51, 53, 64, 66, 87 ([91], [94], [87], [95], [97]).

Taylor J, The Imperial Dictionary of Universal Biography, London [1863], 2.170 ([94]; brief).

Ross J M, Scottish History and Literature, Glasgow 1884, p 208 ([88], [89], [90], [91], [94], [93]).

Schipper J, William Dunbar sein Leben und seine Gedichte, Berlin 1884, pp 300, 303, 307, 312, 317, 319, 349 ([88], [98], [89], [92], [93], [95], [96]).

Veitch J, The Feeling for Nature in Scottish Poetry, Edinburgh and London 1887, 1.235 ([87]).

Mackay Æ J G, Introd, Small edn, l.lxx, cix, cxxx, cxxxv ([88], [87], [96], [97], [98], [89], [94], [90], [93], [91], [92], [95]).

Schipper, edn, pt 4, 42⁴.7, 10, 22, 31, 35, 83 ([88], [98], [89], [91], [93], [97], [96]).

Ten Brink, 3.77 ([94]).

Henderson T F, Scottish Vernacular Literature, Edinburgh 1898; 3rd edn rvsd Edinburgh 1910, p 181 ([92], [96]).

Smith G G, The Transition Period, Periods of European Lit, Edinburgh and London 1900, 4.50 and passim ([92], [96], [90]).

Neilson W A, Studies and Notes in Philology and Literature 6.212 ([89]).

CHEL, 2.291 (group as a whole).

Steinberger C, Étude sur William Dunbar, Dublin 1908, pp 123, 144, 150, 153 ([87], [94], [90], [91], [93], [89], [88], [92], [96]).

Tucker S M, Verse Satire in England, CUS 3, no 2, p 139 ([98]).

Enc Brit, 8.669 ([98]).

Jacobi J B, William Dunbar—an Appreciation, The American Catholic Quarterly Rev 44.311 ([95]; brief).

William Dunbar, TLS Apr 10 1930, p 306 (group as a whole).

Mackenzie A M, An Historical Survey of Scottish Literature, London 1933, p 97 ([92]).

Rait R and G S Pryde, Scotland, N Y 1934; 2nd edn London 1954, p 309 ([92]; very brief).

Smith J M, The French Background of Middle Scots Literature, Edinburgh and London 1934, p 74 ([95]).

Speirs J, William Dunbar, Scrut 7.65, 68 ([98], [95]).

Kerr J, An Almost Forgotten Scottish Poet, Poetry Rev 29.376 ([94], [90]).

Speirs J, The Scots Literary Tradition, London 1940, pp 51, 54 ([98], [95]); rvsd 2nd edn 1962, p 65.

Moore A K, The Secular Lyric in ME, Lexington Ky 1951, p 215 ([92]).

Baxter J W, William Dunbar, Edinburgh and London 1952, p 136 ([92]).

Renwick-Orton, p 417 ([92]; brief).

Lewis C S, English Literature in the Sixteenth Century, Oxford 1954, p 96 ([95], [90], [92], [96], [87], [94], [88]).

Hyde I, Primary Sources and Associations of Dunbar's Aureate Imagery, MLR 51.483 ([90], [95], [96], [92]).

Milner I, Some Aspects of Satire in the Poetry of Dunbar, Philologica (cizojazyčná prioloha Casopisu pro mod* filologii) 8.34, 38 ([98]).

Peter J, Complaint and Satire in Early English Literature, Oxford 1956, pp 51, 190 ([88], [98]; brief reference).

Kinghorn A M, The Mediaeval Makars, Texas Stud Lit and Lang 1.80 ([95], [97]).

McLaren M, The Wisdom of the Scots, London 1961, p 70 ([87], [91]).

Smith Rowland, The Poetry of William Dunbar, Theoria 22.81 ([90]).

Hyde I, Poetic Imagery, SSL 2.184, 193 ([95], [92], [96]).

Scott T, Dunbar A Critical Exposition, Edinburgh and London 1966, pp 62, 81, 84, 147, 238, 253, 275, 338, 342 and passim ([89], [98], [88], [97], [96], [87], [92], [95], [90], [91], [94], [93]).

Kinghorn A M, Dunbar and Villon, MLR 62.197, 201, 203 ([94], [90], [89], [95]).

Bibliography. Robbins-Cutler, nos 470.5 ([94]), 479.5 ([89]), 679.8 ([98]), 865.8 ([88]), 886.5 ([90]), 1356.5 ([87]), 2072.8 ([93]), 2143.5 ([95]), 2587.5 ([96]), 2632.5 ([92]), 3908.5 ([97]), 4110.8 ([91]).

VIII. Religious

(Note: Folios for items [99–105] are listed by MS number, as appropriate, after each title. See under *MSS* below for full listing and information. Titles are from Mackenzie edn.)

[99] ANE ORISOUN.

1, f 40ª; 2, p 326.

[100] OF THE NATIVITIE OF CHRIST.

5, ff 27ª–27ᵇ.

[101] OF THE PASSIOUN OF CHRIST.

2, pp 203–207; 3, ff 168ª–171ᵇ; 4, ff 290ᵇ–292ᵇ.

[102] ON THE RESURRECTION OF CHRIST.

5, f 35ª.

[103] ANE BALLAT OF OUR LADY.

4, ff 303ª–304ᵇ.

[104] THE TABILL OF CONFESSION.

2, pp 199–203; 3, ff 1ª–4ᵇ; 5, pp 9–11, ff 17ᵇ–19ᵇ.

[105] THE MANER OF PASSING TO CONFESSION.

3, ff 161ª–162ᵇ.

MSS. 1, Camb Univ Ll.5.10 (Reidpeth or Moore), f 40ª (1623; item [99]); 2, Magdalene Coll Camb 2553 (Pepysian Libr, Maitland Folio), pp 199–207, 326 (1570–71; lines 1–42, 49–83, 89–168 of [104], [101], [99]); 3, BM Arundel 285, ff 1ª–4ᵇ, 161ª–162ᵇ, 168ª–171ᵇ (1540-1560; items [104–105], [101]); 4, Nat Libr Scot Acc 4233 (Asloan), ff 290ᵇ–

292ᵇ, 303ᵃ–304ᵇ (1513–1542; items [101] and [103]); 5, Nat Libr Scot 1.1.6 (Bannatyne), pp 9–11, ff 17ᵇ–19ᵇ, 27ᵃ–27ᵇ, 35ᵃ (1568; items [104], [100], [102]).

Pinkerton J, Ancient Scotish Poems, 2 vols, London and Edinburgh 1786, 1.v; 2.437, 471 (MSS 2, 5).

Brydges E and J Haslewood, The British Bibliographer, London 1814, 4.183 (MS 5).

Laing D, The Poems of George Bannatyne, Edinburgh 1824, p 3 (MS 5); An Account of the Contents of George Bannatyne's Manuscript, The Bannatyne Club, Edinburgh 1829, 35.43 (MS 5).

A Catalogue of the Manuscripts Preserved in The Library of The University of Cambridge, Cambridge 1861, 4.94 (MS 1).

Small J, The Poetical Works of Gavin Douglas, Edinburgh and London 1874, 1.clxxi (MS 2).

Schipper, edn, pt 1, 40².5ff (MSS 1, 2, 3, 4, 5).

Murdoch J B, ed, The Bannatyne Manuscript, 4 vols, Hunterian Club, Glasgow 1896, 2.43, 69, 94 (MS 5 rptd).

Smith G G, Specimens of Middle Scots, Edinburgh and London 1902, pp lxvi, lxx, lxxiii (MSS 2, 4, 5).

Brown J T T, The Bannatyne Manuscript, SHR 1.136 (MS 5).

Craigie W A, ed, The Maitland Folio, PSTS ns 7, 20, 2 vols, Edinburgh and London 1919–27, 1.224, 393; 2.103, 124 (MS 2 rptd, notes in vol 2); The Asloan Manuscript, PSTS ns 14, 16, 2 vols, Edinburgh 1923–25, 2.242, 275, 282, 284 (MS 4 rptd, notes at end of text).

Ritchie W T, ed, The Bannatyne Manuscript Writtin in Tyme of Pest, PSTS ns 5, 22, 23, 26, 4 vols, Edinburgh 1928–34, 1.13; 2.42, 65, 88 (MS 5 rptd).

Baxter J W, William Dunbar, Edinburgh and London 1952, pp 216ff (MSS 1, 2, 3, 4, 5).

Bennett J A W, ed, Devotional Pieces in Verse and Prose from MS Arundel 285 and MS Harleian 6919, PSTS 3s 23, Edinburgh 1955, pp 1, 257, 266 (MS 3; crit A J Aitken, SHR 36.147).

The Arundel Manuscripts, Catalogue of MSS in The British Museum, ns 1¹.82 (contents of MS 3 listed).

Editions. Laing D, The Poems of William Dunbar, 2 vols, Edinburgh 1834, 1.225, 285, 307; 2.364 (notes in vol 2 and Supplement; MSS 3, 4; Memoirs of William Dunbar preceding text of poems in vol 1 is paginated separately); Supplement, Edinburgh 1865, pp 261ff (continuation of vol 1, with which it was intended to be bound).

Paterson J, The Life and Poems of William Dunbar, Edinburgh 1860 (crit Athen July 14 1860, p 49); reissued The Works of William Dunbar Including His Life, Edinburgh 1863, p 67 (glossings in ftnts).

Small J, Æ J G Mackay, G P McNeill, W Gregor, The Poems of William Dunbar, PSTS 2, 4, 16, 21, 29, 3 vols, Edinburgh 1884–93, 2.65, 156, 239, 267, 280; 3.119, 244, 320, 355, 371 (notes in vol 3; MSS 1, 2, 3, 4, 5).

Schipper J, The Poems of William Dunbar, pt 4, Denkschriften der kaiserlichen Akademie der Wissenschaften, Philo-Hist Classe, Vienna 1892–93, 42⁴.51, 72 (MS sources and variants given in headnotes and footnotes to each poem; MSS 2, 3, 4, 5; crit E Kölbing, EStn 20.439).

Baildon H B, The Poems of William Dunbar, Cambridge 1907, pp 185, 199, 288 (notes at end of text; sources vary, selects reading which seems to him most likely to be correct; crit J H Millar, The Bookman 32.207).

Mackenzie W M, The Poems of William Dunbar, London 1932, p 154 (notes at end of text; MSS 2, 3, 4, 5; crit B Dickins, MLR 28.506; TLS Jan 26 1933, p 55; The Modern Scot 4.63); rptd London 1950; ed B Dickins, rptd and rvsd London 1960 (crit A Macdonald, ESts 43.219); rptd 1970.

Selections. Dalrymple D, Ancient Scottish Poems, Edinburgh 1770, p 83; rptd Leeds 1815, p 104 ([100], [102]; MS 5).

Morison R, Select Poems of Wil Dunbar Part First from the MS of George Bannatyne, Perth 1788, p 87 ([100], [102]; MS 5).

Schipper J, William Dunbar sein Leben und seine Gedichte, Berlin 1884, pp 334, 345 (poems in German scattered through text of discussion; [105], from [104], [99], [100], from [103], [102]; crit E Kölbing, EStn 10.128; M Trautmann, Angl 7.146; The Nation 40.144).

Henderson T F, A Little Book of Scottish Verse, London 1899; 2nd edn 1909, p 69 ([103], [102]; 1 brief introductory note, glossings at foot of page).

Quiller-Couch A, The Oxford Book of English Verse, Oxford 1900; new edn Oxford 1939, p 28 ([100]; glossings at foot of page).

Chambers R, Chambers's Cyclopædia, Phila and N Y 1901–03; rvsd Phila and N Y 1938, 1.200 ([103]; brief excerpt).

Smith G G, Specimens of Middle Scots, Edinburgh and London 1902, pp 14, 271 ([103]; notes at end of text; MS 4).

Dixon W M, The Edinburgh Book of Scottish

Verse, London 1910, pp 28, 52 ([100], [103]; glossings at foot of page).

Metcalfe W M, Specimens of Scottish Literature, London 1913, pp 53, 161 (from [103]; notes at end of text).

Crosse G, Every Man's Book of Sacred Verse, London and Oxford 1923, pp 6, 200 (from [100]; spelling modernized; biographical note at end of text).

Buchan J, The Northern Muse, London 1924, pp 433, 532 ([100], [103]; glossings at foot of page, brief notes at end of text; Small edn).

Leslie S, An Anthology of Catholic Poets, N Y 1925, p 100 ([103]; spelling modernized).

Walsh T, The Catholic Anthology, N Y 1927; rvsd N Y 1932, p 130 (from [103]).

Musser B F, The Chaucer of Scotland, Franciscan Poets, N Y 1933, pp 3, 8 (from [103]; from [100]).

Patterson R F, Six Centuries of English Literature, London and Glasgow 1933, 1.186 ([100]).

Mackie R L, A Book of Scottish Verse, The World's Classics no 417, London 1934, p 65 ([100], [102]; glossings at foot of page); 2nd edn London Glasgow N Y 1967, p 64.

Gray M M, Scottish Poetry from Barbour to James VI, N Y 1935, p 135 ([100], [103]; crit J Speirs, Scrut 6.83; W M Mackenzie, The Scottish Bookman 1, no 4, p 133).

Cecil D, The Oxford Book of Christian Verse, Oxford 1940, p 33 ([100], [102]).

Fergusson J, The Green Garden, London and Edinburgh 1946, p 41 (from [104], [102]; spelling modernized).

Oliver J W and J C Smith, A Scots Anthology from the 13th to the 20th Century, Edinburgh and London 1949, p 37 ([100]; spelling modernized, glossings at foot of page).

Auden W H and N H Pearson, Poets of the English Language, N Y 1950, p 320 ([102]).

[Grieve C M] MacDiarmid H, Selections from the Poems of William Dunbar, The Saltire Classics, Edinburgh 1952, p 7 ([100], [102], [103]; glossings in ftnts; Mackenzie edn); Selected Poems of William Dunbar, Glasgow 1955, pp 15, 34 ([102], [103], [100]).

Kinsley J, William Dunbar Poems, Oxford 1958, pp 1, 67, 108 ([100], [101], [102], lines 1–12, 61–84 of [99]; notes at end of text; MSS 5, 2, 4; crit TLS Apr 18 1958, p 208; D Young, SHR 38.10; E Morgan, RES ns 11.71; J Wordsworth, MÆ 30.128).

Davies R T, Medieval English Lyrics, London 1963, pp 247, 253, 357 (lines 1–12, 61–84 of [103], [102]; glossings at foot of page,

notes at end of text; MSS 4, 5).

Rossi S, I Chauceriani Scozzesi, Napoli 1964, p 210 ([100], [102]; notes at foot of page).

Smith Rowland, The Poetry of William Dunbar, Theoria 22.78 (from [102], from [100]).

Scott T, Dunbar A Critical Exposition, Edinburgh and London 1966, p 302 ([99]; Mackenzie edn).

MacQueen J and T Scott, The Oxford Book of Scottish Verse, Oxford 1966, p 107 ([102], [103]; glossings at foot of page; Mackenzie edn).

Scott T, Late Medieval Scots Poetry, Edinburgh and London 1967, p 126 ([102]; Mackenzie edn).

Ridley F [H], Selected Poems of William Dunbar, Los Angeles 1969, pp 19, 20 ([99], [102]; glossings in margin; MSS 2, 5).

Scott T, The Penguin Book of Scottish Verse, London 1970, p 152 ([102], [103], [100]; glossings at foot of page).

Modernizations. Tytler P F, Lives of Scottish Worthies, London 1833, 3.132 (from [102]; brief excerpts; Laing edn).

Bonar A R, The Poets and Poetry of Scotland, Edinburgh 1864; 2nd edn 1866, p 57 (from [102]).

[Robertson J L] Haliburton H, Dunbar Being a Selection from the Poems of an Old Makar Adapted for Modern Readers, London 1895, pp 40, 48 (from [104], [102]; essentially modernized paraphrase, abbreviated, extremely free; crit R Brotanek, AnglB 6.71).

Scott F G, Rorate caeli desuper, The Modern Scot 4.133 (two stanzas from [100] set to music).

Textual Matters. Laing, edn, 1.307; 2.366 ([101], [104]).

Schipper, edn, pt 4, 42⁴.52, 64, 72 ([105], [99], [101]; see also introductory and ftnts to individual poems).

Mackenzie, edn, p 226 ([99–105]).

Baxter J W, William Dunbar, Edinburgh and London 1952, p 211 ([104], [105], [103], [101]).

Scott T, Dunbar A Critical Exposition, Edinburgh and London 1966, p 298 ([104]).

Language. Dalrymple D, Ancient Scottish Poems, Edinburgh 1770, p 317 (glossary); rptd Leeds 1815, p 367, [added] Glossary, p 1 [separate pagination] ([100], [102]).

Murray J A H, The Dialect of the Southern Counties of Scotland, London 1873 (group as a whole).

Kaufmann J, Traité de la langue, Bonn 1873, p 47 (group as a whole).

Hahn O, Zur Verbal- und Nominalflexion

bei den schottischen Dichtern, Berlin 1887–89 (see especially pt 3, p 17; group as a whole).

Schipper, edn, pt 1, 40².18 (group as a whole).

Gregor W, Glossary, Small edn, 3.401 (group as a whole).

Curtis F J, An Investigation of the Rimes and Phonology of Clariodus, Angl 16.387; 17.1, 125 (group as a whole).

Heuser W, Die Dehnung vor -nd im Mittelschottischen, Die Dehnung -end, Angl 19.401 (brief; group as a whole).

Baildon H B, On the Rimes in the Authentic Poems of William Dunbar, Trans Royal Soc Edinburgh 39³.629; issued separately Edinburgh 1899 (group as a whole).

Flom G T, Scandinavian Influence on Southern Lowland Scotch, diss Columbia 1900 (group as a whole).

Smith G G, Specimens of Middle Scots, Edinburgh and London 1902, pp xi, 325 ([103]; glossary).

Millar J H, A Literary History of Scotland, London 1903, p 687 (glossary; [102], [103]).

Luick K, Studien zur englischen Lautgeschichte, WBEP 17.109 ([100], [103]).

Browne W H, The Taill of Rauf Coilyear, Baltimore 1903, pp 15, 35, 139 (general discussion of Middle Scots, glossary; group as a whole).

Knopff P, Darstellung der Ablautverhältnisse in der schottischen Schriftsprache, diss Würzburg 1904 (group as a whole).

Baildon, edn, pp xxvi, 299 (discussion, glossary; group as a whole).

CHEL, 2.101, 506 (group as a whole).

Dixon W M, The Edinburgh Book of Scottish Verse, London 1910, p 897 (glossary; [100], [103]).

Gray M M, Introd, Lancelot of the Laik, PSTS ns 2, Edinburgh and London 1912, 2.xviii (group as a whole).

Lenz K, Zur Lautlehre der französischen Elemente in den schottischen Dichtungen, diss Marburg 1913 (examples taken from Douglas, Dunbar, Lyndesay, Clariodus; group as a whole).

Metcalfe W M, Specimens of Scottish Literature, London 1913, pp 9, 39, 189 ([103]).

Westergaard E, Prepositions in Lowland Scotch, Angl 41.444 (some examples from Dunbar; group as a whole); Verbal Forms in Middle-Scotch, Angl 43.95 (group as a whole).

Watt L M, Language and Influences, Douglas's Aeneid, Cambridge 1920, p 149 (very generally applicable; group as a whole).

Westergaard E, Studies in Prefixes and Suffixes, London 1924 (group as a whole).

Wilson J, The Spelling of Scotch before 1600, The Dialects of Central Scotland, London 1926, p 168 (group as a whole; attempts to determine pronunciation from spelling, rimes, modern Lothian pronunciation).

Westergaard E, Plural Forms in Lowland Scottish, Angl 51.77 (group as a whole).

Craigie W A, ed, The Maitland Folio, PSTS ns 7, 20, 2 vols, Edinburgh and London 1919–27, 2.135 (glossary; [104], [101], [99]).

Mackenzie, edn, pp xii, xxxvii, 245 ([99–105]; discussion, glossary).

Wood H H, The Poems and Fables of Robert Henryson, Edinburgh 1933; 2nd edn rvsd 1958; rptd 1965, 1968, p xxxi.

Patrick D, Scottish Literature, Chambers's Cyclopædia, rvsd J L Geddie, Phila and N Y 1938, 1.164 (group as a whole).

Fergusson J, The Green Garden, London and Edinburgh 1946, p 228 (glossary; [104], [102]).

Oliver J W and J C Smith, A Scots Anthology, Edinburgh and London 1949, p 497 (glossaries; [100]).

[Grieve C M] MacDiarmid H, Selections from the Poems of William Dunbar, The Saltire Classics, Edinburgh 1952, pp 5, 49 ([100], [102], [103]; brief note, glossary); Selected Poems of William Dunbar, Glasgow 1955, p 60 (glossary; [102], [103], [100]).

Kinsley J, William Dunbar Poems, Oxford 1958, p 139 (glossary; [100], [101], [102], [103], [99]).

Rossi S, I Chauceriani Scozzesi, Napoli 1964, p 261 ([100], [102]; discussion, glossary).

Scott T, Dunbar A Critical Exposition, Edinburgh and London 1966, pp 346, 351; Late Medieval Scots Poetry, London 1967, pp 21, 189 ([102]; discussion, glossary).

Conley J, William Dunbar Additions to and Corrections of OED and DOST, N&Q 213 (ns 15).169 ([103], [105], [104]).

Versification. Schipper J, William Dunbar sein Leben und seine Gedichte, Berlin 1884, p 341 ([103]).

McNeill G P, Note on the Versification and Metres of Dunbar, Small edn, 1.clxxx, clxxxvii, cxcii ([105], [101], [100], [102], [104], [103]).

Schipper, edn, pt 4, 42⁴.67 ([103]; discussion in headnote to poem).

Curtis F J, The Rimes and Phonology of Clariodus, Angl 16.387; 17.1, 125 (group as a whole).

Henderson T F, Scottish Vernacular Literature, Edinburgh 1898; 3rd edn rvsd Edinburgh 1910, pp 156, 161 ([102], [103]).

Baildon H B, Rimes in the Authentic Poems of Dunbar, Trans Royal Soc Edinburgh 39³.629 (group as a whole).

Saintsbury G, History of English Prosody, London 1908; 2nd edn London 1923, 1.273 ([100]).

Abercrombie L, The Theory of Poetry, N Y 1926, p 144 ([103]).

Smith J M, The French Background of Middle Scots Literature, Edinburgh and London 1934, pp 76, 165 ([103]; crit AnglB 45.265; MÆ 4.44).

Renwick-Orton, p 66 ([103]; very brief).

Wittig K, The Scottish Tradition in Literature, Edinburgh 1958, p 58 and passim ([103]).

Baum P F, Chaucer's Verse, Durham N C 1961, p 101 ([103]).

Leyerle J, The Two Voices of William Dunbar, UTQ 31.325 ([103]).

Scott T, Dunbar A Critical Exposition, Edinburgh and London 1966, pp 301, 304, 316, 318, 323, 329, 345 ([102], [103], [105], [104], [101], [100]).

Date. Paterson, edn, p 85 ([101]).

Mackay Æ J G, Introd [and] Appendix to Introd, Small edn, l.lxix, cxxxviii, clxx ([101], [104], [100], [105], [102], [103]).

Schipper, edn, pt 4, 42⁴.51 ([105]).

Baxter J W, William Dunbar, Edinburgh and London 1952, p 124 ([99]).

Authorship. Schipper J, William Dunbar sein Leben und seine Gedichte, Berlin 1884, p 333 ([105], [104]).

Mackay Æ J G, Introd, Small edn, l.lxxi ([100]).

Baxter J W, William Dunbar, p 227 ([99]).

Scott T, Dunbar A Critical Exposition, p 302 ([99]).

Sources and Literary Relations. Laing, edn, 2.365, 368 ([105], [102]).

[Robertson J L] Haliburton H, Our Earlier Burns, In Scottish Fields, London 1890, p 238 ([101], [104], [103]).

Schipper, edn, pt 4, 42⁴.52 ([105]).

Smith G G, The Transition Period, Periods of European Literature, Edinburgh and London 1900, 4.36, 39, 42 and passim ([102]).

Moorman F W, The Interpretation of Nature in English Poetry from Beowulf to Shakespeare, QF 95.144 ([100]).

Jacobi J B, William Dunbar—an Appreciation, The American Catholic Quarterly Rev 44.309 (group as a whole; [105], [103], [104]).

Mendenhall J C, Aureate Terms A Study in the Literary Diction of the 15th Century, Lancaster Pa 1919 (group as a whole).

Smith G G, Scottish Literature Character and Influence, London 1919, p 14 ([103]; brief reference).

Nichols P H, William Dunbar as a Scottish Lydgatian, PMLA 46.219 ([103], [105], [104], [99], [100], [101], [102]).

Nichols P H, Lydgate's Influence on the Aureate Terms of the Scottish Chaucerians, PMLA 47.517, 520 ([103]).

Smith J M, The French Background of Middle Scots Literature, Edinburgh and London 1934, pp 74, 165 ([104], [103]; crit AnglB 45.265; MÆ 4.44).

Patrick D, Scottish Literature, Chambers's Cyclopædia, rvsd J L Geddie, Phila and N Y 1938, 1.166 (group as a whole).

Speirs J, William Dunbar, Scrut 7.62 ([100]).

Hyde I, Primary Sources and Associations of Dunbar's Aureate Imagery, MLR 51.482, 485 ([102], [100]).

Kinghorn A M, The Mediaeval Makars, Texas Stud Lit and Lang 1.73 ([100], [102]).

Leyerle J, The Two Voices of William Dunbar, UTQ 31.320, 327 ([100], [102]).

Smith Rowland, The Poetry of William Dunbar, Theoria 22.78 ([102], [100]).

Hyde I, Poetic Imagery, SSL 2.184 ([101]).

Fox D, The Scottish Chaucerians, Chaucer and Chaucerians, ed D S Brewer, University Alabama 1966, pp 164ff (see especially p 181; [103]).

Scott T, Dunbar A Critical Exposition, Edinburgh and London 1966, pp 37, 282, 302, 326, 329, 358 and passim ([104], [100], [103]; group as a whole).

Woolf R, English Religious Lyrics, Oxford 1968, pp 233, 306 ([101], [100], [102]).

Other Scholarly Problems. Schipper, edn, pt 4, 42⁴.64 (relation of [99] to [107]).

Smeaton O, William Dunbar, N Y (1898?), p 37 ([100], [101], [105], [104]; biographical evidence; crit J W Baxter, William Dunbar, Edinburgh and London 1952, passim; The Scottish Antiquary 13.95).

Teichert O P, Schottische Zustände unter Jacob IV nach den Dichtungen von William Dunbar, Görlitz 1903, p 22 ([101]; contemp conditions; crit O Glöde, EStn 36.267).

Rigg A G, William Dunbar: The Fenyeit Freir, RES ns 14.272 ([101]; biographical evidence).

Scott T, Dunbar A Critical Exposition, pp 283, 344 ([100], [101], [104]; biographical evidence).

Literary Criticism. Tytler P F, Lives of Scottish Worthies, London 1833, 3.132 (group as a whole, [102]).

Laing, edn, 1.58 (Memoirs); 2.365 ([104], [99], [100], [103], [101]).

Paterson, edn, pp 69, 75 ([100], [105]).

Nichol J, A Sketch of Scottish Poetry, ed J Small, 2nd edn rvsd EETS 11, London 1883, p xxxi (group as a whole).

Schipper J, William Dunbar sein Leben und seine Gedichte, Berlin 1884, pp 333, 336, 340, 343 ([105], [104], [100], [103], [101], [102]).

Mackay Æ J G, Introd, Small edn, l.lxix, cxxxviii ([101], [104], [100], [105], [102], [103]).

Minto W, Characteristics of English Poets, authorized American edn, Boston 1899, p 103 ([100]; brief).

[Robertson J L] Haliburton H, Our Earlier Burns, In Scottish Fields, London 1890, p 218 ([101]).

Schipper, edn, pt 4, 42⁴.52, 55, 65, 67, 72, 77 ([105], [104], [100], [103], [101], [102]).

Ten Brink, 3.76 (group as a whole).

Gosse E, A Short History of Modern English Literature, N Y 1897; rvsd edn N Y 1906, p 51 ([103]; brief).

Smeaton O, William Dunbar, N Y (1898?), pp 37, 153 ([100], [101], [105], [104], [102], [103]; considered as a group rather than individually).

Smith G G, The Transition Period, Periods of European Lit, Edinburgh and London 1900, 4.50 and passim ([102]).

Chambers R, Chambers's Cyclopædia, Phila and N Y 1901–03; rvsd J L Geddie, Phila and N Y 1938, 1.199 ([104], [103]).

Baildon H B, Burns and Dunbar, Scottish Art and Letters 2.166 ([102], group as a whole).

Ranken T E, The Scottish Reformation and Vernacular Literature, The Month 103.270 ([103]).

Moorman F W, The Interpretation of Nature in English Poetry from Beowulf to Shakespeare, QF 95.144 ([100]).

CHEL, 2.291 (group as a whole).

Steinberger C, Étude sur William Dunbar, Dublin 1908, p 147 ([100], [101], [105], [103], [102], [104]).

Enc Brit, 8.669 ([102]).

Smith J C, Some Characteristics of Scots Literature, Oxford 1912, p 5 ([103]; brief).

Jacobi J B, William Dunbar—an Appreciation, The American Catholic Quarterly Rev 44.309 (group as a whole, [105], [103], [100], [104]).

Smith G G, Scottish Literature Character and Influence, London 1919, p 14 ([103]; brief reference).

Quiller-Couch A, Studies in Literature, 2s, N Y and Cambridge Eng 1922, p 270 ([100]).

William Dunbar, TLS Apr 10 1930, p 306 ([103]).

Mackenzie W M, edn, p xxxii ([101], [102]).

Nichols P H, Lydgate's Influence on the Aureate Terms of the Scottish Chaucerians, PMLA 47.517 ([103]).

Mackenzie A M, An Historical Survey of Scottish Literature, London 1933, p 95 ([100], [103], [101]).

Mackenzie W M, William Dunbar, Edinburgh Essays on Scots Lit, Edinburgh and London 1933, p 33 ([103]).

Musser B F, The Chaucer of Scotland, Franciscan Poets, N Y 1933, p 2 ([103]).

Grierson H J C, Robert Henryson, The Modern Scot 4.297; rptd Aberdeen Univ Rev 21.206; rptd Robert Henryson, Essays and Addresses, London 1940, p 116 ([102]).

Smith J M, The French Background of Middle Scots Literature, Edinburgh and London 1934, pp 75, 165 ([103], [100], [102], [101]).

Power W, Literature and Oatmeal, London 1935, p 44 ([102]; brief; crit AnglB 48.151; The Scottish Bookman 1, no 4, p 152).

Speirs J, William Dunbar, Scrut 7.62 ([100]); The Scots Literary Tradition, London 1940, p 46 ([100]; crit Scrut 9.193); rvsd 2nd edn 1962, p 62.

Craig HEL, p 169 ([103]; brief).

Moore A K, The Secular Lyric in ME, Lexington Ky 1951, p 198 ([103]).

Baxter J W, William Dunbar, Edinburgh and London 1952, p 211 ([104], [100], [105], [103], [101], [102]).

Morgan E, Dunbar and the Language of Poetry, EC 2.152 ([100], [102], [103], [101], [104], [105]).

Renwick-Orton, pp 66, 417 ([103], [100]; brief).

Wood H H, Scottish Literature, London 1952, p 17 ([103]).

Lewis C S, English Literature in the Sixteenth Century, Oxford 1954, p 95 ([100], [102]).

Kinsley J, The Mediaeval Makars, Scottish Poetry, A Critical Survey, London 1955, p 25 ([101], [102], group as a whole).

Hyde I, Primary Sources and Associations of Dunbar's Aureate Imagery, MLR 51.482, 485, 490 ([102], [100]).

Milner I, Some Aspects of Satire in the Po-
etry of Dunbar, Philologica (cizojazyčná
prioloha Casopisu pro moderní filologii)
8.39, 41 ([102], [100]).
Schlauch M, English Medieval Literature,
Warsaw 1956, p 296 ([103]).
Morrison W S, Some Makars and Makers of
St Andrews and Dundee, Edinburgh and
London 1958, p 8 ([100]).
Kinsley J, William Dunbar Poems, Oxford
1958, pp xiv, xxvi ([103], [100], [102]).
Mackie R L, King James IV of Scotland,
Edinburgh and London 1958, p 180 ([101],
group as a whole; brief comments).
Wittig K, The Scottish Tradition in Litera-
ture, Edinburgh 1958, p 55 ([104], [99],
[101], [102], [105], [100], [103]).
Kinghorn A M, The Mediaeval Makars,
Texas Stud Lit and Lang 1.81 ([100], [102]).
Leyerle J, The Two Voices of William Dun-
bar, UTQ 31.320, 325, 333, 337 ([100], [103],
[102]).
Manning S, Wisdom and Number, Lincoln
Neb 1962, pp 62, 173.
Davies R T, Medieval English Lyrics, London
1963, pp 14, 23, 26, 40 ([102], [103]; brief

references).
Rossi S, I Chauceriani Scozzesi, Napoli 1964,
p 48 ([103], [100], [102]).
Smith Rowland, The Poetry of William Dunbar, Theoria 22.77 ([103], [102], [100]).
Hyde I, Poetic Imagery, SSL 2.184, 195 ([101],
[102]).
Fox D, The Scottish Chaucerians, Chaucer
and Chaucerians, ed D S Brewer, University Alabama 1966, pp 180, 183 ([103], [102],
[100]).
Scott T, Dunbar A Critical Exposition, Edinburgh and London 1966, pp 49, 282, 339,
345, 371 and passim ([103], [100], [101],
[104], [105], [102]).
Wood H H, Two Scots Chaucerians, Writers
and Their Work, no 201, ed G Bullough,
London 1967, p 43 ([103]).
Woolf R, English Religious Lyrics, Oxford
1968, pp 233, 306 ([101], [100], [102]).
Bibliography. Tanner T, Bibliotheca Britannico-Hibernica, ed D Wilkins, London
1748, p 237 ([104]; very brief reference).
Robbins-Cutler, nos 276.5 and 2161.5 ([101]),
688.3 ([102]), 1082.5 ([103]), 2551.5 ([105]),
2831.6 ([100]), 3077.5 ([99]), 3776.5 ([104]).

IX. Attributions

(Note: The following poems are ascribed
to Dunbar by Mackenzie edn, by Small edn,
or by Brown-Robbins. Titles are taken from
Mackenzie when he supplies them, otherwise
from Small or Brown-Robbins. In each case
the source of the attribution is listed with
the title. Folios for items [106]–[126] are listed
by MS number, as appropriate, after each
title. See under MSS below for full listing
and information.)

[106] THE BALLAD OF KYND KYTTOK.
(Mackenzie, no 85; Small, no 5)

10, ff 135ᵇ–136ᵃ; 16, p 192.

[107] BALLATE AGAINST EVIL WOM-
EN. (Small, no 84)

2, ff 39ᵇ–40ᵃ; 4, pp 325–326; 10, f 262ᵃ; 11, p
77.

[108] CRISTES PASSIOUN. (Brown-Robbins, no 2497)

3, f 170ᵇ.

[109] DOUN BY ANE REVER AS I RED.
(Small, no 2 [Attributions])

10, pp 32–34, ff 48ᵇ–50ᵃ.

[110] FAINE WALD I WITH ALL DILI-
GENCE. (Small, no 4 [Attributions])

4, pp 210–211.

[111] FANE WALD I LUVE BUT QUHAIR
ABOWT? (Small, no 3 [Attributions])

10, f 255ᵃ.

[112] THE FREIRIS OF BERWICK.
(Mackenzie, no 93; Small, no 1 [Attribu-
tions]; Brown-Robbins, no 384)

4, pp 113–129; 10, ff 348ᵇ–354ᵇ.

[113] GIF YE WALD LUFE AND LUVIT
BE. (Small, no 5 [Attributions])

10, f 230ᵃ.

[114] GLADETHE THOUE QUEYNE OF

SCOTTIS REGIOUN. (Mackenzie, no 90; Small, no 87)

12, unpaged.

[115] IN ALL OURE GARDYN GROWIS THARE NA FLOURIS. (Small, no 7 [Attributions])

16, p 88.

[116] JERUSALEM REIOSS FOR JOY. (Small, no 8 [Attributions])

10, ff 27^b–28^a.

[117] THE MANERE OF CRYING OF ANE PLAY. (Mackenzie, no 86; Small, no 6 [Attributions])

9, ff 240^a–242^b; 10, ff 118^b–120^a.

[118] NOW GLAIDITH EUERY LIFFIS CREATURE. (Small, no 9 [Attributions])

10, ff 27^a–27^b.

[119] OF FOLKIS EVILL TO PLEIS. (Mackenzie, no 23)

2, ff 3^a–3^b; 10, p 47, f 66^b.

[120] ROS MARY ANE BALLAT OF OUR LADY. (Mackenzie, no 87; Small, no 86)

6, ff 79^b–80^a; 9, ff 301^a–301^b; 13, f 183^b.

[121] THE STERNE IS RISSIN OF OUR REDEMPTIOUN. (Small, no 11 [Attributions])

10, ff 30^b–31^a.

[122] SURREXIT DOMINUS DE SEPULCHRO. (Small, no 37)

10, ff 34^b–35^a.

[123] TO THE CITY OF LONDON. (Mackenzie, no 88; Small, no 88)

1, ff 199^b–200^a; 5, ff 200^a–201^a; 7, f 7^b; 14, ff 45^b–47^a; 15, two unnumbered leaves at end.

[124] TO THE GOUVERNOUR IN FRANCE. (Mackenzie, no 92; Small, no 71)

10, ff 78^b–79^a.

[125] TO THE PRINCESS MARGARET. (Mackenzie, no 89; Small, no 89)

8, ff 17^b–18^a.

[126] TO THE QUEEN DOWAGER.

(Mackenzie, no 91; Small, no 10 [Attributions])

10, f 238^b.

MSS. 1, Balliol 354 (Richard Hill's Commonplace-book), ff 199^b–200^a (1st third 16 cent; item [123]); 2, Camb Univ L1.5.10 (Reidpeth or Moore), ff 3^a–3^b, 39^b–40^a (1623; items [119], [107]); 3, Magdalene Coll Camb 1576 (Pepysian Libr), f 170^b (1470–1490; item [108]); 4, Magdalene Coll Camb 2553 (Pepysian Libr, Maitland Folio), pp 113–129, 210–211, 325–326 (1570–71; items [112], [110], [107]); 5, Cotton Vitell A.xvi, ff 200^a–201^a (1509–1535?; item [123]); 6, Harley 1703 (Forrest), ff 79^b–80^a (1581–1590; lines 1–40, 57–80 of item [120]); 7, Lansdowne 762, f 7^b (1509–1550; item [123]); 8, Royal Appendix 58, ff 17^b–18^a (early 16 cent; item [125]); 9, Nat Libr Scot Acc 4233 (Asloan), ff 240^a–242^b, 301^a–301^b (1513–1542; item [117] with lines 166–173 om, lines 1–24, 41–64 of item [120]); 10, Nat Libr Scot 1.1.6 (Bannatyne), pp 32–34, 47, ff 27^a–28^a, 30^b–31^a, 34^b–35^a, 48^b–50^a, 66^b, 78^b–79^a, 118^b–120^a, 135^b–136^a, 230^a, 238^b, 255^a, 262^a, 348^b–354^b (1568; items [109], [119], [118], [116], [121], [122], [124], [117], [106], [126], [111], [107], [112]); 11, Nat Libr Scot 72.1.37 (Dean of Lismore's Book), p 77 (1512–1526; item [107]); 12, Aberdeen Town Clerk's Office, Aberdeen Minute Book of Sasines, vol 2, unpaged (1503–1507; item [114]); 13, Univ of Edinb 205 (Laing 149, Makculloch), f 183^b (MS proper 1477; Dunbar insertions 1490–1510; lines 1–24, 41–56 of item [120]); 14, Guildhall Libr 3313 (The Great Chronicle of London), ff 45^b–47^a (ca 1450–1513; 292^b–294^a of MS as a whole; item [123]); 15, Morgan Libr MA 717, on two unnumbered leaves (early 16 cent; item [123]). PRINT: 16, Nat Libr Scot 19.1.16 (Chepman and Myllar), pp 88, 192 (1508; items [115], [106]).

Pinkerton J, Ancient Scotish Poems, 2 vols, London and Edinburgh 1786, 1.v; 2.437 (MS 4), 471 (MS 10).

Douce F, A Catalogue of the Harleian Manuscripts in the British Museum, London 1808, 2.176 (MS 6); A Catalogue of The Lansdowne Manuscripts in the British Museum, London 1819, p 168 (MS 7 dated; 1 stanza quoted).

Brydges E and J Haslewood, The British Bibliographer, London 1814, 4.183 (MS 10).

Laing D, The Poems of George Bannatyne, Edinburgh 1824, p 3 (MS 10); The Knightly

Tale of Golagrus and Gawane, Edinburgh 1827, f 10ᵇ (PRINT 16 rptd); An Account of the Contents of George Bannatyne's Manuscript, The Bannatyne Club, Edinburgh 1829, 35.43 (MS 10); The Poems of William Dunbar, edn, 1.303 (MS 12 described in Supplement).

Wright T and J O Halliwell, edd, Reliquiæ Antiquæ, London 1841, 1.205 (MS 7 rptd).

A Catalogue of the Manuscripts Preserved in The Library of The University of Cambridge, Cambridge 1861, 4.94 (MS 2).

Laing D, The Poems and Fables of Robert Henryson, Edinburgh 1865, p 228 (MS 13).

Small J, The Poetical Works of Gavin Douglas, Edinburgh and London 1874, 1.clxxi (MS 4).

Flügel E, Liedersammlungen des XVI Jahrhunderts besonders aus der Zeit Heinrichs VIII, Angl 12.256 (MS 8).

Dickson R and J P Edmond, Annals of Scottish Printing from 1507 to the Beginning of the 17th Century, Cambridge 1890, p 49 (PRINT 16).

Schipper, edn, pt 1, 40².5ff (MSS 2, 4, 5, 8, 9, 10, 12, 13, PRINT 16); Zu Dunbar, Arch 91.241 (MSS 1, 5, 7; variants between MSS listed).

Zupitza J, Zu Dunbar, Arch 90.151 (date of MS 7).

Murdoch J B, ed, The Bannatyne Manuscript, 4 vols, Hunterian Club, Glasgow 1896, 2.67, 71, 80, 93, 133, 180, 215, 337; 3.382, 667, 689; 4.744, 765, 1004 (MS 10 rptd).

Neumann, edn, Arch 101.143 (MS 1).

Smith G G, Specimens of Middle Scots, Edinburgh and London 1902, p lxvi (MSS 4, 9, 10, 13, PRINT 16).

Flügel E, Liedersammlungen des XVI Jahrhunderts, Angl 26.94 (MS 1).

Brown J T T, The Bannatyne Manuscript, SHR 1.136 (MS 10).

Dyboski R, ed, Songs Carols and Other Miscellaneous Poems from the Balliol MS 354 Richard Hill's Commonplace-book, EETSES 101, London 1907, pp 100, 185 (MS 1 rptd, notes at end of text).

Catalogue of Manuscripts and Early Printed Books from the Libraries of William Morris, Richard Bennett, Bertram, Fourth Earl of Ashburnham, and Other Sources, London 1907, 3.167 (MS 15).

MacCracken H N, New Stanzas by Dunbar, MLN 24.110 (MS 6 rptd, discussed).

Borland C R, A Descriptive Catalogue of the Western Mediaeval MSS in Edinburgh Univ Library, Edinburgh 1916, p 291 (MS 13).

Stevenson G, ed, Pieces from The Makculloch and the Gray MSS, PSTS 65, Edinburgh and London 1918, pp 24, 295 (MS 13 rptd, notes at end of text), 156, 262, 302 (PRINT 16 rptd, notes at end of text).

Thurneyson R, Die irische Helden- und Königsage, Halle 1921, p 52 (MS 11).

Warner G F and J P Gilson, Catalogue of Western Manuscripts in the Old Royal and King's Collections, London 1921, 2.394 (MS 8).

James M R, ed, Bibliotheca Pepysiana, London 1923, pt 3, p 16 (MS 3 described, rptd).

Craigie W A, ed, The Maitland Folio, PSTS ns 7, 20, 2 vols, Edinburgh and London 1919–27, 1.133, 237, 391; 2.94, 104, 123 (MS 4 rptd, notes in vol 2); 2.45 (ff 1–8 of MS 2 rptd), 124 (MS 11 rptd); The Asloan Manuscript, PSTS ns 14, 16, 2 vols, Edinburgh 1923–25, 2.149, 271, 281, 284 (MS 9 rptd, notes at end of text).

Nichols P H, William Dunbar as a Scottish Lydgatian, PMLA 46.220 (MS 3 rptd).

Wood H H, The Poems and Fables of Robert Henryson, Edinburgh 1933; 2nd edn rvsd 1958; rptd 1965, 1968, p xxiii (MS 13).

Ritchie W T, ed, The Bannatyne Manuscript Writtin in Tyme of Pest, PSTS ns 5, 22, 23, 26, 4 vols, Edinburgh 1928–34, 1.53, 78; 2.63, 66, 76, 87, 122, 163, 197, 315; 3.10, 303, 323; 4.13, 32, 261 (MS 10 rptd).

Bühler C F, ed, London Thow Art the Flowre of Cytes All, RES 13.8 (MS 15 rptd).

Thomas A H and I D Thornley, edd, The Great Chronicle of London, London 1938, pp xv, 316, 449 (MS 14 rptd, notes at end of text).

Baxter J W, TLS Apr 8 1939, p 208 (MS 12).

Utley C R, p 245 (MS 11).

Chambers OHEL, p 97 (MS 1).

Beattie W, The Chepman and Myllar Prints, Edinburgh Biblio Soc, Oxford 1950, pp viii, 88, 192 (PRINT 16 described, rptd).

Baxter J W, William Dunbar, Edinburgh and London 1952, pp 178 (PRINT 16), 216ff (MSS 2, 4, 8, 9, 10, 12, PRINT 16).

Editions. Laing D, The Poems of William Dunbar, 2 vols, Edinburgh 1834, 1.173, 277, 297, 318; 2.3, 31, 338, 372, 408 ([119], [123], [125], [114], [120], [112], [111], [113], [106], [117], [115], [126], [124], [110], [109], [118], [116], [121], [122]; notes in vol 2 and Supplement; MSS 1, 2, 8, 10, 12; Memoirs of William Dunbar preceding text of poems in vol 1 is paginated separately); Supplement, Edinburgh 1865, pp 261ff (continuation of vol 1, with which it was intended to be bound).

Paterson J, The Life and Poems of William Dunbar, Edinburgh 1860 (crit Athen July 14 1860, p 49); reissued The Works of William Dunbar Including His Life, Edinburgh 1863, pp 89, 297 ([119], [126]; glossings in footnotes).

Small J, Æ J G Mackay, G P McNeill, W Gregor, The Poems of William Dunbar, PSTS 2, 4, 16, 21, 29, 3 vols, Edinburgh 1884–93, 2.52, 154, 237, 266, 272, 285; 3.95, 242, 319, 355, 366, 372 ([106], [122], [124], [107], [120], [114], [123], [125], [112], [109], [111], [110], [113], [117], [115], [116], [118], [126], [121]; notes in vol 3; MSS 2, 4, 5, 8, 9, 10, 12, 13, PRINT 16).

Schipper J, The Poems of William Dunbar, pts 1–4, Denkschriften der kaiserlichen Akademie der Wissenschaften, Philo-Hist Classe, Vienna 1892–93, pt 1, 40².15, 69, 87; pt 2, 40⁴.1, 31, 100; pt 3, 41⁴.80; pt 4, 42⁴.41, 69 ([115], [106], [123], [125], [114], [117], [119], [126], [120]; MS sources and variants given in headnotes and ftnts to each poem; MSS 5, 8, 9, 10, 12, 13; crit E Kölbing, EStn 20.439).

Schipper J, Anonymous Early Scottish Poems Forming a Supplement to the Poems of William Dunbar, pt 5, Denkschriften der kaiserlichen Akademie der Wissenschaften, Philo-Hist Classe, Vienna 1893, 43¹.1ff (glossary and table of contents are for both Anonymous Early Scottish Poems and The Poems of William Dunbar; [112], [111], [113], [115], [110], [107], [124], [109], [118], [116], [121], [122]; MS sources and variants given in ftnts and headnotes to each poem; MSS 4, 10, PRINT 16).

Neumann G, A Treatice of London, Arch 101.143 ([123]; MS 1).

Baildon H B, The Poems of William Dunbar, Cambridge 1907, pp 23, 36, 59, 89, 141, 177, 197, 211, 244, 246, 251, 261, 274, 286, 291, 293 ([106], [123], [125], [114], [117], [119], [126], [120], [112], [111], [113], [115], [110], [107], [124], [109], [118], [116], [121], [122]; notes at end of text; sources vary, selects reading which seems to him most likely to be correct; crit J H Millar, The Bookman 32.207).

Mackenzie W M, The Poems of William Dunbar, Edinburgh 1932, pp 48, 169 ([119], [106], [117], [120], [123], [125], [114], [126], [124], [112]; notes at end of text; MSS 1, 2, 5, 6, 8, 9, 10, 12; PRINT 16; MS 7 [T

Wright and J O Halliwell, edd, Reliquiæ Antiquæ, London 1841, 1.205]; crit B Dickins, MLR 28.506; TLS Jan 26 1933, p 55; The Modern Scot 4.63); rptd London 1950; ed B Dickins, rptd and rvsd London 1960 (crit A Macdonald, ESts 43.219); rptd 1970.

Selections. The Merrie Historie of the Thrie Friers of Berwicke, Printed at Aberdene by Edward Raban For David Melvil 1622 (described J F K Johnstone and A W Robertson, Bibliographia Aberdonensis, Aberdeen 1929, 1.204).

Ramsay A, The Ever Green, Edinburgh 1724, 1.258 ([117]; occasional changes in wording, omits lines 9–24; MS 10); The Poetical Works of Allan Ramsay, ed C Mackay, London and N Y n d, p 257 ([117]).

Poems in the Scottish Dialect by Several Celebrated Poets, Glasgow 1748, p 38 ([117]).

Dalrymple D, Ancient Scottish Poems, Edinburgh 1770, pp 167, 173, 301; rptd Leeds 1815, pp 210, 219, 350 ([119], [117]; notes at end of text; MS 10).

Hawkins J, A General History of the Science and Practice of Music, London 1776, 3.32 ([125]).

Pinkerton J, Select Scotish Ballads, 2 vols, London 1783, 2.75, 184 (from [117]; notes at end of text; Dalrymple, Ancient Scottish Poems); Ancient Scotish Poems, 2 vols, London and Edinburgh 1786, 1.65; 2.195, 394, 424 ([112], [110]; notes in vol 2; MS 4); Scotish Poems Reprinted from Scarce Editions, 3 vols, London 1792, 3.127, 141 ([115], [106]).

Sibbald J, Chronicle of Scottish Poetry, 4 vols, Edinburgh and London 1802, 1.358, 368; 2.349, 372; 3.224 ([106], [111], from [117], [112], from [119]; introductory and end notes; sources not always indicated but include MS 10, PRINT 16, Pinkerton, Ancient Scottish Poems).

Irving J, The Lives of the Scotish Poets, 2nd edn London 1810, 1.419, 422 ([112]; brief excerpts).

Brydges E and J Haslewood, The British Bibliographer, London 1814, 4.191 ([126]).

Wright T and J O Halliwell, edd, Reliquiæ Antiquæ, London 1841, 1.205 ([123]; MS 7).

Rimbault E F, A Little Book of Songs and Ballads, London 1851, p 27 ([125]; MS 8).

Strickland A, Lives of the Queens of Scotland and English Princesses, N Y 1851, 1.52 ([125]; MS 8 with some variants).

Irving D, The History of Scotish Poetry, ed J A Carlyle, Edinburgh 1861, p 291 ([112]; brief excerpts).

Innes, XXVI. Page from the Folio Maitland MS, Facsimiles of National Manuscripts of Scotland, Southampton 1871, vol 3 [unpaged] ([112]; MS 4).

Schipper J, William Dunbar sein Leben und seine Gedichte, Berlin 1884, pp 209, 322, 342 (poems in German scattered through text of discussion; from [117], [126], from [120]; crit E Kölbing, EStn 10.128; M Trautmann, Angl 7.146; The Nation 40.144).

Fitzgibbon H M, Early English and Scottish Poetry, London N Y and Melbourne 1888, pp 112, 115, 432 ([118], [113]; spelling modernized, notes at end of text).

Flügel E, Liedersammlungen des XVI Jahrhunderts besonders aus der Zeit Heinrichs VIII, Angl 12.265; 26.199 ([125], [123]; MSS 1, 8).

Eyre-Todd G, Mediæval Scottish Poetry, Abbotsford Series, Glasgow 1892, p 182 ([123]; glossings in margin).

Oliphant F R, William Dunbar, Blackwood's Edinburgh Magazine 154.420 ([125]).

Flügel NL, p 160 ([125]; MS 8).

Laing D, Select Remains; rvsd W C Hazlitt, Early Popular Poetry of Scotland, London 1895, 2.11 ([117]; MS 9).

Browne W H, Selections from the Early Scottish Poets, Baltimore 1896, pp 133, 190 ([106], [112]; notes at end of text; Small edn).

Henderson T F, A Little Book of Scottish Verse, London 1899; 2nd edn 1909, pp 48, 66 ([106], [123], [125[; brief introductory notes, glossings at foot of page).

Quiller-Couch A, The Oxford Book of English Verse, Oxford 1900; new edn Oxford 1939, p 26 ([123]; glossings at foot of page).

Smith G G, The Days of James iiii, Scottish History by Contemporary Writers, London 1900, p 77 (from [123]; Small edn).

Arber E, English Songs, The Dunbar Anthology, British Anthologies, London 1901, 1.31, 298 ([123]; spelling and some words modernized, identification of source in notes; MS 5).

Smith G G, Specimens of Middle Scots, Edinburgh and London 1902, pp 26, 274 ([106]; notes at end of text; MS 10).

Kingsford C L, Chronicles of London, Oxford 1905, pp 253, 336 ([123]; notes at end of text; MS 5).

Dyboski R, ed, Songs Carols and Other Miscellaneous Poems from the Balliol MS 354 Richard Hill's Commonplace-book, EET-

SES 101, London 1907, pp 100, 185 ([123]; notes at end of text; MS 1).

Murdoch W G B, The Royal Stewarts in Their Literary Connection with Arts and Letters, Edinburgh 1908, p 59 ([125]).

MacCracken H N, New Stanzas by Dunbar, MLN 24.110 (from [120]; MS 6).

Dixon W M, The Edinburgh Book of Scottish Verse, London 1910, p 49 ([123], [125]; glossings at foot of page).

Zupitza J, Alt- und mittelenglisches Übungsbuch, 10th edn, Vienna and Leipzig 1912, p 202 ([106]; variants at foot of page).

Metcalfe W M, Specimens of Scottish Literature, London 1913, pp 51, 58, 160, 163 ([106], [125]; notes at end of text).

Neilson W A and K G T Webster, Chief British Poets of the 14th and 15th Centuries, Boston N Y etc 1916, pp 397, 434 ([106]; brief note at end of text, glossings at foot of page; Small edn).

James M R, Bibliotheca Pepysiana, London 1923, pt 3, p 16 ([108]; MS 3).

Bennett H S, England from Chaucer to Caxton, London 1928, p 109 ([123]; glossings at foot of page; Baildon edn).

Patterson R F, Six Centuries of English Literature, London and Glasgow 1933, 1.192 ([122], [125], [123]).

Gray M M, Scottish Poetry from Barbour to James VI, N Y 1935, pp 123, 130, 134, 148, 153 ([123], [125], [114], [106], from [117]; crit J Speirs, Scrut 6.83; W M Mackenzie, The Scottish Bookman 1, no 4, p 133).

[Grieve C M] MacDiarmid H, The Golden Treasury of Scottish Poetry, London 1940 (crit L MacNeice, The New Statesman and Nation 21.66; TLS Feb 15 1941, pp 78, 84); rptd in The Golden Treasury Series, London 1948, p 191 ([106]).

Sitwell E, A Poet's Notebook, London 1943; rptd Boston 1950, p 237 (from [117]).

Oliver J W and J C Smith, A Scots Anthology from the 13th to the 20th Century, Edinburgh and London 1949, pp 42, 69 ([106], [116]; spelling modernized, glossings at foot of page).

[Grieve] MacDiarmid H, Selections from the Poems of William Dunbar, The Saltire Classics, Edinburgh 1952, p 20 ([106]; glossings in footnotes; Mackenzie edn); Selected Poems of William Dunbar, Glasgow 1955, p 19 ([106]).

Kinsley J, William Dunbar Poems, Oxford 1958, pp 101, 136 ([106], [117]; notes at end of text; PRINT 16; MS 9; crit TLS Apr 18 1958, p 208; D Young, SHR 38.10; E

Morgan, RES ns 11.71; J Wordsworth, MÆ 30.128).

Mackie R L, King James IV of Scotland, Edinburgh and London 1958, p 281 ([123]; MS 14; crit J D Mackie, SHR 38.133); A Book of Scottish Verse, The World's Classics, no 417, 2nd edn London Glasgow and N Y 1967, p 67 ([106]; glossings at foot of page).

Modernizations. Tytler P F, Lives of Scottish Worthies, London 1833, 3.120 (from [112]; Laing edn).

The Friars of Berwick a Scottish Story in English Rhyme, The Dublin Univ Magazine 13.369.

Green M A E, Lives of the Princesses of England, London 1852, 4.178 ([126]; Laing edn).

[Robertson J L] Haliburton H, Dunbar Being a Selection from the Poems of an Old Makar Adapted for Modern Readers, London 1895, pp 51, 89 ([110], from [112]; paraphrase, abbreviated, extremely free; crit R Brotanek, AnglB 6.71).

Schipper J, Die Mönche von Berwick eine altschottische poetische Erzahlung von einem unbekannten Chaucerschuler, Beiträge und Studien zur Englischen Kultur- und Literaturgeschichte, Wien and Leipzig 1908, p 131 ([112]).

Linklater E, A Bawdy Revival, New Saltire, no 9, Sept 1963, pp 21, 24 ([117], [106]).

Textual Matters. Laing, edn, 1.273, 301, 303; 2.338, 378, 384, 389, 411, 413 ([123], [125], [114], [120], [119], [112], [117]).

Schipper, edn, pt 1, 40².4, 21, 27, 70; pt 2, 40⁴.1, 100; pt 3, 41⁴.80; pt 4, 42⁴.70, 86 ([112], [106], [125], [117], [119], [120], [123]; see also introductory and ftnts to individual poems).

Zupitza J, Zu Dunbar, Arch 90.151 ([123]).

Schipper, Anonymous Early Scottish Poems, edn, pt 5, 43¹.4, 44, 47, 50, 65 ([112], [111], [115], [107], [122]).

Schipper J, Zu Dunbar, Arch 91.241 ([123]; variants in MSS).

Brandl A, Berichtingung zu A treatice of London, Arch 102.471 ([123]).

Mebus F, Studien zu William Dunbar, Breslau 1902, pp 7, 50, 77 ([125], [114], [123]; explanation of obscure words and phrases, discussion of references).

Dyboski R, ed, Songs Carols and other Miscellanous Poems from the Balliol MS 354, EETSES 101, London 1907, p 185 ([123]; variants in MSS 5, 7).

MacCracken H N, New Stanzas by Dunbar,

MLN 24.110 ([120]; discussion of MS 6 text).

Mackenzie, edn, pp 208, 227, 240 ([119], [106], [117], [120], [123], [125], [114], [126], [124], [112]).

Bühler C F, London Thow Art the Flowre of Cytes All, RES 13.1, 7 ([123]).

Baxter J W, William Dunbar, Edinburgh and London 1952, pp 142, 178, 217, 222, 225 ([119], [106], [125], [114], [126], [112], [117], [107], [120], 115]).

Jones G F, William Dunbar's Steidis, MLN 69.479 ([117]).

Language. Ramsay A, The Ever Green, Edinburgh 1724, 2.265 ([117]; glossary).

Dalrymple D, Ancient Scottish Poems, Edinburgh 1770, p 317; rptd Leeds 1815, p 367 (glossary), [added] Glossary, p 1 [separate pagination] ([119], [117]).

Pinkerton J, Select Scotish Ballads, London 1783, 1.154; 2.193 ([117]; glossaries); Ancient Scotish Poems, London and Edinburgh 1786, l.cxliii; 2.520 (synorthographic and symphonious words, glossary; [112], [110]); Scotish Poems Reprinted from Scarce Editions, London 1792, 3.227 ([115], [106]; glossary).

Sibbald J, Chronicle of Scottish Poetry, Edinburgh and London 1802, vol 4 [unpaged] (glossary; [106], [111], [117], [112], [119]).

Laing, edn, 2.372 ([112]).

Irving D, The History of Scotish Poetry, ed J A Carlyle, Edinburgh 1861, p 595 (glossary; [112]).

Murray J A H, The Dialect of the Southern Counties of Scotland, London 1873 (group as a whole).

Kaufmann J, Traité de la langue, Bonn 1873, p 47 (group as a whole).

Hahn O, Zur Verbal- und Nominalflexion bei den schottischen Dichtern, Berlin 1887–89 (see especially pt 3, p 17; group as a whole).

Schipper, edn, pt 1, 40².18 (group as a whole); Anonymous Early Scottish Poems, edn, pt 5, 43¹.45, 51, 54, 57, 60, 62, 64, 68 (discussion in headnotes for [111], [107], [124], [109], [118], [116], [121]; glossary to Schipper, edn, pts 1–4, and Supplement, pt 5).

Gregor W, Small edn, 3.401 (glossary; group as a whole).

Curtis F J, An Investigation of the Rimes and Phonology of Clariodus, Angl 16.387; 17.1, 125 (group as a whole).

Bearder J W, Über den Gebrauch der Praepositionen in der altschottischen Poesie, Halle 1894 ([106], [123], [125]; examples from Dunbar; crit EStn 19.410).

Hazlitt W C, Early Popular Poetry of Scotland, London 1895, 2.323 (index, glossary; [117]).

Browne W H, Selections from the Early Scottish Poets, Baltimore 1896, pp 3, 197 ([106], [112]; discussion in introd, glossary).

Heuser W, Die Dehnung vor -nd im Mittelschottischen, Die Dehnung -end, Angl 19.401 (brief; group as a whole).

Baildon H B, Rimes in the Authentic Poems of William Dunbar, Trans Royal Soc Edinburgh 39³.629; issued separately Edinburgh 1899 (group as a whole).

Flom G T, Scandinavian Influence on Southern Lowland Scotch, diss Columbia 1900 (group as a whole).

Arber E, English Songs, The Dunbar Anthology, British Anthologies, London 1901, 1.300 ([123]; glossary, index).

Smith G G, Specimens of Middle Scots, Edinburgh and London 1902, pp xi, 325 ([106]; glossary).

Millar J H, A Literary History of Scotland, London 1903, p 687 (glossary; [123], [117]).

Browne W H, The Taill of Rauf Coilyear, Baltimore 1903, pp 15, 35, 139 (general discussion of Middle Scots, glossary; group as a whole).

Knopff P, Darstellung der Ablautverhältnisse in der schottischen Schriftsprache, diss Würzburg 1904 (group as a whole).

Baildon, edn, pp xxvi, 299 (discussion, glossary; group as a whole).

CHEL, 2.101, 506 (group as a whole).

Dixon W M, The Edinburgh Book of Scottish Verse, London 1910, p 897 (glossary; [123], [125]).

Zupitza J, Alt- und mittelenglisches Übungsbuch, 10th edn, Vienna and Leipzig 1912, p 208 (glossary, definitions in German; [106]).

Gray M M, Introd, Lancelot of the Laik, PSTS ns 2, Edinburgh and London 1912, 2.xviii (group as a whole).

Lenz K, Zur Lautlehre der französischen Elemente in den schottischen Dichtungen, diss Marburg 1913 (examples taken from Douglas, Dunbar, Lyndesay, Clariodus; group as a whole).

Metcalfe W M, Specimens of Scottish Literature, London 1913, pp 9, 39, 189 ([106], [125]).

Taylor R, Some Notes on the Use of Can and Couth, JEGP 16.573 ([112]).

Westergaard E, Prepositions in Lowland Scotch, Angl 41.444 (some examples from Dunbar; group as a whole); Verbal Forms in Middle-Scotch, Angl 43.95 (group as a whole).

Watt L M, Language and Influences, Douglas's Aeneid, Cambridge 1920, p 149 (very generally applicable).

Westergaard E, Studies in Prefixes and Suffixes, London 1924 (group as a whole).

Wilson J, The Spelling of Scotch before 1600, The Dialects of Central Scotland, London 1926, p 168 (group as a whole; attempts to determine pronunciation from spelling, rimes, modern Lothian pronunciation).

Craigie W A, ed, The Maitland Folio, 2 vols, PSTS ns 7, 20, Edinburgh and London 1919–27, 2.135 (glossary; [107]).

Westergaard E, Plural Forms in Lowland Scottish, Angl 51.77 (group as a whole).

Ritchie R L G, Early Instances of French Loan-Words in Scots and English, EStn 63.41 ([123], [117]; examples from Dunbar).

Mackenzie, edn, pp xii, xxxvii, 245 ([119], [106], [117], [120], [123], [125], [114], [126], [124], [112]; discussion, glossary).

Wood H H, The Poems and Fables of Robert Henryson, Edinburgh 1933; 2nd edn rvsd Edinburgh 1958; rptd 1965, 1968, p xxxi.

Bühler C F, London Thow Art the Flowre of Cytes All, RES 13.7 ([123]).

Patrick D, Scottish Literature, Chambers's Cyclopædia, rvsd J L Geddie, Phila and N Y 1938, 1.164 (group as a whole).

Thomas A H and I D Thornley, The Great Chronicle of London, London 1938, p 459 (glossary; [123]).

[Grieve C M] MacDiarmid H, The Golden Treasury of Scottish Poetry, London 1940; rptd in The Golden Treasury Series, London 1948, p 397 (glossary; [106]).

Oliver J W and J C Smith, A Scots Anthology, Edinburgh and London 1949, p 497 (glossaries; [100], [116]).

[Grieve] MacDiarmid H, Selections from the Poems of William Dunbar, The Saltire Classics, Edinburgh 1952, pp 5, 49 ([106]; brief note, glossary); Selected Poems of William Dunbar, Glasgow 1955, p 60 (glossary; [106]).

Kinsley J, William Dunbar Poems, Oxford 1958, p 139 (glossary; [106], [117]).

Scott T, Dunbar A Critical Exposition, Edinburgh and London 1966, pp 346, 351.

Conley J, William Dunbar Additions to and Corrections of OED and DOST, N&Q 213 (ns 15).169 ([126], [116], [120], [117]).

Versification. Laing, edn, 2.375 ([112]).

Schipper, 1.510 and passim ([106], [112]).

Schipper J, William Dunbar sein Leben und seine Gedichte, Berlin 1884, p 208 ([117]).

Mackay Æ J G, Introd, Small edn, 1.lxxxv [112]; brief reference).

McNeill G P, Note on the Versification and Metres of Dunbar, Small edn, 1.clxxiii, clxxx, clxxxv, cxci ([112], [106], [107], [113], [125], [111], [110], [109], [116], [122], [124], [114], [118], [126], [121], [123], [120], [117]).

Schipper, edn, pt 1, 40².69, 88; pt 2, 40⁴.31, 100 ([106], [123], [114], [117]; discussion in headnotes to poems).

Brandl, 2¹.1017 ([117]).

Schipper, Anonymous Early Scottish Poems, edn, pt 5, 43¹.47 ([115]).

Curtis F J, The Rimes and Phonology of Clariodus, Angl 16.387; 17.1, 125 (group as a whole).

Browne W H, Selections from Early Scottish Poets, Baltimore 1896, p 12 ([106]; very brief).

Amours F J, Scottish Alliterative Poems, PSTS 27, 38, Edinburgh and London 1897, p lxxxii ([106]).

Henderson T F, Scottish Vernacular Literature, Edinburgh 1898; 3rd edn rvsd Edinburgh 1910, pp 153, 156, 163 ([106], [123], [114], [117]).

Baildon H B, Rimes in the Authentic Poems of Dunbar, Trans Royal Soc Edinburgh 39³.629 (group as a whole).

Mebus F, Studien zu William Dunbar, Breslau 1902, p 7 ([125]; brief).

Browne W H, The Taill of Rauf Coilyear, Baltimore 1903, p 56 ([106]).

Steinberger C, Étude sur William Dunbar, Dublin 1908, p 157 ([106]).

Saintsbury G, Historical Manual of English Prosody, London 1910; rptd London 1914, pp 163, 303 ([112]).

Oakden J P, Alliterative Poetry in Middle English, Manchester 1930, p 217 ([106]; crit AnglB 42.334).

Taylor R A, Dunbar the Poet, The Poets on the Poets, no 4, London 1931, p 83 ([117]; crit The Criterion 11.331; TLS Mar 17 1932, p 199; YWES 13.124).

Smith J M, The French Background of Middle Scots Literature, Edinburgh and London 1934, pp 76, 155, 158, 166 ([120], [112], [106]; crit AnglB 45.265; MÆ 4.44).

Craigie W, The Scottish Alliterative Poems, Proc of the British Acad 28.217 ([106]).

Scott T, Dunbar A Critical Exposition, Edinburgh and London 1966, pp 36, 168, 318, 323, 326, 329 ([125], [123], [124], [114], [106]).

Date. Pinkerton J, Ancient Scotish Poems, London and Edinburgh 1786, 1.x ([112]).

Laing, edn, 1.35 (Memoirs), 303; 2.373, 410, 415 ([124], [114], [112], [117], [126]).

Paterson, edn, pp 28, 309 ([112], [124]).

Irving D, The History of Scotish Poetry, ed J A Carlyle, Edinburgh 1861, p 291 ([112]).

Schipper J, William Dunbar sein Leben und seine Gedichte, Berlin 1884, pp 116, 213, 321 ([123], [117], [126]).

Mackay Æ J G, Introd [and] Appendix to Introd, Small edn, 1.lxvii, lxx, xci, xciv, cvii, cxxx, cxxxviii, clix, clx, clxiv, clxix ([124], [109], [120], [113], [106], [125], [114], [116], [121], [122], [112], [123], [117], [111], [110], [107], [126]).

Schipper, edn, pt 1, 40².69, 87; pt 2, 40⁴.31, 100; pt 3, 41⁴.80; pt 4, 42⁴.41 ([106], [123], [114], [117], [119], [126]).

Zupitza J, Zu Dunbar, Arch 90.151 ([123]; date of MS 7).

Schipper, Anonymous Early Scottish Poems, edn, pt 5, 43¹.2, 55, 57 ([112], [124], [109]).

Mebus F, Studien zu William Dunbar, Breslau 1902, p 49 ([114]).

Schipper J, Die Mönche von Berwick, Beiträge und Studien zur Englischen Kulturund Literaturgeschichte, Wien and Leipzig 1908, p 149 ([112]).

Bühler C F, London Thow Art the Flowre of Cytes All, RES 13.4 ([123]).

Utley CR, pp 128, 198, 245 ([111], [106], [107]).

Lewis C S, English Literature in the Sixteenth Century, Oxford 1954, p 90 ([123], [125], [126]).

Authorship. Pinkerton J, Ancient Scotish Poems, London and Edinburgh 1786, 1.x ([112]).

Laing, edn, 1.304; 2.366, 372, 408, 410, 415, 455 ([120], [107], [112], [111], [106], [117], [126], [110], [109], [118], [116], [121], [122]).

Green M A E, Lives of the Princesses of England, London 1852, 4.61 ([123]).

Paterson, edn, pp 27, 90, 299, 310 ([112], [119], [126], [124], [117]).

Irving D, The History of Scotish Poetry, ed J A Carlyle, Edinburgh 1861, p 291 ([112]).

Kaufmann J, Traité de la langue, Bonn 1873, p 19 ([112]).

Schipper J, William Dunbar sein Leben und seine Gedichte, Berlin 1884, pp 207, 214, 284, 321, 348 ([117], [119], [126], [124]).

Mackay Æ J G, Introd, Small edn, 1.xxxiii, lxiii, lxvii, lxxxiv, xci, xciv, cxix, cxxix ([123], [126], [124], [112], [113], [106], [107]).

Morley, 7.153 ([112]).

Eyre-Todd G, Mediæval Scottish Poetry, Abbotsford Series, Glasgow 1892, p 151 ([112]).

Schipper, edn, pt 1, 40^2.27, 69, 87; pt 2, 40^4.1, 100; pt 3, 41^4.80; pt 4, 42^4.41, 64, 69 ([106], [123], [117], [119], [126], [107], [120]).

Oliphant F R, William Dunbar, Blackwood's Edinburgh Magazine 154.420, 431 ([123], [106]).

Schipper, Anonymous Early Scottish Poems, edn, pt 5, 43^1.1, 44, 49, 54, 57, 60, 62 ([112], [111], [113], [115], [110], [107], [124], [117], [109], [118], [116], [121], [122]).

Laing D, Select Remains; rvsd W C Hazlitt, Early Popular Poetry of Scotland, London 1895, 2.11 ([117]).

Henderson T F, Scottish Vernacular Literature, Edinburgh 1898; 3rd edn rvsd Edinburgh 1910, pp 175, 277 ([112]).

Browne W H, The Taill of Rauf Coilyear, Baltimore 1903, p 17 ([112]).

Brown J T T, The Bannatyne Manuscript, SHR 1.144, 149, 151 ([118], [116], [121], [122], [109], [119], [117]).

Snell F J, The Poets, The Age of Transition, London 1905, 1.91 ([112]).

Schipper J, Die Mönche von Berwick, Beiträge und Studien zur Englischen Kulturund Literaturgeschichte, Wien und Leipzig 1908, pp 130, 147 ([112]).

Steinberger C, Étude sur William Dunbar, Dublin 1908, pp 81, 117, 130, 176 ([117], [112], [113], [111]).

MacCracken H N, New Stanzas by Dunbar, MLN 24.110 ([120]; discusses and prints text longer than those of MSS 9 and 13).

Enc Brit, 8.668 ([112]; brief).

Watt L M, Scottish Life and Poetry, London 1912, pp 104, 106 ([126], [112]).

Taylor R, Some Notes on the Use of Can and Couth, JEGP 16.589 ([112]).

Mackenzie, edn, p 240 ([123]).

Mackenzie W M, William Dunbar, Edinburgh Essays on Scots Literature, Edinburgh and London 1933, p 50 ([123]).

Bühler C F, London Thow Art the Flowre of Cytes All, RES 13.5 ([123]).

Utley C R, pp 128, 211, 245 ([111], [107]).

Baxter J W, William Dunbar, Edinburgh and London 1952, pp 88, 118, 140, 142, 152, 178, 201, 222 ([123], [125], [114], [119], [117], [106], [126], [112], [111], [113], [110], [107], [109], [116], [118], [122], [120], [115], [124], [121]).

Mackie J D, The Earlier Tudors, Oxford 1952; rptd 1958, p 158 ([123]; brief).

Lewis C S, English Literature in the Sixteenth Century, Oxford 1954, p 99 ([117], [112]).

Kinsley J, The Mediaeval Makars, London 1955, p 14 ([112], [106], [117]; brief); William Dunbar Poems, Oxford 1958, p xx ([123]; brief).

Mackie R L, King James IV of Scotland, Edinburgh and London 1958, p 96 ([123]).

Shire H M, The Thrissil the Rois and the Flour-de-lys, Cambridge Eng 1962, p 26 ([124]).

Scott T, Dunbar A Critical Exposition, Edinburgh and London 1966, pp 67, 137, 167, 228, 246, 267, 302, 304, 324, 361 ([106], [119], [123], [125], [114], [117], [124], [122], [120], [107]).

Johnston E C, The Transmutation of Friar Johine, SSL 5.57 ([112]; brief reference).

Scott T, Late Medieval Scots Poetry, London 1967, p 33 ([106]).

Sources and Literary Relations. Laing, edn, 1.58 (Memoirs); 2.374, 376, 408 ([117], [112], [106]).

Irving D, The History of Scotish Poetry, ed J A Carlyle, Edinburgh 1861, p 298 ([112]).

McElroy J G R, The Thrissill and the Rois, The Penn Monthly 12.541 ([112]).

Mackay Æ J G, Introd, Small edn, 1.lxxxii, civ ([117], [123]).

[Robertson J L] Haliburton H, Our Earlier Burns, In Scottish Fields, London 1890, p 238 ([112]).

Schipper, Anonymous Early Scottish Poems, edn, pt 5, 43^1.3 ([112]).

[Robertson J L] Haliburton H, Dunbar in Burns, Furth in Field, London 1894, p 278 ([123], [114]).

Von Weilen A, Ein Zwischenspiel des Cervantes in moderner Bearbeitung, Beilage zur Allgemeinen Beitung 146.3 ([112]).

Turnbull W R, The Heritage of Burns, Haddington 1896, pp 247, 256 ([112]; brief references).

Smith G G, The Transition Period, Periods of European Literature, Edinburgh and London 1900, 4.36, 39, 42 and passim ([112], [106]).

Chambers R, Chambers's Cyclopædia, Phila and N Y 1901–03; rvsd J L Geddie, Phila and N Y 1938, 1.200 ([112]; brief).

Ritter O, Quellenstudien zu Robert Burns, Palaes 20.51 ([114]; brief).

Mebus F, Studien zu William Dunbar, Breslau 1902, pp 8, 50, 77 ([125], [114]; brief similarities of wording or reference).

Snell F J, The Poets, The Age of Transition,

London 1905, 1.91 ([112]).

Hart W M, The Fabliau and Popular Literature, PMLA 23.329 ([112]).

Schipper J, Die Mönche von Berwick, Beiträge und Studien zur Englischen Kultur- und Literaturgeschichte, Wien and Leipzig 1908, pp 129, 146 ([112]).

CHEL, 2.290 ([106]).

Tucker S M, Verse Satire in England, CUS 3, no 2, p 139 ([107], [124]).

Enc Brit, 8.669 ([106]).

Sandison H E, The Chanson D'Aventure in Middle English, Bryn Mawr Pa 1913, p 141 ([109]).

Taylor R, Some Notes on the Use of Can and Couth, JEGP 16.589 ([112]).

Jacobi J B, William Dunbar—an Appreciation, The American Catholic Quarterly Rev 44.309 ([120]).

Smith G G, Scottish Literature Character and Influence, London 1919, pp 26, 237 ([117], [106]; brief references).

Mendenhall J C, Aureate Terms A Study in Literary Diction of the 15th Cent, Lancaster Pa 1919 (group as a whole).

Schofield W H, Mythical Bards, HSCL, 5.26 and passim ([117]).

James M R, Bibliotheca Pepysiana, London 1923, pt 3, p 16 ([108]).

Spence L, Wee Men in Scots Folklore, The Scots Magazine ns 6.435 ([117]).

Saintsbury G, The Four Great Scottish Poets, A Short Hist of Eng Lit, N Y 1929, p 186 ([112]).

Kitchin G, A Survey of Burlesque and Parody in English, Edinburgh and London 1931, pp 25, 37 ([106], [117]).

Nichols P H, William Dunbar as a Scottish Lydgatian, PMLA 46.218 ([123], [125], [126], [120], [108]).

Smith J M, The French Background of Middle Scots Literature, Edinburgh and London 1934, pp xxvi, 62, 69, 81, 166 ([112], [123], [106], [120]; crit AnglB 45.265; MÆ 4.44).

Patrick D, Scottish Literature, Chambers's Cyclopædia, rvsd J L Geddie, Phila and N Y 1938, 1.116 (group as a whole).

Taylor A, Problems in German Literary History of the 15th and 16th Centuries, N Y 1939, pp 121, 164 ([123]; brief).

Harbage A, Annals of English Drama, Phila and London 1940, p 20 ([117], [125]).

Craigie W, The Scottish Alliterative Poems, Proc of the British Acad 28.217 ([106]).

Utley CR, pp 65, 128, 198, 210, 213, 245 ([106], [111], [117], [107]).

Hyde I, Primary Sources and Associations of Dunbar's Aureate Imagery, MLR 51.486, 489 ([120], [114]).

Maclaine A H, The Christis Kirk Tradition, SSL 2.16 ([106]).

Hyde I, Poetic Imagery, SSL 2.184 ([123]).

Rogers K M, The Troublesome Helpmate, Seattle 1966, p 64 ([107]).

Fox D, The Scottish Chaucerians, Chaucer and Chaucerians, ed D S Brewer, University Alabama 1966, pp 164ff (see especially p 165; [112]).

Scott T, Dunbar A Critical Exposition, Edinburgh and London 1966, pp 69, 326, 329 and passim ([106], [107]); Late Medieval Scots Poetry, London 1967, p 13 ([112]).

Scheps W, William Wallace and his Buke, SSL 6.236.

Other Scholarly Problems. Scott W, Marmion, Edinburgh 1808, p lv ([112]; contemp conditions).

Laing, edn, 1.272, 297, 301; 2.380 ([123], [125], [112]; occasion, setting).

Strickland A, Lives of the Queens of Scotland and English Princesses, N Y 1851, 1.52 ([125]; occasion).

Green M A E, Lives of the Princesses of England, London 1852, 4.61 ([123]; occasion).

Paterson, edn, p 309 ([124]; biographical evidence).

Campbell J F, Popular Tales of the West Highlands, Edinburgh 1862, 4.54 ([117]; contemp conditions, brief).

Ross J M, Scottish History and Literature, Glasgow 1884, p 179 ([112]; contemp conditions).

Schipper J, William Dunbar sein Leben und seine Gedichte, Berlin 1884, p 165 ([125]; occasion).

Mackay Æ J G, Introd, Small edn, l.xxxiii, lxvii, lxxxii, xci, xciv, civ, cxxx ([123], [125], [124], [117], [113], [106], [126]; occasion, identity of subject, setting).

[Robertson J L] Haliburton H, Our Earlier Burns, In Scottish Fields, London 1890, p 236 ([126], [124]; biographical evidence).

Morley, 7.120 ([123]; occasion).

Schipper, edn, pt 4, 42⁴.64 (relation of [107] to [99]).

Oliphant F R, William Dunbar, Blackwood's Edinburgh Magazine 154.420 ([123]; occasion).

Smeaton O, William Dunbar, N Y (1898?), pp 72, 78, 112 ([123], [125], [126]; biographical evidence, occasion; crit J W Baxter,

William Dunbar, Edinburgh and London 1952, passim; The Scottish Antiquary 13.95).

Brown J T T, The Wallace and The Bruce Restudied, BBA 6.79 ([117]; identity of subject).

Smith G G, The Days of James iiii, Scottish History by Contemporary Writers, London 1900, p 76 ([123]; occasion, illustrative quote).

Mebus F, Studien zu William Dunbar, Breslau 1902, p 5 ([125]; musical setting).

Millar J H, A Literary History of Scotland, London 1903, p 50 ([123], [125]; occasion).

Teichert O P, Schottische Zustände unter Jacob IV nach den Dichtungen von William Dunbar, Görlitz 1903, pp 14, 19, 26, 29 ([125], [112], [109], [117], [120]; contemp conditions; crit O Glöde, EStn 36.267).

Powys L, William Dunbar, The Freeman 7.516 ([123]; occasion).

Mill A J, Mediaeval Plays in Scotland, St Andrews Univ Publ no 24, Edinburgh 1927, pp 34, 102 ([117]; contemp conditions, occasion).

William Dunbar, TLS Apr 10 1930, p 305 ([123]; occasion).

Mackenzie, edn, p 242 ([117]; identity of subject).

Bühler C F, London Thow Art the Flowre of Cytes All, RES 13.1 ([123]; occasion).

Baxter J W, William Dunbar, Edinburgh and London 1952, pp 85, 91, 118, 140, 152, 202 ([123], [125], [114], [117], [126]; occasion).

Mackie J D, The Earlier Tudors, Oxford 1952; rptd Oxford 1958, pp 41, 158 ([123]; occasion).

Coldwell D F C, Virgil's Aeneid Translated into Scottish Verse, PSTS 3s 30, Edinburgh and London 1964, 1.15 ([124]; occasion).

Mackie R L, King James IV of Scotland, Edinburgh and London 1958, p 95 ([123]; occasion; crit SHR 38.133).

Dickinson W C, Scotland from the Earliest Times, A New History of Scotland, Edinburgh and London 1961, 1.280 ([123]; occasion).

Scott T, Dunbar A Critical Exposition, Edinburgh and London 1966, pp 68, 169 ([107], [114]; relation between poems).

Literary Criticism. Pinkerton J, Ancient Scotish Poems, London and Edinburgh 1786, 1.xi ([112]).

Ellis G, Specimens of the Early English Poets, 5 edns London 1790, 1801, 1803, 1811, 1845

(5th edn corrected), 1.315 ([112]; very brief).

Irving D, The Lives of the Scotish Poets, 2nd edn London 1810, 1.417 ([112]; largely paraphrase).

Tytler P F, Lives of Scottish Worthies, London 1833, 3.120 ([112]).

Laing, edn, 1.59 (Memoirs); 2.372, 415, 458 ([117], [112], [126]).

William Dunbar, Littell's Living Age 1.383 ([112]).

Wright T, On the Scottish Poet Dunbar, Essays on Subjects Connected with the Literature Popular Superstitions and Hist of England, London 1846, 2.298 ([112]).

Gilfillan G, Specimens with Memoirs, Edinburgh and London 1860, 1.60 ([112]; brief).

Paterson, edn, p 28 ([112]).

Irving D, The History of Scotish Poetry, ed J A Carlyle, Edinburgh 1861, p 292 ([112]; illustrative quotes).

Taylor J, The Imperial Dictionary of Universal Biography, London [1863], 2.170 ([112]; brief).

Kaufmann J, Traité de la langue, Bonn 1873, p 19 ([112]).

Wilson J G, The Poets and Poetry of Scotland, N Y 1876, 1.25 ([112]; very brief).

Mackintosh J, The History of Civilisation in Scotland, London and Edinburgh 1878–88; new edn partly rewritten Paisley 1892–96, 2.309 ([112]).

McElroy J G R, The Thrissill and the Rois, The Penn Monthly 12.541 ([112]).

Ross J M, Scottish History and Literature, Glasgow 1884, p 206 ([112]).

Schipper J, William Dunbar sein Leben und seine Gedichte, Berlin 1884, pp 164, 189, 208, 284, 322, 342 ([123], [114], [117], [119], [126], [120]).

Shairp J C, Sketches in History and Poetry, Edinburgh 1887, p 222 ([112]; very brief).

Skelton J, Maitland of Lethington, Edinburgh 1887, 1.109 ([106]).

Mackay Æ J G, Introd, Small edn, 1.xxxiv, lxvii, lxx, lxxxv, xci, xciv, civ, cvi, cix, cxxiii, cxxix, cxxxvii ([123], [124], [109], [120], [112], [113], [106], [107], [116], [118], [121], [122]).

[Robertson J L] Haliburton H, Our Earlier Burns, In Scottish Fields, London 1890, pp 238, 240 ([112], [123]).

Morley, 7.153 ([112]; largely resumé).

Eyre-Todd G, Mediæval Scottish Poetry, Abbotsford Series, Glasgow 1892, p 151 ([112]).

Schipper, edn, pt 1, 40².69, 88; pt 2, 40⁴.31, 100; pt 4, 42⁴.41 ([106], [123], [114], [117],

[126]).

Oliphant F R, William Dunbar, Blackwood's Edinburgh Magazine 154.420, 431 ([123], [106], [112]).

Schipper, Anonymous Early Scottish Poems, edn, pt 5, 43¹.3, 51, 60, 62, 64, 66 ([112], [107], [118], [116], [121], [122]).

Henderson T F, Scottish Vernacular Literature, Edinburgh 1898; 3rd edn rvsd Edinburgh 1910, pp 153, 165, 170, 175, 278 ([106], [123], [112]).

Smith G G, The Transition Period, Periods of European Literature, Edinburgh and London 1900, 4.50 and passim ([112], [106]).

Chambers R, Chambers's Cyclopædia, Phila and N Y 1901–03; rvsd J L Geddie, Phila and N Y 1938, 1.197 ([106], [123], [112]).

Mebus F, Studien zu William Dunbar, Breslau 1902, pp 7, 49, 58, 76, 83 ([125], [114], [123]; brief comments).

Browne W H, The Taill of Rauf Coilyear, Baltimore 1903, p 17 ([112]).

Millar J H, A Literary History of Scotland, London 1903, p 59 ([117]).

Snell F J, The Poets, The Age of Transition, London 1905, 1.83, 92 ([123], [112]).

Seccombe T and W R Nicoll, The Scots Poets, The Bookman Illustrated Hist of Eng Lit, London 1906, 1.21 ([123]).

Wülker R, Geschichte der englischen Literatur, Leipzig and Wien 1906–07, 1.205, 207 ([123], [114], [126]; brief comment).

Hart W M, The Fabliau and Popular Literature, PMLA 23.360 ([112]).

Schipper J, Die Mönche von Berwick, Wien and Leipzig 1908, pp 148, 152 ([112]; German translation).

CHEL, 2.288, 290 ([117], [112], [106]).

Steinberger C, Étude sur William Dunbar, Dublin 1908, pp 11, 42, 81, 112, 118, 147, 149 ([112], [106], [117], [123], [121], [120]).

Tucker S M, Verse Satire in England, CUS 3, no 2, p 139 ([107], [124]).

Enc Brit, 8.669 ([106], [117]).

Watt L M, Scottish Life and Poetry, London 1912, pp 104, 106 ([126], [112]).

Jacobi J B, William Dunbar—an Appreciation, The American Catholic Quarterly Rev 44.309 ([120]).

Smith G G, Scottish Literature Character and Influence, London 1919, p 26 ([117], [106]; brief references).

Schofield W H, Mythical Bards, HSCL, 5.26, 31 ([117]).

Barfield O, The Scottish Chaucerians, The New Statesman 17.274 ([123], [117]).

Quiller-Couch A, Studies in Literature, 2s, N Y and Cambridge Eng 1922, p 270 ([123]).

Saintsbury G, The Four Great Scottish Poets, A Short Hist of Eng Lit, N Y 1929, p 186 ([112], [106]; brief).

William Dunbar, TLS Apr 10 1930, p 305 ([123], [106], [117]).

Kitchin G, A Survey of Burlesque and Parody, Edinburgh and London 1931, pp 25, 37 ([106], [117]).

Taylor R A, Dunbar the Poet, The Poets on the Poets, no 4, London 1931, pp 35, 43, 47, 69, 79, 83 ([125], [123], [120], [106], [117]).

Elton O, The English Muse, London 1933, p 86 ([112]).

Mackenzie A M, An Historical Survey of Scottish Literature, London 1933, pp 89, 92, 94 ([106], [125], [123]).

Mackenzie W M, William Dunbar, Edinburgh Essays on Scots Lit, Edinburgh and London 1933, pp 35, 49 ([106], [117]).

Smith J M, The French Background of Middle Scots Literature, Edinburgh and London 1934, pp xxvi, 62, 65, 69, 76, 81, 166 ([112], [123], [106], [120]).

Muir E, Scottish Literature, Scott and Scotland, London 1936, p 102 ([117]).

Craigie W, The Scottish Alliterative Poems, Proc of the British Acad 28.230 ([106]).

Grierson H J C and J C Smith, A Critical History of English Poetry, London 1944; 2nd rvsd edn London 1947, p 57 ([106]; brief).

Utley C R, pp 128, 199, 246 ([111], [106], [107]; mainly summary with occasional brief comment).

Sitwell E, A Poet's Notebook, London 1943; rptd Boston 1950, p 236 ([117]).

Moore A K, The Secular Lyric in ME, Lexington Ky 1951, p 213 ([106]).

Baxter J W, William Dunbar, Edinburgh and London 1952, pp 140, 201 ([114], [126]).

Ward A C, Illustrated History of Eng Lit, London N Y and Toronto 1953, p 41 ([123]; brief).

Lewis C S, English Literature in the Sixteenth Century, Oxford 1954, p 98 ([116], [117], [112]).

Kinsley J, The Mediaeval Makars, Scottish Poetry A Critical Survey, London 1955, p 14 ([112], [106], [117]).

Hyde I, Primary Sources and Associations of Dunbar's Aureate Imagery, MLR 51.481, 486, 489 ([120]).

Peter J, Complaint and Satire in Early English Literature, Oxford 1956, p 89 ([107]; brief reference).

Kinsley J, William Dunbar Poems, Oxford 1958, p xix ([106], [117]).

Hyde I, Poetic Imagery, SSL 2.184 ([123]).

Fox D, The Scottish Chaucerians, Chaucer and Chaucerians, ed D S Brewer, University Alabama 1966, p 165 ([112]).

Rogers K M, The Troublesome Helpmate, Seattle 1966, p 64 ([107]).

Scott T, Dunbar A Critical Exposition, Edinburgh and London 1966, pp 67, 136, 168, 267, 302, 304 and passim ([106], [119], [125], [114], [124], [122], [120], [107]).

Johnston E C, The Transmutation of Friar Johine, SSL 5.57 ([112]).

Scott T, Late Medieval Scots Poetry, London 1967, p 33 ([106]).

Shire H M, Song Dance and Poetry of the Court of Scotland, Cambridge 1969, p 17 ([113]).

Bibliography. Henderson T F, Scottish Vernacular Literature, Edinburgh 1898; 3rd edn rvsd Edinburgh 1910, p 277 ([112]).

Geddie W, A Bibliography of Middle Scots Poets, PSTS ns 61, Edinburgh and London 1912, p 206 ([112]).

Brown-Robbins, Robbins-Cutler, nos 2244 ([106]), 2497 ([108]); Robbins-Cutler, nos 442.5 ([112]), 688.5 ([109]), 753.3 ([111]), 753.5 ([110]), 861.5 ([119]), 912.5 ([114]), 1119.3 ([117]), 1440.5 ([113]), 1466.5 ([115]), 1657.5 ([116]), 1933.5 ([123]), 2308.5 ([125]), 2312.5 ([118]), 2497.5 ([126]), 2831.8 ([120]), 3225.5 ([122]), 3306.8 ([107]), 3477.3 ([121]), 3866.5 ([124]).

Utley C R, pp 128, 198, 245 ([111], [106], [107]).

Beattie W, The Chepman and Myllar Prints, Edinburgh Biblio Soc, Oxford 1950, pp xi, xv ([115], [106]).

XI. CHAUCERIAN APOCRYPHA

by

Rossell Hope Robbins

BACKGROUND BOOKS: The following important, frequently listed entries, here given full statement, are referred to in abbreviated form in the pages that follow. For abbreviations not appearing in this list, consult the general Table of Abbreviations.

Brusendorff   Brusendorff A, The Chaucer Tradition, Copenhagen 1925; rptd Oxford 1967 (crit A Brandl, Arch 151.115; V Langhans, Angl 51.323; H R Patch, MP 25.361; A W Pollard, Libr 7.229; M Praz, MLR 22.201; R K Root, JEGP 26.258; C R D Young, RES 3.80).

Hammond EV   Hammond E P, English Verse between Chaucer and Surrey, Durham N C 1927; rptd N Y 1965 (crit F Brie, DLz 51.455).

Lewis   Lewis C S, The Allegory of Love, Oxford 1936.

Neilson   Neilson W A, The Origins and Sources of the Court of Love, HSNPL 6, Boston 1899 (crit G Binz, AnglB 14.364; A Brandl, Arch 106.390).

Seaton   Seaton E, Sir Richard Roos Lancastrian Poet, London 1961 (crit H S Bennett, RES ns 13.174; P Janette, EA 14.232; D Pearsall, MLR 56.576).

Skeat Canon   Skeat W W, The Chaucer Canon, Oxford 1900.

GENERAL.

Selections Generally Available. Chalmers A, The Works of the English Poets from Chaucer to Cowper, London 1810; rptd N Y 1970, vol 1.

Morley, vols 4–6.
Oxf Ch, vol 7.
Hammond EV.
Textual Matters. Oxf Ch, 7.451.
Versification. Hammond E P, The Nine-syllabled Pentameter Line in Some Post-

Chaucerian Manuscripts, MP 23.129.

Friedman A B, Late Mediaeval Ballade and Origin of Broadside Balladry, MÆ 27.95.

Date and Authorship. Tyrwhitt T, The Canterbury Tales of Chaucer, London 1775; rptd 1822, passim.

Oxf Ch 7.ix; Hammond, p 406; Seaton, passim.

Sources and Literary Relations. Schick J, Lydgate's Temple of Glass, EETSES, London 1891, 60.cxviii.

Neilson.

Ainger A, Lectures and Essays, N Y 1905, 2.136 (influence of Chaucer on his successors).

Marsh G L, Sources and Analogues of The Flower and the Leaf, MP 4.23, 281, 319.

Lowes J L, The Prologue to The Legend of Good Women as Related to the French Marguerite Poems and the Filostrato, PMLA 19.593.

Jack A A, A Commentary on the Poetry of Chaucer and Spenser, Glasgow 1920, p 117 (apocrypha).

Kellett E E, Literary Essays, Cambridge 1928, p 1 (Chaucer's influence).

Tuve R, Seasons and Months: Studies in a Tradition of Middle English Poetry, Paris 1933, chap 4.

Bonner F W, Chaucer's Reputation During the Romantic Period, Furman Studies 34.1; The Genesis of the Chaucer Apocrypha, SP 48.461.

Seaton, passim.

Other Scholarly Problems. Sypherd W O, Studies in Chaucer's House of Fame, ChS 2s 39.

Mendenhall J C, Aureate Terms, Lancaster Pa 1919, pp 8, 46.

Whiting B J, A Fifteenth Century English

Chaucerian: The Translator of Partonope de Blois, MS 7.40.

Conley J A, Four Studies in Aureate Terms, diss Stanford 1956; DA 17.353.

Schoeck R J, Goe Little Book: A Conceit from Chaucer to Meredith, N&Q 197.370, 413.

Literary Criticism. Warton T, History of English Poetry, ed W C Hazlitt, London 1871, passim.

Oxf Ch, 1.20; 4.xxv; 7.ix; Neilson, passim.

Smith G G, The Transition Period, N Y 1900, p 22.

Skeat Canon, pp 104, 106, 113, 120 and passim.

Snell F J, The Age of Transition, London 1905, 1.1.

CHEL, 2.197.

Berdan J M, Early Tudor Poetry, N Y 1920, p 59.

Brusendorff; Lewis, p 243.

Légouis HEL, p 162; Baugh LHE, p 249; Bennett OHEL, p 124.

Moore A K, Some Implications of the Middle English Craft of Lovers, Neophil 35.231.

Robbins R H, A Love Epistle by Chaucer, MLR 49.290.

Schlauch M, English Medieval Literature, Warsaw 1956; rptd Warsaw and London 1968, p 290.

Brooke C N L, The Dullness of the Past, Liverpool 1957 (discusses courtly love).

Seaton, passim.

Pearsall D, The English Chaucerians, in Chaucer and Chaucerians, ed D S Brewer, London 1966, p 201.

Bibliography. Hammond, p 406; Utley CR, passim; CBEL, 1.250.

Griffith D D, Bibliography of Chaucer 1908–1953, Seattle 1955, pp 100, 248, 264.

1. EVOLUTION OF THE CHAUCERIAN APOCRYPHA

I. The Influence of John Shirley

MANUSCRIPTS OF JOHN SHIRLEY.

General References. Oxf Ch, 1.25.

Gaertner O, John Shirley sein Leben und Werken, Halle 1904 (crit unfavorably E P Hammond, AnglB 16.360).

Hammond E P, Omissions from the Editions of Chaucer, MLN 19.35.

Snell F J, Age of Transition, London 1905, p 3.

Hammond, p 515.

Kingsford C L, Stow's Survey of London, Oxford 1908, 2.23 (includes rimed epitaph).

Brusendorff, p 207; Hammond EV, p 191.

Baugh LHE, p 298; Bennett OHEL, p 116.

Wright C E, English Vernacular Hands, Ox-

ford 1960, p xiv.
Schirmer W F, John Lydgate, London 1961, p 251.
Doyle A I, More Light on John Shirley, MÆ 30.93.
Pearsall D, John Lydgate, London 1970, p 73.
MSS with Apocrypha in Shirley's Own Hand.
  a. Bodl 6943 (Ashmole 59) (ca 1447–56).
See under [3], [4], [6], [11].
Black W H, A Descriptive Catalogue, Oxford 1845, p 100.
Oxf Ch, 1.53.
Hammond E P, Lydgate and the Duchess of Gloucester, Angl 27.386; Ashmole 59 and Other Shirley Manuscripts, Angl 30.320.
Hammond, p 333; Brown Reg, 1.89; Brusendorff, p 209.
  b. Trinity Camb 600 (1425–50).
See under [7].
James M R, Catalogue (of Western MSS in Trinity Coll Camb), Cambridge 1901, 2.75.
Hammond E P, Lydgate's Mumming at Hertford, Angl 22.364.
Hammond, Angl 30.320.
Brown Reg, 1.240; Brussendorff, p 224.
Stow compiled BM Addit 29729 from this MS, then his property.
  c. BM Addit 16165 (ca 1425).
See under [1], [20], [35], [36], [45].
Hammond, MLN 19.35.
Hammond E P, The Departing of Chaucer, MP 1.331.
Schick J, Lydgate's Temple of Glass, EETSES, London 1891, 60.xxii, lxxii.
Brown Reg, 1.394; Brusendorff, p 207.
Facsimiles of Shirley's Script. Furnivall F J, Autotype Specimens, ChS 1s 48, plate 4.
Robinson F N, On Two Manuscripts of Lydgate's Guy of Warwick, HSNPL, Boston 1896, 5.180.
Brusendorff, p 280.
Orthography. Schick, EETSES 60.xxii; Oxf Ch, 1.76.
Rubrics. Furnivall F J, A Parallel Text Edition of Chaucer's Minor Poems, ChS 1s 21.101, 146; Supplementary Parallel Texts of Chaucer's Minor Poems, ChS 1s 22.47.
Brusendorff, pp 461, 472.
MSS with Apocrypha Showing Influence of Shirley.
  a. Trinity Camb 599 (1500–25).
See under [8], [18], [19], [21], [23], [28], [29], [30], [31], [32], [37], [40], [43], [46], [49].
Oxf Ch, 1.56; 7.lxxii.
James, Catalogue, 2.69.

Greg W W, Chaucer's Attributions, MLR 8.539.
Hammond E P, A Scribe of Chaucer's, MP 27.27.
Brown Reg, 1.239; Manly & Rickert, 1.532.
Robbins R H, A Love Epistle by Chaucer, MLR 49.289.
Seaton, p 93.
  b. Harley 2251 (1460–70).
See under [6], [7], [12], [39], [43].
A Catalogue of the Harleian Manuscripts in the British Museum, London 1808, 2.578.
Flügel E, Chaucer's kleinere Gedichte, Angl 22.511.
Hammond E P, Two British Museum Manuscripts, Angl 28.1 (in same hand as BM Addit 34360, probably derived from Trinity Camb 600).
Oxf Ch, 1.57 (corrected by Hammond, p 329).
Förster M, Shirley-Handschriften, Arch 103. 149.
Kingsford C L, Stow's Survey of London, Oxford 1908, 2.361 (corrected by Hammond, pp 329, 515).
Brown Reg, 1.315; Brusendorff, pp 181, 222.
Hammond E P, A Scribe of Chaucer's, MP 27.27.
Manly & Rickert, 1.241.
  c. Harley 7333 (9 hands; 1450–1500).
See under [5], [7], [8].
Warton T, History of English Poetry, ed W C Hazlitt, London 1871, 3.169.
Catalogue of the Harleian Manuscripts, 3.526.
Gaertner O, John Shirley sein Leben und Werken, Halle 1904, p 19.
Hammond, p 176 (with full bibliography); Brown Reg, 1.355.
Brusendorff, p 219; Manly & Rickert, 1.207.
  d. BM Addit 5467 (1450–75).
Stevenson J, Life and Death of King James I of Scotland, Maitland Club 42, Edinburgh 1837.
Brusendorff, p 213.
  e. BM Addit 34360 (1460–70).
See under [7], [43], [49].
Hammond E P, Two British Museum Manuscripts, Angl 28.1.
Brown Reg, 1.412; Brusendorff, pp 181, 222.

[1] SHIRLEY'S METRICAL INDEX, I.

MS. BM Addit 16165, ff 2ᵃ–3ᵇ (ca 1425).
Brown-Robbins, Robbins-Cutler, no 1426.
Editions. Gaertner O, John Shirley sein Leben und Werken, Halle 1904, p 63.

Brusendorff, p 453; Hammond EV, p 194.
Selections. Bennett OHEL, p 116.
General Reference. Hammond E P, Two Tapestry Poems by Lydgate, EStn 43.12n.

[2] SHIRLEY'S METRICAL INDEX, II.

MS. BM Addit 29729, ff 177b–179a (1558; copied from pages, now lost, in Trinity Camb 600).
Brown-Robbins, Robbins-Cutler, no 2598.
Editions. Brusendorff, p 456; Hammond EV, p 196.
Selections. Hammond E P, Two Tapestry Poems by Lydgate, EStn 43.12.
General References. Hammond, EStn 43.12n; Robbins SL, p xxv.

[3] SHIRLEY'S BOOK MOTTO.

MSS. 1, Bodl 6943 (Ashmole 59), f 59b (ca 1447–56); 2, Trinity Camb 600, p 361 (1425–50).
Brown-Robbins, Robbins-Cutler, no 4260.
Editions. Black W H, A Descriptive Catalogue, Oxford 1845, p 100.
Rel Ant, 2.163.
Hammond E P, Ashmole 59 and Other Shirley Manuscripts, Angl 30.329.
James M R, Catalogue (of Western MSS in Trinity Coll Camb), Cambridge 1901, 2.81 (MS 2).
Gaertner O, John Shirley sein Leben und Werken, Halle 1904, p 23.
Brusendorff, p 460.
Bennett H S, England from Chaucer to Caxton, London 1928, p 160.
Bennett OHEL, p 118; Robbins SL, p xxv.

[4] CHAUCER'S CHRONICLE or THE NINE WORSHIPFULLEST LADIES.

MS. Bodl 6943 (Ashmole 59), ff 38b–39b (ca 1447–56).
Brown-Robbins, Robbins-Cutler, no 1016.
Editions. Furnivall F J, Odd Texts of Chaucer's Minor Poems, ChS 1s 23, Appendix, p vi.
Gaertner O, John Shirley sein Leben und Werken, Halle 1904, p 66.
Date. Hammond, p 333; Utley CR, p 139.
Authorship. Furnivall F J, Trial Forewords to My Parallel-Text Edition of Chaucer's Minor Poems, ChS 2s 6.97.
Ten Brink, 3.272; Oxf Ch, 1.53; 3.lv.
Snell, The Age of Transition, London 1905, 1.4.
Brusendorff, p 236; Seaton, p 366.
Bibliography. Hammond, p 416.

[5] SELLYNG'S EVIDENCE TO BEWARE.

MS. Harley 7333, ff 26a–36b (1450–1500).
Brown-Robbins, no 4074.
Edition. Baugh A C, E&S Brown, pp 176, 168 (authorship, literary criticism).

[6] SCOGAN'S MORAL BALADE.

MSS. 1, Bodl 6943 (Ashmole 59), f 25a (ca 1447–56); 2, Camb Univ Ff.4.9, f 85a (stanzas 2–13; 15 cent); 3, Harley 367, f 86b (first stanza only; 16 cent); 4, Harley 2251, f 153b (a second copy of stanzas 2 and 3 inserted in Burgh's Cato Major at f 178b; 1460–70). PRINT: 5, [Chaucer G], The Temple of Bras [Westminster, W Caxton] (ca 1478) (STC, no 5091).
Brown-Robbins, Robbins-Cutler, no 2264.
Blades W, The Biography and Typography of William Caxton, London 1882, p 202 (PRINT 5).
Editions. Note: for full bibliographical statement of the editions here listed, see below under Black Letter Editions (section III) and Later Editions (section IV) of Chaucer with Chaucerian Apocrypha.
Thynne, Chaucer, 1532, f ccclxxxa.
Stow, Chaucer, 1561, f cccxxxivb.
Speght, Chaucer, 1598, f 334b.
Urry, Chaucer, 1721, p 546.
Bell J, Poets of Great Britain, 1782, 13.159.
Chalmers, Eng Poets, 1.552.
Oxf Ch, 7.237 (Thynne, 1542, collated with MSS 1, 4, PRINT 5).
Date. Oxf Ch, 1.83; 7.xli, 502.
Manly & Rickert, 1.240.
Authorship. Tyrwhitt T, Canterbury Tales, 1822, 1.liii.
Ritson J, Bibliographica Poetica, London 1802, p 97.
Brandl, 2¹.684.
Kittredge G L, Henry Scogan, HSNPL, Boston 1892, 1.109; Lewis Johan, PMLA 16.450.
Lange J H, Zu Scogan und The Court of Love, Arch 110.104.
Snell, Age of Transition, 1.15.
Farnham W E, John (Henry) Scogan, MLR 16.120.
Bibliography. Hammond, p 455.

[7] PRISONER'S COMPLAINT AGAINST FORTUNE.

MSS. 1, Harley 2251, f 271a (1460–70); 2, Harley 7333, f 30b (1450–1500); 3, BM Addit 34360, f 19a (1460–70).
Brown-Robbins, Robbins-Cutler, no 860.

Edition. Hammond E P, Lament of a Prisoner Against Fortune, Angl 32.484 (MS 1).
Date and Authorship. Seaton, p 207; corrected by Davis N, Paston Letters and Papers, Oxford 1971, 1.571.

Jacobs E F, The Fifteenth Century, Oxford 1961, p 485.
General References. A Parallel-Text Edition, ChS 1s 58.449.
More Odd Texts, ChS 1s 77.43.

II. Other Manuscripts Containing Chaucerian Apocrypha

General References. Flügel E, Chaucers kleinere Gedichte, Angl 22.510.
Bonner F W, The Genesis of the Chaucer Apocrypha, SP 48.473.

    a. Bodl 3354 (Arch Selden B. 24) (ca 1486).
See under [12], [24], [25].
Liddell M H, Prosperity, Athen 106(1895). 902.
Macaulay G C, Troilus and Cressida in Prof Skeat's Edition, Acad 47(1905).338.
Skeat W W, Kingis Quair, PSTS 1.xxxvii.
Brown J T T, The Authorship of the Kingis Quair, Glasgow 1896, p 72.
Oxf Ch, 1.47; 2.lxxiv.
Lawson A, The Kingis Quair, St Andrews Univ Publ, London 1910, 8.lxxvii.
Hammond, p 341.
Root R K, The Textual Tradition of Chaucer's Troilus, ChS 1s 99.27.
Summary Cat, 2^1.614; Brusendorff, p 433.
Seaton, p 215.
Scattergood V J, The Boke of Cupide An Edition, English Philological Studies 9.50.
Norton-Smith J, James I of Scotland The Kingis Quair, Oxford 1971, p xxxi.

    b. Bodl 3896 (Fairfax 16) (1425–50).
See under [13], [15], [40], [44], [46].
Warton T, History of English Poetry, ed W C Hazlitt, London 1871, 3.61.
Simmons T F, The Lay Folks Mass-Book, EETS, London 1879, 71.389n.
Hearne T, Remarks and Collections Vol 2, Oxford Hist Soc, Oxford 1885, 7.198.
Schick J, Lydgate's Temple of Glass, EETSES, London 1891, 60.xviii (facsimile p xix).
Oxf Ch, 1.51, vol 3 frntspc (facsimile).
Hammond E P, On the Editing of Chaucer's Minor Poems, MLN 23.20.
Hammond, p 333; Brusendorff, pp 182, 192.
Summary Cat, 2^2.778; Seaton, pp 83, 170, 278.
Scattergood, English Philological Studies 9.50.

    c. Bodl 8113 (Ashmole 781) (ca 1620–31).
See under [11].

    d. Bodl 9914 (Tanner 88) (added in 17 cent hand).
See under [11].

    e. Bodl 10173 (Tanner 346) (ca 1450).
See under [15].
Schick, EETSES 60.xvii.
Krauser E, The Complaint of the Black Knight, Angl 19.211.
Oxf Ch, 1.54; Hammond, p 337; Brusendorff, p 182; Seaton, p 104.
Scattergood, English Philological Studies 9.51.

    f. Bodl 12653 (Rawl C. 813) (1520–40).
See under [54], [55].
Padelford F M, The Songs of Rawlinson MS C.813, Angl 31.309.

    g. Bodl 14526 (Rawl F.32) (1450–1500).
See under [11].
Summary Cat, 3.290; Brown Reg, 1.103.

    h. Bodl Lat misc c.66 (formerly Capesthorne) (1500–35).
See under [11].
Robbins R H, The Poems of Humfrey Newton Esquire, PMLA 65.255.

    i. Camb Univ Ff.1.6 (ca 1500).
See under [41], [46].
Halliwell J O, Thornton Romances, Camden Soc, London 1844, 30.xlv.
Hammond, p 343; Brusendorff, p 187.
Casson L F, Sir Degrevant, EETS, London 1944, 221.xi.
Robbins R H, The Findern Miscellany, PMLA 69.610.
Seaton, pp 85, 107.
Scattergood V J, The Authorship of the Boke of Cupide, Angl 82.138; English Philological Studies 9.51.

    j. Camb Univ Ff.4.9 (15 cent).
See under [6].

    k. Camb Univ Gg.4.27, Ia (1400–25).
See under [38], [45].
Hammond, p 189; Brusendorff, p 200.
Caldwell R A, The Scribe of the Chaucer MS Camb Univ Gg.4.27, MLQ 5.33.
Manly and Rickert, 1.170.

    l. Camb Univ Gg.4.27, Ib (16 cent).
See under [11].

m. Camb Univ Ii.3.26 (1430–50).
See under [11].
Manly and Rickert, 1.295.

n. Camb Univ Ii.6.11 (15 cent).
See under [11].

o. Magdalene Coll Camb 1236 (Pepysian Libr) (ca 1460).
See under [11].
James M R, A Descriptive Catalogue of the Library of Samuel Pepys, London 1923, 3.8.

p. Trinity Camb 595 (ca 1480–1500, additions 1600–25).
See under [10], [11].
James M R, Catalogue (of Western MSS in Trinity Coll Camb), Cambridge 1901, 2.65.
Hammond, pp 193, 348; Manly and Rickert, 1.527.

q. Trinity Camb 601 (1470–80).
See under [39].
James, Catalogue, 2.83; Brown Reg, 1.242.

r. Camb Fitzwilliam Mus 355 (frag, added ca 1400).
See under [11], [22].
Wormald F and P M Giles, A Handlist of the Additional Manuscripts in the Fitzwilliam Museum, pt 3, Trans Camb Bibl Soc 5.367.

s. Cotton Vesp A.xii.
See under [22].

t. Harley 372 (1450–75).
See under [46].
A Catalogue of the Harleian Manuscripts in the British Museum, London 1808, 1.217.
Hammond, p 328; Brown Reg, 1.306.

u. Harley 1337.
See under [11].

v. Harley 7578 (ca 1450).
See under [26], [27], [35].
Catalogue of the Harleian Manuscripts, 3.538.
Oxf Ch, 1.58.
Hammond E P, Omissions from the Editions of Chaucer, MLN 19.38.
Hammond, p 330; Brown Reg, 1.356; Seaton, p 109.

w. Royal 17.A.xvi (15 cent).
See under [11].
Warner G F and J P Gilson, Catalogue of Western Manuscripts in the Old Royal and King's Collections, London 1921, 2.218.

x. Royal 20.B.xv (ca 1450).
See under [12]; Warner and Gilson, Catalogue, 2.367.

y. Sloane 1212 (ca 1450).
See under [45]; Seaton, p 376.
Norton-Smith J, John Lydgate Poems, Oxford 1966, p 143.

z. Sloane 1710 (17 cent).
See under [46]; Seaton, p 95.

aa. BM Addit 5465 (ca 1500).
See under [22].
Briggs H B, A Collection of Songs and Madrigals of the 15th Century, Plainsong and Medieval Music Soc Publ, 1891.
Fehr B, Die Lieder des Fairfax MS, Arch 106.48.
Hughes A, An Introduction to the Fayrfax MS, Musica Disciplina 6.83.
Greene E E Carols, p 330.
Reese G, Music in the Middle Ages, N Y 1940, p 768.
Stevens J, Music and Poetry in the Early Tudor Court, London 1961, p 351.

bb. BM Addit 10303 (1550).
See under [14], [51].

cc. BM Addit 17492 (1529–37).
See under [34], [46].
Seaton E, The Devonshire Manuscript and Its Medieval Fragments, RES ns 7.55.
Harrier R C, A Printed Source for the Devonshire MS, RES ns 11.54.
Stevens J, Music and Poetry in the Early Tudor Court, London 1961, p 405.
Southall R, The Devonshire MS Collection of Early Tudor Poetry 1532–41, RES ns 15.142.

dd. BM Addit 24663 (late 16 cent).
See under [11].
Brown Reg 1.404.

ee. BM Addit 29729 (1558).
See under [2], [9], [12].
Sieper E, Lydgate's Reson and Sensuallyte, EETSES, London 1901, 84.xiii.
Brown Reg, 1.405; Brusendorff, p 227.

ff. BM Addit 31922 (post 1511).
See under [22].
Flügel E, Liedersammlungen des XVI Jahrhunderts, besonders auf der Zeit Heinrichs VIII, Angl 12.226.
Stevens J, Music and Poetry in the Early Tudor Court, London 1961, p 388.

gg. Advocates 1.1.6 (Bannatyne) (1568).
See under [10], [12], [33], [34].
Brydges E and J Haslewood, The Bannatyne MS, The British Bibliographer, London 1814, 4.183.
Murdoch J B, ed, The Bannatyne Manuscript, 4 vols, Hunterian Club, Glasgow 1896, 1.lviii.
Ritchie W T, The Bannatyne Manuscript, PSTS 3s 5.

hh. Univ of Glasgow, Hunterian 230 (early 16 cent).
See under [54], [55].

ii. John Rylands Libr (Manchester)
Lat 201 (late 14 cent).
See under [11], [12].
Fawtier E C, From Merlin to Shakespeare,
JRLB 5.388.

jj. Longleat 256 (ca 1550).
See under [14], [51].
F N, Chaucer's Dream, N&Q 8s 1(1892).467.
Zupitza J, Zu dem Gedichte Chaucer's Dream
oder The Isle of Ladies, Arch 92.68.

kk. Longleat 258 (1460–70).
See under [46], [49].
Furnivall F J, Odd Texts of Chaucer's Minor
Poems, ChS 1s 60.251.
Historical Manuscripts Commission Report
3.188.
Schick, EETSES 60.xxiv.
Hammond E P, MS Longleat 258: A Chaucer-
ian Codex, MLN 20.77; The Eye and the
Heart, Angl 34.235.
Oxf Ch, 7.lix; Seaton, p 92.

ll. Trinity Dublin 516 (1450–75).
See under [11].
Abbot T K, Catalogue of the Manuscripts in
the Library of Trinity College Dublin,
Dublin 1900, p 78.
Robbins R H, Victory at Whitby, SP 67.495.
Harriss G L and M A Harriss, John Benet's
Chronicle, Camden Soc 4s, London 1972,
9.153.

mm. Leyden Voss 9 (1475–1500).
See under [29], [30].
Robinson F N, On Two Manuscripts of Lydgate's Guy of Warwick, HSNPL, Boston
1896, 5.187.
Brown Reg, 1.518.
van Dorsten J A, The Leyden Lydgate Manuscript, Scriptorium 14.315.

nn. Yale Univ 163 (formerly Wagstaff
9, formerly Petworth 8) (15 cent).
See under [12].
Brown Reg, 1.477; de Ricci Census, 2.1902.

oo. Egerton 2257 (19 cent transcript
by Sir Frederick Madden).
See under [20].

pp. Harley 367 (late 16 cent transcript
by John Stow).
See under [6].
A Catalogue of the Harleian Manuscripts in
the British Museum, London 1808, 1.215.

Kingsford C L, A Survey of London by John
Stow, Oxford 1908, 1. xi, xlviii, lxiii.
Brown Reg, I. 306.

qq. Royal 19. A. iii (1450–1500).
See under [47], [48].
Warner G F and J P Gilson, Catalogue of
Western Manuscripts in the Old Royal and
King's Collections, London 1921, 2. 317.

rr. Wells Cathedral fragment (early 16
cent).
See under [22].
Stevens J, Music and Poetry in the Early
Tudor Court, London 1961, p 468.

ss. N Y Public Lib Drexel 4180–4185,
Fragment 9 (early 17 cent).
See under [22].
Stevens, Music and Poetry, pp 426, 464.

[8] PRAISE AND COMMENDATION OF
CHAUCER.

MSS. 1, Trinity Camb 599, f 25[a] (1500–25);
2, Harley 7333, f 132[a] (1450–1500).
Brown-Robbins, Robbins-Cutler, no 2128.
Editions. Note: see sections III and IV below
for full bibliographical statement of the
early editions here listed.
Stow, Chaucer, 1561, f cccxxxvii[b].
Speght, Chaucer, 1598, f 339[b].
Urry, Chaucer, 1721, p 551.
Chalmers, Eng Poets, 1.556 (Stow).
Furnivall F J, A Parallel Text Edition of
Chaucer's Minor Poems, ChS 1s 21.98 (MS
2).
Oxf Ch, 7.450 (MS 1).
Literary Criticism. Oxf Ch, 7.554.
Bibliography. Skeat Canon, p 125; Hammond,
p 446.

[9] BURGH'S PRAISE OF LYDGATE.

MS. BM Addit 29729, f 6[a] (1558).
Brown-Robbins, Robbins-Cutler, no 2284.
Editions. Steele R, Lydgate's and Burgh's
Secrees of Philisoffres, EETSES, London
1894, 66.xxxi.
Förster M, Über Benedict Burghs Leben und
Werke, Arch 101.48, 47 (lists errors in
Steele), 29 (date).
Hammond EV, p 189.

III. Black Letter Editions of Chaucer
with Chaucerian Apocrypha

Pynson. Pynson R, [Chaucer's] The Boke of Fame, London 1526 (STC, no 5088) .

Dibdin T F, Typographical Antiquities, London 1810, 2.515.

Lounsbury T R, Studies in Chaucer, N Y 1892, 1.435.

Oxf Ch, 1.29; Skeat Canon, p 160; Hammond, p 114.

Thynne. Thynne W, The Workes of Geffray Chaucer Newly Printed with Dyuers Workes Whiche Were Neuer in Print Before, London 1532; rvsd 1542 (STC, nos 5068, 5069).

Skeat W W, The Works of Geoffrey Chaucer and Others, Oxford 1905 (facsimile edn).

Furnivall F J, Thynne's Animadversions, ChS 2s 13.xlii.

Maskell J, Chaucer and His First Editor, William Thynne, N&Q 6s 8(1883).381; A Bibliography of Chaucer, N&Q 6s 9(1884).141.

Lounsbury, Studies in Chaucer, 1.265, 431.

Skeat Canon, p 94; Hammond, p 116.

Stow. Stow J, The Woorkes of Geffrey Chaucer Newly Printed with Diuers Addicions Whiche Were Neuer in Printe Before, London 1561 (STC, no 5075).

Dibdin, Typographical Antiquities, 4.469.

Lounsbury, Studies in Chaucer, 1.269, 437.

Oxf Ch, 1.31; Skeat Canon, p 117.

MacCracken H N, Lydgate's Minor Poems, EETSES, London 1910, 107.xxxviii.

Hammond, p 119.

Speght. Speght T, The Workes of Our Antient and Lerned English Poet Geffrey Chaucer Newly Printed, London 1598; rvsd 1602 (STC, nos 5077, 5080).

Lounsbury, Studies in Chaucer, 1.270

Oxf Ch, 1.43; Skeat Canon, p 136; Hammond, p 122.

[10] EIGHT GOODLY QUESTIONS AND THEIR ANSWERS.

MSS. 1, Trinity Camb 595, ff 1ᵃ–2ᵃ (added 1600–25); 2, Advocates 1.1.6, f 45ᵇ and p 29 (1568).

Brown-Robbins, Robbins-Cutler, no 3183.

Editions. Note: see sections III (above) and IV (below) for full bibliographical statement of the early editions here listed.

Thynne, Chaucer, 1532 (preface, unpaginated).

Stow, Chaucer, 1561 (preface, unpaginated).

Speght, Chaucer, 1598 (prologues, unpaginated).

Urry, Chaucer, 1721, (preface, unpaginated).

Bell J, Poets of Great Britain, 1782, 1.ccxlv.

Bell R, Works of Chaucer, 4.421.

Murdoch J B, ed, The Bannatyne Manuscript, 4 vols, Hunterian Club, Glasgow 1896, 2.123 (MS 2).

Ritchie W T, Bannatyne Manuscript, PSTS ns 22.113; 3s 5.48 (MS 2).

Authorship. Skeat Canon, p 115.

Sources and Literary Relations. Todd H J, Illustrations of the Lives and Writings of Gower and Chaucer, London 1810, p 119 (for the Caxton-Thynne scraps).

Dibdin T F, Typographical Antiquities, London 1810, 1.311; 2.514 (for the Caxton-Thynne scraps).

General Reference. Oxf Ch, 7.xv.

Bibliography. Hammond, p 422.

[11] CHAUCER'S PROPHECY.

MSS. 1, Bodl 6943 (Ashmole 59), f 78ᵃ (8 lines headed Profecia Merlini, ca 1447–56); 2, Bodl 8113 (Ashmole 781), p 162 (added ca 1620–31); 3, Bodl 9914 (Tanner 88), p 253 (added in 17 cent hand); 4, Bodl 14526 (Rawl F.32), f 1ᵇ (1450–1500); 5, Bodl Lat misc c.66 (formerly Capesthorne), f 104ᵃ (1500–35); 6, Camb Univ Gg.4.27, Ib, f 4ᵇ (16 cent); 7, Camb Univ Ii.3.26, f 161ᵇ (17 cent scrap); 8, Camb Univ Ii.6.11, end flyleaf (15 cent); 9, Magdalene Coll Camb 1236 (Pepysian Libr) f 91ᵃ (ca 1460); 10, Trinity Camb 595, f 3ᵃ (added 1600–25); 11, Camb Fitzwilliam Mus 355, frag (ca 1400); 12, Harley 1337, f 105ᵇ; 13, Royal 17.A.xvi, f 27ᵇ (added on flyleaf, 15 cent); 14, BM Addit 24663, f 1ᵃ (endorsed Wrytten by Iefferae Chauser, late 15 cent); 15, John Rylands Libr (Manchester) Lat 201, f 277ᵃ (late 14 cent); 16, Trinity Dublin 516, f 118ᵃ (1450–75); 17, MS not identified: illuminated missal flyleaf. PRINT: 18, [Chaucer's Queen Anelida and False Arcite], Westminster, W Caxton, f 10ᵃ (ca 1477) (STC, no 5090).

Brown-Robbins, Robbins-Cutler, nos 3943, 3986.

Facsimile: The Story of Queen Anelida, Cambridge 1905 (PRINT 18).

D'Evelyn C, Peter Idley's Instructions to His

Son, Boston 1935, p 230 (prophecy rptd, PRINT 18).

Editions. Note: see sections III (above) and IV (below) for full bibliographical statement of the editions here listed.

Thynne, Chaucer, 1532 (preface, unpaginated).

Stow, Chaucer, 1561 (preface, unpaginated).

Speght, Chaucer, 1598 (prologues, unpaginated).

Urry, Chaucer, 1721 (preface, unpaginated, MS 2).

Bell J, Poets of Great Britain, 1782, 1.ccxlvii.

Todd H J, Illustrations of the Lives and Writings of Gower and Chaucer, London 1810, p 119 (MS 10).

Dibdin T F, Typographical Antiquities, London 1810, 1.311 (PRINT 18); 2.514 (MS 10).

Brydges E and J Haslewood, The British Bibliographer, London 1812, 2.200 (MS not identified).

British Poets, Chiswick 1822, 5.179 (with Aldine and R Bell adds 4 lines, Ora pro Anglia Sancta Maria, see Hammond, p 442).

[Pickering's] Aldine British Poets, 1845, 6.287;

rvsd edn 1866, 6.307.

Bell R, Works of Chaucer, 3.427.

Furnivall F J, Thynne's Animadversions, ChS 2s 13.xlvi (MS 1).

Gilman A, The Poetical Works of Geoffrey Chaucer, Boston 1880, 3.654.

Skeat W W, Merlin's Prophecy, Athen 108 (1896).874 (MS 1).

Oxf Ch, 1.46; 7.450 (PRINT 18); 7.lxxxi (MS 1).

Skeat Canon, p 115.

Fawtier E C, From Merlin to Shakespeare, JRLB 5.389 (MS 15).

Robbins R H, Poems of Humfrey Newton, PMLA 65.275 (MS 5).

Robbins SL, p 241 (MS 9).

Robbins-HP, p 121 (MS 16).

Literary Relations. Campbell G H, Chaucer's Prophecy in 1586, MLN 29.195.

Literary Criticism. Lounsbury T R, Studies in Chaucer, N Y 1892, 1.435.

Snell F J, The Age of Transition, London 1905, 1.11.

Fawtier, JRLB 5.388.

Bibliography. Hammond, p 447.

IV. Later Editions of Chaucer with Chaucerian Apocrypha

Urry J, The Works of Geoffrey Chaucer, London 1721.

Bell J, The Poets of Great Britain, Edinburgh 1782; rptd London 1807, vols 10–13.

Anderson R, Complete Edition of the Poets of Great Britain, Edinburgh 1793 and London 1795, vol 1.

Chalmers A, The Works of the English Poets from Chaucer to Cowper, London 1810, vol 1; rptd N Y 1970.

Todd H J, Illustrations of the Lives and Writings of Gower and Chaucer, London 1810.

The British Poets, Chiswick 1822, vols 4–5.

Moxon E, The Poetical Works of Geoffrey Chaucer, London 1843.

[Pickering's] Aldine Edition of the British Poets, London 1845; rvsd edn 1866, vols 4–6.

Bell R, Poetical Works of Geoffrey Chaucer, rvsd W W Skeat, London 1878, vols 3–4.

Oxf Ch, vol 7.

[12] WALTON'S PROSPERITY.

MSS. 1, Bodl 3354 (Arch Selden B.24), f 119[a] (ca 1486); 2, Harley 2251, f 152[b] (1460–70); 3, Royal 20.B.xv, f 1[b] (added by Shirley on flyleaf, ca 1450); 4, BM Addit 29729, f 288[b] (1558); 5, Advocates 1.1.6, p 212 (1568); 6, John Rylands Libr (Manchester) Lat 201, f 227[a] (late 14 cent); 7, Yale Univ 163 (formerly Wagstaff 9, formerly Petworth 8), f 29[a] (15 cent).

Brown-Robbins, Robbins-Cutler, no 2820, extract from no 1597 occurring separately.

Editions. [Pickering's] Aldine British Poets, 1866, 6.296 (MS 1).

Murdoch J B, ed, The Bannatyne Manuscript, Hunterian Club, Glasgow 1896, 2.204 (MS 5).

Oxf Ch, 1.47; 7.449 (MS 1).

Brusendorff, p 436 (MS 3).

Ritchie W T, Bannatyne Manuscript, PSTS ns 22.186 (MS 5).

Fawtier E C, From Merlin to Shakespeare, JRLB 5.389 (MS 6).
Lass R, Three Middle English Cautionary Lyrics, Angl 83.174 (MS 7).
Authorship. Warton T, History of English Poetry, ed W C Hazlitt, London 1871, 3.39.

Skeat W W, Walton's Version of The Former Age, Athen 99(1892).565, 600.
Liddell M H, Prosperity, Athen 106(1895).908.
Oxf Ch, 7.lxxxi; Skeat Canon, p 147.
Bibliography. Hammond, p 448.

2. APOCRYPHAL LOVE LYRICS

[13] THE LOVER'S MASS.

MS. Bodl 3896 (Fairfax 16), ff 314ᵃ–316ᵃ (1425–50).
Brown-Robbins, Robbins-Cutler, no 4186.
Editions. Simmons T F, The Lay Folks Mass-Book, EETS, London 1879, 71.390.
Hammond E P, The Lovers Mass, JEGP 7.95.
Hammond EV, p 210.
Date. Seaton, p 290.
Authorship. Hammond, JEGP 7.95.
Sources. Hammond E P, The Lovers Mass in England and in Spain, MP 14.253.
Seaton, pp 291, 293.
Literary Criticism. Brandl, 2¹.692; Neilson, p 233; Hammond EV, p 207; Chambers OHEL, p 118.

[14] BALADE TO HIS MISTRESS, FAIREST OF FAIR.

MSS. 1, BM Addit 10303, f 9ᵃ (1550); 2, Longleat 256, ff 24ᵇ–25ᵃ (1550). PRINT: 3, Speght, Chaucer, 1598, f 365ᵇ (STC, no 5077).
Brown-Robbins, Robbins-Cutler, no 923.
Editions. Note: see section IV above for full bibliographical statement of the early editions here listed.
Urry, Chaucer, 1721, p 587.
Bell J, Poets of Great Britain, 1782, 11.84.
Anderson, British Poets, 1793, 1.479.
Chalmers, Eng Poets, 1.394.
British Poets, Chiswick 1822, 5.138.
Moxon, Works of Chaucer, 1843, p 405.
[Pickering's] Aldine British Poets, 1845, 6.242; 1866, 5.153.
Bell R, Works of Chaucer, 3.508.
Sherzer J B, Ile of Ladies, Berlin 1903, p 116.
Cohen H L, The Ballade, N Y 1915, p 279.
Modernizations. Clarke C C, The Riches of Chaucer, London 1835, 2.232.
Gilman A, The Poetical Works of Geoffrey Chaucer, Boston 1880, 3.651.
Date and Authorship. Skeat Canon, p 138.
Bibliography. Hammond, p 423.

[15] BALADE AND ENVOY TO ALISON.

MSS. 1, Bodl 3896 (Fairfax 16), f 147ᵇ (1425–50); 2, Bodl 10173 (Tanner 346), f 101ᵇ (ca 1450).
Brown-Robbins, Robbins-Cutler, no 2479.
Editions. Note: see sections III and IV above for full bibliographical statement of the early editions here listed.
Thynne, Chaucer, 1532, f ccclxxixᵇ.
Stow, Chaucer, 1561, f cccxxxivᵇ.
Speght, Chaucer, 1598, f 334ᵇ.
Urry, Chaucer, 1721, p 545.
Bell J, Poets of Great Britain, 1782, 11.171.
Anderson, British Poets, 1793, 1.501.
Chalmers, Eng Poets, 1.366.
British Poets, Chiswick 1822, 5.27.
[Pickering's] Aldine British Poets, 1845, 6.128; 1866, 4.85.
Bell R, Works of Chaucer, 4.347.
Ellis F S, The Floure and the Leafe and The Cuckoo and the Nightingale, [Kelmscott Press] Hammersmith 1896.
Oxf Ch, 7.359 (MS 1).
Vollmer E, Das mittelenglische Gedicht The Boke of Cupid, Berlin 1898, p 46 (MS 2).
Modernizations. Wordsworth W, in R H Horne, The Poems of Geoffrey Chaucer Modernized, London 1841, p 52 (omits acrostic).
Gilman A, The Poetical Works of Geoffrey Chaucer, Boston 1880, 3.564.
Textual Matters. Liddell M H, Two Chaucer Notes, Acad 50(1896).116 (notes acrostic).
Oxf Ch, 1.40; 7.529; Skeat Canon, p 113.
Chewning H, The Text of the Envoy to Alison, SB 5.33.
Authorship. Oxf Ch, 7.lxii, 529; Seaton, p 284.
Literary Criticism. Oxf Ch, 7.lxii; Seaton, p 284.
Bibliography. Hammond, p 406.

[16] A GOODLY BALADE TO HIS LADY MARGARET or MOTHER OF NURTURE.

MSS. No MS extant. PRINT: Thynne, Chaucer, 1532, f ccxxxiv[b] (STC, no 5068). Brown-Robbins, Robbins-Cutler, no 2223.

Editions. Note: see sections III and IV above for full bibliographical statement of the early editions here listed.

Stow, Chaucer, 1561, f ccx[a].

Speght, Chaucer, 1598, f 210[a].

Urry, Chaucer, 1721, p 358.

Bell J, Poets of Great Britain, 1782, 13.84.

Anderson, British Poets, 1793, 1.575.

Chalmers, Eng Poets, 1.319.

British Poets, Chiswick 1822, 4.197.

[Pickering's] Aldine British Poets, 1845, 6.255; 1866, 6.275.

Bell R, Works of Chaucer, 3.413.

Oxf Ch, 7.405.

Modernization. Gilman A, The Poetical Works of Chaucer, Boston 1880, 3.565.

Authorship. Oxf Ch 7.lxx.

MacCracken H N, Lydgate's Minor Poems, EETSES, London 1910, 107.xlix.

Seaton, p 201.

Other Scholarly Problems (anagrams). Oxf Ch 7.lxxi; Seaton, p 201.

General References. Lounsbury T R, Studies in Chaucer, N Y 1892, 1.479.

Oxf Ch, 7.lxx; Skeat Canon, p 109.

Bibliography. Hammond, p 440.

[17] TO MY SOVEREIGN LADY.

MSS. No MS extant. PRINT: Thynne, Chaucer, 1532, f ccclxxiv[b] (STC, no 5068). Brown-Robbins, Robbins-Cutler, no 1309.

Editions. Note: see sections III and IV above for full bibliographical statement of the early editions here listed.

Stow, Chaucer, 1561, f cccxxx[a].

Speght, Chaucer, 1598, f 330[a].

Urry, Chaucer, 1721, p 539.

Bell J, Poets of Great Britain, 1782, 13.91.

Anderson, British Poets, 1793, 1.576.

Chalmers, Eng Poets, 1.547.

Oxf Ch, 7.281.

Date. Seaton, p 286.

Authorship. Tyrwhitt T, Canterbury Tales, London 1822, 1.li.

Oxf Ch, 7.lxvii; Skeat Canon, p 103.

MacCracken H N, EETSES, London 1910, 107.xlviii.

Seaton, p 285.

Sources and Literary Relations. Seaton, p 287.

Literary Criticism. Stillwell G, Chaucer's Eagles and Their Choice on February 14, JEGP 53.554.

Woolf R, The English Religious Lyric in the Middle Ages, Oxford 1968, p 278.

Bibliography. Hammond, pp 410, 460.

[18] EPISTLE TO HIS MISTRESS, SIGNED CHAUCER.

MS. Trinity Camb 599, f 160[b] (1500–25). Brown-Robbins, Robbins-Cutler, no 1838.

Editions. Person H A, Cambridge Middle English Lyrics, Seattle 1953; rvsd 1962, p 14 (crit R L Greene, Spec 29.602).

Robbins R H, A Love Epistle by Chaucer, MLR 49.290.

Wilson K G, Five Unpublished Secular Love Poems from Trinity College Cambridge 599, Angl 72.385.

Literary Relations. Robbins, MLR 49.289.

[19] PRAISE OF MARGARET THE DAISY.

MS. Trinity Camb 599, f 160[a] (1500–25). Brown-Robbins, Robbins-Cutler, no 1562.

Editions. Note: see sections III and IV above for full bibliographical statement of the early editions here listed.

Stow, Chaucer, 1561, f cccxliii[a].

Speght, Chaucer, 1598, f 343[a].

Urry, Chaucer, 1721, p 556.

Bell J, Poets of Great Britain, 1782, 13.125.

Anderson, British Poets, 1793, 1.584.

Chalmers, Eng Poets, 1.562.

Modernization. Clarke C C, The Riches of Chaucer, London 1835, 2.311.

Date. Skeat Canon, p 123.

Authorship. Oxf Ch, 7.13.

Bibliography. Hammond, p 428.

[20] WARWICK'S VIRELAI.

MSS. 1, BM Addit 16165, ff 245[b]–246[b] (ca 1425); 1a, Egerton 2257, ff 15[a]–16[b] (19 cent transcript). Brown-Robbins, Robbins-Cutler, no 1288.

Edition. MacCracken H N, The Earl of Warwick's Virelai, PMLA 22.605.

Authorship. Seaton, p 233.

Literary Criticism. Brusendorff, p 208.

[21] VIRELAI.

MS. Trinity Camb 599, f 160[a] (1500–25). Brown-Robbins, Robbins-Cutler, no 267.

Editions. Note: see sections III and IV above for full bibliographical statement of the early editions here listed.

Stow, Chaucer, 1561, f cccxliii[a].

Speght, Chaucer, 1598, f 343[a].

Urry, Chaucer, 1721, p 555.

Bell J, Poets of Great Britain, 1782, 13.123.
Anderson, British Poets, 1793, 1.584.
Godwin W, Life of Geoffrey Chaucer, London 1803, 2.356.
Chalmers, Eng Poets, 1.562.
British Poets, Chiswick 1822, 5.178.
Moxon, Works of Chaucer, 1843, p 439.
[Pickering's] Aldine British Poets, 1845, 6.286; 1866, 6.305.
Bell R, Works of Chaucer, 3.426.
Wülcker R P, Altenglisches Lesebuch, Halle 1874, 2.119.
Morley 5.271; Oxf Ch, 7.448.
Ch&Sidg, p 27; Robbins SL, p 162.
Kaiser R, Alt- und mittelenglische Anthologie, Berlin 1955, p 297.
Kaiser R, Medieval English, Berlin 1958, p 470.
Davies R T, Medieval English Lyrics, London 1963, p 255.
Modernizations. Clarke C C, The Riches of Chaucer, London 1835, 2.310.
Gilman A, The Poetical Works of Geoffrey Chaucer, Boston 1880, 3.652.
Versification. Schipper, 1.365.
Authorship. Tyrwhitt T, Canterbury Tales, London 1822, 1.lvii.
Godwin, Life of Chaucer, 2.356.
Oxf Ch, 7.lxxx; Skeat, Canon, p 122.
Snell F J, Age of Transition, London 1905, 1.7.
Literary Relations. Southall R, The Courtly Maker, N Y 1964, pp 7, 138.
Literary Criticism. Seaton, p 402.
Bibliography. Hammond, p 461.

[22] EARL RIVERS' VIRELAI ON FICKLE FORTUNE.

MSS. 1, Camb Fitzwilliam Mus 355, unnumbered fragment (early 15 cent); 2, Cotton Vesp A.xii, f 170ᵇ; 3, BM Addit 5465, ff 34ᵃ–35ᵇ (1500–50); 4, BM Addit 31922, f 120ᵇ. (ca 1515); 5, Wells Cath, fragment (early 16 cent); 6, N Y Public Libr Drexel fragments, no 9 (early 17 cent).
Robbins-Cutler, no 3193.5.
Editions. Hearne T, Rossi Warwicensis Historia Regum Angliae, Oxford 1716, p 214 (MS 2).
Smith J S, A Collection of English Songs, London 1779, no 9 (MS 3).
Percy T, Reliques of Ancient English Poetry, 4th edn, London 1839, 2.46 (MS 2).
Turner S, History of England, London 1814, 3.465 (MS 2).
The Chronicles of the White Rose, London 1845, p 209 (MS 2).

Ritson AS, p 149 (MS 3).
Flügel E, Liedersammlungen des XVI Jahrhunderts, Anglia 12.254 (MS 4).
Arber E, The Dunbar Anthology, London 1901, p 180 (MS 3).
Stevens J, Music and Poetry in the Early Tudor Court, London 1961, pp 361 (MS 3), 423 (MS 4), 427 (MS 6).
Stevens J, Music at the Court of Henry VIII, Musica Britannica XVIII, London 1961, p 90 (MS 4).
Authorship. Berdan J M, Early Tudor Poetry, N Y 1920, p 150.
Literary Criticism. Snell F J, The Age of Transition, London 1905, 1.8; Berdan, p 150.
General References. Bentley S, Excerpta Historica, London 1831, p 244.
Percy, Reliques, 2.45; Seaton, p 430.

[23] O MERCIFUL AND O MERCIABLE.

MS. Trinity Camb 599, f 161ᵃ (1500–25).
Brown-Robbins, Robbins-Cutler, no 2510.
Editions. Note: see sections III and IV above for full bibliographical statement of the early editions here listed.
Stow, Chaucer, 1561, f cccxliiiᵇ.
Speght, Chaucer, 1598, f 343ᵇ.
Urry, Chaucer, 1721, p 556.
Bell J, Poets of Great Britain, 1782, 13.127.
Anderson, British Poets, 1793, 1.585.
Chalmers, Eng Poets, 1.562.
Language. Skeat Canon, p 123.
Versification. Oxf Ch, 7.xiii.
Authorship. Tyrwhitt T, Canterbury Tales, London 1822, 1.lvii.
Bibliography. Hammond, p 442.

[24] THE LOVER'S COMPLAINT AGAINST FORTUNE AND HIS LADY.

MS. Bodl 3354 (Arch Selden B.24), ff 219ᵃ–221ᵇ (ca 1486).
Brown-Robbins, Robbins-Cutler, no 564.
Edition. Wilson K G, The Lay of Sorrow and The Lufaris Complaynt: An Edition, Spec 29.719.
Textual Matters. Wilson, Spec 29.725.
General Reference. Wilson, Spec 29.708.

[25] THE LAY OF SORROW.

MS. Bodl 3354 (Arch Selden B.24), ff 217ᵃ–219ᵃ (ca 1486).
Brown-Robbins, Robbins-Cutler, no 482.
Edition. Wilson K G, The Lay of Sorrow and The Lufaris Complaynt: An Edition, Spec 29.716.

Textual Matters. Wilson, Spec 29.723.
General References. Wilson, Spec 29.708;
   Seaton, p 225.

[26] COMPLAINT TO MY MORTAL FOE.

MS. Harley 7578, f 15ᵃ (ca 1450).
Brown-Robbins, Robbins-Cutler, no 231.
Editions. Skeat W W, Complaint to My Mortal Foe, Athen 104(1894).98.
Oxford Ch, 4.xxvii.
Skeat W W, The Minor Poems, Oxford 1888;
   rvsd edn 1896, p 468.
Authorship. Kittredge G L, Skeat's Chaucer, Nation 60(1895).240.
Oxf Ch, 4.xxvii.
Skeat, Minor Poems, p 463.
Skeat Canon, pp 64, 148.
General Reference. Seaton, p 429.
Bibliography. Hammond, p 417.

[27] COMPLAINT TO MY LODESTAR.

MS. Harley 7578, f 15ᵇ (ca 1450).
Brown-Robbins, Robbins-Cutler, no 2626.
Editions. Skeat W W, Complaint to My Lodestar, Athen 104(1894).162.
Oxf Ch, 4.xxix.
Skeat, Minor Poems, p 470.
Authorship. Kittredge G L, Skeat's Chaucer, Nation 60(1895).240.
Skeat Canon, pp 64, 148.
General References. Chiarenza F J, Chaucer and the Medieval Amorous Complaint, diss Yale 1956 (cited on p 143 of Index for DA 16).
Seaton, p 429.
Bibliography. Hammond, p 417.

[28] THE NINE LADIES WORTHY.

MS. Trinity Camb 599, ff 110ᵇ–111ᵃ (1500–25).
Brown-Robbins, Robbins-Cutler, no 2767.
Editions. Note: see sections III and IV above for full bibliographical statement of the early editions here listed.
Stow, Chaucer, 1561, f cccxliiᵇ.
Speght, Chaucer, 1598, f 342ᵇ.
Urry, Chaucer, 1721, p 555.
Bell J, Poets of Great Britain, 1782, 13.121.
Anderson, British Poets, 1793, 1.583.
Chalmers, Eng Poets, 1.561.
Sources and Literary Relations. Oxf Ch, 7.xii;
   Skeat Canon, p 122; Utley CR, p 224.
Bibliography. Hammond, p 441.

[29] THE JUDGMENT OF PARIS.

MSS. 1, Trinity Camb 599, f 161ᵇ (1500–25);

2, Leyden Voss 9, f 111ᵇ (15 cent).
Brown-Robbins, Robbins-Cutler, no 3197.
Editions. Note: see sections III and IV above for full bibliographical statement of the early editions here listed.
Stow, Chaucer, 1561, f cccxlivᵃ.
Speght, Chaucer, 1598, f 344ᵃ.
Urry, Chaucer, 1721, p 557.
Bell J, Poets of Great Britain, 1782, 13.130.
Anderson, British Poets, 1793, 1.585.
Chalmers, Eng Poets, 1.563.
van Dorsten J A, The Leyden Lydgate Manuscript, Scriptorium 14.325 (MS 2).
Authorship. Skeat Canon, p 123.
Bibliography. Hammond, p 427.

[30] THE DESCRIBING OF A FAIR LADY.

MSS. 1, Trinity Camb 599, ff 205ᵃ–205ᵇ (1500–25); 2, Leyden Voss 9, f 110ᵇ (15 cent).
Brown-Robbins, Robbins-Cutler, no 1300.
Editions. Note: see sections III and IV above for full bibliographical statement of the early editions here listed.
Stow, Chaucer, 1561, f cccxlivᵃ.
Speght, Chaucer, 1598, f 344ᵃ.
Urry, Chaucer, 1721, p 557.
Bell J, Poets of Great Britain, 1782, 13.131.
Anderson, British Poets, 1793, 1.586.
Chalmers, Eng Poets, 1.563.
Person H A, Cambridge Middle English Lyrics, Seattle 1953; rvsd 1962, p 38.
van Dorsten J A, The Leyden Lydgate Manuscript, Scriptorium 14.324 (MS 2).
Date. Seaton, p 409.
Literary Relations. Kitchin G, A Survey of Burlesque and Parody in English, Edinburgh 1931, p 20.
Literary Criticism. Robinson F N, On Two Manuscripts of Lydgate's Guy of Warwick, HSNPL, Boston 1896, 5.188, 193.
Skeat Canon, p 123.
General References. Utley CR, p 147; Person, Lyrics, p 78.
Bibliography. Hammond, p 428.

[31] O MOSSIE QUINCE.

MS. Trinity Camb 599, ff 205ᵇ–206ᵃ (1500–25).
Brown-Robbins, Robbins-Cutler, no 2524.
Editions. Note: see sections III and IV above for full bibliographical statement of the early editions here listed.
Stow, Chaucer, 1561, f cccxlivᵇ.
Speght, Chaucer, 1598, f 344ᵇ.
Urry, Chaucer, 1721, p 558.
Bell J, Poets of Great Britain, 1782, 13.133.
Anderson, British Poets, 1793, 1.586.

Chalmers, Eng Poets, 1.564.
Skeat Canon, p 124.
Person H A, Cambridge Middle English
Lyrics, Seattle 1953; rvsd 1962, p 40.
Authorship. Skeat Canon, pp 118, 124; Utley
CR, p 213.
Literary Criticism. Seaton, p 415.
Bibliography. Hammond, p 442.

[32] BALADE AGAINST HYPOCRITICAL
WOMEN.

MS. Trinity Camb 599, f 156ᵇ (1500-25).
Brown-Robbins, Robbins-Cutler, no 2661.
Editions. Note: see sections III and IV above
for full bibliographical statement of the
early editions here listed.
Stow, Chaucer, 1561, f cccxliᵇ.
Speght, Chaucer, 1598, f 341ᵇ.
Urry, Chaucer, 1721, p 553.
Bell J, Poets of Great Britain, 1782, 13.115.
Anderson, British Poets, 1793, 1.582.
Chalmers, Eng Poets, 1.560.
Modernization. Clarke C C, The Riches of
Chaucer, London 1835, 2.313.
General References. Oxf Ch, 7.xii; Skeat
Canon, p 122; Utley CR, p 221; Seaton, p
411.
Bibliography. Hammond, p 441.

[33] A PRAISE OF WOMEN.

MSS. 1, Advocates 1.1.6, ff 275ᵃ-276ᵇ (1568).
PRINT: 2, Thynne, Chaucer, 1532, f cccxiᵇ
(STC, no 5068).
Brown-Robbins, Robbins-Cutler, no 228.
Editions. Note: see sections III and IV above
for full bibliographical statement of the
early editions here listed.
Stow, Chaucer, 1561, f cclxxviᵇ.
Speght, Chaucer, 1598, f 276ᵇ.
Urry, Chaucer, 1721, p 456.
Bell J, Poets of Great Britain, 1782, 10.127.
Anderson, British Poets, 1793, 1.444.
Chalmers, Eng Poets, 1.334.
British Poets, Chiswick 1822, 4.295.
[Pickering's] Aldine British Poets, 1845, 6.35;
1866, 6.278.
Bell R, Works of Chaucer, 4.416.
Murdoch J B, ed, The Bannatyne Manu-
script, 4 vols, Hunterian Club, Glasgow
1896, 4.799 (MS 1).
Ritchie W T, Bannatyne Manuscript, PSTS
ns 26.64 (MS 1).
Modernization. Gilman A, The Poetical
Works of Geoffrey Chaucer, Boston 1880,
3.568.
Authorship. Tyrwhitt T, Canterbury Tales,

London 1822, 1.lvi.
Oxf Ch, 7.x; Skeat Canon, p 111.
Literary Criticism. Seaton, p 411.

[34] THE REMEDY OF LOVE.

MSS. 1, Advocates 1.1.6, f 258ᵇ (two extracts
comprising lines 239-45 and stanzas 20-29,
38, 35); 2, BM Addit 17492, f 90ᵃ (extract
comprising lines 239-45). PRINT: 3,
Thynne, Chaucer, 1532, f ccclxvᵇ (STC, no
5068).
Brown-Robbins, Robbins-Cutler, no 3084;
Robbins-Cutler, nos 1409.3, 3648.8.
Murdoch J B, ed, The Bannatyne Manu-
script, 4 vols, Hunterian Club Glasgow
1896, 4. 755 (MS 1).
Ritchie W T, The Bannatyne Manuscript,
PSTS ns 26.23, 24 (MS 1).
Muir K, Unpublished Poems in the Devon-
shire MS, Leeds Philosophical and Literary
Soc Proc 6.278 (MS 2).
Mason H A, Humanism and Poetry in the
Early Tudor Period, London 1959, p 52.
Editions. Note: see sections III and IV above
for full bibliographical statement of the
early editions here listed.
Thynne, Chaucer, 1532; rptd in facsimile W
W Skeat, London 1905, f ccclxvᵇ.
Stow, Chaucer, 1561, f cccxxiᵇ.
Speght, Chaucer, 1598, f 321ᵇ.
Urry, Chaucer, 1721, p 526.
Bell J, Poets of Great Britain, 1782, 12.157.
Anderson, British Poets, 1793, 1.550.
Chalmers, Eng Poets, 1.538.
Authorship. Tyrwhitt T, Canterbury Tales,
London 1822, 1.lvi.
Morley, 5.144.
Other Scholarly Problems. Linn I, If All the
Sky Were Parchment, PMLA 53.951.
Seaton, p 414.
General References. Skeat Canon, p 113;
Utley CR, p 228.
Bibliography. Hammond, p 450; Utley CR,
pp 263, 157 (extracts).

[35] BALADE BY CHAUCER.

MSS. 1, Harley 7578, ff 15ᵃ-15ᵇ (ca 1450); 2,
BM Addit 16165, ff 244ᵃ-244ᵇ (ca 1425).
Brown-Robbins, Robbins-Cutler, no 1635.
Editions. Furnivall F J, Balade by Chaucer,
Athen 57(1871).210 (stanzas 1 and 2, MS 2).
Furnivall F J, Jyl of Breyntford's Testament
and Other Poems, London 1871, p 34 (MS
2).
Hammond E P, Omissions from the Editions
of Chaucer, MLN 19.38 (MS 2).

Brusendorff, p 280 (MSS 1 and 2).
Literary Criticism. Brusendorff, pp 278, 282.
General References. Utley CR, p 170; Seaton,
p 413.

[36] THE PLOWMAN'S SONG.

MS. BM Addit 16165, ff 244^b–245^a (ca 1425).

Brown-Robbins, Robbins-Cutler, no 2611.
Editions. Furnivall F J, Jyl of Breyntford's
Testament and Other Poems, London 1871,
p 35.
Hammond E P, Omissions from the Editions
of Chaucer, MLN 19.37.

3. COURTLY LOVE AUNTERS

[37] THE COURT OF LOVE.

MS. Trinity Camb 599, ff 217^a–234^a (1500–25).
Brown-Robbins, Robbins-Cutler, no 4205.
Editions. Note: see sections III and IV above
for full bibliographical statement of the
early editions here listed.
Stow, Chaucer, 1561, f cccxlviii^a.
Speght, Chaucer, 1598, f 348^a.
Urry, Chaucer, 1721, p 560.
Bell J, Poets of Great Britain, 1782, 12.105.
Anderson, British Poets, 1793, 1.538.
Chalmers, Eng Poets, 1.367.
British Poets, Chiswick 1822, 5.28.
Moxon, Works of Chaucer, 1843, p 333.
[Pickering's] Aldine British Poets, 1845, 6.130;
1866, 4.1.
Bell R, Works of Chaucer, 4.280.
Oxf Ch, 7.409.
Selection. Ward T, Selections from the Eng-
lish Poets, Oxford 1880, rptd N Y 1924,
1.88.
Modernizations. Maynwaring A, Ovid's Art
of Love, London 1709.
Catcott A S, The Court of Love, Oxford 1717
(in heroic couplets).
Purves D L, The Canterbury Tales and The
Faerie Queene and Other Poems by
Chaucer and Spenser, Edinburgh 1870.
Gilman A, The Poetical Works of Geoffrey
Chaucer, Boston 1880, 3.476.
Language. Hochdörfer K F R, Observations
on the Language of the Court of Love, diss
Harvard 1888.
Lounsbury T R, Studies in Chaucer, N Y
1892, 1.497.
Oxf Ch, 7.lxxvii, 540; Skeat Canon, pp 125,
127.
Date. Arnold T, The Date of The Court of
Love, Acad 13(1878).489; 14(1878).66.
Skeat W W, The Court of Love, Acad 13
(1878).512; The Court of Love, Acad 35
(1889).431.
Neilson, p 2.

Fraser R A, The Court of Venus, Durham
N C 1955, p 30.
Seaton, pp 443, 447.
Authorship. Tyrwhitt T, Canterbury Tales,
London 1822, 1.xliv.
Godwin W, Life of Geoffrey Chaucer, Lon-
don 1803, 1.205.
Ten Brink B, Chaucer: Studien zur Geschichte
seiner Entwicklung und zur Chronologie
seiner Schriften, Münster 1870, p 168.
Furnivall F J, The Court of Love and
Chaucer, Acad 2(1870).60.
Waring G, The Court of Love and Chaucer,
Acad 2(1870).61 (reply to Furnivall).
Hall A, Chaucer Restored, N&Q 4s 9(1872)
.32, 70, 109, 155.
Furnivall F J, Note on Chaucer, N&Q 4s 9
(1872).71, 110, 156.
Skeat W W, The Court of Love, Athen 68
(1876).592, 698.
Furnivall F J, Chaucer, Athen 69(1877).417,
512.
Minto W, Chaucer, Athen 69(1877).447.
Swinburne A C, The Court of Love, Athen
69(1877).481.
Furnivall F J, Skeat and Bell's Chaucer, Acad
13(1878).365.
Skeat W W, The Court of Love, Acad 14
(1878).116; Acad 35(1889).431; A Few More
Words on The Court of Love, Acad 40
(1891).56.
Court of Love, Acad 40(1891).56.
Schick J, Lydgate's Temple of Glass, EETSES,
London 1891, 60.cxxix.
Kittredge G L, Henry Scogan, HSNPL, Bos-
ton 1892, 1.109.
Lounsbury T R, Studies in Chaucer, N Y
1892, 1.125.
Morley, 5.125.
Brown J T T, Authorship of the Kingis
Quair, Glasgow 1896, pp 31, 84.
Brandl, 2¹.684; Oxf Ch, 7.lxxv.
Skeat Canon, p 125.
Lange J H, Zu Scogan und The Court of

Love, Arch 110.104.
Piaget A, La cour amoureuse dite de Charles VI, Rom 20.417.
Lowes J L, The Prologue to The Legend of Good Women Considered in Its Chronological Relations, PMLA 20.794.
Seaton, pp 443, 449, 456.
Sources and Literary Relations. Neilson, p 228.
Schick J, EETSES, London 1891, 60.cxxix.
McKenzie W, The Kingis Quair, London 1939, p 32.
Seaton, pp 450, 453.
Wimsatt J, Chaucer and the French Love Poets, Chapel Hill N C 1968, p 65 (Messe des oisiaus).
Literary Criticism. Neilson, p 1 (most complete discussion of poem).
CHEL, 2.220.
Berdan J M, Early Tudor Poetry, N Y 1920, p 68.
Bennett OHEL, pp 136, 303; Seaton, p 450.
Lewis C S, English Literature in the Sixteenth Century, Oxford 1954, p 240.
Pearsall D, The English Chaucerians, in Chaucer and Chaucerians, ed D S Brewer, London 1966, p 229.
General References. Sandras E C, Étude sur Chaucer, Paris 1859, p 56.
Bell R, Works of Chaucer, 4.260.
Rajna P, Le Corti d'Amore, Milan 1890, passim.
Rowbotham J F, The Troubadours and the Court of Love, London 1895, passim.
Courthope, p 358.
Mott L F, The System of Courtly Love, Boston 1896, passim.
Oxf Ch, 7.lxxii.
Campbell T, Specimens of the British Poets, London 1819, 11.15.
Snell F J, The Age of Transition, London 1905, 1.9.
Kitchin G, A Survey of Burlesque and Parody in English, Edinburgh 1931, pp 6, 21.
Lewis, p 256.
Fraser R A, The Court of Venus, Durham N C 1955, passim.
Ferguson A B, The Indian Summer of English Chivalry, Durham N C 1960, p 64.
Stevens J, Music and Poetry in the Early Tudor Court, London 1961, p 190.
Pearsall D, John Lydgate, London 1970, p 110.
Bibliography. Hammond, p 418.

[38] BIRDS' PRAISE OF LOVE.

MS. Camb Univ Gg.4.27, Ia, ff 8^b–10^b (1400–25).

Brown-Robbins, Robbins-Cutler, no 1506.
Editions. Bradshaw H, n p 1864 (privately printed).
Ellis A J, Early English Pronunciation, EETSES, London 1869, 7.463.
ChS 2s 4.463 (first two stanzas only).
Hammond E P, A Parliament of Birds, JEGP 7.105.
Date. Seaton, pp 290, 289 (sources and literary relations), 288 (literary criticism).

[39] BIRDS' DEVOTIONS.

MSS. 1, Trinity Camb 601, ff 196^b–197^a, 246^a (1470–80); 2, Harley 2251, ff 36^b–37^b (1460–70).
Brown-Robbins, no 357.
Editions. Halliwell J O, Minor Poems of Lydgate, PPS 2.78 (MS 2).
MacCracken H N, Lydgatiana, Arch 130.310 (MS 2).
General Reference. Neilson, p 226.

[40] THE TEN COMMANDMENTS OF LOVE.

MSS. 1, Bodl 3896 (Fairfax 16), ff 184^a–186^b (added in 17 cent hand on blank leaves); 2, Trinity Camb 599, ff 109^a–110^a (1500–25).
Brown-Robbins, Robbins-Cutler, no 590.
Editions. Note: see sections III and IV above for full bibliographical statement of the early editions here listed.
Stow, Chaucer, 1561, f cccxlii^a.
Speght, Chaucer, 1598, f 342^a.
Urry, Chaucer, 1721, p 554.
Bell J, Poets of Great Britain, 1782, 13.117.
Anderson, British Poets, 1793, 1.582.
Chalmers, Eng Poets, 1.560.
Robbins SL, p 165.
Date. Oxf Ch, 7.xix; Skeat Canon, p 122 (corrected by Hammond, p 334).
Literary Relations. Seaton, p 383.
General Reference. Neilson, p 207.
Bibliography. Hammond, p 457.

[41] THE PARLIAMENT OF LOVE.

MS. Camb Univ Ff.1.6, ff 51^a–53^b (ca 1500).
Brown-Robbins, Robbins-Cutler, no 2383.
Editions. Furnivall F J, Political Religious and Love Poems, EETS, London 1866, 15.48 (original edn); 15.76 (rvsd edn).
Wülcker R P, Altenglisches Lesebuch, Halle 1879, 2.124.
Literary Criticism. Neilson, p 158; Seaton, p 227.

[42] THE COURT OF VENUS.

MSS. No MS extant. Three separate frag-

ments: PRINT 1, Douce g.3, 15 folios; PRINT 2, Folger Shakesp Libr, 8 folios (includes title page); PRINT 3, Univ of Texas (Stark Collection, formerly Christie-Miller fragment), 2 folios.
Not listed in Brown-Robbins, Robbins-Cutler.
Editions. Griffith R H and R A Law, A Boke of Balattes and The Courte of Venus, Texas SE 10.1.
Fraser R A, The Court of Venus, Durham N C 1955.
Selection. Furnivall F J, Thynne's Animadversions, ChS 2s 13.138.
Date. Lounsbury T R, Studies in Chaucer, N Y 1892, 1.462.
Authorship. Stopes C C, The Metrical Psalms and The Court of Venus, Athen 113(1899). 784; The Authorship of the Newe Court of Venus, Athen 114(1899).38.
Literary Relations. Gregor W, Ane Treatise Callit The Court of Venus, PSTS 3 (for Rolland's Court of Venus).
Literary Criticism. Seaton, p 505.
Stevens J, Music and Poetry in the Early Tudor Court, London 1961, p 190.
Southall R, The Courtly Maker, N Y 1904, p 142.
Bibliography. Hammond, p 443; Griffith and Law, Texas SE 10.6 ftnt.

[43] THE CRAFT OF LOVERS.

MSS. 1, Trinity Camb 599, ff 154ᵇ–156ᵃ (1500–25); 2, Harley 2251, ff 53ᵃ–55ᵇ (1460–70); 3, BM Addit 34360, ff 73ᵇ–76ᵇ (1460–70).
Brown-Robbins, Robbins-Cutler, no 3761.
Editions. Note: see sections III and IV above for full bibliographical statement of the early editions here listed.
Stow, Chaucer, 1561, f cccxliᵃ.
Speght, Chaucer, 1598, f 341ᵃ.
Urry, Chaucer, 1721, p 552.
Bell J, Poets of Great Britain, 1782, 13.110.
Anderson, British Poets, 1793, 1.581.
Chalmers, Eng Poets, 1.558.
Date. Skeat W W, The Craft of Lovers, Acad 33(1888).152.
Authorship. Tyrwhitt T, Canterbury Tales, London 1822, 1.lvii.
Morley, 5.144; Skeat Canon, p 120; Hammond, p 420.
MacCracken H N, Lydgate's Minor Poems, EETSES, London 1910, 107.lxiii.
Schirmer W F, John Lydgate, Tübingen 1952, p 236; trans A E Keep, London 1961, p 275.
Literary Criticism. Moore A K, Some Implications of the Middle English Craft of Lovers, Neophil 35.231; The Secular Lyric in

Middle English, Lexington Ky 1951, p 122.
Robbins R H, A Love Epistle by Chaucer, MLR 49.290.
Seaton, p 183.
Bibliography. Hammond, p 420; Bennett OHEL, p 304.

[44] HOW A LOVER PRAISETH HIS LADY.

MS. Bodl 3896 (Fairfax 16), ff 306ᵃ–312ᵇ (1425–50).
Brown-Robbins, Robbins-Cutler, no 4043.
Edition. Hammond E P, How a Lover Praiseth His Lady, MP 21.384.
Sources and Literary Relations. Seaton, p 136.
Literary Criticism. Hammond, MP 21.379; Seaton, p 132.

[45] SUPPLICACIO AMANTIS.

MSS. 1, Camb Univ Gg.4.27, Ia, ff 509ᵇ–516ᵇ (lines 1–254, 331–562 only) (1400–25); 2, Sloane 1212, ff 4ᵃ–4ᵇ (lines 439–505 only) (ca 1450); 3, BM Addit 16165, ff 231ᵃ–241ᵇ (lacks lines 157–76) (ca 1425).
Brown-Robbins, Robbins-Cutler, no 147.
Edition. Schick J, Lydgate's Temple of Glass, EETSES, London 1891, 60.59 (composite text).
Textual Matters. Schick, EETSES 60.123.
Authorship. Seaton, pp 372, 370, 374 (literary criticism).

[46] LA BELLE DAME SANS MERCY.

MSS. 1, Bodl 3896 (Fairfax 16), ff 50ᵃ–62ᵇ (1425–50); 2, Camb Univ Ff.1.6, ff 117ᵃ–134ᵇ (ca 1500); 3, Trinity Camb 599, ff 98ᵃ–108ᵇ (1500–25); 4, Harley 372, ff 61ᵃ–69ᵇ (stanzas disarranged) (1450–75); 5, Sloane 1710, ff 164ᵃ–176ᵇ (lines 93–140, 191–764 only) (17 cent); 6, BM Addit 17492, f 29ᵇ (lines 717–24), f 30ᵃ (lines 229–36) (1529–37); 7, Longleat 258, ff 120ᵃ–136ᵇ (1460–70).
Brown-Robbins, Robbins-Cutler, no 1086.
Editions. Note: see sections III and IV above for full bibliographical statement of the early editions here listed.
Pynson R, [Chaucer's] The Boke of Fame, 1526 (STC, no 5088) (with Lenvoy de limprimeur, 6 added rime royal stanzas; printed Hammond, p 432).
Thynne, Chaucer, 1532, f cclxxxviᵇ; [for] J Reynes, 1542 (STC, no 5070).
Stow, Chaucer, 1561, f cclᵃ.
Speght, Chaucer, 1598, f 250ᵃ.
Urry, Chaucer, 1721, p 422.
Bell J, Poets of Great Britain, 1782, 10.133.
Anderson, British Poets, 1793, 1.446.

Todd H J, Illustrations of the Lives and Writings of Gower and Chaucer, London 1810, p 296.

Chalmers, Eng Poets, 1.518.

Furnivall F J, Political Religious and Love Poems, EETS, London 1866, 15.52 (original edn of MS 4); 15.80 (rvsd edn of MS 2, collated with MSS 3 and 4).

Oxf Ch, 7.299 (Thynne, collated with MSS 1 and 4).

Versification. Schipper, 1.366.

Date. Dibdin T F, Typographical Antiquities, London 1810, 2.517.

Skeat Canon, p 106; Brusendorff, p 191.

Authorship. Tyrwhitt T, Canterbury Tales, London 1822, 1.lii.

Gröhler H, Über Richard Ros' mittelenglische Übersetzung des Gedichtes von Alain Chartiers La belle dame sans merci, Breslau 1886; Zu Richard Ros, EStn 10.206.

Oxf Ch, 7.li.

Snell F J, The Age of Transition, London 1905, 1.12.

Berdan J M, Early Tudor Poetry, N Y 1920, p 50.

Brusendorff, p 189; Seaton, p 80.

Jacob E F, The Fifteenth Century, Oxford 1961, p 485.

Sources and Literary Relations. Piaget A, La belle dame sans merci et ses imitations, Rom 30.22, 317; 31.315; 33.179; 34.375, 559.

Neilson, p 85.

Timmer B J, La belle dame sans merci, EStn 11.20 (on source of "faire rewtheless").

Hoffman E J, Alain Chartier His Work and Reputation, N Y 1942, pp 52, 80.

Piaget A, La belle dame sans mercy et les poésies lyriques, Paris 1945.

Seaton, p 244.

Fox D, Chaucer's Influence on Fifteenth-Century Poetry, in Companion to Chaucer Studies, ed B Rowland, Toronto 1968, p 397.

English MS with Chartier's poem: Royal 19.A.iii (not in Lansdowne 380).

Literary Criticism. CHEL, 2.216; Lewis, p 245; Bennett OHEL, p 132.

Pearsall D, The English Chaucerians, in Chaucer and Chaucerians, ed D S Brewer, London 1966, p 225.

General Reference. CHEL, 2.389 (Padelford treats MS 5 extract as separate poem).

Bibliography. Hammond, p 432; Utley CR, pp 32, 140.

[47] O BEWTIE PERELES.

MS. Royal 19.A.iii, f 16b (1450–1500).

Brown-Robbins, Robbins-Cutler, no 2386.

Editions. Robbins SL, p 206; Seaton, p 113; Bennett H S, crit Seaton, RES ns 13.175.

Authorship. Seaton, pp 81, 387; pp 245, 387 (literary criticism).

[48] FOR HE IS TRUE.

MS. Royal 19.A.iii, f 16b (1450–1500).

Brown-Robbins, Robbins-Cutler, no 823.

Editions. Warner G F and J P Gilson, Catalogue of Western Manuscripts in the Old Royal and King's Collections, London 1921, 2.317.

Robbins SL, p 288; Seaton, p 114.

Bennett H S, crit Seaton, RES ns 13.176.

Literary Criticism. Seaton, p 387.

[49] THE ASSEMBLY OF LADIES.

MSS. 1, Trinity Camb 599, ff 55a–65b (1500–25); 2, BM Addit 34360, ff 37a–48b (1460–70); 3, Longleat 258, ff 58a–75b (1460–70).

Brown-Robbins, Robbins-Cutler, no 1528.

Editions. Note: see sections III and IV above for full bibliographical statement of the early editions here listed.

Thynne, Chaucer, 1532, f ccxciva.

Stow, Chaucer, 1561, f ccxlviia.

Speght, Chaucer, 1598, f 247a.

Urry, Chaucer, 1721, p 433.

Bell J, Poets of Great Britain, 1782, 10.167.

Anderson, British Poets, 1793, 1.455.

Chalmers, Eng Poets, 1.526.

Oxf Ch, 7.380 (Thynne, collated with MSS 1 and 2).

Pearsall D A, The Floure and the Leafe, London 1962, p 105 (MS 2; crit Elliott R W V, ES 51.57).

Textual Matters. Hammond E P, Ashmole 59 and other Shirley Manuscripts, Angl 30.320.

Pearsall, The Floure and the Leafe, p 7.

Language. Pearsall, The Floure and the Leafe, p 9.

Date. Skeat Canon, p 139; Baugh LHE, p 293; Seaton, p 295.

Authorship. Tyrwhitt T, Canterbury Tales, London 1822, 1.lvi.

Oxf Ch, 7.lxix, 535; Skeat Canon, pp 110, 139.

Snell F J, The Age of Transition, London 1905, 1.5.

Berdan J M, Early Tudor Poetry, N Y 1920, p 65.

Seaton, p 195; Pearsall, The Floure and the Leafe, p 13.

Sources and Literary Relations. Neilson, p 150; Seaton, p 301.

Pearsall D, The Assembly of Ladies and Gen-

erydes, RES ns 12.229.
Literary Criticism. Schofield W H, The Pearl, PMLA 29.659.
CHEL, 2.271; Lewis, p 249; Bennett OHEL, p 134; Seaton, p 296; Pearsall, The Floure and the Leafe, p 58.
General References. Fisher R M, The Flower and the Leaf and the Assembly of Ladies: A Study of Two Love-Vision Poems of the Fifteenth Century, diss Columbia 1955; DA 15.1233.
Pearsall, The Floure and the Leafe, p 20.
Pearsall D, The English Chaucerians, in Chaucer and Chaucerians, ed D S Brewer, London 1966, p 229.
Bibliography. Hammond, p 408; Bennett OHEL, p 302; Pearsall, The Floure and the Leafe, p 79.

[50] THE FLOWER AND THE LEAF.

MSS. No MS extant (text formerly in Longleat 258 but now destroyed). PRINT: Speght, Chaucer, 1598, f 365^b (STC, no 5077).
Brown-Robbins, Robbins-Cutler, no 4026.
Odd Texts of Chaucer's Minor Poems, ChS 1s 60.25 (Longleat 258).
Hammond E P, MS Longleat 258, MLN 20.77.
Lounsbury T R, Studies in Chaucer, N Y 1892, 1.489 (Longleat 258).
Editions. Note: see section IV above for full bibliographical statement of the early editions here listed.
Urry, Chaucer, 1721, p 473.
Bell J, Poets of Great Britain, 1782, 12.83.
Anderson, British Poets, 1793, 1.532.
Todd H J, Illustrations of the Lives and Writings of Gower and Chaucer, London 1810, p 203.
Chalmers, Eng Poets, 1.394.
British Poets, Chiswick 1822, 5.139.
Moxon, Works of Chaucer, 1843, p 405.
[Pickering's] Aldine British Poets, 1845, 6.244; 1866, 4.87.
Bell R, Works of Chaucer, 4.350.
Ellis F S, The Floure and the Leafe, [Kelmscott Press] Hammersmith 1896.
Oxf Ch, 7.361.
Ashbee C R, The Flower and the Leaf, [Essex House Press] London 1902.
Pearsall D A, The Floure and the Leafe, London 1962, p 85.
Selections. Campbell T, Specimens of the British Poets, London 1810.
Hazlitt W, Select Poets of Great Britain, London 1825.

Southey R, Selected Works of the British Poets, London 1831, p 55.
The Book of Celebrated Poems, London 1854.
Ward T, Selections from the English Poets, Oxford 1880; rptd N Y 1924, 1.85.
Modernizations. Dryden J, The Fables, London 1700.
Thurlow E, 2nd Baron, Arcita and Palamon, London 1822.
Clarke C C, The Riches of Chaucer, London 1835, 1.204.
Powell T, in R H Horne, The Poems of Geoffrey Chaucer Modernized, London 1841, p 161.
Gilman A, The Poetical Works of Geoffrey Chaucer, Boston 1880, 3.532.
Briscoe J P, Chaucer's Canterbury Tales, London 1901.
Textual Matters. Pearsall D A, The Floure and the Leafe, London 1962, p 2.
Language. Pearsall, p 9.
Date. Bradshaw H, The Flower and the Leaf, Acad 13(1878).9.
Wordsworth J, The Flower and the Leaf, Acad 13(1878).35.
Furnivall F J, The Flower and the Leaf, Acad 13(1878).55.
Skeat W W, The Flower and the Leaf, Acad 35(1889).448.
Seaton, p 318.
Authorship. Tyrwhitt T, Canterbury Tales, London 1822, 1.xlv.
Sandras E C, Étude sur Geffrey Chaucer considéré comme imitateur des trouvères, Paris 1859, p 95.
Furnivall F J, A Temporary Preface to the Six-Text Edition of Chaucer's Canterbury Tales, ChS 2s 3.107.
Ten Brink B, Chaucer: Studien zur Geschichte seiner Entwicklung und zur Chronologie seiner Schriften, Münster 1870, p 154.
Warton T, History of English Poetry, ed W C Hazlitt, London 1871, 3.8, 29.
Hall A, Chaucer Restored, N&Q 4s 9(1872). 109.
Furnivall F J, Note on Chaucer, N&Q 4s 9 (1872).156; The Flower and the Leaf, Athen 60(1872).49.
Hall A, The Flower and the Leaf, Athen 60(1872).82.
Furnivall F J, Temporary Preface, ChS 2s 3.107.
Marsh G P, Origin and History of the English Language, N Y 1866, p 414.
Hall A, Chaucer Restored, N&Q 7s 4(1887). 167.

Skeat W W, The Flower and the Leaf, Acad 41(1892).592.
Lounsbury T R, Studies in Chaucer, London 1892, 1.489.
Oxf Ch, 7.lxii; Skeat Canon, p 139.
Skeat W W, The Authorship of The Flower and the Leaf, MLQ (London) 3.111; The Authoress of The Flower and the Leaf, Athen 121(1903).340.
Hales J W, The Flower and the Leaf, Athen 121(1903).403.
Snell F J, The Age of Transition, London 1905, 1.5.
Marsh G L, The Authorship of The Flower and the Leaf, JEGP 6.373 (suggests Lydgate as author).
Saintsbury G, A Short History of English Literature, N Y 1929, pp 119, 126.
Pearsall D A, The Floure and the Leafe, London 1962, p 13.
Sources and Literary Relations. McClumpha C F, Origin of The Flower and the Leaf, MLN 4.402.
Neilson, p 149.
Lowes J L, The Prologue to The Legend of Good Women as Related to the French Marguerite Poems, PMLA 19.593.
Kittredge G L, The Flower and the Leaf, MP 1.1.
Marsh G L, Sources and Analogues of The Flower and the Leaf, MP 4.121, 281.
Seaton, p 323.
Pearsall, The Floure and the Leafe, p 20.
Literary Criticism. Schofield W H, The Pearl, PMLA 29.661.
CHEL, 2.217.
Berdan J M, Early Tudor Poetry, N Y 1920, p 62.
Hammond E P, Grass and Green Wool, MLN 40.185.
Bennett OHEL, p 133; Seaton, pp 319, 326; Pearsall, p 29.
General References. Todd H J, Illustrations of the Lives and Writings of Gower and Chaucer, London 1810, p 275.
Sandras E C, Étude sur Geffrey Chaucer, Paris 1859, pp 96, 296.
Morley, 5.249 (with synopsis).
Campbell T, Specimens of the British Poets, London 1819, 2.17.
Skeat Canon, p 139; Lewis, p 247; Baugh LHE, p 293..
Fisher R M, The Flower and the Leaf, diss Columbia 1955; DA 15.1233.
Pearsall, The Floure and the Leafe, p 38.
Pearsall D, The English Chaucerians, in Chaucer and Chaucerians, ed D S Brewer,

London 1966, p 228.
Bibliography. Marsh G L, MP 4.47n; Hammond, p 423.
Pearsall, The Floure and the Leafe, p 79.

[51] THE ISLE OF LADIES.

MSS. 1, BM Addit 10303, ff 1b–9a (1550); 2, Longleat 256, ff 2a–24b (ca 1550).
Brown-Robbins, Robbins-Cutler, no 3947.
Editions. Note: see sections III and IV above for full bibliographical statement of the early editions here listed.
Speght, Chaucer, 1598, f 355b.
Urry, Chaucer, 1721, p 572.
Bell J, Poets of Great Britain, 1782, 11.5.
Anderson, British Poets, 1793, 1.462.
Chalmers, Eng Poets, 1.378.
British Poets, Chiswick 1822, 5.73.
Moxon, Works of Chaucer, 1843, p 389.
[Pickering's] Aldine British Poets, 1845, 6.177; 1866, 5.86.
Bell R, Works of Chaucer, 3.439.
Sherzer J B, The Ile of Ladies, Berlin 1903 (crit B Fehr, EStn 34.295; M Konrath, Arch 112.197).
Modernizations. Clarke C C, The Riches of Chaucer, London 1835, 2.220.
Purves L D, The Canterbury Tales, Edinburgh 1870.
Gilman A, The Poetical Works of Geoffrey Chaucer, Boston 1880, 3.574.
Language. Sherzer, Ile of Ladies, Berlin 1903.
Date. Hertzberg W, Nachlese zu Chaucer, JfRESL 8.133.
Brandl A, Ueber einige historische Anspielungen in dem Chaucer-dichtungen, EStn 12.175 (allegory of match between Henry V and Catherine of France).
McClumpha C F, Chaucer's Dream, MLN 4.129.
Kittredge G L, Chaucer's Dreme, EStn 13.24.
Holzknecht K J, Literary Patronage in the Middle Ages, Phila 1923, p 88.
Seaton, p 140.
Authorship. Tyrwhitt T, Canterbury Tales, London 1822, 1.xliv.
Ellis A J, Early English Pronunciation, EETSES, London 1867, 2.251.
Ten Brink B, Chaucer: Studien zur Geschichte seiner Entwicklung und zur Chronologie seiner Schriften, Münster 1870, p 165.
McClumpha, MLN 4.129.
Hagedorn W, Über die Sprache einiger nördlicher Chaucer-schüler, Göttingen 1892 (crit M Kaluza, EStn 18.228).
F N, Chaucer's Dream, N&Q 8s 1(1892).467.

Brandl A, On the Historical Personages of Chaucer's Squyeres Tale and of the Spurious Chaucer's Dreme, ChS 2s 29.

Hertzberg, JfRESL 8.133.

Sources and Literary Relations. Sherzer, Ile of Ladies, p 32; Seaton, p 144.

Literary Criticism. Sandras E C, Étude sur Geffrey Chaucer considéré comme imitateur des trouvères, Paris 1859, p 81.

Ten Brink B, Chaucer: Studien, p 165.

Lounsbury T R, Studies in Chaucer, N Y 1892, 1.483.

Zupitza J, Zu dem Gedichte Chaucer's Dream oder The Isle of Ladies, Arch 92.68.

Neilson, p 209; Seaton, p 140.

General References. Godwin W, Life of Geoffrey Chaucer, London 1803, 2.576.

Morley, 5.166 (with synopsis); Skeat Canon, p 137.

Pearsall D, The English Chaucerians, in Chaucer and Chaucerians, ed D S Brewer, London 1966, p 229.

Bibliography. Hammond, p 429; Bennett OHEL, p 307.

[52] LETTER OF DIDO TO AENEAS.

MSS. No MS extant. PRINT: Pynson R, [Chaucer's] The Boke of Fame, 1526, ff iiib–viib (STC, no 5088).

Literary Criticism. Seaton, p 363.

General Reference. Hammond, p 436.

[53] THE EXAMPLE OF VIRTUE.

MSS. No MS extant. PRINT: The Example of Vertu, W de Worde [1510] (STC, no 12945); [1520?] (STC, no 12946); 1530 (STC, no 12947).

Robbins-Cutler, no 3954.8.

Modernization. Arber E, The Dunbar Anthology, London 1901, p 217.

Other Scholarly Problems. Knowlton E C, Nature in Middle English, JEGP 20.204.

Literary Criticism. Morley, 3.71 (with synopsis).

Snell F J, The Age of Transition, London 1905, 1.119.

CHEL, 2.258.

Berdan J M, Early Tudor Poetry, N Y 1920, p 78.

[54] THE PASTIME OF PLEASURE.

MSS. 1, Bodl 12653 (Rawl C.813), f 18a (extract lines 2372–2548); 2, Univ of Glasgow, Hunterian 230, f 246b (extract lines 2542–48). PRINT: 3, The Historie of Graunde Amoure and La Bel Pucel Called the Pas-

time of Pleasure, W de Worde [1509] (STC, no 12948); 1517 (STC, no 12949); J Wayland 1554 (STC, no 12950); R Tottel 1555 (STC, no 12951).

Brown-Robbins, Robbins-Cutler, no 4004; Robbins-Cutler, no 2532.5.

Editions. Wright T, The Pastime of Pleasure, PPS 18.

Mead W E, The Pastime of Pleasure, EETS, London 1927, 173 (crit C R Baskerville, MP 27.231).

Padelford F M, The Songs in Manuscript Rawlinson C.813, Angl 31.333 (MS 1).

Robbins SL, p 152 (MS 2).

Selections. Southey R, Selected Works of the British Poets, London 1831, p 76.

Skeat Spec, 3.118.

FitzGibbon H M, Early English Poetry, London 1887, p 128.

Flügel NL, p 15.

Ward T, Selections from the English Poets, Oxford 1880; rptd N Y 1924, 1.178.

Arber E, The Dunbar Anthology, London 1901.

Manly J, The English Poets, Boston 1907, p 59.

Neilson W A and K G T Webster, Chief British Poets of the 14th and 15th Centuries, Boston 1916, p 249.

Hammond EV, p 271.

Textual Matters. Burkhart E A, Stephen Hawes' The Pastime of Pleasure: A Critical Introd to a Proposed New Text, London 1899 (relationship to Nevill corrected by B Cornelius, EETS, London 1928, 179.24).

Literary Relations. Schick J, Lydgate's Temple of Glass, EETSES, London 1891, 60.lxxvi.

Zander F, Stephen Hawes' Passetyme of Pleasure vergleichen mit Edmund Spenser's Faerie Queene, Rostock 1905.

Lemmi C W, Influence of Boccaccio on Hawes' Pastime of Pleasure, RES 5.195.

Wells W, Stephen Hawes and The Court of Sapience, RES 6.284.

Anderson M, The Influence of Renaissance Philosophy on Stephen Hawes, diss Univ Southern Calif 1936.

Bennett OHEL, p 155.

Frankis P F, The Erotic Dream in Medieval English Lyrics, NM 57.237.

Other Scholarly Problems. Furh K, Lautuntersuchungen zu Stephen Hawes' Gedicht The Pastime of Pleasure, Marburg 1891.

Natter H, Untersuchung der Quellen von Stephen Hawes' allegorischen Gedichte Pastime of Pleasure, Passau 1911 (crit O Glöde,

EStn 47.86).

Bühler C F, Kynge Melyzyus and The Pastime of Pleasure, RES 10.438.

Stevens J, Music and Poetry in the Early Tudor Court, London 1961, p 61.

Literary Criticism. Ten Brink, 3.93; Courthope, 1.380; Neilson, p 165; CHEL, 2.224.

Rhodenizer V B, Studies in Stephen Hawes' Pastime of Pleasure, diss Harvard 1918.

Berdan J M, Early Tudor Poetry, N Y 1920, pp 57, 79, 81, 89.

Morley, 7.71.

Saintsbury G, History of English Prosody, London 1923, 1.235.

Hammond EV, p 268; Lewis, p 278; Bennett OHEL, pp 127, 155.

Ferguson A B, The Indian Summer of English Chivalry, Durham N C 1960, pp xi, 6, 59.

Evans M, English Poetry in the Sixteenth Century, London 1967, p 40.

General References. Bale J, Scriptorum illustrium maioris Brytannie . . . catalogus, Basel 1557–59, 1.632.

Ellis EEP, 1.402 (with synopsis).

Warton T, History of English Poetry, ed W C Hazlitt, London 1871, 3.169.

Minto W, Characteristics of English Poets, Edinburgh 1885, p 91.

Smith G G, The Transition Period, N Y 1900, p 24.

Snell F J, The Age of Transition, London 1905, 1.112.

CHEL, 2.223.

Pearsall D, The English Chaucerians, in Chaucer and Chaucerians, ed D S Brewer, London 1966, p 251.

Bibliography. CBEL, 1.253; Renwick-Orton, p 291.

[55] THE COMFORT OF LOVERS.

MS. 1, Bodl 12653 (Rawl C.813), f 24ᵇ (extract of 26 stanzas). PRINT: 2, The Comfort of Lovers, W de Worde [1512] (STC, no 12942.1).

Robbins-Cutler, no 3357.5; Brown-Robbins, Robbins-Cutler, no 2496.

Edition. Padelford F M, The Songs in Manuscript Rawlinson C 813, Angl 31.341 (MS 1).

Textual Matters. Humphreys G S, A Crux in The Comfort of Lovers, TLS June 14 1928, p 400.

Literary Criticism. Berdan J M, Early Tudor Poetry, N Y 1920, p 86 (with synopsis).

General Reference. Burkart E A, Stephen Hawes' The Pastime of Pleasure: A Critical Introduction to a Proposed New Text, London 1899, p 18 (describes original print, now in Brit Mus).

[56] THE CASTELL OF PLEASURE.

MSS. No MS extant. PRINT: The Castell of Pleasure, W de Worde (ca 1517) (STC, no 18475); H Pepwell, 1518 (STC, no 18476).

Brown-Robbins, Robbins-Cutler, no 3811.

Edition. Cornelius R D, The Castell of Pleasure, EETS 179, London 1928.

Selection. Hammond EV, p 289.

Textual Matters. Hammond EV, p 496.

Literary Criticism. Cornelius, EETS 179.9.

INDEX

A bold-face number indicates the main reference in the Commentary; a number preceded by B indicates the reference in the Bibliography. Titles are indexed under the first word following an article. Indexed are all literary works and their authors, names of early printers, and main subdivisions. No attempt has been made to index the names of characters and places in the literary works nor the names of scholars.